Health, Civilization and the State

A history of public health from ancient to modern times

Dorothy Porter

London and New York

First published 1999
by Routledge
11 New Fetter Lane, London EC4P 4EE

Simultaneously published in the USA and Canada
by Routledge
29 West 35th Street, New York, NY 10001

Transferred to Digital Printing 2003

Routledge is an imprint of the Taylor & Francis Group

Typeset in Baskerville by Routledge
Printed and bound in Great Britain by
TJI Digital, Padstow, Cornwall

British Library Cataloguing in Publication Data
A catalogue record for this book is available from the British Library

Library of Congress Cataloging in Publication Data
Porter, Dorothy.
   Health, Civilization and the State: a history of public health from
   ancient to modern times/Dorothy Porter.
      p. cm.
   Includes bibliographical references and index.
   1. Public health–Social aspects–Europe–History. 2. Public health–Social
   aspects–North America–History. 3. Public health–Political
   aspects–Europe–History. 4. Public health–Political aspects–North
   America–History. 5. Social medicine–Europe–History. 6. Social
   medicine–North
   America–History. I. Title.
RA424.P678 1999
362.1'09dc21   98–21836

0–415–12244–9 (hbk)
0–415–20036–9 (pbk)

Contents

Acknowledgements

While writing this book I have accumulated many debts of friendship and
support. First I should like to thank my large family for all the affection and
support that they have always given to me. Among my closest friends the
Abichou family have become almost like extended kin to me. A group of especially dear friends supported me in my worst travails and finest hours: Joanna
Bourke, Sam and Jen Guttenplan, Vanessa Harding, Michael Imlach and
Camilla, Hilary Sapire and Stella Tillyard and her family. All my colleagues and
friends at Birkbeck College have made it a complete joy to work there. No one
could ask for a more intellectually stimulating or profoundly gratifying environment than Birkbeck's history department and no teacher could find finer
students anywhere. The achievements of my research students, in particular,
have given me some of my proudest moments.

My appointment at Birkbeck was made possible through funding from the
Wellcome Trust for which I am deeply grateful. Furthermore, the Wellcome
Institute and Library provide myself and so many colleagues within the discipline of the history of medicine with fantastic research resources. Many
colleagues and friends from within the communities of the history of medicine
and science and the history of social policy have also helped me to develop this
work. My special thanks go to those who read the manuscript at various stages,
including two anonymous referees. I should also like to thank Heather
McCallum for her patience, faith and excellent advice as an editor. The responsibility for the limitations of this work is, of course, entirely my own.

Finally, I wish to thank Brian Dolan for allowing me to experience the
happiest period of my life.

Introduction

Changing definitions of the history of public health

For many students the idea of studying the history of public health provokes a very big yawn since it conjures up an image of investigating toilets, drains and political statutes through the ages. This caricature of public health history was fostered, in part, by administrative histories of public health written in the 1950s and early 1960s which documented parliamentary reforms and technological developments that helped to create healthier environments, which in turn reduced the spread of infectious disease. Historians of public health such as the political biographers Samuel Finer, R. A. Lewis and Royston Lambert (Finer, 1952; Lewis, 1952; Lambert, 1963) and the English public health officers who wrote outstanding administrative histories of public health, William Frazer and Colin Fraser Brockington (Frazer, 1950; Fraser Brockington, 1956) all used a definition of the subject which closely reflected the ideals of nineteenth-century public health reform. They and earlier public health practitioners, such as George Newman and Arthur Newsholme (Newsholme, 1927; Newman, 1932) equated public health with 'the sanitary idea' and methods of preventive medicine, such as vaccination. The limitation of infectious diseases through environmental and preventive reform was represented in this historiographical tradition as the triumphant culmination of a long tradition stretching back to biblical times. In 1952 René Sand, professor of social medicine at Brussels University, wrote an impressive account of what he called *The Advance to Social Medicine* from ancient to modern times (Sand, 1952). Similar themes were subsequently explored by George Rosen in 1958 when he wrote what became the definitive textbook on the history of public health (Rosen, 1958). Both Sand's and Rosen's works were imposing erudite surveys of health regulations from pre-Socratic times to the early years following the Second World War. Both accounts were written at a time when public health appeared to be victorious in achieving massive reductions in mortality rates in the Western world, when scientific medicine seemed to have almost eliminated the menace of pestilence. As a result Sand and Rosen both wrote grand narratives of progress, arising from the technological advance of science and medicine and its capacities to combat endemic and epidemic disease. This heroic vision was reinforced in 1976 by the conclusions of a professor of social medicine, Thomas McKeown, that clinical medicine had played no part in *The Modern Rise of Population*, which had, he claimed, largely resulted from improved nutrition. McKeown also argued that environmental reforms such as the creation of clean water supplies had played a role in population growth (McKeown, 1976a; McKeown, 1976b).

When the parameters of public health history were confined largely to sanitary reforms and the control of infectious diseases, then it was possible to argue that although public health was invented in the nineteenth century it had been preconfigured in technological developments stretching back through time, such as the Mosaic Code and Roman baths and aqueducts (Newman, 1932). In the three decades following the 1960s, social historians of health, illness and disease began to challenge such a view. In 1961 the eminent social historian of nineteenth-century Britain, Asa Briggs, suggested that the story of cholera had been overlooked as a major factor in historical change in Victorian society (Briggs, 1961). Subsequently, historians began to explore not only cholera but the impact of epidemic and infectious disease on historical transformations in early modern and modern European and North American societies. Historians such as Margaret Pelling, William Coleman, Charles Rosenberg, Charles Cippola, Paul Slack, James Riley, Richard Morris and Richard Evans (Pelling, 1978; Coleman, 1982; Coleman, 1987; Rosenberg, 1962; Cipolla, 1979; Slack, 1985; Riley, 1989; Morris, 1976; Evans, 1987) used the economic, social, political and ideological responses to disease to explore the complex ways in which change both caused and was determined by the impact of epidemics. This new historiography investigated the differential experience of epidemics by social classes, professionals, scientific and religious communities and political states and oligarchies (Kiple, 1993). The scope of public health history expanded by the 1980s to include the social relations of ideas and actions taken collectively and individually in response to epidemic disasters. In addition, historians such as William McNeill and Alfred Crosby (McNeill, 1976; Crosby, 1986) began to indicate how disease could influence not only the relations between classes, ruling orders and political states but also the processes of imperialism and colonization. Studies of the relations of health and imperialism have subsequently proliferated, revealing fascinating new insights into the role played by bio-politics in economic, military and political oppression.

At the same time the changing epidemiological and demographic structure of past populations began to be probed by quantitative historians who tried to account, like McKeown, for the modern rise of populations. While numerous studies found McKeown's reasoning about 'hunger and history' to be flawed, the debate continued to rage about the causes of population growth (*Population Studies; Journal of Interdisciplinary Studies*). Quantitative historians added greatly to our knowledge of the social and economic relations of the past, however, by exploring distributions of health and disease and differential patterns of height and weight between social strata, identifying factors encouraging increased fertility, and trying to highlight a wide range of determinants of mortality decline (Barker and Drake (eds) 1982; Szreter, 1988; Szreter, 1996; Wrigley and Schofield, 1981).

From the late 1980s a new world-wide pandemic stimulated yet further directions in public health history. The experience of a contemporary epidemic in times when lethal infections had almost become a lost memory provoked powerful responses, not least among historians, semiological analysts and literary theorists (Gilman, 1988; Gilman, 1989; Gilman, 1995; Showalter, 1986). AIDS revived the historical study of stigma, encouraged new directions in inquiries into the meanings of representation and forcefully added to new debates about the social construction of everyday life (Rosenberg, 1992; Fee and Fox, 1989; Fee and Fox, 1992; Berridge and Strong, 1993; Berridge, 1996). Often stimulated by concerns to understand the historical meaning of AIDS, art historians and literary theorists added their skilful analyses to what sociologists had been interrogating from the late 1970s: that is, the cultural significance of the body in comparative societies (Turner, 1984; Turner, 1992; Outram, 1989; Bourke, 1996). In the 1990s the historiography of health, disease and illness exists within a vastly expanded intellectual discourse on the relations between biology and culture, living and dead bodies.

Intellectual developments in public health history in the 1990s have also been significantly influenced by a range of important philosophical and theoretical movements dating from the 1930s. In the 1960s the French 'archaeologist of knowledge', Michel Foucault, and a variety of Hegelian-Marxist thinkers from the 1930s, such as the Frankfurt School of Critical Theory, highlighted contradictions in the Enlightenment tradition in Western thought (Foucault, 1970; Adorno and Horkheimer, 1972). Such a view fundamentally undermines any heroization of public health as a great achievement of Enlightenment rationalism. Historians influenced by these theoretical perspectives have cross-examined the ways in which public health regulation contributed to the rise of a 'disciplinary culture' which Foucault argued was the defining characteristic of modern society (Armstrong, 1983). Equally, the role played by public health reform in facilitating the development of authoritarian bureaucratic government and the rise of professional power has been interrogated by leftist and Marxist critiques of the repressive nature of modern states (Porter (ed.) 1994; Weindling, 1989). These concerns have fed into a wide variety of new perspectives brought to bear upon what constitutes the history of public health, which now embraces diverse subjects and inquiries from the multicultural politics of the body to examinations of the dramatically changing structure of modern welfare states and social policies.

Over the last four decades or so, historians, social scientists and scholars from a range of intellectual disciplines have extensively broadened the study of the economic, social and political relations of health and society. Accounts of the progressive 'rise of civilization' have long since gone out of fashion and 'grand narratives' themselves have never been more outcast than in the contemporary intellectual climate of postmodernist relativism (Appleby *et al.*, 1994). Heroic accounts of the triumphant emancipation of modern society from the primitive bondage of ignorance can no longer be sustained in a world in which many voices contribute to the reconstruction of the past, within which each has different interests to identify (Eagleton, 1996; Appleby *et al.*, 1996; Topolski,

1994). History writing is no longer dominated by one ideological vantage point even within Western societies, where a new multicultural mix ensures that a huge variety of historical perspectives has been able to gain legitimate authority (Clark *et al.*, 1993).

The attention drawn to relativism by postmodernist theory is, however, only the most recent of many new intellectual and philosophical approaches to the writing of history which have developed since Sand and Rosen wrote their great works. The history of health, medicine and disease has profoundly reflected many different historiographical and intellectual directions between the 1960s and the 1990s. This textbook re-examines the history of public health in Europe and North America by reflecting these trends and using the explosion of work written on the subject in the last four decades. The structure and subject-matter of the book have been dictated by the concerns that historians and others have chosen to explore about the changing relations of health, medicine, disease and society. As a result, what constitutes public health has been redefined within this text beyond the predominantly nineteenth-century concept used by Sand, Rosen and their contemporaries. The stories told here concern *the history of collective action in relation to the health of populations*.

THE HISTORY OF COLLECTIVE ACTION IN RELATION TO THE HEALTH OF POPULATIONS

The broadest history of ideas, beliefs and actions in relation to health and illness would consider traditions of individual health regimens and the experiences of individuals themselves (Porter and Porter, 1988; Porter and Porter, 1989). While individuals and their behaviour are not ignored in the current text, they are a subsidiary analytical category to collective social action in relation to populations and groups. That is, this text is concerned largely with social, economic and political relations of health between classes, social structures and organizations, pressure groups, polities and states. The focus on collective social action does not mean that the behaviour and beliefs of individuals are ignored in this study. They only appear, however, to the extent that the actions, ideas and beliefs held by individuals bleed into the sphere of collective social action. This can mean discussing William Petty's methods of assessing the health of the mercantilist state through 'political arithmetic' in the seventeenth century or examining the role that social reformers such as Henry Griscom played in public health philanthropy in the United States in the nineteenth century. Sometimes the crucial actions of political rulers such as Bernabo Visconti in fourteenth-century Milan, or the massively influential role of civil servants such as the Secretary to the first British Central Board of Health, Edwin Chadwick, have been analysed in some detail.

An exploration of the health of populations can avoid being limited by preconceptions which underlie examinations of 'public health' as defined in nineteenth-century terms (Frazer, 1950; Finer, 1952). The first chapter, for example, investigates how the concern of ruling elites in some ancient Mediterranean societies with their own comfort generated political actions derived from abstract theories and practical codes of health behaviour. This form of collective action in relation to health is differentiated, however, from statutory or voluntaristic comprehensive public health systems developed in much later periods that aimed to reform the conditions of existence and levels of mortality of all the social strata within a society. Subsequent collective actions explored in different chronological periods have been identified according to the significance they held for population health. It is for this reason that discussion of population health in medieval times is concerned on the one hand with social welfare provided for the sick, especially the sick poor, and on the other hand with plague, since this constituted the most serious threat to population health at that time. In the same way that it could be legitimate to argue that 'public health' was invented in the nineteenth century, it could be possible to defend an assertion that 'population' was invented in the seventeenth and eighteenth centuries. The development of population as a subject of study by demographers or other 'quantifiers' has, therefore, been given considerable attention, while confining the discussion largely to the context of the health of populations specifically. Nevertheless, this text does not intend to use the term 'population' in a narrow academic or mathematical way. Rather, it is a term which, as mentioned above, is used here to facilitate the discussion of health and disease in relation to classes, groups, nations and societies.

The concern with collective social action involves an analysis of the structural operation of power, which makes the political implications of population health in different periods and in different societies a persistent theme throughout the book. In pre-modern societies this means paying attention to a wide variety of different theatres of power including city states, fiefdoms and dukedoms, monarchical realms and large social organizations such as the Church. In the modern period, the study of the operation of power in relation to population health necessarily involves an examination of the rise of the modern state as an autonomous political sphere. The book has paid special attention, therefore, to the implications of health citizenship as a 'right of man' within democratic states from the late eighteenth century. The later chapters attempt to draw out different interpretations, made in different periods, of the rights and obligations of citizens within the 'social contract' of health between the state and civil society in modern democracies.

The subject of this study is health as distinct from therapeutic medicine. However, this book is concerned with the way in which population health is influenced by biomedical theories and practices, and the way population health is influenced by access to therapeutic medicine. From the early chapters, therefore, medicine is discussed within the context of the social organization for health. In ancient Mediterranean societies, for example, medical theory is explored in terms of the insight it provides into the emergence of rational material beliefs about health and illness, thereby making it possible to distinguish how hygiene regimes influenced practical codes of settlement and colonization of what were perceived to be healthy environments. Towards the end of the book, the economic and political organization of access to medical care is discussed in societies where it became crucially significant to health levels among populations which have increasing numbers of longer-living yet chronically sick individuals. Population health has always depended upon collective provision of social welfare in different societies. Because of changing demographic structures in advanced or post-industrial societies, social policies aimed at providing welfare to relieve social and economic disadvantage have become inherently linked to the costs of medical care. The mechanisms developed for meeting the costs of care are compared in a variety of national contexts in the latter chapters of this book. Population health is discussed here within the broader history of social policy in industrial and post-industrial societies in the twentieth century.

While the subject matter of this text has been dictated by the work of historians, the interpretations and arguments offered in this account are guided by analytical themes which are inspired by the work of two sociologists, Norbert Elias and Max Weber.

CIVILIZATION AND THE STATE

As mentioned above, postmodernist intellectuals are perplexed by the problem of relativism in relation to the interpretation of communication and language, contemporary social relations and historical events. Negotiating epistemological relativism and determinism had, however, preoccupied earlier generations of historians and social scientists in the twentieth century (Bernstein, 1983). Norbert Elias and his friend, the sociologist Karl Mannheim, both addressed this philosophical and methodological dilemma in various works. When they were colleagues at Heidelberg University in the 1920s and early 1930s, the sociological community there attempted to grapple with the problem of relativism when they were analysing the sociological basis of beliefs and values (Mennell, 1989). Mannheim believed he had resolved this dilemma by suggesting that all beliefs were 'relational' ideologies determined by the structural position of individuals and groups within society. All values were the product of sociologically determined 'bias' or 'one sidedness' (Mannheim, 1991). In 1939 Norbert Elias used his study of the long-term transformations in social structures and personality structures in European societies which defined their 'civilising process' to investigate the sociological basis to belief from a somewhat different point of view. He argued that the correct path through the epistemological minefield of relativism was to be found in understanding 'the order of historical changes, their mechanics and their concrete mechanisms' (Elias, 1994: xv). In his studies of the history of manners and the operation of power, state formation and civilization, Elias attempted to elucidate what Max Weber had referred to as the unintended consequences of intended actions (Weber, 1979). That is, Elias investigated the structural roots of changing standards of behaviour and how, in turn, individual actions unintentionally formed social institutions. He tried to do this by investigating the sociogenesis and psychogenesis of what different societies identified as civilized behaviour. Elias's work stimulated what might now be called the historical sociology of feelings and experience. He focused, for example, on historical transformations in the social construction of shame, delicacy and fear and the psychogenesis of the experience of ageing. He asked how the process of 'growing up' in Western societies changed. Elias explored how such sociogenic and psychogenic processes were related to the historically constituted parameters of civilization. In particular, he was interested in how historical transformations in these processes affected structural differentiation and integration within different societies. For this reason he was especially concerned with the way in which historical transformations in the sociogenesis of civility were linked to the formation of the state in European societies (Elias, 1939: 335–421). He accepted Max Weber's view that the state emerged in post-medieval European societies as a social organization which instituted a monopoly of the exercise of physical force. Elias believed that it was possible to investigate why such a centralization and monopolization of physical violence had occurred, by exploring the intersection of a multitude of social interactions which shaped individuals by permitting and prohibiting different behaviours. He argued that the centralization of power in the institution of the state through the sociogenesis of civilization subsequently brought about transformations in the psychogenesis of behaviour (Elias, 1939: 449–524).

Health, Civilization and the State explores how collective actions which aimed to regulate or improve the health of populations were involved in changing the historical relationship between the civilizing process and state formation in European and North American societies. It explores the question: how did population health feature in the sociogenesis of civility, civil society and the state? Like Max Weber, and many contemporary social scientists who would identify themselves as Weberians, I accept the idea that the state is a distinctive social organization with a degree of autonomy which functions as one of the defining characteristics of modern societies (Evans, Rueschemeyer and Skocpol, 1985). Also like Weber, I accept that it is a social organization which institutionalizes the operation of centralized power and that it consists of a constantly changing structure of political processes. Therefore, this study examines the way in which collective action to improve and regulate population health has been an historical political process which has definitively contributed to the formation of autonomous states.

These investigations are explored within the restricted social, economic and political history of European and North American societies which make up what has frequently been referred to as the 'Western tradition'. In this respect this textbook reproduces the scope of Sand's and Rosen's studies. The abundance of new scholarship on the history of imperialism, health, medicine and disease could not be incorporated into such a small study. Furthermore, the vast range of expertise required to explore the historical transformation in collective action on population health in societies beyond the narrow scope of Europe and North America is far beyond the knowledge and capabilities of this author. It is, however, a tragic inadequacy of the study presented here which must be rectified by other historians who have the skills to do so. The relationship between the history of 'Western traditions' in population health actions and those of Eastern European, South American, African and Asian societies raises profoundly innovative questions.

A further disclaimer for the current study is that it discusses collective actions regarding population health but does not analyse the massive scholarship which has quantitatively investigated historical demographic change.

This study is designed as a textbook for students of the history of public health, whether they have been trained in history, public health or medicine. It is written as a set of analytical arguments which synthesize and interpret the wide range of historiographical sources available on the subjects it covers. It has been organized to be used as a teaching tool, and each chapter is referenced and provided with a bibliography of the most relevant further reading. The References section at the end of the book aims to provide tutors with a choice of material to set for course reading-lists and a range of materials which students can use to pursue various subjects in greater depth.

Earlier generations of historians and historical sociologists who have attempted studies of social transformations over long periods of time often did so on the basis of huge erudition complemented by a wide range of linguistic reading skills. Some of their 'grand narratives' would certainly be accused by contemporary intellectuals in many fields of being historiographically old-fashioned and philosophically naïve. Even the attempt to explore transformations over long periods of time may now justly receive similar criticism. The present study, therefore, may be considered by some to be an intellectual endeavour which is hopelessly out of step with current trends. I believe, however, that Elias's recommendation to study long-term transformations still has much merit.

Part 1

Population, health and pre-modern states

In Part 1 we consider the influence of the health of populations upon the social organization, operation of power and system of beliefs and values in European societies from ancient to early modern times. This is not an attempt to find the early origins of modern systems of public health provision. Rather, the relative significance of population health is examined in different contexts. Chapter 1 investigates how and towards whom ancient societies applied their moral codes and practical advice about health and hygiene. Did the health of the poor play a role in the expansion of Christian charity in the period of late antiquity? Chapter 2 documents the increasing concerns with the economic, political and social significance of epidemic and pandemic infectious diseases in medieval and early modern European societies, especially leprosy, plague and syphilis. Chapter 3 explores the changing discourses surrounding population health in early modern societies after widespread shock invasions of diseases such as plague began to decline. Here we draw out the role of population health in the ideological interpretations of market economies, consumer societies, mercantilist states and Enlightened political constitutions. Chapter 3 documents the development of the study of population health as an early modern social science and analyses the extent to which it featured in democratic theories in both the United States and in Europe at the end of the eighteenth century.

1 Health and morality in the ancient world

In the ancient world the pursuit of bodily and environmental cleanliness had both spiritual and material justifications (Temkin and Temkin, 1962; Temkin, 1977; Edelstein, 1967). Concern over individual health was a patrician preoccupation, a cult of the educated and leisured (Wear, 1993; Rather, 1968; Jarcho, 1970). The rules guiding the creation of healthy settlements and early forms of sanitary engineering were a practical expression of this cult for the well-being of the ideal community, consisting of a self-governing elite (Lloyd (ed.), 1983; Miller, 1962). Health and cleanliness helped to eliminate the danger of spiritual defilement from material corruption and provided for patrician comfort. It enhanced the lifestyles and social status of the governing classes, who perceived themselves to be the bearers of civilization in an otherwise barbarian world. Repelling the stigma of disease from the community removed the symbol of spiritual backwardness from civilization (Glacken, 1967). Political concern with public health and the ideology of the civilizing process continued to be interrelated. From the time of the late Roman empire, new pagan patrician preoccupations with charity began to be concerned with the health of the poor (Horden, 1985). This was exploited further by Christianity, aiding its hegemonic expansion throughout the late ancient and early medieval world (Numbers and Amundsen (eds), 1986; Sheils (ed.), 1982). Christian charity concerned itself with the health of non-elite populations which expanded the perception of society by the powerful.

There can be no positivistic account of linear development in healing practices or in the provision of health for individuals, social groups or the population at large in the long period dating from classical Greek society to late antiquity and the early middle ages. For example, the provision of public physicians by Greek city-states was imitated and expanded with the Hellenization of the defeated Persian empire and, later, the Roman world (Jackson, 1988). Amid the social and cultural transformations which took place between late antiquity and the early medieval period, followed by the break-up of the empire in the West and the disintegration of towns, less and less opportunity existed for either the public or private practice of 'learned' medicine. In the Byzantine East the institution of the public doctor continued, such as those civic physicians supported in Egypt by two measures of corn per year, according to Diodorus of Sicily. Town physicians who survived at all in the West were confined to some of the few cities remaining in northern Italy and southern Gaul (Nutton, 1981b).

Collective concern about the health of populations did, nevertheless, shift ground. The institution of Roman hospitals for slaves and soldiers was absorbed into Pagan and Christian charity in late antiquity (Amundsen and Ferngren, 1986). The benefit of welfare provision as a social source of power was subsequently exploited to its fullest by the Church and the poor took on a new political significance (Greer, 1974). The Church subsequently enhanced its social authority by adapting ancient codes of spurning the spiritually unclean from society into the institutionalized isolation of the contagious (Pelling, 1993). From the ancient to the early medieval period, collective concerns about the health of populations shifted from providing a salubrious environment for patrician comfort to the provision of care for the poor (Miller, 1985; C. Jones, 1993). This chapter charts the journey from health codes designed to provide salubrity for the spiritual and material comfort of patrician elites to the early institutionalization of health and welfare provision for the needy. In the following chapter we will see how providing care established a legitimate authority for regulating social behaviour as a method of containing the spread of sickness and contagion among the urban and rural poor.

PURITY OF BODY AND SOUL

When our prehistoric ancestors replaced hunting and gathering with domestication of animals and crops to sustain regular food supplies, they also created a new disease regime for human societies (Cohen, 1989; McKeown, 1988). Shortening the food chain by protecting animals and crops from large predators also enhanced the opportunity for microparasitic forms to proliferate. Agricultural settlement reconstructed the ecosystem and the door opened for hyperinfestation. For example, human settlements offered greater opportunity for constant contact with intestinal parasites carried through human faeces, whereas a band of hunters constantly on the move were much less at risk from such infections. Settlement, domestication of animals and plants and urbanization altered the disease environment of the human species for ever (Cohen, 1989; Cockburn, 1977). From the most ancient times of recorded history all societies have been affected by the contingencies of sickness and health (McNeill, 1976). From ancient times human societies used various means to ward off the dangers of sickness which were often imbued with spiritual symbolism as much as they were the product of rationalist thought (Douglas, 1974).

There has been much speculation about diseases of early agricultural societies which has largely assumed that the settlements of Mesopotamia, and those surrounding the Indus river and the Peruvian coastal region, were plagued by classical tropical diseases such as malaria and schistosomiasis – a blood fluke parasite (Cohen, 1989). Little is known about the disease regimes of prehistoric societies but ancient health and cleanliness protocols, along with relics of ancient civil and sanitary engineering, indicate that cleanliness and godliness were closely linked in many early cultures. Ancient medical systems depended heavily upon mystical and religious explanations for disease and used empirical as well as philosophical and spiritual methods for healing. Many ancient belief systems stressed the importance of warding off sickness through divination; ritual and practical methods of prevention linked spiritual and temporal purity through various codes of behaviour and dietary protocols (Lloyd, 1979).

Chinese doctors under the Chou Dynasty (1122–250 BC) advocated health preservation through exercise, deep breathing and temperance. Wine was forbidden. They linked physical health to moral well-being and spiritual serenity, which led to cosmic harmony. Intermarriage between people of different ages and physical types was thought to produce a healthy lineage. In ancient India, health regimes were equally based on a mixture of dietetics, physical and spiritual exercises and the advocated daily care of the body, paying special attention to the mouth, tongue, teeth, hair and nails (Unschuld, 1985; Epler, 1988). Ancient Egyptian medicine was similarly based upon a belief that sickness resulted from an imbalance between temporal and spiritual existence and that health could be restored by prayers, magic, rituals or through the use of an extensive pharmacopoeia of empirical cures (Whitney, 1996). The body was believed to be controlled by a system of vessels carrying the blood, urine, sperm and tears which, like Egypt's system of canals, had to be kept clean and free of obstruction. Purgings were used as preventive medicine. Bodily cleanliness, both within and without, aimed to achieve spiritual purity, so that regulations about clean food, clothes, bathing and sexual relations were largely ritualistic (Risse, 1986). In Mesopotamian health cultures, including Babylonian, Assyrian and Hebrew codes, spiritual purity and prevention of disease were given priority (Ritter, 1965: 299–321). The fundamental aim of these hygiene customs was to purify the body before God. The rabbi-physicians of the Talmudic period formulated elaborate rules for disease control based on the belief that some diseases were communicable through foods, bodily discharges, clothing, beverages, water and air. Plagues were believed to be spread through contaminated water (Preuss, 1978). But the Hebrews and the Babylonians also connected epidemics to rats, flies, gnats and other creatures, although the significance of animals was probably magical. Individuals were isolated during epidemics and their houses and belongings fumigated and disinfected. The laws against leprosy set out in Leviticus chapter 13, which were also shared by the Babylonians, were derived from magical belief as much as from an aetiological explanation of the disease (Weymouth, 1938). Ritual cleanliness demanded that no well was to be dug near a cemetery or a rubbish dump, and water was to be boiled before drinking. Food had to be clean, fresh and thoroughly cooked. The Talmudic code continued to influence the development of public health throughout Europe, especially as Jewish, together with Muslim, physicians played a crucial role in transferring the traditions of classical medicine during the middle ages (Conrad, 1992).

In the ancient world the environment was both natural and supernatural.

Like Mesopotamian medicine, ancient Mexican and Peruvian medicine relied upon astrology and sorcery for diagnosis and used magical and ritualistic therapeutics. Both the Aztecs and the Incas had a supernatural concept of disease-bringing winds – the wind gods sometimes brought pestilence. Both systems did observe, however, the seasonal nature of epidemic disease and crop blight. The Incas instituted an annual health ceremony which included cleaning all homes (Garrison, 1929).

Mysticism dominated many ancient health and healing cultures, but temporal and divine causes of disease began to be separated in the natural philosophy of ancient Greek culture. Priestly medicine flourished in pre-Socratic Greek society. The Homeric epics identified Apollo as the god of disease and healing until he was replaced by Asclepius, his son, who was an heroic warrior and 'blameless physician'. Asclepius's sons were also warriors and healers. Asclepius was portrayed with a staff and a serpent, which were common symbols of magical medicine among numerous ancient Semitic cultures. By the third century BC, temples of Asclepius were set up throughout the ancient world where healing was practised through 'incubation'. The patient slept at night in the temple, waiting for the god to appear and prescribe a cure (Edelstein and Edelstein, 1943).

Between the seventh and the fifth centuries BC, new schools of philosophy, at settlements on the periphery of the Hellenic world at Cnidus in Asia Minor, Crotona in Sicily, Rhodes, Cyrene and Cos, developed a secular conception of medicine and a non-priestly medical tradition (Longrigg, 1993). Various explanations have been offered for the rise of secular rationalism in the provincial societies of the Greek colonial world. The societies on the Aegean fringes absorbed a multiplicity of intellectual influences from the Mediterranean, Asian and Oriental cultures, and avoided the limiting rigidity of religious dogmatism. Hellenic religious traditions themselves were largely mythical and non-dogmatic because they were not linked to the political stability of the state. Greek civilization was not organized around a strong central government or priesthood, but it was primarily a trading society in which the city-state was the most important political unit (Longrigg, 1993).

A new natural philosophy of medicine emerged among the pre-Socratic schools of thought. A number of the first pre-Socratic Greek philosophers were also physicians who began to develop natural explanations of health and disease but still retained mystical elements of belief. Physicians at Cnidus established an elaborate system of disease classification and Thales of Miletus (639–544 BC) identified water as the fundamental element of life. The founder of the 'Italic' school of philosophy at Crotona, Pythagoras (580–489 BC), applied the lore of numerical harmony to medicine which was absorbed into the Hippocratic concepts of 'critical days' and crisis in sickness. Pythagoras's pupil, Alcmaeon, developed a theory of disease based on the idea that cosmic harmony resulted from the blending of opposites. For example, too much heat caused fever and too much cold caused chills. This line of reasoning was taken further by Empedocles of Agrigentum (504–443 BC) who applied the theory of harmonious balance to the four physical elements, fire, earth, air and water, as the basis of health (Lloyd, 1987).

In the fifth century BC on the island of Cos, various features of pre-Socratic philosophy were absorbed into the Hippocratic tradition of medicine (Smith, 1979). Hippocrates was probably an historical figure who lived some time between 460–361 BC. His ancient biographers, including Aristotle and Plato, praised him as a great and honoured physician, but it is uncertain whether he authored any of the collection of essays and texts known as the Hippocratic Corpus. The Corpus was compiled by many authors and absorbed the traditions of many of the Greek medical communities. The famous oath, for example, was probably Pythagorean (Lloyd, 1983). Hippocratic medicine radically departed from the religious and mystical traditions of healing and stressed that disease was a natural event, not caused by supernatural forces. For example, one treatise claims that epilepsy was not a sacred affliction but the result of natural causes (Longrigg, 1993).

The Hippocratic tradition concentrated on the patient rather than the disease and emphasized prevention. It used a system of dietetics to preserve and restore health through appropriate regimens for acquiring fitness and treating sickness. Its emphasis on health regimens was linked to a culture which revered an idealized body in a cult of athletics. Many Hippocratic authors linked their therapeutic regimens to the health of athletes. The Hippocratic tradition represented medicine as an empirical craft which adapted methods and healing regimens and whose prime therapeutic function was prognosis based on clinical observation (Smith, 1979). Greek doctors were identified to a great extent through their reputation, especially for their ability to predict the course of disease (Edelstein, 1967a). Hippocratic physiology assumed that the four essential elements of the physical universe were mirrored in the body by four fluids or humours: blood, black bile, yellow bile and phlegm. Each of the cosmic elements possessed certain qualities: fire was hot and dry, earth was cold and dry, air was hot and moist and water was cold and moist. Bodily health was maintained through the correct balance of humours and qualities controlled by the body's heat, which was generated through *pneuma*, or breath, and fuel, food and drink (Smith, 1979).

The Hippocratic tradition also recognized that health and disease were affected by season and the quality of environments. Several books on *epidemics* (visitations) provided clinical observations of numerous diseases and examined their external causes (Longrigg, 1992). The central Hippocratic text which analysed the environmental determinants of disease, *On Airs, Waters, Places*, discussed the effects of winds, the properties of waters and the effect of season upon human constitutions and the development of disease (Lloyd, 1983). The treatise divided diseases into those which were 'endemic', always present, and 'epidemic', which only occurred occasionally and excessively. The text resembled a 'how to' book, providing advice on environmental determinants of local endemnicity as a guide for colonization, suggesting that climate, soil and water were crucial. New settlements should avoid marshy lowlands and houses should be built on elevated areas to be warmed by the sun and catch salubrious winds (Longrigg, 1992). From about 800 BC, Greek expansion slowly edged along the Aegean towards the Black Sea and westward into Italy, Sicily and Spain. The treatise suggested that physicians should help to choose sites for settling new communities by judging their salubrious qualities. *On Airs, Waters, Places* served Greek physicians, who were itinerant craftsmen, as a reference work to help them cope with local diseases and assist successful prognosis as they travelled from one town to another (Edelstein, 1967a).

In post-Hippocratic times the conquests of the Macedonian king, Alexander the Great (356–323 BC) of the former Persian empire, reconfigured the political and social order of the ancient world. The influence of Greek culture and institutions spread from the borders of India to Libya. Hellenization was accepted by local elites in exchange for being allowed to maintain their political authority. Greek philosophy and medicine were spread by wandering philosophers and itinerant doctors throughout the Hellenistic world through institutions such as the gymnasium, a sort of club/academy, which became a common feature of even small cities. Itinerant doctors delivered lectures and spectacular demonstrations at the gymnasium (Philips, 1980). The intellectual and cultural metropolis of the Hellenistic world moved to the city of Alexandria, where the ancient lore of Egypt and the most dynamic elements of Greek civilization fused into one culture. In Alexandria innovative investigations into anatomy and physiology revealed new knowledge of the internal organs of the body (Staden, 1989). Hippocratic traditions continued to influence various Hellenistic medical sects, collectively described as rationalistic or dogmatic because they opposed one sect which rejected the role of theory altogether and stressed the need for therapeutics based purely on observation and experience. The Empiricists rejected humoralism and advanced the study of symptomatology, pharmacology and surgery (Edelstein, 1967c).

Under the influence of Greek physicians, Roman medicine equally emphasized the importance of personal regimens and dietetics to ward off disease. This was promoted, above all, by the most famous Greek physician of the Roman empire, Galen (c.129–200 AD), in his discussion of the 'natural' (innate constitutional), 'non-natural' (environmental), and 'preternatural' (pathological) causes of health and disease which produced variations in the pulse and affected the balance of humours within the body (Bylebyl, 1971). Galen adapted the philosophy of the humours into a system of physiology and pathology in which blood was regarded as the primary humour; all disease could be controlled or treated by its regulation. Dietetics, the system of dietary rules and protocols of personal hygiene, behaviour and exercise, was the way healthy humoral balance could be maintained. According to Galen, both innate causes of variation in the pulse – such as sex, temperament, weight, age, pregnancy, sleep, awakening, ambient air – and 'non-natural' or optional causes, such as hot and cold baths, large meals, wine and water, all had the potential to become pathological. Thus, he advised that regimens should be designed for the successful manipulation of the determinants of health such as air, food and drink, motion and rest, sleep and wakening, inanition and repletion, and accidents of the soul – or the passions (Nutton, 1981a).

Ideas about health and illness in the ancient world were concerned with the purity of both body and soul. Pre-Hippocratic cultures of mystical healing aimed to achieve states of grace through bodily cleanliness. Greek rationalism provided regimens to produce idealized forms of physical beauty. Considerations of health figured in the most utopian representations of the human condition in learned ancient cultures. Philosophies of health were developed by and for learned elites. Ancient environmentalism was also linked to mystical theories of salubrity until Greek rationalism turned it into a practical art to assist colonial settlement (Longrigg, 1993).

PUBLIC MEDICAL SERVICES

From ancient times, political states have been involved in the organization of medical services and the institutionalization of medical practice and education. Individual practitioners have been sponsored and regulated by political authorities in a number of different ways. In ancient Egyptian society, for example, a hierarchical organization of medical practice was controlled by the state with the court physicians at the top, led by the chief physician and a group of superintendents. Each was a specialist in particular diseases and each court physician was in charge of a single illness. Other types of physicians existed, including sorcerers, dentists, physicians to the military and physicians to the pyramid builders. At least one chief woman physician is known to have been an overseer to the pyramid builders (Estes, 1989). In China under the Chou Dynasty the government regulated medical education by providing provincial medical schools and annual examinations for those who wished to practise. The Chou imperial service employed salaried physicians to serve the imperial army or become specialist food physicians, physicians for simple diseases, ulcer physicians and physicians for animals (Garrison, 1929; Bray, 1988).

Collective medical services have also been institutionalized from antiquity. In ancient Mediterranean cultures temple precincts served as hospitals. In Egypt there were special institutions known as 'the House of Life' where medical texts were compiled and physicians received training (Estes, 1989). Similarly, in ancient Indo-China medical aid was available in temples and schools, and early travellers recorded hospitals, supported by the state and private endowment, which provided care and shelter for the sick and the poor (Garrison, 1929). In India, Buddhist charity made medical care widely available and the edicts of King Asoka (273–232 BC) suggest that he provided hospitals and dispensaries throughout his kingdom. Later travellers to India also told of hospitals for animals. Buddhism carried the Indian system of Ayurvedic medicine and the charitable provision of services to many other parts of the world which adopted it (Zysk, 1991). Buddhist missionaries travelled to Syria, Egypt, Greece, Tibet and China, but in India itself Ayurvedic medicine remained intimately linked to the Hindu religion (Zysk, 1985).

In Mediterranean Europe from about 600 BC individual cities began to appoint a physician who was paid an annual salary from local taxation, the *Iatricon*, but was still allowed to work for private fees. The earliest recorded is Democedes of Croton, who was appointed by Aegina, then Athens and later to the Persian court in the late sixth century. Physicians were appointed by the Assembly at Athens a hundred years later. It is not clear whether Democedes or any other civic physicians of the ancient world were required to provide any services by the civic authorities who employed them (Nutton, 1988). Plato stated that his doctors were appointed to public service after they had addressed the Assembly of Athens, but probably more for their rhetorical rather than their practical skills. Municipal doctors were provided with an *Iatreion* where they lived with their families and servants and had a consulting room, operating theatre and a dispensary. Ostensibly, town doctors were hired largely to serve the needy and it is possible that at the height of the Periculean democracy in the middle and late fifth century civic doctors in Athens provided free treatment to the poor (Cohn-Haft, 1956). The comic poet Aristophanes claimed that the payment of civic doctors ceased with the defeat of Athens by Sparta in 404 BC. The employment of public physicians, however, was continued by the civic authorities in the Hellenistic world which replaced the city-states of classical Greece. The services of these municipal doctors also included public health and legal medicine (Nutton, 1988; Nutton, 1981b).

Greek physicians emigrated throughout the ancient world, but from about the third century BC they began to fulfil a unique role in the rising European power following the death of Alexander, Rome. Initially a republic of yeoman farmers, Rome grew into an imperial power with a complex and vigorous combination of Greek and Roman culture forged through centuries of war. Unlike Greek urbanized bourgeois merchants and adventurers, Roman farmers preferred the practical over the abstract and idealized the pastoral life, even though they constructed cities of unprecedented size and complexity. Early Roman society despised the practice of medicine for fees and Latin authors such as Cato and Pliny recorded that émigré Greek physicians were treated with great suspicion (Jackson, 1988). Cato described indigenous Roman medicine as based on charms, chants, prayers and herbs and vegetables, including cabbage. It was a craft practised by slaves and women (Jones, 1957). However, the influence of Hellenistic medicine in Latin urban centres allows us to make a distinction between urban medical sophistication and traditional rural healing. Greek medicine practised in the countryside was as magical as that of Roman rural communities. In rural Latin households the patriarchal head of the household was responsible for supervising the medical affairs of his family, slaves and animals. Cato (234–149 BC) thundered in the Senate against Greek physicians, accusing them of poisoning the sick. He claimed that Greek doctors were dedicated to killing all barbarians through the administration of drugs, and that they considered Romans barbarians. Despite Cato's warnings, Greek physicians became increasingly influential in Roman society as it became more affluent and diverse. Roman citizens eagerly purchased the therapeutic services and health advice of consulting physicians, some of whom flourished, such as Asclepiades, the founder of the methodist school of medical thought (Jackson, 1988). Methodist therapeutics were based upon the efficiency of systematic inference as opposed to using the healing power of nature. Asclepiades rejected humoralism in favour of solidism, and developed the corpuscular theory into an atomistic analysis of health and disease. Methodism was a holistic doctrine of medicine which advocated the classic Coan regime of air, light, dietetics, exercise, hydropathy and massage as the principal route to health maintenance. It opposed the empiricist emphasis on the locality of the disease and its local treatment, and stressed the importance of understanding the health of the whole patient (Jackson, 1988).

PATRICIAN COMFORT AND THE ROMAN ADMINISTRATION

Perhaps it was the practical turn of the Roman frame of mind which made it suspicious of the conceptual abstractions of medicine and instead to favour the direct effect upon health of sanitary improvement. Sanitary reform was facilitated in Roman society by the growth of a bureaucratic imperial state and the development of sophisticated civil engineering to provide rapid communications. The stability of the vast expanding empire required bureaucratic organization and direct routes of communications. Road-building enhanced the science of civil engineering and bureaucratic government enhanced the science of public administration (Robinson, 1992). Both of these made the unprecedented development of Roman technology in water supply engineering and sanitary administration possible. By the second century AD Rome had fresh water delivered to it via aqueducts. Many ancient Roman cities had sophisticated baths, piped water, drainage systems and public pay lavatories located in the busiest sections of towns (Bruun, 1991). Care was taken about the salubrity of settlement sites. In *On Architecture* (27 BC) Vitruvius Pollio stressed the need to test the environmental quality of an area before establishing new communities. To test the soil, animals were often left to graze on the land of a prospective site and then slaughtered. If their livers appeared to be greenish-yellow the area was regarded as unhealthy. The Romans were especially concerned with the bad effects of swampy grounds and marsh air. The poet Marcus Terrentius Varro – a contemporary of Vitruvius – noted in 36 BC that tiny creatures bred in these places which were beyond the naked eye but entered the mouth and nose and caused disease. Vitruvius added that when sea water mixed with marshes, towns located near them might remain healthy (Nutton, 1983). The Roman historian Pliny pointed out that some diseases resulted from the hazards of various occupations, the dull pallor of gold-miners, for example, or the varicose veins of augurs and the diseases of blacksmiths. Galen treated copper-sulphate miners working in Cyprus who almost suffocated from the overpowering stench of the vitriolic fluid that they transported from the mine (Rosen, 1958).

The administration of public health services in Rome extended to the government supervision of public baths, water supply, street cleaning and the regulation of the sale of spoiled food. However, the Roman state provided a salubrious environment for the rich and privileged only (Robinson, 1992). The poor lived in overcrowded squalid conditions in burgeoning cities. In the same way, in the early empire only the rich and privileged employed the émigré Greek physicians, while the poor continued to rely on folk and religious healing which had been the characteristic medical care of the Republic. Slaves were served by healers who themselves were slaves. The employment of physicians differed in the eastern and western halves of the early empire. More opportunity for employment existed for doctors among the bourgeoisie of the more highly urbanized East. The social and economic opportunities improved for doctors in the western empire, however, as Greek culture enjoyed a renaissance. In the early years of the empire Greek doctors obtained Roman citizenship in the East. With Hellenization doctors began to achieve citizenship in the western empire as well. The move from non-citizen to citizen doctors also reflected the general reduction of slaves and the devaluation of Roman citizenship throughout the empire. By the second century AD the number of physicians had expanded, aided by privileges given to doctors such as exemption from having soldiers billeted upon them and tax immunities. The expansion of medical practice encouraged specialization and local civil authorities became involved in the recognition of qualified practitioners. In the early second century doctors were given immunity from taxation by most civil authorities. From about 150 AD Antoninus Pius decreed that no more than five to ten doctors in a large city should be eligible for tax immunity. Doctors employed by municipalities were salaried to administer to the poor but could also undertake private fee-paying practice (Nutton, 1981b).

CHARITY, FAITH AND THE SICK POOR

From the late second century to the early fourth century, the dominant belief in the location of divine power shifted. Access to the deity was equally available to all who believed that pagan gods might converse with humans personally through their dreams or through the oracle (Brown, 1978). If someone believed that they might possess special access to heavenly powers, however, then they kept it to themselves in Antonine society. In a social order driven by a relentlessly competitive culture of ambition but controlled by a model of parity, it was wise to fear the envy of enemies (Brown, 1992). For example, the advantages of accumulating vast wealth were hidden behind face-saving humility expressed through beneficent construction of public institutions. Equally, acquiring the status of divine preference led to walking a fine line to avoid the accusation of sorcery. Within such a social structure of belief, the relationship between healing and religion was tricky. Ascelpius regularly visited Aelius Aristides in his dreams and provided him with all the health and therapeutic advice he needed to turn him into a profound hypochondriac. Aristides was able to boast about the superiority he gained through his special relationship to the god, but he had to pay for it by succumbing to the crippling regime of an invalid (Brown, 1988).

By the time of the death of the first Christian emperor, Constantine, social disruption caused by the culture of *philotimia* resulted in the breakdown of the model of parity as a force of social regulation (Brown, 1978). Under these circumstances a religious system which was based on the idea that one man was God made flesh, and which also believed that some humans were endowed with special access to heavenly powers, flourished. Within a less rigidly traditionalist atmosphere, some individuals could now claim to act as special mediums between earthly and heavenly powers and escape the accusation of sorcery. A hierarchy of the 'friends of God' could begin to form, with distinguished status reserved for bishops and holy men (Brown, 1992). Healing, particularly in its quintessential Christian form through miracles which imitated those of the physician to the world himself, was just one possible expression of the new domi-nant idea of holiness. Healing acquired a new status in Christian doctrine as an act of charity, an art practised out of religious devotion rather than a technical speciality and a subject of objective enquiry. Above all, curing was an act of divine benevolence and faith was the ultimate therapeutic resource. Disease became a punishment for sin, demonic possession or witchcraft. While the Greeks had revered the healthy body, Christian doctrine despised the flesh and physical desires. However, the body was the temple of the soul and therefore it was important to strengthen it physically as much as possible in order to resist evil (Brown, 1988). Christ's performance of healing miracles took place within a long tradition of Jewish medicine. The Mosaic Law advocated bodily and spiri-tual health, and King Solomon was credited with magical and medical powers. By 400 AD many Jewish communities were served by a physician. Christianity extended the Jewish tradition of healing, although the New Testament promoted a number of different new attitudes towards the subject. While healing was regarded as an act of pious charity, suffering was a divine trial, a privileged opportunity to demonstrate devout faith. Hippocratic medicine could easily be absorbed into the model of charity, but Christian emblems could equally be used as magical amulets, such as the miraculous powers of holy oil, relics or marks of special providence. Monastic medicine used the power of prayer, incantations and the miraculous therapeutics of the deity itself on the one hand, and earthly dietetics, hygienic regimens, drugs, bleeding and simple surgery on the other. Monks practised as doctors both within and beyond their communities. Secular healers were sometimes employed by monastic orders. Earthly medicine prac-tised within the Christian world, however, more often took the form of the provision of shelter, nursing and general care of the sick, the destitute and the shunned (Ferngren, 1992).

The Romans established *valetudinaria*, infirmaries, for sick slaves from the first century AD. Occasionally these institutions were also used by free Romans. Military hospitals were established at large fortresses mainly in the less urbanized western half of the empire and at the Danube frontier in the early third century (Davies, 1989). After 250 AD, when Augustus's mobile army, backed by local levies, no longer needed such bases, the sick and wounded were treated in temporary field hospitals (Miller, 1985). While hospitals were provided for slaves and soldiers there was hardly any provision for the poor in Roman society apart from the availability of shrines. Roman administration disintegrated with the decline of the empire and was succeeded by the development of new kingdoms in western Europe with an increasingly reduced centralized state remaining in Byzantium. In the West from the fifth century a vast array of complex geographical, ethnological and political changes took place in which the culture of Barbarian invaders, classical heritage and the teachings of Christian religion awkwardly moulded together. In the period from about 500–1000, the Church came to dominate 'learned' healing, and magical beliefs and folk medicine flourished within Paganism (Kroll and Bachrach, 1986).

Under the influence of Christianity, institutionalized charity expanded, providing various forms of care and shelter for the poor and sick. A long Jewish tradition of hospitality was extended by Christian care of the lonely and needy through the distribution of alms, supervised by special deacons, and the provision of food, shelter and nursing for the destitute and the sick. After the legalization of Christianity in the fourth century, Bishop Leontius (344–358) founded a number of hostels (*xenodokeia*) in the eastern empire at Antioch and the nearby spa of Daphne. Outside the walls of Caesarea, St Basil created a sort of village-annex which received the sick, the leprous and the poor. Strangers could also receive care there. By the fifth and sixth centuries, such institutions had become widespread, with average towns in the East possessing at least one or two hospitals. Sometimes these establishments were no larger than one room in a large house, but occasionally they were considerably more elaborate (Allen, 1990).

In the West the first institution devoted to medical care was founded by Fabiola in Rome in the fourth century after he had seen similar establishments in the East. Few hospitals were subsequently established throughout Italy or beyond. In the East hospitals became ever larger and more specialized. Edessa possessed a women's hospital in 400 AD and in 600 AD Antioch and Constantinople had hospitals with up to 600 beds, divided into male and female wards. After the death of Charlemagne in 814, larger hospitals began to decline through loss of revenue, and in their place monasteries began to provide small accommodations for the sick within their own grounds. The tiny monastic infirmaries were often simply a small house which provided shelter, food and general nursing for the poor and the lame. The monastery infirmaries also had a pharmacy and garden of medicinal plants and gave safe haven and care to travellers and pilgrims (MacKinney, 1937).

Various levels of medical care were available in a number of different institutions, and surgery was performed in some of them, at least from the seventh century. Their various names – hospice, hostel, poor-house, sick-house, hospital, etc. – reflected how a diversity of establishments were developed under the order of Christian charity in this period, with overlapping functions but all providing some form of welfare or other. Later, in the Islamic world, hospitals were created by rulers and public officials in urban centres, such as the Caliph Harun-al Rashid and Caliph al-Muktadir of Baghdad. Both set up hospitals there in the ninth and tenth centuries. A third hospital, founded at Baghdad in 970, had a staff of twenty-five physicians who taught medical students as well as caring for the sick. One hospital, founded in Cairo in 1283, had separate sections for fever patients, the wounded and those with eye diseases, and special rooms for women. However, if under Islam hospital provision and political power were clearly linked, then for Christianity in Byzantium, and to some extent in the West, the provision of welfare became a source of social power facilitating its ideological expansion and rise to cultural domination (Miller, 1985). Within this context a broader conceptualization of society included the poor as significant social actors. The social relations of access to political power changed shape as the Christian Church became increasingly involved in the formation of states in the aftermath of Roman decline. As a result, providing welfare for the sick-poor may have been one route to power; controlling their ability to spread disease was another.

2   Pestilence and public order in medieval Europe

Cities emptied out following the disintegration of the Roman empire in the west (Nicholas, 1997a). In the high middle ages urbanization, however, gathered momentum. From the eleventh to the fifteenth centuries new patterns of economic relations began to reconfigure the structure of European societies as feudalism gave way to the rise of social systems based upon free exchange (Britnell, 1986). The trading societies of the late medieval world encouraged the growth of towns and cities (Nicholas, 1997b). Cultural preoccupations with health in this period began to focus less upon the comfort of elites and more upon the dangerous diseases of denser populations. The diseased poor were more than simply an ideological threat to elite civilization, and health care acquired a new political status with the rise of urbanization. They had already become the objects of Christian welfare provision; now their behaviour in relation to the spread of disease became subject to regulation by civil states (Palmer, 1982; Richards, 1977).

The welfare of the needy was taken up by devout secular philanthropists with the approval of the Church. Philanthropists and political rulers began to found hospitals in the late medieval period with the sanction of the Pope. In 1145, Guy of Montpelier founded the Holy Ghost Hospital, which was approved by the Pope in 1198. Pope Innocent III himself built a hospital of the Holy Ghost in Rome in 1204 and sanctioned their establishment throughout Europe. Hospitals were also established by several knightly orders along routes taken by Crusaders, the most famous of whom were the Knights of St John, or Hospitallers, who set up hospitals from Malta to Germany (Miller, 1978). Cities and guilds of the late middle ages established hospitals as symbols of civic pride and progress. In the late medieval period, hospital philanthropy acquired special social status. It became a goal of many princes and counts to found a shelter for the poor, the infirm and the disabled (Horden, 1988).

MEDIEVAL INSTITUTIONALIZATION OF MEDICAL
LEARNING AND REGULATION OF PRACTICE

With the decline of the Roman empire, the classical tradition of learning survived in the Byzantine empire based at Constantinople. From here the Greco-Roman tradition of medicine was passed on to Arab physicians through Syriac translations prepared by Nestorian and Monophysite Christians, sectarians who were driven out of Byzantium because of their heresies and settled in Persia. By the tenth century the majority of Greek medical works had been translated into Syriac, Hebrew or Arabic (Scarborough (ed.), 1983). By this time, however, Arab medicine was undergoing transformations of its own. New generations of Moslem physicians began to establish their independence from the classical tradition while still drawing upon ancient doctrines (Rosenthal, 1990; Conrad, 1995). The Persian physician Rhazes (865–925) is perhaps the most famous of all for differentiating smallpox from measles and other exanthemata and for developing radically new therapies such as mercurial ointment and using animal gut for sewing up wounds. Rhazes produced numerous texts which contained some of the first original and innovative medical analyses since classical times (Conrad, 1992). Equally renowned was another Persian physician, Avicenna (980–1037), who was as much a philosopher as a medical theorist. He attempted to synthesize the medical doctrines of Hippocrates and Galen with the biology of Aristotle in a five-volume work which he called *Canon*. As its title indicates, it was intended to be a definitive work of immutable medical law, an absolutely authoritative dogma. He illustrated his conceptual synthesis with clinical histories and their therapeutic indications. The *Canon* became an authority for medical teachers and practitioners until the end of the seventeenth century (Cameron, 1930; Siraisi, 1987). Jewish medicine also flourished in the medieval period, with innovative theorists such as the Rabbi Moses ben Maimon, Maimonides (1135–1204), from Cordova in twelfth-century Islamic Spain. Maimonides wrote a treatise on personal hygiene for the Sultan Saladin which became a model for self-help health manuals up to the nineteenth century (Bar-Sela, Hoff and Faris, 1964). He wrote other advice books, such as *Ars Coeundi* on sexual intercourse and another on poisons and antidotes with descriptions of clinical cases. All of his works were independent of the classical tradition and critical of Galen. The advances made in Arabian chemistry in the medieval period were reflected in numerous new texts on *materia medica* (Conrad, 1995).

Throughout the late middle ages, the Greco-Roman and medieval Arabic medical traditions were introduced into western Europe through scholastic latinization of Arabic editions of classical medical texts (Siraisi, 1990). The most notable translators were Constantius Africanus (1020–1087), who worked at Salerno, and Gerard of Cremona (1140–1187), who worked at Toledo. In this period the practice of medicine gained a new professional status and institutionalized training (Bullough, 1966). Medicine was studied by lay students at the school at Salerno from the middle of the tenth century, probably as the result of the hospital founded there by the Benedictines in the seventh century (Kristeller,

1945). By the middle of the eleventh century, Salerno, in co-operation with the Benedictine monastery at Montecassino, began to emerge as a centre of theoretical learning based on Greek and Roman medical sources. Like Montpellier, the second centre of medical education founded in 1181 close to the borders of Islamic Spain, it combined Arabism with an empirical orientation. Its standards were widely revered and its curriculum imitated, for example by the University of Paris, founded in 1110 (Kristeller, 1945). The first universities established in the twelfth and thirteenth centuries extended learned study beyond the walls of the monasteries and were run by the lay clergy as well as the monastic orders. They taught law, theology, philosophy and medicine. Celibacy was required of university teachers in some cases, such as Paris, until 1452. The universities set new scholastic standards for medical education which dominated the future structure of medical practice in Europe (Coban, 1975). Scholastic medicine in the late middle ages was almost entirely derivative of the classical tradition, the only innovative influence coming from Islamic theory (Ottosson, 1984). But the institutionalization of medical education imposed a new professional structure on practice. Medical men trained in the universities were the first to attain the title 'doctor' and they established new professional guilds and associations. All university-trained physicians were clerics, and thus when the Council of Tours declared in 1163 that 'the church does not shed blood', surgery was relegated to a manual craft practised by barbers and other craftsmen (Amundsen, 1979; Allbutt, 1905). While university medicine established a new professional hierarchy, learned physicians remained a tiny minority among medical practitioners, most of whom still acquired their skills through apprenticeship and practical experience (Siraisi, 1990).

Along with university training the late medieval period witnessed the development of the first medical legislation regulating practice. King Roger II of Sicily, for example, ruled that those wishing to practise medicine should pass state examinations (Garcia-Ballester *et al.*, 1994). Similar legislation covering qualifications and licensing was passed elsewhere in Italy, Spain and Germany (Park, 1985). Licensing and qualification became increasingly important as the practice of hiring town physicians spread throughout the late medieval and Renaissance periods. In Italy, many small towns and rural districts employed municipal physicians by the fourteenth century, largely because there was an insufficient supply of indigenous private practitioners and therefore local authorities had to attract physicians from outside. As the supply of trained private practitioners increased in post-medieval times, the practice of employing *medici condotti* dramatically declined. Town physicians were employed for attending wounds and injuries and providing health advice (Palmer, 1981). But in late medieval German provinces, university-trained *physicus* were employed by local authorities to do more than simply attend to individuals. The *physicus* had to make medical reports on injuries and other forensic issues for the local courts and to supervise public health administration. In fourteenth-century Spain, the municipalities of the kingdom of Aragon made extensive contracts with physicians to provide health advice to the local community and to remain permanently in residence (Lopez-Pinero, 1981).

Despite the slow expansion of the medical profession and the sporadic employment of town physicians, by far the majority of the population dosed themselves and tried to keep themselves healthy. After the establishment of printing, traditional health advice and healing remedies were reproduced in many popular manuals which flooded the market. Apart from reproducing all the classical theories about diet and personal hygiene, they also offered advice on domestic cleanliness and healthy housing. 'Moderation in everything' was the essence of their philosophy (Arano, 1976; Palmer, 1991). Another resource for individual hygiene was public bathhouses, which became widespread by the thirteenth century, often as places of amusement with wine, women and song. As we shall discuss below, during the course of the syphilis epidemic from the end of the fifteenth century, the bathhouse fell into disfavour and was gradually abandoned until it was revived in the modern period (Vigarello, 1988).

DISEASE AND THE SOCIAL ORDER

Methods of personal and public hygiene were interwoven into schemes for preventing the spread of disease and warding off sickness in ancient societies, in an effort to provide a salubrious spiritual and material environment for elites. Both individual and collective behaviour was regulated for the benefit of elite community health. As social orders began to change in the late medieval period, approaches to disease prevention faced new challenges. Leprosy and, later, epidemics of plague and syphilis threatened to destabilize more than just the comfort of the patrician classes. The diseased poor began to take on new significance as their numbers grew and densities increased in urban environments, leading to new attempts to isolate the infectious from healthy society through the excommunication of lepers from the community.

The diseases of the ancient world are difficult to determine, but evidence points toward the persistent prevalence of smallpox, typhoid, diphtheria, cholera, typhus, anthrax, scarlet fever, measles, epilepsy, trachoma and gonorrhoea. Malaria was a prominent disease, frequently referred to by numerous witnesses (Grmeck, 1989). As new methods of agricultural production developed in northern Europe from the early middle ages, however, new disease regimes began to dominate. The population of Europe is believed to have increased threefold between 800 to 1300. Increased agricultural production supported this demographic growth, but larger populations placed greater demands upon resources and diseases of dietary deficiency expanded throughout the middle ages for the majority of the poor peasantry, who were often hungry and lacked sufficient housing, clothing and fuel. Populations were sometimes devastated by famines caused by crop failures. In antiquity and the early middle ages, there is evidence that while as many females and males reached the age of fifteen overall, the life expectancy of females was much lower. A combination of death in childbirth and higher undernutrition probably accounts for this. In the late middle ages a surplus of women developed over men. Throughout the period between

500–1500, the average age of death remained around thirty-five years. Malnutrition and undernutrition do not necessarily enhance the spread of infectious disease but do account for other types of sicknesses reaching epidemic proportions, such as rickets, scurvy and pellagra (Walter and Schofield, 1989). One disease directly produced by crop disaster was ergotism, St Anthony's Fire, which resulted when whole communities consumed rye infected with the ergot fungus. Epidemic waves of this disease occurred from the ninth century, but it flourished in the tenth, especially in the Loire and eastern French provinces (Haller, 1993).

Changing patterns of agricultural production in the medieval period produced greater density of population in the West. Urbanization also expanded as a result of increased trade with the densely urbanized societies of the Middle East (Flinn, 1981; Rotberg and Rabb (eds), 1985; Kunke, 1993). These social, economic and demographic factors combined to create new opportunities for the spread of infections, the most prominent of which throughout the middle ages were plague, leprosy, tuberculosis and the 'English Sweats', now widely accepted as influenza, which first appeared in 1485 at the time that Richard III was defeated at Bosworth (Wear, 1995). Evidence from excavations of skeletons in Germany supports the argument that tuberculosis increased with urbanization between 1000 and 1348. The custom among French and English kings to cure scrofula by touching its victims testified to its significance. Tuberculosis of the lymph nodes in the neck became commonly known as 'the king's evil' or 'the royal disease'. Edward I of England touched 1,736 scrofula victims between 1289 and 1290, 983 between 1299 and 1300, and 1,219 between 1303 and 1304 (Bloch, 1973). Tuberculosis is caused by *Mycobacterium tuberculosis*, which is the same genus as the agent which causes leprosy, *Mycobacterium leprae*. Exposure to TB confers immunity against leprosy, and one explanation for the decline of leprosy in the late medieval period may have been increased contraction of tuberculosis among small children who survived to adulthood. Thus the increase in tuberculosis, resulting from urbanization, could have caused the decline of leprosy (Carmichael, 1993).

Leprosy, however, was responsible for some of the greatest suffering throughout the medieval period. It afflicted many societies from biblical times, but was relatively rare. It could possibly have been brought to the West by Alexander's army, returning from India in 327–326 BC. It spread from the sixth century as trade increased, reaching very high levels by the twelfth and thirteenth centuries and then declining throughout the fourteenth. Numerous chroniclers, such as Gregory of Tours and Marius, Bishop of Avrenches, record epidemics of leprosy in the sixth century. Skeletons from fifth- and sixth-century England display signs of lepromatous leprosy in the skull and limbs. Gilbertus Anglicus wrote of squinantia in the twelfth and thirteenth centuries, and John of Aberdeen identified a similar epidemic of 'death by suffocation' in the fourteenth century. According to some estimates it affected 1 per cent of the population of western Europe (Richards, 1977).

Among Leviticus's elaborate rules governing spiritual and physiological uncleanness, there are many instructions about contact with individuals afflicted with skin diseases. Lepers were segregated from the ancient Hebrew community. The Talmudic code for isolating the contagious was applied by the medieval church authorities to control the spread of leprosy. The Council of Lyons restricted the free association of lepers with the community in 583, and church councils elsewhere thereafter followed suit. Anglo-Saxons did not necessarily separate lepers, however, because the bones of victims are found in general cemeteries, although some leper houses were established by the eleventh century. The disease reached its peak in England in the first half of the thirteenth century when 53 hospitals were constructed. Altogether 200 institutions were established in England but no new ones were built after the fifteenth century (Richards, 1977).

Pest houses, or lazarettos, were set up throughout western Europe; in France alone there were about 2,000 by the thirteenth century. In the Danish cemetery at Naestved 650 patients were buried between 1250 and 1550. An estimated 19,000 lazarettos existed in Europe as a whole. Lazar houses were built downwind from towns; they usually lodged six to twelve people but could be built for one victim alone. Bishops and abbots endowed leprosaria with income from tithes, rents and tolls, and in some areas, such as northern Italy, lepers were a civic responsibility (Palmer, 1982). The social consequences of contracting leprosy were as fearful as the disease itself. The Third Lateran Council in 1179 ordered lepers to be segregated from the rest of society. Outcast from society for life, lepers were considered socially dead long before they actually experienced physical death. This was ritualized in a ceremony where the leper would stand in a grave as a priest threw earth over him and declared him 'dead unto the world but alive unto Christ'. A distinguished fourteenth-century novel by Edith Simon describes the solemn mass which ritualized a leper's pitiful excommunication. The leper lived on but was legally and socially dead. His relatives inherited his property, and he was covered in a cloak. carried a bell and kept his distance from the community on penalty of death. A healthy wife could not, however, divorce an infected husband (Brody, 1974).

The decision to diagnose leprosy was taken extremely seriously and anyone under suspicion was examined by special commissions consisting of a bishop and several other clerics, together with a leper considered to be a 'specialist'. Eventually physicians were included in these commissions. John of Gaddesden suggested in the fourteenth century that only once the face had been destroyed by the disease should an individual be judged a leper (O'Neill, 1993). Because the diagnosis had such serious consequences it is possible that it was actually conservative. The leper cemetery at Naestved showed that 80 per cent of the 650 skeletons had lepromatous leprosy, whereas only a very small proportion of cases in modern times involve the bones, occurring only among the most severely affected (O'Neill, 1993). Excommunication from the community was not necessarily motivated by fears of physical contagion as much as the reputation of leprosy as being a punishment for lechery and other sins (Gilman, 1988; Pelling, 1993). Its association with unusually sexually active behaviour may have resulted from its confusion with syphilis, along with a variety of other skin diseases. Modern lepers also show a high incidence of syphilis, which suggests an unknown affinity between the two diseases. While the Black Death has traditionally been used to explain the decline of leprosy in the fourteenth century, it is unclear how this could have occurred. Lepers in the advanced stage can be immune to plague. It is more likely, as mentioned above, that the rise in tuberculosis in urban centres was directly related to the decline of the disease.

Isolation of victims of lethal infectious diseases continues to be a prophylactic tool up to the present day. The figure of the leper remained a powerful metaphor for the social stigma which continued to penalize victims of infectious diseases. The corruption of the flesh was to persistently viewed as the physical mark of a corrupt soul (Camporasi, 1988; Gilman, 1988). Nowhere was this more powerfully represented than in the rise of epidemic syphilis at the end of the fifteenth century. But methods of isolation, and the political impact of controlling the spread of disease among the poor, expanded significantly as the late middle ages and early modern period faced an even greater demographic threat, bubonic plague.

Some medieval towns grew up around old Roman settlements and others moved to new sites for political reasons (Nicholas, 1997a). Every city depended upon its encircling fortifications for security and consequently suffered from overcrowding as their populations expanded within the confined space (Nicholas, 1997b). With the decline of Roman municipal administration the task of providing a public water supply was often taken up by the Church. The Franciscan friary, for example, supplied Southampton with water from 1290. But various municipalities claimed to have been at least partially responsible for ensuring the water supply, such as Dublin, Basel and Bruges. Municipalities attempted to limit pollution of drinking water by preventing citizens from throwing dead animals or refuse into streams and rivers. Tanners were not permitted to wash animal skins and dyers were prohibited from emptying their dye residues into drinking water sources. By the late middle ages, municipal sanitary regulations covered street cleaning, refuse removal and restrictions on the slaughter of animals. Urban dwellers still kept livestock in their dwellings, which exacerbated the problems of refuse accumulation. Some municipalities tried to introduce systematic sewage removal. Milan, for example, had ordinances regulating the building of cesspools and drains. Rules to govern general social and commercial behaviour were also instituted by some urban medieval communities to regulate the sale of food, clothing, pottery and the cleanliness of the market-place. By the fourteenth century some cities, such as Zurich, Florence and Strasbourg, enforced commercial hygiene through a municipal inspectorate of the market-place (Rosen, 1958).

If leprosy had indicated the possible threat which contagion might pose to expanding urban societies, epidemic bubonic plague produced a new relationship between disease and social disorder in late medieval Europe. Bubonic plague arrived in western Europe when its existing economic and political structures were already fracturing (Cambell (ed.), 1991). The social upheaval caused by the initial impact of the epidemic powerfully reinforced these trends, bringing about major economic and political changes (Ziegler, 1997; Gottfried, 1983). The intermittent return of epidemic plague throughout the following three hundred years stimulated the growth of bureaucratic government dedicated to maintaining social stability and public order, which enhanced the power of civil political authorities. Epidemic syphilis drew out an equally stark relationship between disease and moral pollution in Renaissance culture. Syphilis stimulated moral as well as social panic in Renaissance societies, which responded with new values regarding behavioural discipline (Quetel, 1990; Arrizabalaga, 1993). If ancient societies sought to banish disease in order to banish barbarism, late medieval and early modern societies pursued the civilizing process through the creation of new forms of cultural and political discipline.

THE BLACK DEATH AND THE END OF FEUDALISM

Some of the greatest suffering in the middle ages was caused by bubonic plague, which continued to haunt western Europe until the eighteenth century (Park, 1993). Plague also stimulated the earliest direct involvement of civil government in the control and prevention of epidemic disease. It links the late medieval with the early modern world in a unique way, demonstrating a powerful continuity over a period of four hundred years.

Plague is caused by the bacillus *Pasteurella pestis* or *Yersinia pestis*, named after Alexandre Yersin (1863–1943) who first described it in 1894. It is an internal parasite of rodents, which is transmitted from host to host via fleas. When feeding on the blood of an infected rodent, the feeding tube, or proventriculus, of some fleas becomes blocked with *Y. pestis*. Unable to imbibe, the flea then regurgitates the bolus of bacteria and infects another host. Other fleas which do not have a feeding tube excrete the bacteria, which enters the blood stream of a host when it scratches. Some rodents can survive and reproduce while still being infected with the disease, but when an ecological disturbance occurs it brings susceptible animals in contact with the disease and an epizootic – an epidemic among animals – results. Transmission to human hosts occurs when an epizootic has produced high mortality among rodents and the flea population seeks new feeding grounds. The rodents and fleas largely involved in human plague are the black rat, *rattus rattus*, and its fleas, *xenopyslla cheopis*, although the human flea, *pulex irritans*, can transmit severe septicaemia plague from human to human. Healthy humans cannot normally carry *Y. pestis* and cannot pass it on to other hosts, thus plague cannot be sustained in human populations and become endemic. Human epidemics of plague require a rodent epizootic to precipitate them. The action of *Y. pestis* in humans can rapidly lead to complete circulatory collapse and defeats both cellular and humoral immunity, which means that 60 per cent of those infected will normally die within ten days if not treated. Once the organism enters a human host, the area of the flea bite blackens and produces a carbuncle. The lymphatic system drains the infection to the regional lymph gland, which becomes gorged with blood as macrophages and white blood cells attempt to ingest the organisms. This process produces the characteristic buboes in the neck, armpits or the groin. If the organism reaches the lungs, the victim coughs up highly virulent bacteria which will be rapidly absorbed by the mucous membranes of any other person close by. When bubonic plague takes a pneumonic form, the spread of the disease is extremely rapid and nearly 100 per cent fatal. The disease can proceed in an individual too rapidly for the body's defence mechanisms to even begin to counter it. It then becomes a bloodborne, or septicaemia, plague and the patient becomes comatose and dies without any buboes having had time to form. Epidemics of bubonic plague often involve some pneumonic and septicaemia expressions of the disease which necessarily spread more rapidly and fatally (Arno, 1995; Carmichael, 1993a).

Vaccines against plague were developed in the 1920s and 1930s, and were sufficiently effective to reduce mortality to a minimum among the Allied forces during World War II, despite the fact that troops were often occupying plague-infected areas. Pesticides became a major feature of prevention once the true mechanism of transmission was known. Unfortunately, early pesticides were also lethal to humans and domestic and farm animals, but DDT, developed in 1938, killed rat fleas and was not toxic to other populations. Yersin developed an anti-plague serum from horses which remained the only therapeutic until sulphonamide drugs were developed in the 1930s. Penicillin cured plague in the laboratory but was ineffective against the live disease in the body. The antibiotic streptomycin, developed in 1941, finally proved lethal to the plague bacillus and by 1950 two further antimicrobials, tetracyclines and chloramphenicols, were used to supplement streptomycin (Arno, 1995; Carmichael, 1993a).

Records of plague exist from biblical times, but the first well-documented epidemic occurred in 542 during the reign of the Byzantine emperor Justinian, and is consequently referred to as the Plague of Justinian. The epidemic reached western Europe by 547, when it was described by Bishop Gregory of Tours. It continued to appear in virulent bursts for the following two hundred years. A second wave began in the middle of the fourteenth century and initiated four hundred years of sporadic epidemic episodes throughout Europe. The first episode of this cycle appeared in the Crimea in 1346 and shortly afterwards at Constantinople. It spread through the Middle East, the Mediterranean, western and northern Europe by 1350 and moved on through Eastern Europe between 1350 and 1353. Witnesses described the dramatic impact of the epidemic, which became commonly called the Black Death (Ziegler, 1997; Bridbury, 1973). There was extensive mortality, with whole villages being either wiped out or abandoned. Rapid high mortality made smaller settlements no longer viable and surviving populations relocated to towns and cities (Ziegler, 1997; Gottfried, 1983). One of the best accounts of the fourteenth-century epidemic was made by the medieval physician and surgeon Guy de Chauliac, who described the presence of all three forms of plague (Park, 1993).

Population growth from the early middle ages led to the clearing of arable land and rapid development of overcrowded cities (Smith (ed.), 1984). The epidemic could have been stimulated by the after-effects of a series of crop failures and famines, when rats abandoned empty granaries and fled to human households in urban centres, where they thrived in the squalid and overcrowded conditions. The human population, weakened by hunger, became easy victims to the disease, which could account for the devastating impact of the fourteenth-century epidemic (Arno, 1995). But this explanation is not entirely satisfactory, since the hearty and strong succumbed as frequently as the weak (Twigg, 1984).

Some early studies of mortality from the Black Death have suggested that in 1348 over 42 million Europeans perished. Recent estimates believe this to be greatly exaggerated, placing mortality rates closer to 20 million and ranging between 30 and 50 per cent in different areas of Europe, with towns such as Florence, Sienna, Orvieto and San Gimigniano probably losing about 50 to 60 per cent of their population (Park, 1993). The traumatic effect of losing one-third of the population brought about major changes in the social and economic order of European societies. The Black Death arrived in Europe at a time when medieval populations had outgrown their productive capacity. Feudalism was already in a crisis, which was exacerbated by the epidemic. These conditions maximized the disease impact, which subsequently assisted in undermining traditional political authority, thinning out existing oligarchies, levelling feudal barriers to economic growth and creating a demand for labour. Plague thus assisted in intensifying the structural forces of transition in Europe (Ziegler, 1997; Gottfried, 1983). The Black Death contributed to the disintegration of feudalism in England by creating a labour shortage. Traditional land–labour relations were never the same again. Landowners could not tie their workers and prevent them moving on to better-paid employment. With depopulation from such high mortality, the demand for labour raised its economic value and encouraged geographical mobility. As traditional systems of authority broke down with the disappearance of villeinage, serfdom and vassalage, the basic economic conditions for free-market labour mobility began to emerge (Ormrod and Lindley (eds), 1996). Apart from the broad effects of demographic change upon the political and economic order of feudal society, the Black Death stimulated a wide variety of social responses, including brutal persecution of scapegoat populations, and new initiatives in disease prevention by civic governments.

For those who could afford it, the immediate response to plague was to migrate to a safe haven until the epidemic had passed. Christian authorities endorsed flight, but the Islamic doctrine forbade it, claiming that the plague was the will of God to which believers must subject themselves (Dols, 1977). Even so, in the Islamic world flight was often resorted to (Conrad, 1992). For Muslims the plague was the will of God, but for Christians it was the wrath of God, divine retribution for the sinfulness of men. Plague thus stimulated ever more elaborate rituals of Christian penance, such as a new cult of public flagellation (Camporasi, 1988). Beginning in Italy but later throughout Europe, little processions of flagellants whipped themselves in public and preached repentance. Pope Clement VI denounced them as heretical because of their radically critical view of the Church. Flagellation was intended as a prophylactic against the disease and was sometimes associated with another Christian response to the Black Death, the horrifying persecution of Jews. In southern France, Spain, Switzerland and southern Germany and the Rhineland, Jews were accused of poisoning the wells. The Pope protested against pogroms, but Christians continued to burn and destroy hundreds of Jewish neighbourhoods and districts, and to imprison, torture and exile individuals. As a result, the European Jewish community moved eastward to escape (Park, 1993).

NEW FORMS OF POLITICAL INTERVENTION

The social disruption and threat to social order posed by the Black Death produced extensive intervention of political authority into the social and economic relations of late medieval society. When plague first appeared in southern Italy in 1347, Italian port authorities began turning away vessels travelling from suspect areas. In 1348 this ad hoc measure was formally codified in Venice on 20 March, when it closed its port to all suspect ships and instituted systematic isolation of travellers and ships in the harbour, initially for a period of thirty days. In 1377, Venice's Adriatic colony at the port of Ragusa (Dubrovnik) set up stations where travellers and merchandise from infected areas were isolated likewise. At Marseilles (1383), Venice (1403) and Majorca (1471), the period was extended to forty days, hence the term 'quarantine'. The period of forty days was believed to separate acute and chronic forms of disease. The subsequent development of Italian administrative measures to prevent the importation and spread of plague in the fifteenth and sixteenth centuries provided a powerful model which was gradually copied by the rest of Europe (Palmer, 1978).

The reason for the institution of quarantine in Venice and Dubrovnik may not, as it might first appear, be directly related to an idea of plague being spread by person-to-person contact. The medical theory of contagion, from antiquity to the Renaissance, remained largely an atmospheric one (Pelling, 1993; Hannaway, 1993). The Hippocratic notion of polluted air producing pestilences was reaffirmed by Galenic notions of generalized atmospheric corruption producing humoral corruption within the body. Nevertheless, the aetiology of pestilences was believed to result as much from the corruption of the soul as the body (Pelling, 1993).

Lay beliefs about various diseases such as leprosy and gonorrhoea clearly acknowledged dissemination through contact. The idea of contagion through person-to-person contact, however, confronted the difficulty of accounting for the substance that was transmitted. In *On Contagion, Contagious Diseases and their Treatment* in 1546, Girolamo Fracastoro (1478–1553) put forward a theory that contagion might consist of tiny seeds which could be passed from one person to another. But it is possible that in 1546 Fracastoro built a theory which incorporated long-held popular beliefs about disease transmission (Howard-Jones, 1977; Nutton, 1990).

There was clearly no singular idea about the aetiology of plague in the late medieval period. Any combination of causes could account for it: sin, particular stellar configurations, seasonal influences or direct contact with plague victims or the atmosphere, clothing, bedding, merchandise which they had contaminated. While rats were never singled out, there were popular beliefs that domestic animals such as cats and dogs might spread the disease. The response to epidemic plague by Italian states from the fourteenth to the end of the fifteenth century displayed a wide variety of beliefs about the mechanisms of plague transmission (Carmichael, 1986; Henderson, 1988). At Venice and Ragusa the initial institution of quarantine was a passive measure which allowed the authorities to wait and see if hidden plague developed on board incoming ships or travellers and their goods. The Venetian authorities believed that if plague developed it would produce a general corruption of the air, and they promptly turned the infected away. Neither Venice nor Ragusa made any provisions for the isolation of the ill or the healthy who had contact with the disease. None of the original quarantine regulations set up at these ports were motivated by an idea of the specific contagiousness of the disease (Carmichael, 1993a).

Elsewhere, the response of Italian rulers reflected a different understanding of the mechanism of plague diffusion. In both Milan and Mantua, greater emphasis was placed upon the isolation of the sick and those who had contact with them. Milan was the first city-state which followed the Venetian example. In 1350 and in 1374 Bernabo Visconti, ruler of Milan, issued orders to the Podestà of Reggio that all victims of the plague and anyone who had nursed them should be sent to a pest-house established beyond the city walls. Bernabo Visconti's regulations were later extended by Gian Galeazzo Visconti, ruler of Milan at the time of the epidemic of 1398–1400. When plague appeared in Soncino, 1,398 travellers from there were banned by Gian Galeazzo from entering Milan. He used the River Adda as a natural *cordon sanitaire* by stopping all travellers at bridges and ports, and in 1400 he created alternative routes for pilgrims journeying to Rome to keep them outside the city. In 1399 Gian Galeazzo decreed that all who fell sick were to be removed to two plague hospitals, their houses shut up and their contacts sent out of town. He rejected the idea of his city council that the sick should be kept in their houses, but insisted that in the hospitals patients be separated and provided with medical care. Families of victims were quarantined in monasteries outside the town (Palmer, 1978).

In Mantua in 1374, Ludovico Gonzaga declared that any Mantuan who had travelled through a plague-ridden district would not be allowed to re-enter the city. All Mantuans were forbidden to travel to areas of pestilence or lodge any visitor from such a place, on penalty of death. By 1400, anyone who passed through Mantua during times of plague required an official licence (Palmer, 1978).

The emphasis on controlling the movements and lodging of healthy and sick individuals reflected a clear belief in the spread of plague through direct contact. The rulers of these inland city-states had sufficient power to impose strict policing upon their citizens, enforce it through armed militia and by using the religious authorities to provide surveillance and intelligence. In Florence the political authorities also instituted emergency powers during the 1348 epidemic. But these largely took the form of setting up a temporary board of health to enforce existing sanitary legislation which had been developed in the thirteenth century. This consisted of an array of ad hoc measures, including street cleaning, preventing the pollution of drinking water, and controlling noxious trades and the sale of adulterated food. All of these measures were based on the Galenic principles of maintaining pure air and water and healthy food to prevent disease. In the last chapter, we discussed the way medieval towns commonly developed such regulations even if they did not enforce them. As the epidemic was approaching, Florentines were ineffectually ordered to comply with this traditional legislation. Once the epidemic arrived, the health board compelled compliance through fines and forcible removal of putrid matter or persons which could corrupt the air. Few new measures were created, except for dispensing charity to the plague-stricken who could not leave the city (Carmichael, 1986).

By 1383, when Florence faced a fourth epidemic, new measures were instituted, aimed not at preventing the spread of the disease but at maintaining civil order. Many of the wealthy fled the city. The authorities feared revolt among the poor who were unable to leave. Taxing those wishing to flee failed to discourage them, and the chancellor, Coluccio Salutati, posted guards to protect the property of the absent. Florence had recently experienced a revolt among day-labourers in the large wool industry at Ciompi in 1378, and the remaining ruling elite believed that the political dissidents who led it might turn the desertion of the plagued city to their advantage. Seventy years later, in 1448, a Florentine political magistracy, 'Eight Custodians', which had been created in 1378, was given specific powers for three months to control the spread of yet further plague epidemics. Civil policing to suppress panic and disquiet grew incrementally in this way in Florence and in other Italian city-states throughout the fourteenth and fifteenth centuries (Carmichael, 1986).

Florentine authorities created no new measures to deal with the prevention of plague, beyond those aimed at maintaining social order and protecting property, until the end of the fifteenth century. Initially the proposal for a plague hospital was an entirely charitable enterprise directed towards the poor who were unable to flee the city and were perceived to be the main victims of the plague (Pullan, 1988; Henderson, 1989). But by the time the *spedale del morbo* was first used in an epidemic in 1497, it was being designated as a lazaretto in which to house the infected for fear of their contagiousness. Other new measures to prevent the sick from mixing with the well were instituted by the Florentine authorities in the 1490s. A new health committee was set up in 1493, when it was feared an epidemic in Rome might spread to Florence. The committee posted guards outside the city to prevent travellers from infected districts from entering the city, and banned markets, festivals and processions. They instituted new provisions for confiscating suspected contaminated goods, killing dogs – thought to be plague-carriers – and ordered that each new victim and their family be removed to the *contado* to prevent them spreading the disease to others. Their measures were relaxed only once the epidemic subsided in Rome, but they prevented Florence from being affected (Carmichael, 1986).

From the fourteenth century, then, measures taken to prevent the spread of plague were aimed at containing the panic, civil disorder and social breakdown which the epidemic threatened to create. Understanding the way in which the disease was spread was only relevant inasmuch as it affected the means of containing social disorder. Protecting health was only considered in relation to the economic and political survival of the status quo. The political interventions enacted to prevent the spread of plague, however, served the interests of some but penalized the interests of others among the ruling elites. This conflict of interests was exacerbated as Italian city-states expanded civil administration to monitor, prevent and control plague in the sixteenth and seventeenth centuries (Cipolla, 1976). Quarantine greatly interfered with trade and was vigorously resisted by merchants and their labourers, both groups being adversely affected. Such tensions increased throughout the early modern period.

The Black Death was only the beginning of continuing epidemic visitations of plague over the next three hundred years. New civil administrative structures to deal with plague were created in Renaissance and early modern Italian city-states which became a model for public health administration throughout Europe.

PESTILENCE AND EARLY MODERN POLITICS

Numerous Italian city-states began providing lazarettos to house plague victims in the late fifteenth century and, like Florence, created semi-permanent public health officials or health boards to institute new plague regulations. The actions of the boards reflected growing acceptance of the transmission of plague through person-to-person contact. Preventing contagion was, however, only one aim of plague control measures. More elaborate regulations were developed in order to control the behaviour of the urban poor, whose swelling numbers were viewed as an increasing risk to social stability. The poor and the socially deviant were perceived as the prime victims and bearers of plague (Pullan, 1992). The rich escaped the impact of plague by moving to a safe location and thus plague became a disease of the poor who could not flee (Pullan, 1971; Pullan, 1992). The political authorities in late fifteenth-century Italian city-states recognized that economic deprivation, social deviance and plague were a potentially volatile cocktail (Martines, 1983). Health legislation was targeted at restricting the movements of the morally outcast, such as prostitutes and sodomites, 'ruffians' and beggars, as well as the plague sick-poor, who were assumed to pose equally serious threats to civil order. While the health authorities justified their actions as necessary steps to prevent the spread of plague from person to person, their primary goal was maintaining social stability by controlling the mobility of the anarchic, unpredictable underclass (Pullan, 1992; Brucker, 1977; Cohn, 1980).

Permanent health boards began to be established in most major Italian cities in the early sixteenth century. Florence created one in 1527, followed by Pisa, Pistoia, Pontremoli and Leghorn. In smaller towns, 'local gentlemen' were appointed as public health officers in times of epidemics. In Milan, a permanent health magistracy had been created in the fifteenth century. By the seventeenth century, the Italian city health boards, especially some of the most efficiently run such as Venice, were admired and imitated elsewhere in Europe (Cipolla, 1976). While physicians were consulted for their advice, the health boards were entirely political bodies administered by the local nobility or their patrician delegates. Eventually physicians and lawyers were appointed as health commissioners, but the boards remained entirely under the control of the political authorities. The health boards functioned partly as intelligence services to gather as much information as possible about the progress of plague in neighbouring and distant towns and locations. They also functioned as city immigration authorities who demanded health licences from visitors and their merchandise or goods. Health passes were issued by local health authorities to confirm that the individual and their merchandise were infection-free at the time of their departure. Migration and trade was impossible between some city-states without valid health licences. In some city-states, all travel between areas within the state required health licences (Cipolla, 1981).

During epidemics, most health authorities had the power to isolate plague victims and their families and confiscate and destroy suspected goods and merchandise (Cipolla, 1973). They used watchmen at city gates, who checked all entering and leaving and used household isolation, pest-house quarantine and *cordons sanitaires* to contain epidemics. It is important to view the development of Italian plague administration within the context of broader cultures of social control and political authority (Cipolla, 1981). Regional identity was paramount in a society of dukedoms where strangers and travellers were suspected of espionage or treachery. The primacy of regional political authority and loyalties helped to reinforce restrictions on geographical mobility and exchange. Thus the system of port quarantines and military sanitary cordons fitted into an existing political culture of keeping local populations in their place and dissuading travel and travellers (Cipolla, 1976).

By the seventeenth century, the power and prestige of many city health boards grew to the point where they were able to challenge the authority of the Church (Cipolla, 1979). Festivals, religious assemblies, processions and other public gatherings were often banned in epidemic times despite the vigorous opposition of the clergy. Health authorities justified their actions on the basis of experience. In Florence, for example, in 1633 the health magistrates closed schools and prevented religious assemblies because they believed that experience had demonstrated that public gatherings advanced contagion. Even in small settlements, such as the village or castello of Monte Lupo, the civil authorities challenged the power of the Church in trying to enforce total quarantine of every household and prevent any religious processions. In doing so the civil authorities asserted the value of experience over faith as the most efficient means of fighting the epidemic. In response, church authorities fought vigorously to establish the priority of religious observance. In Monte Lupo the local clergy staged a procession of devotion to the crucifix in defiance of the health ordinances, provoking popular resistance which the civil authorities barely managed to contain. Similar conflict occurred elsewhere. During a severe epidemic in 1630, a local bishop accused the health commissioner of Volterra of illegally trying to enforce restrictions upon ecclesiastical affairs and of heresy for accusing citizens of believing in priests above the will of the Lord. The bishop reported the patrician health commissioner, Luigi Capponi, to the Florentine health magistrates, but was rebuffed by the grand duke and his officials. In all similar local conflicts, the civil authorities supported their health officials, with armed force if necessary, putting the need to maintain social order and limit the spread of contagion above ecclesiastical demands to maintain freedom of action. For the Church, plague was the result of divine wrath which could only be assuaged by penance and observance. For health officials, the divine origin was less significant than the miasmas which spread the disease, along with the anarchy which it threatened to provoke. Preventing unrest, however, often required subtlety as well as force. Knowing that quarantine and other restrictions could cause the economic collapse of a community, health authorities often made concessions to local economic interests, such as agreeing to fumigate confiscated merchandise, such as silk or wool, instead of destroying it. This would not only appease local mercantile interests but would also prevent rebellion amongst their workforces. Merchants and their labourers were sometimes offered compensations for their losses. Health authorities attempted to raise funds to pay for the costs of containing the epidemic through emergency local taxes which were frequently vigorously resisted, as in Monte Lupo (Cipolla, 1979).

Italian health authorities instituted constant intelligence and surveillance measures to limit the damage caused by a local outbreak of plague. In seventeenth-century Florence, the health board used physicians and surgeons to inspect and report on mortality in surrounding districts in order to monitor general levels of contagion (Cipolla, 1981). The authorities were concerned with other contagious outbreaks, such as typhus. They did not recognize typhus as a disease in itself but believed it was a kind of 'stage' in rising levels of contagiousness which, if it reached critical levels, might turn into plague. The health authorities believed that by monitoring the levels and character of mortality in surrounding districts they would have sufficient warning to prevent plague migration at the earliest possible moment. Apart from surveillance by central authorities, like the Florence health board, local monitoring, such as communities under Florentine jurisdiction, became equally vigilant. Once cases of plague began to appear, local health authorities went to great lengths to play down its significance as long as possible to prevent the economic disaster that emergency health measures inflicted upon a community. Communications between health authorities stressed the reciprocal value of the free exchange of information (Cipolla, 1981).

Developing health administration and imposing emergency measures upon local communities created major conflicts. But the political elites of early modern Italian city-states succeeded in enforcing draconian legislation despite opposition. The political elites of these princely states consisted largely of the landowning nobility, and their priority was to preserve the status quo. They developed health bureaucracies and methods of enforcing their goals in order to preserve the existing structure of power when the economic and social dislocation and disorder caused by plague threatened to undermine it (Cipolla, 1976). Nevertheless, the economic and civil order of early modern Italy was seriously compromised by the impact of repeated plague epidemics. The severe and widespread outbreaks of 1597 and 1630, in particular, interrupted the economic development of this region and led to social and political stagnation in preindustrial Italian society (Cipolla, 1981).

DEARTH, DISORDER AND SOCIO-ECONOMIC DEVELOPMENT: PLAGUE AND MODERNIZATION

Plague administration in Italy became a model throughout Europe. In France elaborate ordinances against plague were issued in the early sixteenth century, and the temporary health boards appeared first at Lyons in 1580 and later in Agenais. Emergency health boards were created in times of plague in Switzerland in the early seventeenth century; in Brussels from the late sixteenth century doctors were hired as *pestmeetsers* to take charge during epidemics (Carmichael, 1993a; see also Alexander, 1980).

England lagged behind the Continent in developing plague administration. The civil authorities did not begin to institute any plague regulations until the sixteenth century. From the time of the Black Death which ravaged England in 1349, frequent visitations of plague continued up to the later half of the seventeenth century (Hatcher, 1994). In the period from 1486 to 1666 a plague crisis happened nationally about once in every seventeen years. This took place within a society which probably experienced a mortality crisis about once in every decade from some cause or another, such as crop failure and famine, other infectious diseases or war. Plague was, of course, not experienced everywhere at the same time but slowly moved from place to place (Platt, 1986).

England lacked the urban political structures which had imposed plague regulations upon Continental city-states. It did have a centralized form of government, which meant that once a health policy began to be taken up it developed a steady momentum. The response to plague in Tudor and Stuart England took place on a number of different levels. Central government had to take into account the interpretations of plague by ecclesiastical and secular intellectual authorities as well as the ability of local political authorities to implement regulations. Furthermore, both local and central government had ultimately to cope with the reaction of the general populace to the impact of the epidemic and the imposition of policy (Slack, 1985).

Before 1518, England, unlike many other European countries, had no fixed plague regulations. New orders were developed in 1518, in 1578 and in 1630, but none of these dates coincides with great plague outbreaks, such as those which occurred in 1563 or 1603. Rather, they were developed when milder outbreaks exacerbated moments of extensive urban crises. Various political figures, including Henry VIII, wished to increase the social and political sophistication of English society, putting it on a par with the Continental city-states. Numerous features of social policy were directed at this aim, such as institutionalizing medical practice through the creation of the College of Physicians in 1518, commissions of enquiry into enclosures and new measures to control vagrancy. Much of this was instigated by Cardinal Wolsey, who also designed the first local plague orders which were issued in London in 1517. The Continental practice was copied of requiring houses infected with plague to be identified by hanging bundles of straw from their windows for forty days and making their inmates carry a white stick when they walked through the streets. Plague orders were subsequently reissued in London during every epidemic up to 1563, but often without much urgency (Slack, 1985).

Similar orders were instituted in Oxford in 1518 by the humanist Thomas More, who shared the goal of modernizing English society. These first measures in 1518 could be viewed as the beginning of English public health policy. Additional measures aimed at halting miasmatic infection were taken, such as street cleaning and forbidding the use of clothes and bedding from infected houses. Effort was concentrated on preventing contagion between individuals, such as marking houses containing plague victims and preventing the inmates from leaving except to obtain provisions (Slack, 1985).

In provincial districts, various local authorities established plague houses outside town walls. By 1550, segregating plague victims in pest-houses was widely established, but few local authorities developed economic policies to cover the costs of caring for the sick or appointing watchmen to police them. Many town and city corporations throughout the country instituted some form of plague orders by the 1570s.

Sixty years after the first orders of 1518, the central government issued new national directions for combating contagion. Elizabeth I's chief minister, William Cecil, adopted further European plague controls and devised a new set of orders which he issued in 1578 as orders of the Privy Council, which then dictated plague policy up to the middle of the seventeenth century. They were made statutory in a Plague Act in 1604. Under the Act, justices of the peace were to meet every three weeks during an epidemic to receive reports on the progress of infection from the 'viewers' or searchers of the dead in each parish. Local authorities were allowed to raise a tax for the relief of the sick, extending to villages and areas surrounding the infected zones. All the clothes and bedding of plague victims were to be burnt, and funerals were to take place at dusk to reduce the number attending them. The most important clause, however, was the order to shut up the households of plague victims, isolating them, together with their families, for six weeks. Watchmen were appointed to enforce the order and officers were to supply the house inmates with food. Any criticism of the orders was to be punished. In 1604 the Plague Act added penal punishment for anyone attempting to disobey the orders (Slack, 1985).

The rationale underlying the house-arrest of plague victims and their families coincided with the aims of the Poor Law and other measures to deal with disorder arising from dearth. Social policy under the Tudors and Stuarts aimed to maintain social stability in an economically developing and socially volatile society by restricting movement. The most popular response to plague matched that of populations facing crop failure and unemployment: that is, to flee to safe havens or greener pastures. Migration stimulated by panic or hunger was perceived by the early modern English state as a grave threat to social stability, creating mass disruption of local communities. The purpose of house-arrest was to keep people in their place at moments of crisis in the same way as the Elizabethan Poor Law enforced local settlement when communities faced periods of economic failure and shortage. The English plague regulations, however, stimulated violent opposition and thereby contributed to increasing disorder. By the end of the 1665–1666 epidemic in London, the plague orders were seen to have failed and were replaced by new 'Rules and Orders' which recommended the removal of the sick to pest-houses away from their families and the isolation of family relatives in their houses for forty days (Slack, 1985).

The great epidemic of 1665–1666 was vividly described in the Diary of Samuel Pepys and later in the fictional account by Daniel Defoe written in 1722 (Defoe, 1990). High mortality had been experienced in previous epidemics, but in London in 1665 the rate more than doubled. At the height of the epidemic as many as fifty burials per day took place in some parishes, and overall about 55,000 probably died of plague in a city containing approximately half a million. The common geographical distribution of the plague was repeated again and again in London; the eastern parishes always suffered first and worst. The parishes of the poor consistently took the brunt of plague. In 1665, however, parishes much further west and north suffered badly, such as St Giles-in-the-Fields. But this was the last major plague epidemic experienced in England.

THE DISAPPEARANCE OF PLAGUE

After such a long history, plague began to disappear in western Europe with the last major epidemic occurring in Marseilles in 1720–1722. Much historical debate has attempted to identify what caused its disappearance. Did the disease itself lose its pathological virulence? Was there some alteration in the flea vectors, or the rat population? Did political regulation see it off? Were climatic changes responsible?

The 'quarantine model' has suggested that although it was falsely aimed at the prevention of person-to-person transmission it interrupted the transportation of infected fleas and rodents through the passage of human goods, vessels and luggage. From the early eighteenth century a great sanitary cordon along the Austro-Hungarian border, with over a hundred manned checkpoints, restricted the passage of a third wave of epidemic plague being transmitted from the Ottoman empire (Slack, 1981). Even if the quarantine regulations managed only to act as a partial barrier, they may have saved Europe from a pandemic which spread eastwards over Asia and eventually landed on the west coast of America in 1900, setting off an epidemic in San Francisco in 1904.

Quarantine regulations may well have acted in conjunction with climatic changes which occurred from the early eighteenth century. A cooler period, 'a little Ice Age', may have reduced the number of infected rodent colonies in Asia which permanently harboured the disease. Fewer infected rodents would have thereby been imported to Europe. On the other hand, a new orientation towards trade with the western colonies of the New World shifted markets away from the Mediterranean and the Far East and may have reduced the opportunity for importation of plague to Britain, Scandinavia and the Low Countries. Trade had traditionally passed from east to west out of the Mediterranean, and the relatively late survival of plague in Italy and Spain after it had disappeared from western Europe may support this view (Carmichael, 1993).

The disappearance of plague from western Europe probably resulted from a combination of a number of causes (Appleby, 1980). If maritime quarantine and *cordons sanitaires* did contribute to the prevention of reinfection, many of the other draconian measures instituted against plague probably did nothing but assist its mortality toll. Isolating families in their own houses infested with plague-ridden rodents prevented them from escaping the infection. Isolating the healthy with the sick in pest-houses increased the opportunity for human transition of the disease, especially the pneumonic form (Slack, 1985).

But the central goal of the plague regulations begun in Italy and later imitated throughout Europe was the elimination of the threat to the political status quo posed by the economic and social breakdown caused by the epidemic. Plague founded public health as a function of the modern state, aimed at the management of the relationship between disease and social disorder.

SICKNESS AND SIN

In the Renaissance and early modern world, fears of social disorder were matched by the dread of moral corruption which could result from disease (Gilman, 1989). In the late fifteenth century the disease which came to be identified as the French disease, *morbus gallicus*, was believed to be a new contagion (Arrizabalaga, 1993). Numerous contemporary observers wrote accounts of a new epidemic pox appearing in Italy in 1495, following Charles VIII's campaign against the Spaniards for control of Naples. His army, which consisted largely of mercenaries from Belgium, Germany, southern France, Italy and Spain, was believed to have spread the disease. The Italians called it 'the French sickness'; the French called it 'the Neapolitan sickness'. The earliest descriptions of the disease came from its appearance among the French army at the Battle of Fornovo on 5 July 1495. The *morbus gallicus* was spread throughout Europe as the mercenary army disbanded and returned to their homelands. Numerous famous accounts of the disease were given by poets and authors, such as Jean Molinet, official historian to the House of Burgundy, Sebastian Brant, who had authored the famous satirical fable *The Ship of Fools*, and Joseph Grunpeck of Augsburg and Ulrich von Hutten of Franconia, who both contracted the disease (Quetel, 1990). Brant provided the first illustrated account, with wood engravings by Dürer, who depicted the syphilitic as a French fop (Gilman, 1988). Within a decade of the first outbreak noted at Fornovo, epidemic syphilis had spread throughout Europe. Although national cultures frequently identified it as the disease of their enemy, it was most commonly referred to as *morbus gallicus* (Quetel, 1990). In 1530 Girolamo Fracastoro first called this disease 'syphilis' in his allegorical poem about a shepherd who contracted it. The term 'syphilis' was rarely used, however, and often referred to an indeterminate range of conditions until the late nineteenth century, when the specific bacterial origin of the disease had been identified.

The *morbus gallicus* was recognized to be spread venereally. Christian ideology accounted for it as divine retribution for licentiousness, but contemporaries such as Grunpeck also attributed it to astrological sources (Gilman, 1988). From the sixteenth century, the American origin of the disease was the source of much controversy and remains so even today (Crosby, 1972). Some historical epidemiologists have suggested that there is one micro-organism which has mutated and been expressed in related diseases according to various ecological and sociological conditions. The organism responsible for syphilis is *Treponema pallidum* subspecies *pallidum*, which is a spirochetal bacterium, the only known host of which is the human being. There are a number of different spirochetal genera, and the *Treponema* genus includes several species responsible for four different human diseases: pinta, yaws, endemic syphilis and venereal syphilis. While scholars such as E.H. Hudson have claimed that the appearance of these diseases has occurred at various moments in history according to changing social and ecological circumstances, others, such as C.J. Hackett, have suggested that these four diseases emerged separately from one common ancestor. Both theories deny the direct transmission of venereal syphilis from the Americas to Europe, though the transmission of a mutation of endemic syphilis is still considered a possibility. Nevertheless, venereal syphilis was perceived as a new disease in Europe by those experiencing the epidemic at the end of the fifteenth century, and new measures to control both its spread and the contagion of immorality which it symbolized were instituted (Arrizabalaga, 1993).

Isolation of sufferers was attempted by some authorities, the syphilitic being subjected to similar stigmatization as lepers in medieval times. Stricter controls were instituted against beggars and vagrants in France, which also converted old leper houses into accommodations for 'incorrigible paupers'. The Hôtel-Dieu overflowed with emigré pox victims in the 1520s, and they were provided with money to enable them to return home. In France, inspection and stricter regulation of prostitutes was established from 1500. In Edinburgh in 1497 the city council required patients sick of the 'gradgor' be removed to the island of Inch until they were completely cured. Anyone resisting the regulations faced the penalty of complete exile and the branding iron (Quetel, 1990).

Changing attitudes towards sexual practices were already evident in Renaissance societies. The late medieval tradition of the steam baths, which were part of a cult of pleasure rather than cleanliness or hygiene, began to decline in the sixteenth century. Many famous hotels offering the steam bath as a main attraction disappeared throughout Europe. The custom of visiting the steam bath to conduct a discrete liaison or simply to enjoy free and easy frolicking among naked men and women also began to decline. The pleasure dome of the steam bath became an increasing target of the guardians of public morals, but their decline coincided with the rise of epidemic syphilis. The epidemic significantly affected changing attitudes towards libertine pleasure, adding caution to the justification for new codes of moral discipline. The aims of public authorities to control syphilitic contagion were assisted by broader changes in cultural beliefs and social behaviour towards the pursuit of pleasure. What public policing may not have successfully achieved through coercion was perhaps accomplished through new ideologies regarding moral perpetuity (Vigarello, 1988; Gilman, 1989).

3 Enlightenment discourse and health

With the decline of plague the disease profile of western Europe changed focus. Geographical exploration, urban development and imperial expansion created new patterns. Epidemic diseases of isolated communities became endemic in urban environments. By the eighteenth century shock invasions were replaced by rising levels of endemic infections and chronic sickness which occasionally became epidemic, such as malaria, smallpox and gout (Kiple, 1993). The absence of catastrophic disasters meant that emergency disease control was no longer a priority. Instead, the Age of Enlightenment became a period in which a new interest in the social scientific analysis of the health of populations developed (Fox *et al.*, 1995). The eighteenth century also witnessed the development of innovations in sanitation and immunization.

IMPERIALISM AND BIOLOGY: DISEASE AND CONQUEST IN THE EARLY MODERN PERIOD

From the fifteenth century the western world rose to global dominance in wealth, trade and military power. But as the West grew wealthier it did not grow healthier. The West's populations were, from time to time, decimated by pandemic waves (Flinn, 1981). The disease regimes of the West and the societies which it had contact with changed dramatically during the eighteenth-century period. The early modern transportation revolution in oceanic travel precipitated a new global order in the ecology of disease. Columbus's arrival in the Americas signalled an age of exploration and discovery of new worlds by the old. But the meeting of far-flung peoples who had never previously had any contact had major consequences for epidemic infections (Kiple, 1993).

Europeans devastated Amerindian populations by bringing them into contact with the common diseases of the Old World. Infections such as smallpox, measles, mumps, chickenpox and scarlet fever had a massive impact upon populations which had never experienced them before. The vulnerability of this 'virgin population' meant that pandemics decimated the Caribbean Indians and then swept through urbanized societies in Mexico and Peru at a catastrophic rate (Ashburn, 1947; Crosby, 1972; Crosby, 1986). Smallpox, in particular, facilitated the Spanish conquest of the Inca and Aztec empires (McNeill, 1976). The progress of infection through the nomadic societies of the northern continent was more gradual but equally destructive. The estimated size of the pre-Columbian American population is between 50 and 100 million. Possibly 90 per cent of this original Amerindian population was wiped out by the diseases transmitted by Europeans and the slaves they transported from Africa (Ashburn, 1947; Crosby, 1972; Crosby, 1986).

When the Amerindian population began to die out, Europeans replaced their labour power with African slaves, which set in motion a three-way disease exchange. West Africans, who have a degree of immunity to falciparum malaria via the genetic sickle-cell trait, brought the disease with them to America through their forced migration. The water casks on the slave ships brought the mosquito that carried yellow fever. The milder vivax malaria was also transported because it was indigenous among European populations. By the late seventeenth century the European and Amerindian populations began to die of the diseases indigenous to West Africa, the first outbreaks of yellow fever appearing in Boston in 1693 (Duffy, 1990; Carrigan, 1988).

The absence of diseases common among European, African and Asian populations in the American continents resulted from their isolation and the pattern of their agricultural production and consumption and urbanization. Herd animals domesticated by Amerindian societies, such as llamas, did not suffer the same infections transmissible from animal to man as the cattle herds domesticated in the Old World. Those Amerindian societies which lived primarily on diets of agricultural produce rather than from hunting and gathering appeared to balance vitamin content through a combination of maize, beans and pulses. Thus, they would have avoided deficiency diseases such as pellagra or scurvy. Only few pre-Columbian societies had reached the density threshold required to sustain a chain of human infection indefinitely. So, with only a limited amount of contact between human and domestic animal populations, dietary sufficiency and low density of urban or nomadic societies, it seems unlikely that endemic or epidemic infections had developed. Evidence from skeletal remains exists of fractures, arthritis and a disease which may have been analogous to tuberculosis amid the pre-Columbian Amerindian population. Trephination was also performed by pre-Colombians but the reasons for it may have been spiritual rather than therapeutic (Buikstra, 1993).

In the previous chapter we discussed how syphilis was perceived as a new disease in Europe by contemporaries who attributed it to a Colombian exchange. It was also regarded as a new disease in India and in Japan, where it arrived in 1505. Whether this was transported from the Americas is difficult to determine. Little evidence exists of infectious diseases among the indigenous pre-Columbian populations of the American continents (McNeill, 1976). Evidence does exist of a non-venereal form of the disease present among the pre-Columbians, which means that even if it did migrate to Europe it mutated into the venereal form experienced from the end of the fifteenth century. Whatever its origin, the impact of syphilis upon sixteenth-century European societies was significant inasmuch as it thinned out numerous ruling European oligarchies, making room at the top of otherwise rigidly autocratic societies. By the end of the century syphilis began to recede, with the more virulent strains being replaced by attenuated milder longer chronic forms as a result of the adjustment between parasite and host (Arrizabalaga, 1992; Quetel, 1990).

From the sixteenth century other new epidemics began to appear throughout Europe, such as typhus. The first contemporary accounts of typhus suggested that it began to appear from 1490 among Spanish soldiers fighting in Cyprus, and then in Italy as the French and Spanish fought for control of the peninsula. The disease appeared again when the French besieged Naples in 1526 and it ravaged the area (Zinsser, 1942). It subsequently followed troop movements and began to haunt 'lousy' institutions such as jails and poorhouses (Delacy, 1986). Typhus was a disease of overcrowding and poverty, and it expanded along with the urban expansion of the European trading cities and centres. It was thus only one of a host of new infections indigenous to urban poverty and its demographic impact therefore was only partial (Flinn, 1981).

A puzzling infection among the English began to be chronicled after Henry VII won the English crown at the Battle of Bosworth. An initial outbreak was identified in London in 1485, brought back by Henry's mercenaries from France and Flanders (Carmichael, 1993b). What precisely the 'English Sweats' was is uncertain, and various historians have speculated it could have been anything from scarlet fever to influenza. Historical epidemiologists currently suggest, however, that it was probably some form of airborne infection which was novel to the English but endemic among children in other parts of Europe. While contemporaries such as the court historian Polydore Vergil gave graphic accounts of its sudden and rapid effects, the 'sweats' did not have any major demographic impact. Initially spread among English soldiers and courtiers, by the mid-sixteenth century it had become endemic in England among children and its impact was thereby reduced (Carmichael, 1993b; Wylie and Collier, 1981).

Between 1500 and 1700 the most significant effect of the expansion of oceanic travel and international trade upon world ecology was to domesticate and homogenize epidemic diseases. Infections which at one time ravaged isolated susceptible populations in catastrophic waves now became endemic within densely crowded urban environments with high levels of demographic immunity. Diseases which at one time were responsible for high levels of mortality among adults in secluded communities were reduced to attacking new susceptibles: that is, infants and children. Throughout the communications network binding Europe to the rest of the world the frequent circulation of infections established a new stable pattern of disease. Catastrophic epidemics only affected remaining isolated populations or resulted from genetic mutation of disease organisms (Stannard, 1993).

Within Europe a stable pattern of familiar endemic infections was established which occasionally rose to epidemic levels among new generations of susceptibles. Endemnicity spread slowly from urban and port trading centres into the countryside. Among the urbanized trading world the scene was set for massive demographic rise perpetually dogged by endemic sicknesses and high rates of infant mortality (Stannard, 1993).

THE STRENGTH OF THE STATE

The relationship between the health and wealth of nations was not lost on political and economic thought in the eighteenth century. The early modern political philosophy of mercantilism stressed the need to measure the strength of the state by assessing levels of health (Rosen, 1974). The growth of public health paralleled the rise of centralized government in this period. As the modern state began to emerge from the late sixteenth century, so incipient ideas of national health slowly gained ground (D. Porter, 1994). What was the relationship between the changing power structures of the body politic and the health of the subjects under its domain?

The development of what the French *ideologue* Condorcet called 'social mathematics' was highly significant in the development of the relationship between the emergent modern state and the health of its subjects (Baker, 1982). Various methods of counting the subjects of the state and measuring its size and strength in terms of their number and their health were introduced in the early modern period. In the sixteenth century, Italian cities made elaborate statistical inquiries into population, economic activity and epidemic disease (Rosen, 1974; Brucker, 1977). Eighteenth-century Sweden used its Episcopalian ministry to collect information on births, deaths, cause of death, levels of literacy and levels of ill health (Johannisson, 1994). English intellectuals in the late seventeenth century developed the idea of a political arithmetic (Greenwood, 1948). France established a bureau of statistical investigation during the Napoleonic era. Imperialism encouraged the development of censuses. The Spanish made a census of Peru in 1548 and of their territories in North America in 1576. Nova Scotia and Quebec instituted censuses in the 1660s. The Caribbean islands reported on trade and populations to their French, Spanish and English rulers. The Constitution of the United States continued colonial practice and wrote in a required decennial census. The English produced an arithmetical account of Ireland in 1679 (Hacking, 1990). Counting and evaluating the strength of the state was supported by the political philosophy of mercantilism which viewed the monarch's subjects as his paternalistic property and equated the entire well-being of society as coterminous with the well-being of the state, as embodied by the sovereign. It was based on a form of political book-keeping which enabled the state to measure its strength in terms of the size of its healthy population and which guided its administrative goals and objectives.

Methods for assessing the strength of the state by counting the population were developed by the late seventeenth-century physician, wealthy landowner and early social scientist, William Petty (1623–1687). In the preface to his *Political Anatomy of Ireland*, he claimed to have been inspired by Francis Bacon's observation that the preservation of the body politic and the body natural were linked and that the strength of the state could be anatomized statistically. Petty produced a political arithmetic of social facts to enhance the state's chances of military defence, commercial and technological expansion and social reform. He collected data on population, trade, manufacture, education, diseases and revenue. He was the earliest market researcher: 'What are the books that do sell most?' (Rosen, 1974: 180). He studied the conditions under which prosperity flourished and was impeded. Petty attempted to project the number of lives – and economic wealth – which might be preserved for the crown if the supply of qualified medical practitioners was to increase. Petty's contemporaries, such as Nehemiah Grew (1641–1712) produced similar quantitative analyses (Rosen, 1974).

Petty's friend, a mercer and fellow of the Royal Society, John Graunt (1620–1674), began to calculate health and disease. He scrutinized the London Bills of Mortality to discover the regularities of life-events such as births and deaths – noting the excess of male over female births and excess male over female deaths – and the proportion of individual disease mortality to the whole. He highlighted the higher urban over rural death rates (Greenwood, 1948).

These were the early foundations of 'vital statistics' and epidemiology which, by the nineteenth century, became a prerequisite for systematic disease prevention. Quantitative methods continued to develop in the eighteenth century. One of the most important tools of vital statistics was the 'life table' which was first devised in 1693 by the English astronomer Edmund Halley (c.1656–1743) (Greenwood, 1948). The English advanced the use of social statistics, but the idea that the modern nation-state was inherently characterized by its statistics and therefore required a statistical office to define itself and its power was developed within the eighteenth-century German states, above all Prussia. In the seventeenth century the co-discoverer of the calculus, Gottfried Wilhelm Leibniz, had proposed that the Brandenburg-Prussian state should measure its true power in terms of its population, and suggested that a central statistical bureau should be created. Leibniz proposed a central office of statistics in the 1680s which could serve various branches of military and civil administration and maintain a register of births, marriages and deaths. He devised a 56-category evaluation of the population, including sex, social status, the number of able-bodied men for bearing arms and marriageable women for bearing children. Brandenburg-Prussia became a kingdom in 1701, but although Frederick I had been impressed by Leibeniz's proposals a statistical office was not created until the reign of Wilhelm I (1713–1740). The study of statistics was subsequently advanced in Germany both by amateurs and within the universities (Hacking, 1990; T. Porter, 1986; Frängsmyr *et al.* (eds), 1990).

The term *Statistik*, meaning statecraft, was invented by the professor of law and politics at Göttingen University, Gottfried Achenwall, to describe catalogues and surveys illustrating 'the condition and prospects of society'. Achenwall developed the idea of a university course which would combine this with the study of law, largely for students hoping to become civil servants. They would explore the comparison between states in terms of their populations, geography, climate, natural resources, trade, manufacturing, military strength, education, religion and constitution. But statistics within the German universities remained descriptive and non-numeral, in the sense that it was not quantitatively evaluative. Quantitative analysis, however, developed outside the universities in Germany among public amateurs (T. Porter, 1986).

Numerous late eighteenth-century German travellers and cataloguers collected data and completed statistical analyses, to such an extent that Goethe commented in 1786 that he lived in 'statistically minded times' (Hacking, 1990: 18). The most systematic attempt was undertaken by a cleric, J. P. Süssmilch, who calculated various aspects of the material world to demonstrate the regularity of divine order in nature. Süssmilch's natural theology studied births, deaths and sex ratios to reveal divine providence at work (Gigerenzer *et al.* (eds), 1989). To an extent Süssmilch mirrored the work of John Graunt and the English physician John Arbuthnot, who claimed to have proved in 1710 that providence produced a greater number of male than female births in order to compensate for the loss of men in war (Gigerenzer *et al.* (eds), 1989; Hacking, 1990). In the 1740s Süssmilch presented an analysis of population management demonstrating the relationship between marriage ages, birth rates, population growth and the use and availability of farmland (Hacking, 1990). Süssmilch, like other eighteenth-century writers on probability, argued against chance and supported instead the argument for design, which was equally taken up in discussions on natural history by authors such as John Ray and William Paley (Brooke, 1991). Süssmilch represents what Michel Foucault suggested was the growing science of bio-politics at the end of the eighteenth and beginning of the nineteenth centuries, which produced systematic assessments that facilitated increasingly disciplinary interventions upon the individual and social body as a whole (Foucault, 1990). Such disciplinary knowledge was focused on the body itself, its biological processes and functions, disease propagation, birth and mortality, levels of health and morbidity, life expectancy and longevity (*Ibid.*). Süssmilch's demographic theology was a part of the development of eighteenth-century quantitative social science, which was grounded in the discussion of 'population' (Tomaselli, 1989; Whelan, 1991). Demography, however, took a pessimistic turn in the work of the English cleric, the Reverend Thomas Malthus (Wrigley, 1989).

Malthus argued against the optimism of the eighteenth-century view of perfect balance being achieved through divine order. Alternatively, he contended that the human population inevitably increased in a way which outstripped food supply, and thus poverty and starvation would always remain constant. Malthus denounced extending the system of outdoor relief under the English Old Poor Law, and suggested that poverty, like war and disease, should be allowed to follow its natural course towards reducing the population and thereby increasing prosperity (James, 1979; Winch, 1987). The impact of Malthus's philosophy in undermining optimistic Enlightenment belief in the capacity of reason and reasonable government to solve all human and social dilemmas was profound

(Hilton, 1988; Bonnar, 1966). Equally the impact of his philosophy upon the institutional solutions to the cost of poverty sought by the English state was extensive (Hilton, 1988; Himelfarb, 1984). These had direct consequences upon the development of public health in the nineteenth century. Above all, Malthus placed the importance of demographic change at the heart of the discussion of social amelioration which was to directly influence philosophies of government both within and beyond the English state (Wrigley, 1989).

Early modern exploration of probability and population (Daston, 1988; Porter, 1986; Gigerenzer *et al.* (eds), 1989) had a powerful influence on the development of public health. Statistics provided essential methods for enquiring into the health and disease profile of populations; it also prompted new philosophical concerns and facilitated a new metaphorical exchange between the biological, physical and social worlds in which the contradictions of 'organic' nature figured prominently (Hacking, 1990). Malthusianism continued to figure prominently in debates surrounding preventive medicine and public hygiene up to the twentieth century (Soloway, 1982). It is clear from its early history that statistical science was never a neutral enquiry; but was embedded in a broader metaphysic laden with value judgements about the rational rather than the mysterious mind of God and the natural order of human society. Statistics contained mixed messages characteristic of Enlightenment social science which were critical to the subsequent relationship between knowledge and power in the politics of disease prevention and procuring public health.

THE SCIENCE OF ADMINISTRATION AND MEDICAL POLICE

Later we shall discuss how probabilistic statistics was incorporated into the early nineteenth-century study of social-physics by Adolphe Quetelet (1796–1874). Social-physics was used to quantitatively analyse the social and economic determinants of disease distribution. The mercantilist philosophy of government which underpinned the political arithmetic of the late seventeenth-century English gentlemen-scholars William Petty and John Graunt was used to justify the creation of a new eighteenth-century science of health administration called medical police (Rosen, 1974). The conceptual theory of medical police was outlined by the Austrian physicians Johann Peter Franck, Wolfgang Thomas Rau and Anton Mai, but it was Franck who first proposed a comprehensive system (Rosen, 1974). Franck (1745–1821) was physician to the late eighteenth-century Hapsburg court and director of the General Hospital in Vienna. In six large volumes he outlined methods for regulating intimate individual behaviour which might spread or engender disease, such as marriage, pregnancy and personal hygiene (Lesky, 1976). Equally he proposed public hygiene measures of drainage, pure water supply, street cleaning, control of vice and overcrowding and the sanitary order of hospitals. Franck's system reflected the paternalistic political philosophy of 'cameralism' of the Hapsburg Empire, headed by enlightened despots from the reign of Maria Theresa (1717–1780) who saw the role of the monarch as akin to that of the parent of the people (Evans, 1979; Dickson, 1987). Cameralism, the specifically German expression of mercantilism, also viewed a growing healthy population as an inexhaustible source of power for the monarch seeking agricultural, industrial and military expansion. The body and behaviour of the individual was the economic and political property of the state, to be utilized for its benefit through the science of police, *policey*, a form of civil service administration (Raeff, 1983; Gawthrop, 1993). Franck's elaborate discussion of medical police, however, was not original. The practice of health administration under the banner of medical police had already been institutionalized elsewhere in Europe earlier in the century.

From 1648 in Brandenburg-Prussia, the science of civil administration was linked to the modernization of the state, replacing feudal overlords with paid civil servants, even if many of the most powerful were still recruited from the nobility (Melton, 1995; Oestreich, 1982). The early philosophers of the German Enlightenment, such as Samuel Pufendorf (1632–1694), Christian Thomasius (1655–1728), Gottfried Wilhelm Leibniz (1646–1719) and Christian Wolff (1679–1754) all analysed the concept of *policey* as a system of modern government which would facilitate the foundation of social welfare by the state (Raeff, 1983; Whaley, 1981; Riley (ed.), 1981; Carr (ed.), 1994). For all of these theorists the function of *policey* was to establish state policies for ensuring a healthy population. As discussed above, Leibniz had been a major advocate for the development of state statistics and state health policies. In 1661, he, together with various court physicians, had requested the setting up of a 'Collegium Medicum' to regulate the medical profession and the sale of drugs. The Collegium Medicum was created by the Elector Frederick William in 1685 and issued edicts which imposed new regulations on medical practice and pharmacy. The Collegium Medicum decided who should be admitted to the medical profession and established a state examination system and preparatory courses. They policed unlicensed practice through a legal system administered by local health bureaucracies. Town and district physicians which, as we saw in the last chapter, were set up throughout the German provinces from the fifteenth century, were now officially appointed as servants of the state. Their function was to oversee the institutionalization of medical police in their localities. They were responsible for supervising qualified practice and for prosecuting unlicensed quacks. They also administered the new laws on the sale of pharmaceuticals. Town physicians made sure that a standardization of fees was established among local practitioners. Medical police was extended throughout the eighteenth century in the Prussian state, but its focus continued to be the legal regulation of the healing market. Preventive health measures to avoid epidemic disease were not part of its remit. Instead, the cameralist state perceived the route to population growth was through an efficient state regulation of medical practice and the standardization of pharmaceutical preparations and sales. The ideology of medical police justified dominance of public health administration in Germany by legally trained civil servants almost until the end of the nineteenth century (Munch, 1995; Lindemann, 1996).

The practice of medical police in eighteenth-century Prussia contrasted with its institutionalization in Sweden, where a different approach to state health intervention was developed before 1800 (Johannisson, 1994). Health reform in Sweden was made possible through the creation of a national census in 1749 which, together with that of Finland, was the first in Europe. Shockingly low levels of population in Sweden galvanized the state into action on health and pronatalism (Johannisson, 1988). Sweden's homogeneous society and universal Episcopal bureaucracy enabled the state to institute the first comprehensive system in Europe of population registration and census-taking. The promotion of fertility and personal hygiene education, the policing of sexually and socially transmitted diseases through policies of isolation and treatment, and the development of municipal hospitals were instituted in eighteenth-century Sweden in the name of strengthening the state through population growth (Johannisson, 1994; Johannisson, 1988). These policies were administered in Sweden through local secular and Episcopal bureaucracies long before Johann Peter Franck included such measures in his theoretical system of medical police.

The concept of medical police also helped to found some preliminary forms of health administration under the *ancien régime* in France, initiated by Louis XIV's minister of finance, Colbert. The Société Royale du Médecine was created in 1772 to police medical nostrums and quackery, distribute medicine chests to rural health authorities and set up a network for reporting local epidemics. The principles of medical policing continued to fit well with a post-revolutionary centralized state in nineteenth-century France which had little regard for civil liberties but equally little enthusiasm for collective intervention. Political and economic individualism in France supported the policing of individual hygienic responsibility and avoided addressing the collective needs of the community (Ramsey, 1994; Hannaway, 1972).

Although the practice of medical police varied, throughout Europe mercantilist concerns over healthy population levels promoted ever stricter enforcement of port quarantines, border sanitary cordons and the policing of public nuisances and civic disorder. But mercantilism and medical police were not the only intellectual forces stimulating innovation in public health practice prior to the nineteenth century. Enlightenment humanitarianism emphasized the role of philanthropy in encouraging self-help and civic improvement (R. Porter, 1991). This was linked to the revival of ancient philosophies of individual and environmental health improvement (Wear, 1993).

AVOIDING DISEASE AND CREATING A RENAISSANCE OF HEALTH

Town improvement commissioners in late eighteenth-century England sought to bring about the 'civilizing process' among the wretchedly squalid poor by inducing self-improvement through environmental improvement (Borsay, 1989; Corfield, 1982). The largest commercial economy in Europe also made civic environmentalism a profitable trade, spawning new commercial enterprises in night-soil collection, street widening, paving and lighting (Porter, 1991). When combined with the theories of political economy, sanitary reform and evangelical piety, this Enlightenment humanitarianism emerged as a sort of 'moral ecology' among nineteenth-century public health reformers such as Thomas Southwood Smith, the Unitarian doctor who was the closest ally of the founder of English public health, Edwin Chadwick. But equally the Parisian *parti d'hygiène* of the 1830s, who took the lead in developing theories of public health, drew upon such ideological resources.

Enlightenment doctors revived the Hippocratic philosophy of prolonging life and preserving individual health through dietetics, regimen and exercise (Smith, 1985; Wear, 1993). The massive increase in health advice books throughout Europe in the eighteenth century reflects the popularity of personal health cults (Porter and Porter, 1988; Porter and Porter, 1989; Wear, 1987; Beier, 1987). The same revival of classical values encouraged concern with environmental health regulation. The predetermined environment of disease contained in the Hippocratic doctrine of *On Airs, Waters and Places* was scrutinized by seventeenth-century physicians and scientific thinkers. Robert Boyle deduced from meteorological observations that local weather could be linked to epidemics and the salubrity of the air. Equally he reinforced the idea that disease might be caused from inorganic corpuscular emanations beneath the earth's surface mixing with other atmospheric elements (Riley, 1989). The great disciple of Hippocratic environmentalism, Thomas Sydenham, built upon Boyle's assumptions with observations of the relationship between changing seasons, local conditions and epidemic occurrences. By chronicling London's major diseases between 1661 and 1675, Sydenham identified what he considered to be five distinct epidemic constitutions, each associated with a season in the year, for example the dysenteric constitution of 1670–1672. While Sydenham constructed a disease matrix which he thought underlay the conditions under which epidemics occurred, he believed that its complexity made it impossible to predict. Nevertheless, he identified five elements which were worth monitoring: heat, cold, moisture, dryness and emanations from the bowels of the earth. The latter one was the chief element of an epidemic constitution but was, Sydenham believed, beyond scrutiny. On the basis of his observations, Sydenham classified diseases into those produced primarily by environmental constitution, those produced purely by atmospheric constitution and those resulting from humoral imbalance (Dewhurst, 1966).

Despite the new environmentalism, theories of contagious disease persisted throughout the eighteenth century. Boyle incorporated particular elements of contagion into his corpuscular theory, and environmentalists such as Sydenham accepted that diseases such as smallpox were transmitted through Francastorian agents passing directly between individuals or through the atmosphere. But in the eighteenth century the boundaries between environmental and contagious theory of disease were not distinct. Rather, conceptions such as the epidemic constitution blurred the relationship between the origin and means of propagation of disease (Riley, 1989).

Medical environmentalism spawned new enquiries into medical meteorology and medical geography, and encouraged the quantitative analysis of disease. It also supported a new interest in preventive medicine. In the light of these new medical enquiries eighteenth-century health investigators began to correlate dirt with disease. John Bellers (1654–1725), a Quaker cloth merchant who lived in London, wrote extensively on the health of towns in 1714, emphasizing the importance of population density to the propagation of disease. He recommended municipal street cleaning, refuse collection, regulation of dairies, abattoirs and noxious trades. He was especially concerned with the replacement of intermittent with constant water supply to towns (Clarke, 1987). The philanthropist John Howard (c.1726–1790) studied gaols, bridewells, lazarettos and hospitals in Britain and on the Continent in the 1770s and 1780s. He concluded that their filthy conditions and closed contaminated atmospheres were lethal because they caused such endemic conditions as 'gaol fever' – typhus. The naval and military physicians James Lind (1716–1794) and John Pringle (1707–1782) campaigned for ship and camp cleanliness to eliminate typhus – also referred to as 'spotted fever'. The political radical, religious dissenter and physician, John Haygarth (1740–1827) argued that typhus fever's contagiousness was responsible for its prevalence among the urban poor living in their congested slums. Eighteenth-century health campaigners equally believed that stench spread disease. When Pringle and the physiologist and inventor, the Reverend Stephen Hales (1677–1761), were commissioned in 1750 to try and purify the noxious air of Newgate Prison, they recommended the introduction of ventilators. Hales had first devised new mechanisms for the ventilation of ships and gaols in the 1740s, consisting of hand-operated bellows. Later he devised a type of windmill device to be placed on roofs (Riley, 1989; R. Porter, 1991).

In Enlightenment England, the campaign to avoid disease was based on social as well as environmental analysis. It was only sporadically translated into public policy through the haphazard proliferation of urban improvement commissions. Philanthropic individuals set up commissions with responsibility for improving paving, lighting and street cleaning in local areas. No central government policy was developed. In this laissez-faire society public health did, however, become a commercial enterprise. Various trades began to service the selective cleaning of the surface of towns. Scavenging, street cleaning, night-soil collection, the design of 'airy' dwellings, grew as profitable enterprises (R. Porter, 1991).

But the most successful of all eighteenth-century disease prevention campaigns was inoculation against smallpox (Hopkins, 1983; Razell, 1977). The wife of the British ambassador to Constantinople, Lady Mary Wortley Montagu (1689–1762), first introduced inoculation into Europe in 1718 when she reported on its common practice in the Ottoman Empire. First practised on condemned prisoners and orphaned children, it was popularized by the inoculation of the royal family. High-ranking intellectuals such as Sir Hans Sloane (1660–1753), President of the Royal Society, endorsed it, together with Charles Maitland (1668–1748) a leading surgeon (Miller, 1981). From the 1760s it was commercialized with great success by operators such as Robert (1707–1788) and Daniel

Sutton (1735–1819) who inoculated whole towns and villages at the same time. John Haygarth promoted a complete system of smallpox eradication for the poor (Hopkins, 1983).

THE HEALTH OF DEMOCRATIC CITIZENS

By far the most important ideological influence on late eighteenth-century rhetoric about health and the political state was the Enlightenment philosophy of democratic citizenship. Democratic revolutions in America and France asserted new principles regarding the state and the health of its subjects. Thomas Paine did not include health among the property rights to which all free men are innately entitled, but Thomas Jefferson declared that sick populations were the product of sick political systems (Rosen, 1952). According to Jefferson, despotism produced disease, democracy liberated health. Jefferson believed that a life of political 'liberty and the pursuit of happiness' would automatically be a healthful one. He told his co-signer of the Declaration of Independence, the physician and patriot Benjamin Rush, that the iniquity of European absolutism was reflected in its people's wretchedly unhealthy and demoralized condition. Democracy was the source of the people's health. Democratic citizens, self-educated in exercising their political judgement, would secure a healthful existence. Jefferson claimed that the healthiness of the American people reflected the superiority of democratic citizenship (Rosen, 1952).

But it was French revolutionaries who added health to the rights of man and asserted that health citizenship should be a characteristic of the modern democratic state. In 1791 the Committee on Mendicancy, directed by the Duc de la Rochelle, declared work to be a right of man. If the state could not provide it, then it must ensure a means of subsistence to the unemployed. In 1791 the Constituente Assembly's Committee on Salubrity added health to the state's obligations to its citizens. The Committee believed this could be achieved by establishing a network of rural health officers who, while trained in clinical medicine, would also become responsible for reporting on the health of communities and monitoring epidemics among both humans and farm animals (Weiner, 1970; Weiner, 1974; Weiner, 1993).

The citizen's charter of health, however, was double-sided. The *ideologue*, Constantine Volney (1757–1820), raised the issue of the citizen's responsibility to maintain his own health for the benefit of the state. In the new social order, the individual was a political and economic unit of a collective whole. It was a citizen's duty to keep healthy through temperance, in both the consumption of pleasure and the exercise of passions, and through cleanliness (Jordanova, 1982).

Democratic rhetoric on health citizenship failed to translate into reality in any late Enlightenment state. But it was still idealistically burning in the hearts of the German and French revolutionaries of 1848 (Chapter 6). The mantle of health reform was inherited, instead, by utilitarian political economy. It was the economic value to expanding industrial societies of preventing premature

mortality which was ultimately responsible for public health reform in early nineteenth-century Europe.

HEALTH AND THE PURSUIT OF HAPPINESS

If political and economic freedom was one dominant theme of Enlightenment
philosophy, the pursuit of happiness, as announced by the American Declaration
of Independence, was another (Quennell, 1988; Gay, 1967–1969). This philosophical theme produced a theory of government which legitimated the
involvement of the nineteenth-century state in the development of public health
policy. Understanding the eighteenth-century social and political philosophy of
Utilitarianism is essential, therefore, for analysing the rationale of subsequent
social policy.

The pursuit of happiness as a justifiable philosophical goal was based upon
the new psychology of association first elaborated by David Hartley but initially
addressed by John Locke, John Gay and David Hume (Ogberg, 1976). In *A
Dissertation concerning the Principle and Criterion of Virtue and the Origin of the Passions*
(1730) John Gay suggested that all men seek pleasure and the avoidance of pain,
and thus the normal law of action identifies the path which leads to happiness.
While this end may be universally agreed upon, men differ regarding the means
to it because the association of ideas varies from individual to individual.
Utilitarian morality attempted to resolve the dilemma of personal and general
interest created by the psychology of association with the quantitative concept of
the 'greatest happiness of the greatest number'. The idea that this felicific
calculus could provide the basis for a theory of government was first articulated
by the English political philosopher Jeremy Bentham. Utilitarianism attempted
to apply the universality of law to the realm of politics and morals. It was moral
Newtonianism in which the principle of the association of ideas and the principle of utility took the place of the principle of universal attraction (C. Smith,
1987; Leslie, 1972).

But Bentham's felicific calculus synthesized various concepts in the eighteenth-century philosophy of moral utility (Scarre, 1995). The professor of
moral philosophy at Glasgow, and friend of both Adam Smith and David Hume,
Francis Hutchinson, developed the Earl of Shaftesbury's concept of innate
human 'moral sense' into a Utilitarian philosophy (Manuel (ed.), 1965).
Shaftesbury had attacked Thomas Hobbes's pessimistic philosophy of human
nature by asserting instead that it was characterized by a natural moral sense and
universal harmony. Hutchinson suggested that it was possible to measure the
moral evil or vice of an action by the degree of misery it created for the number
of sufferers (Scott, 1900; Taylor, 1965). Thus the action which was 'best' was
that which 'accomplishes the greatest happiness for the greatest number'.
Hutchinson also described elements of a system which Bentham was later to call
'moral arithmetic'. David Hume equally attacked Hobbes by suggesting that
egoism and social feeling could be compatible. Hume claimed that if the

predominating motives in human nature are egoistic then the fact that the human species lives and survives indicates a degree of harmonization of egoisms. So it was possible for individual interests to be identified with general interests. It could be argued, therefore, that the aim of government should be to bring this identification about. Hume proposed that the art of politics consisted of governing individuals through their own interests by creating artifices which facilitated their co-operation for the public good (Livingston and Martin (eds), 1991; Flew, 1986). Bentham based his concept of utility upon this principle of the artificial identification of interests. The legislator's function was to solve the problem of morals and to identify the interests of the individual with that of the community through a well-regulated application of punishments (Letwin, 1993).

But this method of government had been first explored by the French philosopher Claude-Adriane Helvétius. Helvétius, like Hume, wanted to establish a science of morals as well as physics. He believed that the differences between individuals, as indeed the differences between men and women, were entirely socially constructed rather than physiological. He promoted the late Enlightenment belief in the power of education to mould human behaviour. The purpose of a moral science was, Helvétius believed, to identify the interests of the public, 'that is to say of the greatest number'. Since society and history were morally rather than physically determined, then morals and legislation were 'one and the same science' because it was by good laws only that virtuous men could be made. Rewards and punishments should be constructed to bind individuals together in the general interest. The principle of law must rest on its public utility: 'that is to say, of the greatest number of men subject to the same form of government'. Helvétius's concept was taken up and elaborated by an Italian legal theorist, Cesare Beccaria, who attempted to mathematize this Utilitarian principle. Bentham, like Gay, Hume, Helvétius and Beccaria, believed that morals could become an exact science if based upon the principle of utility (Halévy, 1972). In *A Fragment of Government*, Bentham gave Hume the credit for originating the concept of utility but he did so because his theory of government was intended to be a Humean form of social science (Dinwiddy, 1989).

Bentham built upon the work of Helvétius, Beccaria, Hume and others to develop a theory of government which was intended as a practical guide to administrative action. Happiness in the felicific calculus had very specific meaning as far as Bentham was concerned: 'Subsistence, abundance, security, equality – to these heads may be reduced the fruits of good government' (Einstein, 1991). The provision of social welfare came under the heading of security which included the liberties of the subject, i.e. security against injury to the person, property, reputation or condition of life, security against oppression from government, community or neighbours. Bentham's theory of government hinged on the security of expectation. Such expectation underlay the Utilitarian principle that governments should strive after the welfare of their subjects, which included the welfare of the poor as much as the rich (Halévy, 1972).

Bentham perceived the welfare of the poor and the indigent a necessary obligation of Utilitarian government. He made a clear distinction between the poor, who worked for wages to achieve their subsistence, and the indigent, who were destitute and in need of relief. Bentham believed a country was rich or poor according to the condition of the majority of its inhabitants and 'the vast majority of the inhabitants of every country is constituted by the poor'. The rights and interests of the poor must be safeguarded as much as those of any individual. It was the duty of the government to refrain from doing anything which made the condition of the poor man any worse than that of the rich regarding his 'liberty, his reputation, his life or his domestic or political rights'. Wages were the foundation of security for the poor – the only property they possessed. When wages were unobtainable, relief of indigence was a necessity, a duty of government which could not be left to the whims of charity. Relief of destitution, however, if undertaken by the government was done so at the expense of the labouring poor, and therefore their condition must never be made superior to that of the labouring classes. However, he did not recommend that their condition be made deliberately worse (Halévy, 1972). The principle of less eligibility was invented later by Bentham's disciples, Edwin Chadwick and Nassau Senior (Finer, 1952). Bentham's answer to the relief of indigence was the creation of industry houses.

Originally Bentham conceived of industry houses as administered by government, but he later believed they would be more economically and efficiently managed if they were to become part of a joint stock corporation similar to the East India Company, called perhaps the National Charity Company. Profit would be an incentive for frugal management but public inspection and good book-keeping would ensure that the inmates received humane treatment and that standards were kept up (Bahmueller, 1981). The architecture of the industry houses should mirror the panoptican of the prison or the asylum (Foucault, 1977). The industry houses were not just a solution to the relief of destitution, but were a 'social experiment' in the scientific management of communal life, regimentation of labour and provision of economic security – a miniature society organized for the production of wealth and the improvement of living standards (Bahmueller, 1981).

The social experiment within the industry houses would include the provision of health care, which should be primarily concerned with the prevention of disease. A regime of life should be imposed within the community to produce a healthful existence, with attention paid not only to hygiene and cleanliness but also to diet, exercise and occupation. Bentham believed that apart from the production of profit, work was essential to the maintenance of healthy spirits. The industry houses would also act as dispensaries, and would replace the country hospital with the appointment of medical curators, who would minister not only to the inmates but to the independent poor living in the district surrounding it. Doctors should tender for these positions, the best being those who worked for the lowest pay or without a salary altogether, because their motive would be that of service rather than money. The gains for the doctor, Bentham believed, would be enhanced experience and reputation which would improve his ability to attract private paying patients (Semple, 1993).

The industry houses would also provide the opportunity for a range of medical experiments and the gathering of socio-medical statistics. Case records would provide new insight to the effectiveness of different therapies and drugs. Statistics on health and morbidity could be correlated with diet, alcohol consumption, occupation and living standards to found the basis of a comprehensive epidemiology. Normal health as well as disease was to be studied, along with the stages of child development – at what age they first cut their teeth, started to walk and talk. Their height and weight gain should be recorded and their strength tested at various intervals. The industry houses should also be places of medical education where the curators would give lectures on not only human but also veterinary medicine. All domestic animals found dead in the houses should have an autopsy to determine the cause of death. The industry houses should become the centre of scientific study of all kinds (Semple, 1993).

The Utilitarian welfare provision for the poor constituted the social scientific management and study of communal life. Bentham drew up his plans for the relief of poverty with an eighteenth-century optimistic belief in the economic value of population growth. The dismal science of political economy, stimulated by Malthus's pessimistic warning about the downside to demographic explosion, did not play a part in Bentham's conception. The principles of both classical political economy and Utilitarianism contributed to the reconstruction of state provision for the relief of poverty and the provision of public health measures. But the Benthamite conception of the social scientific management of communal life was a powerful force in the state provision of public health in nineteenth-century Britain.

Part 2

The right to health and the modern state

We have seen in Chapter 3 how population health figured in Jeffersonian democratic theory and how French Revolutionaries declared health to be a right of citizenship. French *idéologues*, however, argued that the right to health also implied obligations for democratic citizens. These tensions within the social contract of health between modern states and their citizens are explored in the next two sections of the book.

In Part 2 we focus on nineteenth-century conceptions of health as a civil right to equality under the law to protection from assault by disease. The next six chapters, therefore, discuss the influence upon state policies of political and social thought and biological and social scientific theories about population health, in order to chart the changing parameters of the social contract of health in this period.

Chapter 4 explains how, in the first half of the nineteenth century, new methods of quantitative and social scientific analysis reconfigured perceptions of population health. These new analytical languages facilitated the professionalization of disease prevention. Chapter 5 discusses the epidemic consequences resulting from the social, economic and political upheavals of industrialization. It highlights the way in which economic and urban expansion produced massive levels of social dislocation, provoking the spread of the epidemic diseases, such as typhus and cholera, which came to characterize nineteenth-century industrial societies. Chapters 6, 7, 8 and 9 then examine the response in continental Europe, in Britain and in the United States to the new landscape of disease in urbanized industrial societies. These chapters draw out the comparative impact of disease prevention upon the development of the modern state within different national histories and cultures.

The chapters in this section discuss how the right to health for some meant the loss of civil liberties for others within the emerging social contract of health in the modern state. They highlight the way in which the politics of health contributed to the rise of bureaucratic within democratic states, and investigate how differential levels of health reflected the economic and social inequalities that characterized nineteenth-century industrial societies. The history of collective action in relation to population health in this period sheds special light upon changing political and social perceptions of poverty and deprivation. Public health, therefore, is examined in this context in terms of the transformations taking place in social and civic consciousness in the nineteenth century.

4 Social science and the quantitative analysis of health

Late Enlightenment thought made a connection between social improvement and environmental reform. As the industrial age emerged at the outset of the nineteenth century, the ecological and social relations of disease dramatically changed (Kunitz, 1993). Nineteenth-century society responded on many different levels to the paradoxes of industrialization and extensive urbanization. The Enlightenment study of political arithmetic and human longevity evolved into the statistical study of human aggregates and their consequences for both the moral and physical environment. The enumeration of human misery was linked to the social physics of human improvement, inspired by both the Enlightenment pursuit of happiness through the felicific calculus and an Evangelical and philanthropic moral imperative. In the nineteenth century, public health reform interwove Victorian social science with Enlightenment political economy and was integrated into philosophical radicalism and the politics of social amelioration.

Nineteenth-century analyses of society aimed to replace 'opinions' with empirical 'facts' (Young, 1977). Social science appealed to the domination of 'reason' above ideological bias. The neutrality which the social sciences of man and society aimed for was, however, never realized. From its inception social science was bound to a prescriptive mission (D. Porter, 1997). The earliest attempts to develop a 'social mathematics' and 'social physics' of society were directed at reforming the political operation of power and restructuring of social relations (T. Porter, 1986). The reform impulse of early 'social physics' carried over into the first attempts to make medicine a social science of health and welfare in the mid-nineteenth century. Advocates of 'social medicine' at this time invented the physician as an attorney to the poor and encouraged him to take up his duty to participate in the political planning of society. Furthermore, nineteenth-century sociology was born out of a medical metaphor which compared the analysis of social order to the analysis of living organisms. Sociology, like its social scientific predecessors, was wedded to reordering society, but its prescriptive goals were derived from an analogy which compared society to a functioning organism (D. Porter, 1997; Gordon, 1991). The intellectual objective of the new 'positive' science of the social organism was to identify the laws which governed the harmonious functioning of its organs. Its method was to differentiate normal from pathological social states. The prescriptive nature of the organic analogy continued to have a powerful influence on the development of medicine as a social science of the management of the health of populations (D. Porter, 1997).

THE SOCIAL PHYSICS OF HUMAN AGGREGATES

Before the nineteenth century, an Enlightenment tradition applied Newtonian philosophy and Lockean empiricism to the analysis of society as a mechanism. The *philosophe* Ambroise Condorcet (1743–1794) believed that society was made up of homogeneous individuals all born equal under the law (Baker, 1982). The homogeneity of individuals made it possible to discover the mathematical laws which governed the social mechanism. He thought that government should become the realization of natural social laws, making it a technocratic exercise rather than an act of will, and that correct state action could be guided by scientific truth. Although he espoused the philosophy of natural rights he did not consider the general populace sufficiently expert to contribute to decision-making. Instead, Condorcet devised an anti-democratic theory of government ruled by experts. He supported widespread scientific education in order that a system of elections could be instituted in which voters could discriminate between the most ably qualified experts for government (Baker, 1982).

Condorcet set a precedent for creating a science of society analogous to the physical sciences, the principal motor-force of which from the seventeenth century was the development of mathematical measurement (Daston, 1981; Daston, 1988). His reduction of diversity and inequality to a social mechanism made up of homogeneous individual parts made a science of social statistics possible (Hacking, 1990; Gigerenzer *et al.*, 1989). The quantitative analysis of social physics was taken up in the early nineteenth century by Lambert-Adolphe-Jacques Quetelet, a Belgian astronomer who devised the theory of the normal frequency distribution curve (Ackerknecht, 1952). A generation younger than Condorcet, Quetelet (1796–1874) dropped the moral science of precepts and made a transition to a social science of laws. But he still believed that social science could provide the basis for reform. While setting up an observatory in Brussels in 1823, Quetelet began to apply the routine methods of mathematical analysis used in astronomical observation to some of the demographic questions which had been investigated by the French mathematicians Pierre Simon Marquis de Laplace (1749–1827), and Joseph Fourier (1768–1830). This led him to found a social mathematics based upon the concept of the average man being equivalent to the concept of the centre of gravity in celestial physics (T. Porter, 1986; Gigerenzer *et al.*, 1989). He believed that humans were fundamentally alike and that the deviant effects of the peripheral members of the social body cancelled each other out. Virtue was a just mean between two vicious extremes. Quetelet assumed a direct equivalence between the statistical laws of society and the mechanical laws of the heavens, and that the historical path of society could be deduced in the same way as that of the planets. The idiosyncrasies of the behaviour of individuals formed general regular patterns on aggregate. Thus, he saw that there was a 'law of large numbers' which could predict the regularities of social behaviour, such as the relationship of suicide to climatic seasons. His theory of the normal distribution of human variation became a measurement of error, a set of accidental fluctuations from a golden mean (Gigerenzer *et al.*, 1989). He believed that social statistics could provide the basis of the scientific management of society which chimed with Bentham's notion of scientific government achieved through a felicific calculus.

In France in the early nineteenth century the application of social physics did not lead to social reform. Instead it created a new academic enquiry into the conditions which determine health and disease. There had been a long tradition of the use of 'number in medicine' in France. The celebrated philosopher-physician Cabanis had first pointed the way to the possible use of statistics in the investigation of the social origins of disease. The numerical regularities observed by Laplace in astronomy were applied by the alienist Philippe Pinel in the evaluation of therapeutic effectiveness, and developed further with regard to physiological inquiries by French clinician Pierre Louis (1787–1872) (Shryock, 1979; Gigerenzer *et al.*, 1989). An ex-army surgeon, Louis René Villermé, who was a friend of Quetelet, translated social physics into elaborate studies of the differential mortality of the rich and poor and the health conditions of the proletariat and their average expectation of life (Ackerknecht, 1952). The result was a definitive identification of death as an economic and social disease. The revelation of this relationship, however, did not stimulate political action. Villermé warned against the involvement of the state in health reform and suggested instead that the remoralization of the poor would eliminate epidemic disease and premature mortality.

In France there was no institutionalization of social statistics or health reform in learned societies or political organizations, but a distinct group of sociomedical investigators emerged in the early nineteenth century, a *'partie d'hygiène'*. Few among them were practising physicians, official bureaucrats or revolutionary political agitators. Most were university-trained 'hygienists' and they completed commissioned studies for a range of agencies, from the Ministry of the Interior to the Royal Medical Academy and the Academy of Moral and Political Sciences. Most hygienists studied under Jean Noel Hallé within the Department of Hygiene of the new Royal Academy of Medicine, set up at the end of the Napoleonic Wars. Numerous students became leading lights of the *partie d'hygiène*, such as Parent-Duchatelet, Michel Lèvy and Villermé himself (Coleman, 1982).

Quantitative analysis of social conditions was also supported by a bureau for statistics, set up in 1800 in the Ministry of the Interior but abolished in 1812. While J.A. Chaptal in the Ministry of Manufacture and Commerce attempted to set up a national census, this failed to be realized for the first quarter of the century. Failure to establish a national census led the Prefect of the Department of the Seine, G.J.G. Chabrol de Volvic, to create a municipal statistical office to produce a census of Paris. Chabrol employed Frederic Villot as director of the bureau and his old teacher from the Ecole polytechnique, J.B.J. Fourier, as its mathematician. The first census of Paris was completed in 1817, and in 1821 the bureau produced the first large-scale use of social statistics in France in a massive analysis of the demographic structure of Paris, the *Recherches statistiques sur la ville de Paris*. Second and third volumes of the *Recherches* were published in 1823 and 1826. The Royal Academy of Medicine created a statistical commission to examine the health implications of the Chabrol-Villot tableaux and employed Villermé to produce an official report (T. Porter, 1986; Gigerenzer *et al.*, 1989).

Louis René Villermé served as an army medical surgeon during the Napoleonic Wars. On his return to Paris he completed a doctoral thesis in the newly founded hygiene department in 1814. He never again practised clinical medicine but devoted himself to the social diagnosis of disease. He became a full member of the Academy of Medicine in 1835, but prior to that was elected to the Academy of Moral and Political Sciences in 1832, and was made its president in 1849. Villermé completed a study of prison life in 1820 in which he developed many of the statistical techniques which he later used in his studies of differential mortality and the health of the working class (Ackerknecht, 1952).

In his review of Villot's *Recherches* Villermé attempted to correlate the differential mortality between *arrondissements*, or districts of the city, with a range of variables. He first tested various environmental features as determinants of different levels of disease and mortality, such as elevation of the soil, movement of prevailing winds and other meteorological conditions. None, however, showed any patterns which coincided with mortality. The Commission then turned to the question of congestion, but found that densities were so mixed within *arrondissements* that again no clear pattern emerged, and similarly distribution of open spaces did not fit the facts. Having exhausted the traditional environmental factors, the Commission turned to social conditions, beginning with an analysis of the overall financial condition of city inhabitants, using rent levels as an indicator of wealth. The Villot study had already provided information on the distribution of rents in each *arrondissement* and tax liabilities (Coleman, 1982).

The result revealed that untaxed renters, who represented the poorest inhabitants, consistently showed the highest levels of mortality throughout the city, which explained the differential levels between *arrondissements*. Furthermore, detailed area studies of quarters and streets demonstrated that the Rue de la Mortellerie, which heaved with some of the poorest Parisians, had a death rate of 30.6 per thousand, while a short distance away across the river, the higher-taxed residents of the quays of the Ile-Saint-Louis had a death rate of only 19.1 per thousand. In his final *Rapport* in 1828, Villermé presented these data together with further correlations on births and marriages and the ratio of illegitimacy with poverty and wealth. The *Rapport* demonstrated that wealth tended to reduce the number of births, increase abandonment of natural children and preserve life; the poor had higher birth rates, lost more children to death, recognized their natural children and overall died younger. The poor not only died at a far greater rate than the wealthy, but they died most frequently at the prime age of life. In this first study of death in Paris, Villermé thus asserted that the primary determinant of differential mortality was socio-economic conditions. From this he went on to study broad patterns of life and death, using the Quetelet frequency distribution to discover patterns of vitality such as the conjunction of births with season, the average duration of diseases at different ages and the age-specific influence of marshes on human mortality. After 1835 Villermé concentrated on creating life tables for the working class, studying the textile industry in particular, and actually correlating mortality to income. Occasionally he collaborated with his fellow student from Hallé's department, Benoiston de Chateauneuf (Coleman, 1982).

The 1828 *Rapport* demonstrated that the aetiology of disease could be successfully investigated through statistical methods, which allowed Villermé and his hygienic associates to believe that they could be used to solve the problem of the health of populations. The *partie d'hygiène* shared an economistic philosophy grounded in their faith in the science of political economy. The ideas of the Swiss economist J.-C.-L. Sismondi, the French political economist J.B. Say and Thomas Malthus governed their vision of the progressive nature of a modern industrial free-market economy (Gigerenzer, 1989; Blaug (ed.), 1991a; Blaug, 1991b). Their allegiance was above all to liberty, the freedom of action for individuals, which they believed was the true legacy of the French Revolution, and the supreme right of property. In opposition to Jean Jacques Rousseau, they did not perceive 'civilization' to be a regressive force for humanity but saw it as the emancipation from ignorance and responsible for superabundant productivity and prosperity. The imperfections of progress, the social costs of unequal mortality and disease visited upon the poor, could be corrected through the correction of the individual behaviour of those who bore them (Coleman, 1982).

The moral regeneration of the poor would put an end to destitution and its cohorts, disease and death. In this the masters of industry should bear the greatest responsibility. It was up to the entrepreneur to see that his workers lived in a respectable way and were educated in moral habits, through Christian example and instruction. The economist hygienists perceived no role for the state nor legislative reform which would fundamentally undermine individual freedom and initiative. They feared the rise of socialism and the overthrow of the rule of property. They sought instead a programme of amelioration through religious indoctrination of the poor into the ways of moral behaviour. Their answer to the claim that civilization produced the ills of society such as poverty was simply to say that the poor were as yet uncivilized. Their answer to the question of poverty was that it was caused by the poor themselves, and that once they were educated into the ways of civilized behaviour it would be eliminated. Thus, French hygienist analysis of the social origins of disease identified the poor as a 'race apart', a barbarian, uncivilized multitude which bred in abundance and died equally excessively. The answer was to civilize them into the ways of moral correctness and responsible citizenship (Coleman, 1982).

STATISTICAL THINKING AND SOCIAL REFORM IN BRITAIN

The 'geography of health' was examined in Britain as part of the discovery of the social conditions of the poor. In the 1830s a fashion developed for attempting to transfer the treatment of social issues from a polemical to a statistical basis (Cullen, 1975). As the new tool for measuring social inequality, statistics was embraced by Victorian social reform movements (Metz, 1984). Statistics as a numerical science of society was explored in England in the 1830s by a group of scientists and gentlemen of letters with Whig reforming principles, who set up a separate section 'F' of the British Association for the Advancement of Science (Morrell and Thackray, 1981; Macleod and Collins, 1981). Later this group founded the Statistical Society of London (Cullen, 1975).

The ethos of the Society was based on the neutrality of *facts* and the Baconian spirit of enquiry. The substitution of 'facts which can be stated numerically and arranged in tables for opinion' (Eyler, 1979: 15) was a fundamental goal echoed and restated many times by the Society members and in its annual reports and the first editions of its journal. It was a direct attempt to end politics as a process of conflict and replace it with scientific government (Abrams, 1968). However, from the outset the ambiguity of facts was guided by a moral bias for improvement and reform. Nowhere was this more evident than in the large proportion of the work completed on the investigations of 'the condition of the people' (Chinn, 1995; Easson and McIntyre, 1978; Disraeli, 1983; Harrison, 1979) which became an investigation of 'social pathology' resulting from assessments of the social costs of industrialization (Cullen, 1975).

The composition of the founding membership of the Society ensured a synthesis of perspectives from political economy, demography and mathematical calculation, together with a Benthamite spirit of reform (Cowherd, 1977). The influence of Benthamite Utilitarianism was found throughout the studies undertaken by Society members, typified by W.R. Devell, who suggested that

> facts are statistical only inasmuch as they can be shown to have a direct relation to the ostensible end for which social union is established – the greatest happiness of the greatest number and that all national and even local legislation can be just and equitable only as it proceeds upon the general average principles obtained from statistical documents.
>
> (Eyler, 1979: 21)

Despite the attempts of the statisticians to emancipate themselves from the traditional relationship that political economy had to 'moulding policy', investigation into the 'the conditions of the people' repeated well-worn assumptions. For example, in his study of the education of pauper children, James Kay-Shuttleworth concluded that special schools of industry would prevent future dependency by training them in the 'correct social habits', which would enable them to 'discharge their social duties' (Abrams, 1968: 21–22). The Society conducted large-scale studies on many aspects of the condition of the poor and developed the technique of local surveys. The programme of empirical social research, however, sacrificed the development of innovative mathematical rigour. Francis Galton later described the work of William Farr, for example, as representing the 'poetic' side of statistics, and accused social statisticians of generally hindering the development of statistics as·a pure science (Eyler, 1979).

Statistical studies of health and the social determinants of disease were brought together in another reforming scientific society of the mid-Victorian period, the Epidemiological Society of London (ESL) (Watkins, 1984). The Society was formed under the presidency of Lord Ashley, seventh Earl of Shaftesbury, on 30 July 1850. The inadequacies of public health provision had been demonstrated during the cholera epidemic of 1848–1849. Despite the establishment of the first Public Health Act, the mortality was higher than that of the 1831 epidemic (Pelling, 1978). The Society was set up partly in response to the shocking effects of the epidemic, but also for the broader objective of the need to study the process of epidemics as a whole. The founders of the Society were equally concerned with the study of the 'constant and active prevalence of the ordinary epidemics of this country'. It aimed to investigate the progress and development of what it classified as diseases 'connected with the soil and climate' such as ague, remittent and yellow fever; 'epidemics' such as typhoid fever which were continuously prevalent; 'epidemics like cholera, appearing in a locality, and spreading thence to distant countries'; and last, a class of disease they called 'eruptive fevers', such as scarlatina. The aim was not simply to seek out the causes of epidemic diseases and study the determinants of their spread, but also to assess the effectiveness of different methods of prevention, such as quarantine, vaccination or preventing the sale of contaminated foods. As important as research was its role as a pressure group, aiming to influence government, health boards, medical corporate bodies, public institutions and medical societies (Metz, 1984; Watkins, 1984).

Leading medical and scientific men rather than political figures dominated the ESL. Among its presidents were William Jenner, Joseph Fayrer, George Buchanan, Richard Thorne Thorne, Thomas Crawford, Shirley Foster Murphey, John Lane Notter, John Tathum, Patrick Manson and William Corfield. The general membership was a mixture of medical officers of health, ex-army and naval MOs and civil servants from the Local Government Board. It also had a large body of foreign corresponding members. Some of the most significant epidemiological studies of the mid-Victorian period were first presented through the forum of the ESL. John Snow (Shepherd, 1995) in 1853 presented to the Society a study of 'Comparative Mortality of Large Towns and Rural Districts, and the Causes by Which it is Influenced', which prefigured the methods he used two years later to demonstrate the water-borne contagiousness of cholera. Benjamin Ward Richardson published a seminal paper in 1858 in the *Transactions* which outlined the use of the experimental method in the study of epidemiology, and Gavin Milroy demonstrated before the Society, 'The Influence of Contagion on the Rise and Spread of Epidemic Disease' in 1861.

Other major papers were given by leading lights of the Victorian medical profession and sanitary reform movement, such as Edward Sieveking, James Bird, Sir William Pym, T. Spencer Wells and Headlam Greenhow (Watkins, 1984).

The study of health and disease as part of the study of the state of society flourished within English learned societies in the early nineteenth century (Metz, 1984). This social science, while purporting to be entirely factual, was in reality bound to political and moral philosophies of reform and active philanthropy. Epidemiology as a science of social statistics sought to eliminate the spread of disease by destroying the environment which bred it. That environment was partly physical and structural and partly social and moral (Watkins, 1984). This reforming epistemology was exemplified in the work of one of the most significant sanitary reformers, William Farr.

Villermé asserted that the social origins of disease and premature mortality lay among the poor as a 'race apart' who needed to be civilized (Coleman, 1982). It was a belief shared by William Farr as he studied the distribution of disease and mortality in England. Farr was against the indiscriminate expansion of financial assistance to the destitute, but he did not believe that the poor were beyond reform. He thought that good hearts and willing souls often lay beneath the superficial appearance of vicious depravity. The presence of God's charity among them meant that the poor could be reformed through the influence of enlightened humanitarianism. He had a vision of the poor as wretched but redeemable creatures. Unlike his French counterparts, Farr attributed a much greater role to environmental determinants of health and pursued a different programme of disease prevention and social amelioration (Eyler, 1979).

Farr used social statistics to construct social reforms through an analysis of mortality and urban salubrity. The compulsory registration of births, marriages and deaths and the Registrar General's Office (RGO) were created in Britain under the 1836 Registration Act, with T.H. Lister as the first registrar. On the recommendation of Edwin Chadwick, William Farr was appointed Compiler of Abstracts, in charge of statistics. Farr studied medical statistics under Louis in the early 1830s. In his annual reports at the RGO, Farr demonstrated that mortality increased with density, and he stressed that overcrowding was the main determinant of high mortality from what he classified as zymotic diseases. Farr argued that crude mortality rates could direct public health policy by using the 'life-table' as a 'biometer' of health and a measure of salubrity, comparable to a barometer for meteorological measurement or the thermometer for measuring heat (Eyler, 1979).

In his first five annual reports, Farr highlighted the unhealthiness of the urban over rural environments, and compared poor with wealthy registration districts. He identified insanitation rather than poverty as the primary cause of higher urban mortality, because he believed that the price of the necessities for subsistence had to completely outstrip the ability to purchase them before income had any influence on death rates. As a result, he advocated the keeping of statistics, education in basic hygiene for the general public, and the reform of medical education to make physicians more aware and responsible for preventing illness. He was a great enthusiast of vaccination and supported the campaign for the provision of uncontaminated water (Eyler, 1979).

Farr showed that the life-table could demonstrate how life expectation at different ages varied according to occupation, wealth and hygienic conditions. Subsequently it became the basic tool of every English public health officer, analysing the health of a district through infant mortality, the most important vital measure. 'Vital statistics' became the primary subject of all public health education (Newsholme, 1923).

THE ORGANIC ANALOGY: SOCIAL SCIENCE AND THE SCIENTIFIC MANAGEMENT OF SOCIETY

Statistics in England in the 1830s and 1840s was only one of a number of new sciences of social management and amelioration which emerged in the nineteenth century. As noted above, social amelioration had lain at the heart of the early social sciences from the late eighteenth century (Zeitlin, 1968). The mechanical metaphor derived from Newtonian physics had supported the development of social mathematics as the primary method of social enquiry (Daston, 1981). Natural history, by contrast, promoted an organic analogy of social order based on the new Enlightenment theories of physiology. Understanding society as an organic system provided another model of scientific management. The organic analogy based the social management of society on the division between the normal and the pathological (Canguilhem, 1989). This concept added a further dimension to nineteenth-century public health reform which had significant consequences for social medicine in the twentieth century (D. Porter, 1997).

The mechanistic model of social physics was not universally accepted by its contemporaries. It was dismissed, for example, by Edmund Burke, who used a chemical metaphor to explain the volatile, indeterminate vitality of social and political change (Stanlis, 1991). Others believed that society was a functioning organism rather than a physical machine (T. Porter, 1990). In *The Order of Things*, Michel Foucault suggested that the social sciences succeeded the natural sciences at the turn of the nineteenth century by replacing static analytical taxonomies with functional organic systems (Foucault, 1970). Thus wealth, natural history and grammar transmuted into economics, biology and philology by redefining life, labour and language in terms of the functional discourse of scientific rationality in a modern capitalist society. In what Foucault chose to call the Classical Age of Knowledge, the subject of objective enquiry was divinely ordained 'nature', but the modern *'episteme'* consisted of the human sciences, which focused on the history of man himself. The human sciences reconstructed the functional relations of organic systems hidden beneath classifiable observable characteristics (Foucault, 1970). Foucault argued, therefore, that objective study of the order of human society translated the language of the natural sciences to the social sciences through an organic metaphor. Organicism was linked to scientism as a defining cultural characteristic of modern society (Foucault, 1970; Foucault, 1972).

The organic metaphor of a functional society powerfully advanced a division between the sociologically normal and the pathological, which first emerged in the work of Auguste Comte (T. Porter, 1990; Thompson, 1976). Comte's intellectual predecessor in utilizing the organic analogy, Claude-Henri de Saint-Simon, wanted to replace Catholicism and superstition with Newtonian rationalism, applying natural philosophy to the study of social order to discover its natural laws using the methods of Lockean empiricism (Manuel, 1956; Ionescu, 1976). Unlike Condorcet or Quetelet, he did not believe that society was made up of homogeneous equivalent individuals, but was divided into ruling parasitical and industrial classes because humanity consisted biologically of thinkers, artists and workers. Society had its own physiology, just like the human body (Manuel, 1956; Ionescu, 1976). His concept of social science, therefore, was one which he frequently referred to as social physiology, which Comte later condensed into the term 'sociology'. It is clear from the relationship that Comte's work bears to Saint-Simon that European sociology is grounded in analogical organizist reasoning (Hacking, 1990). The goal of 'the true Organic Doctrine', Saint-Simon pointed out, was to help European society to achieve complete harmony. The pursuit of a science of society was subsequently linked to the search for political prescriptives, and the creation of sociology was part of a programmatic doctrine of positive social unity (Hawthorn, 1976).

Positive social unity was the central goal of sociology as it was defined by Auguste Comte. Like Saint-Simon, Comte rejected all social philosophies of negation which led to social instability and revolution, such as Hegelianism, and sought to identify the mechanisms of social integration and harmony (Pickering, 1993). He viewed society as an organism governed by laws that resulted in the harmonious functioning of its interdependent organs. The task of a positive science of the social organism was to observe the laws governing social stability. The identification of these laws would synthetically produce a new intellectual order that would result in human unity. The task of sociology was to realize the true positive spirit in history, ending war, conflict and diverse antagonisms. Sociology was a prescriptive as much as a descriptive science, that would inaugurate a new era in human history (Pickering, 1993), the era of positive philosophy which would replace religion as the dominant ideology upon which the social order depended. Sociology was the course through which the system of positive philosophy would become what T.H. Huxley was later to aptly describe as Catholicism with Christianity taken out (Hacking, 1990).

In England, J.S. Mill and Herbert Spencer criticized Comte's appropriation of the positivist method. They both suggested that the method of 'inverse deduction' was simply a characteristic of the scientific spirit of the age, a feature of the rampant demand for scientific inquiry. Both Spencer and Mill refused to acknowledge this as an invention of Comte alone and claimed that they had already employed this method in their own analyses of social relations. While they welcomed the historical and cross-cultural analysis of social organization to discover the laws of social evolution, they rejected positivism as a secular ethic, a 'positive polity' (Mill, 1961; Spencer, 1969; Spencer, 1996). In England this led to separate analytical theories of social evolution, the most prominent of which were those developed by Spencer himself (Peel, 1972).

Despite his critics, Comte remained an important influence in British and American sociology. British sociologists such as L.T. Hobhouse and Patrick Geddes, who were among the founders of the Sociological Society, were all positivists whose reaction to Comte had been formative in their development (Abrams, 1968). British sociology shared with Comte a positivist model of scientific inquiry dedicated to analysing the laws of social evolution with a view to the creation of an harmonious society. But the most significant consequence of Comte's use of the bio-physiological model of positivist inquiry into organic systems was the transfer of the idea of the normal and the pathological into the discourse on social behaviour (Canguilhem, 1989). Positivist social inquiry aimed to identify the normal state of social order determined by the general laws of human unity (Hughes, 1979). Comte used a physiological model of pathological inflammation as a deviation from 'the normal state' of an organ to construct the idea of the sociologically normal. When the doctor, phrenologist and medical theorist François Joseph Victor Broussais challenged the ontological notion of illness with a sliding scale between the normal and the pathological, he provided Auguste Comte with the conceptual apparatus for developing a science of the norms and standards of behaviour that made up the basis of society (Canguilhem, 1989). The fundamental proposition of positivist sociology is that all behaviour is caused, and the laws which determine it can be empirically identified and experimentally predicted. Normal social behaviour is that which has followed its determined path. Pathological social behaviour is that which deviates: that is, a variation of the 'normal state'. The term 'normal' can, in the empirical sense, mean 'typical' – quantified, statistically significant, average, median – but it also implies a prescriptive value (Canguilhem, 1989).

The analysis of normative belief brought the relationship of facts and value into question within sociology but in Comte this relationship was most starkly demonstrated. The 'normal state' of social order, that which creates social unity, became not simply an analysis of what existed, but that which should be sought for through the institution of a positivist ideal. Positivism was, especially in Comte's latter years, a science of social pathology striving to obtain a state of purified social normalcy (Hacking, 1990).

The organic metaphor of normal and pathological states was extended by Emile Durkheim into an analysis of the causes of normativity itself as the basis of social cohesion, integration and stability (Lukes, 1973). In this context Durkheim explored the normative construction of individuation. He suggested that in modern society, characterized by increasing division of labour, social unity depended upon the successful social construction of individualism. When the socialization of the individual broke down, patterns of social pathology resulted, such as suicide. Suicide, Durkheim argued, was not just an expression of individual despair, but a symptom of social disintegration (Lester (ed.), 1994; Giddens, 1990).

Differentiation between the normal and the pathological remained central to the subsequent sociological analysis of social integration in the nineteenth and twentieth centuries. In socio-medical enquiry the social-biological determination of normal and pathological states remained, however, problematic. The conceptual tensions inherent within the organic metaphor continued to loom large in the development of social medicine and medical sociology in the twentieth century as disciplines derived from the analysis of social integration and deviance (D. Porter, 1997).

In England a prescriptive social science of social unity was pursued in the mid-nineteenth century by the National Association for the Promotion of Social Science (Goldman, 1986; Goldman, 1987). As the British Association had constituted itself a 'Parliament for Science', the Association set itself up as a 'Parliament for Social Causes', assisting policy formation by replacing political bias with empirical research. The political identity of the great majority of its members, however, belied its neutrality, being overwhelmingly made up of reforming and radical Liberals and Liberal-Conservatives. Its founding patrons included Lords John Russell, Stanley, Shaftesbury, Brougham, Trevelyan and William Gladstone, as well as Christian Socialists, Charles Kingsley and F.D. Maurice. There was a natural affinity between the objectives of the Association and that of the Liberal Party, namely 'social amelioration' (Goldman, 1986; Goldman, 1987). Edwin Chadwick described it as an organization which brought educationalists, sanitarians, law reformers, and political economists together to struggle with the social concerns of the period. These produced five departments dealing with law amendment, education, crime, public health and social economy. To direct the aims of these departments, the Association attracted not only leading political figures of the day but also leading intellectuals from the professional and scientific classes, such as John Stuart Mill, Chadwick, Farr, Southwood-Smith, Kay-Shuttleworth, William Guy, John Simon and George Hastings, the son of the founder of the B.M.A., Charles Hastings. There was considerable overlap with the membership of the London Statistical Society and the Epidemiological Society (Watkins, 1984).

Social research was driven by a moral imperative directed by the ideology of ameliorism. George Hastings expressed the quintessential ethic of social science as effective philanthropy (Grey-Turner and Sutherland, 1981). As a result, the subject for analysis was the social relations of individuals rather than social structure. The studies published in the *Transactions* of the Association frequently concentrated on the state, the individual and occasionally class, but never dealt with the social system or the relations between these various components of it. Social pathologies were studied as single causes to social breakdown, identified from the analysis of data on institutional provision, crude mortality rates, drunkenness and crime. There was a special concentration by these middle-class investigators on alcoholism as being the fundamental social pathology of the working classes. The means of ameliorating the causes and effects of social pathology was legislation. Within the Association social science never developed into sociology during the early nineteenth century in England, but remained more closely allied to 'social work'. With a mixture of Comtean positivism on the one hand and Christian Socialism on the other, the Association attempted to emancipate social science from the amoral approach of the 'dismal science' of political economy (Goldman, 1986; Goldman, 1987).

The empirical methodology employed by British social scientists within the Association and beyond it was heavily influenced by the work of Frederick LePlay. Like the English ameliorists, he believed that the study of society should be dedicated to the alleviation of human suffering, and 'a social science was necessary for the cure of the ill'. That science should be built upon an empiricist inductive method. Individual social behaviour should be observed and understood in terms of its institutionalization within social structures such as the family. Social peace depended on social institutions adapting to historical and environmental changes. Sociological enquiry investigated the means by which this could be brought about. Thus, LePlay provided the ameliorists with a sociology of social reform offering a middle path between the anomie of disordered capitalism and the tyrannies of socialism. One of the central research tools LePlay developed for achieving these ends was the social survey, and his influence in this regard was evident in the works of Rowntree, Booth, Geddes and Mrs Webb. Patrick Geddes based his unique system of evolutionary determinism on a mixture of Comte, Huxley and LePlay, turning sociology into what he termed 'civics'. Geddes claimed that the research methods of LePlay provided access to the roots of the organic integration of society (Boardman, 1978).

The organic integration of society was the object of social enquiry in the social science investigations of the nineteenth century. Population health had figured prominently in this agenda, both within the context of the Association for Social Science and in the London Statistical Society. The Health Section of the Social Science Association was dominated during the early years by Chadwick, Farr and Simon and later presided over by Lyon Playfair (Hardy, 1993). But George Hastings brought many of the members of his father's organization with him, and the Association became a useful vehicle of mobility for aspiring medical men seeking improved social and professional status (Matthews, 1995). The co-operation of the BMA and the British Association resulted in the formation of the Joint Committee on State Medicine (1867–1881) which became an important public health pressure group. The Committee persuaded the government to set up a Royal Commission into the state of the English public health system in 1867. The report of the Commission led to the creation of the Public Health Acts of 1872 and 1875 (Macleod, 1968).

Public health reform as one expression of a broader programme of rational social reform had its nineteenth-century critics. On the one hand it was widely criticized by the Tory press, who claimed that any interference from the state into the lives of its citizens was gross paternalism which undermined the whole philosophy of individual freedom under a system of liberty (Roberts, 1979). On the other hand it was criticized by doctors, such as Henry Rumsey, who wanted to see a much expanded concept of 'state medicine' put into practice, with far greater powers of intervention and a much more substantial bureaucratic health administration (Chapter 7). From still yet another direction, the science of social amelioration was refuted by the challenge of socialist analysis of the ills of society resulting from the inherent conflict of interests between labour and capital. This view saw the whole enterprise of empirical research into the social and environmental causes of disease and differential mortality as being harnessed to a futile philosophy of correcting what could not be corrected, namely the dialectically historical contradictions of capitalism which would inevitably be resolved by its overthrow as the proletariat fulfilled the role which that system historically ascribed to them (Engels, 1985).

Social statistics, social science and epidemiology were clearly never the neutral fact-gathering pursuits which their practitioners and advocates claimed them to be. They were demonstrably linked to particular philosophies of political, social and moral reform. But despite their own confusions and contradictions, the health reformers who participated in these movements assisted the development of new practices of disease prevention. These practices varied widely in their national contexts, ranging from broad legislative changes and substantial state administrations to individual and local reforms. These will now be examined in the following chapters.

5 Epidemics and social dislocation in the nineteenth century

An epidemic is a sudden disastrous event in the same way as a hurricane, an earthquake or a flood. Such events reveal many facets of the societies with which they collide. The stress they cause tests social stability and cohesion (Slack, 1985; Slack, 1992). Epidemics, however, have their own characteristics, one of which is that while they cause social upheaval they are also caused by it. The massive dislocation brought about by the transformation of agrarian into industrial societies in the nineteenth century produced its own patterns of epidemic invasions.

In England up to the late seventeenth century population grew gradually. The early modern period witnessed new surges in population growth in a society with an exponentially expanding economic base (Wrigley and Schofield, 1981). Epidemic diseases caused massive levels of mortality in the first industrial society in the nineteenth century, and yet population growth soared (Woods and Woodward (eds), 1984). Towards the end of the nineteenth century Britain began to see a dramatic decline in premature mortality and increased length of the average life (Winter, 1982). In other Western industrializing societies, similar patterns were reproduced (Kunitz, 1983; Kunitz, 1984). Changing patterns of economic development were a major factor in bringing about demographic change from the early modern to the modern period, allowing earlier marriage and rising standards of living which led to increased fertility and less hunger. Can the modern rise of population be accounted for purely by the reduction in famine and malnutrition and improved overall levels of nutritional status (McKeown, 1976; Razell, 1974)?

Studying the epidemic streets of the nineteenth century provides one with insight into this question (Hardy, 1993). The sprawling urban world of high-density masses massacred innocents more than anything else. Infant death was responsible for a huge proportion of preventable mortality in the nineteenth-century industrial city. Infants died in their millions among the most economically deprived, who had least access to the facilities which would provide an hygienic environment for infant life. Infants died of measles, whooping cough, smallpox and, above all, of diarrhoea. Children and young adults died of diphtheria and tuberculosis. Everyone, from all age groups, caught fever – typhoid and typhus – and the great grim reaper, cholera, brought periodic devastation. A population like England's urban proletariat were largely well-fed enough throughout the nineteenth century to remain above the level of malnutrition which would affect immunity to these diseases, yet they gradually declined as the century wore on (Hardy, 1993). After 1870 in Britain, mortality from infectious diseases declined dramatically, so how can this be explained if improved nutrition does not provide the whole answer (Szreter, 1988)?

The prevention of infantile diarrhoea depended upon a clean water supply for washing utensils and maintaining sufficient levels of domestic hygiene. This gradually became available in Britain from the late nineteenth century and coincided with the period of mortality decline. Diphtheria, on the other hand, needed the temporary isolation of the disease from the school population in order to prevent the disease from spreading. British local health officers had the power to close schools and isolate victims and their siblings from the 1870s. At this time a number of factors began to converge, which increasingly provided a protective environment for all against infectious disease. Newer levels of social stability created the opportunity for masses of the population to settle and control their immediate environments as the pace of industrial growth and urbanization slowed and infrastructural developments became fixed and functional (Hardy, 1993). Direct interventions to halt the routes of infection had also been operating for a continuous period by this time, i.e. the environmental and preventive medical reforms of the sanitary and state medical movements. In Britain the preventive idea had been proselytized by new bearers of a professionalized hygienic ideology, medical officers of health (MOHs) (Porter, 1991), and this began to have an effect upon domestic consciousness by the turn of the century, reducing the apathy towards infectious disease and encouraging new practices within the home. Above all, a century of massive economic, social and technological transitions was beginning to solidify and learn to cope with the penalties of expansion. Displaced populations were beginning to settle, social dislocation was reduced, public health intervention had begun to take effect and infectious disease began to decline (Hardy, 1993).

Two epidemic diseases of the nineteenth century illustrate this process more than any other and have come to characterize the costs of the level of urbanization which accompanied industrialization. Typhus is a disease which flourishes among populations who live under the circumstances of refugees without access to hygienic shelter, clean water and enough food. It became a persistent feature of poverty among inner-city populations, especially among the migrant and itinerant poor (Risse, 1985). Typhus is transmitted to humans through the vector of body-lice (Woodward, 1973). It attacks people who live in dirty conditions without access to clean surroundings and clothes. It was traditionally associated with gaol inmates, armies and famine victims who all lived under such conditions (Zinsser, 1935; G. Foster, 1981). In the nineteenth century it was the migrant urban populations who most suffered from typhus. Migration became a defining demographic characteristic of early industrial societies. Agricultural labourers migrated to become industrial workers and members of the industrial proletariat and lumpenproletariat often moved more than once during a lifetime to follow the geography of the business cycle. But the populations who 'got on their bike' to look for work became the poorest and most deprived in the urban environment. They were last in line and had least access to the facilities that the city could offer – a stable roof over their heads, clean water, regular employment and a sufficient income to provide them with an adequate subsistence. They were dirty, hungry and, in the winter, cold. They became louse-ridden. They were attacked by typhus in their droves.

Typhus became a disease that the migrant poor always had with them, but among epidemic disasters of the nineteenth century cholera was king (Longmate, 1966). Asiatic cholera swept through Europe and the United States from India like an avenging angel. Cholera revealed its own story about the social, political and economic relations of industrial societies (Evans, 1988). It demonstrated the dysfunction of mass aggregation in the urban environment and the tenuous stability of class relations. It stimulated governments into creating policies to improve the environmental conditions which had facilitated its massive pandemic spread. Cholera killed with shocking speed and vicious regularity. At its peak it could wipe out communities in a week. The social-psychological effect of cholera on the nineteenth-century mentality was devastating (Chevalier, 1958). It became the symbol of the human costs of expo-nential industrial and economic growth.

Understanding epidemic disease in industrial society and how to control it required a rethink. Following traditional patterns of quarantine and isolation employed in the control of plague proved inadequate. For one thing, cholera seemed to defy the contagionist theory of disease. It bypassed quarantine proce-dures and isolation measures, cutting across all traditional barriers erected to protect the community (Ackerknecht, 1948). Miasmatic aetiology seemed to offer a more plausible explanation. It could explain its transmission across *cordons sani-taires* and suggested the answer might be to clean up the environment rather than operate quarantine, which stopped the economic life-blood of the free-market trading societies. As cholera raged among urban communities, politicians, doctors and disease theorists fought over how it was caused and how it could be eliminated (Pelling, 1978).

Here we examine the way in which epidemic disease and disease theory took the question of population health to a high point on the political agenda of the nineteenth-century state, and how it became the definitive symbol of the disloca-tions of industrial societies.

AETIOLOGY AND ACTION

The explanation of disease causation was a controversial subject in the first half of the nineteenth century. The theory of contagion is an ancient belief that disease was spread through contact. There is no evidence of this theory in the Hippocratic *Corpus* but there are abundant ancient biblical references to contam-ination through contact with leprosy (Chapter 1). There were no ancient theories as to what might constitute the substance of contagion until Roman times, when

Varro and Cicero both speculated that fevers might be contaminations by 'tiny animals' that were carried on the wind. The clearest account of this idea was provided much later by Girolamo Fracastoro, who published his famous treatise *On Contagion* in 1546. Fracastoro asserted that contagious diseases were probably caused by living disease seeds which could be communicated, and he strongly recommended quarantine, sequestration and fumigation to prevent their spread. In the seventeenth century this theory was reinformed by sightings of microscopic 'animalcules' by the inventors of the microscope in 1659, Athanasius Kircher (1602–1680) and Anton van Leeuwenhoek (1632–1723). This theory remained little modified until the middle of the nineteenth century (Pelling, 1993; Hudson, 1993).

By 1804, physicians such as Thomas Trotter, the naval physician who identified alcoholism as a disease of the mind, were suggesting that the theory of contagion was a relic of the past (Delacy, 1986; Risse, 1979). By the mid nineteenth century, some physicians and health reformers held it up to ridicule as a kind of futile mythology from the dark ages of medicine. Jacob Henle, the German biologist who taught Robert Koch, remained one of the serious scientific thinkers investigating contagionist aetiology through a new fungoid theory of disease (Baldry, 1976; W. Foster, 1970).

As we discussed in Chapter 3, from Hippocratic times there had been various theories of foul contaminated air being responsible for propagating disease. In the seventeenth century, Thomas Sydenham developed a theory of atmospheric contamination in which the ultimate agents of disease were the poisonous effluvia thrown up at various times from movements of the bowels of the earth. By the nineteenth century, miasmata were believed to be inanimate particles produced from decaying organic matter. Some nineteenth-century public health reformers and hygienists, such as Thomas Southwood Smith, subscribed strictly to this view of aetiology. It is unclear exactly to what extent Chadwick himself studied the subject of aetiology, but his basic policy was guided by a generalized philosophy that filth was responsible for producing all diseases indiscriminately. The most important feature of the miasmatic theory made quarantine redundant. Miasmatism indicated that environmental improvement would be the most effective method of preventing disease (Hannaway, 1993).

By the early nineteenth century, diseases which appeared to defy quarantine measures and progressed in healthy communities increasingly undermined the theory of contagion. The miasmatic explanation was employed to justify the abolition of quarantine of shipping and isolation of towns and individuals (Ackerknecht, 1948). In the 1831 cholera epidemic in France, health authorities were divided between advocates of sanitarianism, defined as quarantine, and public health, defined as methods of eliminating environmental pollutions (Delaporte, 1986). In England also, Chadwick and Southwood Smith limited the use of quarantine and instituted policies for sanitary improvement (Pelling, 1978).

In the United States, repeated epidemics of yellow fever enhanced the belief in the miasmatic theory (Blake, 1968; Duffy, 1966). In the 1793 epidemic,

Benjamin Rush abandoned contagionist explanations and rejected quarantine measures. Instead, he indicted a cargo of rotting coffee in the docks at Philadelphia as being responsible for the disease. Rush was a leader of medical opinion and many Philadelphia physicians followed his lead. Subsequently controversy raged in the United States for the next sixty years about the contagiousness of yellow fever and the necessity for quarantine (Duffy, 1990).

In Europe, yellow fever occurred in Gibraltar in 1821. Both the Spanish and the French authorities immediately set up quarantine restrictions along their border. However, a Dr J.A. Rocheaux of France and Charles Maclean, chief army surgeon from Britain, published a manifesto in 1822 attempting to persuade the quarantine authorities of the anti-contagious nature of the disease and to withdraw their regulations. They were successful in getting the Spanish authorities to comply. In France, the physician Nicolas Chevrin, who had spent a decade practising medicine in the United States, lobbied the French authorities to follow the Spanish withdrawal of quarantine restrictions. The French government requested the Academy of Medicine to investigate the issue. The Academy accepted the anti-contagionist argument and persuaded the authorities to eliminate quarantine regulations. This perhaps was anti-contagionism's greatest moment of triumph (Coleman, 1987).

During the cholera epidemics, anti-contagionists made similar gains. In the first epidemic of 1831–1832, cholera broke through all attempts at isolation of infected areas and districts. Riots in Russia, Prussia and New York demonstrated the explosive potential of restrictive policies (McGrew, 1965). By the second epidemic in 1848, anti-contagionist views had a dramatic effect on reducing the use of quarantine regulations. The division between contagionist and anti-contagionist theories of disease was influential in determining preventive strategies during the first half of the nineteenth century. It would be a mistake, however, to presume that the intellectual divisions were clear-cut or the ideological and political matrix anything other than blurred and murky. Intellectual and ideological changes took place between the 1830s and the 1850s, shifting the focus between different aspects of disease theory. The thinking of some individuals exemplifies those changes. In England, for example, the statistical work and sanitary vision of William Farr, as discussed in the previous chapter, was guided by an atmospheric theory of disease. Farr modified his views, however, in order to adapt to mid-century demonstrations of water-borne contagion and evidences of the germ theory.

Early on in his work at the Registrar General's Office, Farr was confronted with inadequately recorded causes of death both by medical practitioners and in coroners' reports. The registration system as a whole received its most severe criticism over the methods used to record deaths. Henry Rumsey, a mid-century spokesman on public health and statistics, consistently demanded a complete reform of registration, with the appointment of full-time registration officials trained in numerical medicine together with the replacement of coroners with medical superintendents. Farr attempted to reform the system by making it at least easier for medical practitioners to register deaths in a revised nosology of diseases. Initially the registration system was based upon the traditional nosology of William Cullen. Farr began by grouping diseases into categories of contagious, epidemic and epizootic. He eventually described these collectively as 'zymotic' (Eyler, 1979). Farr was able to arrive at this description via the chemical theory of disease developed by Justus Liebig. During the 1830s, Liebig had identified the nature of contagious matter in the atmosphere as poisonous substances responsible for transmitting specific diseases by producing putrefactions, or fermentations in the blood. This considerably modified the theory of atmospheric transmission by replacing the idea of generalized inanimate miasms, responsible for all diseases, with the idea of specific poisons whose fermentations produced different disease conditions in the blood. Specific poisonous contaminations could derive from a number of different sources, including exhalation of human breath or the shedding of diseased skin particles. In this schema, contagiousness was contingent upon the atmospheric conditions favouring the production of individual poisons, and the conditions which either did or did not favour putrefaction in the blood of the victim of the disease. Without committing himself to a generalized theory of miasmatic pollution, Farr was able to use an atmospheric theory of poisonous contamination and blood fermentation to eliminate the difficulties of classifying smallpox with typhus fever in the registration system (Hamlin, 1990; Baldry, 1976; W. Foster, 1970).

The mid-century demonstrations of water-borne transmission of cholera by John Snow and William Budd ended any uncritical reign that miasmatism may have enjoyed, however (Pelling, 1978). Farr's chemical theory, which was held by a number of his contemporaries among the English medical profession, such as Edmund Parkes, easily accommodated the idea of water-borne contagions (Porter, 1985). Chemical substances could retain their disease-producing properties in different media, both water and air. But the correlation made by Farr between density and increased mortality was fundamentally inspired by a theory of polluted vitiated contaminated air as the primary environment of disease transmission, and his whole aim to demonstrate the insalubrity of urban life was guided by this principle.

When cholera hit the Prussian states, they reacted to it with traditional methods of quarantine. These were abandoned because they became politically impossible to implement. Miasmatism was forcefully advocated by Max von Pettenkofer. Other influential German health reformers, such Rudolf Virchow, remained committed to a multi-causal theory of disease. Even after 1880 Virchow refused to accept bacteriological aetiology because he believed that there could be no single agent of disease. He claimed that the exciting causes of disease were derived from a matrix of relations which favoured its spread or hindered it. He never promoted a miasmatic or contagionist theory but followed the direction of the French Hygienists in believing that disease resulted from both biological and social causes (Evans, 1987).

For Villermé and his contemporaries, as we have seen, the numerical investigation of epidemics led them to conclude that the major determinant of disease was the socio-economic conditions of existence. The issue of contagiousness was of secondary importance to economic and moral reasons as to why diseases flourished, where and among whom. Alleviation of suffering from disease, therefore, was to be found not so much from environmental sanitarianism as from moral reform of the economic class among which it festered (Coleman, 1982).

It is not clear that contagionism and anti-contagionism were thought to be mutually exclusive theories by the majority of medical theorists in this period. The controversy only concerned a small number of diseases: cholera, plague, the various epidemic fevers and yellow fever. Other diseases which became targets for prevention, such as consumption and rickets, were still presumed to be caused by a mixture of hereditary and contagious factors. Furthermore, the categories of contagions were confusing. In early nineteenth-century medical textbooks it was possible to find descriptions of 'contagious miasms'. The author John Mason Good, for example, discussed the way in which miasms were a form of corruption and how this corruption could be applied to the body (Hamlin, 1992). This idea, as discussed above, was later capitalized on by William Farr.

Despite attempts at extensive classification of disease at the end of the eighteenth century, disease was still characterized not in terms of ontology but rather in terms of physiological changes: the clinical symptoms displayed by the patient during the course of a disease. In this sense the nature of disease was actually perceived as a deviation from health; disease was thought to be a condition of less or more healthfulness. The concern with cause was thus expressed in terms of proximate causes which actually referred to the essence of the disease itself: that is, inflammation, the febrile nature of the disease and such like. Although a disease could be identified in the patient, they would not be considered to *have* a disease in the modern sense. Continued fever, for example, was simply identified as a collection of clinically observable symptoms, which might or might not be communicable but was determined by the physiological changes that it brought about rather than its external cause (Hamlin, 1992).

The proximate cause was the pathological process which characterized the disease. The other category of causation, following the Galenic schema, was the remote causes which were divided into general programmatic causes, called 'predisposing', and specific and occasional causes, called 'exciting'. There was never presumed to be any one single exciting cause to a disease, however, and equally the division between exciting and predisposing causes was often blurred. Wet and cold together, for example, could be characterized as an exciting cause. However, early nineteenth-century physicians wanted to know how this exciting cause could produce different diseases in different individuals and, indeed, not produce any disease at all in others. Exposure to wet and cold might give some people rheumatism, others a fever, and others still would not experience any reaction of sickness at all (Hamlin, 1992).

Given the multiple ways in which an exciting cause could operate upon different individuals, medical theorists looked to the predisposing causes to explain the differences between them. In other words, what circumstances had predisposed some patients to get sick and others to remain well when both had been attacked by the exciting cause? Predisposing causes were usually defined in terms of the environmental and social antecedents of ill health, although later in the century much more interest was taken in heredity, which produced a diathesis, a tendency, towards the contraction of certain types of ill health. These were the conditions which sapped the strength of the individual and rendered them susceptible to disease. Poverty, malnourishment and filth could all predispose different populations to become susceptible to a variety of exciting causes. This complex model of disease causation, therefore, attempted to draw up a totality of the disease experience and its determinants (Hamlin, 1992).

Concepts of disease causation, emphasizing the relationship between predisposing and exciting causes, were widespread among English physicians and medical authors in the early nineteenth century. However, they were differentiated from those theorists who rejected the significance of predisposing causes in favour of those who wished to identify only the exciting cause as significant in the disease process. This latter orientation characterized those who, for want of a better word, we can call the Chadwickians. These were doctors such as Neil Arnott, James Philip Kay and Southwood Smith, who continued to promote the idea of atmospheric poisons as being the singular cause of all diseases (Pelling, 1978).

The most important difference between what we might call predisposing-orientated theory and poison-orientated theory was that they implied completely different methods of disease prevention. Predispositionist prevention had to identify those conditions which would maintain the integrity of health and those which undermined it. Thus, vitiated air was not dangerous simply because of the poisonous material it contained, which produced ill health, but also because of the lack of oxygen in it, vital to the maintenance of health. Lack of fresh air would slowly debilitate the constitution, thus making an individual less able to resist the effects of the poisonous material. Similarly, poverty could undermine health by causing continual anxiety, prolonged malnutrition and exposure to the cold, which would wear down vitality. The theory of predisposing causes implied a much more general level of prevention, which began with the creation of the conditions that would maintain health. The miasmatist view, by contrast, focused on only one singular cause of disease, miasmatic poisons, and thus prevention simply meant the removal of the putrefying material which caused it. Prevention could thus become a single-minded campaign simply to clean up filth (Hamlin, 1992).

Rudolph Virchow clearly represented a predispositionist argument in his analysis of the causes of typhus in Upper Silesia in 1848 (Ackerknecht, 1953). He saw poverty, slum housing, ignorance and political subjugation as the predisposing causes which undermined the vitality of the population, leaving them vulnerable to the typhus when it arrived. He advocated major social and political change as the best means of preventing its recurrence. In England the predispositionist theory of causation and prevention was inhibited and excluded from the field of public health by the anti-contagionist group of Chadwickians. Among the doctors whom Chadwick used to compile his 1842 Report were some who opposed his views. Many of these doctors were contagionists who identified poverty as the main cause of its spread. They denied that drainage alone was a sufficient measure to actually prevent the spread of epidemic disease (Hamlin 1992).

But Chadwick and Southwood Smith's response to such doctors was to attempt to push their arguments into the background by focusing upon exciting causes alone (Pelling, 1978). According to Smith, predisposing causes simply aided the spread of disease. The exciting cause of atmospheric poison would, in a law-like manner, effect a disease response in all individuals who were exposed to it for a certain amount of time. The difference between individual response was dependent simply on the length of exposure, which of course varied the intensity of the dose of poison they received. Thus, both the robust and the feeble alike would succumb. Smith was willing to accept that these exciting causes might produce the later predisposing causes which would assist the progress of the disease. For example, the malarial poison might upset the digestive system and therefore the inability to eat would cause the patient to suffer malnutrition, which in turn would affect their ability to recover. In this context, much of the immorality that often accompanied poverty, such as drink and bed-sharing, could also be explained by an infection by a disease poison (Hamlin, 1990).

Within the Chadwickian schema, poverty was to be seen not as a cause of disease but as an effect. The miasmatist orientation of the Chadwickians advocated the removal of filth as the single measure which would eliminate disease. This left the integrity of the Poor Law intact. The predispositionist theory of causation, however, implied that the perpetuation of poverty by the Poor Law was itself a cause of disease, and that the remedy was first and foremost a new policy for eliminating poverty itself.

From the mid-nineteenth century, new investigations into the nature of organic fermentations led to new insights into the possible origins of disease. This is not the place to retell the history of bacteriology (see Baldry, 1976, and W. Foster, 1970). Suffice it to say that the new theory was gradually adopted by health policy-makers and administrators throughout the last two decades of the nineteenth century. It stimulated new directions in preventive strategies and was more influential in some national contexts than others. The impact of bacteriology in various contexts will become part of the stories discussed in later chapters. The most important consequence of the bacteriological revolution was to expand the parameters of the concept of the environment. The environment in which disease was perceived to flourish now included social behaviour. Individuals and their social behaviour were now understood to be the bearers of the social relations of sickness.

DISEASE, DISLOCATION AND SOCIAL ORDER

Numerous scholars who have looked at disease in history, such as William McNeill and Alfred Crosby, have discovered how it has frequently precipitated widespread social disruption and upheaval and has been a factor in bringing about revolutionary changes (McNeill, 1976; Crosby, 1986). Disease has subsequently been examined as a test of social cohesion at different periods. Much of the work on nineteenth-century cholera, for example, has set out to demonstrate the link between pandemic waves and revolutionary uprisings. Other scholars have suggested that cholera was the spur to the development of public health administration throughout Europe and the United States. However, more recent studies have challenged this view and have demonstrated how a much broader set of events combined with epidemic episodes to stimulate the growth of public health administrations (Slack, 1992).

Did disease precipitate social disruption or was it precipitated by it? Certainly, cholera pandemics coincided with times of severe disorder and unrest in nineteenth-century Europe. The first European epidemic in 1831–1832 followed the tail end of the revolutions on the European continent in 1830, and took place during the most violent period of civil disorder resulting from political agitation for Parliamentary reform in Britain in 1832. The second pandemic, in 1848–1849, occurred in the year of revolutions in Germany and France, and the 1854 epidemic coincided with the outbreak of the Crimean War. The 1866 epidemic occurred as the German Federation was demolished after Bismarck's war with Austria, and the Second Empire fell in France as cholera spread during 1871. At the time of the last wave of cholera in 1892, there were major disturbances in Russia and Poland (Evans, 1988).

Cholera created violence and rioting, especially during the 1831–1832 epidemic. In Russia the peasant masses rioted against their feudal lords in the belief that there was a deliberate campaign to poison the water, as part of a Malthusian conspiracy to kill off the poor and relieve the state of the financial burden of poverty. Riots occurred in Paris against medical officials for similar reasons (Delaporte, 1986; Bourdelais and Raulot, 1987). In England the cholera riots of 1831 were directed at doctors, this time in the belief that the medical profession was encouraging the spread of cholera to obtain bodies for anatomical dissection (Durey, 1979; Morris, 1976).

It is easy to understand why cholera should have created such unrest if we consider how European authorities generally responded to it. Most authorities, when faced with the prospect of the epidemic in 1831, simply employed the old quarantine procedures used in feudal times against the plague. That is, they set *cordons sanitaires* with military enforcement, closed down public meeting-places, and sealed off cities and towns. But these measures, which were passively accepted by the masses living under absolute states in the seventeenth and eighteenth centuries, were not so easily imposed upon a generation which had witnessed the rise of radical democratic popular movements, following the lead of the American and French Revolutions. The coincidence of inexplicable mass mortality and the sudden appearance of government officials, medical officers and military troops aroused popular suspicion and unrest. The bourgeois authorities became the object of conspiracy theories among the poor and were attacked as the agents of a class war. The homes of noblemen and the offices of health authorities were ransacked throughout Prussia, and officials were murdered in Paris (Evans, 1988). In Britain, doctors were attacked in Bristol, not for being agents of the state but as the result of the popular conceptions about their sinister macabre trade in dead flesh (Durey, 1979; Morris, 1976).

Cholera, however, spread through Europe largely as an effect of social disorder rather than as the cause of it. First, it did follow dearth and famine, but there is only limited evidence that malnutrition lowers the stomach acid level and weakens resistance. Much more significantly, it followed the movements of troops and the disruption of war. Cholera was first transmitted from its original home in India by the military campaign fought by the Marquis of Hastings against the Marathas in 1817. In 1831, the Russian war against Poland spread the disease from Asia to Europe. British troops spread it to Portugal, and in 1866 cholera was spread by the war between Austria and Italy. In 1854, French troops transferred the disease again eastwards when they landed in Gallipoli during the Crimean War. It is easy to understand why troop movements spread the disease. War produces mass movements of refugee populations who abandon their homes only to end up living in appalling insanitary encampments. Troops themselves are cramped and confined in grossly insanitary camps which rapidly spread disease to the nearest civilian settlement. Demobbed soldiers carry disease back to their civilian homes. Above all, overcrowded prisoner-of-war camps became fever hubs (Evans, 1988).

Apart from war, the increasing mobility of population through the expansion of trade during the nineteenth century was the most important vehicle for the spread of cholera. The water-borne disease followed canal routes and rivers, and was carried by sailors, traders and shipping workers. Service occupations involving water were always the first groups to succumb, such as cleaning and washing and inn-keeping.

Cholera coincided with crisis in nineteenth-century Europe, but often conditions were made ripe for its spread by social upheaval. Cholera was spread by social dislocation and subsequently exacerbated it. This pattern of social dislocation and epidemic spread is equally demonstrated for another acute infection characteristic of the times, typhus. Typhus has a long history of being associated with war and famine, frequently flourishing in military encampments and gaols. Typhus, however, became almost endemic among some urban populations during the nineteenth century. It was repeatedly associated with individual urban localities. It reflected the social dislocation occurring in the everyday life of towns and cities (Harrington, 1965; Luckin, 1984; Harden, 1993b).

The pattern of typhus epidemics in Victorian London is not immediately easy to explain. A steady decline of the disease occurred without any apparent correlation to hygiene or nutrition. There is no nutritional basis to immunity to typhus, although hunger is connected with it indirectly, and it consequently followed periods of dearth and famine in the eighteenth century. Urban typhus, however, did not follow the slumps of the business cycle in Victorian Britain, and therefore different circumstances must account for its unpredictable pattern. Typhus epidemics in Victorian London were precipitated by the much more complex phenomenon of urban crisis rather than nutritional crisis. Urban crisis describes the combination of a number of features of deprivation, which include hardship from political and economic conflicts, such as strikes and lockouts, and homelessness and overcrowding resulting from slum clearance and demolition for the construction of railways. Such forces can produce urban stress, which a disease like typhus can exploit (Hardy, 1988).

Continuing outbreaks in London occurred between 1861 and 1869. Throughout the late 1850s, the workers in the building trade in London had been locked out by their masters for refusing not to join a union. The industrial unrest caused widespread hardship and malnutrition. It coincided with a massive programme of housing clearance for the construction of the railways. Certain areas of London were, by the 1860s, filled with families living in grossly over-crowded conditions, with anything up to twelve in one room, hungry and without a clean or regular water supply (Hardy, 1988).

Typhus is a rickettsia disease which is spread by the human body-louse. The rickettsi multiplies in the body of the louse and is ejected in its faeces. Humans contract it from scratching and breaking the surface of the skin. The disease can remain active in the faeces dust of the louse for a long period, and therefore can be breathed in from house dust in a dwelling which has not been disinfected. Hungry people feel the cold more and in the middle of winter are less likely to change their linen or wash their clothes, and typhus flourishes in the winter months. In these conditions they are much more likely to harbour lice and increase the opportunity for infection (Harden, 1993b).

It was in the areas of great overcrowding where typhus became epidemic in 1860–1869 and then suddenly and dramatically declined after 1870. What accounted for the decline? First, the demolition programme of the railway building ceased, and municipal building programmes began distributing the slum populations to new housing. The fever-nest slums were subsequently demolished. Second, a clean and constant water supply became available from the end of the 1860s, which enhanced the chances of improved personal and domestic hygiene. Third, London's economy stabilized and the labouring poor experienced a comparative period of minimum prosperity. Typhus clearly followed the social dislocation which resulted from urban crisis in Victorian London. The pattern of infection among Irish immigrants demonstrates this relationship most clearly. Contemporary moralists and medical investigators presumed that typhus was indigenous to the Irish and referred to it as 'Irish fever', but the epidemics occurred in London before they occurred in Dublin. The fact that many Irish immigrants lived in infected localities reflects the way that this group, more than any other, suffered the deprivations of urban crisis and were the most vulnerable to its ravages (Hardy, 1988).

Typhus and cholera reveal how disease is a multifaceted phenomenon. Its biological existence was directly determined by social, economic and political conditions, and it in turn brought about historical changes in those relation-ships. Epidemic cholera also revealed other features about nineteenth-century society, in particular the social relations of inequality and the extent to which different societies were socially stable and cohesive. It is to this topic we shall now turn.

CHOLERA, SOCIAL STABILITY AND HISTORICAL TRANSITION IN INDUSTRIAL SOCIETY

Cholera and typhus illuminated the relationship between disease and social change in nineteenth-century Europe. More than anything, these epidemic diseases reflected nineteenth-century society in transition. Major epidemics were one facet of the processes of historical transition, but how did they frame change? How did epidemics contribute to social change by stimulating political, economic and ideological responses? How did disease mediate changing social values and scientific beliefs and become a resource for the legitimation of social actions (Rosenberg, 1992)? Cholera, the shock-horror disease of the nineteenth century, had a unique impact on the social psychology of the time with the suddenness and surprise nature of its attack, its relentless and ruthless capacity to kill and the speed with which it achieved this end. Worst of all was the way in which it killed.

A victim of cholera first feels symptoms of nausea, vomiting and diarrhoea, which within hours can become so violent as to severely dehydrate the body. Nineteenth-century medical accounts of cholera recorded rooms of patients awash with vomit and rice-water stools up to the ankles. In the stage of severe dehydration, the patient takes on the bluish pallor which uniquely distinguishes the disease. This is followed by violent cramps and uncontrollable muscular spasms. In the final hours before death, the patient becomes comatose. Muscular spasms continue after death, which nineteenth-century doctors could often only determine after the irreversible process of putrefaction had begun. Cholera kills anywhere between a few hours up to three days. Few have the Herculean constitution to survive a virulent attack, and even fewer in the nineteenth century received any medical therapy that was effective. In modern times it can be treated with massive doses of antibiotics and constant rehydration. None of these were available to nineteenth-century victims, who might instead have their condition and agony exacerbated by bleeding or the administration of a favourite remedy, the emetic calomel and tobacco enemas, which are an extremely strong purgative. Levels of acidity or alkalinity in the stomach can affect the infectiousness of the disease in an individual. Alcoholics were especially vulnerable. The elderly were sometimes protected by low levels of gastric acidity (Howard-Jones, 1972). The social-psychological impact of such a disease, spreading like wildfire seemingly overnight amid a community, was intense, and these experiences translated into broader ideological and social responses.

In Britain, the distribution of death from cholera mirrored the distribution of wealth in reverse. Cholera killed the economically vulnerable and dispossessed first and the economically secure only as an afterthought. If cholera mortality was a measure of massive social inequality between classes, it was even more a reflection of the political cultures of classes. In Britain in 1831, the ruling and middle classes were divided in their response to cholera. Some believed it would divert the poor from their agitations for political reform, weakening their constitutions, undermining their resolve and distracting them from the arena of political conflict. A contrary view believed cholera would incite insurrection and violent revolution, and breed anarchy. Other members of the ruling elite, notably the aristocratic government, believed that cholera was the answer to their Malthusian prayers. It would eliminate huge numbers of the destitute and dependent, and resolve the most pressing issue of the times, the crisis in the cost and operation of the Poor Law. It would kill two birds with one stone, eliminating poverty and political unrest by eliminating the poor and their demands for reform (Durey, 1979; Morris, 1976).

But the response of the middle classes in Britain, overall, demonstrated a remarkable lack of panic and some degree of genuine empathy and charity. The middle classes rarely fled towns which became infected. Often they stayed and set up health boards and charitable relief funds. Voluntary subscriptions escalated during the cholera epidemics. Temporary fever hospitals were set up and staffed by armies of ladies bountiful, secular sisters of mercy. The cholera victim soon became incorporated into the stereotype of the suffering deserving poor who warranted free soup, blankets and other doles (Morris, 1976; Durey, 1979). Cholera carriers, however, were another matter. The middle classes singled out a special group of the poor as eminently blameworthy for the spread of cholera. This was the itinerant worker and the wandering vagabond. They were represented by middle-class commentators and moralists as filth-spreading disease-carrying wasters. Their economic worthlessness was equated with moral depravity and many of this group of the poor were seen as biologically racially inferior (Himelfarb, 1984).

Amid the poor, cholera in 1831 engendered suspicions of conspiracy among the medical profession rather than the ruling oligarchs of the state. The poor believed that the medical profession manufactured cholera to obtain the corpses of paupers for anatomical dissection. The cholera riots were also an expression of a much broader discontent among the British working classes, which demanded that social justice be placed on a new premise. Cholera was assimilated into a new worldview which intended to undermine the traditional values about poverty itself. The new demands for social justice expanded beyond the traditional boundaries of simply more requests for more doles. Instead, new concepts challenged the contemporary, conventional perception of the culture of poverty as a whole (Richardson, 1988).

Rioters protested that not only were their lives exploited but that even in death their bodies were not sacrosanct. They protested the translation of their vital health into cannon fodder for war and industrial production, and the translation of their death into a medical utility. The cholera rioters insisted that a new social justice must at least acknowledge that the bodies of the poor had a right to the dignity of being mourned, buried and religiously ritualized. Until 1834, only the bodies of executed murderers were legally allowed to be dissected because they were lost souls and denied burial in hallowed ground. The poor believed that cholera victims who had been forcibly removed from their homes as a quarantine measure, and who died in the workhouse infirmary and were dissected, were being damned on a level with godless murderers.

In the United States, cholera highlighted the relationship between religious piety and political values in mid-nineteenth-century American culture (Rosenberg, 1962). Cholera crossed the Atlantic in 1832 to course through American cities, but its effects were far more limited than those of the epidemic that followed it in 1848–1849. On 1 December 1848 the *New York* docked at New York harbour containing 331 steerage passengers from Le Havre, packed tightly below decks. Seven immigrants had died during the journey and others were sick with the unmistakable symptoms of cholera. The passengers were removed and quarantined in makeshift barrack-like hospitals in warehouses on Staten Island. Over half of these, however, escaped into New York City and New Jersey. Within weeks the first cases of cholera appeared in the city. The progress of the disease was halted by the freezing conditions of the winter but reawakened in the spring. Between May and October 1849, 5,017 people had died of cholera in New York City (Duffy, 1968). The city did not suffer as much as the cities of the southern states. Ships carrying immigrants from Hamburg and Bremen sick with cholera brought the disease to New Orleans in December 1848. The mild winter weather allowed the disease to travel to all the towns and landing spots on the Mississippi, the Arkansas and the Tennessee.

Throughout the United States little or no effective public health administration existed at this time to prevent the spread of the disease. The few local health boards which existed in some areas had neither the funds nor the mandate to enforce sanitary regulations such as street cleaning and the removal of refuse. Squalor persisted in towns where the local government was either impotent or corrupt. New York City, for example, had a permanent health board by 1849 but employed contractors to undertake street cleaning. The contracts were political spoils and consequently were never completed sufficiently. In the absence of government, voluntary associations of citizens became the most organized force during the epidemic. They set up their own health committees which arranged for refuse removal and street cleaning by volunteers from the community. They also provided emergency hospital facilities (Duffy, 1990). More than this, they preached hygienic reform to the diseased and their neighbours. The motives which drove the volunteer effort were critical to the success of its endeavour. It was in this context that the relationship between beliefs in science, providence and progress became crucial to the course of the cholera epidemic.

As far as President Zachary Taylor was concerned in 1849, cholera was the exercise of God's will. In 1832 Andrew Jackson had hesitated before offering a day of fasting as a prophylactic against the epidemic. Taylor had no such inhibitions. He ordered a day of fasting for the first Friday in August 1849. It was ordered as an attempt to atone for the vice, viciousness and undefined appetites which had brought the miserable retribution of cholera upon the land. Cholera was nothing other than a plague of Egypt visited upon infidels, Sabbath-breakers and atheists who had challenged God's laws and turned America into a godless Babylon. Among the pious, sin was believed to be the primary predisposing cause of cholera – the sins of intemperance, non-churchgoing and immorality among the reckless feckless poor. Perhaps above all, the sin of materialistic avarice among the wealthy was at the root of the epidemic. God-fearing and enterprising industry had turned America into a land of plenty. But enterprise had turned into ambition and material greed. Moralists warned that the exploitation of the South by the northern states, the enslavement of Africans and the frenzied lust for gold had brought the hand of providence in the form of cholera. Thus, while it was a fearful scourge, it was also an angel of mercy, chastising intemperance out of its vicious ways and leading souls back to the way of truth and light (Rosenberg, 1962).

Cholera was perceived as divine retribution among most pious evangelical sects, and a just punishment for popishness, which explained its prevalence among the Irish immigrants. If the pious believed sin to be the primary cause, they also believed that this gave rise to secondary exciting causes such as filth – next only to vice as the worst of mortal sins – poor drainage and lack of ventilation. The orthodox ministries began preaching the gospel of hygiene. Prayer was a necessary but not sufficient remedy. Practical measures were also needed against the epidemic. Orthodox piety was opposed by Unitarianism and Universalist religious sects, who were as much a part of the voluntarist movement. These believed that the supernatural explanation of the cause of cholera was mere superstition and that fasting was a ridiculous prophylactic. The Unitarian sects placed their faith not so much in the direct providential hand of God as in the laws by which he governed nature. Cholera was in their view the result of the contravention of the laws of nature. This must be corrected through sanitary reform as a prevention against cholera (Rosenberg, 1962).

All were agreed that, for whatever reason, the poor suffered most from the epidemic. Whether as a punishment for sins against God or against nature, they had now brought the terrors of cholera upon themselves. The way to combat the disease was to re-educate and remoralize the poor into the gospel of godliness, cleanliness and temperance. Most especially the ignorant helpless immigrant poor were in need of the hygienic gospel. Another goal of the health mission among the poor was to re-create the conditions of rural life among the urban masses and to encourage as many as possible to return to the sunlight of the cornfields (Rosenberg, 1962).

Nineteenth-century cholera epidemics drew out the contrasting cultures which lay on either side of the Atlantic. In Britain, and in most of Europe, cholera heightened tensions between social and economic classes and mediated their political values. In the United States it gave expression to dominant cultures of religious piety and individualistic voluntarism. But in both cases cholera was a catalyst for change, to greater and lesser extents.

The cholera epidemics in the United States did not contribute to any lasting developments in the creation of public health administrations. The latter arose, as we shall discuss in Chapter 9, from a set of complex processes. The influence of cholera on the development of British public health was more significant, providing additional legitimation for sanitary reform which was stimulated by the need to address the relationship between poverty and disease more generally. In France, cholera assisted the implementation of the sanitary method of disease prevention. The experience of cholera in Paris in 1831 facilitated the triumph of the miasmatic over the contagious explanation of disease and helped to stimulate the introduction of new methods for environmental reform. France's public health reformers divided according to their theory of the aetiology of the disease. The quarantine-contagionists lost, and the atmospheric-sanitarians won the day to lay the foundations of the French public health system as a whole (Delaporte, 1986; Bourdelais and Raulot, 1987).

Cholera epidemics, while revealing social and ideological divisions, demonstrated the underlying stability of nineteenth-century industrial society. But Hamburg in 1892 proved to be an exception. The city-state of Hamburg in late nineteenth-century united Germany was a little island of laissez-faire rule in the middle of an autocratic and hugely bureaucratic state. It was a city which politically resembled eighteenth-century England more than nineteenth-century Germany. Hamburgers did not believe in government and public institutions. But by the 1890s Hamburg stood on the edge of an historical transition which took on an inevitable momentum. This transition was brought about by the experience of cholera in 1892 (Evans, 1987).

Hamburg was a city of merchants. Trading and commerce dominated its economic and political life. The needs of trade were paramount. For that reason, the chief medical officer of the town, Dr Kraus, had a definite plan of action should the town ever experience an epidemic. That plan was to keep it secret as long as possible and avoid the alarm and the regulations which inevitably followed: every merchant's worst dread, quarantine. When cholera arrived in Hamburg in late August 1892, Kraus concealed the outbreak for a vital number of days during which the population could have been warned not to drink from the infected water supplies and to boil all water for washing. As it was, the delay in the public admission of the presence of cholera led to a catastrophe in which 17,000 people caught the disease by the end of October and over 8,500 of them died (Evans, 1987).

The wave of cholera which crossed Europe in 1892 had a negligible effect elsewhere. Even in the town which bordered Hamburg, Altona, the impact was small. Why did it spread so rapidly? The reason was that Hamburg had delayed and squabbled over instituting sand filtration for the water supply, a measure which had been taken by all major European cities from the early 1870s. This failure, together with the deliberate delay, caused massive unnecessary mortality. However, the city's government justified their refusal to effect sanitary reforms by claiming that cholera was transmitted through the atmosphere and not through water.

The political status of Hamburg as a city-state had allowed it to escape control by the Prussian government under unification. The Prussian authorities used the outbreak to invade Hamburg's political autonomy, by sending Robert

Koch to investigate the cause of the epidemic and institute measures to control it and prevent its recurrence. Hamburg's medical authorities used the belligerent assertion of miasmatism by Max von Pettenkofer to challenge the most famous of all bacteriologists' pronouncements on local negligence. Pettenkofer attempted to disprove Koch's assertion of the bacteriological origin of the epidemic by notoriously drinking a glass of cholera-contaminated water and surviving to tell the tale. The melodrama, however, was to no avail, because Koch and the power of the Prussian authorities he represented overwhelmed Hamburg's resistance. Sanitation and bacteriology triumphed over miasmatism and neglect, and Hamburg was finally forced into developing a public health system. Hamburg lost its political autonomy as the result of the epidemic and subsequently came under the direct control of the Prussian administration. A new system of public health regulation was set in motion by Koch (Evans, 1987).

Cholera was a catalyst for change. It did not create social revolutions or public health systems, but contributed to the process of historical transition in industrial society. Perhaps its role in bringing about the downfall of laissez-faire in Hamburg in 1892 is the best example of this. Rather than directly stimulating an uprising, it was a vehicle, a medium, for acting out an historical tale whose stage had already been set. It provided a frame in which social actors and forces expressed conflicts but also resolved them.

EPIDEMICS AND INTERVENTIONS

Epidemic diseases characterized the downside to economic and urban growth. They also revealed some of the intricate social changes taking place in industrial society. They declined towards the end of the nineteenth century. The interventions of the state into the means by which they were transmitted among mass urban populations and declining and impoverished rural populations played a crucial role in that decline. What is more, the role of the state in providing for the public health altered its profile. The relationship between the health of populations and the changing shape of the modern state is what we now turn to in the next few chapters.

6 Public health and the modern state: France, Sweden and Germany

New models of policing population health had been developed in the eighteenth century, including voluntaristic efforts to improve the environment and the civil administration of quarantines, inoculation, regulation of medical practice and the sale of drugs. Health as a right of citizenship had been declared an ideal of modern democracy by the French Revolution. The early nineteenth century witnessed the rise of new sciences of socio-medical inquiry which expanded the possibilities for investigating the health of populations. To what extent did these developments bear fruit in systematic health regulation in the nineteenth century? Did the health of populations enter the agenda of high politics of the nineteenth-century state, and to what extent were the ideals of health citizenship realized within liberal democracies? How did industrialization and urbanization accelerate the necessity for disease regulation? In this chapter we examine a selection of nineteenth-century European states which had already begun to institute population health controls in the eighteenth century. How much was public health subsequently moulded in each society by its particular political culture and how much was it influenced by contemporary developments elsewhere?

FROM MERCANTILISM TO INDUSTRIALIZATION: SWEDEN

The public policy of medical police, introduced into Sweden in the eighteenth century, began to have the desired effect of reducing mortality and stimulating population growth from the early nineteenth century. After 1810, deaths no longer exceeded births and the population almost doubled between 1750 and 1850, reaching 5.2 million by 1900.

Medical provision grew only slowly, and until the late nineteenth century few districts employed public physicians; private practitioners were spread thinly across a wide sparsely populated territory. Nevertheless, the Collegium Medicum continued to represent state medical interests by receiving reports from district physicians, who described the disease profiles of local areas, the level of medical treatment and drug therapy available and the lifestyles of the population, including nutrition, housing conditions, levels of alcoholism and literacy, along with local climatic changes. A prominent feature of these reports was the account of resistance to medical intervention by the agrarian population, who were reluctant to seek the services of a doctor when they fell sick, giving their fate up to the will of God. Furthermore, medicine was perceived as a government authority outside the local community of lay practitioners and their traditional healing methods. Within the slowly expanding urban environments, however, the emergent bourgeois classes increasingly embraced professional medicine, integrating the consumption of medical services into their growing commercial economies. Also, from 1813 the Collegium Medicum was transformed into the National Board of Health, and this provided the medical profession with a new authority in public policy. Gradually throughout the nineteenth century, doctors became increasingly influential in political and community life, taking on the role of new secular 'priests' of society, incorporating both physical and moral welfare within the legitimate boundaries of their observation and practice. But the annual reports of the National Board of Health, published from 1850, demonstrated that the new political role of the medical profession failed to prevent the spread of a persistently brutal regime of epidemic diseases among children and adults, including malaria, dysentery, cholera, typhoid and pulmonary tuberculosis. Doctors used the eighteenth-century ideology of personal health care to explain the continuing high levels of morbidity and premature mortality. The new industrial proletariat were blamed for their 'poor health behaviour', including their inadequate dietary habits, alcoholism, immorality and parental neglect (Johannisson, 1994).

In the early nineteenth century more emphasis was placed on acute care provision, and the number of hospitals expanded, along with the network of district physicians, urban private practitioners and midwives. The number of physicians serving the population increased from 550 in 1850 to 1,131 by 1900. When pandemic infections struck, however, such as cholera in 1834, the state employed traditional methods of quarantine and compulsory isolation of individual victims to prevent the spread of disease. When these measures appeared to encourage the spread of cholera, quarantine policy was relaxed and the state relied instead on the creation of temporary dispensaries and more voluntary hospital provision. As elsewhere in Europe, cholera stimulated class suspicion and social unrest with a fervent belief among the proletariat of a government conspiracy against them.

Economic growth slowly increased in Sweden, until by the last two decades of the nineteenth century an agrarian society was transformed into a modern industrial nation. Urban expansion encouraged the state to become increasingly involved in public health policy from 1867, when Parliament created the first professorship of public health. The first chair was appointed to the Karolinska Institute at the medical school of Stockholm in 1876. Bacteriology further enhanced the academic acceptance of the discipline of public hygiene; a special 'Hygiene Section' was created within the Swedish Medical Association in 1899 and a National Laboratory for Bacteriology was established in 1907. The first

Public Health Act was passed in Sweden in 1874, establishing local boards of health responsible for setting up local sanitary infrastructures by establishing clean water supplies and efficient sewage and refuse removal systems. Doctors employed as local health officers were charged with the duty to control local air pollution and the sale of adulterated foods, inspect unfit housing and monitor the personal health habits of the local population, including domestic hygiene, alcohol abuse and immorality (Johannisson, 1994).

In the latter decades of the nineteenth century, population growth increased as a result of these reforms. By the turn of the century, infant mortality had declined by 17 per cent and, while infectious diseases were still the main cause of death, their levels among the adult population had discernibly declined. The earlier mercantilist concern with population scarcity became reversed into a preoccupation with the problems created by surplus. The first response to this was a liberalization of the emigration laws, which resulted in a dramatic exodus between 1860 and the First World War in which 1 million – the equivalent of one-fifth of Sweden's population – emigrated, largely to the United States. Most of these were agricultural labourers unable to survive Sweden's transition to an industrial economy (Brandstrom and Tedebrand (eds), 1988; Wilson, 1979).

As in the rest of Europe, the United States and the colonized world, the population debate in Sweden in the early twentieth century began to concentrate on the 'quality' as well as the quantity of the national stock. This stimulated new directions in public health policy, comparable to social hygiene movements found elsewhere on the Continent, for example in France and Germany, characterized by a new biologistic interpretation of social relations. These developments, however, will be explored in Chapter 10.

Sweden's experience of public health reform in the nineteenth century illustrates the resilience of the eighteenth-century concept of medical police, which continued to contribute to the policing of personal hygiene among local communities. Public hygiene and sanitary reform only slowly replaced medical police in public policy in the latter half of the nineteenth century. If the life of this concept was perpetuated in the Swedish context by the slow pace of industrialization until the end of the nineteenth century, then the same could not account for its survival in the context of both French and German public health reform, to which we shall now turn.

CENTRALIZATION AND INERTIA IN FRANCE

France led the development of public hygiene as an academic discipline in the first half of the nineteenth century. The 'birth of the clinic' in Paris, following the end of the Napoleonic Wars, was matched by the birth of a public hygiene movement. But unlike clinical medicine, preventive medicine remained largely an intellectual pursuit focusing upon the analysis of social conditions and the way in which they influenced the spread of disease. The translation of public hygiene theory into public policy was restricted by a commitment to a liberal political-economic philosophy, which was shared by politicians, public servants, the medical profession and the *partie d'hygiène*. Social analysis of health conditions did not translate into the construction of a state apparatus of disease prevention as it did in England. Instead, the central state relied on old structures of health surveillance set up under the *ancien régime* and left reform to local initiative.

Before the Revolution, the campaigning Vic d'Azir had institutionalized a national network of monitoring epidemic and epizootic conditions by using local provincial physicians to submit reports to the Royal Society of Medicine. This system was restored when the Royal Academy was established in 1820. The Academy also funded research, and while this facilitated the growth of public hygiene as an academic subject it remained a specialist interest, confined to a small group of social investigators who were not linked to any larger movements of social reform or to the medical profession as whole (Hannaway, 1981). Conceptual interest in public health reform became institutionalized in the establishment of the journal *Annales d'hygiène publique et de médecine légale* in 1829. Some public hygiene researchers, however, did become active policy advisors, at least in a metropolitan context within the Paris Council (La Berge, 1984).

At the outset of the century, responsibility for various public health functions was distributed among various government departments. The Ministry of the Interior, plus its statistical bureau, provided support for epidemiological and demographic inquiries. The Ministry of Agriculture was concerned with epizootics and the Ministry of Commerce was officially responsible for public health as it affected economic activities, although there was no policy or legislation covering such issues. Public health at the local level was the duty of prefects, sub-prefects and mayors of districts and towns. The most active local authority was the Health Council of the *département* of the Seine, established in 1802, which was staffed by salaried permanent officials drawn from leading members of the academic hygiene movement. The *département* of the Seine investigated persistent chronic public health issues such as noxious industries, quacks, garbage, sewage and adulterated food, and was not limited to the control of epidemics. It remained an advisory body only, with no powers of enforcement, but was nevertheless a model for other municipal health authorities both nationally and internationally (La Berge, 1992).

Maritime quarantine was administered by municipal health boards in port-cities, the most powerful of which, the Intendancy of Health at Marseilles, controlled the quarantine of merchant shipping in the Mediterranean. In 1820, when France faced an invasion of yellow fever from Spain, the central state created a High Council of Health to co-ordinate quarantines, *cordons sanitaires* and lazarettos, along with local sanitary commissions to implement HCH regulations. The High Council of Health operated entirely on the eighteenth-century model of medical police against contagion, and was not connected to the new public hygiene movement (Coleman, 1987).

Apart from operating quarantines during epidemics, the French central government remained largely inert in the first half of the nineteenth century and public health reform depended largely upon local initiative. Local physicians were appointed as 'health officers' to co-ordinate state action during epidemics, but full-time salaried employment of doctors by the state was limited to medical relief for the poor (Ackerman, 1990). Medical relief reached only a fraction of the population in need. Most provincial districts instituted few health reforms, but a local prefect could make a difference. In the Alsatian department of the Bas-Rhin region, Adrien Lezay-Marnésia had served in an annexed territory of the Rhineland and reproduced the German model of the district physician in his own area. In 1810 he set up a network of public physicians in each canton who served both as public health officers and as public physicians to the poor. These doctors remained in private practice but received 500 francs as a stipend for their public office. Two further *départements* in the north-east reproduced this system after the Restoration (Ramsey, 1994).

The Paris Health Council was the most active public health body in France in the early nineteenth century. The Paris prefect of police was responsible for the control of pollution, the inspection of markets and slaughterhouses, street and sewer cleaning, public lighting, monitoring and authorizing industrial establishments, the supervision of animal slaughter, maintaining the salubrity of public places and the control of quackery. Health ordinances were issued by the prefect but, as the Health Council reports demonstrate, few of these powers were ever enforced. From 1802 the Paris Health Council compiled medical statistics and mortality tables and produced reports on epidemics, rivers, cemeteries, slaughterhouses, refuse dumps, dissection rooms and public baths. When it was expanded in the 1830s, some of the major figures of the hygiene movement, such as Villermé and Parent-Duchatelet, were appointed to it and undertook innovative research into social and sanitary conditions within the city. But, as mentioned above, the Council remained an advisory body only, and many of its recommendations were never taken up by the Paris political administration because they were costly and they challenged an ideological allegiance to economic liberalism. Numerous programmes proposed by the Health Council were never adopted, such as the creation of new municipal drainage and systematic refuse removal systems. Nevertheless, the Council was able to have some effect on industrial development in Paris through its power to authorize commercial establishments, and after 1848 it gained the power to regulate the salubrity of private dwellings (La Berge, 1984; La Berge, 1992).

Although early nineteenth-century French politics were dominated by economic and philosophical liberalism, France was the breeding ground for socialist theory in the 1830s, and the Saint-Simonians incorporated public health reform into their critique of economic individualism and their belief in a new industrial order based upon brotherhood. Revolutionaries in 1848 identified a new social and political role for medicine when the editor of the *Gazette médicale de Paris*, Jules Guérin, promoted a 'brotherhood of physicians' dedicated to 'social medicine'. Guérin believed it was time for medicine to participate in government itself through the establishment of a Ministry of Public Health. The radicalism of 1848 matched that of the 1789 Revolution, but withered as the Revolution failed. Napoleon III suppressed the left after 1851. While he liberalized trade and took a new interest in alleviating the conditions of poverty, the central state continued to remain largely inactive in terms of health reform (Faure, 1989; Ramsey, 1994).

By the mid-nineteenth century, the state had begun to take some active role in individual areas. For example, in the 1850s new regulations were created to control the conditions of work for textile workers and the employment of child labour. Factories with more than twenty employees were banned from employing children younger than eight and restricted in the hours that other children were allowed to work. Some attempt to regulate housing conditions was made with the Melun housing law of 1850, which empowered communes to appoint inspection commissions to identify unhealthy rented lodging houses and prosecute neglectful landlords. Few local authorities adopted the law, but a precedent had been set allowing public authorities to intervene in the sanctity of the private property market. While no new measures were taken by the central state to prevent the spread of infectious disease in Paris, the prefects of the Seine, Rambuteau and later Baron Haussmann, improved the city's stench. The major Paris slaughterhouse was removed to the outskirts of Aubervilliers in 1839, and in 1841 the Montfaucon refuse dump in the city centre was closed. Haussmann also improved sewage and drainage engineering in the city which substantially expanded the clean water supply. Such sanitary reforms continued in Paris throughout the century, so that by the end of the period the city celebrated its modern status by hosting a world fair (Ramsey, 1994).

In the late nineteenth century, public hygiene began to take on a new profile when the Third Republic, established in 1870, made an ideological commitment to the health of the people (Elwitt, 1986). Although the Republic continued to prioritize the political rights of private property, socialists and moderate republican progressives all believed that public health programmes would help sustain social stability. Bacteriology provided renewed ideological legitimation for public hygiene stimulated by the impact of Louis Pasteur's discoveries and his political influence within French society. Responsibility for the disparate features of health policy was brought together in a new Bureau of Public Health and Hygiene created within the Ministry of the Interior. This brought medical assistance and public health control under one administration headed by a Pasteurian-minded politician, Léon Bourgeois. In addition, the Consultative Committee on Public Health (CCPH) which maintained jurisdiction over quarantine, headed by the dean of the Paris Medical Faculty, Paul Brouardel, was moved from the Commerce Industry to the Ministry of the Interior (Steudler, 1986).

As elsewhere in Europe, new voluntary associations concerned with the prevention of tuberculosis, alcoholism and the spread of venereal disease were also established, as preventive medicine in France increasingly focused on 'regeneration' of the population. In France the eugenic creed was heavily influenced by Lamarckian beliefs in the inheritance of physiological improvements from one generation to another. Thus, eugenic reformers campaigned for improved public welfare provision and promoted pronatalism, ante-natal care, maternal and infant 'puericulture' and the value of breast-feeding. Academic hygiene theory itself, however, remained dominated by its early identity as a social and political rather than biologically determinist science.

The central government health authorities were dominated by Pasteurian disciples, and Pasteur himself was recruited to the CCHP from 1881 to his death in 1895. Henri Monad, a career civil servant who headed the bureau for two decades from 1886 as the Director of Assistance and Public Health, and Brouardel formed the nucleus of an activist lobby. The CCHP promoted new legislation making vaccination, notification of infectious disease and death registration compulsory, and making disinfection services and pure water supply universally available. No national system of public health administration was created comparable to that developed in England by the 1875 Public Health Act, but three-quarters of the regional *départements* had active health councils even though they still remained advisory bodies to the prefect. From 1888, regional inspectors of hygiene services, recruited from among the professors of the medical faculties, were appointed to supervise public health services. By the end of the century, twenty large cities had created municipal hygiene bureaux with laboratories and disinfection services. Research was elaborately supported through the establishment of the Pasteur Institute itself and its replicas in Le Havre, Lille, Nancy, Lyons, Grenoble, Marseilles, Montpellier and Bordeaux. Pasteurian science replaced the earlier methods of indiscriminate quarantines with focused isolation of infectious individuals, disinfection and extermination of parasites and vermin, especially as animal vectors were discovered. In 1884 France battled cholera with systematic environmental improvement and the closure of places of public congregation. By the time of the 1892 epidemic, individual patients were isolated and their surroundings decontaminated (Latour, 1986).

Within a new context of political collectivism, represented not only by socialism but by other factions such as solidarism, support for state health care provision expanded. Both liberals and socialists feared the rising industrial and social strength of the unified German state, with its state-supported systems of comprehensive health and welfare provision. In the 1890s, new laws were introduced which revived the 1789 principles of rights and obligations of health citizenship, transferring medical assistance from poor relief into a system of national insurance. For the first time France established a national health code. The medical assistance act of 1893 made the *départements* and communes obliged to provide medical assistance to the destitute, funded by regional and local budgets with state subsidy. Numerous rural communes applied for exemption from the scheme but were resisted by legislatures who believed this was an opportunity to bring modern medicine to the countryside. The medical profession co-operated with the scheme, but resisted any form of salaried employment by representing their interests through the medical syndicates which had replaced the earlier loose federation of mutual aid organizations known as the General Association of French Physicians (Hildreth, 1987). Most regions adopted a system whereby patients freely chose their doctor, who would be subsequently reimbursed for his services. Initially the scheme was intended to serve 3–6 per cent of the population, but by 1895 1.3 million citizens had enrolled. By 1904, this had increased by 50 per cent, and the costs of the scheme had risen to 100 million francs by the beginning of the First World War (Mitchell, 1991). The growth of the state system was matched by the rise of private insurance schemes and the rapid expansion of mutual aid societies, which will be discussed in Chapter 11.

Together with the law on medical assistance, a law imposing universal standards of hygiene maintenance upon all regions and local districts was introduced in 1893. It finally came into force in 1904, making vaccination and notification to the mayor or sub-prefect compulsory and requiring local authorities to deal with insanitary sites and buildings. Any commune with a mortality rate which exceeded the national average for more than three years was compelled to undergo inspection and to provide sanitary reforms at the expense of the local authority. Every commune with more than 20,000 inhabitants was obliged to create a health office, although this public health bureaucracy had no coercive powers and remained under the jurisdiction of the mayor or the prefect. Local health council members were not paid and no salaried inspectorate was enforced, although individual prefects were allowed to create one if they wished. Thus, the central state avoided creating a national professional public health service but opted to use a mixture of compulsion and encouragement of local agencies to be responsible for health provision (Ramsay, 1994).

Throughout the nineteenth century, the French state chartered a course which it perceived to lie somewhere between the laissez-faire Anglo-Saxon model and German statism. Fearing both revolution and despotism, the French state remained centralized but non-interventionist, delegating its responsibilities for achieving national reforms to the individual operations of local and regional authorities. It did not fail to react to population health needs on the same level as some of the Swiss cantons or the city of Hamburg, but did not stimulate the opposition of libertarian movements such as the anti-vaccination league in England. Hygiene reform was restricted by the defence of private property rights throughout the period. By the first decades of the Third Republic, a new collectivist political will supported the expansion of public health policy as a means of invigorating the national stock and encouraging social stability. Hygiene reformers promoted their public health policies as a matter of life and death, but they had to compete in a pluralistic political system in which their interests were balanced against those of other groups.

POLICING THE GERMAN STATE

As we saw in Chapter 3, German Enlightenment theory of the absolute state incorporated the idea of the regulation of population health. The interventionist model of medical police outlined by J.-P. Franck was impossible to realize, even under the political system of absolutism. The cost alone of introducing a system of regulating the health and social life of all the monarch's subjects would have been prohibitive. Nevertheless, numerous German states gradually adopted medical regulations to control quackery and the sale of drugs, and established a machinery to contain epidemics whenever they occurred. The theory of medical police continued to dominate public health administration throughout the nineteenth century. As a result, the health bureaucracy was run by legally trained civil servants, and doctors took a secondary role. It took the triumphs of bacteriology to legitimate a medical take-over of the direction of health policy in unified Germany after 1871 (Weindling, 1994).

The German states established the tradition of municipal physicians from the late medieval period, but in 1817 Prussia created the office of a district doctor, the *Kreisphysickus*. The *Kreisphysickus* acted as a forensic expert, sanitary inspector and health advisor to the local authority. His duties often involved all those of a police doctor, such as examining corpses found under suspicious circumstances or adjudicating rape cases. He was also responsible for reporting on the health of military recruits, conducting state qualifying examinations of doctors, surgeons, apothecaries and midwives, certifying lunatics, prosecuting quacks and dealing with epidemics. In the early nineteenth century, a number of German states, such as Prussia and the city-state of Hamburg, introduced legislation making the notification of diseases, the isolation of patients and the fumigation of effects compulsory. Forensic medicine and population health policy together formed what was identified as *Staatsarzneikunde*, or state medicine in the German provinces.

While state medicine remained subservient to the goals of civil service administration, the medical profession was increasingly challenging this system by the middle of the nineteenth century. For example, in Hamburg a health committee was created in 1818 which was dominated by civil servants and members of Hamburg's Senate. No full-time medical officers were members of the committee, and its policies persistently reflected the interests of Hamburg's mercantile community rather than the priority of disease prevention. By the end of the 1860s, Hamburg's medical profession demanded a bigger say. Gustav Gernet, one of the city's two medical officers, insisted that reform was unavoidable because the amateur nature of health administration was inadequate for a large industrial city and seaport. He compared the situation in Hamburg with the comprehensive system in Britain based on 'scientific' principles and administered by full-time specially trained medical officers of health. The Senate replaced the health committee in 1870 with a medical board on which the medical profession had a clear majority, but it was solely an advisory body with no power to introduce regulations itself (Evans, 1987).

The Hamburg medical profession was divided over goals and objectives. The physicians on the health committee wanted a board, led by a Senator, to continue the existing general approach. The majority of the city's leading physicians, represented by the Doctors' Club, wanted to separate state medicine from policing and establish sanitation as a separate function of government. Furthermore, they demanded that this function required scientific leadership directed by specialist physicians. Such demands by the Hamburg medical elite reflected those which were being made by physicians in many other parts of Germany by the 1860s, but the dominance of the bourgeois entrepreneurial classes on the one hand and the power of the autocratic civil service bureaucracy on the other were major obstacles to them achieving their goals. Nevertheless, a growing movement for the establishment of 'political medicine' had been gathering momentum in the German states since the European revolutions in 1848 (Evans, 1987).

Radical doctors in both France and the German states in 1848 wanted medicine to play a role in national government. As mentioned above, in France this role was called 'social medicine' by the *Gazette médicale de Paris*. Within Prussia a similar philosophy was outlined by the physician who became the founder of cellular pathology and a liberal politician, Rudolph Virchow. Early in 1848 the Prussian government employed him to investigate a severe epidemic of typhus fever in the mill district of Upper Silesia, an area lying on the borders of Northern Prussia and Poland but ruled by Prussian occupation. Virchow had no remedy for the disease, but identified the insanitary conditions in which the weavers lived as the cause of the epidemic. He developed what he chose to call a 'socio-logical' epidemiology, which led him to conclude that the strength of the disease among the Upper Silesians was due to their subjugated political state. Poor and oppressed for decades by the imperial exploitation of Prussia, they had failed to rebel because of widespread ignorance and the social-psychological apathy which results from the culture of poverty and political slavery. The impoverished conditions and levels of squalor in which they lived would never have been tolerated by citizens living in a 'free-democracy with general self-government'. Therefore, Virchow concluded that 'free and unlimited democracy' was the only way to prevent typhus (Ackerknecht, 1953; Boyd, 1991).

> The logical answer to the question as to how conditions similar to those that have unfolded before our eyes in Upper Silesia can be prevented in the future is, therefore, very easy and simple: education, with its daughters, liberty and prosperity.

Virchow suggested that

> We have thus reached with the logical argument the stand-point …[that] medicine has imperceptibly led us into the social field and placed us in a position of confronting directly the great problems of our time.

For this reason Virchow had no hesitation in saying that the elimination of famine and ignorance would lead to the prevention of population decimation from virulent diseases. A well-fed and politically emancipated population would produce a society in which both capital and labour had the same rights to health.

These are the radical methods I am suggesting as a remedy against the reoccurrence of famine and of great typhus epidemics in Upper Silesia…. May therefore the next interval be used to preserve from the repetition of such scenes of horror by liberal institutions for the benefit of the people, which to the shame of the government has so far been inhabited only by poor and neglected people.

(Virchow, 1986: 319)

Because the investigation of disease led medicine into the social relations of health and illness, Virchow believed that medicine should become political (Weindling, 1984). Political medicine was essential to the operation of modern democratic states and the health of populations in industrial societies. Within this context, Virchow outlined a political role for the physician as an ambassador for the poor, with the responsibility of identifying and recording sickness and devising measures to prevent it.

Virchow's programme was supported by other revolutionary doctors, such as Salamon Neuman of Berlin, who put forward a similar programme in 1847 which he justified by the fact that

Most diseases which either prevent the full enjoyment of life or bring about premature death in a large proportion of the population are due, not to natural causes but to social causes…. In its inmost core, in its essence, medical science is a social science; but until this potentiality is realized, we shall not taste the fruits, but must be content merely to feel and gaze.

(Sand, 1952: 203)

Like Virchow, Neuman believed that health standards were 'primarily the effect of means and education on the one hand, of poverty and ignorance on the other'. Neuman also called for the political mobilization of medicine in order to allow science to determine the organization of medical care (Sand, 1952: 206).

The revolutions of 1848 failed, but the political role of medicine in the state regulation of health expanded, albeit incrementally and largely on a localized basis. Virchow encouraged Berlin to build sanitary infrastructures to supply pure water and remove sewage and refuse, all by the end of the 1860s. In Munich, reform was led by the first German professor of public hygiene, Max von Pettenkofer. Pettenkofer was a major figure in the development of the academic study of public hygiene and sanitary reform in the nineteenth century. Trained in medicine and pharmacology, Pettenkofer studied with Justig Liebig, the founder of organic chemistry, at Giessen. Early in his career he made a number of notable inventions and discoveries, such as devising a copper amalgam for filling teeth and preparing meat extract, which ultimately led to the development of the Oxo cube. His main interest, however, was always public hygiene, on which he published a vast amount of material. He was persuaded by the contemporary fungal germ theories of disease transmission, but remained a determined opponent of both contagionism and bacteriology to the end of his days. His opposition to bacteriology led to a famous showdown with the discoverer of the cholera bacillus, Robert Koch, during the Hamburg epidemic of 1892, when he drank a weakened solution of the bacillus to refute Koch's theory. This heroic effort did not, however, make a sufficient impact to dissuade the Hamburg authorities from following Koch's instructions to introduce sand filtration of the water supply in order to halt the cholera infection of the town (Evans, 1987).

Pettenkofer was appointed associate professor of medical chemistry at Munich University in 1847 and became court apothecary to King Maximilian II of Bavaria in 1850. He was made professor of hygiene in 1865 and persuaded the Bavarian government to create an Institute of Hygiene in Munich in 1878 under his direction. His influence became widespread throughout the medical academic community, and by the end of the century over thirty chairs and institute directorships in hygiene had been created throughout Germany. He and his pupils disseminated their ideas through two journals which they edited, *Sietschrift für Biologie* and the *Archiv für Hygiene* (Beyer, 1956).

His allegiance to a contingent-contagionist theory of disease transmission based on chemical fermentation led Pettenkofer to oppose the direct interventionist policies of the contagionists and support a broad-based agenda for disease prevention. In the 1870s he pushed the Munich authorities into acquiring a fresh mountain water supply and installing a modern sewage removal system. He believed that, whatever the medium of disease transmission, it required favourable local conditions to be effective, including climate and soil quality. Thus, he thought that sewage must be removed downriver in order to preserve the purity of the local soil from contamination. He argued that quarantine was a useless measure against epidemic invasion and instead advocated improved housing and education of the population in healthy diet, exercise and temperance. As a pioneer of prevention, he was highly influential in German health policy regarding infectious diseases. The sanitary reforms instituted in Berlin and Munich were adopted in other major German towns throughout the nineteenth century (Sand, 1952). A notable exception to this pattern, of course, was the city-state of Hamburg, where rugged economic and political liberalism prevented collective action for the creation of a modern sanitary urban infrastructure.

Pettenkofer influenced national public health organization, becoming the leading member of the Cholera Commission for the German Empire, which was the forerunner of the Imperial Health Office, created in 1873 and operating from 1876. This, however, had only limited powers of monitoring health conditions and co-ordinating actions in the face of epidemics. The Office collected statistics and eventually established a laboratory. Pettenkofer's achievements in establishing hygiene as an academic discipline legitimized the medical professionalization of public health administration, which increasingly challenged the traditional civil service domination of policy formation and execution in the last quarter of the century. The German Association of Scientists and Doctors founded a National Society for Public Health in 1873, and local associations were created in rural areas such as the Ruhr. Pettenkofer's influence over policy continued until it was overtaken by the champion of the new discipline of bacteriology, Robert Koch, who, based in Berlin, was embraced by the Prussian state's power within the Second Reich of unified Germany. Koch, together with Bismarck's physician, Heinrich Struck, was joint director of the Health Office from 1881, but they were both succeeded by two legally trained administrators. The Office was not directed by another medically trained man until 1925, but the medical profession continued to assert its expert status through the establishment in 1900 of an advisory health council, the *Reichsgesundheitrat*, which consisted of seventy-seven doctors (Evans, 1987).

Bacteriology facilitated a new administrative centralization of public health, but with a less economic interventionist approach focusing instead on the isolation of infectious individuals and disinfection of effects. Prussia established full-time medical officers of health in 1899, but the replacement of part-time state doctors throughout Germany took place over a long period. Various municipalities such as Berlin, Charlottenburg, Schöneberg and Neukölln soon created full-time medical departments. As in other European states, bacteriology was succeeded by the Darwinian-inspired science of eugenics, which aimed to explain disease and biological degeneration by understanding the mechanisms of heredity. Eugenics inspired the creation of two new movements in Germany, social hygiene and racial hygiene, which will be discussed in detail in Chapter 10. Nevertheless, the rise to prominence of social hygiene, along with new concerns over social assistance and health insurance, demonstrated the level of political importance which population health had reached in Germany by the end of the nineteenth century. The various Enlightenment philosophies of population health had been explored in the German context throughout the nineteenth century, in terms of both medical policing and health citizenship. And yet, despite the traditional autocratic bureaucracy, centralized interventionist health policy remained extremely limited among the German states. Even after unification in 1871, wide variations in health regulations depended upon local political contexts. Nevertheless, the growing pace of industrialization had spurred ever greater concern with population health, moving it beyond the ideal rationalizations of the eighteenth century into a more pragmatic and politically orientated practice.

HEALTH AND THE MODERN STATE

The gradual adoption of political measures to prevent epidemic disease and preserve population health by European societies was determined both economically and politically. Enlightenment concepts of health as a social value and a political right provided a rationalization for reforms dictated by the economic costs of premature mortality from epidemic disease, created by rapid urbanization as the pace of industrialization increased. Reforms were shaped, however, by national cultures, even though a distinctive discourse on environmental health policy emerged which crossed national boundaries. Disease prevention high-lighted different forms of political tension in different European states. In Sweden, the Enlightenment perspectives on health survived late into the nine-teenth century as the transition from an agrarian to an industrial society took place slowly, resulting in a failure to balance population scarcity and surplus. In France, the translation of advancements in the science of public hygiene into public policy was restrained by the conflict between political-economic liberalism and centralism. Towards the end of the century, an enthusiasm for liberal-collec-tivism allowed the French state to resolve this conflict through a mixed policy of state intervention and voluntary action in the prevention of disease and provi-sion of health services. In Germany, autocratic bureaucracy resisted the rise of medical statesmanship and thus public policy could only gradually be informed by new expertise and become innovative. The importance of national context is drawn out even further when the above examples are compared with the devel-opment of public health in Britain and the United States.

7 Public health and centralization: the Victorian British state

The British state was relatively slow to begin considering issues of population health. As we have seen, powerful civil and maritime quarantine laws had been developed by a number of European states since the time of the Black Death. In Tudor England, Cardinal Wolsey had looked enviously at governmental modernization on the Continent and was the first British administrator to imitate it when he encouraged the development of preliminary plague regulations. By the seventeenth century, complex civil plague controls had been established by sophisticated administrations in city-states such as Florence and Venice. From the late seventeenth century, interest in population health escalated in Britain, promoted largely by philanthropic gentlemanly scholars concerned to apply social theory to a practical object. Political arithmetic, theories of the health advantages of ventilated interiors, civil administration of smallpox inoculation and the environmental improvement of towns as the basis for self-improvement of individuals were all subjects explored to various degrees within the enlightened culture of the fastest-growing consumer society in Europe. England pioneered mass inoculation for profit, along with commercial refuse removal and street improvements.

From the end of the eighteenth century, the question of the people's health in Britain became bound to the changing role of the state in the transition to an industrial society. After 1815, the public purse, relieved of the burden of massive military expenditure on war, became increasingly dedicated to domestic social policy. Public health policy was a beneficiary of this development. In Britain, rapid industrialization transformed the demographic structure and geographical distribution of the population and escalated urbanization (Woods and Woodward, 1984). An urban proletariat and lumpenproletariat expanded with the industrial economy, and one of the most pressing social costs of growth became the burden of destitution created by the business cycle and epidemic disease. The British state explored new directions for the relief of poverty and distress which relied on the Victorian expansion of voluntary effort to provide services in health, education and housing. The mixed economy of social welfare in nineteenth-century Britain reflected the values of a society which wished to keep the size of the state to a minimum.

Despite the pervasive rhetoric of liberal individualism, the promotion of the economic ideology of laissez-faire and the reliance upon voluntary effort to provide social services to those in need, the Victorian state in Britain nevertheless continued to expand and become increasingly interventionist. Expansion was justified by Utilitarian beliefs that the profitable operations of a market economy could be maximized if it was protected by a political, legal system which created the best conditions for its freedom. Nowhere were the contradictory tensions of Victorian political and economic philosophies more obviously reflected than in the growth of public health intervention. Public health policy in Britain exemplified the growth of a bureaucratic within the liberal democratic state. The British state sought solutions to the epidemic costs of economic expansion through the creation of an interventionist bureaucratic system of health administration. Initially the role of the state was to 'enable' local authorities to intervene to protect their environments. But the grammar of public health legislation increasingly adopted the syntax of compulsion. The architects of state intervention justified it by assuming that a large proportion of poverty – and its costs upon solvent individuals, industry and society in general – could be reduced by preventing premature mortality of breadwinners caused by epidemic disease (Porter, 1997; MacDonagh, 1958; Clark, 1959; Lubenow, 1971). As we shall see, in the United States public health intervention was driven, designed and dominated by local and voluntaristic initiatives in the nineteenth century. By contrast, in Britain the initiative for public health intervention was driven by the actions of central government but relied on local government for its practical application. In this respect, public health provision continued to be open to a degree of local government discretion and accessible to public participation in local democratic processes. However, the opponents of public health intervention in Britain perceived it as a threat to local government autonomy and an unacceptable intervention by the central state in their affairs. Public health intervention was perceived by early Victorians as the most infamous growth of authoritarian, paternalist power of central government on the one hand and the growth of the despotic influence of a particular profession – the medical profession – on the other (Roberts, 1979; Porter and Porter, 1988). These accusations gained force as the interventions of the state became more extensive and mandatory, for example in the area of compulsory smallpox vaccination. While the dominance of voluntary provision in the mixed economy of welfare in Victorian Britain has encouraged contemporary historians to describe it as a 'weak' state, the Victorian opponents of public health would not have agreed. Perhaps instead, therefore, we should employ more credibly the views of Victorians themselves in exploring the growth of bureaucratic intervention in public health, as one way in which state power increased in areas which the Victorian government had given priority. The next two chapters examine both of these themes in the Victorian state's management of population health.

URBANIZATION AND SQUALOR

Industrialization exponentially multiplied environmental threats to health primarily through the massive growth of towns. London had 800,000 people in 1801, and there were only thirteen towns with populations of over 25,000. By 1841, London's population had risen by one million, and forty-two towns contained over 25,000 people. By 1861, six British cities contained more than a quarter of a million inhabitants. In the early 1800s, approximately 20 per cent of the population of England and Wales lived in towns of over 5,000; by 1851 over half the population did so, and by 1901 almost 80 per cent. By contrast, in rural areas some counties contained a lower population in 1901 than they did in 1851 (Woods and Woodward, 1984).

These patterns were repeated in Europe and the United States as industrialization gathered momentum. No urban development could accommodate such a demographic explosion which resulted in mass overcrowding, inadequate housing, dramatic accumulation of human, animal and industrial waste products together with rising levels of industrial and domestic atmospheric pollution, and deadly pollution of insufficient potable water supply (Hamlin, 1990). In Britain and on the Continent, the grotesquely squalid conditions imposed upon the slum-dwelling proletariat were revealed by a host of observers, from social reformers to investigative journalists, and soon produced dramatic rises in infant mortality, rising levels of epidemic diseases, such as 'fever' – both typhoid and typhus – and rising levels of dependency created through sickness (Wohl, 1984).

The physical expansion of the cities could not keep pace with the population influx and growth. Existing building stock became grossly overcrowded with huge densities of people. The amenities designed for vastly smaller numbers were totally inadequate. The need for new housing led to building methods which sacrificed quality for speed. The notorious jerry-built housing degenerated into slums as quickly as it was erected. Back-to-back housing favoured by northern British towns was a classic example (Wohl, 1975).

Sanitary facilities designed for less dense levels of population were the most serious failure. Traditional methods of waste disposal, such as cesspits and middens, served more sparsely distributed populations adequately but became dangerously overburdened under these new conditions. Cesspools turned into manure swamps and seeped into the local water supplies and wells. Dry middens and their consequent dungheaps turned into mountains infested with flies and vermin. Existing levels of intermittent water supply could not possibly serve the expansion of demand (Wohl, 1984; Hamlin, 1990).

The traditional life of a market town became fatally hazardous under these new pressures. Transportation was horse-drawn. Animals were brought into markets for sale and slaughter. Whereas these activities had once produced pollutions which were relatively harmless, their escalation among the new density of population made them deadly. Traditional scavenging had coped with the removal of refuse of small communities. These methods were hopelessly inadequate for the new levels of manure, animal and human wastes.

The defining feature of the heavily overstressed towns in the nineteenth century was their stench. Little wonder that atmospheric theories of disease were popular with some: the stink of the urban environment must have seemed strong and foul enough to kill, or at least induce vomiting. The most deadly feature of the new towns was the close proximity of human beings to each other. For example, the report of a health officer for Darlington in the 1850s found six children, aged between 2 and 17, suffering from smallpox in a one-roomed dwelling shared with their parents, an elder brother and an uncle. They all slept together on rags on the floor, with no bed. Millions of similar cases could be cited, with conditions getting even worse as disease victims died and their corpses remained rotting among families in single-roomed accommodation for days, as the family scraped together the pennies to bury them (Wohl, 1984).

These conditions convinced health statisticians such as William Farr that mortality increased with density. For Farr, the spatial distribution of mortality revealed the facts. Later surveys appeared to support his assumption. In London in 1892, where there was 15 per cent overcrowding per total population, the mortality rate was 17.5 per cent – where overcrowding exceeded 35 per cent, mortality rose to 25 per cent. In Glasgow in 1901, families living in four-roomed accommodation had a death rate of 11.2 per thousand – families living in one room had a death rate of 32.7 per thousand. In 1907, a national survey showed that districts with average densities of 136 persons per square mile had a mean death rate of 11.63 per cent – districts with an average of 55,000 persons per square mile had a mean death rate of 34.82 per cent. The rapid growth of towns produced areas with staggering densities. Some sections of Liverpool had 300 people per acre in 1881. In the same year, central Glasgow had 1,000 people per acre. With such densities, the demand for new housing stock was intense and led to new buildings being built closely together, packing as many people into every inch as possible. The slums were labyrinths and mazes of close courts and narrow alleyways. The new accommodation had no sanitary facilities or regular water supply, and hardly any ventilation or sunlight. Such intensive building produced parallel rows of dwellings separated by only six feet, and the infamous back-to-backs (Frazer, 1950; Fraser Brockington, 1956).

Victorian middle-class society believed these conditions not only produced disease but also fostered immorality, drunkenness, crime, incest and fornication among the poor. It destroyed the sanctity of the home and the families within. It bred political danger, disposing the poor to socialism and nihilism, and encouraged them in atheism (Jones, 1983). Urbanization brought the workers to the factories and trade to the town, but its consequences were seriously disconcerting to the ruling classes.

THE IDEA OF THE POOR

Industrialization and urbanization changed the character of the poor from dissipated agricultural labourers and country vagabonds into agglomerated masses crowded into sprawling urban slums. A culture of fear and suspicion surrounded the urban proletarianized poor. The creation of an urban proletariat by an industrial economy generated more than just increases in production. It bred more sharply defined economic class division, potentially threatening underlying social stability. As the British landowning aristocracy struggled to maintain their rule of Parliament through political reform, radical elements of the proletariat challenged the entire political structure and, while revolution was never a threat, flashpoints of civil unrest heightened unease (Thompson, 1970; Jones, 1983; Hollis, 1973). In France, political economists like J.B. Say feared the population would continue to expand at the same level as industrial production, threatening prosperity. Friedrich Engels described the desperate state of the urban proletariat family under capitalism, and Karl Marx propagated the dialectical materialist theory of inevitable revolution. In the United States, Evangelical leaders feared providential retribution for the wickedness created by urbanism among the dissolute poor (Rosenberg, 1962).

Many competing views of the poor existed in the early nineteenth century. A fundamental distinction was made between the poor and what Jeremy Bentham called the 'indigent'. Poverty consisted of labouring for a meagre living. Indigence was destitution – either through unemployment or through infirmity. The poor were labouring for low wages, the destitute were unable or unwilling to work. A common middle-class Victorian belief was that the labouring poor were deserving of charitable empathy, as were the impotent indigent. The able-bodied unemployed, however, were seen as idlers and wasters, and were frequently believed to become itinerant vagrants and vagabonds – scrounging from the industrious, and undeserving of assistance. Poverty created problems on a number of different levels. It was a financial burden on the commonwealth, it demoralized through immiseration, and it finally threatened to breed ideological disaffection and political and social instability. Poverty stimulated numerous types of social response (Himelfarb, 1984). Evangelicalism in Britain and the United States and Catholicism in France attacked the question of remoralizing the poor.

In Britain, Evangelical philanthropists promoted educational reform and the reform of factory employment. In his study of the establishment of pauper schools, the Unitarian physician and educationalist James Phillips Kay-Shuttleworth (1804–1871) concluded that they would prevent dependency by educating the poor to 'discharge their social duties' through training in 'correct social habits' as much as providing workers with technical skills. The great Evangelical reformer, the seventh Earl of Shaftesbury, Lord Ashley, began a movement to establish charity schools for 'ragged children' of the labouring and indigent poor, and campaigned for the statutory reduction of the daily hours of factory work. Other Evangelicals believed self-improvement could be achieved through the assertion of political rights. In an *Address to the Working Classes* in 1847, Thomas Southwood-Smith, the Unitarian doctor and one-time secretary to Jeremy Bentham who became central to the early public health movement, declared that government apathy was responsible for the appalling conditions in which the labouring poor had to live, and he urged them to command the attention of the legislature (Porter, 1997).

The question of human improvement was equally central to the concept of the pursuit of happiness in political economy, especially in the context of the British philosophy of Utilitarianism. The eighteenth-century physician Bernard de Mandeville had claimed that all successful economies ran on the principles of unbridled self-love. Adam Smith, along with many of his contemporaries, denounced Mandeville's vulgar amoral philosophy and replaced it with a systematic analysis of the 'wealth of nations' being achieved most successfully in a free market economy, in which the realization of self-interest created sufficient surplus value, or profit, to provide the best possible subsistence for all. In Smith's system, self-interest guided by the hidden hand – the autonomous mechanisms of the free exchange of goods in the market-place – was a means to a greater, more just and moral end which was to the benefit of all (Webb, 1993).

This moral ethic, however, was superseded by the disciples of Smith and replaced by a new scientific rationality contained within philosophical radicalism, especially as it was expressed in the felicific calculus of Jeremy Bentham. The Reverend Thomas Malthus had countered Smith's optimistic vision of the productive capacity of the free market economy with a dismal scenario resulting from the law of population. This law proposed that as society became more affluent the labouring classes would increase in number geometrically and would out-populate the capacity of the market to provide a subsistence for them. The classical economist David Ricardo modified both Smith's and Malthus's vision with the iron law of wages, whereby the increasing profitability of the market would necessarily drive the wages of labour down to subsistence level, eventually impoverishing them below the point of survival. Together, the law of population and the iron law of wages meant that the success of the market economy depended upon the immiseration of the labour force and the expendability of the poor (James, 1979).

In response to the laws of political economy, Jeremy Bentham placed his faith in the rule of civil law to ensure the conditions whereby economic relations of the market could function with the greatest degree of freedom and benefit the greatest number of people at any one time. The driving force behind the reforming 'spirit of the age' was the Utilitarian goal of achieving the greatest happiness of the greatest number by acting, in accordance with the laws of political economy, in the interests of those who could not or would not act for themselves (Roberts, 1969).

It was within this context that remedies for the rising costs of poverty were discussed in Britain. Numerous factions were concerned about the increasing costs of the poor. Farmers and parishioners, burdened by ever rising rates, had the sympathies of the intellectual radicals such as Bentham, who shared their concern, not merely because of the severe financial burden under which they laboured but, more importantly, because in political economic terms the old Elizabethan Poor Law had become an obstacle to the free movement of labour, economically and geographically. In Britain the agricultural poor and the indigent became an increasing financial problem as the result of changes in the agricultural economy at the end of the eighteenth century. The war with France, new techniques of agricultural production and successive bad harvests depressed the agrarian economy from 1795, with farmers having diminishing wages to pay their labourers. The crisis led to the introduction of an allowance system administered through the old Poor Law. The Elizabethan Poor Law had mostly provided outdoor relief in kind to the hungry poor living below subsistence. This method became extended into what became known as the Speenhamland system, wherein agricultural labourers had their wages subsidized by the Poor Rates to bring them up to the level of subsistence, according to the price of bread. Poverty had thus become increasingly pauperized and wages depressed through the allowance system. The price of poverty escalated to levels which were perceived as critical, from £3–7 million pounds per annum (Fraser, 1973; Rose, 1991).

By the 1830s it appeared to be the most pressing problem of the British state and it was attacked using the most systematic and modern methods of analysis yet introduced into government. A study of poverty was made by two assistants to the central Poor Law Commission, two disciples of Bentham, the economist and lawyer Nassau Senior and the petit-bourgeois, upwardly socially mobile lawyer Edwin Chadwick, who had been Bentham's secretary. The Report of the Poor Law Commission in 1832 concluded that the allowance system was the worst of all threats to the free market economy. It artificially depressed the price of labour and removed the incentive of the fear of hunger to the poor to help themselves. Furthermore, the old settlement laws prevented the geographical mobility of labour essential to the emergent industrial economy (Rose, 1991).

The answer, Chadwick believed, was to deter pauperdom by making it less eligible than the lowest paid labour. He believed the way to achieve this was to deprive the pauper of his liberty, split up his family and incarcerate them in a workhouse. The new Poor Law was instituted under the Poor Law Amendment Act in 1834 and it remained intact until 1929. It was the most hated and dreaded of all the harsh Victorian impositions upon the poor and the destitute. While successful in reducing the poor rates, however, it proved to be unworkable in the northern industrial areas, where periodic destitution resulted from the fluctuations in the business cycle of the manufacturing industry (Crowther, 1981; Edsall, 1971).

The Poor Law investigators had been largely concerned with agricultural pauperism, but the problem of destitution among the urban proletariat in Britain, France and the United States proved to be inherently related to disease. In different ways, in France, Britain and the United States, the elimination of poverty through the remoralization of the poor became bound to the question of health reform.

POLITICAL CURES FOR DISEASE AND DESTITUTION

The social-physics of disease, poverty and urbanism was taken up throughout Europe in the first half of the nineteenth century. Its influence upon governments varied. As we saw in Chapter 6, in France little systematic or comprehensive state action was enforced until later decades. In united Germany after 1871, the state programme for health reform was extensive. Public health reform in Europe and America resulted from a mixture of philanthropic relief, political expediency, new faith in the possibility of 'rational' government and, in Britain and France, from principles of political economy and Utilitarianism.

The murderous mortality of the 1832 cholera epidemic in Britain especially highlighted the problem of disease and its connection with the increasing costs of poverty upon tax-payers. Chadwick believed that separating the labouring from the dependent poor would prevent them from the contamination of pauperization (Williams, 1981). He also explored many other avenues beside less-eligibility, to prevent destitution, investigating causes of pauperism like alcoholism, crime, overcrowding and violence, and concluded that a great proportion resulted from disease. In 1837 he appointed three doctors sympathetic to sanitary reform, Neil Arnott, James Phillips Kay-Shuttleworth and Thomas Southwood Smith (1788–1861), to investigate London districts with the highest typhus mortality. In their 1838 reports, they revealed the full squalor of the London rookeries where medical officers to the Poor Law as well as the local inhabitants lost their lives from rampant 'fever'. Chadwick followed these studies with an investigation of insanitary areas throughout Britain (Finer, 1952; Lewis, 1952).

Chadwick loathed Poor Law medical officers because he thought they exploited the relief system by prescribing useless philanthropy, but he used hundreds of their reports to compile a massive survey of *The Sanitary Conditions of the Labouring Classes of Great Britain* in 1842. The conditions described in London in 1838 were matched in Glasgow, Birmingham, Leeds, Manchester and other major urban centres. The 1842 Report recommended implementation of what Chadwick called 'the sanitary idea', beginning with the creation of a central public health authority to direct local boards to provide drainage, cleansing, paving, potable water and the sanitary regulation of dwellings, nuisances and offensive trades. The local authorities should appoint a medical officer of health to supervise and co-ordinate all local sanitary work, and an inspector of nuisances. Sanitary regulation would be assisted by strengthened nuisance laws and building laws, and local authorities would be allowed to raise a rate for large engineering projects to provide new sewage drainage and water supply (Wohl, 1984).

Chadwick was convinced that the construction of massive new drainage and sewage removal systems was of primary importance. He believed that existing square bricked sewers with large tunnel pipes that did not flush or empty should be replaced by small egg-shaped sewers lined with glazed brick and connected by small earthenware pipes, which would be constantly flushed by high-pressurized water (Hamlin, 1997). Liquid sewage could be recycled as manure fertilizer to outlying farming districts. Street-widening, the removal of cesspools and all other noxious nuisances, together with an end to intermittent drinking water, were fundamental.

Chadwick built his sanitary idea upon a miasmatic theory of disease aetiology which he interpreted as causation through non-specific contamination of the atmosphere by gaseous material given off by putrefying, decomposing organic matter – thus, for Chadwick, disease was smell. Victorian social reformers rallied to the cause of urban sanitation in the Metropolitan Health of Towns Association, founded in 1844 by Southwood Smith, and in scholarly forums such as the National Association for the Promotion of Social Science, the Royal Statistical Society and the London Epidemiological Society. As we discussed in Chapter 4, these clubs brought reformers together with influential policy-makers and cabinet ministers. The Health of Towns Association was supported by aristocrats and politicians such as the Marquis of Normanby (1819–1890), who was its first president, Viscount Morpeth (1802–1864), Lord Ashley (later the seventh Earl of Shaftesbury) (1801–1885), Benjamin Disraeli (1804–1881), and elite doctors such as Sir James Clark and John Simon (1816–1904). Their supportive propaganda, such as a Health of Towns Association's report in 1847, became crucial in the fight for new legislation (Finer, 1952; Lewis, 1952).

Following Chadwick's 1842 report, a Royal Commission on the Health of Towns was set up in 1843–1845, which reinforced its recommendations and added new clauses regarding interments. In 1846, Liverpool created the first sanitary authority under a local Act and appointed the first medical officer of health, a local physician, William Duncan. The Liverpool administration provided a model for national legislation. The first British Public Health Act was passed in 1848. While comprehensive, it remained permissive. The potential for a national sanitary bureaucracy was available but left largely to the discretion of individual local authorities. The Act created a central authority, the General Board of Health, consisting of three members: the seventh Earl of Shaftesbury as its first president, Viscount Morpeth (Earl of Carlisle) who had been responsible for introducing the Act into Parliament, and Chadwick, its only salaried member. Southwood Smith was appointed as its medical advisor under the Nuisance Removal and Disease Prevention (Cholera) Act 1848 (Hamlin, 1997).

Any one-tenth of the ratepayers within a locality could petition the General Board for the adoption of the Act, or it could be imposed by the Board upon a local authority with an annual death rate above 23 per thousand living. The local town council or corporation became the sanitary authority, as a local board of health. The local board of health was responsible for sanitary supervision and inspection, drainage and water and gas supplies, and could increase the local rates or raise mortgages to cover costs (Wohl, 1984). They were to appoint local medical officers of health. Local boards had the power to regulate offensive trades; remove 'nuisances' as defined under the 1846–1848 Nuisance Acts; regulate cellar dwellings and houses unfit for human habitation; and provide burial grounds, public parks and baths. The Act applied to all districts outside the metropolitan boroughs of London. The London boroughs had their own

Metropolitan Commission of Sewers, set up in 1848; the City of London obtained its own private Sewers Act 1848, to keep it outside the jurisdiction of the General Board, and appointed its own medical officer of health, a consultant surgeon from St Thomas's Hospital and a member of London's elite medical community, John Simon (Lambert, 1963).

Chadwick believed that metropolitan London was more important to sanitary reform than all other localities. The internal conflicts and incompetence of the Metropolitan Sewers Commission, however, led to Chadwick's removal from it in 1849. He still attempted to bring London's interments system and water supply under the control of the General Board. He wanted to 'nationalize' burial and set up state cemeteries, but was opposed by the Treasury and the metropolitan vestries. Ultimately an Interments Act of 1852 allowed the Home Secretary to close any metropolitan burial ground and empowered local parishes to purchase new graveyard sites, but the General Board had no power to intervene (Brundage, 1988).

Chadwick aimed to municipalize the private water companies and link water supply to drainage under one public authority. He was effectively opposed by the Metropolitan Sewers Commission and the water companies, who were a powerful parliamentary lobby. A Water Act of 1852 allowed the metropolitan water companies to retain their separate existence, but forced them to abandon all sources below Teddington, to provide a constant supply, to cover their reservoirs and to filter their water. In both the interment and water questions, private interests and municipal government resisted public ownership and central control (Luckin, 1986; Hardy, 1984).

Between 1848 and 1853, 284 districts applied to adopt the Public Health Act, and it was established in 103 towns. Vigour varied between sanitary authorities. Some failed to make any improvements to mains drainage or to implement the Board's engineering schemes. In other districts, the same insanitary conditions persisted whether they adopted the Act or not. Some authorities, however, took up their new responsibilities and powers with a vengeance and instituted model reforms under the direction of the Board's inspectors (Wohl, 1984).

Opposition to the whole measure came not just from 'metropolitan radicals' but from outraged defenders of local government autonomy and those who opposed 'despotic interference' into the lives of individuals and the free relations of the economic market. The Tory press raged against 'paternalistic' government. The *Herald* believed that 'A little dirt and freedom may after all be more desirable than no dirt at all and slavery', and the *Standard* suggested that the country had 'heard enough of the effect of centralization in the New Poor Law'. Local ratepayers resented being dictated to by a 'clean party' (Roberts, 1979). The Institution of Civil Engineers disclaimed the arterial system and supported the alternative designs of Joseph Bazalgette (Hamlin, 1990).

The General Board's immense unpopularity forced its members to resign in 1854. A first chapter in the English experiment in state health regulation closed. A new professional health management, however, followed Chadwick's downfall, directed not by an engineering but by a medical model and run not by philosophical lawyer-reformers but by doctors.

THE PHILOSOPHY OF STATE MEDICINE

The creation of a public health system in Britain was founded upon a political economic philosophy which intended to use statutory regulation to enhance the free operation of market relations. Reducing the cost of destitution and poverty by preventing the premature mortality of breadwinners was one feature of a new theory of government which asserted that efficiency and justice could only be obtained through the scientific and rational organization of the affairs of state. Policy-making should become a managerial practice. Edwin Chadwick was the central figure in bringing this approach to the management of public health with his 'sanitary idea'. The sanitary idea was based on a simple model of disease caused through general filth, which could be remedied by the construction of civil engineering works providing efficient sewage and drainage and the supply of clean water. The sanitary idea did not expand much beyond these boundaries except to address questions of interment and the recycling of human manure for agricultural fertilizer. It was not based on any systematic analysis of the details of policy. It recommended the widening of streets but did not define 'wide'. Chadwick's sanitary code was independent of medical analysis (Brundage, 1988; Hamlin, 1997). Even before he had left office, however, his conception of health reform was already being challenged by members of the medical profession. After he left, a philosophy of medical management of the public health succeeded him. A new concept of 'state medicine' came to dominate central government health policy and eventually local government practice.

A shift from the sanitary idea to medical management took place as Chadwick was succeeded by a doctor, John Simon, as Britain's chief health administrator. Simon's term to describe his form of health administration was 'state medicine', but what was it and how did it differ from the 'sanitary idea'? What were its aims and goals? What did it achieve in the development of health policy in the latter half of the nineteenth century?

In 1856, a prominent public spokesman for the medical profession, Dr Henry Rumsey, published a series of *Essays on State Medicine*. Rumsey admitted that although the essays were published in 1856 they had been delivered as public lectures several years previously. They predominantly addressed the failings of health administration under the General Board of Health. Rumsey bemoaned the fact that the nation's health had been made the responsibility of two barristers and a lawyer, with no medical guidance. The Board could never successfully manage health, Rumsey claimed, without the contribution of medical expertise (Porter, 1997).

What were the limitations of a sanitary idea which did not include medicine? Rumsey believed that it lacked a comprehensive vision of health care which integrated preventive and palliative medicine into one unified system. Second, its system of prevention was based upon simple generalizations and did not investigate the multiple determinants of sickness and disease. Medical prevention was concerned not just with filth in the external urban environment, but insanitation and unhygienic practice within dwellings, factories and public buildings. It focused upon the spread of infectious disease by contact as well as atmospheric pollution, and involved the isolation of sufferers and their contacts, and systematic disinfection. A medical analysis of the hazards of population density examined the multivariable relations of disease and overcrowding instead of assuming simple equations of ill health.

Rumsey claimed that medical prevention attacked a broad range of causes of disease and had a wide scope of methods for their elimination. Rumsey also developed an elaborate administrative scheme of disease prevention, beginning with a permanent medical official in central government and a civil service of medical health officers throughout local government districts. His idea of the local health officer was based upon the German example of a physician who abandoned private practice to serve only the duties of his state appointment. Rumsey's local health officers would also be superintendents of the registration of births, deaths and disease incidence, and would be responsible for integrating both preventive and palliative medical services.

Rumsey's views were never directly realized in Victorian sanitary administration, but he was influential in medical politics until his death in 1876. His *Essays*, however, were not entirely original, but reflected a medical approach to disease prevention which had already been established in the public health administrations of the cities of Liverpool and London by their respective medical officers of health. It was one of these officers who translated the theory of state medicine into a pragmatic, practical programme of reform throughout the mid-Victorian period (Porter, 1997).

Chadwick's style of management at the General Board of Health had met with political resistance largely from the advocates of local government autonomy, and had reached a critical point during 1854. The Board was dissolved and reconstituted under the presidency of Benjamin Hall, who chose to appoint John Simon to the newly created medical officership to the Board in 1855. Simon was a surgeon at St Thomas's Hospital who had taken an interest in public health since he had been a founding member of the Health of Towns Association in 1844. He became a local medical officer of health when, during 1848, the City of London Corporation pre-empted the Public Health Act with one of its own, and subsequently appointed him to the post. Simon had previously worked for the first General Board of Health during 1853 as a commissioner of inquiry into the cholera outbreak at Newcastle and Gateshead, and was later asked by Hall to join the Medical Council to advise upon the epidemic. Simon was Hall's choice for the new medical post, and his decision was carried out by William Cowper, who succeeded him to the presidency in 1855 (Lambert, 1963).

Before leaving the City of London, a collection of the reports made by Simon to the authority were published commercially with a new preface added by him.

Simon took the opportunity 'to express ... some thoughts on sanitary affairs in a fuller sense of the term than had yet become usual'. He did not wish to limit his analysis to the City itself,

> but speaking of the country in general, and pleading especially for the poorer masses of the population, I endeavoured to show how genuine and urgent a need there was, that the State should concern itself systematically and comprehensively with all chief interests of the public health. I submitted, as the state of the case, that except against wilful violence, the law was practically caring very little for the lives of the people.
>
> (Quoted by Porter, 1997: 25)

From the earliest years of his career in public office, he discovered that the health of the community was part of a matrix of social, economic and political relations. From 1854 to 1890, he stated that public health was bound to the politics of poverty. Low wages resulted from unlimited competition together with excessive demand for accommodation and food, which pushed their prices higher and higher and forced the labouring population below subsistence. They lived in ever more decrepit and inadequate dwelling spaces sold at exorbitant rates by unscrupulous landlords, and they bought the cheapest, inedible and adulterated foods. Squalor and malnutrition produced disease and disease produced destitution.

> If such and such conditions of food or dwelling are absolutely inconsistent with healthy life, what more final test of pauperism can there be, or what clearer right to public succour, than that the subject's pecuniary means fall short of providing him other conditions than those? It may be that competition has screwed down the rate of wages below what will purchase indispensable food and wholesome lodgement. Of this, as fact, I am no judge; but to its meaning, if fact, I can speak. All labour below that mark is masked pauperism. Whatever the employer saves is gained at the public expense. When, under such circumstances, the labourer or his wife or child spends an occasional month or two in the hospital, that some fever infection may work itself out, or that the impending loss of an eye or limb may be averted by animal food; or when he gets various aid from his Board of Guardians, in all sorts of preventable illness, and eventually for the expenses of interment, it is the public that, too late for the man's health or independence, pays the arrears of wages which should have hindered this suffering and sorrow.
>
> (Quoted in Porter, 1997: 26)

The first law of all political economy was that wages should not be interfered with. But the conditions of physical existence could be controlled. Apart from those which protected the individual from personal violence, there were no laws, Simon pointed out, which protected his physical welfare. Disease was not spread passively, but through deliberate actions. There was, therefore, the need for laws to protect physical welfare and for a legislative parliamentary authority, a special Minister of Health. And since the question of physical health was the province of medical expertise, then the health minister and his department should be guided by doctors-turned-statesmen (Porter, 1997).

Public health could play an important part in solving the question of how to make the 'poor less poor'. The political economy of labour was beyond the jurisdiction of medical expertise in government, but public policy on health and physical welfare could be guided by it in numerous ways: for example, through sanitary controls on housing stock and laws prohibiting the sale of adulterated food and chemicals and poisons; regulations regarding the industrial health of workers; preventing the spread of epidemic diseases with vaccination and isolation of the infectious; supervision of noxious trades; procuring environmental cleanliness by minimizing atmospheric pollution and building efficient sewage and drainage infrastructure; ensuring standards of pure water supply; and, not least, legislating against unqualified medical practice and varying standards of medical training to prevent the grossest inadequacies of some medical treatment.

By the end of his career, this conception of state medicine was articulated within Simon's broader political philosophy, which approximated an almost Saint-Simonian socialism. Health conditions of life would enable the labouring classes, together with universal education, to be independent and self-supporting, to strengthen their ability to fight for higher wages through trade unionism and to procure security against sickness, unemployment and old age through a state insurance system. While he believed that existing medical relief should be given to all without question or means-testing and acknowledged the achievements of the 'socialistic' Elizabethan Poor Law, he felt it was well time to replace it. Through compulsory insurance, medical treatment, financial need during periods of unemployment and retirement support given as poor relief could thus be abolished. Along with this vision of emancipation of the labouring classes from poverty, Simon also shared some of the prejudices of late nineteenth-century socialism against the residual poor. He abhorred indiscriminate, 'eleemosynary' philanthropy, believing it was an evil substitute for legislation. Apart from charities competing among each other to use 'relief' as a means to proselytize some ideology or other, it also encouraged dependence and wilful idleness. While Simon fully recognized that the despair of the labouring classes who were forced into destitution pushed them also into immorality, depravity and crime, he believed there was a residue of 'staunch mendicants' and idlers who would always perpetuate pauperism and raise their children to such a way of life. These should be discouraged at all costs, and he believed that Parliament had an unviable right to prevent the 'hereditary continuance of pauperism' by taking into state care all those children whose parents 'cannot, or will not, bring them up otherwise than into pauperism, or presumably crime'. All forms of 'sham poverty' and parasitism should be discouraged to the utmost by the institution of a communal politics of self-help. Simon saw this communal politics as the defining characteristic of late nineteenth-century civilization.

The constantly increasing care of the community at large for the welfare of its individual parts is an eminently characteristic and influential fact in our present stage of civilisation.... It is something curiously unlike what Machiavelli taught as politics. It is socialism of the sort which consists with social justice, and tends to social consolidation ... the religion of mutual helpfulness....Stronger now than ever in the history of the world, and of wider range than ever in that history, thoughts of loyalty to his kind are gaining sway with him [man]. And surely in the years to come, so far forward as man's moral outlook can reach, they who shall be in the front will more and more have to count it sin and shame for themselves, if their souls fail of answering to that high appeal, and they strive not with all their strength to fulfil the claims of that allegiance.

(Quoted by Porter, 1997: 26)

Therefore, while he did not share Rumsey's concern for joint superintendence of prevention and treatment in one department of health, he did believe that medical administration of the 'conditions of physical existence' could reduce preventable sickness and death and, in its wake, destitution. This would ultimately replace the need for the Poor Law as a whole, and put unemployment, old age and sickness into a system of self-support through higher wages and compulsory insurance. Public health administration could achieve this end by combating poverty rather than through unification with the Poor Law medical relief.

STATE MEDICINE IN PRACTICE

As Simon entered central government service at the General Board of Health, the first experiment in sanitary administration was coming to an end. The first attempt at sanitary reform through a system of central government interference in local affairs had foundered. The defence of local 'democracy' had resisted the capacity of central government to bring about change through coercion. This was a fundamental lesson which Simon internalized in his subsequent strategy for reform. He believed he could avoid the mistakes of his predecessor by devising a new basis for the development of public health through the persuasive power of scientific research and information, keeping the power of coercion as the last resort.

Simon became the first doctor to hold a high-ranking government appointment. In 1858 the General Board was abolished by a new Public Health Act and its functions divided among a number of different government departments. The central focus of health administration was moved to a new medical department created under the domain of the Privy Council. Simon was appointed as the Chief Medical Officer to the department and was given the power only to inquire and report into health conditions. He was also made responsible for the administration of smallpox vaccination. He was the only appointee of the department, but was given the opportunity to hire temporary and part-time staff. Within a decade, Simon used the terms of his appointment to create a department with a continuous staff of about forty officers and inspectors, and used the power of inquiry to authorize a substantial body of legislation which laid the foundations of subsequent British health policy (Lambert, 1963).

The 1830s to 1850s witnessed the foundation of English public health, but reform did not slow down subsequently, even if it did change direction. The legislative base of public health expanded dramatically after 1848. The growth in legislation during this period was, however, unrelated to its implementation. It was haphazard and piecemeal. It was too chaotic to be executed by local authorities, or else too disparate for them even to be aware of all the various new duties and powers which it bestowed upon them. What it may have provided comprehensively in theory was neutralized by its incoherence in practice. Its chaotic and unmanageable state required rationalization and codification, which led to the need for a Royal Commission in 1868 and the Public Health Act of 1875 (Wohl, 1984).

Chadwick had considered himself leading a vanguard in scientific policy-making. But his conception of scientific statesmanship reflected the indeterminate idea of social science as social reform, which pervaded the Utilitarian models of government of the early nineteenth century. The model of scientific specialism in the Medical Department at the Privy Council had a much narrower definition, derived from the experimental method of laboratory research and governed most of all by the empirical and theoretical models of clinical medicine. Mid-century public health reform developed along two lines. On the one hand there was the anarchic growth of *legislation*, on the other there was the development of precision in *administration* developed by John Simon at the Privy Council. It was the eventual domination of the former by the latter in policy implementation that changed public health reform in England into the practice of state medicine.

From the outset Simon aimed to pursue a comprehensive approach to disease prevention and set up investigations into a wide range of issues, from the regulation of food contamination and drug adulteration to hygienic standards of environmental planning. He managed to recruit, on a part-time basis, the most senior scientists of the day to complete both field research in local areas and laboratory research on the nature of the disease process. The initial surveys covered the multivariate determinants of health and epidemic and endemic diseases in different localities, including the social and economic relations of poverty. He wished to identify specifically which aspects of the lives of the poor generated the conditions in which different diseases flourished, and to use the new documentation to pressure Parliament into new legislation. In this way he redefined the meaning of a 'public nuisance' and revised the law to cover everything from pollution from human waste, industrial effluent, river and atmospheric pollution to the illegal transportation of infected persons. He introduced the first legislation for the control of the sale of contaminated food and adulterated drugs, and the first housing and municipal planning laws. But the most significant legislation that Simon generated was the Sanitary Act of 1866. This Act contained the first compulsory public health laws which empowered central government to prosecute a local authority for failing to fulfil its duties under the nuisance laws (Lambert, 1963).

Although he never implemented it, Simon used the threat of sanction, together with the shameful exposure of neglect through a government inspection, to coerce local authorities into public health reform. He also used the power of his department to vet requests from local authorities for low interest loans for sanitary works, to induce them into following his department's recommendations. State medicine in central government progressed in a pragmatic fashion during the 1860s, but the multiplication of sanitary law became so chaotic that even enthusiastic local authorities found it too bewildering to implement. After pressure from the British Medical Association and the Association for the Promotion of Social Science, Parliament set up a Royal Commission to investigate unifying the law. The 1875 Public Health Act codified all existing sanitary legislation, but also made its adoption compulsory (Macleod, 1968). Every local authority was subsequently compelled to create a local board of health and employ a local health officer. The medical department of the Privy Council was amalgamated with the Poor Law administration into a new structure called the Local Government Board. However, this was not a happy marriage and the new Board was dominated by the Poor Law authorities and starved of funds by the Treasury. Simon found it impossible to continue to run a programme comparable to that achieved under the Privy Council and resigned his position as Chief Medical Officer in 1876. With his resignation, the influence of state medicine in central government declined (Macleod, 1968). The focus of health policy, however, shifted to its implementation in the local districts and the professionalization of public health in a national bureaucratic state service. But before discussing the consequences of this shift, it is necessary to examine briefly some of the responses of Victorians to the creation of compulsory health laws.

Appendix

Mid-nineteenth-century public health legislation for England and Wales

Nuisances Removal and Diseases Prevention Act, 1848; City of London Sewers Act, 1848; Metropolitan Sewers Act, 1848; Lodging Houses Act, 1850; Common Lodging Houses Act, 1851; Vaccination Act, 1853; General Board of Health Act, 1854; Diseases Prevention Act, 1855; Metropolis Local Management Act, 1855; Nuisances Removal Act, 1855; Local Government Act, 1858; Public Health Acts, 1858 and 1859; Nuisances Removal Act, 1860; Vaccination Act, 1861; Nuisances Removal Act, 1863; Sewage Utilisation Act, 1865; Nuisances Removal Act, 1866; Sanitary Act, 1866; Sewage Utilisation Act, 1867; Sanitary Act, 1868; Local Government Act, 1871; Public Health Act, 1872.

8 The enforcement of health and resistance

The interventionist state in Britain was built largely on adoptive rather than compulsory legislation. Intervention was implemented, however, by officials whom local government authorities were initially induced and later compelled to employ. The growing number of local government officials directing the implementation of public health policy became increasingly qualified in exclusively specialized training (Porter, 1991a). This group of professionals had an ideological investment in the growth of a statutory bureaucratic public health system. Public health officers constantly demanded greater compulsory powers, first provided for them under the 1866 Sanitary Act. From this point public health legislation acquired an ever greater vocabulary of systematic enforcement. The imposition of the law was not straightforward in mid-Victorian society, highly suspicious of paternalistic despotism. Victorians were forced to decide whether legislation designed to protect them against themselves was tyranny or salvation. The battles over the enforcement of health, however, were eventually superseded by the professionalization of the relationship between doctors and the state.

THE POLITICS OF PREVENTION

While general sanitarianism was aimed at the limitation of the whole genre of infectious diseases based on the principle of raising 'health standards' as a whole, the earliest intervention directed specifically at one such disease in particular was the case of smallpox prevention (Baxby, 1981; Hopkins, 1983). Free vaccination was made available through the administration of the Poor Law medical services in 1840. In 1853 the state took the unprecedented step of making vaccination compulsory for all children within the first year of life. Failure to comply with the law meant prosecution and fines for parents, and these penalties were made more severe when a new Vaccination Act was passed in 1867. Parents were now liable to repeatable fines and imprisonment for either neglecting to have their children vaccinated or objecting to it on grounds of conscience. Compulsory health laws did not end with the control of smallpox, but continued to be introduced in relation to other socially and sexually transmissible diseases throughout the nineteenth century in Britain. Smallpox vaccination was the first step taken in this direction; compulsory inspection and isolation of prostitutes to control venereal (contagious) diseases was the second; and finally the Notification Acts covered almost the complete list of endemic infectious diseases which occasionally erupted epidemically (Porter and Porter, 1989). The ideological justification for compulsory prevention was articulated by mid-century advocates of 'state medicine' such as Rumsey and Simon. They suggested that the sovereign right of the individual to contract, die of and spread infectious disease should be suspended for the benefit of the health of the community as a whole (see Chapter 7).

For these reasons, Simon was the greatest advocate of vaccination, as well as its chief administrator during the mid-century period. He also recognized the need for reform of the system of administration, admitting that poor quality lymph and inadequate training and supervision of local vaccinators caused injury and death, which contributed to opposition to vaccination. Expert inspection, training for vaccinators and new 'vaccination officers' with the task of co-ordinating notification and enforcement were created in the local authorities in 1871, and the supply of lymph was reorganized and supervised by Simon's department. In his own words, Simon instituted 'medical management' of the system, which had previously been undertaken as an extension of some of the secretarial duties of Poor Law authorities (Lambert, 1963).

While improving the quality of vaccination, these reforms did not eliminate the risks of vaccination entirely. During an epidemic in 1871, a number of cases of syphilis were transmitted to children via the method of arm-to-arm vaccination, and one of Simon's own inspectors, Jonathan Hutchinson, had the unenviable task of reporting the incidences to a Parliamentary Committee of Inquiry. Hutchinson recommended vaccination with calf lymph to replace the old method, which always held the danger of transmitting additional human infections. Overall, however, the vaccination campaign was successful in vastly reducing the incidence of smallpox in Britain, and indeed throughout Europe and America by the end of the nineteenth century (Porter and Porter, 1988).

Resistance to compulsory vaccination had occurred from the outset. John Gibbs, a hydropathic operator who owned an establishment in Barking, published a pamphlet in 1854 called *Our Medical Liberties*, and forwarded extracts from it in protest to the General Board of Health in 1856. His cousin, Richard Gibbs, helped to found the Anti-Compulsory Vaccination League in 1867 after the extension of the law. Provincial associations became the focus of activity during the 1870s. During the early 1870s several Boards of Guardians refused to implement the law. The most notable events took place at Keighley, where imprisonment of recalcitrant Guardians resulted, inspired by the 'martyrdom' tactics advocated by the Reverend William Hume Rothery and his wife Mary, who founded the National Anti-Compulsory Vaccination League at Cheltenham in 1874. In 1880 William Tebb established the London Society for the Abolition of Compulsory Vaccination, and began a journal, *The Vaccination Inquirer*, in 1879. Its first editor was William White. After his death in 1885, he was succeeded by Alfred Milnes. The London Society was the focus of activity during the 1880s and early 1890s in lobbying parliamentary support. The local organizations of the movement gravitated towards the metropolitan leadership, and in 1896 Tebb amalgamated the provincial and London organizations into one National Anti-Vaccination League (Porter and Porter, 1988; compare with Kaufman, 1967; Leavitt, 1976).

Against a general background of distrust of the medical profession and of its capacity to dupe Parliament and the public, the anti-vaccination movement targeted its attack on the principle of compulsion in respect of laws relating to the health of the individual. The first issue of the journal clearly stated that the aims of the organization were to combat medical despotism in its worst forms, the Compulsory Vaccination Acts. Anti-vaccinationism offered various 'alternative scientific' arguments about the dangers of vaccination and the benefits of other methods of prevention. But the driving principle of their ideology was a resistance to the growth of government intervention into the civil liberty of the individual (Porter and Porter, 1988; Mooney, 1997).

The anti-vaccination movement launched a propaganda campaign and a war of civil disobedience against the public health authorities from the 1860s, using their journal, *The Vaccination Inquirer*, as their main weapon. Some local groups were more influential than others. In Leicester, successful infiltration of local government agencies resulted in widespread unprosecuted failure to comply with the law (Fraser, 1980). Similarly, in Gloucester anti-vaccinationists who were influential members of the community, such as the local newspaper proprietor, waged a successful campaign against the medical officer of health (MOH) until an epidemic in 1896 eventually resulted in a mass vaccination of the town (Porter and Porter, 1988).

Anti-vaccinationism never achieved its goal of abolishing compulsory vaccination completely but did achieve a modification of the law in 1907. The Act was then amended to include a conscientious objection clause, allowing parents to opt out of the system. By this time, however, the battle against smallpox had largely been won and universal vaccination of infants was so nearly complete that the necessity for stringent compulsory laws no longer existed.

Anti-vaccinationism shared an opposition to centralizing interventionist government with the campaign to repeal the Contagious Diseases Acts, designed to control the spread of sexually transmitted diseases. But the political organization to repeal the Contagious Diseases Acts had more than one ideological foundation. The organization itself was a mixture of sometimes strange ideological bedfellows pursuing the aim for contradictory reasons. However, the opposition to the social control of sexually transmitted diseases still reflected the dilemma faced by Victorian society concerning health and citizenship (Mchugh, 1982; Walkowitz, 1980).

In 1864 Parliament passed the first Contagious Diseases Act, which provided for the compulsory examination by a naval or military surgeon of a woman believed by a special police superintendent sworn before a magistrate to be a 'common prostitute'. Initially the Act was in force in eleven garrison towns in the southern counties. If the woman was diagnosed as venereally diseased, she became liable to detention, on the order of two magistrates, in a locked ward, and could be held there for up to one year and subject to regular fortnightly inspections. She had no right of appeal to habeas corpus (Mchugh, 1982; Walkowitz, 1980).

The Act had been drawn up by a committee of the House of Commons consisting of representatives of the army, the Admiralty and medical experts. Why was this Act deemed necessary? In 1854–1856 Britain had repulsed the attempt to overthrow the Turkish Empire by Russia, trying to get access to ports in the Black Sea. During the Crimean campaign an army sanitary commission had, for the first time, gathered accurate statistics about the level of mortality resulting from disease rather than on the battlefield. In 1861, after the war, a Royal Commission was set up to investigate the health of the army. The Royal Commission's report highlighted the high incidence of venereal disease among enlisted men. It also focused attention on the appalling conditions in which the troops lived alienated and distressed lives, making them more inclined to visit prostitutes as a means of escape and relief. The report recommended that new measures be taken to change the boredom and filthy living conditions of army life (Mchugh, 1982; Walkowitz, 1980; Mort, 1987).

However, during the 1860s, as we noted, earlier legislation to regulate health conditions in civilian life had expanded extensively. Thus, a precedent had been set for the use of the state administrative control of the relations of sickness and disease. The Royal Commission recommended that the army appoint a statistician to continue to monitor conditions. A Dr Bryson, an army MO, was appointed and it was his reports which encouraged opinion within the medical profession for legislation for the control of venereal disease. By 1864 Bryson had demonstrated that one in every three cases of sickness in the army was a case of venereal infection, representing 290.7 per thousand. The naval statistics were only slightly less sensational, amounting to 125 per thousand. The financial loss in manpower – each case meant a sick leave of about two to three weeks – created an urgent need for something to be done (Mchugh, 1982; Walkowitz, 1980; Mort, 1987).

The 1864 Act was extended by a second in 1866 to cover further garrison districts, and then in 1867 new proposals were made by advocates of the Act to have them extended to the northern counties and to the civilian population. This campaign was undertaken by the Association for the Promotion of the Extension of the Contagious Diseases Acts, which had been formed after the Harvarian Society had produced a report in 1867 showing the high incidence of venereal disease among civilian and military populations and the totally inadequate facilities for dealing with it. The Association acquired 400 members, published pamphlets and lobbied Parliament. Tories supported extension because they believed it served the interests of the military. The Anglican clergy were also recruited to the cause since they believed the Acts represented the interests of the established civil order. The police also supported it for similar reasons. The leading civilian doctors who promoted extension were either from the elite medical fraternity who had studied in Paris and had been impressed by the system of regulated prostitution there, or they were doctors who worked among the poor and were familiar with the appalling insanitary and unhealthy environments in which they were forced to live. But the fundamental rationale behind the extension of the Acts was that in order for them to work efficiently they needed to cover further districts, to prevent prostitutes from evading the police by migrating to unregulated areas (Mchugh, 1982; Walkowitz, 1980).

The extension Act was passed in the autumn of 1869, but by December organized opposition had signed a petition listing eight charges of injustice. Opposition had already been voiced, however, before the Act had been passed. This came from John Simon. In 1868 Simon had produced a report which condemned the extension of the Contagious Diseases Acts to the civilian population on all grounds. First, he questioned their effectiveness in reducing venereal diseases, even within garrison towns. Second, he identified the impossibility of administering the Acts among the general population. He believed that not only were there too limited resources for such large-scale policing and inspection but that, more significantly, the Acts would be unworkable because of the resistance they would meet among the poor. Building sewers and drains, cleaning streets, inspecting homes and condemning contaminated meat were one thing, but invading the most intimate and clandestine activities of personal lives was another. Simon, the staunch advocate of state intervention, paradoxically objected to its extension into this realm of privacy. He dismissed the moralists' arguments that policing public morals led to their improvement, and emphasized instead the immoral impropriety of the execution of the Acts themselves. So, despite the fact that the supporters of the Acts modelled their legislation on that of Simon, he dismissed their validity and rejected them morally. In this respect, however, he reflected a much broader view held by the public health profession generally. The majority of public health officers dreaded having the responsibility for implementing the Acts imposed upon them. As long as the Acts remained a military affair they could leave it to those authorities. If they were to be applied to the civilian population, however, then they would immediately become additional duties for the MOH, who had no resources to implement them and would have to face the unbridled hostility of local populations. Without doubting Simon's sincerity, it is clear that he was concerned primarily with the practical chaos the Acts would cause if they were extended to the local districts (Mchugh, 1982).

The initially ad hoc opposition became organized by the end of 1869 into the National Association for the Repeal of the Contagious Diseases Acts. It never became a very large pressure group. By the 1880s its membership was fewer than 800 and its annual budget only £3,000 per annum. The body of the Repeal Movement consisted of a mixture of social and religious purity advocates, feminists and civil libertarians, but the boundaries distinguishing between these various ideologies were extremely blurred within the National Association (Walkowitz, 1980). The leaders of the opposition were the political economist Harriet Martineau, aristocratic philanthropic social workers Josephine Butler,

Sarah Robinson and Mary Hume Rothery, and the crusading lady of the lamp Florence Nightingale, and their voice in Parliament, the radical Quaker Liberal MP Sir James Stansfeld. Among this group, the central figure around which the movement revolved was Josephine Butler. Butler was a feminist and moral reformer but was also self-obsessed and uncompromising. By one of her own contemporaries and fellow-Repealers, Mary Priestman, Josephine Butler was described as 'a woman Christ to save us from our despair'. The upper-class philanthropic reforming women who led the Repeal campaign were a hard-working band of women devoted to female emancipation and moral reform, but were also 'ladies bountiful' who imposed their conservative values upon the objects of their charity (Smith, 1990).

The Repealers wanted to end the double standard of morality applied to the sexual licence afforded to men and the repression placed upon women. They protested the Acts were a gross invasion of privacy and believed they legitimated an autocratic rule of medical expertise. Equally, however, the Repeal campaigners stressed their opposition to the growth of state responsibility for any forms of social welfare as a mortal sin against the system of individual freedom and self-reliance. The female philanthropic leaders of the opposition called themselves the 'Lords Scavengers', sent out to rescue fallen women from their unholy plight. The main aim of the rescue work was to morally reform prostitutes into giving up their trade for an honest life, or death from starvation. They believed that the law would make prostitution safer and encourage self-esteem among those who continued to ply their trade. Their philanthropic aim was a mission of social purity, aiming to achieve the salvation of the poor and unrighteous through their remoralization. Butler and her associates did espouse the rights of women to equal education and rights to property before the law, but they still insisted that the woman's separate sphere was the domestic bliss of the house and hearth, even though most of them were hardly ever in it. These upper-class angels of mercy wanted to reclaim the women of the night, not by curing venereal disease but by recapturing their souls for Christ. For this reason the Contagious Diseases Acts horrified them, because they discouraged prostitutes to aspire to respectability. Sarah Robinson, the Evangelical temperance worker, was aghast when she failed to reform what she called a 'well-to-do' prostitute who told her, 'You see, Miss Robinson, you get your income in one way and I get mine in another. I pay my tradesmen's bills the same as yourself, and I do not see why I should be excluded' – excluded, that was, from working for the Temperance Society (Smith, 1990).

However, these mixed motives and political messages succeeded in marshalling an extremely vocal campaign against the Contagious Diseases Acts. The Repealers charged that the police frequently arrested innocent respectable women and subjected them to the most degrading inspection and detention. They were horrified by what they called the legalized rape of women who were forced to submit to internal gynaecological examinations by male physicians. They claimed that women were infected by unhygienic inspections by the surgeons and were imprisoned without trial to prove whether they were guilty or innocent. The Repealers emphasized that the Act failed to properly define what constituted a 'common prostitute'; more often than not this was left to the discretion of the police, who were influenced by rumour and corruption. They also claimed that the Acts failed to influence any reduction in the rates of syphilis and gonorrhoea (Walkowitz, 1980). They were supported in their claim that the Acts were an infringement of civil liberties by John Stuart Mill (Mill, 1986) who gave evidence to a Royal Commission of Inquiry in 1871. He proposed an alternative system, in which both men and women could voluntarily undergo inspection and receive treatment in state-supported clinics. He was opposed to compulsory inspection on the grounds that it reduced the responsibility that each citizen should possess for their own health as a duty to the commonwealth. It thereby impaired the individual moral will upon which a society ultimately rested. Though Mill opposed the Acts, he deplored the activities and ideology of the members of the Repeal campaign (Smith, 1990).

The Repeal campaign met with little success, however, until a woman who was not a prostitute drowned herself after having been falsely accused and subjected to the examination and detention in 1875. Josephine Butler was almost grateful for the death of Mrs Percy because she thought, 'Every good cause requires martyrs...and this poor woman's death will...be the means in the hands of Providence, of shaking the system.' The campaign's fortunes began to revive, only to slump again by 1883. In 1886 Gladstone's Liberal government was fighting for its survival against attacks from within its own ranks. The tireless work of James Stansfeld finally paid off when the government agreed to repeal the Acts as a token gesture towards the radical northern Liberal dissenters in exchange for their acceptance of Home Rule for Ireland. The repeal of the Contagious Diseases Acts, therefore, while representing a triumph of individualist opposition to compulsory health policies, was equally the result of the Machiavellian machinations of 'business as usual' parliamentary politics (Smith, 1990).

STATUTORY NOTIFICATION: THE LONGER ARM OF THE LAW

The most powerfully interventionist policies went unopposed in England, however. These were the infectious diseases laws, created at the end of the nineteenth century. These laws were developed as the result of the bacteriological discovery of disease causation and were aimed at controlling socially transmissible infections which had endemically effected high morbidity and mortality within local communities throughout Britain during the nineteenth century (Watkins, 1984). Under the Local Government Act of 1875, MOHs were granted powers to remove sufferers of such diseases from the community and place them in isolation or fever hospitals, as 'nuisances'. As early as 1876, MOHs claimed that these were insufficient powers to effectively identify and isolate infectious diseases which threatened the community, but from the outset, general practitioners voiced vigorous opposition to notification. It involved additional unpaid work on their part and put them, to a degree, under the scrutiny of the local public health authority, the MOH, who might be a rival general practitioner.

Individual local authorities gradually adopted notification measures on an ad hoc basis over the following decade, and eventually a permissive Act for notification was passed in 1889. This enabled local authorities to adopt a dual system of notification in which either the householder or the medical attendant of a patient was obliged to inform the local public health authority of the incidence of a (listed) infectious disease. The diseases listed included not only life-threatening diseases such as smallpox, typhus, typhoid, diphtheria, eresipilis and scarlet fever, but also diseases often simply treated by the family, such as measles and whooping cough. On receipt of notification, the MOH was subsequently empowered to isolate the patient at home or remove them to an isolation hospital when he considered it necessary, and to carry out disinfection of households, clothing and bed-linen. In certain diseases, such as diphtheria or scarlet fever, the siblings of infected children could be excluded from school during the incubation period and occasionally, when an epidemic outbreak threatened, the MOH was empowered to close public establishments such as schools (Watkins, 1984).

By 1896 the Act was in force in 1,405 provincial sanitary districts with an aggregate population of 18,878,441. After 1891, London had compulsory notification in all the metropolitan boroughs, serving a population of 4,232,118. Throughout the 1890s, forty-nine small towns and forty port authorities had adopted the Act, and in 1899 a new Act made the adoption of notification of infectious diseases compulsory throughout England and Wales. The preventive methods of the Acts were based upon a bacteriological model of disease causation. Notification identified the location of an incidence of infectious disease and the possibility of immediate isolation. The long-term advantage was the information gained, which made statistical mapping of disease movements possible, especially with regard to comparative analysis of districts (Watkins, 1984).

The whole system as a means of prevention depended upon sufficient hospital provision. Hospitals for infectious diseases were provided by the sanitary authority in the provincial districts of England and Wales and by the Metropolitan Asylums Board in the London boroughs. The authorities were empowered to build isolation hospitals under the 1872 Public Health Act and to recover costs through charges made to patients. Some hospitals did not make charges, however, but entered patients under the Poor Law provision, thus pauperizing patients, entailing their disenfranchisement. MOHs were constantly frustrated by the failure, especially of some of the smaller and rural districts, to provide isolation hospitals, and the whole pauperization principle used by others. The Society of MOHs advocated that admission should be free of charge and free of pauperization, with charges only for 'private patients' who paid for special accommodation. Arthur Newsholme believed that the basic principle of non-payment had not been grasped by the majority of local authorities and that isolation was not an issue of improved treatment but primarily a function of the prevention of disease dissemination. He emphasized that they should be maintained for the benefit of the community and not individual patients.

The Notification of Infectious Diseases legislation represented the greatest infringement of the individual's freedom to be sick and spread disease, and it emphasized more than any other the superior priority of the needs of the community. It also interfered in the most highly valued and sacrosanct area of medical practice, the private relationship between a doctor and his patient. The Acts met with continued opposition from GPs, who objected to secondary diagnosis of their patients by the local MOH and to the onerous duty imposed upon them of having to comply with the notification procedures. Thomas Crawford, Chairman of the Sanitary Institute, pointed out that the insistence upon bacteriological diagnosis of cases by MOHs undermined the GPs' authority, and prosecutions for default of notification simply infuriated the clinical branch of the profession. He believed that the outrage of many GPs was matched by hostility of families who objected to the law.

> The English people are not afraid of risking either their lives or their health in the interests of those whom they love and they are consequently not easily persuaded to part with any member of their family simply because he or she happens to be suffering from an infectious disease.
>
> (Quoted in Porter and Porter, 1989: 108)

There was some objection, specifically to the 'dual system' which placed an equal duty upon the head of household as well as the medical attendant of a case of infectious disease to inform the authorities. Mr D. Biddle, for example, correspondent to the *BMJ* throughout 1889, pointed out the consequences of high insurance premiums for inhabitants of districts where dual notification was instituted.

William Corfield, president of the SMOH and professor of hygiene at University College, believed much opposition could be overcome if the notification system was operated with sensitivity by the MOH. Even so, conflicts did arise. Alfred Bostock Hill, MOH for Birmingham and professor of toxicology at Queens University, discovered that fourteen cases of diphtheria in his area had not been notified to him by a medical attendant. The GP in question informed Hill that since there was no chance of improving the sewers, which was the only method he believed could prevent infectious disease, there was no point in informing the MOH of the cases which he attended. Hill replied that preventing the spread of diphtheria involved measures of isolation and disinfection which depended entirely on knowing where incidences occurred. The GP's final response was to say that, first, he did not believe in disinfection, second, he did not see why he should do Hill's work for him, and, last, he felt that it was the responsibility of the MOH to discover cases of infectious disease through efficient inspection of the district (Watkins, 1984).

The Infectious Diseases Acts, however, met with little or no public opposition.

The public health service claimed that once the Acts had been established in a district and were seen to work efficiently, they did not meet with resentment from the local GPs. There were no repeal movements, no record numbers of prosecutions for default or even any organized rebellion from the clinical profession against the Acts. This lack of opposition is noteworthy given that, when comparable powers of removal had first been introduced during the 1832 cholera epidemic, there had been extensive rioting. This suggests that by the last quarter of the nineteenth century, the British public was becoming acclimatized to a new medical rationality which might involve the trimming of its liberties (Porter and Porter, 1989). Also, the combination of nutritional improvements and environmental health measures throughout the century had helped to reduce the levels of lethal epidemic diseases, and the frequency for the necessity of invoking the compulsory powers of the Acts was greatly reduced (Mooney, 1997b).

Despite subsequently continuing reduction of infectious diseases throughout the twentieth century, the compulsory powers of notification and isolation remained on the British statute books. The real impact of infectious diseases upon the British system of public health, therefore, was not simply to stimulate the creation of sanitary law, but ultimately to legitimize the power of the state to override the freedom of the individual in the reduction of the threat from diseases perceived to be preventable.

EXPERTISE AND LOCAL ADMINISTRATION: THE GROWTH OF A NATIONAL BUREAUCRACY

The demand and design of the infectious diseases laws were driven by the increasingly powerful officers of a nationally distributed British local health service, MOHs. Edwin Chadwick institutionalized the utilitarian ethic of expert scientific management of government in the Victorian British state with his appointment to the Poor Law Board and the General Board of Health. Simon reinforced the role of the expert recruited from the professions as a government administrator. The role of the professions is central to understanding the development of community health care in Britain. From the mid-nineteenth century, the construction and execution of health policy was increasingly determined by professionals legitimated by the authority of specialized knowledge not only in central but also in local government. One professional group crucial to Victorian public health administration was the MOHs. Both Chadwick and Simon believed that district health officers were indispensable to an effective system of disease prevention. By the end of the nineteenth century, they constituted a national bureaucratic public health service and a distinct professional group with its own goals and values. As the power of medical influence declined in the Local Government Board following Simon's resignation, the power to direct policy development shifted to this group of local government administrators with a collective identity. The subsequent period in disease control has been characterized as an era of 'preventive medicine'. This was a much broader movement than state medicine, outside the central corridors of power and beyond the elite provinces of the medical and scientific communities. It was not, however, a 'lay' organization, but was associated with the growth of prevention as a professional practice distinct from cure. It was centred around doctors whose primary function was the provision of health in the community and who relinquished the treatment of illness in individuals. The struggle for economic and social security by MOHs during the 1890s helped them to develop a separate identity from the clinical profession as preventive practitioners (Porter, 1991a). There was also what might be called a 'community' of interests surrounding preventive medicine, which was communicated through journal literature and high-profile conferences and embodied in a variety of institutions set up for educational and research purposes (Watkins, 1984). The ideological development of preventive medicine demonstrated how the economic and social values which underlay the environmentalist philosophy of sanitarianism were slowly replaced by a technical imperative.

The compulsory appointment of MOHs, first to metropolitan sanitary districts in 1855 and later to provincial districts throughout England and Wales in 1872, created a national service of doctors responsible for the health of the community rather than the treatment of individuals. They were employed by local sanitary authorities to monitor health conditions through inspection and report. They were responsible for the removal of nuisances, and implemented the sanitary regulation of overcrowded lodging houses, building standards, the condition of bakeries, dairies and slaughterhouses. From 1889 they enforced prevention of infectious diseases through notification and isolation procedures. By the turn of the century they increasingly supervised expanding local social services, such as health-visiting. The annual reports of MOHs are a rich historical source of information on 'the people's health' during the nineteenth and twentieth centuries. Karl Marx was one of the first to use this material in his analysis of the living conditions of agricultural workers. Modern social and economic historians have used the same materials to analyse the impact of social policy upon Victorian health and the role of state intervention upon local economies. The function of public health officers was structured by Parliament, but the interpretation of policy was governed by professional ideology (Porter, 1991a).

From the time they were universally appointed throughout British sanitary districts in 1872, MOHs were a mixed and stratified occupational group. In the metropolitan and large urban provincial districts, highly qualified and professionally ambitious doctors became full-time salaried servants of the state and abandoned private clinical practice altogether. Other MOHs worked part-time with more or less of their professional time devoted to preventive rather than clinical medicine, depending on their circumstances in their local districts. Others combined a number of appointments in various sanitary districts to make up full-time employment in the state service. For yet others their appointment as an MOH was merely nominal, and their professional identity remained entirely within general medical practice. The stratification of MOHs led to intra-professional conflicts and a general failure to consolidate their social and economic position with either their employers, the Local Sanitary Authorities, or their political masters, Parliament, and the Local Government Board. Lacking any political force, however, a professionalizing caucus of the occupational group sought to use standards of expertise to enhance their economic security. This strategy did achieve a limited success. Through the influence of their professional association, the Society of MOHs, upon the regulation of the Diploma in Public Health, the supply of expertly trained and specially qualified officers was limited, which enhanced the market monopoly of the group over its own labour power. The failure, however, of the professional caucus to control the aims, goals and practices of the entire group undermined the overall influence of MOHs in the political and economic development of the public health system. Despite these limitations, the professional strata of MOHs developed an ideology of prevention which significantly influenced the discourses on health care by the turn of the century. It was founded on the professional hegemony of MOHs and their occupational investment in the expansion of the British public health system (Porter, 1991).

THE PREVENTIVE IDEAL

In 1881 Chadwick addressed the Social Science Association on the relative merits of prevention and cure. He praised the achievements of preventive science and bemoaned its poor standing in the eyes of the medical profession, government and public at large. He also constructed a definition of prevention in 'sanitary' terms, focused on the deaths which had been avoided by the environmental regulation of water pollution, sewage disposal, street widening, and all the other modern civil engineering works. A decade later the response to such a view among the preventive profession was that it characterized an era of disease control producing a type of knowledge which, for future progress, must be unlearned. The first British professor of hygiene appointed to the Army Medical School at Netley, Edmund Parkes, noted in his *Manual of Hygiene* that prevention had, in the past, worked with generalized assumptions about the nature of disease causation and had used generalized methods, moving haphazardly in the dark. He believed that the scientific future of prevention lay in the discovery of the specific causes of individual diseases. Without the principle of specificity, the science of hygiene was only 'working with shadows'.

The historiography of medicine and science has rightly warned against assuming that what, with hindsight, looks to have been a revolution in knowledge was perceived as such at the time. The developments in bacteriology, however, which took place during the 1880s, were embraced by the preventive profession during the 1890s and used directly in new claims to legitimate authority for what they viewed as their separate branch of medicine. The discussion concerning infectious disease dominated the journal literature up to 1900, and was overwhelmed by the bacteriological explanation of disease. Most of the journals allocated separate sections of their publications to new bacteriological research from England and the Continent, having the most recent papers translated. All were concerned to encourage the usefulness of bacteriology to public health work, as a diagnostic technique and method of tracing the mode of transmission (Watkins, 1984).

There is an historiographical discussion of the effects of bacteriology on procedures of disease control which suggests that a shift in emphasis took place from the environment to the individual as the vector of transmission (Porter and Fee, 1992). The carrier problem in disease did become a new line for preventive action, and this was most clearly demonstrated in the development of systems of notification and isolation. In the English case it is not clear, however, that this transition was a simple one. Individual hygiene, or domestic hygiene, was an ancient philosophy of health. In England during the eighteenth century it expanded with the proliferation of 'advice books' (see Chapter 3). But there was no great revival of this tradition as the result of bacteriology. The new shift in public health during the Edwardian period began to categorize individuals into 'risk populations'. The 'sanitary era' had treated the health of an undifferenti-ated 'public'. It possessed a generalized concept of the population as well as a generalized theory of disease propagation. The new target populations of preventive medicine resulted from a new analysis of the disease process based on what Edmund Parkes had termed 'the great principle of specificity' (Porter, 1985). During the 1890s, preventive medicine divided the population into TB victims; potential sufferers of post-partum puerperal fever; infants at risk from diarrhoea; and schoolchildren vulnerable to diphtheria. This pattern became increasingly pronounced as new concerns developed about the physical deterio-ration of the nation during the early years of the twentieth century.

The bacteriological revolution had provided preventive medicine with an understanding of disease from what Arthur Newsholme called the 'social stand-point'. A new concept of the environment of disease lay at the heart of the late nineteenth-century preventive ideal. By the last decade of the nineteenth century, MOHs were deeply entrenched in a structure of public policy-making, legislation and administration, which gave them a massive identification with a professional ideology of preventive medicine. The rhetoric of late Victorian preventive medicine launched its own energetic critique of the deficiencies of earlier sanitarianism. Crude sanitarianism – with its focus upon drains, sewers and nuisances – had failed to move beyond a partial myopic understanding of community health; hence it had achieved nothing but piecemeal gains. In the eyes of late Victorian preventive medicine, responsibility for the scandalous continuation of chronic ill health among the Edwardian poor must be laid at the door of the failure of Parliament to pass more comprehensive legislation, for neither Parliament nor the sanitarians had grasped the relationship between urbanism, poverty and disease. What did this charge entail?

There is no denying, of course, that the reciprocal relationship between poverty and disease had long been acknowledged by public health reformers (Eyler, 1997). From early Victorian times, public health had developed as one of a variety of social initiatives directed towards solving the problem of poverty. Edwin Chadwick had sought to prevent what he saw as the diseases of 'filth' in order to reduce destitution's burden upon the rates. After Chadwick, John Simon contended that the role of 'state medicine' was to ensure that housing was fit for habitation, food was free of adulteration, dangerous trades were regulated, industrial pollution controlled, environmental cleanliness maintained through proper sewage and drainage, and, not least, the spread of epidemic diseases checked through vaccination and quarantine.

Edwardian MOHs recognized that poverty was still the main challenge of preventive medicine. James Niven, MOH for Manchester for over forty years and one-time president of the SMOH, pointed out in 1909 that poverty was a complex and protean entity. In one area at one time, there might be high levels of unemployed labour temporarily thrown out of work by the trade cycle. Elsewhere, the poor might mainly comprise orphans, widows and the aged. Other areas might have a large itinerant population. Sometimes the causes lay beyond the control of the individual: old age and chronic sickness. Yet alcoholism and deliberate idleness were also to blame, leading to the vagrant lifestyles of the common lodging-house, public house and brothel (Porter, 1991b).

For Niven, preventive medicine should aim to reduce poverty caused by ill health. Even so, he accepted that there would always be 'incurable loafers, incapables, and degenerates'. His remedy was the popular, punitive Edwardian variation on the workhouse theme. Incurable loafers should be sent to 'detention colonies [and] labour colonies'. Niven approved detention of the feeble-minded in the model colonies set up by Mary Dendy, a member of the Manchester school board. Her 'farms' for the feeble-minded were designed to take them out of the city and provide them with a rural working life in permanently 'secure' institutions. The Victorian 'residuum' was thus still seen as a special problem for Edwardian public health reformers. But they continued to insist that the relationship between poverty and sickness could best be addressed by measures to prevent disease among the labouring industrial classes.

Take, for instance, the many discussions on poverty and tuberculosis staged by the SMOH. John Barlow, 1906 president of the north-western branch of the Society, was staggered at the levels of pulmonary tuberculosis among what he termed the 'poorer classes and the very poor'. Rejecting the idea of hereditary diathesis, he reminded his colleagues that some members of the poorest classes must possess the strongest constitutions in order to survive the persistent threat of tuberculosis within their communities. The predisposing conditions favourable to tuberculosis were, he suggested, those most closely connected with poverty; 'damp, dark, dirty, and overcrowded rooms and alcoholism' – conditions which inevitably led to its rapid spread throughout families. These same conditions were equally the source of high infant mortality from diarrhoea, pneumonia, and perinatal mortality resulting from maternal malnutrition. Poverty, he claimed, also bred bad moral habits such as poor childcare and intemperance. The relationship between poverty and disease, Barlow stated, inevitably involved the medical officer of health in moral and social questions (Porter, 1991b).

The response of Edwardian preventive medicine to the dilemma posed by poverty and disease was to expand its vision of what Simon had identified as the environmental influences upon the 'physical conditions of existence'. For example, Simon had urged that the housing of the working classes should be the primary target of public health reform. In the event, however, Victorian legislation to reduce urban slums and overcrowding had been piecemeal and lacking in coherence. Recognition of this provided new stimulus from the 1890s for the formulation of a more holistic understanding of the urban system. New proposals were floated for decentralizing the city, redistributing industry, and taking industrial workers, metaphorically and even literally, 'back to the land'.

In a significant new alliance from about 1907, preventive medicine began to join forces with the aspirations of town planners for housing reform. Town planners began to contribute to the preventive medical journals, especially *Public Health*, and participate in the annual congresses of the professional preventive medicine community. Thus, in 1908, such leading members of the planning movement as Henry Vivian (a Liberal MP who led the national Tenant Co-Partnership Movement) and Raymond Unwin and Barry Parker (joint architects of the first garden city, Letchworth) directed the housing debate at an annual congress of the Royal Institute of Health. They argued that overcrowding exacerbated physical degeneration by being a prime agent in the spread of communicable disease. The housing question was thus no longer simply a matter of the sanitary standards of buildings, but had turned into the much wider issue of redistributing a population of potential disease-carriers. Planned regulation of city growth was presented as a means of controlling individual health, in order to prevent the physical deterioration of the community.

Unwin and Parker accused the sanitarians' perspective on housing regulation of being hopelessly blinkered. True, the advent of a sanitary infrastructure had helped to remove major sources of disease propagation, just as building by-laws had ensured a minimum quantity of adequate housing stock. But such sanitary improvement of dwellings had failed to tackle the haphazard growth of towns: no rational distribution of population had been sought, no account taken of the historic evolution of a settlement. Such questions had finally been addressed, they suggested, in the pioneering City Survey methodology advocated by Patrick Geddes. The ultimate result of the holistic urbanism which Geddes advocated, they argued, would be 'vigorous and happy citizens' (Porter, 1991b).

The spokesmen of Edwardian preventive medicine criticized earlier generations of sanitarians for failing to tackle the structural relationship governing urbanism and health. Older campaigns for housing reform needed to be transformed into forward-looking concepts of town planning. In so doing, environmentalist ideologies co-opted the language of degenerationism into arguments for comprehensive holistic social planning. The fundamental assumption was that overcrowding spread infections and caused chronic weaknesses in each generation, whether or not these were subsequently transmitted genetically. Health levels could be raised only by a holistic approach to environmental development.

In the same way as the Victorian housing debate became broadened into the Edwardian ideology of urban planning, so concerns with malnutrition also acquired a new focus, a broader programme. Simon had suggested that, apart from housing, public health regulation of food standards must be central to securing the physical welfare of the labouring poor. Victorian legislation thus prohibited the sale of substandard and adulterated food and dangerous drugs. Edwardian public health reformers went further. Legislation was passed establishing free school meals and setting up a medical inspection service for schoolchildren. The statutory introduction of ante-natal care and stricter regulation of midwifery were similarly aimed at preventing underfed mothers from producing constitutional weakness in their offspring.

The bacteriological revolution broadened an understanding of what constituted the environment of disease. No longer restricted to the physical milieu, it now included the social behaviour of individuals. Bacteriology demonstrated that the greatest agent of disease dissemination was the *human* carrier. Hence the individual could no longer be seen as an isolated health unit; he was rather the bearer of the social relations of health and illness. Just as town planners vested their faith in creating a new civic consciousness, public health reformers believed they could eradicate habits of hygienic inefficiency and forge citizens who would safeguard health. It was no longer enough for individuals to heed their own health, as had been urged by the Enlightenment ideology of individual hygiene; they must be made conscious of the social impact of individual behaviour upon the health of the community. Campaigns were thus launched early in the twentieth century by MOHs for compulsory education of schoolchildren in hygiene, to indoctrinate them in the creed of personal responsibility for community health (Porter, 1991b).

Thus, the individual was sociologically redefined as the bearer of the relations of health and illness. This new perspective validated the Edwardian philosophy of preventive medicine as the panoptic overseer of communal life. In his 1910 report to the Local Government Board, its medical officer, Arthur Newsholme, thus emphasized that infant mortality was not a 'weeding out' process of eugenic value, but simply represented the 'preventable wastage of child life' (quoted in Porter, 1991b: 171). The phrase Newsholme chose echoed the calls of William Farr and other nineteenth-century sanitarians for the reduction of preventable mortality. A new philosophy of prevention, Newsholme pointed out, had, however, to be implemented to achieve it (Eyler, 1997).

Techniques of preventing disease within the community had evolved, he claimed, in two stages. The first had involved 'a crude idea that local insanitary conditions, irrespective of specific infections, caused epidemic disease'. This was, at best, he said, only 'a first approximation of the truth', comparable to the empirical methods employed in traditional clinical medicine. But just as scientific medicine had superseded empiricism, so a new rational concept of prevention had *emerged* from, but also *emancipated* itself from earlier sanitarianism, as a result of new knowledge of the specific aetiology of diseases. By identifying the origin of specific diseases, it had revealed the interdependence of those social and biological conditions which furthered their propagation. Prevention could at last mount what Newsholme described as a 'causal attack' upon disease, thanks to the redefinition of the environment from a 'social standpoint' (Porter, 1991b).

Newsholme contended that this new definition of the environment afforded a vision of how the whole range of the 'physical, mental, and moral life of mankind may be brought within the range of preventive medicine'. Social efficiency would depend upon a method 'which should govern the supervision and control of communal life'. If it were to function as a tool of corporate management of communal life, it followed that preventive medicine must possess a 'vision of the whole'. In the evolution of this approach, he emphasized, 'the collective have gradually overshadowed the personal' (Porter, 1991b).

Conceived thus as 'social efficiency', preventive medicine became synthesized into a specific policy agenda. From 1905, the Society of MOHs joined forces with Sidney and Beatrice Webb in a campaign for establishing a unified health service, to replace the existing fragmented public health and Poor Law medical services. The SMOH was already campaigning for the establishment of a Ministry of Health and a state medical service. The Society demanded a unified health service, administered by a Whitehall department, managed by a full-time tenured staff of specially qualified district MOHs. They wanted a new service paid for out of the Exchequer's purse and not the local rates (Porter, 1991a; Porter, 1991b).

The Royal Commission on the Poor Law, which sat from 1905 to 1909, produced a Majority and a Minority Report, the latter authored by the Webbs. Alongside many other proposals for revising the social services (including labour camps for the unemployed to replace the workhouse), the Minority Report proposed a national health service, uniting both clinical and preventive medicine, and financed from central taxation. This service was to be managed by MOHs, through an expansion of their existing bureaucracies. It was to be directed by the principles of preventive medicine, interpreted as a philosophy of rational comprehensive planning for the health needs of a community. In formulating this concept, the Webbs were assisted by Arthur Newsholme, and they received the wholehearted support of the Society of MOHs.

Though there were moments when it appeared close to becoming a reality, the unified health service was not endorsed by Asquith's Liberal government. In fact, health policy took another direction entirely in the National Insurance Act of 1911. This instituted compulsory health insurance for working men. The Poor Law remained intact to deal with their dependants. In the wider arena of Westminster party politics, the goals of comprehensive planning for the social, economic and physical environment of health were only very partially realized before the First World War (Porter, 1991a; Porter, 1991b).

PUBLIC HEALTH AND THE BIRTH OF THE
BUREAUCRATIC BRITISH STATE

In the mid-nineteenth century, Britain initiated central state control of population health. Continental-wide concerns about industrialization and epidemic disease stimulated a state interventionist resolution in the British context which was legitimated by a Utilitarian philosophy of scientific management of government. The Utilitarian doctrine of political economy required the free market economy to be maintained by the elimination of waste. The new Poor Law had been designed to enhance competition in the labour market. But, in Edwin Chadwick's view, if competition was less economically efficient than monopoly then the amalgamation of tiny capitals into one ownership under the control of the state should be adopted. The nationalization of water was more economically efficient than private enterprise by this criteria, so too was state control of the gas supply, the telegraph system, or London transport systems, cabs and bread shops. In aggregate, the small entrepreneurial operations to supply these services used an excessive amount of equipment and fixed capital than was necessary; by their consolidation huge sums could be saved.

Despite the apparent contradiction between 'individual freedom' and 'bureaucratic State intervention' Chadwick retained the whole-hearted support and admiration of the most noted defender of 'liberty' in nineteenth-century English philosophy, his friend John Stuart Mill. The solution to the burden of poverty and epidemic disease upon capital-accumulating societies had led the Utilitarian philosophy of political economy from the justification of the free market to the justification of the bureaucratic state.

The systematic management of British health policy entered a professionalized phase with the appointment of an elite physician, John Simon, as its chief central government administrator. The medical professionalization of public health continued with the development of a national service of health officers who sought to establish their status as trained specialists in preventive medicine. Simon had believed that the new collectivist politics emerging in the late Victorian era marked the most advanced form of civilization. The preventive health agenda of the late Victorian and Edwardian period reflected these intellectual commitments. For explanations of ill health, preventive medicine looked to the historico-sociological determinants of social development, above and beyond the biological basis to human existence. The preventive medical community expanded the environmentalist platform to include social behaviour. This platform allowed them to secure substantial legislative gains, yet they failed to achieve the institution of a unified rational-comprehensive system of health care. They did manage, however, to achieve some comprehensive features within social policy legislation during this period, such as Sanatorium Benefit under the National Health Insurance Act, 1911. The Society of MOHs viewed the Act itself as a major setback to the progress towards a unified health service. Nevertheless, their role in the organization of local health services greatly increased after the First World War. The expansion of their practical responsibilities was not matched, however, by the growth of a coherent public health philosophy which grasped the new challenges presented by the epidemiological transition taking place in British society from infectious to chronic disease. When a unified health service was introduced in 1946, the public health community lacked a theory of chronic disease prevention. As a result, the power to determine the structure of the new health service was superseded by the profession who claimed to have a prerogative on chronic disease management, clinical medicine.

The growth of a state apparatus for regulating population health in Victorian Britain demonstrated liberal democracy's need for bureaucratic government. The contradictions of the free market economy established the limits of liberal individualist philosophy as an organizing principle of laissez-faire society. Collectivist intervention into the social relations of health, however, highlighted the tensions between the ideological goals of civil liberty and community benefit. The enforcement of health cost individual freedom and Victorians articulated their hostility to bureaucratic compulsion by opposing the Vaccination and Contagious Diseases Acts. The tension between democratic and bureaucratic politics continues to be a central dilemma in the construction of contemporary health policy, not only in Britain but in developed and developing countries everywhere.

9 Localization and health salvation in the United States

In Victorian Britain, public health innovation was driven through the expansion of an interventionist central state. The establishment of a national bureaucratic public health service extended the principle of professional managerial control to local government. A starkly contrasting model of public health development occurred in the United States. Here reform was dominated by local voluntary effort which was not initiated by aspiring specialist professionals. Instead, reform was promoted by Puritan moral codes regarding social cleanliness and godliness. By the turn of the century a new technocratic ideal of social progress became influential, but this never succeeded in overcoming the persistent American suspicion of central government paternalism and a belief in the superior claims of local rights. The contrast with the British and other European models of reform highlights the multidimensional nature of the relationship between public health administration and the modern state.

FROM A RURAL TO AN URBAN WORLD

At the outset of the nineteenth century, the new republic was still predominantly a rural society. There were only thirty-three cities in the United States with populations over 2,500 (Brogan, 1985). Conditions in these small towns reflected the agrarian lifestyle which surrounded them. Town dwellers kept livestock in their homes; stray pigs, goats, and dogs roamed the streets; horse manure littered unpaved byways; garbage and human wastes were dumped in the streets and thrown on to undrained vacant lots; slaughtered animal carcasses and entrails were thrown casually into the thoroughfares; primitive cesspits served as the most efficient form of sanitation. Under these conditions, subsoils became saturated and polluted and water supplies from local wells and cisterns became contaminated (Porter and Fee, 1992). Malaria raged almost everywhere except in New England, enteric fevers were endemic and imported yellow fever returned repeatedly in one epidemic after another. In southern ports, it became almost endemic (Duffy, 1966; Duffy, 1990).

Tiny towns began to grow rapidly in the first half of the century, with rural migration to industrial centres and European immigration swelling urban settlements. The public health needs of these large urban populations vastly outstripped the primitive amenities available. Furthermore, industrialization deepened the divide between the prosperous and the poor who moved socially, economically and geographically further apart (Brogan, 1985). Paternalism was replaced by repulsion towards the alien urban poor. Poverty was no longer seen as a charitable estate by the wealthy, who increasingly blamed the poor for their condition. The poor were idle, reckless, heathen, immoral and therefore undeserving of altruism, charity or sympathy. Paternalism gave way to a rising tide of rugged individualism in which community responsibility was dismissed in favour of the importance of individual self-sufficiency. The prevailing political philosophy in Jacksonian America advocated that government should be kept to a minimum, maintaining law and order so that each man could fend for himself (Rimini, 1976; Rimini, 1984).

At the end of the eighteenth century, a series of severe yellow fever epidemics had stimulated emergency government action to enforce quarantine regulations. The temporary health boards set up in cities such as Washington and New Orleans did not outlast the epidemics and were not revived until cholera replaced yellow fever as the grim reaper of the early 1830s (Duffy, 1966). Most towns were virtually without any health organization during this period, but New York City set up a health office to regulate quarantine which continued as a state authority throughout the early years of the new century. In addition, the city appointed a permanent health inspector in 1804 who gathered information and reported nuisances. He was given no power, however, to implement any measures to correct them. The first New York City Board of Health was appointed in 1805 and consisted of five aldermen and three officials from the state health office. The Board operated largely in times of emergency only. Its activities declined during the first decades of its existence. Initially it had a budget of $8,500, but it was receiving only $500 by 1819. By 1830, the Board of Health, like the remaining Boards in all other US cities, was appointed every summer to organize street cleaning before the season of epidemics began (Duffy, 1968).

The early Boston Board of Health was the singular exception to this pattern. The official Board was created by the General Court in 1798, but consisted of local representatives elected from each of the twelve wards of the city. As a representative body it was given authority to order the removal of nuisances at the expense of the owners. Consisting of elected members, the Board was more responsive to the opinion of the general public and was often able to resist the special interests of the business community, especially when called upon to enforce quarantine restrictions (Rosenkrantz, 1972).

The experience of New Orleans provides a stark contrast. The first Board was appointed during a yellow fever epidemic in 1804 as a quarantine and sanitary authority, but was abolished immediately after the emergency ended. It was not revived during the next epidemic in 1809 but was appointed again after a major flood in 1818. In 1819 it was again abolished until more yellow fever outbreaks led to a third Board in 1821. By 1825 the city's business lobby succeeded again in getting it dismissed (Ellis, 1970; Duffy, 1968; Harrell, 1966).

The existence of temporary city health boards did establish the beginnings at least of quarantine and sanitary regulations. Individual cities also began to pass ordinances for street cleaning and nuisance regulation, even though no health or municipal police authority existed to enforce them. For example, Pittsburgh began with orders requiring owners of hogs and horses to prevent them from running freely in the streets, and preventing the slaughter of animals at public markets. A twenty-cent fine was later set for letting a horse run wild, and an ordinance was passed forbidding the tossing of garbage and human waste into the streets. The ordinances, however, were little regarded and no one was ever prosecuted under them. Street cleaning was left largely to the residents themselves but, in 1830, the city council appointed a street commissioner to employ municipal workers to work in cleaning gangs. Pittsburgh appointed its first health authority in 1832 as cholera threatened (Duffy, 1990).

Similar patterns of the growth of early sanitary measures could be told for Washington, Baltimore and many of the major US cities that, by 1830, all had some form of temporary health authorities which met either in an emergency or once every summer to organize an annual clean-up. If no health board existed, nearly all cities appointed a commissioner of street cleaning. As towns grew the water supply became more problematic. Without proper sewage and drainage, local wells became increasingly polluted. Philadelphia, Madison, New Orleans, Pittsburgh and St Louis all began to have water piped from distant clean sources by the 1840s. Often the early piping systems intermittently failed, so that the supply was haphazard. But the need for continuous water supply grew increasingly urgent as the burgeoning populations increased the risks of fire and disease (Anderson, 1984).

The first decades of the nineteenth century witnessed only limited developments in public health in the US. A sanitary movement could be said to have barely begun in most major towns. The onset of the Civil War, paradoxically, proved to have a galvanizing effect on subsequent developments.

WAR AND REFORM

The American Civil War claimed the lives of 600,000 soldiers. A large number of these actually died from typhoid and dysentery in grossly insanitary encampments rather than by a bayonet or a bullet. In 1861 a voluntary organization, the Women's Central Relief Fund, run by a physician and sanitary reformer from New York, Elisha Harris, pressured the secretary of war, Simon Cameron, into creating a Sanitary Commission to distribute voluntary relief medicine and food and to investigate the health and hygienic conditions of the troops. The Commission consisted of nine civilians and three army officers. Elisha Harris was appointed as its corresponding secretary and Frederick Law Olmstead, the landscape architect, executive secretary. The Commission discovered appalling lack of fresh food and medicine supplies, pitiful levels of medical care for the sick and wounded and precious few hospital facilities. It distributed fresh fruit and vegetables throughout all the regiments and ensured the regular supply of vital medicines. More important than this volunteer effort was its effects on reforming the Army Medical Corps itself. Initially faced with total hostility from the medical officers, the Commission shamed the army into cleaning up the conditions of the camps. They produced damning reports demonstrating the correlation of high mortality with insanitary practices, such as the failure to enforce the use of latrines and the mounting levels of human excrement turning camps into cesspits. The Commission exerted pressure upon the leading military authorities to institute hygiene reforms and the Army Medical Corps began adopting new policies to prevent typhoid and ensure the plentiful supply of fresh vegetables to prevent scurvy. Isolation to prevent the spread of infections was also introduced (Duffy, 1990).

The sanitary reform of the army had a direct impact on the civilian population. As Union troops began to occupy southern towns they imposed new sanitary programmes upon the local authorities. General Benjamin Butler, for example, occupied New Orleans from April 1862 and enforced sanitary regulations in the city with military police. He employed a labour force of 2,000 men to clean and drain the entire city and inspect stables, slaughterhouses and nuisance industries and supervise garbage collection and cesspit cleaning. The city authorities maintained Butler's programme after the war and improved their quarantine organization (Duffy, 1990).

Other cities such as Charleston and Memphis benefited from wartime sanitary programmes. The chaos that ensued with post-war reconstruction, however, made it difficult to maintain. Freed slaves became virtually a refugee population and suffered all the massive deprivations that traditionally accompany such social and geographical dislocation. The problems vastly outstripped the capacity of the Freedmen's Bureau to deal with them, and destitute black populations desperately required employment, housing and medical services. However, not until a new cholera threat and the return of yellow fever did local communities begin to respond to the need (Duffy, 1990).

The post-war era brought new challenges for sanitary reform created by the need to reconstruct a society torn apart by civil war, and a rapidly industrializing economy attracted ever larger numbers of immigrants from the European continent. The sanitary programmes established during the war and the activities of the US Sanitary Commission offered possible models of reform. Some individual localities continued to expand the programmes they began before the war. These reforms, however, were set in motion not by wartime marshal health law, but by philanthropic individuals. The role of John Henry Griscom in New York exemplified the relationship between the philosophies of hygiene and Evangelical piety which characterized the development of public health consciousness in the United States in the nineteenth century.

DISEASE IS SIN IN GOD'S OWN COUNTRY

European state sanitary reform had little impact upon the consciousness of US citizens. Individual US reformers were drawn into the public health movement not by political radicalism but by Evangelical piety. In 1842 John Henry Griscom, the health inspector of New York City, conducted a large-scale survey which he published in 1845 as a pamphlet called *The Sanitary Condition of the Labouring Population of New York*. He was not typical of his profession since most physicians at that time were uninterested in health reform and were divided over the theory of the causation of disease. Griscom's interest in health reform came from his pious devotion as a Quaker (Rosenberg and Smith-Rosenberg, 1968).

Raised in a household with a Quaker father who was committed to science education, Griscom was a member of the well-connected elite of New York's scientific and philanthropic communities. He qualified as a physician at the Pennsylvania School of Medicine and took up an appointment at the New York Dispensary. Later he became an attending physician at the New York Hospital and was a founding member of the New York Medical Academy and Medical Society. He believed that the popularization of physiology and hygienic knowledge 'would...have a greater meliorating influence upon the human condition than any other'. Hygiene and physiology had a spiritual as much as a material message, because morality and the physical world were all part of God's design of nature. In Griscom's natural theology, high mortality could not be the result of providence because the Deity could never have been so clumsy. It was man's neglect of the divine laws of nature which created abnormalities such as epidemic disease. The solution for man was to identify nature's dictates and follow them.

Where was man to find the rules of nature which applied to his own health? They were exemplified in the lives of noble savages and contravened in the degenerate life of the urban dweller. Griscom made a Rousseauvian idealized comparison of the healthy muscular native American Indian with the stunted degenerate New York inhabitant. But Griscom believed that civilization was redeemable. There was no reason why civilization could not create a healthy environment. Man only had to follow the most basic rules of nature such as the obvious need for clean air and ventilation. The failure to follow God's natural law was a sin. The rules of hygiene were a moral and religious duty and the sanitary regeneration of modern life was a religious crusade. Griscom also pointed out how the consequences of sanitary degeneration bred moral depravity. For example, the shocking tenement housing where the poor lived several families to a room and in basement, cellar hovels prevented the possibility of a virtuous existence. Such conditions could only lead directly to fornication, incest, alcoholism and crime. Sanitary reform would solve numerous social problems at once. Give the poor habitable living conditions and the threat of disease, immorality and crime will be reduced (Rosenberg and Smith-Rosenberg, 1968).

Griscom, like many of his contemporary American physicians, subscribed to the miasmatic theory of disease transmission and believed that even diseases which began as contagious could be turned into atmospheric infections through such unhealthy conditions. Air constantly contaminated by the breath of the diseased became vitiated with more and more effluvia to infect all who breathed it. Like Villermé in France and Farr in England, Griscom believed that the solution to the problem of insanitation and moral degeneration was to educate the poor into moral and hygienic salvation. Their religious denominations were different but their moral messages of public hygiene were remarkably similar. Griscom worked with philanthropic organizations such as the New York Tract Society to disseminate the gospel of hygiene to the poor. Other religious missionary societies also played an important role in the public health reform of New York as a whole. The New York Association for Improving the Condition of the Poor was a prototype social welfare agency that became directly involved in the campaign for pure milk, housing reform and the supply of free medical treatment for the poor. It also campaigned for general public health measures such as the improvement of the city's sewers, the regulation of slaughterhouses and the prevention of tenement dwellers from keeping pigs, goats and cows in their apartments (Brieger, 1966).

The pious logic of Griscom's philosophy of health reform was reproduced by many early US health reformers, such as Lemuel Shattuck (1793–1859), Griscom's contemporary, who was the pioneer of public health in Massachusetts (Rosenkrantz, 1972). The significance of religious moralism for US health reform was reinforced in the American response to cholera. Its greatest impact was in the cities, towns and landing spots along the Mississippi, the Arkansas, and the Tennessee. Cholera spread like wildfire from New Orleans during the mild southern winter weather (Waring, 1966). In the absence of government authorities, voluntary associations of citizens organized refuse removal, street cleaning and emergency hospital facilities. Evangelical volunteers preached hygienic reform to the diseased and their neighbours. While they believed that sin was a primary cause of the epidemic, they also believed that this gave rise to secondary exciting causes such as filth – next only to vice as the worst of mortal sins – poor drainage and lack of ventilation. Evangelicals began preaching the gospel of hygiene. Prayer was a necessary but not sufficient remedy. Practical measures were also needed (Brewer, 1979).

Individualistic voluntarism, missionary zeal and militarism subsequently characterized the development of US health policy. A society which prized self-sufficiency recoiled from paternalistic government which undermined the sovereignty of individual rights. Challenged by escalating urban squalor and disease this predominant ideology was supplemented by moralistic and militaristic sanitary reform.

THE LIMITS OF LOCAL ADMINISTRATION

The earliest efforts at public health reform in the US were largely rearguard reactions to epidemic disasters guided by a pious philosophy. Early public health campaigns aimed to regenerate American society by remoralizing the poor using the divine laws of nature designed to induce health. The work of the Sanitary Commission during the Civil War introduced significant new developments into occupied cities and towns which laid the foundation for the institutionalization of a more systematic approach to disease prevention. After the war, new city health boards and state boards of health were developed and a new concern with public health began to emerge within the context of changing ideologies of social reform in the late nineteenth century.

New York City established a health department prior to the Civil War during the cholera years. After the Civil War, however, it languished during the depression of 1873 and its budget was continually cut. Appointments to the department were always political spoils, so there was little opportunity for professionalism to be introduced into disease control. Despite this, the Board remained effective in promoting vaccination and improvements in child health. The director of the department from 1873, Dr Charles Chandler, managed to introduce laboratory testing of the city's milk supply and begin a Summer Corps of physicians who visited children living in the tenement areas and provided free medical care. The vaccination of schoolchildren also created the opportunity for the inspection of schools, but the reports of the health department on the appalling conditions in them were ignored. By the 1890s the New York City Health Department had expanded its activities into the inspection of meat and milk and began to promote sanitation in schools. From 1866 the state of New York established a sanitary bureau which was responsible for the surveillance and control of communicable diseases which dealt with sanitary inspections, contagious diseases, public drainage and food inspection and the inspection of offensive trades. Laboratories were also established in both the city and state departments (Duffy, 1966).

In other eastern cities similar health departments developed during the 1870s and 1880s. Newark established a Board of Health in 1857 but by 1870 it was still spending only 7 cents per head on health regulation. In 1892 it finally appointed two full-time health officers and established an effective agency for the first time (Galishoff, 1988). Among the cities of the mid-west St Louis was one of the leaders in health reform, appointing a board in 1867 consisting of the mayor, the police commissioner, a health officer and two physicians. In 1871 a sanitary police force, recruited from the regular force, was incorporated into the health department and used to assist in investigating contagious diseases, sanitary standards, the quality of milk, quarantine and smallpox hospitals and the city's poorhouse. The department's spending budget in 1871 was $17,056. The total costs of the health department, including its budget for hospital provision, rose to $272,801 by 1880. St Louis was the first Board of Health to be involved in the control of venereal diseases through a system of licensing and medical inspection of prostitutes, begun in 1870. Church members were, however, outraged by this public endorsement of sin and the Social Evil Ordinance, as it was called, was repealed in 1874; the Social Evil Hospital, which had been financed out of the licensing fees, was closed. Chicago established a Board of Health in the late

1860s, but by 1894 conditions were worse there than in many of the eastern cities. Louisville, Kentucky and Cleveland, Ohio, were more successful and, despite massively increased levels of population, managed to reduce their overall mortalities from around 23 per thousand in 1870 to 16.4 by the 1880s (Duffy, 1990).

The South experienced the greatest difficulties in recovering from the effects of the Civil War. Louisiana was the first state to establish a Board of Health but it functioned only haphazardly as a quarantine authority. It did nothing to assist individual towns such as New Orleans, Memphis and others from the Mississippi valley to co-ordinate their efforts, especially when it was most needed during yellow fever epidemics which raged in 1878. In 1872 Memphis had an average annual crude mortality of 46 per thousand. In theory it had a Board of Health, but this was completely ineffectual. The death toll in the 1878 epidemic was the final straw which pushed the Memphis business community into seeking sanitary reforms (Ellis, 1970). By this time the briefly existent National Board of Health had been set up, headed by John Shaw Billings, and the city applied to it for assistance. Billings brought a group of sanitary experts to the city in 1879 who recommended the construction of a sewer system and recruited eight physicians and twenty-six other inspectors to begin a house-to-house sanitary survey (Chapman, 1994). Subsequently the city constructed a filtered water supply system and established a Board of Health with new powers to inspect and remove nuisances.

In the west the first city health authority was established in San Francisco in 1870 and consisted of a five-man health board: a health officer, secretary and three inspectors. The department's programme was comprehensive. The rising mortality from diphtheria and smallpox was continually blamed on the insalubrity of the immigrant Chinese community. The health authority was efficient and progressive, establishing a complete sanitary infrastructure by 1876. The sheer size of immigration created all the familiar difficulties which follow displaced and dislocated populations, but the health department did succeed in reducing the crude mortality rate to around 18.7 per thousand by 1877 and 11.5 per thousand by 1891 (Duffy, 1990).

From 1870 most major cities established some form of health regulation, but it became ever clearer that none could operate in isolation from each other and that at least co-ordination of activities was required by the states, if not some form of regional or national government. The portability of epidemics defied the capacity of city governments to prevent them passing along the River Mississippi and the trade and train routes between north, south, east and west. The continual movement of population equally demonstrated that no city community could any longer consider itself isolated.

The need for State Boards of Health was only slowly met, however. The first State Board, established in Louisiana in 1855, was an ineffectual quarantine authority. The first effective one was established in Massachusetts in 1869. Fifteen years earlier, Massachusetts had recruited a Boston statistician, Lemuel Shattuck, to complete a survey of the health of the commonwealth. Shattuck was a pious reformer who originally saw no need for state intervention and believed that health regulation could be achieved by simply imposing the rules of health, clean and godly living upon the poor. By the time he had completed his report in 1850, however, he understood how the problems of mass immigration and industrialization demanded a much more systematic and rational response. His report recommended institutional reform and eventually led to the creation of a State Board in 1869. The Board was given powers to investigate but not to implement reforms. Once created, it attempted to institute new hygiene regulations upon slaughterhouses and noxious trades and successfully persuaded the Massachusetts legislature to pass an Offensive Trades Act in 1871. This gave the Board its first authoritative powers to prosecute violators of the nuisance law throughout the state. Under the direction of the first chairman of the Board, Dr Henry Bowditch, the Board used the local health authorities to gather state-wide vital statistics and provide general supervision of water supplies and pollution. The Board was given additional powers in 1886 but continued to use persuasion rather than sanction to enforce new regulations. By the 1890s Massachusetts had the most efficient water supply and drainage system and uniform sanitary regulations of any state authority. Many state boards created during the 1870s and 1880s were modelled on the Massachusetts example (Rosenkrantz, 1972).

The majority of the state boards established by 1900 were largely powerless and ineffective. The chief function of many of them became the licensing of physicians. The need for collective action regarding health increased as the pace of industrialization, urbanization and immigration escalated. The response to this need came largely from outside municipal and state health administrations as part of a new philosophy of scientific government. The new philosophy of scientific rational government was reflected in the health sphere in the demand for professionalization to replace charitable and moralistic reform.

NATIONAL HEALTH

The belief that epidemic disease posed only occasional threats to an otherwise healthy social order was shaken by the industrial and economic transformation of the US in the late nineteenth century. Death rates among the itinerant and immigrant urban populations escalated from high levels of lethal infections. Pious beliefs about poverty and moral failing no longer explained or offered a means of dealing with the environmental consequences of industrialization and urbanization. Economic growth cost social stability. Major strikes between 1877 and 1892 and the assassination of President Garfield in 1881 indicated the potential for civil disorder. In such an atmosphere social reform took on a new urgency. New political movements such as the American Association for Labour Legislation – with a membership of 700,000 – campaigned for income tax, an eight-hour day, social insurance, labour exchanges for the unemployed, the abolition of child labour, workmen's compensation and public ownership of the railroads. Democratic machine politics challenged the ruling order of old elites (Porter and Fee, 1992).

Increasing numbers of social reform movements developed during the last quarter of the century aimed at ameliorating social crises and preventing revolution and anarchy. Health reform played a significant role in this context which exemplified the new social consciousness. For example, a group of engineers, physicians and public-spirited citizens formed the American Public Health Association in 1872. The APHA was not a professional organization in any sense, but rather a body of informed persons of goodwill interested in devoting their energies to social reform. Even the physicians who were members were contributing their sense of responsible citizenship more than their medical skills. By 1884 the Association had spread its influence throughout the United States and beyond, attracting members from Canada and later from Mexico and Central America. Its main aim was to encourage co-ordination and standardization of public health practice among the dissipated authorities throughout the country. It was difficult, however, to agree upon standards when no one speciality dominated public health practice at this time (Rosenkrantz, 1974; Rosenkrantz, 1985).

Towards the close of the century a new spirit of scientific management of social and political reform directly influenced health. The ideological aim of the Progressive movement was to achieve scientific management in government through an increased role of specialist professionals in the construction and execution of public policy. The Progressives formulated a politically radical analysis of the crisis of industrialism and its injustices to the poor and disadvantaged but did not advocate the complete overthrow of the existing social order (Thompson, 1979; Colburn and Pozzetta (eds), 1983). Instead they supported reform based on scientific and humanitarian principles. Health reform was an excellent target for Progressivism because sanitary improvement alleviated the conditions of poverty without restructuring society. Progressives such as Henry Welch, the founder of the Johns Hopkins Medical School and School of Public Health, argued that health reform made sense economically. Investing in a healthy population cost less than paying the price for premature and unnecessary mortality among the labouring classes (Fee, 1987).

The Progressive movement stressed the need to emancipate public health practice from its unsystematic and ad hoc basis. Universal standards of public hygiene must be administered by a uniform system of public health organization throughout the national community. The inadequate patchwork provision of health regulation among the various states was amateur. Charles Chapin, the superintendent of health of Providence, Rhode Island, argued that public health should become a profession with appropriate training (Cassedy, 1962).

Public health leaders were arguing for central planning in health policy on the one hand and the scientific construction and execution of policy on the other. Progressive reformers wanted questions of health to be removed from the politics of interest and to be governed instead by rational and official public administration. This reflected the general aim of the Progressive movement to reduce the influence of political interests in government and increase the role of professional administrators. Social reform was to become a science of social administration (Colburn and Pozzetta, 1983; Davis, 1984). A centralized federal health department was critical to achieving these aims. Developments in the southern states and beyond the shores of the US helped to support these goals (Wasserman, 1975; Marcus, 1979; Watson, 1982).

As the US expanded its international trade it became embroiled in territorial conflicts in the defence of trade routes. Such a dispute brought the US into the Spanish–American war in 1898. Of the 250,000 troops that were sent to Cuba, 968 men died on the battlefield and 5,438 men died from infectious diseases. In 1900, an Army Commission was sent to Cuba under the direction of the military bacteriologist Walter Reed to investigate yellow fever. He demonstrated that it was spread by mosquitoes, that there was an incubation period in the mosquito and that the mosquito itself bred in close proximity to human habitats. Following Reed's discoveries, Surgeon Major William Gorgas conducted a quasi-military campaign aimed at eliminating mosquitoes with pesticides and succeeded in preventing a further epidemic. The experiences of the military abroad illustrated the importance of effective public health measures. The French abandoned an attempt to build a canal across Panama because of enormous mortality among its workforce. The United States faced the same problems when it took over the project. In 1904 William Gorgas took control of the campaign to prevent malaria and yellow fever and persuaded the Canal Commission to systematically eliminate the mosquito. It worked, and the canal was completed in 1914 (Delaporte, 1991).

The lessons learnt in Cuba and Panama had resonances for public health in the southern states. The army's methods were used by the Marine Hospital Service, working in conjunction with the Louisiana State Board during a yellow fever epidemic in New Orleans in 1905, and managed for the first time to bring the epidemic under control before the cooler winter months began (Warner, 1985; Ettling, 1981). The southern states of the US were economically depressed and technologically less developed than the North at the end of the nineteenth century. The progressive Roosevelt administration sought to eliminate what they perceived as 'backwardness' by creating a Commission on Country Life consisting of a number of experts in different fields who were to travel through the South and assess levels of literacy, poverty and malnutrition. Two members of this Commission were Charles Widdell Stiles, a zoologist who worked at the Marine Hospital Service hygiene laboratory, and William Hines Page, a publisher and editor. Stiles had been investigating the disease of hookworm for many years and was convinced that it was responsible for widespread lethargy and stunted growth among the sharecrop community. He believed it could be eradicated from the South through simple drugs and sanitary measures which would eliminate the parasite. During the travels of the Commission, Stiles managed to persuade a number of his colleagues about the possibility of eradicating hookworm, or what he called the 'disease of laziness'. Walter Page used his connections with the press to get Stiles's plans for eliminating hookworm to be considered by the General Board of Education at the Rockefeller Foundation. In 1909 the Board responded by agreeing to set up the Rockefeller Sanitary Commission for the eradication of hookworm (Ettling, 1981). The Board appointed Wickliffe Rose, the Dean of George Peabody College and the University of Nashville and executive secretary of the Southern Education Board, as its director (Fee, 1987).

This was the first step in what became a massive national and international investment in public health by the Rockefeller Foundation (Brown, 1979). Rose went beyond the task of simply trying to control hookworm and attempted to institute permanent and effective health agencies throughout the southern states. At the end of the five-year period, although the campaign had been effective, it had not eradicated hookworm. The Commission did succeed, however, in greatly enlarging the role and function of the southern health agencies. Between 1910 and 1914 the average annual budgets for health rose from hundreds of dollars to hundreds of thousands of dollars. In 1914 the experience gained in the southern hookworm campaign enabled it to extend its operation to the Caribbean and Central America (Ettling, 1981; Brown, 1979).

The health actions of the military in Cuba and the Rockefeller Foundation in the South strengthened the Progressives' demand for the establishment of a national health agency. In 1906 a group of Progressive intellectuals within the American Association for the Advancement of Science (AAAS) led by J. Pease Norton, Yale Professor of Political Economy, began a campaign to establish a federal health department. Earlier that year Norton's colleague at Yale, the economist Irving Fisher, had written to President Roosevelt proposing the creation of a federal health department. Roosevelt replied that before he would consider the issue there would have to be evidence that a real demand existed among the general public. The AAAS created a Committee of One Hundred to study the subject and elected Fisher as its president. Once Roosevelt became aware of the existence of the Committee he wrote to Fisher stating that while he was sympathetic to the cause he would be completely opposed to a new department with cabinet status. The Committee began a publicity campaign, and the American Health League was formed to promote education and provide financial support (Wasserman, 1975).

From the outset the campaign was opposed by advocates of states' rights. But Fisher believed that national health more than any other area of policy justified centralization and planning and that the states' autonomy issue was an inevitable fight which would have to be overcome sooner or later. He did not, however, anticipate opposition that would arise from within the federal health agencies themselves.

A federal agency had existed from the late eighteenth century which co-ordinated health activities. This was the Marine Hospital Service. The Marine Hospital Service was set up in 1798 when the federal government provided hospital facilities for the merchant marine. In the 1870s the service established a commissioned corps of medical officers who began to play a broader role beyond the care of sailors alone, providing public health advice to communities during periods of crisis. Gradually the commissioned corps expanded in numbers and began to function as a federal agency which could be called upon by any city or state health authority during times of crisis (Mullan, 1989).

By 1902 the Marine Hospital Service was the largest single agency in public health administration. Other government departments did have specific responsibilities. The Interior Department dealt with the sanitary conditions of schools and school hygiene. The Census Bureau and the Department of Commerce and Trade dealt with health relating to factories and housing; the War Office, through the Surgeon-General, dealt with military health and maintained a library and conducted laboratory and epidemiological research. The duties of the Marine Hospital Corps had become so extended that in 1902 it was renamed the Public Health and Marine Hospital Service. The Service was limited and controlled by the Secretary of the Treasury, who determined policy as much as the director of the Service, the Surgeon-General (Mullan, 1989).

Surgeon-General Wyman had directed the Marine Hospital Service since 1891 and was determined not to have the service's role diminished by the creation of a new federal bureau. Wyman repeatedly thwarted the efforts of the committee to get legislation passed during the Roosevelt administration. With the election of President William Taft in 1909 Fisher had new hope for the Committee's campaign. Taft was much more sympathetic than Roosevelt, but when new legislation was introduced into the Congress it was effectively hindered by the opposition of the National League for Medical Freedom. This organization opposed the American Medical Association (AMA), claiming that it represented a medical monopoly and was trying to impose universal standards upon medical practice, inhibiting the freedom of individual practitioners and specialists. The League claimed that the health legislation, which was strongly supported by the AMA, was simply a means of setting up a private medical trust to be controlled by a medical elite with federal authority. They waged an expensive high-profile newspaper campaign opposing what they termed the Health Primer Bill. Ultimately the collective opposition defeated the legislation and in 1912 Congress passed a measure which expanded the functions of the Marine Hospital Service, changing its name to the United States Public Health Service, and raised the pay of its officers. The revised agency was authorized to study health conditions and 'from time to time issue information in the form of publications for the use of the public' (Mullan, 1989). By 1915 the US Public Health Service and the Rockefeller Foundation became the major agencies involved in public health activities, supplemented on a local level by a network of state and city health departments, many of whose members were organized in the American Public Health Association.

THE NEW PUBLIC HEALTH AND PROFESSIONALIZATION

A further contributing factor for the move from a local to a national outlook in public health was the influence of bacteriology in the US (Marcus, 1979). The development of the bacteriological theory of disease coincided with the Progressive reform movement in health and was crucial in the aim of planning public health on a scientific and professional basis. The clarity and simplicity of bacteriology identified the enemy of disease decisively and it facilitated a new universalism based upon the precepts of the experimental scientific method. American physicians who studied the experimental method in Berlin laboratories in the 1880s applied it to the prevention of disease and used it to challenge the dominance of empiricist clinical medicine. Although bacteriology was embraced by the American medical profession and many public health reformers, it did not have an uncontested revolutionary impact. Even enthusiasts were extremely sceptical about its immediate usefulness. In the hunt for the yellow fever germ in the 1890s, internal disputes over the validity of methods of explanation and testability often meant no progress was made at all with regard to practical questions of prevention (Fee, 1987).

Despite this, some leading Progressive health reformers used bacteriology to legitimate the creation of what they advocated as an entirely new science of public health. Charles Chapin established public health laboratories in Providence, Rhode Island, in the 1880s; Victor C. Vaughn created a hygienic laboratory in Michigan, and William Sedgwick established bacteriological examination of Massachusetts water supplies at the St Lawrence Experiment Station. For some Progressives, bacteriology differentiated the 'New Public Health' from the old. Charles Chapin believed that the management of sewage and drainage and other environmental issues should be relegated to municipal departments of engineering because sanitary environmental control no longer had a place in the work of the medical team, who should be running a health department. The medical team should concentrate instead on methods of identifying cases of infection, isolating individuals and their contacts, and implementing the use of the latest technologies of immunology. Herbert Winslow Hill, the director of epidemics at the Minnesota Board of Health, popularized Chapin's philosophy as *The New Public Health* (Cassedy, 1962).

Charles Chapin believed that the methods of the New Public Health could completely stamp out individual infections. He put his theory to the test in a campaign to eliminate diphtheria in Providence after he became the superintendent of health in 1888. He believed that effective isolation of all bacteriologically tested victims and health carriers of the disease, plus a comprehensive programme of disinfection of dwellings of victims, could rid the community of the disease. Chapin began using William H. Park's method of diagnosing diphtheria in 1893, making it necessary for two negative cultures to be obtained from patients before they were allowed to leave hospital. In 1896 he took the additional step of requiring negative cultures from every family member where there had been a case of diphtheria before the placard isolating their dwelling could be removed. Through these strict measures he believed he could achieve perfect isolation of the disease. Later, he used the Chick test to identify healthy carriers and isolate them. In 1894 he began employing compulsory treatment with antitoxin and a vigorous disinfection campaign. His optimistic hopes for stamping out diphtheria, however, were dashed when he observed that during the period of strictest control the disease flourished greatest. This led him to drop his programme back to the previous level of voluntary hospitalization and temporary quarantine of siblings. Using these methods, Chapin found that he improved the reduction of diphtheria morbidity and no longer had the problem of enforcing extensive levels of quarantine (Cassedy, 1962).

While this narrow bacteriological view of prevention dominated some of the public health leadership, it did not go unchallenged. Charles-Edward Winslow at Yale asserted the need for a more holistic approach. Winslow saw public health as still requiring a mixture of skills outside medical expertise, such as those of public health nurses and professional administrators. Joseph Goldberger demonstrated how pellagra was a disease of nutritional deficiency, the only prevention of which was economic security. The researchers into the importance of vitamins and healthy diet challenged the narrow biochemical model of disease (Roe, 1973).

The idea of the New Public Health and the adoption of a bacteriological model of disease prevention nevertheless dominated the subsequent development of public health training. The largest and most important school of public health, at Johns Hopkins, was set up with the aim of producing prestigious research in the biomedical sciences rather than for providing training in public health administration. By the second decade of the twentieth century the New Public Health had become a new specialization. It was not a model, however, which induced consensus. It was challenged from within the public health reform movement and from those whom it excluded or those with whom it conflicted. The New Public Health aroused opposition from the professionals who had previously played an equal role in public health, such as sanitary engineers. However, by the early twentieth century more and more qualified public health workers were required by an ever expanding health system in both the local and the federal agencies. By this time health reformers were looking to the reform of therapeutic medicine for new directions in prevention (Fee, 1987).

FROM PIOUSNESS TO PROGRESSIVISM

As the United States made the transition into the largest industrial society in the world, urban squalor escalated out of control. Unlike in Europe, the high levels of mortality that it caused did not provoke a major political response. The politically motivated philosophies of European reform made little impact upon the general civic consciousness of the majority of US citizens. Instead, a society which prized individual industry and self-sufficiency above all else, and in which the rich became increasingly separated and alienated from the poor, recoiled from collective community policies required for sanitary reform. Such political aims were associated with the paternalistic charity of a past generation and were replaced by a system of values which were wedded to the virtues of the absolute sovereignty of the individual.

At least two things began to challenge this predominant ideology. First, the hygienic reform of the army during the Civil War brought major institutional change to territories which it occupied. And second, a new pious gospel of the relationship between cleanliness and godliness galvanized philanthropic missionary campaigns into improving the moral life of society through the sanitary regeneration of the poor.

Collectivism emerged as a new faith in technical expertise gripped American culture. This faith was reflected in the Progressive reform movement and in new practical directions in public health administration. Community control of epidemic diseases was driven by technological imperatives rather than the politics of interests. To a limited extent the one usurped the other in the history of public health in the United States.

Part 3

The obligations of health in the twentieth century

The next three chapters deal with the development of health citizenship in the twentieth century. In the twentieth century the health of populations became bound to the question of how social solidarity and cohesion could be maintained in advanced industrial societies that were divided by systems of economic and social stratification. The question of social solidarity was politically expressed in liberal democracies in the twentieth century in the concept of social citizenship which became identified with the welfare state as the mechanism for eliminating inequality through policies designed to reduce economic and social disadvantage.

Chapter 10 investigates how new discourses surrounding the quality of population encouraged the development of personal health and welfare services before the Second World War. Chapter 11 then provides a comparative analysis of the role of health policy in the creation of 'the classic welfare state' in Britain, Sweden, France, Germany and the United States. At various stages of their development, welfare states attempted to provide health services, both therapeutic and preventive, for an ever more comprehensive range of social strata. Chapter 12 discusses why such goals became compromised by changing economic conditions after the Second World War and explores the prospect for publicly and privately funded health services in shrinking as opposed to expanding welfare states. Whether state-funded or market-determined, health services became crucial to levels of health as they affected the quality of life in twentieth-century societies which experienced an epidemiological and demographic transition to longer-living populations with higher levels of chronic illness.

10 The quality of population and family welfare: human reproduction, eugenics and social policy

The social science of population health was a product of Enlightenment rationalism created in an effort to calculate the strength of the state in terms of the health of its subjects. The process of industrialization in the nineteenth century made the prevention of epidemic infections, rather than the pursuit of health, the focus of this science. Nineteenth-century disease prevention became a political and economic science and was translated into social movements for sanitary reform. Increasingly, disease prevention was absorbed into the operations of the modern state under terms such as state medicine or political medicine. Sanitary reform and state medicine were based on a belief in the environmental determinants of disease, the remedy for which was political intervention followed by new bureaucratic measures of administration for regulating the health of communities. In the last quarter of the nineteenth century bacteriology altered the environmental model of disease prevention promoted by the sanitary idea by focusing attention on the social behaviour of individuals. The methods employed by the 'new public health' were compulsory notification of infectious diseases, isolation of sufferers and their families, tracing contacts, laboratory diagnostic testing of 'carriers' and voluntary immunization. Bacteriology expanded the concept of the environment to include social action (Porter, 1991a).

Another late nineteenth-century science introduced the idea that social behaviour itself was determined biologically. This was the emergent science of human heredity informed by Darwinian evolutionary theory. At the end of the nineteenth and the beginning of the twentieth century, the investigation of heredity was linked to a set of philosophical goals for racial improvement and the prevention of evolutionary degeneration through planned human reproduction. This was the science of eugenics. Eugenics placed the links between demography and degeneration at the centre of a new discourse on the quality of population. In this chapter we will explore the impact of concerns about demography and degeneration upon social policy and health care provision up to the Second World War. But we need to begin by outlining the theoretical sources of beliefs about the influence of biological forces upon the social world.

GALTON'S CREED

Industrialization in the nineteenth century was accompanied by population explosions throughout Europe. This demographic rise did not receive a mercantilist welcome but inspired concern about the expansion of hungry, diseased and degenerate hoards. In the two decades before the First World War, as European imperialism was at its height European societies were haunted by darkest cultural doubt. From the late nineteenth century European intellectuals contemplated the worm in the evolutionary bud that could lead to the biological degeneration of their assumed racial supremacy (Pick, 1989). Eugenics used new knowledge about heredity and the process of evolution through natural selection to address the question of degeneration. The founder of this science was Francis Galton, a cousin of Charles Darwin. Eugenics was a statistical as much as a biological and social science, and during the course of its development Galton invented the measure of probabilistic significance, the 'correlation co-efficient' (Forrest, 1974).

Galton was born in the same year as the Augustinian monk from Moravia, Johann Gregor Mendel (1822–1884), who produced the famous study of the inheritance of biological characteristics in sweet peas which founded the science of genetics. Mendel first read a paper on his study of sweet peas before the Brunn Society for the Study of the Natural Sciences in 1865, but his work was not acknowledged until after his death in 1900 when this paper was simultaneously rediscovered by William Bateson from England, Hugo DeVries from Holland, K. Correns from Germany and E. Tschermak from Austria. By that time a German biologist, August Weismann (1834–1913), had shown that only innate and not acquired characteristics could be transmitted through the mechanism of inheritance. This was a significant departure from previous beliefs about inheritance, which had been influenced throughout the nineteenth century by the work of Jean Baptiste Lamarck (Kevles, 1985). In the late eighteenth and early nineteenth century Lamarck had developed a pre-Darwinian theory of the transmutation of species which was based upon the idea of acquired characteristics. Darwinian evolutionary theory, based upon the principles of natural selection, had not analysed what the mechanism of inheritance could be (Bowler, 1989). Darwin himself remained vague on the issue and retained some Lamarckian perspectives (Geison, 1969). Weismann conducted an experiment in which the tails of white mice were cut off in numerous generations for over a year. But no evidence was produced that any characteristics of tail-lessness had been transmitted to any future mouse generation. Weismann posited that there was a fundamental division between body cells and germ cells. The germ cells contained a precious substance – the germ plasm with chromosomes and what he termed 'ids', or what were later to be called genes. He insisted that no characters acquired by body cells during the life of experience of an organism could be transmitted to future members of the species. After the publication of Weismann's findings some evolutionary theorists such as E. D. Cope and Alpheus S. Packard asserted that variations were not random but resulted either from direct environmental introduction, orthogenesis or long-maintained habits.

According to this neo-Lamarckian philosophy natural selection weeded out the weakest, but acquired characteristics were responsible for creating the fittest (Kevles, 1985).

Francis Galton, however, had attempted to develop a method of analysing the effects of inherited characteristics long before Mendelian theories of genetics had been made public. When developing evolutionary theory, Charles Darwin had been inspired by observing the way in which animal and plant breeders cross-fertilized different breeds to obtain various physiological characteristics. Galton posited that the human species could also be improved by selective breeding and take charge of their own evolution. He published his first investigations into these questions in 1865 in a two-part article in *Macmillan's Magazine* which was subsequently expanded into a book, *Hereditary Genius*, published in 1869. Galton traced family links between individuals listed in a contemporary biographical encyclopaedia, the *Dictionary of Men of Our Time*. He drew up a sample population spanning two centuries who were related to each other, and concluded that ability was inheritable. This conclusion was based on the assumption that reputation, or renown, indicated ability. Galton thus claimed that not only physical characteristics but also talent and character – or personality – were inheritable and not the result of social conditioning (Kevles, 1985).

Darwin approved of his cousin's approach and Galton's work attracted great interest throughout the rest of the century, producing some brilliant protégés such as the statistician Karl Pearson, who took up the first Galtonian Chair of Biometry at University College London. Galton continued to expand his study of heredity in his anthropometric laboratory in South Kensington. It was in the course of his study of height, weight and the measurement of skulls that he developed the analysis of mathematical regression and the tests of significant correlation between variables. Galton's science of eugenics was aimed at the 'possible improvement of the human breed' through the production of a race of supermen by fertilization between partners of exceptional ability. The late nineteenth century also witnessed a growing cultural preoccupation with the inheritance of regressive qualities of degeneration and with the idea that modern society was on the road to inevitable biological decline (Chamberlin and Gilman (eds), 1985; Kelly, 1996).

Herbert Spencer, the social theorist and founder of English sociology, applied the propositions of natural selection to an analysis of social evolution. Spencer believed that consciousness created society and that the human species then became subject to social as much as biological evolution. He argued that social evolution was subject to the same mechanisms as biological evolution, but unlike Darwin he did not believe that the outcome was limited simply to survival. Instead, Spencer argued that natural selection produced 'the survival of the fittest', a phrase coined by him but often mistakenly attributed to Darwin. For Spencer, the mechanism of natural selection in social evolution was progressive and resulted in social improvement. He believed that this process produced ever increasing differentiation in social organization so that society became increasingly heterogeneous. Interference in this progressive mechanism of social development would reverse the civilizing process and bring about a social backwardness and decline into barbarism (Peel, 1972; Andreski (ed.), 1971). His philosophy was elevated into a fashionable ideology in the last quarter of the nineteenth century called 'social Darwinism' (Bannister, 1979). Social Darwinists claimed that attempts to ameliorate conditions of social disadvantage had interfered in this natural self-regulation of society and had given rise to conditions which allowed artificial selection to flourish. It was within this context that biological degeneration had been facilitated and social regression became inevitable (G. Jones, 1986; Evans, 1997).

Numerous theorists of degenerationism proliferated towards the end of the nineteenth century. The first to use the term was a French psychologist, Max Nordhal (Nordau, 1993). The studies of the Italian criminologist Cesare Lombroso on the physiological characteristics of the criminal type were equally influential (Pick, 1989; Chamberlin and Gilman (eds), 1985). In 1875 the Reverend Richard Dugdale completed a study of a family called the Jukes which traced the ancestry of a group of criminals, prostitutes and social misfits back through seven generations to a single set of forebears in upstate New York. Although Dugdale himself had stressed the importance of the role of social and environmental disadvantage in the family history, his study was used to support theories of hereditary degeneration (Haller, 1984).

Galton's new science provided, in the mind of eugenists, the statistical means by which degeneration could be documented and regeneration could be planned. Thus when Galton, now an old man, addressed the British Sociological Association in 1904 about his 'science of the improvement of the human breed', he was already talking to the converted, who saw the future of eugenics as a kind of new religion. At this meeting Galton claimed that eugenic marriage could 'do providentially, quickly and kindly' what nature did 'blindly, slowly and ruthlessly'. If eugenics could become 'a new religion' then the 'general tone of domestic, social and political life would be higher' (Farrell, 1985).

The British Eugenics Education Society, founded in 1907, attempted to translate these ideals into legislative measures for controlling marriage and the reproduction of the 'unfit'. Unfitness included many different categories of deviant behaviour such as alcoholism, promiscuity and criminality, plus what they termed 'the feebleminded', by which they meant the mentally retarded, and 'moral imbeciles', such as single women who had children. Eugenists in Europe and the United States hoped to introduce birth control and voluntary sterilization among the working class and compulsory sterilization for certain groups such as the insane, the mentally retarded and criminal. Selective breeding was the only route, they believed, to the survival of the 'civilized races' (Farrell, 1985).

EUGENICS IN NATIONAL CONTEXT

Enthusiasm for eugenics crossed national boundaries. It became an international ideology which highlighted the significance of demographic change in modern societies and created a new discourse on the relationship between quality and quantity of population. Eugenists believed that modern economies encouraged dysgenic differential birth rates by facilitating the survival of 'unfit' mental and moral defectives, the chronic sick, residual idlers, recidivist criminals and the unemployable. The productive had to bear ever greater tax burdens in order to support the growing numbers of degenerates and higher fiscal exactions naturally persuaded the prudent middle classes to practise family limitation. Declining fertility among the professional and middle classes, rising birth rates among the working classes, and massive reproductive surges among the lumpenproletariat had to be corrected in order to avoid race suicide (Soloway, 1990).

The self-appointed mission of eugenists was to 'protect the unborn' through a programme of selective breeding. Positive eugenics aimed to achieve racial improvement by encouraging the fit to breed while the goal of negative eugenics was to prevent breeding among the unfit. In Britain, Europe and the United States, eugenic reformers advocated marriage regulation, sequestration of the mentally deficient and sterilization – voluntary or compulsory – of the unfit. Methods for controlling human reproduction and directing demographic change were applied, however, in different ways in different national contexts.

Before the First World War, eugenists in Britain concentrated on obtaining the sequestration of the 'feebleminded', which included the mentally retarded, alcoholics and women who had more than one illegitimate pregnancy. British eugenists also advocated voluntary and compulsory sterilization for various social categories and some flirted with the idea of the 'lethal chamber' for ridding society of its unwanted, but this idea had its most profound expression in Germany in the inter-war period (Porter, 1991a). In Germany and elsewhere, however, negative eugenics can be seen to have accommodated rather than invented a set of political goals with origins in a much broader cultural base (Proctor, 1988).

Eugenism combined with other ideological cults in Germany during the 1930s and 1940s to produce a murderous science which legitimated the 'final solution' implemented under the Third Reich. When Hitler held a meeting on 20 August 1942 to appoint Otto-Georg Thierack as Reich Justice Minister and Roland Freisler as President of the 'People's Court', he raged about the need to reconstruct the criminal justice system. He held a tirade about the dysgenic effects of war which left only the poorest stock to breed for the future. The justice system had to be used to re-balance the equation by killing off the 'negative' elements of the population. Punishment was subsequently used to cleanse the 'body of the race' of its undesirable members. Criminals who, according to the Führer, included the frivolous and the irritable, were not, of course, the only undesirables who were being referred to. Cleansing also meant targeting Jews, gypsies, the mentally ill and political dissenters for elimination. The relationship between eugenics, social Darwinism, racial hygiene and the Nazi policies of elimination is highly complex and fiercely debated by historians (Evans, 1997). Some historians agree that Nazi population policy was a mixture of science and pseudo-science which informed but did not solely determine the murderous ideology of Fascism. However, although eugenics may not have led directly to the construction of the 'Final Solution', it played a significant role in providing it with a rationalist authority. It provided similar legitimate authority to the debate about population quality elsewhere (Weindling, 1989).

Eugenics won enthusiastic disciples during the Progressive era in the United States, appealing to both the conservationist and the technocratic ideas of the movement. Eugenics was embraced by a number of reform movements which espoused the ideas of Progressivism (Pickens, 1968). Sex educationalists in the social hygiene movement believed that 'eugenics will destroy that sentimentalism which leads a woman deliberately to marry a man who is absolutely unworthy of her and can only bring disease, degradation and death'. Margaret Sanger supported her leadership of the birth control movement with eugenic arguments about stemming the tide of the reproduction of the unfit. In the United States and elsewhere, however, other eugenists were extremely cautious about the question of birth control. Some were concerned that those whom they wanted to breed actually used contraception most, namely the middle-class economically prudent family (Pickens, 1968). In Britain, the Eugenics Education Society were hostile to the activities of the Neo-Malthusian League because they feared that the widespread availability of contraception would simply enhance the decline of the middle-class birth rate, which was already fearfully low (Soloway, 1982).

The temperance reform and prohibition movements used eugenic arguments to suggest that the Weismann 'germ cell' could be damaged by alcohol, causing 'blastophoria' which would produce feebleminded offspring. Temperance reformers argued that alcoholics should be sterilized. The zoologist president of Indiana, and later Stanford, University, David Starr Jordan, supported his leadership of the American peace movement with a Darwinian argument that proved the dysgenic effects of war. He claimed that ancient Rome fell after it scattered its best blood throughout its far-flung imperial campaigns, leaving behind only slaves and stable-boys to sire the next generation. War, he claimed, resulted in the slaughter of the best stocks of all combatants. The famous Yale economist, Irving Fisher, echoed Jordan's view that 'the tragedy of war is its waste of germ plasm' (Kevles, 1985).

In the United States, eugenics successfully influenced three other policy areas: marriage regulation, sterilization of the unfit and immigration restriction. By 1914, thirty states had passed laws preventing marriage of the mentally handicapped and the insane, together with laws restricting marriage between people suffering a venereal disease or those from various categories of feeblemindedness. The first state sterilization law was passed in Indiana in 1907. By 1917 fifteen other states had followed suit. Sterilization was legal for habitual criminals plus various categories of the insane, mentally handicapped and epileptics. Apart from this, eugenics in the United States provided ideological justifications for immigration restriction and the development of intelligence testing (Kevles, 1985).

The French psychologist, Alfred Binet, another Galton devotee, was employed in 1904 by the French government to devise a method for detecting mental deficiency in children. He drew up a series of tests which assessed memory, articulation and other mental activities, and in collaboration with a colleague, Theodore Simon, he developed a method for assessing 'mental age'. An American psychologist, Henry H. Goddard, brought the Binet–Simon tests to the United States in 1908 and completed research on measuring grades of feeblemindedness. Goddard's work was taken up by other psychologists such as Lewis Terman, who introduced the term 'IQ' (intelligence quotient) into the language of intelligence testing. A comparative psychologist, Robert Yerkes, developed a new IQ test and was employed by the military in 1917 as head of a team to design an army testing programme to classify men, in order to place them in their most effective roles as soldiers. The programme was extensive and over a million and a half recruits had been tested by the end of the First World War. The use of IQ testing within the military gave it a new authority. One of the team of army testers, Carl Brigham, applied his experience to testing among the civilian population, and his work was published in time for consideration by the hearings on immigration in 1923. The methods of testing developed within the military were a major tool for restricting immigration at the Ellis Island clearing house (Kevles, 1968).

Concerns over Asian immigration had led to the Chinese Exclusion Acts of 1882 and 1902. The federal government was pressurized for further action by various groups such as representatives of organized labour, social workers, businessmen and 'nativists', who thought that immigrants would pollute the American character. Apart from the nativists, the other groups objected to unlimited immigration for fear of economic competition and the encouragement of political radicalism among the lower orders. All of these considerations were powerfully voiced by a group of students and intellectuals based at Harvard University who were instrumental in getting new immigration legislation enacted in 1921 and 1924. Eugenics played an increasingly prominent role in immigration restriction, largely as the result of the efforts of Harry H. Laughlin who, in 1910, was appointed by Charles Davenport as Superintendent of the Eugenics Record Office at Cold Spring Harbor. Charles Davenport, a Harvard-trained biologist, was Galton's greatest disciple in the United States. He set up a station for the experimental study of evolution at Cold Spring Harbor with a $10 million endowment from the Andrew Carnegie Foundation, which helped make Cold Spring Harbor the centre of eugenic research in the United States. Although Davenport did not believe that research should be recruited into policy-making, he supported Laughlin's participation in the creation of new immigration restriction legislation. Laughlin presented the results of various eugenic research projects and a collection of petitions by eugenists to the House Committee on Immigration and Naturalization in 1920, when it was set up to develop emergency restriction legislation. After this was passed in 1921, the Chairman of the Committee, Republican Congressman Albert Johnson, appointed Laughlin an 'Expert Eugenical Agent'. Laughlin made a report to the Committee in 1922 with an analysis of the immigrant inmates of asylums. He inaccurately concluded that immigrants constituted a large proportion of this group, and that therefore Ellis Island must be used to discriminate who should be allowed to become 'carriers of the germ plasm of the future American population'. The American Eugenics Society itself made a report to the Committee in 1923, endorsing extensive new restrictions on immigration through the use of intelligence testing and physical examination. After the new immigration law was passed in 1924, intelligence testing became a crucial feature of restriction (Ludmerer, 1972).

Eugenics in the United States was popularized in mass culture through the press and through film. Eugenic aesthetics were popularized as methods of assessing 'fitness' and degeneracy. Richard Dugdale opened his book on the Jukes with the ironic anomaly that the first member of the family he encountered was an attractive but feebleminded young woman in a local asylum. This apparent contradiction – the appearance of normality in a feebleminded subject – drew his interest and led him to his subsequent investigations. In 1912, the psychologist Goddard used data he had acquired from field studies on mental deficiency in families to construct a pseudonymous family, 'The Kallickaks', which he used to demonstrate the way in which he believed feeblemindedness was hereditary. Such investigations popularized support for compulsory sterilization, publicized famously by the legal case of *Buck* v. *Bell*. In 1927 the United States Supreme Court upheld a Virginia law permitting the sterilization of Carrie Buck, an 18-year-old inmate of the Virginia State Colony for Epileptics and Feeble Minded, who was the daughter of a woman designated as feebleminded and had given birth to a mentally defective child. The opinion of the court was immortalized by Justice Oliver Wendell Holmes, when he declared that three generations of imbeciles was enough (Pickens, 1968; Haller, 1984; Kevles, 1985).

Eugenics was politically influential in the United States before the Second World War. While the laws on marriage and immigration restriction were not reproduced in exactly the same way elsewhere, the United States was not the only nation to adopt compulsory sterilization laws. In Sweden, compulsory sterilization was a feature of the demographic focus of its twentieth-century politics. In Germany, sterilization policy was extended into policies on euthanasia for the 'hereditarily unhealthy' and became inherently bound up with policies of genocide under the Third Reich.

By the inter-war years eugenics in Britain focused on the declining birth rate, the changing demographic structure of the population, family allowances and family tax relief, voluntary sterilization, popularizing the idea of the eugenic marriage and raising a eugenic consciousness throughout society. The British biologist, Julian Huxley, and the long-serving secretary of the Eugenics Education Society in the 1920s and 1930s, C. P. Blacker, suggested that eugenics should become a form of social consciousness which elevated the needs of the community above those of the individual, thereby facilitating the creation of a planned utopian society (Macnicol, 1989).

'Reform' eugenics in Britain and Europe in the inter-war period claimed that social systems and philosophies based upon individualism, such as capitalism and

nationalism, were dysgenic because rigid social stratification failed to
the reproduction of hereditary talents which were distributed throug.
social divisions. Capitalism, for example, failed to provide favourable cond.
for the most able among the labouring classes to rise to higher social a
economic status and reproduce their hereditary endowments. Equally, the leasi
able in all classes were not prevented from reproducing their inadequacies in
their offspring. In place of the class system, a eugenic utopia would be a unidi-
mensional society which would provide an equalized environment maximizing
the possibility for the expression of desirable genetic qualities (Freeden, 1979;
Paul, 1984). Improvement of the social environment was crucial if a eugenically
sound society was to be achieved (Macnicol, 1989; Soloway, 1990).

While concern over the differential birth rate remained central among
eugenic thinkers, the demographic debate broadened to include discussions of
the changing age structure of the population (Glass, 1936). The transformation
of the demographic structure of modern industrial societies with fewer productive populations supporting expanding numbers of ageing, chronically sick and
unproductive dependants led eugenists in Britain and Europe to advocate the
introduction of family allowances and tax relief to encourage large families
among both the working and the middle classes in order to combat the declining
birth rate (Macnicol, 1980). The broadening of the demographic debate was
accompanied by the modernization of discussions about sterilization. The
eugenic campaign for voluntary sterilization in Britain and elsewhere in Europe
now suggested that the people most likely to be enthusiastic about legal voluntary sterilization would be working-class mothers with no other access to reliable
birth control (Macnicol, 1989; Soloway, 1990).

Eugenism in this period became a loose synthesis of widely divergent ideologies. The *Eugenics Review* reflected the broad cross-section of eugenic
interpretations of demography and degeneration. British eugenists were enthusiastic about the first sterilization laws set up in Germany in 1933, admired the
Nazi policy of family allowance and tax relief which assisted 'Aryan' early
marriage and large families, and approved of the courage of the new regime in
introducing compulsory sterilization of the mentally defective. However, British
eugenists were at pains to point out the differences between German and British
proposals for legal sterilization. The British Eugenics Society wanted a law based
on consent with legal protection for the 'liberty of the individual'. Blacker in
particular perceived the need, early on, to publicly separate the identity of
British from German eugenics, although he was privately aware of the members
of the Society who wholeheartedly approved of the German measures.

THE QUALITY OF POPULATION AND THE HEALTH OF
MOTHERS AND CHILDREN

Anxieties over population quantity and quality stimulated political interest in
maternal and child welfare. The provision of welfare since the early modern

period was inherently bound to the politics of the family economy. The primary recipients of doles and alms were mainly poor women and children. As discussed in Chapter 7, Edwin Chadwick recognized this when he tried to reduce the costs of poverty by trying to reduce premature mortality among male breadwinners from infectious disease. From early modern times, poor women had drawn upon numerous resources in addition to state provision to negotiate family poverty. Poor wives were often the main family agent who sought relief either from the state or private charity in times of economic stress. Husbands were reluctant to experience the humiliation of seeking relief and would continue to try and find work at any price. For wives and mothers, managing access to relief was an extension of managing the household economy (Digby, 1996).

Policy-makers also began to understand welfare provision in terms of family economy in the modern period, and by the late nineteenth and early twentieth century maternalism and child welfare became the central platform of social policy (Cohen and Hanagan, 1991). Some historians and political scientists have argued that in 'weak states' such as the United States and Italy, the only welfare provision that was made at all focused on maternalist concerns (Skocpol, 1992). The social security of mothers and their offspring increasingly determined policy in Britain as well. This resulted, not least, because women were able to 'domesticate' politics at the local level. The systematic management of social assistance to relieve household poverty was claimed by middle-class women as their proper domain (Lewis, 1996b). By claiming knowledge of the domestic household economy as their special province of expertise, middle-class women professionalized systematic social assistance as 'women's work' (Lewis, 1996a; Hollis, 1987; Lewis, 1991). Maternalist social security offered a route for middle-class women to move from the private sphere of managing their own households to the public sphere of administrating social security. Opportunities which were lacking in central government were often available for women in local government policy-making. In England reforms such as rules allowing women to become members of local school boards from 1870 and Poor Law Guardians from 1875 made this possible (Hollis, 1987). In Britain, Europe and the United States, within the context of local government and organized philanthropy women used a language of service and duty to identify a type of gendered citizenship which allowed them to participate in the public sphere (Lewis, 1994; Koven and Michel, 1990). The public focus on human reproduction encouraged by eugenic concerns about degeneration placed the health and welfare needs of women and children centre-stage of social policy-making in the early years of the twentieth century. It also gave added authority to the claims of middle-class women that they were the most appropriately qualified specialists to administer the public provision of family welfare.

In Sweden, demographic shifts created fears about degeneration and differential population growth. The concept of social hygiene which emerged in Sweden after 1900 aimed to improve population quality as part of a broad social project to address the 'people's health' in order to achieve national efficiency, strength and modernization. Reducing tuberculosis, venereal disease, alcoholism and the social scourges of feckless slum-dwellers was linked to the improvement of health of mothers and children, soldiers and workers. Attacking these questions led to the development of maternal and child welfare provision, sanatoriums for tuberculosis sufferers, industrial hygiene laws, the regulation of prostitution and the integration of the Temperance Movement into adult education programmes (Johannisson, 1994).

Anxieties about population growth were directly linked to concerns about efficient colonial rule in the British dominions in the early 1900s. These prompted the first moves towards state medicine in Canada and the Antipodes, beginning with the creation of infant and maternal welfare designed to ensure continued imperialist domination (Cassel, 1994; Bryder, 1994). Though both European and Colonial eugenists feared that proletarian fecundity threatened to outstrip the reproductive rates of the middle classes, contraception and abortion were almost universally outlawed on the assumption that the prudent and thrifty would use it and the feckless and reckless would go on breeding like rabbits.

In the Second World War, the application of positive eugenics to social policy in Germany created a system of special ante-natal clinics and orphan homes for the progeny of SS officers with suitably Aryan women. The attempt to breed a blond-haired blue-eyed race was supported by a broad sweep of policies providing public financial and tax incentives for early marriage and the production of large families among 'Aryan types' (Bock, 1997; Bock, 1991).

Elsewhere in Europe, positive eugenics played a part in the development of ante-natal and baby clinics, school inspection services, free school meals and family allowances. It did not, however, set an agenda of its own, but served as a rhetorical resource to support preventive medical programmes which already had their own momentum. The reduction of infant mortality, for example, had been a major public health priority of the nineteenth-century sanitary idea. This priority was recast in the biologistic language of social Darwinism in the twentieth century, even though the political goals of maternal and infant welfare programmes everywhere, with the exception of Germany, remained the same.

Concern about depopulation and demographic differentiation also stimulated a social hygiene movement in France which, as in Sweden, focused on tuberculosis, venereal disease and maternal and infant welfare. In 1917 the founder of the National Alliance for French Population Growth, André Honnorat, sponsored a parliamentary bill to build sanatoriums in all *départements*. In 1923 a joint initiative by the American Red Cross and Rockefeller Commission, to establish tuberculosis prevention where rates were high, transferred its responsibilities to the French National Committee for Defence against Tuberculosis, headed by Honnorat until 1925. By 1924 national expenditure on TB prevention exceeded 20 million francs, and in 1936 even private sanatoriums came under government supervision. The tuberculosis service also helped to professionalize public health, since all their medical functionaries, as in the state mental asylums, were salaried government employees (Ramsey, 1994).

Concern over population levels and France's declining birth rate put pronatalism and infant and maternal welfare high on the political agenda at the end of the First World War. A massive public education campaign encouraged its demobbed sons to procreate as fast and as often as possible (Offen, 1991). The pronatalist campaign followed a period of rapid expansion in public health and social welfare legislation. Experimental programmes of public assistance during the war were extended into peacetime campaigns for national social insurance. But French social hygiene movements continued to concentrate on population issues such as differential birth rates and campaigns against venereal disease. A Government Commission on Venereal Disease was created in 1920, which was elevated to a High Council of Social Hygiene in 1938. This organization continued to promote positive eugenics, but as the recovering birth rate surpassed that of Britain and Germany in the economically depressed 1930s Malthusian concerns were revived. The French government resisted eugenist calls for pre-marital and medical examinations (Ramsey, 1994).

In Britain anxieties over the quality of the national stock and the future of the 'imperial breed' stimulated new social concerns with the survival of infants and the health of mothers and schoolchildren (Davin, 1978; Dwork, 1987). The British debate on motherhood, infancy and childhood mirrored many of the issues raised in other national contexts. British maternalist welfare policy is a useful heuristic device, therefore, for understanding the issues involved in state welfare for mothers and infants more generally.

Britain's humiliations in the Boer War stimulated a debate on 'national efficiency' which eugenists seized as an opportunity to spread the gospel of racial improvement through selective breeding. In South Africa, the Imperial Army had almost faced defeat at the hands of an opposing force that was barely trained; largely, the Boers were simply farmer volunteers. At the same time as Britain was witnessing the decline of its economic and military might, it watched the massive growth in the German, American and French economies. The rise of Germany in particular was perceived as the greatest threat. When Major-General Frederick Maurice published an account of the difficulties experienced by the army in trying to obtain satisfactory recruits in 1902, his report seemed to confirm the worst nightmare of the Edwardian paranoia. Fears of national decline stimulated the development of a new reform movement dedicated to the ideology of national efficiency. This was a political 'quest' for national efficiency which crossed all traditional party lines. Enthusiasts for national efficiency were to be found in the Tory, Liberal and Socialist parties, but its clearest expression was represented by a faction which had split within the traditional Liberal Party. These were the Liberal Imperialists, led by Lord Rosebery, who described themselves as the party of national efficiency. Some of the ideals of the Liberal Imperialists were similar to those of the Progressive movement in the United States. They shared a belief in the creation of efficient government, and indeed general management of all social affairs, through the adoption of expert guidance and scientific rationality. But the Liberal Imperialists also stressed the importance of maintaining and preserving a vigorous empire in order to ensure Britain's captive market for its industrial output and endless supply of cheap natural resources. Continued imperial exploitation was regarded as essential to the economic survival of the nation itself. It was Britain's only bulwark against the competition of the rapidly developing industrial market economies of the United States, Germany and France (Searle, 1971).

Support for imperialist preservation went hand in hand with support for national efficiency and became widespread throughout the Edwardian period. Concern about the physical stature of the national stock was central to both goals. Amid this general cultural malaise, special attention was drawn to the health of mothers, infants and children – the nation's hope. In the last quarter of the nineteenth century, the crude mortality rates for the general population in Britain steadily declined. From this date, however, the rates of infant mortality remained constantly high and just before 1900 began to increase. In 1876, the crude death rate was 21 per thousand; by 1897, it had dropped to 17.4 per thousand. The infant mortality rate, by contrast, was 146 per thousand in 1876 and rose to 156 per thousand in 1897, an increase of nearly 6.8 per cent (Szreter, 1996). There were those, such as Galton's disciple Karl Pearson, who thought that high levels of infant mortality were a healthy sign that the evolutionary mechanisms were functioning well. They thought that the weakly were well and truly being weeded out of the population before they had a chance to grow up and reproduce their degenerate qualities in a future generation (MacKenzie, 1981).

The British public health profession, however, took high infant mortality as an indicator that preventive medicine had not received the governmental support that it needed. Environmentalists countered eugenic arguments with demands for wider programmes of preventive medicine. For example, medical officers of health, who considered themselves professionals in preventive medicine, began to include social behaviour as much as the physical environment among the determinants of health. In the pre-bacteriological era, the 'sanitary idea' depended upon epidemiological methods to identify the environmental determinants of disease. MOHs now asserted that bacteriology demonstrated that individual behaviour and habits were crucial to spreading infection (Porter, 1991b). The Chief Medical Officer of the Local Government Board, Arthur Newsholme (1857–1943), stated in 1910 that 'from the social standpoint', public health depended upon changing habits of domestic hygiene, reinforcing public hygiene education and identifying groups at risk in terms of both their physiological and sociological characteristics. The solution to 'social efficiency', Newsholme claimed, was the public health management of all community life (Eyler, 1997). The Edwardian agenda advocated by the public health service included welfare programmes for pregnant and post-natal mothers, tiny infants, schoolchildren, men and women at work, the acutely sick, the chronically infirm, the tubercular and the aged. This agenda culminated in public health officers demanding a comprehensive health system integrating preventive and therapeutic services, administered by local health authorities and funded by taxation (Porter, 1991b). The British debate about an integrated service continued throughout the years leading up to the Second World War and finally was partially realized in the creation of the National Health Service in 1946. The introduction of maternal and child welfare, however, prefigured the structure of the national health system, the origins of which were established before the First World War.

The public health profession was able to use imperialist concerns about national efficiency and eugenic anxieties about human reproduction to mobilize support for an expansion of their demands for health services. Newsholme argued that high maternal and infant mortality were linked in an inexorable chain of poverty, deprivation and environmental disadvantage (Eyler, 1997). Other health professionals, however, such as the Medical Officer to the Board of Education from 1907 to 1918, George Newman, believed by contrast that the source of infant mortality was inadequate, ignorant and feckless mothering (Lewis, 1980). Different remedies were offered by different factions within the public health and social services. Newsholme believed that the way to reduce infant mortality was through the creation of a maternal and child welfare system within a broad programme of public health provision. Newman, on the other hand, believed that the more direct solution lay simply in the creation of something called 'mothercraft', or the public health education of mothers in the arts of domestic hygienic management and the proper methods of child-rearing (Eyler, 1997; Lewis, 1980).

The main cause of infant death, however, was diarrhoea. No bacterial organism had been identified as the direct cause of this epidemic, and thus it remained open to speculation and a variety of theories were put forward by the medical profession. Arthur Newsholme maintained that infant diarrhoea was the result of general unhygienic conditions. In his reports on infant mortality written between 1908 and 1911, he described conditions of subsoils overloaded with accumulated wastes, inefficient night soil collection, inadequate housing stock and other amenities as the forces which undermined infant survival (Eyler, 1997).

Newman attributed the deaths to unhygienic domestic conditions which were perpetuated by inefficient mothers. He pointed out that in areas where general sanitary conditions had been improved, infant mortality remained high. Instead, he cited the specific causes of infant mortality as dirty bottles, infant clothing and bedding. Newman believed that the unhygienic conditions which caused infant deaths were within the control of a conscientious mother who managed to maintain a clean domestic environment. Equally, he believed that the diarrhoeal epidemic was the result of improper methods of feeding and inadequate infant diet. As the MOH for the district of Finsbury in north London, he completed a study of infant death between 1902 and 1923. He discovered that thirty infants had been breast-fed, fifty-five had been bottle-fed and sixty-one had been fed with a mixture of methods. He used his study and the statistics from other MOH reports to argue that breast-feeding would dramatically reduce infant mortality (Eyler, 1997; Lewis, 1980).

Domestic dirt was clearly a major hazard to infant lives. It was not clear, however, that mothers living in impoverished conditions could do a great deal to improve them. Newman continued to maintain that these conditions resulted largely from working-class ignorance and carelessness in the mismanagement of their environment. As he stated in 1913, infant mortality was 'simply a question of motherhood and ignorance of infant care and management'. By 1916 it had been accepted as a truism by the health service at large that infant mortality was due to the people themselves rather than their surroundings. The concept of maternal inefficiency was further promoted by Karl Pearson, who claimed that inefficient mothers were biologically incapable of child-rearing due to a hereditary low intelligence and what he believed to be other inherited traits such as fecklessness and lack of affection for their offspring (Lewis, 1980).

The main tactics in the mothercraft campaign were the institution of home visiting and inspection and the education of the mother in baby and domestic management. Home visiting for the purposes of education had been conducted by charitable organizations from the mid-nineteenth century. In 1862 the Ladies Sanitary Association of Manchester and Salford had been founded to preach the gospel of public health to the poor. They used public lectures and freely distributed pamphlets and leaflets to proselytize their cause, and also began health missionary work in the slums. Health missionary work spread to other districts throughout England and Wales, and some MOHs capitalized upon it by incorporating the lady helpers into a health department's administration. In Buckinghamshire in the 1880s, the MOH, Dr De'ath, began training his voluntary workers and suggested to the SMOH that a system of certification be introduced (Watkins, 1984). The aims of the early health visitors were to change what were perceived as the inadequate child-rearing practices of poor mothers. The health visitor brought a new philosophy of domestic hygiene and mothercraft which assumed that poor infants died of the neglect and ignorance of their mothers. As a result, health visitors were initially viewed as a police force rather than a resource by poor mothers, who resisted their advice and dreaded their inspections. Understanding between health visitors and mothers increased, however, as the system of health visiting developed. As health visitors replaced theory with experience, they increasingly perceived the obstacles faced by mothers caring for infants in conditions of dire poverty. Much of the advice offered by health visitors could not be followed in such circumstances even if mothers wished to co-operate. Sympathy for the plight of poor mothers on the part of the health-visiting profession was matched by reduced hostility from mothers themselves. Mothers began to value the health visitor as a means of support, not only for the advice she could offer but for the free milk and other baby products to which she could help gain access (Davies, 1988; Marks, 1996).

Apart from the employment of inspectors, other health departments experimented with the idea of milk depots as a means to provide maternal education. The milk depot idea had originated in France, and in England they were used to provide guaranteed clean milk, together with feeding and hygiene instruction for mothers. The depots met with limited success, since the milk they offered was too expensive. In the London borough of St Pancras, another variation on the outreach scheme was implemented in conjunction with the local voluntary effort. The health authority set up a Baby Welcome Clinic in 1907, run by a female physician twice a week. Here babies were weighed and classes on mothercraft were provided, covering everything from home economics and cookery to baby bathing. Extremely low-cost meals were also provided for mothers, a penny-ha'penny each. The Baby Welcome became a kind of mothers' union club (Dwork, 1987).

But such schemes could not operate without the initial contact which was facilitated by the operation of compulsory notification of births. Without this, no scheme could hope to make any real impact on infant mortality. Where it was adopted, there was clear statistical evidence of its effect in reducing mortality rates. From a survey conducted by the Women's Section of the Labour Party in 1935, it was clear that the uptake of services depended heavily upon the promotion given to them by health visitors. This survey, however, also revealed the hostilities which existed between poor mothers and patronizing middle-class health visitors. The reports of health visitors themselves suggested that initial hostilities diminished after they were seen as a resource rather than a policing agency. Letters from mothers to the Women's Co-operative Guild seemed to support this view to some extent. Where Baby Welcomes and infant welfare centres were set up there was generally a positive response among mothers, who enjoyed the club community and other facilities available to them. Nevertheless, the levels of attendance depended upon the location of the centre and its individual character in different localities. Working-class women in Woolwich showed a preference for a centre located in a shabby building in the poorest area rather than an improved facility in a more affluent area. The local MOH discovered that working-class mothers' resistance resulted from them feeling uncomfortable in their poor clothes in front of middle-class mothers. Most successful of all were the attempts to provide some ante-natal and delivery services which helped to reduce the fear of the very common hazards leading to high levels of maternal mortality (Marks, 1996).

The basis of an infant welfare system, therefore, was in place in Britain before the First World War. The advent of war increased the urgency for the need to systematically expand and develop these services. New fears about the necessity for replacing the massive slaughter taking place on the fields of France was the main impetus to reform. The central focus still remained the preservation of infant rather than maternal life. Even when systematic attempts to introduce universal ante-natal care were established in the 1920s, the focus was still the preservation of healthy mothers for the purposes of raising the next generation, more often than not of future cannon-fodder. Despite the mixed motives for establishing a system, state health care for mothers and infants was often created against the desires of the medical profession, who saw the advent of more and more municipal clinics as posing ever greater threats to a major source of their livelihoods, namely sickly children (Marks, 1996). This conflict was further exacerbated through the establishment of a further state medical service for the care of the health of schoolchildren.

By comparison to the complicated issue of infant health, the ill health of schoolchildren seemed relatively straightforward. Infants died of indeterminate causes. Infant diarrhoea was largely the subject of highly speculative reasoning, and competing explanations only served to complicate the options for public health policy. By contrast, the diseases experienced by schoolchildren were well known and understood. Also, they were rarely life-threatening except for the case of diphtheria, which was at least somewhat combatable after the introduction of anti-toxin. Thus the health of the school child seemed to pose a much simpler challenge to the public health authorities (Smith, 1979).

The first major impetus to child welfare reform came after the publication of the *Report of the Physical Deterioration Committee*. The committee showed that general levels of malnourishment were the major cause of physical insufficiency among recruits, especially teenagers. This coincided with new arguments among the medical profession that learning capacity was linked to nutritional status. In a series of articles in the *Manchester Guardian* between April and June 1903 on 'National Physical Training', leading health spokesmen and social reformers argued that teaching and training were impossible among hungry students. Sir George Arthur noted that physical stature was the central concern of public opinion following the Deterioration Report. 'There are many significant indications,' he stated, 'that public opinion is being sharply aroused to the subject of the physical decadence of the English Masses', and he suggested that no one could be taught or trained who was not properly fed. Winston Churchill echoed this sentiment in a later article in the series when he said that 'good food must be the foundation of any system of physical training' (Dwork, 1987).

After the publication of the 1904 Report, the *BMJ* editorialized, 'There can be little doubt that one of the chief causes of this degeneracy amongst young people is to be found in the insufficient food on which it seems to be expected that the hard work of school life should be prefaced.' The *BMJ* suggested that the answer to the dilemma was 'an intelligent employment of the food factor'. This intelligent employment was eventually translated into the practical institution of free school meals. One of the chief advocates of school meals was Sir John Gorst, who was until 1902 the Vice-President of the Committee of the Privy Council on Education. In 1903 he became an Independent MP in the House of Commons, where he campaigned for the plight of impoverished children. 'If a child is not fed,' he wrote in 1903, 'neither must it be taught.' Gorst's argument was that if the state chose to make universal education compulsory then it was obliged to provide sufficient food for students to prevent hunger and educational failure (Smith, 1979).

The Paris communes offered a model for school feeding in a system of school restaurants or canteens which provided free meals. The London School Board attempted to imitate the model of the commune by systematizing the existing voluntary efforts. Thomas Manamara, the Chairman of the London School Board, proposed that the municipal authority institute the French system of school restaurants or canteens. He explained that: 'All of this sounds like socialism – a consideration which doesn't trouble me very much. But as a matter of fact it is in reality first-class imperialism' (Dwork, 1987).

As a measure of first-class imperialism, Parliament in 1906 passed an Education (Provision of Meals) Act which empowered a local education authority to establish canteen committees in all local schools to serve meals daily.

The Act was only permissive and was only slowly taken up by local authorities, but it was made compulsory on the eve of the First World War in 1914. A grant-in-aid system was then created to support the scheme and remove the burden from the local rates (Smith, 1979).

Following the 1907 School Meals Act, a second education bill was introduced establishing a health inspection service for children. The new service was placed under the jurisdiction of local MOHs who appointed medical inspectors and nurses for each district. Frequently, in practice, the local school medical officer was in fact the MOH himself, operating with the assistance of a nursing staff. Inspection was valueless without treatment centres, and thus school clinics were simultaneously instituted. The chief civil servant in charge of the new service as the Medical Officer to the Board of Education, George Newman, believed that school inspection was simply an expansion of the broader public health system (Eyler, 1997). He did not share the view of some school MOs, such as John Kerr at the London County Council Board, that school inspection should be a separate state medical service (Hirst, 1981). Instead, Newman, like Newsholme, believed that there was a need to create a unified health service in which all the different state health functions were co-ordinated and regulated.

By the beginning of the First World War, the health of mothers, infants and children in Britain had been linked in a new system for the provision of health welfare. The model of health service supply established for these groups was to prefigure institutionalization of general health care provision created under the National Health Service in 1948. The development of maternal and child welfare was thus critical to the process which led towards the establishment of a state health service funded by taxation.

WOMEN, CITIZENSHIP, AND THE MATERNALIST STATE

In the early twentieth century, new discourses focused on the influence of human reproduction in the construction of population health. Eugenics offered one among numerous interpretations of the role played by biology in the construction of the social world. There were some interpretations of the relationship between health and behaviour, however, which rejected the concept of the biological basis of social structure. The exponents of a new sociological environmentalism put their faith in nurture rather than nature as the determinant of human development (Porter, 1991a; Armstrong, 1983). Nevertheless, the focus on reproduction promoted social policies which made motherhood more efficient and the life of infants and children more secure.

Maternalist welfare benefited mothers and children as consumers of services. Motherhood and childhood were also used as a political strategy by women to expand their rights, including the right to challenge traditional values about the sexual division of labour (Lewis, 1994). Maternalist welfare offered women increased occupational opportunities which allowed them to professionalize the provision of health and social services as a female speciality (Ladd-Taylor, 1994;

Digby, 1996; Koven and Michel (eds), 1993). Women acted as either paid or unpaid providers of welfare in both state and voluntary social services (Lewis, 1996; Ladd-Taylor, 1994). In Britain they were employed as health visitors, nurses, housing managers, doctors and, increasingly, MOHs and assistant MOHs. Within the hierarchy of the public health service female doctors fought a long battle to gain equality. Fully qualified medical women were often employed by male MOHs as sanitary inspectors and given special responsibility for the maternal and infant welfare services. Men employed as sanitary inspectors were often qualified only with a Royal Sanitary Institute Certificate. Female doctors did slowly begin to gain appointments as assistant MOHs and MOHs through the inter-war and post-war years, but did not start to gain parity within the public health service until the last quarter of the century (Watkins, 1984; Porter, 1991b). Although formal routes to equal opportunity were blocked, women found various routes to participation in the political sphere and in social policy formation and administration.

Italian feminists used motherhood as a strategy in their battle to obtain political equality and full citizenship for women. Women such as Paolina Schiff who led the *Unione Femminile Nazionale* (National Women's Union) based women's claim to citizenship upon their role as the bearers and nurturers of future citizens. After the unification of Italy a group of women from Lombardy identifying themselves as 'Cittadine Italiane' petitioned Parliament for political emancipation on the grounds that child-rearing was largely a female responsibility whose civic importance should receive constitutional recognition. The *Unione Femminile Nazionale* campaigned for maternity benefits for working mothers by identifying the social value of motherhood as an occupation which the entire nation depended upon for its survival. Maternity funds had been set up by mutual aid societies of women workers from the 1890s in Italy, to provide insurance which would cover absence from work or cessation from work during confinement and the months immediately following. The battle to get a partnership between employers, the state and employees in a national maternity fund succeeded in getting a law passed in 1912. The operation of the National Fund was flawed, inasmuch as it left the responsibility of administering it to employers and it did not prevent women who did not return to work after the minimum period from losing their benefits (Buttafuoco, 1991).

The expanded employment of women during the First World War greatly increased the numbers of women who came under the law, but less than half the women eligible for insurance actually registered for it. Following the war, the campaigns for maternal welfare expanded, including proposals to obtain payment for housework from the state. Feminists such as Laura Casartelli believed that state remuneration for maternal labour would acknowledge the financial value of women as household managers, housewives, spouses and mothers. Feminist and other social reform movements were of course abandoned and closed down once the Fascist regime succeeded to power. The *Unione* was finally banned in 1938 on the grounds that independent insurance was no longer needed, since the state now provided for all social security (Saraceno, 1991).

In Sweden, women within the Social Democratic Party also argued for maternity insurance to support women during a period of leave from work which had been made statutory in 1900. The Labour Protection Law of 1900 gave women a statutory right to leave from industrial labour for four weeks after giving birth, but did not provide any financial assistance to support her, on the assumption that she would be provided for by her husband. Social Democratic women campaigned for maternity insurance on the grounds that poor families could not support themselves on one income and that the law ignored the needs of single mothers. The radical campaign of the Social Democratic women highlighted the plight not only of widows but also of women abandoned by male partners. Both categories of women became solely responsible for the financial support of their families. At the 1905 Social Democratic Party conference, delegates Emma Danielsson and Anna Sterky proposed that men who abandoned women carrying their children were equivalent to strike-breakers who had double-crossed their comrades. In their support for single mothers, Social Democratic women expressed a radical revision of the concept of marriage and family, seeking to gain state financial support for maternity without marriage. In 1908, Ruth Gustafsson, one of the first Social Democratic Members of Parliament, called for 'free marriage' and 'conscious marriage' in order to revise the marriage laws which put women under the tutelage of their husbands (Ohlander, 1991).

The initial maternity insurance laws passed in 1908 were heavily criticized by Social Democratic women as inadequate. They argued that financial assistance should be universally available to all classes regardless of marital status, and should be paid until the child was old enough to care for itself. Childbearing and child-rearing should thus be considered by the state in the same terms as extra-domestic employment. Such a law was eventually passed in Sweden in 1931, although the general interests of the Social Democratic Party had changed focus by that time. Specific concern with maternity had been replaced by a broader agenda on family policy as a whole. This was influenced by new discourses on population quality stimulated by the work of the famous Swedish sociologists Alva and Gunnar Myrdal (Ohlander, 1991).

In Britain, campaigns for women's political rights had been located within broader public debates from the 1870s, about the legal rights and obligations which bound citizen, state and society together. Throughout Europe in the years leading up to the Second World War, the role of states and the definitions of citizenship were being dramatically renegotiated, and at a rapid speed. In Britain, feminist campaigns used the role of women as mothers and housewives to demand equal political rights for female citizenship, which included not only the vote but the rights to social security. Women in political associations in Britain, such as the Women's Labour League, argued that a male-dominated state ignored the social deprivation experienced by women and children. They argued that a vital political role for women lay in placing the values of women at the centre of the state's concern to serve the needs of all its citizens (Lewis, 1983).

Women claimed special expertise in the management of social welfare from their experience gained in voluntary and charitable organizations from the mid-nineteenth century (Lewis, 1996a). They continued to provide maternal and infant welfare through either waged or voluntary labour in both voluntary and state organizations. Women's groups, such as the Women's Labour League and the Women's Co-operative Guild, provided independent baby clinics which offered ante-natal and infant-care advice and access to medical assistance for poor women. Independent baby clinics were often preferred by poor women over the local authority welfare clinics because of the greater range of services offered, which often included free milk and food for pregnant and nursing mothers and their children, along with free medical treatment. Some of these facilities were sometimes so popular that they were envied by middle-class women. By the First World War, 154 towns in England and Wales employed 600 health visitors, either voluntary or salaried, and meals for pregnant and nursing mothers were available in 27 towns. By the late 1930s the number of health visitors had risen to over 5,000, and 409 welfare authorities supplied either free or low-cost milk to pregnant mothers. Some authorities also provided cheap meals and home helps to assist pregnant women with heavy housework. There were, by this time, over 3,000 welfare centres for mothers and babies (Marks, 1996).

In the inter-war years, Labour women in Britain increased their campaign to improve maternity and child welfare services. In 1917, new state funding was provided for midwifery and ante-natal care in an attempt to reduce the continued high levels of deaths in childbirth. Despite new legislation, maternity and ante-natal services remained grossly inadequate in some poor areas, such as Rochdale and the Rhondda Valley. As a result, the maternal mortality rate rose by 22 per cent between 1923 and 1933. A new Midwives Act in 1936 compelled all local authorities to provide salaried qualified midwives to meet the needs of their communities. Maternal mortality, however, did not begin to decline until the introduction of sulphonamide drugs in 1935, which reduced death from puerperal infection (Loudon, 1992). The Maternity and Child Welfare Act in 1918 enabled local authorities to create Maternity and Child Welfare Committees, which would include at least two women. These were to receive government subsidy, with the rest of the funding being raised from local taxes. The Committees could provide a range of activities, from hospital services for children under five to maternity hospitals, home helps, food for expectant mothers and children under five, and crèches for the infants of widowed or single mothers at work. From 1919 government subsidies were also available for voluntary agencies providing similar services. Labour women campaigned throughout the inter-war years to press for the implementation of this legislation by local authorities (Digby, 1996). Although services were seriously cut back during the years of the Depression, provision was greatly increased between 1918 and 1939. During the 1930s, however, women in Britain and elsewhere in Europe contextualized the campaign for women's social security rights within a

broader ideological debate about demography and the politics of family structure.

THE BIRTH RATE AND FAMILY POLICY

By the inter-war years debates surrounding human reproduction and population
quality had broadened. One strand of eugenics in Europe and the United States
now revised views on the class structure of the population, believing that a level
playing-field was necessary in order for talent to thrive. Improvement of the
social environment was promoted by eugenists who advocated welfare reform,
claiming that it was crucial if a society of equal opportunity was to allow eugenic
forces to flourish. For example, Julian Huxley agreed with his contemporary,
leading British nutritionist Sir John Boyd Orr, that the diet of the working classes
was completely inadequate. Other environmental obstacles to progress were the
existing patterns of sedentary lifestyles among the middle classes and unequal
educational opportunities throughout society. Eugenic planning of human reproduction in an equalized environment could, Huxley claimed, raise the average
IQ of a population by 1.5 per cent, resulting in a 50 per cent increase of individuals with IQs of over 160 (Macnicol, 1989; Freeden, 1979; Paul, 1984).

Pronatalist arguments supported the development of family policies in
Sweden during the 1930s. The work of the Myrdals highlighted the importance
of demographic decline and the need to encourage fertility. This had a major
impact, for example, on the question of abortion. In 1935, the Swedish Minister
for Justice drafted a bill to allow abortion for social reasons which was forcefully
supported by the women of the Social Democratic Association (SDA). The surge
of pronatalism, however, resisted such reform, and instead the Swedish government set up a Population Commission in 1935 to investigate ways in which to
facilitate demographic increase. As a result, a range of new policies were introduced to encourage Swedish couples to produce large families, which included
marriage loans, maternity benefit and a bonus, a 'motherhood penny', paid to all
childbearing mothers. State housing was provided for 'child-abundant' families
and a new law made it illegal for employers to dismiss a woman on the grounds
that she was pregnant. In 1945 Sweden introduced universal state child
allowances (Ohlander, 1991).

Opposition to pronatalist policies stimulated an ideological shift among Social
Democratic women who now saw the state as reinforcing a view of women as
child-producing machines. Although they welcomed the fact that the new state
benefits were paid directly to women, enhancing their financial independence
within the family structure, women in the SDA saw pronatalism as turning childbearing into women's primary social duty. Pronatalism had elevated the needs of
society above the personal needs of the individual. By contrast, they asserted that
citizenship must be about the right to decide, especially about questions of
reproduction (Ohlander, 1991).

Pronatalism was supported in Britain by the arguments of demographers such as Enid Charles and David Glass, which helped to legitimate the establishment of family allowances. Glass brought attention to the changing age structure of the population. The Eugenics Society commissioned Glass to study *The Struggle for Population* in 1936. In it, he argued that the transformation of the demographic structure from a pyramid to a shape which resembled the lower half of an hour-glass resulted in a less and less productive population supporting more and more ageing unproductive dependants. Glass advocated the introduction of family allowances and tax relief to encourage large families among both the working and the middle classes in order to check these population trends. He also believed that the changing social role of women meant that large families could not be encouraged without the state provision of full crèche facilities and additional systems of childcare support (Glass, 1936).

Certainly family allowance extended the concept of the 'endowment of motherhood' which, on the one hand, had been used to justify the idea that women should be given the choice to work outside the home. On the other hand, the 'endowment of motherhood' was accused by some feminists as elevating 'home-making' as a woman's highest duty. Debates raged in the 1930s in Britain between and within political parties, women's groups and the trade union movement about the value of family allowance (Thane, 1991; Macnicol, 1980). The chief promoter of family allowances, Eleanor Rathbone, who led the Family Endowment Society which included members such as William Beveridge, proposed a scheme which made family allowances the responsibility of employers. She claimed it would facilitate the creation of equal wages because men would no longer be able to argue that they needed higher wages to support a family. Rathbone also believed that family allowances provided payment for what had been previously unpaid labour: homemaking and child-rearing. Women in the Labour movement insisted, alternatively, that family allowances should be paid for by the state, from taxation (Pederson, 1993). Labour women and the Women's Co-operative Guild (WCG) fiercely argued for payments to be made directly to women in order to enhance their financial independence within the family. The WCG had vehemently opposed the way in which national insurance covered only waged manual workers, leaving out their wives and children and the unemployed (Thane, 1991).

Pensions for widows and mothers with incapacitated husbands received a consensus of support following the First World War and were vigorously campaigned for by the National Union for Equal Citizenship. After 1918, the women's vote made politicians in all parties more sympathetic to such issues. The extension of such schemes into universal family allowances, however, was opposed by some trade unions. These saw non-contributory universal state benefits as a threat to the wage-bargaining power of employees, and they were concerned that if family needs were increasingly met by the state then this would be a disincentive for workers to join unions. Members of the Conservative Party, who agreed with this point of view, supported the development of state welfare. The idea that welfare was a more economical way of meeting need rather than high wages was also supported by the Macmillan Committee on Finance and

Industry, set up in 1929 and used by coal-mine owners to justify the long lock-out of workers between 1926 and 1927. By 1930, however, there was an opinion among some members of the Trades Union Council (TUC), notably the mining union, that state family allowances could enhance trade union bargaining power by providing a family income during strikes. Although the TUC refused to endorse family allowances at their congress in 1930, they gave the idea increasing support towards the end of the decade (Thane 1991; Stewart, 1996).

Support for family allowances in Britain was not simply limited to questions of the gendered division of labour and income. The 'endowment of mother-hood' had always been justified by concern for the health of offspring, and this became even further emphasized in the inter-war years. The eugenic overtones of the demographic debate continued to emphasize the role of children in the building of national futures. This was supported by the new science of nutrition, which examined the effects of food upon health and growth. These ideas were taken into account within the British Labour Party, which increasingly separated out women's issues from those which affected children in the development of social policies (Stewart, 1996).

In France, the combination of pronatalism, social Catholicism and employer perceptions of the advantages of voluntary assistance established a system of family allowances for workers in the 1930s. These were provided by employers on an individual voluntary basis and distributed differentially to male wage workers according to the size of their families. The first *caisses de compensation* were established by employers such as Emile Romanet, the devout Roman Catholic managing director of the Grenoble engineering firm of Régis Joya. Social Catholics like Romanet viewed the *caisse* as a religious and social duty of indus-trialists and employers to contribute to the regeneration of French society. Another devout Catholic, the textile manufacturer Louis Deschamps, set up the *Caisse Patronale de Sursalire Familial* among his fellow textile employers in Rouen in 1919 (Pederson, 1993). The motives of these social Catholics echoed those of nineteenth-century health reformers such as Villermé who believed that employers should take responsibility for sanitary reform and thereby encourage the remoralization of the poor.

Other employers in different industries began to follow the Romanet–Deschamps example, but were influenced less by the motives of social Catholicism than current anxieties about demographic decline. Employers iden-tified their schemes as a sacrifice made in the name of patriotism, but they also perceived direct advantages it gave them in relations with their labour forces. Family allowances allowed employers to stabilize wage costs by providing a disin-centive to industrial action for wage increases. The cost could be contained, since there were fewer employees with large families than single men. Worker solidarity would be fragile in times of proposed strikes, when wives urged married men and fathers to go into work in order not to lose benefits as well as wages. For the same reasons, wives would also put pressure on husbands not to take time off unnecessarily. French employers believed that a family policy would improve attendance, keep wages low and reduce workers' negotiating power.

French employers fiercely resisted attempts to institute state allowances, however. They justified their position on the grounds that the state bureaucracy would only make the scheme more costly, and which they would be asked to finance. Social Catholics, on the other hand, increasingly perceived the need for state intervention, realizing that employer-led family allowance was an institution which they could support but not control (Pederson, 1993).

Family allowances were gradually adopted in a variety of European states under different state and voluntary schemes during the 1930s and 1940s. The debate on health, the quality of population and family values, however, extended beyond the realm of welfare policy and into the social conventions which governed family life as a whole. One of these areas was birth control. As noted above, while some birth control campaigners supported their demands with eugenic arguments, other eugenists were extremely apprehensive. Some birth control sympathizers, such as the founder of population genetics in the United States, Raymond Pearl, supported birth control on both libertarian and eugenic grounds (Allan, 1991). Some feminists in Britain and Sweden separated the rights of women to control their own fertility and eugenic concerns about racial improvement. The SDA in Sweden included birth control among their demands for the state to support female independence. Women within the British Labour Party campaigned for women's rights to limit their own families (Hoggart, 1996).

As we saw above, Swedish feminists wanted to use welfare rights to redefine conventional views of marriage. In Britain, eugenic concern about racial purity and breeding powerful stock led to radical discussions among intellectuals which also challenged the existing social mores of marriage. British eugenists began to speculate that monogamy might become redundant as a social institution. They began to experiment with ideas about the eugenic value of polygamy and polyandry. Some British eugenists enthusiastically encouraged women to choose their partners eugenically. Others, such as Anthony Ludovici – author of *The Future of Woman* (1936) – and his reviewer, R. Austin Freeman, heavily criticized the dysgenic effects of contemporary ideas about female emancipation which allowed women to reject their 'natural' and necessary responsibilities of breeding and raising offspring. In 1933, Ludovici instituted an even more radical discussion within the Eugenics Society about the eugenic value of consanguineous marriages and the desirability of removing the social and legal barriers against incest. In a paper read before the Society in July, he argued that inbreeding in animals produced superior stock and was a model for positive eugenics in the human population. Consanguineous marriage in earlier societies had produced superior racial strains such as the Ptolemaic dynasties. The biological arguments against consanguinity were based on the harmful effects of inbreeding in tainted streams. Much more clearly harmful, however, Ludovici claimed, were the mental and moral problems which arose from miscegenation. Random breeding destroyed mental harmony by combining in one individual conflicting emotional reflexes. Outbreeding led to biological and psychological disharmony. The laws against incest were superstitious custom and their removal would allow the biological and sociological benefits of consanguinity to flourish in future super-breeds. While few inter-war eugenists agreed with Ludovici about consanguinity, many, such as the British geneticist and professor of social medicine at Edinburgh University, Francis Crew, and Raymond Pearl, believed that marriage conventions and the stigma surrounding birth control needed to be radically revised. Crew thought that the rigidity of the divorce laws in Britain was a substantial barrier to both eugenic procreation and human happiness in general.

Eugenism influenced the development of social medicine in the inter-war years. Francis Crew suggested that health was determined by man's function as a member of an ecological system. Health was the product of the evolutionary relationship between the biology of the species and its adaptability to its environment. Human society moulded its environment to a considerable extent, and therefore health depended upon the social actions taken to provide the optimum conditions for human development. Crew believed the most important of these was increased economic standards of living as well as the kind of sanitary control of the environment which prevented infectious disease. Equally, however, human health depended upon the widest distribution of genetic variety among the population, and therefore social medicine had to address the question of the way in which this was reflected in the demographic structure of a population and the social institutions which determined human reproduction. Furthermore, in a society in which the threat of infectious disease to human betterment had been largely conquered, the hereditary basis to population health was crucial (Porter, forthcoming).

Crew argued that planning population health had to begin with the demographic structure of a society. In Western Europe, falling birth rates and increased life expectancy presented new obstacles to maintaining biologically healthy and economically viable social systems. Ideological and social policy reform needed to address this question, such as the elimination of stigma about and the provision of care for illegitimate births. Crew believed that the state should provide economic security for unmarried mothers and that they and married mothers should have equal access to state childcare facilities to enable them to pursue their own economic efficiency and vocational skills. Ideas about the structure of the family needed to change as social values regarding sexual and economic relations changed, including increased levels of divorce. Above all, the state needed to provide economic and social support which encouraged the production of large numbers of offspring and ensured their economic security. The study of the hereditary basis to health and the identification of the social actions necessary to enhance it were critical to social medicine.

By the inter-war years new debates concerning the social relations of human reproduction and the quality and quantity of population pointed towards new directions in social policy, preventive medicine and the revision of social mores and conventions about family structure and social function. All of these issues were influential in another context within Europe, but were also contextualized within a political culture which sought unique solutions to improving racial breeding and preventing degeneration.

BARBARISM AND THE CIVILIZING PROCESS

Demographic change and declining birth rates were an international concern by the inter-war years. From the end of the First World War race hygienists in Germany believed it was critical to 'Aryan' strength and survival. When the National Socialists came to power, they attempted to correct this trend with a range of powerful pronatalist policies all aimed at removing women from the work-place into the home, making maternity the prime female function and paternity their civic duty. Modern trends of education and employment outside the home for women were perceived by leading Nazis as seriously undermining racial strength, and social policies were devised to find a 'solution to the woman question'. These included banning women from academic and other professional work, and making it either illegal or extremely difficult for them to become lawyers, judges or doctors (Proctor, 1988).

Racial hygienists believed that the average healthy woman could easily bear about fifteen children during her lifetime, and developed policies to encourage women to believe that this was their social obligation and to encourage men to assist them. Government loans equivalent to one year's salary were offered to men whose wives agreed to give up working outside the home, and for every child born the amount owing on the loan was reduced by a quarter. In 1938, Hitler established the Honour Cross of German Motherhood, awarded in bronze for four children, silver for six and gold for eight. In 1938, male public officials were sacked if they did not marry and anyone without a child within the first five years of marriage received a penalty tax. Mass marriages of SS and SA officials took place even before the Nazi seizure of power. New laws were passed to allow single Aryan women to become mothers. Special orphanages were set up to adopt and raise these children, especially the illegitimate children of SS officers. Abortion of German children was identified as an act of race treason against the 'bodily fruit of the German *Volk*' and could be punishable by death. Selective abortion was available if the mother's life was in danger or, of course, on eugenic grounds (Bock, 1991; Bock, 1997; Proctor, 1988).

The effect of these laws was to promote considerable rises in the birth rate, but this was accompanied by an equal rise in the number of women in paid employment. As the Nazi war machine removed more and more men from industrial jobs into the military, women, with or without children, were increasingly employed to keep Germany's manufacturing going. Despite the Nazi loathing of females taking up careers such as medicine, the number of women practising medicine greatly increased between 1933 and 1945. This resulted from a large shortfall of physicians as Jewish doctors were removed from the profession and others were recruited into the military and state medical service (Proctor, 1988).

While demographic anxieties led to the development of radical family policies to increase the birth rate of those whom the Third Reich identified as desirable, they led to a much more dramatic radicalization of policies to prevent the reproduction of those whom they deemed unfit. Fears of biological degeneration grew in the years of social and economic crisis in Germany following the First World War. Throughout the period of the Weimar Republic, preventive medicine, along with other forms of social amelioration, was indicted by race hygienists for having saved the weakly with the robust and allowed the unfit to survive, breed and burden the biologically vigorous. Policies for countering medicine's interference in the process of natural selection were explored even during the period of the war itself. Inmates of psychiatric hospitals were either starved to death or medically killed and after the war experimental sterilization was secretly practised on selected poor women. The best method of eugenic intervention to annihilate and prevent 'lives not worth living' was prominently debated within Germany from 1920, and resulted in the Prussian Health Council drafting a sterilization bill in 1932 which was never enacted. By this time, Nazi views on compulsory sterilization were well known, but ideas of eugenic intervention were widely shared by many groups, including representatives of the medical and psychiatric professions. Weimar's Expert Advisory Committee on Population and Race Policy drew upon a broad consensus in its support for the imminent sterilization law (Weindling, 1990).

Racial hygiene was a science that originated in nineteenth-century Germany as Darwinian theories of evolution and the new sciences of heredity began to influence German medicine and biology. Leading German social Darwinists, such as Wilhelm Schallmayer and Alfred Ploetz, popularized the idea that the struggle for existence needed to be maintained if evolutionary improvement was to continue. They feared that Social Democratic movements placed an obstacle to racial improvement. In 1895 Ploetz published a founding document of what came to be identified in Germany as 'racial hygiene'. Ploetz warned of the effects of counterselection brought about by improved medical care for the weak and social amelioration helping the unfit to survive. Racial hygiene would consider the health, not only of individuals, but of the race as a whole. War often destroyed the best germ plasm. Poor relief should only be provided to those past childbearing age and breeding among the very young and very old should be discouraged. Most of all, medical care for the weakly should be discouraged so that they did not survive to reproduce. In 1904 Ploetz founded the *Journal of Racial and Social Biology*, and together with a group of similarly minded intellectuals set up a Society for Racial Hygiene in 1905. The German Racial Hygiene movement promoted selective breeding to encourage the reproduction of the fit and a host of measures to counter 'counterselection', such as sterilization (Weindling, 1989).

Darwinian theories of evolution in Germany were also incorporated into another branch of social biology which identified itself with, rather than against, preventive medicine. This was a theory of social hygiene which was developed by a physician who was also trained in the social sciences, Alfred Grotjahn. Grotjahn believed that social hygiene should be an interdisciplinary science which used the social, economic and eugenic analysis of what he called 'social pathology' for its prevention. He rejected the term 'social medicine', since it had become associated with social insurance in Bismarck's Germany. Public hygiene in the nineteenth century had used the physical and biological sciences to understand the noxious environmental factors which affect health. Social hygiene should analyse the effects of social conditions upon health and mortality in order to plan qualitative and quantitative population growth. Grotjahn wanted social hygiene to be included in the training of physicians, who should become pivotal in educating patients, society and governments in planning future social organization (Weindling, 1989).

Social hygiene provided a rationale for the professionalization of health and welfare. From the 1890s, Prussian initiatives were developed in infant and child health along with a new focus on the prevention of chronic diseases. These initiatives were always restrained by the finance ministry, however, which left a space for voluntary agencies, dominated by physicians, aristocrats and senior civil servants, to develop dispensaries, *Fürsorgestellen*. The *Fürsorgestellen* not only promoted infant welfare but also attempted to combat what they perceived as 'racial' poisons such as alcoholism, tuberculosis and venereal diseases. These agencies were centralized by the Prussian ministry during the First World War, which developed wide-ranging health and population reforms administered through an inter-ministerial council. State health offices were set up and services were combined into integrated health centres. After the war, the Weimar Republic made social welfare a formal branch of government which was realized in the creation of a comprehensive welfare state. Eugenic ideology, however, provided a rationale for medical intervention in a wide range of welfare services and was employed by both left- and right-wing public health professionals and reformers. While its use by the left and the right may not have been identical, both nevertheless shared a common view of the need for planned interventions into human reproduction. Thus, while radical social hygiene reformers promoted the use of the public health system to provide primary health care linked to birth control, welfare services and education, this was set within a consistently nationalistic and racial context. German social hygiene up to the end of the Weimar Republic did make significant innovations in the amalgamation of medicine and the social sciences. These innovations were achieved, however, within the context of promoting the science of racial hygiene. The focus on eugenic and racial issues in Weimar social hygiene had an impact upon the subsequent Nazification of public health after 1933 (Weindling, 1989; Weindling, 1990).

The Nazis turned racial hygiene into a central political agenda. Doctors and others who enthusiastically supported sterilization before 1933 testified to the fact that it was only Hitler's rise to power which allowed them to make their dreams come true. In 1933 the National Socialist regime declared that life, marriage and the family in Germany were, from now on, to be controlled by the state in order to prevent the generation of hereditarily diseased offspring. Three laws were passed in 1935 to put state racial policy into practice: the Sterilization Law, the Blood Protection Law and the Marital Law. The Blood Protection Law made sexual intercourse between non-Jewish Germans and Jews, gypsies or people from other 'alien races' illegal. The Marital Law made marriage between these categories illegal and the marriage between eugenically undesirable Germans with 'hereditarily healthy Germans' illegal. The compulsory sterilization law aimed to prevent 'worthless life' by preventing the eugenically undesirable from breeding. It operated through a system of courts, each of which consisted of three judges made up of two doctors and a lawyer. Physicians were obliged to identify candidates for sterilization among their patients, who would then be examined by the courts and sent for sterilization. By 1945, approximately half a million people in Germany and its annexed territories were sterilized under this law (Bock, 1997; Proctor, 1988).

By 1939, the Third Reich had shifted its goals, not simply to prevent 'worthless life' but to annihilate it through what was euphemistically referred to as 'euthanasia'. The policy of euthanasia eliminated approximately 200,000 inmates of psychiatric hospitals and other institutions by the end of the war. Killing the ill subsequently became interlinked with a policy of genocide of the Jews which reached the level of approximately 6 million murders (Bock, 1997; Proctor, 1988).

As we have seen, family policy to encourage population growth and sterilization as a form of either voluntary or compulsory birth control was established in numerous societies during the inter-war years. How the *prevention* of 'lives not worth living' transmuted into the *annihilation* of 'worthless lives' in Germany is the subject of wide historiographical debate. Perhaps the most chilling feature to explain is that these policies were pursued as the most rational route to the political goal of modernizing the German economy and society. The eugenic and ethnic racism enacted under the Third Reich can be seen, therefore, to reflect the ambivalence of the twentieth-century conceptualization of modernity. A modernizing process dedicated to human improvement may, in the process, contribute to human destruction. It is what was referred to by Norbert Elias, a Jewish intellectual who lived in occupied France, as the potential of the civilizing process for creating barbarism (Bock, 1997).

ENGINEERING THE FUTURE

The revelations of mass murder under the Third Reich temporarily undermined the authority of eugenics. General increases in demographic growth and the imagined 'population boom' following the Second World War also reduced the appeal of pronatalism. A revolution in values surrounding the social relations of sexuality and gender in the 1960s resulted in a liberalization of laws concerning human reproduction which allowed women much greater control of their own fertility. Birth control became universally available, abortion was legalized and fertility treatment for those with difficulty conceiving became more easily available. After the Second World War genetic science, which had attempted to intellectually distance itself from eugenism since the 1920s, continued to pursue a theoretical and experimental analysis of the molecular basis to organic life. Following the discovery of DNA in 1953, genetics and molecular biology concentrated on the analysis of the genetic component to various diseases. The human genome project begun in the 1970s has, however, reawakened interest in the biological analysis of human behaviour. Sensational claims have been made by some genetic scientists who suggest they have discovered the genetic origin of homosexuality, aggression and other behaviours and emotions. Whatever these behaviours might consist of, their determinants remain highly disputed between the natural and the social sciences, and indeed by religious, political and other public moralists. The politics of molecular biology is the focus of some of the most fierce ideological conflicts in late twentieth-century society. The new techniques of analysis and manipulation of the genetic basis to organic life promise to make these conflicts continue to dominate cultural discourses of, and about, the foreseeable future.

11 Health and the rise of the classic welfare state

From the end of the nineteenth century, changes in the economic and social structures of industrial and industrializing societies were shadowed by ideological shifts. These changes resulted in a renegotiation of the relationship between the state and civil society which had significant implications for the meaning of citizenship in modern societies. The relationship between the state and its citizens was intensely contested in the question of social security provision. Various attempts have been made to explain why modern systems of welfare began to emerge during the last two decades of the nineteenth century. One popular argument has suggested that social welfare is the outcome of the 'logic of industrialization'. When industrialization moved families from the land to the city, networks of mutual aid became redundant as wage-earning employment required a nuclear, more isolated and anonymous family to be socially and geographically mobile. The social dislocations experienced by families as the result of industrialization left them unable to cope with the effects of disabling accidents at work, major episodes of illness, periods of unemployment, or dependent elderly or physically or mentally compromised relatives who were unable to work. Nation-states responded by creating policies to provide social security to meet these needs without forcing respectable citizens to accept aid under the demeaning and disenfranchizing rules of traditional poor laws (Fraser, 1973). The 'logic of industrialization', however, does not explain why societies at very different stages of development, such as between Sweden and Britain, developed similar systems of social security at the same time (Weir *et al.* (eds), 1988).

Some analysts have attempted to modify the industrialization thesis with explanations about the influence of national cultures upon the development of welfare systems. So, for example, the development of social security legislation in Bismarck's Germany was facilitated by the weakness of liberalism, the strength of a patriarchal social ideal and the influence of the Christian social ethic in the late nineteenth century. By contrast, in the United States the dominance of liberal individualism and the commitment to self-help led to tenacious resistance to social protection. However, this does not explain why Britain rapidly established public social assistance by 1920, even though it too had been dominated by laissez-faire values up to the end of the nineteenth century (Gilbert, 1966).

The ideological transformations within liberalism in Britain which led to the collectivist values of 'new liberalism' also developed within American liberalism during the same period. In Britain and America sufficient cultural transformations occurred within liberalism to legitimate support for social welfare. The Progressives, however, did not manage to institute a social insurance programme in the United States until 1935. Also, the social security legislation passed in that year left out health insurance and created a patchy system with uneven standards administered by state and local governments in the United States which contrasted sharply with the centrally administered system created in Britain (Weir *et al.* (eds), 1988).

Yet further explanations for the rise of the welfare state have highlighted the importance of the changing relations of class in industrial societies. This argument has suggested that, where the power of largely homogeneous working classes grew on the basis of organized solidarity, as perhaps in Germany or Britain, states responded to the demand for social security as a means of preventing social upheaval. In the United States a divided and ethnically fragmented working class allowed industrial capitalists to resist the development of social protection. Ideological splits among the French working class hindered political mobilization and slowed the pace of social security development. It is difficult to demonstrate, however, decisive links between class conflict and the development of welfare policies. The expansion of working-class political representation brought new influences, such as collectivist liberalism and socialism, into the governing systems of modern societies, but that fails to account for continuities and contrasts between welfare structures in different national contexts (Weir *et al.* (eds), 1988).

Finally, some political scientists have suggested that welfare policy has arisen historically in its various forms as the result of different patterns of state formation in industrial societies (Skocpol, 1985). The strength or weakness of modern political states can be measured in the extent to which government machinery consists of a coherent apparatus of bureaucratic institutions that can act with a degree of autonomy. To this extent the state is identified as an institutional political process which enacts policy that rationalizes political and class struggles. In this context welfare is understood as a form of rational policy-making achieved to an increasing or lesser degree by states that have a greater or lesser degree of political autonomy from the influence of the most powerful interests groups in civil society (Skocpol, 1985).

Whatever its determinants, social welfare provision contributed to redefining the boundaries of the state and the political meaning of citizenship in modern societies (Esping-Anderson, 1997; Culpitt, 1992; Vogel and Moran, 1991). State intervention in the delivery of health services and medical care played a significant role within these broad social changes. Here we continue to examine the renegotiation of health citizenship in the twentieth century by comparing the changing structure of health care provision during a period in the twentieth century which has been identified by some historians as witnessing the initial foundation of the 'classic welfare state'.

COLLECTIVISM AND AN ORGANIC SOCIETY

At the beginning of the twentieth century, modern states had little involvement
with the delivery and organization of medical care. In France and Britain
medical care was purchased either through private practice or through voluntary
insurance funds organized through mutual aid societies and friendly societies. In
Sweden, although the state had a long involvement in hospital provision, voluntary health insurance provided by the guild system in the eighteenth century was
continued by industrial workers' organizations in the late nineteenth century. In
the United States medical care was financed through private practice, hospitals
run for profit and voluntary organizations (Hollingsworth *et al.*, 1990). In
Germany models of private medicine, voluntaristic and charitable health care
provision were challenged, however, by a new philosophy of state intervention in
the 1880s. In Germany in the 1880s statutory social security against the misfortunes created by sickness, disability, old age and unemployment was established
and it subsequently influenced industrial societies throughout the twentieth
century (Hennock, 1987).

The first initiatives in German social insurance were designed to arbitrate the
disputes between employers and employees about liability for industrial injury
(Milles, 1990). From the early nineteenth century various European states introduced legislation to regulate the health and safety conditions of factory work. In
Britain the Earl of Shaftesbury had pioneered the statutory regulation of child
labour and adult working hours in the industrial production process. The
Prussian state also introduced legal protection for child factory labour in 1839.
Both Britain and Prussia developed systems of factory inspection although it
remained ineffective in the German context until it was made compulsory and
was universally applied after the unification of the German states in 1871
(Weindling, 1994). Factory inspection in Britain was aimed at the regulation of
safety standards in order to reduce the hazards to life and health inherent in the
industrial production processes and was, in principle, preventive. Nevertheless,
legal battles between employers and employees over liability for industrial injury
escalated. Laws to regulate the terms of employer liability were introduced in
Germany and Britain in the 1870s. In 1884, Reich Chancellor Otto von
Bismarck created compulsory accident insurance. The law compelled employers
to form trade associations which would settle compensation claims. The inadequacies of the workmen's compensation laws to cover needs created by the
disabling effects of sickness led the German Reich to consider the more comprehensive measure of health insurance. Compulsory health insurance for industrial
workers was established under the Health Insurance Law of 1883 and state
support for old age and disability was established by a further statute in 1889.
Together this legislation allowed Bismarck to create a model of social insurance
which became highly influential throughout the industrializing European
community. The rationale underlying the Bismarckian policy was the prevention
of a socialist challenge to the authority of the state by the industrial proletariat.
For this reason the representatives of organized labour were highly suspicious

and saw state social security as a means of 'buying off' the impetus for a prole-tarian revolution (Hennock, 1987).

German health insurance, established in 1883, was compulsory and financed by one-third contributions from employers and two-thirds contributions from employees. Funds were collected and distributed by local compulsory health organizations, *Krankenkassen*, or through trade health insurance organizations. Independent health insurance, organized by trade unions, *freie Hilfskassen*, had been legalized since 1876 and were allowed to continue as an alternative form of compulsory health insurance after 1883. The *freie Hilfskassen* allowed a degree of self-managed health insurance by labour (Hennock, 1987; Mommsen and Mock (eds), 1981). The health insurance law set up the principles of health security which have continued in Germany up to the present day. From 1883 health insurance in Germany has been compulsory, premiums are paid as advance concessions, members have a legal claim to services without a means test and rates are dependent upon levels of gross income and not upon risk factors such as the age or medical history of an individual. A health certificate was not required in order to join a health insurance organization and the services used did not have to be paid back. Employers have continued to be compelled to pay towards the premium for each worker (Altenstetter, 1982; Lawson, 1996).

The services provided by the *Krankenkassen* were largely cash benefits to workers unable to work when they were sick, money paid to families of insured workers when they died, and maternity support for female workers. Under the law, material support included free medical treatment and medicines, and free medical aids such as glasses and surgical supports. Although the main aim of the health insurance law was to prevent destitution in times of sickness through the payment of 'sick money', health insurance organizations were compelled to provide medical services. These largely consisted of employing doctors to sign certificates of sickness to qualify claimants for benefit. Until the end of the nine-teenth century, medical treatment was infrequently provided. However, as the number of insured patients rose and the medical labour market flooded with rising numbers of recruits, doctors increasingly found themselves competing for *Krankenkassen* work. Small *Krankenkassen* usually employed only one doctor; larger organizations employed several. Employment contracts were determined by the health organizations who dictated the extent and type of medical treatment for which they would pay. Contracted doctors were salaried and unable to set indi-vidual fees. Increasingly forced into health organization employment, the German medical profession began to act collectively to try and shift the balance of power. Acting occasionally as a trade union, threatening a general strike in 1913, 'panel' doctors eventually secured the Berlin Agreement, which resulted in a universal contract to apply to all doctors employed by *Krankenkassen* and elimi-nating the employer autonomy of individual organizations. The terms of the *Krankenkassen* contract were negotiated collectively through a contract committee (Labisch, 1997).

The role of the state in social welfare provision expanded extensively in Germany following its defeat in the First World War. Economic and political crises stimulated the rise of an 'organizist' view of society and the necessity for interdependence and co-operation in order to save the German nation. An organizist state socialism was institutionalized in the formal inauguration of the Weimar Republic in 1919. During the period of the Republic, up to 1933, the finance-economy was viewed as an organism which could be managed by the state which would redistribute wealth through welfare benefits. The Weimar constitution removed the primary responsibility for welfare from the voluntary sector and placed it within the jurisdiction of state and municipal administration. A comprehensive welfare state emerged under Weimar which combined insurance, state, municipal and some remaining voluntary agencies (Weindling, 1990).

Weimar welfare facilitated the socialization of health which prioritized the goals of the social hygiene movement, focusing on the prevention of chronic disease, the health of mothers and children and combating psychiatric disorders. The socialization of health also legitimated new forms of health professionalism. Apart from increasing the political influence of the medical profession itself, it also facilitated the professionalization of social assistance by trained social workers. Responsibility for social hygiene, maternity benefits, war pensions and occupational medicine became the responsibility of the Ministry of Labour in 1919, and the Ministry of Interior became responsible for public health, mental hospitals and statistics. Leading social hygienists, such as Alfred Grotjahn, lobbied all the political parties to try to establish a single Ministry of Health headed by a doctor. This campaign failed, and health and social welfare remained linked to the largely federal structure of public administration in Germany directed by the states, the *Länder*, and municipal governments. This meant regional and local health administrations varied widely but all were compelled to provide a comprehensive package of services (Weindling, 1990).

Prior to the war, competing local strategies had tried to provide welfare through either municipal welfare clinics or district health centres. These ideas were fused in the Weimar system of combined health, youth and welfare offices (Harvey, 1993). In towns these functions tended to be separated, and some municipalities established health centres that employed salaried doctors and other health care workers with wide-ranging programmes of social medicine, including the health of infants and children, the prevention of tuberculosis, venereal disease, alcoholism and mental disorder, and the provision of ante-natal care and genetic counselling. Sometimes these activities overlapped with the Youth and Welfare Offices who often dealt with the blind, deaf, dumb and 'feeble-minded' (Harvey, 1993). Health and welfare clinics dispensed supplements and hygiene education, and began to provide mass screening for the early diagnosis of diseases such as tuberculosis, venereal disease and diphtheria. Between 1919 and 1921 in Prussia, 823 district and local authority clinics had been established employing 133 full-time district and communal doctors, 294 part-time doctors and 2,344 social workers (Weindling, 1990).

Clinics also played a major role in gathering new information on population health. Health officials argued that mortality figures did not accurately reveal levels of ill health and deprivation. Local clinics began to gather data on children to illustrate the levels of chronic ill health. Clinic staff recorded levels of malnutrition, measured heights and weights and noted domestic hygiene conditions, such as whether a child had its own bed, linen and clothing. Clinics identified numbers suffering from rickets, skin conditions like eczema, diarrhoea, worms and tuberculosis. High levels of malnutrition – between 25 and 75 per cent of children in some districts – led to changes in the way national health statistics were recorded. In 1931 the Reich Health Office moved from a disease index to a health index based upon the monitoring of selected social groups, including the unemployed, and their families.

The development of health services under Weimar was motivated by organizist collectivist social ideology, which included beliefs in regenerationist biology. The leading influential social hygienists viewed the new system of health and welfare clinics and health surveillance as an opportunity for institutionalizing goals of biological improvement. Grotjahn campaigned not only for a ministry of national health but also for new social insurance and population policies. The main thrust of his programme was a nationalization of all medical services, including hospital services, and the introduction of a pronatalist 'parenthood insurance'. Medical reformers were convinced that nationalization of medical welfare would rejuvenate the social order of defeated Germany. Social hygiene reform legitimated its goals within an appeal to nationalist revival. A powerful feature of the social crisis within German society following the war was a fear of its consequences upon the vitality of the German *volk*, or race. The social hygiene movement promoted its goals within the context of eugenic and racial hygiene concerns about the hereditary nature of social-biological decline. Through the combined influence of racial and social hygiene, eugenics continued to play a significant role in the development of health care under Weimar, often providing an additional underlying rationale for reform. Health measures designed to reduce unnecessary ill health were instituted with a view to improving the health of future generations. Eugenic ideals about the need to plan population development were highly compatible with organizist ideals about collective responsibility for welfare (Weindling, 1990).

Demographic concerns had also stimulated social policies in Sweden from early modern times. Social welfare had been consistently provided for the needy in Sweden through the parishes, which had employed provincial physicians from 1700, and the state had subsidized hospital provision from the late eighteenth century. Although Sweden remained largely an agrarian economy, industrialization began to develop in the later nineteenth century centred in village workshops, the *bruks*, owned by small-scale entrepreneurs. As the population increased by 50 per cent during the nineteenth century, the parish system became inadequate to supply relief to an ever expanding landless unemployed and impoverished proletariat. The destitute posed a threat to social stability, especially as consumers of grain and potato spirits. Distillation, indeed, began to dominate agricultural production in the late nineteenth century. Paternalistic owners of the *bruks* provided some social welfare for local communities, but in large urban areas such as Stockholm the concentration of industrial workers produced political organizations demanding reform and a new party in 1889, the Social Democratic Party. The SDP became, and remained until the present day, the only trade union affiliated party in Sweden. Its initial revolutionary goals became tempered by the failure of the 1909 general strike to bring about major structural economic changes. Subsequently the SDP worked within the emerging capitalist system, substituting the creation of welfare and security for their original goal of a totally planned economy. The SDP gained increasing political strength in the Swedish political system from the early twentieth century, and from the 1930s remained in power continuously in either majority or coalition governments until the late 1980s (Wilson, 1979; Heidenheimer and Elvander (eds), 1980).

Constitutional reform in 1886 replaced a *Stänerriksdag* made up of four estates – nobles, the Church, burghers and peasants – with a bicameral parliament and a limited franchise. The 1886 reforms also created new units of local government, county councils, which were given the powers to raise taxes. The county councils were given responsibility for the provincial hospitals which had been created with government subsidies from the middle of the eighteenth century. In the 1920s the county councils became responsible for providing hospitals in localities where there was no other provider. In the nineteenth century, constitutional reforms had little effect on poor relief and the most popular solution to escaping destitution became mass emigration to the North American continent. Over 1 million Swedes, out of a total population of about 5 million, emigrated between 1870 and 1910 (Wilson, 1979; Heidenheimer and Elvander (eds), 1980).

Influenced by the German social insurance system, Sweden adopted initial health insurance legislation in 1891. Unlike the German system, however, in Sweden health insurance was made available on a voluntary rather than a compulsory basis. Voluntary sickness insurance funds which had been established by the guild system in the eighteenth century were now taken over by industrial workers in new urban areas. Voluntary sickness funds, however, largely provided only cash benefits to skilled workers when unable to work through illness. Medical services still had to be purchased from private practitioners. The Swedish medical profession remained wary of insurance medicine and therefore no collective negotiation took place with the insurance funds to regulate the costs of medical services. Instead, services continued to be purchased on an individual fee-for-service basis. Between 1891 and 1931 amendments to the insurance laws simply maintained income levels in times of illness. This contrasted with Denmark, where workers' voluntary insurance was adopted in 1892 with the co-operation of an organized medical profession. The Danish medical profession played a significant role in the construction of the Insurance Law in 1892, because the Denmark Medical Association assumed that the physician–patient relationship improved with the elimination of direct payments. After 1892, medical services in Denmark were supplied to insurance patients on a tariff basis which was negotiated by local medical associations and the federation of local sickness funds (Heidenheimer and Elvander (eds), 1980).

Voluntary insurance funds in Sweden could not cover many features of need arising from illness, industrial injury, unemployment and old age. In 1901 new laws covering workmen's compensation made employers legally liable for injury at work. Old-age pensions had been continually debated from the mid-nineteenth century. Industrial insurance for old age had been blocked by the Farmers' Party, which represented self-employed farmers and which held the majority in the *Riksdag* until the 1930s. In 1913 a contributory pension scheme was created in Sweden which, unlike Germany and Britain, made citizen status the basis for receipt of a pension which was widely supplemented from government and local relief funds. No further progress in social welfare reform was achieved by a succession of minority governments in Sweden until economic depression, new concerns about the declining birth rate and the election of a majority SDP government revived the social security debate in the 1930s (Wilson, 1979; Heidenheimer and Elvander (eds), 1980).

Voluntary insurance against loss of income during times of sickness had also been a nineteenth-century tradition in France. Exclusive groups of workers had organized voluntary health funds through mutual aid societies from the time of the late Napoleonic empire. The early societies were formed for individual occupational groups in different localities, but by the time of the Second Empire, mutuals became increasingly multi-professional and regional. Largely they were voluntary associations of wage-earners with similar social and economic status. Mutual society memberships were often small and restricted usually to about fifty to sixty members. Larger mutuals with 100–150 members were rarer, but later in the nineteenth century they sometimes became as large as 500 members. Members paid an induction fee to join and a monthly premium; they would be fined or expelled if they failed in their payments. The purpose of mutual aid societies was to provide funds for medical diagnosis and income during times of illness. New members were restricted to workers between the ages of twenty-five and forty-five. Older workers were refused because risk of sickness was greater. Mutual aid societies were organizations designed to protect stable, relatively prosperous breadwinners against the misfortunes of illness. They were not aimed at rescuing paupers from destitution and disease. After the revolutions of 1848, mutuals frequently required their members not to engage in political agitation or raise religious issues at meetings. In many respects the mutualist movement represented the values of the artisan and shopkeeper classes in France, and as a result mutualism became separated from the syndicalism and trade unionism of the industrial proletariat (Mitchell, 1991a; Mitchell, 1991b).

A mutual employed its own physicians who would be resident in the commune or *arrondissement* where it was based. Occasionally some mutuals extended benefits to old-age pensions, but those which did were often the first to fail financially when mutualism was greatly disrupted by war in 1870. Mutualism flourished under Louis Bonaparte, who made himself 'Prince President' of the movement in 1852. By the 1860s the emperor could boast that mutual membership reached almost 1 million, and he declared mutualism to be the basis of a French *Etat-Providence*. During the war of 1870 the membership of the mutuals became dislocated and many societies failed or struggled to survive in the early years of the Third Republic. Throughout the nineteenth century the mutual aid movement was regarded as a liberal organization of welfare which avoided the extreme philosophies of English laissez-faire on the one hand and German statism on the other. However, by the 1880s the example of compulsory German state insurance challenged the claims of the mutualist movement to provide comprehensive welfare. Furthermore, while mutualism provided protection against sickness, very few could cope with making provisions for the permanently disabled or the retired. Liberalism flourished initially under the Third Republic, which enacted widespread deregulation, such as unrestricted licensing of drinking establishments. Mutual societies were also assisted by relaxed governmental requirements for chartering new societies, and the movement grew to 3.5 million members by 1901. By the 1890s, however, the values of laissez-faire began to be challenged by new organic metaphors of society and trade union activism which stimulated changes in French liberalism. Solidarism emerged as a new philosophy of increased state intervention to achieve social security and justice which would prevent the spread of socialism. Solidarists had their greatest influence in the Radical Party, whose leader, Leon Bourgeois, became prime minister and the most prominent spokesman of solidarism. Solidarism sought to balance the right to individual freedom with the claims and obligations upon the individual by society. Voluntary health insurance provided by mutualism fitted well with such solidarist ideals. Solidarism also created new protective laws for the indigent. For example, the Medical Assistance Act of 1893, which was first implemented in 1895, provided care for the destitute in an equivalent way to medical relief received by paupers under the English Poor Law (Mitchell, 1991a; Mitchell, 1991b; Ramsey, 1994; Weiss, 1983).

German compulsory social insurance nevertheless forced the French state into re-evaluating its voluntarist policies in social welfare. In 1901 Leon Bourgeois suggested that, although the mutual societies provided medical insurance for 3.5 million members, English Friendly Societies covered 11 million members, and 18 million Germans were covered by state social insurance. In the period of the *Belle Epoch*, leading French intellectuals and political figures debated the merits of the voluntary or compulsory route to social welfare provision. A reformist Parisian barrister, Albert Crochard, argued in 1902 that France must choose between the German and English models. He concluded that English friendly societies provided insufficient security and that the German state system was far more comprehensive. The director of the Musée Social and president of the National Federation of Mutual Societies, Léopold Mabileau, retorted in 1904, that mutual insurance was a uniquely Gaelic mixture of voluntary and obligatory systems of social welfare and avoided the worst evils of state sponsored charity which created a culture of dependency. Mutualism represented both liberty and solidarity. The rhetorical debate over mutualism versus state intervention delayed the development of comprehensive welfare provision in France, but was partially resolved in the creation of universal state retirement pensions in 1910. The establishment of state old-age pensions indicated the drift towards the German model of welfare provision in France which left the future of voluntary insurance and mutualism unclear. After the First World War, the partial coverage offered by mutualism to exclusive groups of workers was inadequate to the task of creating a national system of health care. While they could preserve the status of the few, they were unable to provide for the many, and in this respect were unable to pioneer new models of social security which emerged in France by the middle of the twentieth century (Mitchell, 1991a; Mitchell, 1991b).

After the First World War, the tensions between statism and liberalism, centralization and localism, voluntarism and individualism was still evident in French policy towards health care. Despite the efforts of solidarism to resolve these conflicts and strike a balance between competing ideologies, it failed to secure a clear path for welfare provision in France. In a number of ways the French ideal of avoiding both English liberalism and German statism had by the early twentieth century become a rather empty rhetoric which no longer matched reality. Imperial Germany was more federal than the Third Republic, with extensive powers invested in the *Länder*. German administration of social insurance was devolved and controlled through local representative bodies. In Britain the ideology of laissez-faire was increasingly challenged from the end of the nineteenth century. More power had become vested in a centralized state, especially in the area of public health policy. France maintained a centralized state, but one which recoiled from intervening to act collectively on behalf of the community as a whole (Ramsey, 1994).

In contrast to either France or Sweden, Britain sacrificed the principles of liberalism and voluntarism with much greater readiness once state social security had been established in Germany. Before the end of the nineteenth century, officers in the expanding British public health service had visions of the unification of the health services of the Poor Law and the public health service. MOHs such as Arthur Newsholme attempted to influence the ideas of Fabian socialists such as Beatrice Webb with schemes for a unified service funded by the exchequer rather than through local taxes (Chapter 8). Although such collectivist programmes would have been unacceptable to the values of mid-Victorian liberal governments, collectivism gained increasing political support from the 1880s. From this period up to the early 1920s, a new set of ideological attitudes took shape in Britain which shifted emphasis away from individual freedom and towards collective responsibility of the state for its citizens. As in Germany, new perceptions of society as an organic whole were articulated by the founder of English sociology, Herbert Spencer. The notion of the interdependent social organism replaced the idea of society as a collection of freely competing atoms. The crisis in laissez-faire free market economic concepts in the 1870s was reflected in the extent to which John Stuart Mill changed his mind about immutability of workers' wages and in the popularity of Henry George's ideas about land nationalization among workers' movements. The ideological shifts within bourgeois liberal thought were typified by the new resonance which the economic ideas of the art critic, John Ruskin, found among middle-class intellectuals. Ruskin was a conservative thinker but aimed to promote class harmony based upon the duties rather than the rights of citizenship. Ruskin encouraged the idea that the state was responsible for social welfare and he managed not only to inspire liberal reformers but also to influence the socialist movement emerging from the 1880s in Britain (Rowbotham, 1994).

Advocates of larger state irresponsibility had many supporters within the state machinery, apart from the obvious leading voice of Lloyd George (Harris, 1992; Harris, 1994; Harris, 1996). For example, both Winston Churchill and William Beveridge supported the new vision of liberalism from within the Board of Trade. Working-class radicalism also began to see the value in the extension of state intervention in education, training and universally establishing working-class demands, such as the eight-hour day campaigned for by 'new unionism' from the 1880s. Enthusiastic imperialism, as we saw in Chapter 10, also believed that a stronger British state could strengthen the survival of the Empire. As in Germany, Britain's Liberal and Conservative politicians grasped the advantage of the insurance principle as a means of expanding the role of the state in the provision of welfare and for reducing the threat of socialism as a political force. Winston Churchill, president of the Board of Trade in 1908, suggested that Prime Minister Asquith 'thrust a big slice of Bismarckianism over the whole underside of our industrial system'. Herbert Spender, radical Liberal editor of the *Contemporary Review*, urged Asquith's Chancellor, Lloyd George, to use the German strategy to undermine the growth of socialism (Harris, 1992; Harris, 1994; Harris, 1996).

Unlike in Germany, British law had continued to focus on individuals and did not introduce compulsory trade association for employers or compulsory insurance to cover workmen's compensation. The statutory regulations, however, made opting out of voluntary insurance schemes an unattractive option for employers, and the Workmen's Compensation Law of 1898 did establish systematic financial coverage for injured workers. In 1907 the Liberal administration expanded the categories of injuries eligible for compensation to include various diseases induced by industrial processes, but coverage was inadequate to meet the needs of workers laid off through sickness and disability. The need for some form of universal worker insurance against both the medical costs and loss of livelihood through sickness and disability became ever more pressing by the early years of the twentieth century (Weindling (ed.), 1985).

Almost twenty years of Tory rule came to an end in 1905 when Arthur Balfour's administration collapsed in disarray. A landslide victory in a general election in 1906 put the Liberals in power until after the First World War. It was the moment in which a radical reforming politician, Lloyd George, who had built his career on his identification with the 'people's plight', could press forward his programme for social policy. Free school meals, old-age pensions and a 'People's Budget' which redistributed wealth through graduated taxation, and the introduction of capital gains tax and land duties, were the first provisions towards creating a safety net of economic welfare. The majority report of a Royal Commission on poverty between 1905 and 1909 believed that the principles of the 1834 Poor Law should be upheld, making the poor bear the responsibility for their misfortune or wilful idleness through an extension of means-tested doles. A minority report, architectured largely by the Fabian socialist Beatrice Webb, wanted a complete restructuring of policy by creating a comprehensive system of social welfare funded through taxation to eliminate the possibility of destitution regardless of its cause (Thane, 1985).

By the time the reports were published in 1909, Lloyd George had already begun to construct a policy which ignored the rhetoric of both. A visit to Germany during 1908 had convinced the British Chancellor of the advantages of the insurance system for funding welfare policy (Hennock, 1987). The cost upon taxation was prohibitive, but extracting compulsory payments from both sides of industry would provide the funds needed not only for health and unemployment benefits but also for old-age pensions. Furthermore, the insurance principle eliminated the old discriminations against the deserving or undeserving poor. Contributing to the system qualified the individual for benefits regardless of the cause of his loss of income, whether it be self-induced or not. As Churchill observed, anyone who earned the right to benefit was entitled to it even if he had been the cause of his own destitution, and the insurance fund would simply have to 'stand the racket'. Similarly, entitlement to medical benefit was dependent on being sick regardless of how the illness or injury was contracted. Lloyd George explained that medical treatment had to be provided for all illnesses regardless of their cause (Thane, 1985).

Even the British Tories saw the strategic value of national insurance. It provided an economic minimum which was persistently demanded by the Fabian socialists but made the labouring classes pay for it. Making the proletariat pay for their own welfare system reduced the appeal of socialism by limiting the disadvantages imposed by the free-market economy without restructuring society. As Keir Hardie, the founder of the Independent Labour Party, observed, the Liberal party did 'not uproot the cause of poverty but ...[provided] a porous plaster to cover the disease that poverty causes'.

Health and unemployment insurance were provided under Parts One and Two of the 1911 National Insurance Act. Lloyd George intended to make the British insurance system more self-governing than the German one by employing large affiliated friendly societies to administer the scheme. While the small *Krankenkassen* allowed workers participation in governing the insurance system, Lloyd George believed they would be less efficient than the large friendly society organizations. Friendly societies were run by elected officers from among their affiliated membership and would ensure democratic participation but, Lloyd George hoped, make the English system less bureaucratic than the German. By the time of the First World War, however, the nature of the friendly societies was changing. At one time, election to a society committee was a mark of status and respectability among the working classes. By the First World War, however, the growth of their membership made the friendly societies large centralized collecting agencies, operating bureaucratically by post from a central office, and deposit societies for savings as well as insurance. The democratic ideal was even further eroded by giving commercial insurance companies the status of 'approved societies' for administrating the statutory scheme. The large industrial insurance companies, such as the Prudential, had a vast army of agents collecting pennies from poor clients every week who paid into funeral schemes to avoid the dreaded stigma of a pauper's burial. Lloyd George had to sacrifice his hopes for widows' and orphans' benefit and allow the commercial insurance companies to participate in administering national insurance to get them to comply with the scheme (Daunton, 1996).

Lloyd George hoped to retain democratic participation in state social insurance by having it administered through the friendly societies. As in Sweden the friendly societies were an organizational extension of the guild tradition which had provided voluntary health insurance. They operated schemes which offered both cash payments and covered medical bills for large groups of skilled and semi-skilled workers. The friendly society method of employing doctors on fixed salaries was hated by the medical profession who claimed that 'club practice' exploited them. Lloyd George secured the co-operation of the friendly societies by making them 'approved societies' under the Act, and he secured the co-operation of the medical profession by replacing 'club practice' with a panel system managed by local health committees made up of representatives from the approved societies and the medical profession. The insured individual would be attended by a panel doctor of his choice, who was paid a capitation fee for all patients on his list, and thus the private nature of the doctor–patient relationship, so highly treasured by the profession, was retained. When it came into operation the health insurance scheme took contributions of 4d per week from all employees earning less than £160 per annum. Employers contributed 3d and the state 2d. Lloyd George described the scheme with his famed arithmetic as workers receiving 9d for 4d (Fraser, 1973; Gilbert, 1966). But the limitations of the insurance scheme were obvious. While providing benefit for employed workers it did not cover their dependants. As far as the preventive health authorities were concerned, the insurance scheme defeated the possibility of creating a unified health system to provide both preventive and therapeutic services under one public administration.

A new organic vision of society supported a larger role for the state in undertaking collective responsibility for welfare in numerous European societies. The ideologies of welfare in Europe underwent further changes after the First World War, leading towards the establishment of the 'classic welfare states' of the 1940s and 1950s (Harris, 1996). Many features of the European ideologies of welfare were also present within political organizations in the United States. Despite the fact that the United States became the most rapidly advanced industrial society in the twentieth century, the establishment of welfare provision took place much later than in Europe. The reason for the differences between Europe and America lies in the historical political determinants of classic welfarism.

UNIVERSALISM AND THE CREATION OF THE CLASSIC WELFARE STATE

The spirit of voluntarism which had dominated Swedish and French health care provision up to the First World War began to shift towards compulsory state insurance and universal welfare provision by the early years following the Second World War. In Sweden, health insurance was mandated to provide medical care in addition to cash benefit payments under a new law covering sickness funds in 1931. The Social Democrats revived the question of social welfare when they were elected to power in 1932. In 1934 the publication of *The Crisis in the Population Question* by Gunnar and Alva Myrdal boosted the Social Democrat programme for welfare reform. This, together with the influence of Keynesian theories of a managed economy upon the Stockholm School of Economics, provided the SDP with a new ideological foundation for their goals. Social welfare was now advocated by Social Democrats as critical to economic progress which would stimulate demand and investment in periods of recession and reduce unemployment, boost production and raise national income. The new SDP programme for welfare reform in the 1930s was characterized by Prime Minister Per Albin Hansson as 'The People's Home'. Government subsidies and supervision were introduced for sickness and unemployment benefit societies and a new law introducing both insurance-based and means-tested old-age pensions was passed in 1937. A Social Services Commission was set up in 1938 which proposed a comprehensive and integrated structure of state funded and administered social welfare which became the basis of reforms instituted after the Second World War (Heidenheimer and Elvander (eds), 1980; Wilson, 1979).

A separate commission was set up on health care in 1943 under the chairmanship of Axel Höjer, the director of the Board of Health. Many of the principles contained in the 1942 Beveridge Report in Britain were matched in the Höjer Report. Höjer suggested that medical services should be made universally available free at the point of delivery and that it should be the duty of community authorities to co-ordinate a regulated organization of public health, hospital care, preventive and ambulatory medicine. The 1943 report recommended that such a system should be implemented through county council administration and that preventive and therapeutic health care could be integrated through health centres created around local hospitals. Despite the fact that the report was widely criticized by the Swedish Medical Association, who feared the creation of a salaried service, the state gradually implemented most of its principles (Heidenheimer and Elvander (eds), 1980; Wilson, 1979).

By the mid-1950s the Swedish state had transformed its system of welfare from one which had provided a basic security against destitution to one which gave universal equal access to basic services, such as medical care, as a right of citizenship. Universal old-age pensions were introduced in 1947, along with family allowances. Pensions were eventually supplemented by a state system of superannuation for all, including manual workers, following the example of earnings-related pensions created in Germany. The large funds accumulated in government pensions were eventually used to purchase equities in private Swedish companies, but as a result the SDP were accused of introducing nationalization through the back door. A Labour Market Board had been set up during the war and began to supervise public works once peace was declared. In the 1950s the Labour Market Board was transferred into a sophisticated manpower management agency run by representatives of government, employers and employees which tried to regulate regional imbalances of supply and demand for labour. The Labour Market Board earned Sweden the status of a full-employment post-war welfare state (Heidenheimer and Elvander (eds), 1980; Wilson, 1979).

Compulsory state health insurance was introduced in 1955, and Sweden was divided into seven hospital administrative regions which each contained a major teaching and research hospital. The county councils took over the regulation of hospital outpatient care in the 1960s, along with the functions of District Medical Officers. Central government responsibility for health was transferred to the Ministry of Health and Social Welfare in 1963 which became responsible for planning all new hospital development and the regional distribution of ambulatory care in the 1970s. In 1975 'total responsibility' for the delivery of all state medical services was transferred to the county councils. Throughout the century Swedish doctors had developed a common practice of combining public employment in hospitals with private practice, using hospital outpatient facilities. In 1970 the 'Seven Crowns Reform' made all doctors servicing health-insured patients in either in-patient or out-patient practice salaried employees of the county councils (Heidenheimer and Elvander (eds), 1980); Wilson, 1979).

After the First World War, in France the recovery of territories in Alsace and Lorraine lost to the Germans in 1871 highlighted the limitations of voluntary health insurance. The successfully implemented German state insurance system in the occupied territories stimulated new debates surrounding state welfare provision in France. A commission on national insurance in 1920 accepted the principle of compulsory state insurance for a limited number of occupational groups. The establishment of a national system in France was consistently blocked for a decade, however, by the Communist Party and the medical profession. The Communists saw state social insurance as a hindrance to major economic transformation. The medical profession wished to guard what the Congress of Medical Syndicates identified in 1927 as four major principles which they called the 'Medical Charter'. These included the free choice of a doctor by patients, no third-party payment of fees, freedom to diagnose and prescribe according to professional judgement and a direct contract between patient and practitioner. When compulsory state health insurance was established in 1930 all of these principles were preserved. Health insurance was introduced for all wage-earners below a specified maximum; their payroll deductions, plus employer and state contributions, funded the scheme, which provided cash benefits for unemployment during illness and funds to cover medical treatment. Patients made a direct contract with their chosen physician, paid his fees and were reimbursed by an insurance fund also chosen by the individual. The insurance funds continued to be administered by voluntary and commercial approved societies. A fee scale was agreed between the state and the medical profession but individual doctors were not obliged to stick to it. It was thus a state system which was not run by a government bureaucracy and retained the liberal economic model of medical practice intact, but not for long (Hollingsworth *et al.*, 1990; Ramsey, 1994).

The end of the Second World War and Nazi occupation witnessed dramatic changes in the direction of French social policy. The spirit of universalism which produced the Beveridge Report in Britain was equally influential in post-war France. An ordinance by the National Resistance Council in October 1945 created the basis of a comprehensive social security system which included old-age pensions, sickness, disability benefits and family allowances. A decentralized self-governing national health system was established and administered by regional boards, independent of the central state, made up of representatives of contributors: employers and employees. The proportion of the population covered under the nationalized insurance scheme expanded to cover the great majority within the first few decades following the war. The expanded role of government in social security provision was signified by the creation of a national social security office with increasing authority over regional offices. Fee scales were now negotiated by local medical syndicates and *départements* which reduced the power of the medical profession to maintain competitive fees through 'direct contracts' with the patient. After 1960 the system was again revised, with *départements* continuing to negotiate fees but now within a government model convention. Doctors whose local *syndicat* had failed to reach an agreement with the *département* could now operate according to the national model, and this virtually ended the system of direct contract apart from private practice, which remained outside the scheme, defended by the breakaway Federation of Physicians of France (Ashford, 1986; Hollingsworth *et al.*, 1990; Ramsey, 1994).

A national fee scale was introduced in 1971 as one measure aimed at containing the costs of health care. The national plan, negotiated through the Confederation of Medical Syndicates, applied to all physicians, and in return the government agreed not to promote health maintenance organizations. After a long and successful resistance to centralized state intervention, a social security and health care delivery system was established in France which was able to accommodate many of the liberal values which had opposed it since the nineteenth century. Voluntarism maintained a significant organizational role in administering the financial structure of health care delivery. Professionals, such as the medical profession, preserved strong powers of self-determination against the force of the state (Hollingsworth *et al.*, 1990).

In France, liberalism successfully resisted centralized state intervention and compulsion. In Sweden, Social Democratic collectivism was realized in a managerial full-employment welfare state. In Britain, the balance of the mixed economy of voluntary and state welfare shifted dramatically in the twentieth century as the liberal collectivism of the Edwardian period gave way to a new philosophy of universalism by the Second World War (Harris, 1992; Finlayson, 1994). These ideological shifts also redefined the boundaries of citizenship in Britain (Harris, 1996). Voluntarism had encouraged a citizenship of service through participation in the delivery of welfare (Finlayson, 1994). The growth of central state welfare provision, justified as means of achieving social equality, legitimated a citizenship of rights and entitlement which had been first articulated in the political philosophies of the Enlightenment (Daunton, 1996). The citizenship of voluntary service was replaced by a citizenship of rights to statutory relief in times of need (Harris, 1996). In the nineteenth century many of the basic welfare services, in areas such as education and housing, had been provided through voluntary organizations. Some historians have claimed that, when the state became the principal provider of basic services in the twentieth century, the opportunity for democratic participation was reduced (Finlayson, 1994). Supporters of centralized welfare in the inter-war years in Britain, however, believed that democracy could only be achieved through equality, and that this in turn could only be achieved through universal values being applied to all. Centralizers argued that universalized standards of welfare would equalize social justice and provide equal access to basic needs which, they claimed, was the prerequisite for truly universal democratic participation in the political process (Daunton, 1996).

Through the inter-war years, the British Labour Party argued for the expansion of the tax-funded basis of welfare, believing that it would provide more rather than less democratic control. Social insurance was administered through 'approved societies' which included not only friendly societies, accountable to their membership, but also commercial insurance companies which were not. As demand for insurance grew in the inter-war years, friendly societies had to compete with commercial companies for members by becoming large anonymous collecting and savings deposit organizations. The scope for democratic participation in social insurance administration was extensively reduced as all the approved societies became increasingly bureaucratized and remote. Furthermore, the range of benefits that societies could offer was strictly controlled by the central government and therefore it was extremely difficult for them to be innovative. While the autonomy and the democratic basis of the approved societies was compromised, their efficiency was also limited. A diverse pattern of benefits between societies was often divisive within local communities and did not always fit well with the structure of services offered by different local authorities. The most striking inadequacy of national health insurance in Britain, however, was the fact that it only covered ambulatory medical services for largely healthy workers and did not provide care for their dependants, or hospital care (Webster (ed.), 1991).

Health care became an issue of social reconstruction following the First World War. During the war, Lloyd George encouraged national morale by promising 'homes fit for heroes' and the creation of a Ministry of Health once peace was won. The Ministry was established in 1919 and the first Minister of

Health was a doctor and liberal MP, Christopher Addison, who had helped Lloyd George introduce the National Insurance Act in 1911 (Honigsbaum, 1993). The Ministry's first Permanent Secretary was Sir Robert Morant, a civil servant recruited from the education department who had long since sympathized with the views of Sydney and Beatrice Webb on the need for a unified state medical service. The first Chief Medical Officer was Sir George Newman, an MOH who had become the Chief Medical Officer in the Department of Education before the war (Honigsbaum,1989).

The inadequacies of national insurance were recognized by Addison and both his chief civil servants, all of whom wanted a unified service run by elected local authorities together with a nationalized hospital service manned by a salaried service. Addison recognized that this would be massively resisted by the medical profession, and aimed instead to extend the panel system to provide GP services to workers' families and bring hospital services into the public domain gradually. Addison thought that this might be achieved by combining the interests of the four consultative councils, representing doctors, patients, local authorities and approved societies, which had been provided for the new Ministry. He asked the head of the Medical Consultative Council, Bertrand Edward Dawson, later Lord Dawson of Penn, who became the President of the Royal College of Physicians in the 1930s, to publish an interim report in 1920. Addison and Newman were disappointed in the results, which resisted unification under local authorities (Honigsbaum, 1993; Honigsbaum, 1989). Instead, the Dawson Report recommended a system of hospitals connected to local health centres which would give GPs as well as consultants access to beds. The report suggested that these services should be 'available' but failed to discuss whether they should be free (Webster (ed.), 1991). All plans for a unified service, however, collapsed in the face of growing economic crisis. Means-tested Poor Law medical provision remained intact even after the Poor Law was officially abolished under the 1929 Local Government Act. The system of public assistance which replaced it was in practice a return to a form of outdoor relief based upon means-testing.

As economic recession deepened, the need for comprehensive health cover increased. The bottom was falling out of the market in private medical practice, with the vast majority of employees receiving insurance medicine and their families dependent upon public assistance and municipal hospital services. Voluntary hospitals were also in a financial crisis. Hospital charity had been an important arena for local politics from the eighteenth century (Webster (ed.), 1991). Local elites excluded from political participation because of their religious affiliation or their lack of patronage were able to acquire notability and social influence through philanthropy (Cavallo, 1991). Participation in philanthropy, however, became less significant for the middle classes as politics became increasingly secularized and the Conservative Party became more associated with property and commercial interests. Furthermore, structural changes to the organization of capital, with a shift to large public companies, changed the structural composition of local economies and the social relations of local elites. The voluntary hospital was a casualty of these changes. Hospitals were supplanted by local clubs such as Rotary or organizations like the Freemasons as vehicles for gaining social influence. As middle-class philanthropic support eroded, voluntary hospitals became financially vulnerable. By the late 1930s, many of the large voluntary hospitals were only saved from bankruptcy through municipal subsidies which cost them a degree of autonomy, bringing them under the control of local health authorities (Pickstone, 1985). Furthermore, as labour relations were taken over by direct negotiations between unions and employers, philanthropy became a less effective means of regulating class relations (Daunton, 1996).

In 1938 the BMA produced a report on the introduction of a nationally funded and organized system of medical care, but the planning process for a unified health service began within the Ministry of Health in 1936. From the outset the Ministry had aimed at the construction of one comprehensive system administered through local government. An attempt had been made to create a unified medical service under local government control through the Local Government Act of 1929. This had transferred the control of Poor Law medical services, including hospitals, to the local authority. Local authorities subsequently controlled both the public health services and the delivery of medical services. After 1929, however, the profusion of local authority services had led to a chaotic and inefficient system, often with unnecessary overlapping and duplication of functions. Where local authority control had been successful, as under the Manchester Board, it had largely been the result of intervention from the influence of the university and medical elite in its organization (Honigsbaum, 1989; Webster (ed.), 1991).

Local government became a battleground within the Conservative Party in the inter-war years. On the one hand, Conservatives feared Labour taking over local government. On the other hand, Conservatives such as Neville Chamberlain wanted to preserve the strength of local government democracy. Since the end of the nineteenth century, local government taxation had increasingly failed to cover the costs of administration. Lloyd George had tried to help solve this fiscal crisis through the creation of new land taxation, but it had fed central rather than local government funds. Municipal trading had also failed to produce necessary revenues because the technologies of services such as gas and electricity supplies required broader geographical distribution. Chamberlain had introduced a redistributive system of block grants to help strengthen financially weak local authorities, but these efforts had been completely undermined by Winston Churchill's measures of derating industry. The loss of revenue from industrial rating and the decomposition of local industrial economies had left local authorities in a greater fiscal crisis than ever before. The growth of joint stock companies, industries on a national scale and centrally regulated welfare all substantially reduced the financial and political power of local authorities by the 1930s (Daunton, 1996).

After 1931 the Labour Party believed that it could capture the central state and saw this as the quickest route to reducing inequality through the control of the national budget fuelled by taxation. Labour argued, for example, that welfare funded by taxation would be more democratic than social insurance distributed through bureaucratic approved societies. The Labour Party still perceived local government to be critical to maintaining democratic participation in the political process, but only if neighbourhood organizations were co-ordinated within larger planning structures. The Labour Party believed that regionalization would maximize democratic control while at the same time facilitating rational planning on a national scale. Labour's two planning documents published on health care and local government in 1943 proposed a system of twelve elected regional authorities which would co-ordinate the activities of local health centres regulated by local authorities. In this way the control of health care would be removed both from the approved societies on the one hand and from the medical profession on the other (Daunton, 1996; Webster (ed.), 1991).

If the Labour Party envisaged regionalization as a means of obtaining a democratically accountable nationalized health system with a salaried medical service, the medical profession supported similar plans for entirely different reasons. More than anything else, the medical profession wanted to avoid their twin enemies: a salaried service and local government control. The British medical profession viewed salaried service as a direct attack upon their autonomy and wished instead to continue to contract into a state-funded service through capitation fees. The voluntary hospitals were equally hostile to the Ministry's proposals. Great rivalry had developed between the clinical profession and the public health service before the war. Clinicians bitterly resented doctors employed by the state undermining private practice through the maternal and child welfare services and the public health control of municipal hospitals. Furthermore, each time a voluntary hospital went bankrupt it was taken over by municipal administration. GPs and the voluntary hospitals hated their experience of local health authority interference (Digby, 1996; Fox, 1986).

The profession believed that the best route to escaping municipal control was through the construction of a regional administration system governed by appointed committees dominated by medical representatives. GPs aimed to gain local control by replacing insurance committees with newly appointed bodies directed by local doctors (Fox, 1986). A precedent for regionalization had been set during the war when the Emergency Hospital Service was organized into twelve regional administrative bodies. By the time it came to finalize the legislation to institute the service after the war in 1946, the battle between the government and the medical profession became the main threat to implementation. GPs threatened non-co-operation with the service through a strike. The Minister of Health in the post-war Labour government, Aneurin Bevan, resolved the issue by nationalizing the hospital service administered through delegated regional boards directly controlled by central administration in Whitehall. Primary care remained organized on the panel principle but the old insurance committees, dominated by the approved societies, were replaced by new local Family Practitioner Committees run by doctors, which became responsible for the distribution of medical practice within an area. The final structure of the British National Health Service was the result of a negotiated compromise between a Labour government determined to create a comprehensive service, funded by taxation and free at the point of delivery, and a medical profession which preferred nationalization to multipurpose local government control (Webster, 1988; Webster (ed.), 1991; Digby, 1996).

The creation of the National Health Service was also the result of a new ideological shift towards universalism in welfare provision which went beyond either party or sectional interest politics in Britain. Universalism was the outcome of new perceptions of the relationship between the economic structure of civil society and the state. The advantages of state intervention in economic relations had been promoted through the new economic theories in the 1920s by the Cambridge economist John Maynard Keynes. Keynes invented a philosophy of a professionally managed economic system (Clarke, 1990). His mission was to rescue capitalism from its own vices by abandoning laissez-faire for an actively managed economy which encouraged investment and aimed for the full employment of capital and labour in optimal production. Keynes believed that capitalism could be preserved only by transforming it into a professionally operated system. The Keynesian revolution took hold during the war and afterwards swept all before it. It became the basis of a political consensus surrounding the whole question of reconstruction. Belief in the professional manipulation of the economy was a prerequisite of a comprehensive welfare state which involved incorporating social and economic logic into the corporate planning of society (Deakin, 1994). The idea of welfare corporatism was built upon what the eminent sociologist T.H. Marshall called 'social citizenship'. Social citizenship justified interventionist planning by the state in order to achieve a level of 'national efficiency'. The idea of social citizenship was crystallized in the Report on Social Insurance and Allied Services produced by the principal of the London School of Economics, Sir William Beveridge, in 1942. Beveridge's report represented ideological universalism as the defining characteristic of the 'classic welfare state' in which benefits and services were to be open to all and used by all. The Second World War fostered an unprecedented sense of social unity and engendered a national mood which was intolerant of privilege. Social problems were being redefined, not as individual failings, but as the product of pathologies in social organization. Universalism and corporate welfare planning assumed that the state had an obligation to release the majority of people from the fear of poverty. Social citizenship assumed that the guarantee of subsistence by government was not a threat to but a precondition of personal responsibility (Deakin, 1994; Clarke *et al.*, 1992).

With the outbreak of war and the threat of invasion, Britain's coalition government used planning for post-war reconstruction as their main strategy for stimulating a spirit of national unity and boosting morale to resist defeat. Wartime emergency made socialism a pragmatic necessity wherein the state took over the organization and co-ordination of national life. For example, wages were fixed at high levels in order to maintain high levels of productivity. In addition, a forced distribution of the labour force placed workers in the most necessary industries, and all eligible males were drafted into the fighting forces.

The reconstruction campaign was centred around the creation of a new system of social security. William Beveridge was employed to analyse needs and to devise a system to meet them. His 1942 Report advocated a national health service, funded from taxation and free at the point of delivery, which would cover each individual from the cradle to the grave. Within the Ministry of Health, Sir John Maude, the permanent secretary, and Sir William Jameson, the Chief Medical Officer, translated Beveridge into policy. Their plans to create a salaried medical service under local government control and organize community services around hospital access were, however, successfully resisted by the medical profession. The National Health Act was passed in 1946 and the system came into operation on the appointed day of 5 July 1948. The Labour government succeeded in establishing a national system of health care but sacrificed the original planning aims of the Ministry of Health. In doing so, the Labour government secured the nationalization of health but failed to realize the rationalization of services based upon preventive rather than therapeutic goals. As a result, the structure of health care and the delivery of medical services remained unchanged but access to it became universal and free. The state, in effect, funded the existing system (Webster, 1988).

The greatest loss of power in the new system was experienced by the public health sector and the local health authorities. Municipal hospitals were integrated into the regional hospital organization system, which was dominated by the major teaching hospitals. The local health authorities were left with control over existing municipal services providing for maternity, infants, schoolchildren, the insane. Local health authority services expanded after the war with the changing structure of the demographic composition of the community as more municipal services were needed for the elderly and chronically sick, such as nursing homes, meals-on-wheels and old people's homes. Social work developed extensively after the war as local health authorities took over the care of various groups within the community, such as neglected, abused and abandoned children and one-parent families. The Ministry's plans for primary health care administered through local health centres were relegated to experimental programmes undertaken by a few local authorities, but non-co-operation of local general practitioners made them inoperable (Webster, 1988).

The most immediate result of the implementation of the service was that millions of people got free dentures, eye glasses and hearing aids. The National Health System was subsequently supported by a broad consensus from 1945 to the 1980s, but it did not come into existence as the result of consensus (Webster, 1988). The service was created out of bitter political dispute between the medical profession, the civil service, the public health service and different political interests. Once established, however, it appeared for a while to make everyone happy (Honigsbaum, 1989). The medical profession was pleased with guaranteed income and employment in a society where the bottom had fallen out of the healing market. Hospital medicine got a big boost and promotion to centre-stage. The need to control costs by rationing services ensured the survival of general practice as the largest sector of medical delivery. General practitioners kept themselves in business by becoming the policemen of the service, monitoring and controlling access to specialist hospital acute care. Hospital medicine retained its elite status, eliminating the possibility of access to hospital facilities by general practitioners. The consultant elite were saved from the threat from the growing band of so-called 'consultoids', GPs who had developed hospital practices in the municipal hospital system before the war (Honigsbaum, 1989). Patients got free and unlimited access to medicine. Health care costs were directly controlled by the Treasury, which made sure the system was structured so that excess was never allowed to occur. For nearly forty years following the war, the National Health System remained a cheap system of health care delivery with no one sector being allowed to make a profit out of it. Private practice remained an available option for patients and practitioners, but the existence of a comprehensive service meant that there was nothing much to buy until queuing became an inefficient system of rationing use of service. Private practice could then sell faster access to expert elite medicine for acute and elective care. The system did eliminate, however, the escalation of costs stimulated by a third party, such as private health insurance companies with the need to pursue ever greater profits (Webster, 1988; Honigsbaum, 1989).

The Treasury mentality permanently undercut the need to expand services to meet the requirements of a changing population structure. Also the failure to build a system around preventive principles led to an ever larger demand for increasingly elaborate and technologically sophisticated therapeutic procedures with high costs. The system became increasingly inefficient, resulting from the accumulating effects of underfunding. Inefficiency allowed an assault on the organization – and, indeed, the principles – of the service by the politics of the New Right in the 1980s and 1990s. The success of the right-wing reform in dismantling the National Health Service will be discussed in the following chapter.

SOCIAL SECURITY AND HEALTH IN THE UNITED STATES

The rise of the classic welfare state is often described as having two historical stages. First, the creation of social insurance systems, which largely took place in most European states by the First World War. These did not differ radically, however, from traditional forms of public assistance. They served to ease the extreme poverty of the least privileged members of society but provided only small benefits to a limited population. Second, after the Second World War new forms of social security were established in numerous European societies based upon the principles of universality and substitutive benefits. Social security now provided comprehensive benefits and services available to all and was related to earnings. Benefits in modern systems of social security went beyond basic subsistence and substituted wages lost through unemployment, sickness, disability or old age. Social security was set at levels that were sufficient to allow continuity in living standards. Universality and earnings substitution have been the defining characteristics that divide modern welfare from traditional public assistance. Modern social security programmes were designed not simply to provide subsistence for the poor, but also to provide income security for the expanding middle strata of post-war societies. Standards of living were protected for manual workers with average incomes and regular employment and the professionals and managers of the new middle class. The gradual incorporation of the middle class into the welfare state created a cross-class coalition in favour of public provision. The middle classes became allies, rather than enemies, of the welfare state (Esping-Anderson, 1990; Ashford, 1986).

The historical pattern which underlay the development of modern welfare states in Europe was not followed in the United States. Social insurance was not established until 1935 and then it did not include health insurance. Even after the Second World War, modern social security was limited to the creation of old-age pensions as a retirement wage. In post-war America, the welfare state continued to be a welfare state for the poor alone with no universality in health care provision, unemployment benefits or family allowances. Partial systems such as Medicaid and Aid to Families with Dependent Children provided assistance to the very poor only. The only social security which incorporated the middle classes was old-age pensions. However, because the political base of the retirement wage was not the poor but the better-off – industrial workers and the broad middle class – old-age pensions were able to resist attacks made upon them by the New Right in most recent times (Weir *et al.* (eds), 1988).

The unique pattern of social security development in the United States cannot be described as simply historically lagging behind the evolution of European welfare. Public policy has been determined by specific features of American politics. Specific characteristics of the American political universe failed to bring about the cross-class coalition between elites, the middle classes and industrial workers that was a prerequisite for the formation of welfare states elsewhere. State formation in the nineteenth and twentieth centuries was a major determinant of the United States' social policy reform, and did not provide the political structure necessary for the construction of a welfare state on the European model. Confidence in the institution of new social policies depended upon the capacities of states to implement them. Implementation required professional rather than patronage systems of administration. In Europe, state administrations gradually shed patronage and replaced it with a professionalized civil service with bureaucratic autonomy. In most European states, the bureaucratization of the administrative state took place before mass democratization of the executive. This pattern of state formation was a prerequisite to the institution of social policy reform. For social insurance to succeed, state administration had to have the capacity to plan and administer complex programmes. Influential public officials could then play key roles in formulating new social policies with existing administrative resources, press them on executives and work out compromises with interest groups. Contributory social insurance was a difficult negotiation which provided benefits but taxed workers and employers and meant that the state had to intervene in what had previously been the domain of working-class voluntary associations. While popular support for non-contributory pensions could be used by policy makers to overcome opposition, elite support for reform depended upon the administrative capacity of the state to implement policy initiatives efficiently and honestly. Elite support could only be recruited if the state administrative apparatus inspired confidence that policies would be workable (Weir *et al.*, (eds), 1988).

The sequence of bureaucratization and democratization has been critical to the process of state formation. In most European states, state bureaucratization preceded democratization. As a result, when modern European political parties emerged and sought electoral support, they could not offer the spoils of office as an inducement to voters and party activists because access to jobs in civil administration was controlled by established bureaucratic elites. Instead, parties had to offer ideological programmatic appeals or promises about how state power might be used to promote policies supported by various interest groups. By the mid-nineteenth century, international economic and military competition had encouraged industrializing societies in Europe to develop a more efficient and professionalized bureaucratic state administration. Where states continued to be governed by patronage, struggles to overcome 'political corruption' and create a professionalized civil service were paramount. The geopolitical isolation of the United States meant that the political system escaped such pressures. In the United States, mass democratization preceded state bureaucratization and as a result civil administration was not protected from partisan use. The franchise was extended to all white males in 1830. Political parties could, however, continue to use government jobs and resources for patronage, and so did not develop programmatic or ideological appeals to mobilize their constituencies. The electoral calculus of party politicians dominated the operations of state organizations, making them less able to use bureaucratic resources to plan autonomous state interventions into civil society. Without a coalition for bureaucratic autonomy American politics continued to be dominated by a system of spoils (Weir *et al.*, (eds), 1988).

Throughout the nineteenth century, democratized patronage became firmly rooted in the American political system. 'Political corruption' was subsequently difficult to overcome when, in the twentieth century, new political forces emerged dedicated to transforming the American state into a technologically professionalized and efficient institutional process. Turning government into a professional operation was a central goal of the new political philosophy of Progressivism which emerged in the United States in the early years of the twentieth century. Progressives wanted to replace democratized patronage with a technologically efficient state apparatus, making the state what they understood as an ethical agency. Instituting social security was at the heart of the Progressive political agenda, but it was continually overshadowed by the task of overcoming 'political corruption' (Weir *et al.*, (eds), 1988).

The ideological transformations which had taken place within European, especially British, liberalism, had also resulted in changing the ideological direction of liberalism in the United States in the early twentieth century. United States liberalism began to move away from beliefs in self-help and distrust of state intervention and began to accept that independence could be thwarted by necessity. New Progressivist liberals in the United States believed that government could support individual liberty by providing security against socially caused misfortune and regulating competition to allow for individual initiatives. There was broad support for Progressive reform in the United States before the First World War. In the 1912 Congressional election, the Progressive Party, led by former president Theodore Roosevelt, won 4 million votes and Woodrow Wilson's Democratic Party won 6 million, edging Republican President William Taft effectively out of power (Ekirch, 1974; Cadenhead, 1974). The Progressives stood on a platform of protecting home and life against the hazards of sickness, irregular employment and old age through social insurance (Thompson, 1979).

Progressivism shared many of the collectivist goals of 'new liberalism' in Europe. Progressivism had a number of collectivist foci, one of which was ecological conservation. President Theodore Roosevelt was greatly concerned with environmental conservation and protection of the integrity of large areas of the country. The conservation of nature equally created a new enthusiasm for the conservation of the health and vigour of the American population. As we discussed in Chapter 9, the Committee of One Hundred grew out of such Progressive enthusiasm. The Committee of One Hundred submitted a number of reports on the conservation of health to the Natural Conservation Commission, which had been created in 1908. The most influential of these was the *Report on National Vitality: Its Wastes and Conservation*, authored by the Yale economist, Irving Fisher. Fisher suggested that it was bad economic and political policy to leave the protection against ill health to voluntary charity or to the philanthropy of physicians. He proposed that a national public health service be created which would also provide a comprehensive system of medical care (Numbers, 1978).

A precedent for state intervention had been set in new laws governing Workmen's Compensation which were established in thirty states before 1915. Workmen's Compensation was the first government-sponsored programme in the United States which involved the services of hospitals and physicians and went beyond traditional concerns with the destitute, the mentally ill and the military. In Europe, the establishment of Workmen's Compensation was soon followed by the creation of social insurance against sickness, disability, unemployment and old age. In the United States, however, the Progressivist support for social insurance was hindered by concerns over continuing 'political corruption'. Those who had led the drive for Workmen's Compensation began to pursue the issue of state health insurance for the general population. The compensation laws had made injury and illness legitimate objects for social assistance, and thereby shifted the economic burden of unemployment created by sickness from the individual worker to the industrial system. The campaign for Workmen's Compensation was led by the American Association for Labour Legislation, which was founded in 1906 after the Paris meeting of the

International Association for Labour Legislation in 1900. The AALL was headed by Progressivist labour economists and intellectuals, and by 1913 its 3,000 members consisted of academic social scientists, social workers and Progressives interested in social reform. While not militantly radical, the AALL believed in using the regulating power of the state for the public benefit beyond simply the domain of the military, the police and the postal services. Supporters of individual enterprise, they nevertheless believed that there were circumstances in which the social system rather than the individual must become responsible for social welfare (Numbers, 1978).

The AALL scheme for state health insurance aimed to provide support for the costs of illnesses and accidents which occurred outside the workplace. In 1912 the Association created a Committee on Social Insurance, consisting of three members recruited from the American Medical Association's Social Insurance Committee. These three doctors, Alexander Lambert, I. M. Rubinow and S. S. Goldwater, became the driving force behind the campaign. At the first American Conference on Social Insurance, held in Chicago in 1913, Rubinow took a strong position against what he called 'the fetishism of self-help' which led to the preference for voluntary insurance and the growth of charity and commercial benefit organizations. He suggested that alternatively the European experience had demonstrated the superiority of compulsory state insurance in bringing about a uniform system in which all workers were equally well covered.

The AALL presumed that the easy passage of the Workmen's Compensation campaign into law would be repeated with health insurance. Rubinow and his associates believed that the persuasive power of the successful slogan for Workmen's Compensation, 'Safety First', would be matched by the idea of 'Health First'. In his presidential address to the Association in 1916, Irving Fisher optimistically urged the United States to reproduce the 'Great German Miracle' of exponential economic growth since the adoption of social insurance in 1883. But the Association did not anticipate the force of opposition health insurance would arouse. The initial support of the American Medical Association and representatives of the private insurance industry was short-lived. Once both groups perceived that health insurance was not inevitable, they fiercely campaigned against it. Opposition from powerful lobbies was not the only reason, however, why health insurance in particular and social insurance generally was not introduced in the United States before the First World War (Numbers, 1978). Progressivism was unable to build the cross-class coalition necessary to generate political support for public spending on social security. Middle-class support for public spending could not be recruited as long as the state administration failed to inspire confidence. Anxieties over the continuation of 'political corruption' had been heightened by the massively abused and politically corrupted system of military pensions set up for veterans of the Civil War. Civil War pensions had demonstrated the continued existence of democratized patronage in the American political system which undermined middle-class confidence in the capacity of the state to implement social policy and public spending efficiently and honestly. Unable to mobilize support for implementing reforms through central government, Progressives attempted instead to institute reforms at state government level, where a patchwork of social insurance policies were implemented. The experience gained by Progressivist reformers in state government, however, had an important influence upon the structure of social security eventually set up as the New Deal in 1935 under the Social Security Act (Weir *et al.*, (eds), 1988).

Progressive reformism lost its momentum with the entry of the United States into the First World War, but the creation of centralized federal administration to mobilize American resources for war led reformers to believe that these could be extended to peacetime. For example, the AALL hoped that the US State Employment Service could form the basis for unemployment insurance in the same way as unemployment insurance had been created in Britain after the establishment of national labour exchanges. However, whereas in Europe the First World War stimulated political support for social insurance, in the United States emergency war organizations were dismantled after demobilization. In the post-war era, an anti-bureaucratic state was promoted by Presidents Warren Harding, Calvin Coolidge and Herbert Hoover. Hoover developed the idea of an 'associative state' which would encourage research, planning and co-opera-tion by private groups and encourage enlightened capitalists to provide for the needs of citizens in an industrial society without government interference. In the associative state, social security would be provided by 'welfare capitalism'. Welfare capitalism, however, only gave protection to a tiny proportion of the workforce, those employed by industrialists who established welfare programmes for their employees. Welfare capitalism remained a powerful ideological force against public social spending until it was utterly discredited by its total failure to cope with the depravation caused by economic depression in the 1930s (Weir *et al.*, (eds), 1988).

The Great Depression of the 1930s dramatically changed the context of American politics and set in motion changes which facilitated the creation of New Deal social welfare legislation. By 1932, four years of economic depression had shattered the belief that corporate welfare programmes and private charity could substitute for public provision in a period of economic downturn. Hoover had responded to the crisis by trying to continue to work within a voluntarist framework encouraging expanded philanthropic efforts. Their blatant failure meant that demands for federal intervention mounted, and again popular and expert interest was revived in using public policy to solve social and economic problems. Franklin Roosevelt won the 1932 presidential election promising inter-vention which would respond to the demands of mass movements such as Huey Long's 'Share our Wealth' movement, Father Coughlin's National Union for Social Justice, and Dr Francis Townsend's Old-Age Pensions movement. Public sentiment was reinforced by the marches of the unemployed, sit-down strikes, increased voting among new-stock urban dwellers and farmers' protests (Weir *et al.*, (eds), 1988).

Mass movements and pressure groups made reform a necessity and popular support made Roosevelt's policy initiatives possible. Roosevelt worked to build a cross-class coalition for social policy using intellectuals and activists who had received their political training through the Progressive movement to study and plan social security policy. The Committee on Economic Security (CES), set up in 1934, was chaired by Labour Secretary, Francis Perkins, and consisted of Progressives who believed in good government and fiscal responsibility. The Committee members had gained their experience of government running expert agencies in state administrations. State agencies were the enduring legacy of Progressivist state-building and social reform efforts. The New Deal reformers had to balance the demands for federal reform against the persistent articulation of 'states' rights', especially by Southern Democrats. While not subscribing to the reactionary philosophy of the 'states' rights' lobby, Franklin D. Roosevelt and his colleagues nevertheless valued state administrations even though they were trying to develop a national system. National uniformity versus state autonomy was a persistent tension which accounted for the shape of the New Deal. The Social Security Act in 1935 provided national contributory old-age pensions for covered industries and a federal–state contributory insurance system for the unemployed, in which the states were induced but not compelled to participate. Benefit levels and eligibility requirements were set by the states. States were given the option of establishing non-contributory means-tested social assistance for dependent children with only one parent and for the elderly who did not qualify for insurance benefits. The costs of public assistance programmes would be shared between federal and state funds (Weir *et al.*, (eds), 1988; Starr, 1982).

Health insurance was omitted from the Social Security Act because Roosevelt and his aides, such as Edwin Witte of the CES, believed that opposition to its inclusion would have led to the defeat of the Social Security Act. Witte also believed that health insurance benefited doctors rather than patients by providing government subsidy to the medical profession, allowing patients to purchase more and more medicine. The omission of health insurance from the Social Security Act, however, was a legacy of the failure to get health insurance passed in the Progressive Era. The opponents of health insurance massively increased their influence following the first defeats of health insurance, which allowed them to resist its inclusion in the New Deal (Weir *et al.*, (eds), 1988).

Although support for health insurance withered, the popular interest in the progress of medicine expanded in the inter-war years. Popular novels, journalism and film production all raised the public profile of 'The Men in White', who were represented as heroes of the age, pushing back the boundaries of knowledge and winning the battle against disease and chronic illness. Medical progress appeared to be a politically neutral investment for philanthropic organizations. From the beginning of the century, large financial foundations such as the Rockefeller and Carnegie trusts poured money into both biological and social-scientific medical research and health policy. In 1910 the Carnegie Foundation funded Abraham Flexner to conduct an inspection of the state of American medical education. This study was followed up by a Rockefeller initiative to reorganize American medical education into a system of hierarchical schools and institutions in order to try and place it on a scientific basis. Organized medicine responded by endorsing further studies into the organization of medical practice and care (Fox, 1986; Fox, 1993).

In 1926 a Commission on Medical Education (CME) was endorsed by the American Medical Association (AMA) and funded by the Carnegie, Macy and Rockefeller Foundations. In the same year a Committee on the Costs of Medical Care (CCMC) was set up, also endorsed by the AMA and funded by eight foundations. The CCMC was dominated by the same coalition which had antagonized the medical profession during the campaign for compulsory health insurance. It consisted of forty-two members, of whom fourteen were private practitioners, six were public health officials, eight were doctors from hospitals and representatives of the AMA, five were economists and nine academic social scientists ostensibly represented the general public. The CCMC targeted the blame for the disorganization of medical care upon the medical profession itself. William F. Ogburn of the University of Chicago developed a sociological theory of cultural lag which the CCMC used to explain why institutional change based on scientific advance was resisted by a medical profession who stuck to outmoded customs and habits. A vanguard movement was required to ensure that technology was fully utilized and progress promoted. The leading academics on the CCMC considered themselves to be this vanguard. Ogburn and his CCMC colleagues, such as Michael Davis, a social scientist, and I. S. Falk, a public health administrator, characterized the majority of the medical profession as handicraftsmen clinging to traditional individualistic practice. But scientific progress had made medical care the key to the development of health and it must therefore be organized collectively in order to exploit fully the advantages of technology. Doctors needed to take on a new role as health evangelists to society, distributing new knowledge as well as treating disease (Hirshfield, 1970).

The Progressivist campaigners for compulsory health insurance before 1920 had focused their attention on establishing sickness benefit, which would cover the loss of wages resulting from a period of illness. The CCMC, however, demonstrated that the costs of medical treatment now far outweighed the loss of earnings. For families earning under $1,200 per year, the costs of medical care were 20 per cent more than the loss of earnings. For families with incomes higher than this, the cost of medical care was 85 per cent higher than the loss of earnings. Medical expenses were thus becoming a much larger feature of a family's budget. The CCMC believed that medical care was the key to improving health because the advances of science meant that it could be much more effective in reducing the burdens of illness (Fox, 1986).

The Final Report of the Majority of the Committee, published in 1932, argued that a greater proportion of national wealth should be spent on medicine. The Progressives had envisaged insurance as a means of covering the existing costs of illness. The CCMC now viewed insurance as a way of budgeting for ever larger expenditures. The CCMC envisaged medical insurance as a form of advanced credit purchase. Insurance should take on an expansionary function, going beyond the maintenance of incomes during illness to provide funds to support the expanded use of medical care. The committee did not explore, however, the implications that this expansion of medical expenditure would have for those who controlled the supply of medicine. Its recommendations for the reorganization of medical provision were based upon assumptions about the benevolent power of the medical expert to determine the right structure of a new system. Basically, their analysis of the requirement for reorganization was aimed at reducing the barriers to access to medical care by enhancing the power of professionals and organizing medicine on a bureaucratic basis. The Committee believed that the structure of provision could be changed first by voluntary insurance and then through compulsory insurance. Voluntary insurance schemes would encourage group practice and medical co-operatives. The Committee recommended that hospitals be converted into comprehensive health centres serving a local area. Each health centre would include general inpatient and out-patient medical services and be the centre for public health administration. Medical stations within the area would be administratively attached to the health centres. The Committee suggested that the system would be most efficiently funded through a prepayment scheme (Fox, 1986; Hirshfield, 1970).

Thirty-five members of the Committee signed the Final Report. Some members dissented from recommending voluntary rather than compulsory insurance because they believed that it would inhibit the creation of a national system. Liberal Committee members Edgar Sydenstricker and Walter Hamilton refused to sign because they felt the Report was ill conceived and too conservative. The main dissenters, however, were doctors who were offended by the tone of the Report and the blame it assigned to the medical profession for the current state of disarray. The AMA responded negatively to the 1932 Report, and from then onwards the editor of *Journal of the American Medical Association (JAMA)*, Morris Fischbein, accused academics and the medical elite of trying to reorganize medicine into a collective hierarchical practice. He claimed this was 'socialized medicine' and equated it with revolutionary socialist politics. The division between the elite specialist and rank-and-file generalists within the American medical profession was starkly revealed by the reaction to the CCMC 1932 Report. The lone general practitioner felt threatened by both the scientific advance of medical education and proposals for reorganizing medical care into group practice funded by prepayment. The determination of the rank-and-file practitioners to resist changes which would affect their livelihoods, autonomy and status hardened and influenced all subsequent debates concerning health care provision in the United States until after the Second World War (Fox, 1986; Starr, 1982).

The exclusion of health insurance from the New Deal legislation meant nevertheless that doctors found it harder and harder to get their bills paid as the recession deepened. Support grew within the medical profession for some form of reform of funding for medical care, in particular funding which would eliminate the economic uncertainty created for families by hospitalization. It was the rising costs of hospitalization rather than idealistic notions about socialized medicine which stimulated the development of prepaid medical care. In the

1920s, hospital groups established a variety of non-profit-making prepayment schemes for individuals and families to reduce the costs of hospitalized illness. Group hospital insurance covered the costs of hospital residence but did not include the costs of medical care. Other schemes for comprehensive hospital care coverage for employees and their families were organized by employers, the farmworkers' and other unions, and mutual aid societies (Grey, 1989). Some of these schemes extended coverage to general medical care and the services of physicians, and were an expression of 'welfare capitalism', in which employers provided systematic social security for employees. Physicians who were engaged by employment groups, however, were often banned from the local and state medical societies, which meant that they were excluded from hospital privileges in their area. Some state medical societies nevertheless began their own schemes for group hospital insurance. Group hospital insurance stimulated the establishment from 1929 of Blue Cross Plans throughout the United States. By 1946, over 21 million Americans were enrolled in this form of voluntary health insurance. A Blue Cross Plan was a non-profit corporation community organization which accepted members and equal payments from groups of members which covered the expenses of their bills for a period of hospitalization. These plans were supplemented by medically sponsored Blue Shield Plans, which provided coverage for medical and surgical services. The initial cost of plan membership was roughly 75 cents a month per person and $2 per family. Rates for doctors' services were about the same. The benefits of the plan were paid to members in terms of services provided rather than in cash payments. Membership was encouraged by tax exemption for contributions. Blue Cross Plans were established through enabling Acts and were supervised by an approval programme organized by the American Hospital Association and by the insurance department of individual state administrations (Law, 1976; Anderson, 1975; Anderson, 1985).

The Second World War revived political interest in social policy and health planning. New enthusiasm for reorganization of medical services and government subsidy developed among the medical profession as a result of their wartime experience. Military medicine, organized hierarchically and collectively, achieved prominent successes in saving soldiers' lives. As a result, American doctors who had served as military MOs became aware of the benefits of group practice based on scientific principles. The new enthusiasm for legislative reform was supported by the American Hospital Association and the United States Public Health Service. President Roosevelt also made a new commitment to the introduction of health reform. Wartime social policy planning in Britain extended the pre-war focus on insurance as the basis of social security; in the United States, wartime social policy extended the New Deal emphasis on obtaining full employment. The National Resource Planning Board (NRPB), set up in 1942, produced *Security, Work and Relief Policies*, an equivalent document to the Beveridge Report, in 1943. The report identified full employment as the central goal of social policy. NRPB advocated the nationalization of the United States employment service and unemployment insurance, and the creation of disability and health insurance. The report also wanted to uncouple benefits from contributions and wanted social security to be funded by taxation. The Social Security Board, however, was only lukewarm towards the report. The Progressives in this agency objected to nationalization of general assistance because they believed that replacing contributory insurance with aid funded by taxation would transform it into a guaranteed income and encourage dependency (Fox, 1986; Fox, 1993; Starr, 1982).

The NRPB planning proposals were not defeated by bureaucratic rivalries, however, but by political changes taking place during the war. Full-employment policies had wide support during the Depression, but when employment soared during the war they lost popular appeal. The British parliamentary system had facilitated a formal coalition, and the Emergency Powers Act of 1940 gave the government the capacity to conscript property, control labour distribution and ration food. These powers were extended to be in effect two years after the war. Wartime mobilization established planning for industrial location, employment and housing which supported a vigorous social policy programme by the post-war Labour government. In the US, political coalition was only informal and elections continued during the war as normal. American defeats in the Pacific theatre and wartime emergency measures made the Democrats unpopular, and they lost fifty seats in the Congressional elections of 1942. Roosevelt's enthusiasm for social security reform was now limited by the weakened Democrat executive. Congress eliminated some of the executive planning committees, such as the NRPB, and policy initiatives were left to liberals in the Senate and the House of Representatives. The Wagner–Murray–Dingell Bills were drawn up in 1943 by liberal senators with the aid of the Social Security Board. In 1943, emphasis shifted back to social security rather than full employment, and mirrored many of the proposals of the Beveridge Report. Before his death, President Roosevelt finally gave his full support to the establishment of a national health programme, and in 1944 he asked Congress to agree to the establishment of a whole new charter supporting economic opportunity after the war. However, by that stage a conservative Congress had overtaken post-war planning and Congressional committees became so weighted with conservatives that Republican Robert Taft became head of a key Senate sub-committee. By the time Harry Truman became president in 1945, Congress had already become unfavourable to the liberal social policy planning of the late New Deal and early war periods (Starr, 1982).

After Roosevelt's death, President Truman introduced his own new programme for national health into Congress. Truman's programme repeated the main principles of the Wagner–Murray–Dingell Bill but made hospital construction and expansion the primary reform. He also proposed that a federal system of universal compulsory insurance should be introduced regardless of income or employment status. Those who were unable to pay would have their contributions made by public agencies. This universal federal system was intended to by-pass previous proposals for schemes administered at the individual state level. Under the federal system, the organization of medical care would remain unchanged and patients would retain the freedom to choose any doctor or hospital, with the dollars following the patient. Truman emphasized that this was not socialized medicine, because no interference was made into the delivery of services or the freedom of the physician to set and charge fees. Truman characterized the new programme rather as a government subsidy for the purchase of existing services (Poen, 1979; Starr, 1982; Fox, 1986; Jacobs, 1993).

Despite bending over backwards to accommodate the interests of the medical profession, however, the Truman programme was rejected by the AMA, who announced that the new system would 'make slaves' out of doctors. Alternatively, the AMA proposed an expansion of the public health services for the indigent and the further development of voluntary insurance. When Truman's Bill was entered into Congress, Republicans insisted that it constituted the greatest piece of socialist legislation ever to be put before the house. In 1946 the Republicans replaced the Democratic majority and Senator Taft replaced Senator Thomas Murray as the head of the Social Security and Labour Committee. He proposed an alternative programme for the expansion of a means-tested public health service for the destitute and support for the development of voluntary insurance for the employed. When the liberals objected that this would divide Americans into stigmatized paupers and freemen, Taft replied that the unemployed must suffer the consequences of their misfortune. Taft's programme, however, was never translated into realistic legislative proposals. Within the atmosphere of the Cold War, health insurance became labelled as Communist treachery. Taft insisted that government propaganda for the scheme should be investigated. Suspicion fell upon a member of I.S. Falk's staff who had written a favourable report about socialized medicine in New Zealand. He was accused of being an agent of Moscow toeing the party line. An inquiry by the FBI cleared his name but the stigma of Communist sympathy was subsequently linked to the federal insurance issue (Poen, 1979; Starr, 1982).

Despite this propaganda war, Truman persisted with his aim and after his surprise re-election in 1948 the AMA believed they had arrived at Armageddon. They hired public relations experts to mount a savage war of words in which health insurance was depicted as a Soviet plot to overthrow the American way of life. They used pamphlets, the press and public speakers to support 'voluntarism' as the American Way, and to claim that the socialization of medicine would lead to the socialization of every other aspect of American life. The AMA campaign managed to exploit the weaknesses in public support for the Truman programme. The greatest support came from the lower income groups. Middle-class workers – those with far more influence in community agencies, the media and local government – demonstrated a preference for voluntary insurance over the introduction of federal contributions. The AMA was able to appeal to these differences in opinion and link the federal system of health insurance with the Soviet threat, thus undermining public support. As anti-Communist feeling increased, the support for federal insurance dropped in the public opinion polls from 56 to below 30 per cent (Starr, 1982).

With the election of Republican President Eisenhower, federal policy on national health care was largely abandoned until it was revived under the Johnson administration in the 1960s. In the meantime, government subsidy for post-war hospital construction was achieved through the Hill-Burton Act, which provided local areas with grants-in-aid to subsidize hospital building. This Act was supported by conservatives and liberals as a non-threatening means of support for the development of the hospital as the primary agency for advancing medical progress in American society. The consensus surrounding the Hill-Burton Act echoed one of the main themes of the 1930s studies on the costs of medical care (Fox, 1986; Fox, 1993).

Wartime economic mobilization differed in Britain and the United States. In Britain, centralization of control was achieved through permanent ministries. In the US, centralization used temporary ad hoc bureaucratic agencies to co-ordinate federal and state government. The weakness of federal controls over wartime economy meant that centralization could not be converted into a post-war practice. Social security and health planning were casualties of the inability of the federal government to maintain the momentum of its wartime economic and social mobilization in the post-war period.

HEALTH AND HAPPINESS FOR ALL

From the early twentieth century, a new collectivist political will promoted increased state intervention in the provision of welfare in industrial societies. In European states, the balance of mixed economies of public and private voluntary protection shifted up to the end of the Second World War. When the role of the central government in welfare provision expanded at the expense of private or voluntary organizations, it was legitimated by an ideological faith in the capacity of the state to generate greater social equality. European states instituted comprehensive welfare systems after the war in the belief that the principle of universalism would turn public protection into a citizenship entitlement and end the stigma of means-tested public and private charity. Ideological transformations within liberalism in the United States also facilitated the development of the provision of social security beyond a subsistence minimum for some groups, such as the retired. However, structural forces within the institutional political process in the United States prevented the development of universal welfare after the Second World War. Health care was not included in federal welfare provision until partial coverage was created for the poor and the elderly in the Medicaid and Medicare programmes of the 1960s. Beyond the United States, comprehensive coverage and universal entitlements were to be challenged as economic conditions and social attitudes changed among increasingly affluent post-war industrial societies.

12 Conditional citizenship: the new political economy of health

After the Second World War, European states and the United States consolidated and expanded their systems of public protection. Those systems based upon the principle of universalism aimed to provide security without stigma. Within this context, the first three decades following 1945 witnessed the establishment of welfare states, with social policies designed to reduce disadvantage and maintain social solidarity and cohesion in advanced industrial societies divided by systems of economic and social stratification. According to some social policy analysts, three different models of liberal, corporatist-statist and decommodified social democratic welfare states emerged in this period (Esping-Anderson, 1990). These three worlds of welfare relied on more or less bureaucratically administered state funding, voluntary and compulsory insurance, or market mechanisms for the provision of services and social security. A significant division developed between the generous insurance-based social security systems operated in parts of continental Europe and the lower level of insurance plus tax-funded means-tested state benefits operated in Britain (Flora (ed.), 1986). Further divisions occurred between the universal statutory insurance-based systems constructed in Europe and the private insurance plus means-tested welfare provision operated in the United States (Girod *et al.* (eds), 1985). A fourth model of welfare provision developed separately in the Antipodes, involving means-testing without social stigma (Castles and Mitchell, 1991). Classic welfare states were constructed within an epoch of exceptional economic growth enjoyed by societies which adopted a Keynesian model of economic management based upon the principle of full employment (Deakin, 1994).

Within these broad frameworks, different rates of welfare expansion continued for the first three decades following 1945, until international economic crises in the mid-1970s ended what has been eulogized as a 'golden era' of political consensus, economic growth, rising living standards and social justice (Esping-Anderson, 1997; Lowe, 1993). Some historians have suggested that the political consensus surrounding the construction of post-war welfare states was symbolized by the emergence of 'Butskellism' within the British context (Lowe, 1990). 'Butskellism' represented a set of common agreements which emerged between the two British political parties identified with R.A. Butler, a Tory Chancellor of the Exchequer, and Hugh Gaitskell, leader of the Labour Party, in the late 1950s. However, other historians have argued that the appearance of consensus, especially within the context of British politics, thinly masked deeply embedded conflicts about the purpose, objectives and value of public welfare which were to become powerfully influential when economic downturn began to change the political maps of advanced industrial societies (Kavanagh and Seldon, 1989). Although the end of the era of welfare expansion in Europe was driven by economic change, it also stimulated significant ideological shifts (Clarke *et al.*, 1992). In the United States, social welfare provision increased after the Second World War, but was not based upon the principle of universal public protection without stigma. American suspicions of public provision gained force in the development of social policy on both sides of the Atlantic from the mid-1970s (Girod *et al.*, 1985). The idea of Keynesian-managed modern economies supporting full employment was dramatically undermined as growth rates declined, governments' deficits soared and the costs of public provision surpassed the capacity of industrial societies to afford them (Apple, 1980). From the late 1970s to the 1990s, welfare states faced new economic and ideological challenges (Deakin, 1994; Mishra, 1990; Mishra, 1984). Some historians have suggested that a new political consensus emerged from this period, resulting in a universal shift towards right-wing neo-liberal economic and political policies (George and Miller, 1994; Seldon, 1994).

The health of ageing populations in advanced industrial societies was significantly determined by these sea changes in welfare policy, which affected the provision of medical services throughout the period following the Second World War. Equally, the issue of health care service provision became critical to the changing nature of the welfare debate. Outcomes of this debate remain uncertain.

The period following the Second World War up to the mid-1970s has been identified as the era in which the classic welfare state flourished (Digby, 1989; Lowe, 1993; Deakin, 1994). It was a period in which governments in advanced industrial societies actively promoted individual welfare by trying to slay William Beveridge's 'five giants' of idleness, squalor, disease, want and ignorance (Timmins, 1995). The method which most democratic governments chose was to use progressive taxation to maintain full employment and allocate scarce resources efficiently in order to prevent the wastage caused by unregulated markets. Unregulated markets were held responsible by Keynesian economic theory for causing the economic crises of the 1930s in that they inefficiently allocated resources, since it was impossible to measure the consequences of decisions taken by individuals or firms within the market. Therefore, the market was unable to provide sufficient necessary common services, public goods like public health which are in everybody's interest and which cannot charge a price. Unregulated markets misallocated resources because it was not possible to justify theoretical assumptions about the perfect knowledge of consumers and perfect competition between producers in the real world. In England, the spectre of economic disaster in the 1930s underlay an early cross-party post-war determination to ensure that it should never happen again (Hennessy, 1992). Similar perceptions encouraged the view among other post-war Western governments that state intervention would maximize economic efficiency, and they also adopted the Keynesian route to sustained economic growth and prosperity through corporately managed economies (Hall, 1989). Keynesian theory was built upon the principle that, in Keynes's words, if you 'look after unemployment...the budget will look after itself' (Timmins, 1995). William Beveridge had stressed the way in which full employment was the lynch-pin of universal social security. Full employment was necessary to pay for the welfare state by maintaining the solvency of the social insurance system. As important, however, was the role that full employment played in allowing universal public protection to create an equal society, not least because it prevented the alienation which results from social rejection (Cutler *et al.*, 1986).

Governments engaged in expanding their welfare states believed that public protection would help to establish equality in the social status of their citizens (Harris, 1992; Harris, 1996). This was not the same thing as achieving an equality of outcome, in the sense of a direct redistribution of wealth (Offe, 1984; Gough, 1979). The politics of post-war equality were more in line with what the British sociologist T.H. Marshall had described in 1949 as a new type of 'social citizenship' in which equal social status was accorded to all through the establishment of social rights (Marshall, 1950). Marshall suggested that, although it originated in ancient societies, modern citizenship had evolved in three stages from the end of the eighteenth century, when citizenship first became defined in terms of the civil right to equality under the law. The right to equal political participation was developed in emergent democratic nation-states in the nineteenth century but, as Karl Marx had pointed out, neither civil nor political rights eliminated economic and social inequality (Barbalet, 1988). According to Marshall, from the early twentieth century the demands of organized labour, through collective bargaining, addressed the issue of inequality by establishing the social right to a prevailing standard of living and the social heritage of a society. In Marshall's account, social rights grew out of industrial rights as an extension of civil rights. Reducing inequality was a prerequisite of achieving social rights, and Marshall argued that a social policy which established a national minimum was thus inherently linked to the institutionalization of social citizenship. The concept of social citizenship subsequently became identified with that of the welfare state (Barbalet, 1988).

Marshall differentiated welfare as a social right from earlier systems of state or charitable provision for the poor which often incurred the loss of rights. The nineteenth-century New Poor Law system in England, for example, deterred applicants by making them 'less eligible' than those in work for civil freedoms and political participation. Receipt of Poor Law relief entailed the loss of whatever civil and political rights an individual may have possessed (Heater, 1990). Marshall claimed that when welfare was provided as a social right it did not involve the sanction of stigmatization. In the 1960s, the American sociologist Erving Goffman's work (Goffman, 1968) on social stigma was highly influential upon the work of theorists of social welfare such as the British professor of social administration at the London School of Economics, Richard Titmuss (Titmuss, 1968). Titmuss dominated the post-war academic study of social policy. He believed that the pursuit of equality would lead to increased social integration and harmony. The welfare state would, Titmuss suggested, restore community and mutual care in society. Social harmony based upon mutual care could only succeed, however, if welfare provided universal rather than selective benefits, since targeting provision used means-testing, which created stigma. Those identified as 'the neediest' through selection obtained, in Goffman's terms, a 'spoiled identity' which facilitated discrimination. Selection resulted in social rejection for a variety of groups which experienced discrimination on the basis of their ethnicity, class, gender or mental fitness (A. Deacon, 1996).

Marshall's concept of social citizenship and Titmuss's prescriptions for social policy have been much criticized. The sociologist Bryan Turner has argued that Marshall's teleological account of citizenship as an historically accumulative process incorrectly assumes that citizenship is an inevitable process which accompanies the development of industrial capitalism (Turner, 1986; Turner, 1993). This is contradicted by the development of industrial economies in East Asia and South America without welfare states in the late twentieth century (Esping-Anderson, 1997). Furthermore, the idea that social rights were an outgrowth of civil rights ignores, according to Anthony Giddens, the extent to which they have actually resulted from class conflict and have been fought for by the industrial proletariat in its battles with the bourgeoisie (Giddens, 1982). The concept of universalism underlying Beveridge, Marshall and Titmuss's view of welfare as a social right has been criticized for actually applying to male bread-winners only and ignoring the rights of both women and ethnic minorities (Lister, 1997). For Beveridge, Marshall and Titmuss, welfare was a social right earned by participation in the labour process, the opportunity for which was often denied to both women and members of ethnic minorities who have been historically discriminated against (Lister, 1997). Feminists especially have argued that the universalism of the Beveridgean welfare state and Marshallian social citizenship contained exclusionary features which masked the politics of difference. Universalism in the classic welfare state recognized the citizenship of earners, who were mostly men, but ignored the rights to citizenship of carers, who were mostly women (Lister, 1997).

Titmuss's work was, nevertheless, highly influential among policy-makers both within and beyond Britain after the Second World War because there was widespread acceptance among Western social democratic political parties that the causes of poverty were structural and not the result of personal failing (A. Deacon, 1996). Up to the 1970s, social democratic governments designed policies to redress the inequalities caused through economic and industrial organization. In Britain, social security was distributed as a social right to those who obtained it through participation in the labour process. It continued to be doled out on a means-tested basis as handouts to those unable to work, who remained perceived as public burdens rather than as individuals engaged in unpaid work. In Britain, the insurance principle guaranteed public protection to workers and their dependants against the misfortunes of unemployment, sickness and old age (Lowe, 1993; Glennerster, 1995). In other European countries, however, the universal principle was extended to citizenship itself (Castles, 1978; Flora, 1986; Esping-Anderson, 1990). In Sweden and France, benefit was distributed from central funds according to citizenship status rather than based on participation in the labour market. However, where Beveridge interpreted universalism in terms of flat-rate contributions and benefits, Sweden, France and Germany soon developed earnings-related schemes, which turned social security into replacement wages rather than subsistence doles (George and Taylor-Gooby (eds), 1996).

In the period of welfare expansion, expenditure on the public sector of the economy and social security provision was perceived as a stimulant rather than a drain on economic growth. State intervention was believed to increase efficiency, and social policy played a constructive complementary role to economic policy. In Britain, William Beveridge had attacked the pessimistic fatalism of the Treasury department, who saw social security as an unproductive expenditure. On the contrary, Beveridge argued, increased social expenditure would produce economic benefits, and social security was a precondition of economic growth. Employers and the macro-economy got a healthier, better educated, more mobile and, as a result, more highly productive labour force. Employees paid contributions into a comprehensive state system, which gave them much greater value for money than a mixture of voluntary and state insurance. Eliminating poverty was not only a crusade against a moral scandal within modern civilization, but it also constituted sound economic judgement (Cutler *et al.*, 1986; A. Deacon, 1996).

These basic principles underlay post-war economic thought that supported public sector and social security expansion up to the early 1970s. In this period welfare provision was believed not only to stimulate economic growth but also to expand individual liberty. Welfarism struck a fine balance between collectivism and individualism. The right to benefits depended upon contributions made to social funds, so that social security was earned by individuals fulfilling their responsibility to the collective good. Since it universally covered the rich, who could not contract out, as well as the poor, universal welfare eliminated stigma and equalized risk and maintenance. Public protection was a social right earned by fulfilling social responsibilities, which eliminated the anarchic individualism of the market-place that allowed the weak to go to the wall and guaranteed security without the authoritarianism of a totally planned economy. Within the social democratic philosophies that dominated Western politics in this period, the welfare state was represented as creating a constructive rather than confrontational relationship between economic and social policy, individualism and collectivism (A. Deacon, 1996; Deakin, 1994; Clarke *et al.*, 1992).

SOCIAL DEMOCRACY AND CORPORATE-STATISM: THE ROLE OF HEALTH IN FULL-EMPLOYMENT WELFARE STATES 1945–1975

The most extensive interpretation of the concept of universal comprehensive welfare policy was made in post-war Sweden (Heclo and Madsden, 1987; Olson, 1990; Allardt, 1986; see also Graubard (ed.), 1986). Here the Social Democratic Party's project of the 'People's Home' became a national agenda resulting in what Gosta Esping-Anderson has suggested has been a decommodified welfare state based upon public management of the labour market to maximize the potential of full employment (Esping-Anderson, 1990). Sustainable political stability in the negotiations between capital and labour had been established in the 1930s in the model of collective bargaining established between the Swedish Federation of Manual Workers' Trades Unions (LO) and the Employers' Association (SAF). This, together with neutrality during the Second World War, established the basis for sustainable economic growth in the post-war period. Substantial growth rates in the 1950s and 1960s and high levels of exports allowed the Social Democratic Party, now perceived as the 'natural' party of government, to expand social and economic welfare (Gould, 1996).

By the end of the 1970s, Sweden was regarded by social scientists and some Western governments as the prototype of an advanced modern society (Castles, 1978). Impressive growth of Sweden's capitalist economy had given Swedes almost the highest standards of living in the world. This had been achieved along with a major commitment to full employment and rationalized state management of the labour market. Sweden also achieved greater labour mobility and a more extensive system of social security than anywhere else. By the 1970s, Sweden had universal systems of health insurance, income-related old-age pensions, sickness and unemployment benefits, a comprehensive system of schooling based upon mixed-ability teaching and a high-quality state-housing programme. Social security benefits and pensions supplied unemployed or sick workers and retired pensioners with up to 90 per cent of their previous earnings. By the early 1970s, Sweden was perceived as the world's most comprehensive modern welfare state, not just for the quantity but for the quality of the programmes offered and the resources allocated to them. Poverty appeared to have been eradicated and the Swedish political system had developed a consensual approach to political decision-making by using an elaborate system of parliamentary commissions which maximized participation. Policy areas would be investigated by a commission for up to ten years. The results of investigations would then be subjected to the *remiss* process whereby they were sent out to various interested parties for discussion. At the end of this process the results would be debated by the opposition political parties. Conflict was substituted with compromise through these procedures (Gould, 1996).

In the early 1970s, the Social Democratic government sought to push Sweden even further towards being the first democratically achieved comprehensive socialist state by introducing radical reforms in higher education, making employers solely responsible for the social insurance contributions of their employees, giving trade unions a greater role in industrial management and by inventing 'wage-earner' funds. The wage-earner funds would require employers to use a proportion of profits for the future benefit of their workforce. Trade union representatives as well as employers would manage the funds. As the Social Democratic Party moved further to the left and the Swedish economy began to experience economic stagnation following the oil crisis in 1973, the Swedish voting population moved to the right for the first time in 44 years and elected a conservative government coalition of the Conservative, Liberal and Centre Parties. The Bourgeois government, however, was disunited and unable to change radically any of the welfare institutions securely established over the previous post-war decades. They continued with many programmes which had been set up by the SDP government, with the exception of the wage-earner funds. Nevertheless, capital investment began to move abroad and the national deficit began to grow. When the Social Democratic Party returned to power in 1982, they inherited an economic disarray exacerbated by the incompetence of the conservative coalitions. Despite adverse economic indicators, the SDP government devalued the krona by 14 per cent to bring the economy under control and succeeded in dramatically reducing the budget deficit with a series of strict economic measures. By the mid-1980s Sweden remained the most successful left-wing Western democratic state, proving that large public-sector investment contributed to economic growth (Gould, 1996; Lewin, 1988; Heclo and Madsden, 1987). At the very end of the 1980s, however, international events began to undermine the Swedish economy in the same way as they had done at an earlier time in other Western societies. In the 1990s, when Sweden was facing an economic crisis, its public sector and social security expenditure posed a major obstacle to recovery (Stephens, 1996).

One of the largest areas of growth in public expenditure in Sweden up to the 1990s was health insurance and health care services. The reasons for this were not unique to Sweden but were the common forces driving up the costs of medical care in all advanced industrial societies. The increasing cost of technological medical treatments, increasing numbers of longer-living chronically sick individuals and ever higher expectations all contributed to increased proportions of gross national products being spent on health care throughout the developed world. The health care system in Sweden, however, although funded by central and local taxes and compulsory health insurance, used charges to ration use. After health insurance was made compulsory in 1955, the cost was removed from employee to employer in 1974, when a new law made employers responsible for four-fifths of the insured person's contribution and the central state responsible for the remaining fifth. This provided the individual with the right to cash support of up to 90 per cent of earnings in periods of sickness, which was subject to taxation to avoid workers being better off when sick than in employment. Individuals were charged when they used services but were entitled to refunds of medical expenses from the insurance system for treatments certified as necessary by a medical practitioner. Various forms of preventive medicine, such as ante-natal services, were free. Hospital out-patient care was also provided without charges by county councils, along with free public ward in-patient care for an unlimited period of time. Pensioner in-patients were charged for treatment after one year in either a county or a municipal long-stay hospital or nursing home. The majority of out-patient care was provided by hospitals and medical centres, which virtually eliminated the function of the family practitioner until the idea of recreating them was proposed in the 1970s. The Liberal Party first introduced the concept of the *husläkare* in 1976 but it failed to be taken up by the Riksdag until it was reintroduced in 1993 by the minority Conservative government. Opposed by the socialist block on the grounds of the expense of creating 4,000 new doctors during a time of enforced public-spending austerity, the law failed to be passed in 1994. By that time, however, 70 per cent of the population had registered with a family practitioner (Heidenheimer and Elvander (eds), 1980; Wilson, 1979).

A serious shortage of medical personnel after the introduction of compulsory health insurance was rectified by the government breaking professional control over training and recruitment. A major rise in the number of medical students and an expansion of medical education took place in Sweden between 1953 and 1973. The government also developed incentives to attract doctors to rural, less well-served areas to try to achieve a more even distribution of general and specialist medical care throughout the country. Swedish doctors had largely maintained a mixed income from public and private practice, but after the 'Seven Crowns Reform' in 1970 all doctors serving insured patients in in- or out-patient care became salaried state employees. Patients could still purchase private practice, but only with doctors in their private surgeries and not in public hospitals or medical centres. The advantages of private purchase of medical care, which included free choice of doctor and more rapid treatment, continued for a small minority of Swedish patients (Heidenheimer and Elvander (eds), 1980; Wilson, 1979).

The Swedish health system used a mixture of central, regional and local organization which attempted to maintain a degree of democratic participation in a large bureaucratic edifice. Insurance funds were administered by the local societies of the National Insurance Boards, which were the successors of voluntary sickness benefit societies. Hospitals and hospital care supplied by county councils, funded through local taxation, continued to expand until the national government imposed tax restrictions upon the county councils in order to limit spending in the 1970s. Planned distribution of services was attempted through the creation of regional hospital areas which tried to achieve a balanced distribution of specialist and general hospital services at the county, district and municipal level. The costs of the expansion of the hospital system in the 1960s and 1970s limited the supply of domiciliary services. Together, these factors increased the use of in-patient hospital services, which in turn increased costs. These developments meant that, by 1975, Sweden spent more of her GNP, 10.2 per cent, on nationalized health services than many of her Western counterparts, which ranged from 3.5 per cent in the USA to 5.2 per cent in the UK, 7.1 per cent in Germany, 6.0 per cent in France and 8.6 per cent in the Netherlands. This expenditure gave Sweden the lowest infant mortality rate among the twelve leading industrial nations in 1975 and almost the longest average life expectancy (Gould, 1996; Heidenheimer and Elvander (eds), 1980). The high share of GNP devoted to health care, however, led to re-evaluation of priorities and restructuring of services in the 1990s (Stephens, 1996).

Sweden's expansive welfare state was only partially imitated by other European governments after the war. In Germany, 'social Keynesianism' was adopted in the state management of the labour market and training, according to the Swedish model. The German post-war social state, however, continued a Bismarckian tradition of providing social and labour programmes to maintain social stability but without pursuing the goal of establishing social equality (Leibfried, 1993). The Christian Democrat coalition which remained in power up to the mid-1970s expanded policies of social protection but promoted job security and power-sharing in industry rather than attempting to redistribute wealth or directly create social egalitarianism. Economic liberalism ensured that all social interventions remained 'market conforming'. As a result, social security was provided through transfer payments rather than through public social services. Social insurance schemes were work-orientated, based upon strongly reinforced principles of self-help. Social and health security were designed to maintain a worker's position in the labour hierarchy acquired through work. Accordingly, the German state was the first to introduce earnings-related benefits and pensions to supply replacement wages instead of universal flat-rate subsistence. Social insurance administration continued to be decentralized through local organizations and was largely funded by employers and employees rather than the state. These measures were underpinned by full employment obtained through co-operation between employers and employee organizations. Trade unions accepted wage restraint in exchange for substantial job security and increased participation in industrial organization along with welfare benefits provided by employers (Lawson, 1996).

But Germany made a much smaller commitment to the public provision of social services. In health care, social insurance provided guaranteed access but medical services and goods were provided by private suppliers. Doctors remained independent practitioners rather than public employees and, with the exception of a small number of public hospitals, hospital care continued to be provided by private and voluntary trusts. Medical expenses and fees were covered by compulsory insurance. While a substantial proportion of GNP was spent on health care, therefore, a small amount of it was paid by the state. The system was little subsidized by taxation. Access was funded through compulsory insurance and services provided by the private and voluntary sectors. The market orientation of public provision was similarly reproduced in both housing and education. An initial drive to build public housing after the war was changed to a public policy of providing housing allowances to tenants in private rented accommodation along with legal rent and rate controls (Lawson, 1996).

For those outside the insurance system social assistance continued to be provided by a mixture of public and voluntary agencies. The principle of 'subsidiarity' allowed the social state to stress family responsibility to provide self-help followed by voluntary relief as a second resort. Public assistance was provided only as a last, and stigmatized, resort for those who had access to no other resources. Up to the mid-1970s only a peripheral minority claimed public assistance. In the early post-war period, therefore, the German social state appeared to have eliminated poverty to the margins of society. Migrant workers who were increasingly employed in the least attractive and least well-paid forms of work in Germany had little access to social services and were not able to claim security from the social fund. The 'guestworkers' facilitated a substantial degree of upward mobility for native German workers without making demands upon the social state (Lawson, 1996).

France, like Germany, founded its post-war welfare state on the insurance principle but also provided assistance to those who fell outside the eligibility criteria or who ran out of their statutory benefits. Compulsory social insurance was set up immediately after the war between 1945 and 1946 and provided cover for health and pensions. Unemployment insurance was not made compulsory for all industrial and commercial workers in the private sector until 1958. Public sector workers were guaranteed continued employment. Unlike anywhere else in Europe, unemployment was and continued to remain outside the social security system and was funded instead by individual schemes set up between employers and employees. Social insurance and benefits were established on an earnings-related basis by the end of the 1970s (Hantrais, 1996).

A specific feature of French social security has been its corporatist administration. Central government decided policy and established the rules of administration, but policy was implemented through a decentralized system of corporatist organizations comprised of elected representatives of employers, unions and the insured themselves. Conflicts arose between central and local goals and objectives, and the pluralistic nature of the French system led to significant variations and discrepancies in service provision between different areas. While the French welfare state provided expansive comprehensive coverage for the first thirty years following the Second World War, its pluralist corporatist nature made it one of the most complex systems in Europe. During the period of progressive expansion France was governed largely by centre-right coalitions which appeared to have little effect upon this trend. When the socialists were elected to power in the 1980s, different economic circumstances required new policies of restraint in public expenditure.

Like pensions and unemployment, sickness benefit in France was placed on a wage-related basis administered by local funds. Additional benefits were paid to individuals who held extra insurance with mutual societies or commercial companies. From the time that the health insurance system was created, medical services were charged for at the point of delivery, but 70 per cent of doctors' fees and 40–100 per cent of treatment costs were reimbursed by insurance cover. All ante-natal and maternal care was free, along with treatment for some long-term chronic conditions. Hospital fees were paid directly from insurance funds and the costs of surgery were covered fully. The medical profession avoided state employment and retained all the principles of private practice, including free choice of doctor by the patient and, in non-hospital care, direct payment between patient and doctor. While doctors remained independent, however, the increasing costs of treatments and drugs became subject to statutory regulation under the insurance system. The biggest increase in health service costs became the growing numbers of the elderly sick requiring long-term care. Many of the elderly qualified for free treatment by virtue of their low incomes. Although the entire working population was covered by health insurance, by 1978 benefits in cash and kind varied for different occupational groups. These inequalities were exacerbated in old age, especially as a multitude of complementary and supplementary pension schemes were established for those in the higher-earning professions and occupations.

The British system of public protection was based on the insurance principle and was substantially funded by taxation. As in Germany and France, universal rights to social security rested upon participation in the labour market, in the case of either workers themselves or their dependants. For those outside the labour force, or those who ran out of their statutory benefit rights, however, a system of Poor Law means-tested public assistance remained. Universalism was interpreted in terms of flat-rate contributions and benefits, and earnings-related replacement wages were not introduced until the 1970s. Sustained growth in public housing and state primary, secondary and higher education was maintained into the 1970s, along with a commitment to full employment. Within this period, however, the British economy grew at a much slower rate than many of its European counterparts (Lowe, 1993; Glennerster, 1995).

Behind an apparent consensus underlying a political commitment to full employment and the welfare state, distinct ideological values divided government social policy (Webster, 1994). Within the Labour Party, a debate continued over the interpretation of equality. The post-war Labour ideologue and one-time Minister of Education, Anthony Crosland, argued in *The Future of Socialism* in 1956 that equality did not depend upon the redistribution of wealth but upon the quality of life that individuals led. Crosland maintained that further nationalization of industry would not influence the progress of equality. Corporate regulation of the economy through a coalition of government and both sides of industry, on the German or Swedish model, could ensure prosperity and full employment. Equality depended instead upon education and personal security. The post-war leader of the Labour Party, Hugh Gaitskell, fought a battle to try and get the Labour Party to abandon its commitment to public ownership; this failed, but Crosland's arguments became a driving force behind social policy when Labour took power (Glennerster, 1995).

The British Conservative Party's endorsement of the welfare state was articulated in a pamphlet called *One Nation* written in 1950 by a group of then young Conservative MPs including Iain Macleod, Angus Maude, Enoch Powell and Edward Heath. A coalition White Paper on *Employment Policy* which committed the government to 'high and stable' unemployment reflected an incipient cross-party acceptance of Keynsianism, captured above all in a report authored largely by the Conservative coalition Minister for Education and post-war Chancellor, R.A. Butler, on the *Industrial Charter*. The post-war party leader and Conservative prime minister, Harold Macmillan, guided policy in the Conservative governments from 1951 to 1964, based upon an acceptance of a mixed public and private sector economy managed by state intervention according to his philosophy of *The Middle Way*, of which he had written in 1938. This apparent acceptance of some of the Labour Party's ground by Conservatives who participated in the consolidation of the post-war welfare state led to a revision in Conservative philosophy which R.A. Butler claimed could never again be called 'reactionary' (Timmins, 1995). Some historians have recently identified the Labour and Conservative participants in the establishment of the post-war welfare state as founders of a mythical utopian New Jerusalem. The 'New Jerusalemers', led by Beveridge, Butler and Bevan, have been accused of erecting what turned out to be a nanny state, which undermined rather than built Britain's long-term prosperity (Barnett, 1986). As Michael Fraser, a Conservative research worker in 1946 who became party chairman as Lord Fraser of Kilmorack under Margaret Thatcher, observed in 1987, 'one nationism' may have placed the two parties on trains running on parallel tracks, but they were always aimed at different destinations (Timmins, 1995).

Nowhere was division between the two major post-war British political parties more clearly evident than in health policy. Problems with providing a tax-funded universally accessible health service arose in the early years of its establishment. In 1951 charges were introduced for dental and opticians' services and prescriptions, which caused the minister responsible for negotiating and introducing the 1946 Act, Aneurin Bevan, to resign, along with his cabinet colleague Harold Wilson, then the Minister for Trade and later to be prime minister (Webster, 1988; Webster, 1991). Once the Conservative Party returned to government in 1951, despite the fact that the 'one nation' Tories publicly wanted to claim the NHS as much their own invention as that of the Labour government, they were already privately searching for ways to reduce health expenditure which they feared would escalate out of control (Webster, 1994; Webster, 1996). This fear was exacerbated when the new government was bound to a doctors' pay rise legally arbitrated by Mr Justice Dankwerts. The Dankwerts settlement threatened to send NHS spending beyond the Conservative government's ceiling of £400 million. Numerous ideas circulated in Conservative quarters for containing costs, such as increasing existing prescription charges and charges for dental and opticians' services, or abolishing them on the NHS altogether, introducing hospital hotel charges and ambulance charges, restricting the types of drugs available on NHS prescription and extending paybeds in hospitals. Before putting any of these theoretical proposals into practice, the Minister for Health, Ian Macleod, launched a review of the NHS headed by Claude Guillebaud, a Cambridge economist. However, the Guillebaud Report, published in 1956, demonstrated that the NHS was a remarkably economically efficient method of paying for and delivering health care. The cost of the service was dropping as a proportion of GNP. Inflation and extra services rather than inefficiency and extravagance accounted for the rising bill. Nevertheless, the Conservative government still explored the idea of funding the NHS entirely through insurance payments rather than taxation, but this was dropped in 1957 when increasing contributions would have set off new demands for improved pensions (Timmins, 1995; Glennerster, 1995).

When Enoch Powell became Minister of Health in 1960, he proposed to raise NHS charges so that they recovered 5.6 instead of 4.5 per cent of NHS spending, and again planned to shift a proportion at least of NHS funding to increased insurance contributions. This was denounced by one of his own Cabinet colleagues, John Boyd-Carpenter, the Minister for Social Security, as a 'hypothecated regressive poll tax', since as a flat-rated tax it greatly disadvantaged the lower income groups, who at that time were largely exempt from income tax altogether. Powell was eventually stopped by a censure motion in Parliament brought by the Labour Party in 1961, but he retained a reputation as a 'would-be' welfare state dismantler. Powell was committed to reducing public expenditure and had already resigned from his post at the Treasury in 1958 when Macmillan had refused to introduce cuts. As Minister of Health, Powell intended to use part of the increased NHS charges to fund a Hospital Plan, launched in 1962, to build 90 new hospitals, remodel a further 134 and provide a further 356 improvement schemes costing £100,000 each. This resulted in the biggest renewal programme of the NHS and was responsible for creating many of the new district hospitals, built in the 1960s, which continue to be used by the NHS up to the present day (Timmins, 1995; Webster, 1996).

Powell's second attack was upon long-stay institutions for mentally ill and retarded patients. New drugs and changing attitudes made it possible to begin considering reorientating policy in this field. The 1959 Mental Health Act had ensured that patients would be largely voluntary rather than compulsorily detained, but Powell proposed developing a policy which would remove inmates from institutions and return them to the community. Later scandals, such as the revelations which broke in 1969 of horrifying cruelty and abuse to long-stay mental patients at Ely Hospital in Cardiff, gave added impetus to this policy. Powell, however, acknowledged the fact that institutional care could not be closed down without sufficient funds being available to put community care services in their place. The gap between these two strategies became responsible for widespread homelessness of mental patients in the late 1980s and early 1990s (Timmins, 1995; Webster, 1996; Glennerster, 1995).

Despite Conservative plans to change it, the economic structure of the NHS remained intact throughout their administration. The major change which they brought about, however, was to reorganize the administration of public health and health service delivery in 1974. Ironically, the Conservative reorganization of local government and the NHS marked a high point of faith in 'planning' which had characterized the Labour administration between 1964 and 1970. This was the period when Prime Minister Harold Wilson promised to place Britain at the forefront of the white heat of the technological revolution and when the role of experts in advising and constructing government policy had never been greater. Consideration of restructuring the organization of the NHS had begun in 1968. The split between hospital, general practitioner and local authority health services had created inefficiencies and professional rivalries within the service. In addition, new social patterns which demanded new community services, plus the rise of an independent profession of social work, made it necessary to provide a separate administration for social services (Timmins, 1995; Webster, 1996).

Sir Keith Joseph, the Conservative Minister of Health and Social Security from 1970 to 1974, set up a multidisciplinary study group to search for ways of instituting new managerial efficiency into the great edifice of the NHS. Reorganization was planned to be co-ordinated with the reorganization of local government under the Environment Minister, Patrick Walker, which replaced 1,700 local authorities with 400. In the NHS 700 hospital boards, boards of governors, management committees and executive councils were replaced by 14 regional health authorities, 90 area health authorities linked to family practitioner committees, and 200 district management teams, each attached to a community health council. The environmental responsibilities of the local public health authorities were separated from a newly created long-term strategic planning function. Local medical officers of health were replaced by newly styled 'community physicians' who became members of a new professional organization, the Faculty of Community Medicine, which provided them with the equivalent 'consultant status' to their clinical counterparts, all within the Royal College of Physicians. Despite its apparent simplicity, the new organization became massively unwieldy and the attempt to create a two-way system of decision-making and accountability simply resulted in an administrative maze in which no one seemed to be in charge. The NHS 1974 reorganization was remembered by those who had the burden of implementing it as creating 'tears about tiers'. The reform did, however, integrate hospitals into their local area health organizations more fully, and the community health councils did allow patients to have some voice in the system, even if it remained minimal and largely ignored (Timmins, 1995; Glennerster, 1995; Webster, 1996).

In contrast to Britain and Europe, national health insurance and federal funding of health care had been eliminated from the political agenda in the United States in the immediate post-war period. President Truman's single success in the Hill-Burton Act did, however, begin to change the organization of medical practice. The federal subsidy to hospital building and the expansion of medical schools began to make hospital medicine the primary site of medical care. As a result, as in Sweden, family practice began to diminish substantially by the 1970s, but high-tech hospital medicine and prestigious bio-medical research flourished. In the post-war period of the Truman years, the United States enjoyed prosperity and full employment, and celebrated its achievements. By the end of the 1950s, however, a slow-down in economic growth and rising unemployment began to depress this spirit towards the close of President Dwight Eisenhower's administration. John F. Kennedy fought the presidential election in

1960 with a promise to get the economy and American society moving again. Despite its radical rhetoric, the Kennedy administration achieved little in terms of social policy reform, but by this time a movement for creating a contributory hospital insurance programme for the elderly was gathering force. Those campaigning for it within and outside central government administration used a different strategy from the earlier ones used to support comprehensive universal health insurance. The health lobby, who largely came from within the public health profession, academic medicine and the social security administration, contextualized their proposals within the more general concern for providing public protection for the retired as a group. Social security in retirement had been the one welfare policy area which had managed to recruit the support of the middle class, who saw it as a legitimate field for government intervention, as much on their own behalf as on that of lower income groups and the poor. Social security in retirement did not carry the same stigma as welfare provision for the unemployed or public assistance to the poor who fell outside the labour market. Pensions graduated into a fully modern system of welfare in the United States when the Nixon administration placed the federal system on an earnings-related basis which allowed social security to provide replacement wages in retirement. The increased supply of hospital medicine, boosted by the Hill-Burton programme, had created its own demand. Many conditions such as heart failure, fractures and deliveries which would at one time have been dealt with in the patient's home were now treated in hospital wards. Hospital insurance, therefore, became the second focus of the proposed health reform for the elderly (Starr, 1982; Fox, 1986; Fox, 1993).

Another development during the Kennedy administration was a policy which was considered not long before his assassination. When Kennedy's proposed tax cuts came into effect in 1964, they boosted the American economy into a further year of expansion. This contrasted sharply with the sluggish economic years of the Eisenhower period. When he had first considered it in 1962, Kennedy had feared that economic expansion might not reach the entire population, and the year before his death he asked his advisers to begin planning an anti-poverty programme. At that time, the civil rights movement was changing the face of race relations in the United States and emphasized the critical importance of economic issues. In 1963 Kennedy's successor, Lyndon Johnson, made 'war on want' a central platform of his administration, and set up the Office of Economic Opportunity as a first step towards building a 'Great Society'. Federally assisted medical care for the elderly and the poor became two further central features of these reforms (Starr, 1982; Fox, 1993; Jacobs, 1993).

The growth of group prepaid practice, the desire to expand the supply of specialist medical services and the new relations between labour and medicine created a new environment for the discussion of national health policy by the time that Johnson became president. All concerned believed that those outside the system who needed services most should be supported through federal funding. The commercial and prepaid health insurance organizations, as much as labour unions and doctors themselves, all perceived the advantages of having federal funding pay for the supply of medical services to the elderly and the very poor, who were the most costly burdens upon the health care system. The Democratic landslide election of 1964 gave Johnson the opportunity to institute his expansive programme for the 'Great Society', and his special political skills enabled him to steer an unprecedented amount of radical legislation through the House of Representatives between 1964 and 1969. A new political consensus allowed Johnson to implement Medicare and Medicaid, to provide means-tested state-funded medical services for the elderly and the poor, with amazing speed and without resistance from Congress (Starr, 1982; Fox, 1993; Jacobs, 1993).

From the beginning of the century, health care in the United States was shaped by accommodation and compromise achieved through a 'negotiated balance of competing interests that persisted for many years' (Fox, 1993: 56). However, that balance of interests consistently focused upon providing services to treat acute rather than chronic illness and ignored the significance of the epidemiological transition in Western societies from acute infectious to chronic diseases as a health policy priority. The alliance between business, the medical profession and the state from the end of the nineteenth century formed a consensus about the need to develop the scientific and technological basis of care. This consensus aimed to provide increased success in the treatment of acute illness episodes, whether they were infectious diseases or the acute stages of chronic disease. Long-term care and rehabilitation for chronic illness was left out of the equation by everyone, including social scientists who portrayed the social relations of illness and health within the context of social actors playing an acute 'sick-role'. As a result, the epidemiological and demographic transition of the twentieth century towards an increasingly ageing and chronically sick population was never addressed and continued to loom as a crisis which baffled all who attempted to reduce it. Prevention of chronic illness was ignored, while ever more attention and investment of resources were poured into the technology of invasive and acute therapeutics. The focus on acute illness led to spiralling costs, not only of technological investment but also of increasing patient demand for more treatment as it became available (Fox, 1993).

From the 1980s the costs of the old compromise based on the acute model began to be seen by all as failing. A sense of disarray in American health care subsequently developed as the old compromise of health care provision in the United States began to crack and fall apart. For both providers and consumers of medicine, a no-win situation appeared to be developing. The only benefits gained were massive fees enjoyed by malpractice lawyers and ever greater profits achieved by the medical insurance sector. All the actors of the old alliance began to become dissatisfied, aggravated by a better-informed patient population with new mechanisms for making themselves heard in forums such as law courts with sympathetic juries. In the early 1980s the main political strategy employed for addressing this smouldering time-bomb was largely to ignore it (Fox, 1993). By the beginning of the 1990s, a president sought a second term of office making health reform a central platform of his campaign. By that time, however, the debate surrounding the role of government in public protection and the premises on which the concept of the welfare state was based were being seriously challenged, not only within America but by liberal democracies throughout the world.

HEALTH CITIZENSHIP ON CONDITION

Throughout the period of its expansion the welfare state was the subject of critical debate. Marxists attacked it for failing to bring about any real redistribution of wealth and diverting attention away from the task of achieving complete economic reorganization and social transition (Offe, 1984; Gough, 1979). Marxism also occupied common intellectual ground with right-wing critiques of the bureaucratic nature of the welfare state (Klein, 1993). The unwieldy democratically unaccountable welfare bureaucracy was determined, Marxists claimed, by technocratic experts who pursued the internal logic of their own professional ideologies. The welfare state was one expression of the way in which the 'logic of domination' of scientific rationality was institutionalized within the liberal democratic state, bringing about a monolithic level of social integration which negated all forms of opposition and created 'one-dimensional man' (Marcuse, 1972; Wilensky, 1976).

Even the architects of the welfare state, however, had expressed caution about some of the principles on which they founded it. In 1942 Beveridge had qualified the concept of welfare as a universal right of citizenship with certain conditions. Welfare was a right that was earned by fulfilling the obligations of citizenship. The contributory principle made social security a right belonging to those who had paid for it. For those who remained outside the contributory scheme, the principles of the Poor Law continued to be enforced. The generosity and accessibility of public assistance had to be downgraded, in Beveridge's view, so that the scheme

> would leave the person assisted with an effective motive to avoid the need for assistance and to rely on earnings or insurance....Further, an assistance scheme which makes those assisted unnameable to economic rewards or punishments while treating them as free citizens is inconsistent with the principles of a free community.
>
> (A. Deacon 1996: 194)

Comprehensive welfare should provide a secure minimum for all, but it should also be designed to ensure that it did not condone a 'breach of citizen obligations'. The qualifications which Beveridge placed on the universal principle became the central focus of a renewed ideological onslaught upon the welfare state in Western societies which began when affording it became an ever greater dilemma from the end of the 1970s (A. Deacon, 1996).

Two factors triggered a major re-evaluation of strategies which post-war governments in industrial societies had employed to manage their economies.

First, in 1973 the world's oil-producing countries collectively restructured their markets, resulting in an exponential rise in prices. The second factor was the emergence of Japan as the world's leading competitive industrial economy for a period in the 1980s. Japan had ignored the idea that industrial societies required a public sector maintained by social expenditure. Japan's diverse economy provided workers with job security and company welfare, at least for those employed in large-scale enterprises (Mishra, 1984). Health and pension schemes varied widely. With a highly disciplined and largely healthy workforce creating high levels of productivity, Japan's strong economy with low levels of public expenditure recovered from the effects of the oil crisis far quicker and more easily than most of-its Western counterparts. In the West, the end of sustained economic growth plus the example of a formidably successful competitor put an end to policies of full employment and made governments re-evaluate the virtues of the welfare state (Ringen, 1987; Gilbert, 1983).

In the 1980s critics began attacking the welfare state with new vocabulary which recast old concepts (Friedman and Friedman, 1980). Universalism was accused of failing to discriminate in favour of those in greatest need. By the 1980s, some left-wing economists, such as Julian Le Grand, demonstrated that those who benefited most from a universal service, such as the British NHS, were the middle classes, who used it most (Le Grand, 1982). Since the 1950s, conservative economists had used similar arguments to justify introducing selective benefits targeted only at the neediest. More significantly, in the 1980s universalism was accused of creating a dependency culture in which welfare became a way of life and rights were claimed without regard to obligations (Dean and Taylor-Gooby, 1992). This thesis was forwarded by two American theorists whose work became highly influential among Western policy-makers, Charles Murray and Lawrence Mead (Murray, 1984; Mead, 1986).

Murray suggested that universal welfare created a dependency culture which gave individuals perverse incentives for bizarre behaviour. In a publication called *Losing Ground* (1984) he argued that the 1960s 'War on Poverty' in America deepened the problems it aimed to solve because it created conditions which made poverty a rational choice. Aid to single mothers via the Aid to Families with Dependent Children (AFDC) programme gave women an economic incentive for single motherhood. In turn this eliminated the responsibilities of paternity. Without the motivation of caring for a family, welfare dependency and crime were better options for single men than low-paid employment. The lack of necessity to gain employment reduced the penalties for ignorance and thereby reduced the need for education and training. Thus, according to Murray, the alleviation of poverty created a poverty trap. A dependency culture resulted which made it 'dumb' to take low-paid work when crime and/or welfare could be more profitable (Murray, 1984). Murray claimed that in the 1980s the statistical indicators of unemployment, crime and collapse of the family proved the way in which welfare disadvantaged the poor. Underlying Murray's arguments was an assumption that poverty could be caused or perpetuated as much by individual behaviour as through structural organization. Individualist assumptions which theorists of universal welfare, such as Titmuss, had assigned to Dark-Age Victorian bigotry, were reasserted therefore in this new critique of the welfare state. Titmuss had argued that welfare should be administered universally without judgement of the individual, to avoid stigma. Murray, and later Lawrence Mead, argued that, because individual behaviour was fundamentally self-interested rather than co-operative, welfare should be distributed selectively and on the condition that, as Beveridge had stated, individuals fulfilled their obligations. Furthermore, benefits should only be distributed to those who were judged not to have brought their difficulties upon themselves (Murray, 1984).

An American policy analyst, Lawrence Mead, had specific agendas for making public provision both conditional and judgemental. In *Beyond Entitlement* (1986) Mead argued that the poor either refused or were unqualified to work, either way meaning that they could not be competent citizens. A successful civil society needed competent citizens who had the capacity to learn, work, support their family, respect the rights of others and thereby meet their social obligations. In America in the 1980s, Mead claimed, a growing proportion of the population were unable to fulfil these obligations. They constituted an underclass who combined 'functioning problems' with low incomes. Failing to function as competent citizens could not be solved by providing cash benefits as entitlements given without regard to behaviour. Benefit should be used instead to improve the character of the poor. The fault, Mead asserted, was not with the poor but with the political authorities who refused to govern them properly. Workfare should be introduced, which required the unemployed to work for benefit, and the poor should make their own arrangements to provide childcare. Governments should introduce work requirements into benefits but should not be responsible for determining the value of work or training or whether it would lead to permanent employment. This was because, Mead argued, governments should not play the role of providing useful work or constructing careers, but should undertake the responsibility of changing social values. Job inducements, such as childcare arrangements, could only be offered to non-workers who accepted jobs, because only functioning citizens could claim economic rights (Mead, 1986).

Murray and Mead's analyses of and remedies for the contradictions of the welfare state became highly influential in New Right thought about social policy, which interpreted the welfare state as a maternalist nanny which had sapped the spirit of independence within Western societies, drained their economies and created a 'why work?' culture. The New Right philosophies of welfare remarkably resembled high-Victorian moralism, and some of the new ideologues proudly declared the analogy. New Right philosophy in 1980s Britain, identified under the umbrella term of 'Thatcherism', claimed to be consciously trying to reinvigorate British society with Victorian values (Green, 1993; Lowe, 1994). Throughout Europe and America the New Right managed to gain a consensus on the need for 'mutual responsibility' in the provision of welfare. By the early 1990s, both liberals and conservatives accepted that Beveridge's original principle of 'conditionality' had to be instituted in a way that made individuals fulfil their social obligations in order to enjoy their rights to benefits, jobs and training

(Culpitt, 1992). Critics of the new consensus claimed that the terminologies of conditionality and judgementalism were a crude resurrection of Chadwickian principles. Entitlements on condition distinguished between the deserving and undeserving poor by using modern forms of less-eligibility as a mechanism of deterrence (A. Deacon, 1992).

Little of the New Right philosophy of welfare and social policy promoted by American policy intellectuals in the 1980s was very new. The need for targeting and selectivity in a benefits system had been asserted early in the 1950s by Britain's 'one nation' Tories. The young Tories who had written the pamphlet distinguished themselves from the ideologues of consensus such as Harold Macmillan and the post-war Tory prime minister, Anthony Eden. In 1953 Enoch Powell said that whereas socialism wanted to supply a set of average welfare services to all, Tory policy wanted to target those in greatest need. He claimed that the ideals of universal equality repressed opportunity and undermined independence. This was later to be restated by Margaret Thatcher, who offered members of British society 'the opportunity to be unequal' in her famous 'Let them grow tall' speech, made when she was first elected as the Conservative Party leader in 1975. From the time that the Institute for Economic Affairs was founded in Britain in 1957, it was dedicated to attacking the Keynesian consensus and promoting the monetarist economic theories of the then little-known economics professor at Chicago, Milton Friedman. By 1961 the IEA advocated many of the fundamental ideas which were later employed to try and break up public provision, such as tax reliefs, the introduction of vouchers for public services and abolishing a health system funded by taxation in favour of one funded through private insurance and fees. Means-tested benefits and services would remain for any who could not provide for themselves. The attack on universalism continued within British Conservative think-tanks, such as the Conservative Political Centre, and in the writings of the 'one nation' group who published *The Responsible Society* in 1959 (Timmins, 1995).

A pamphlet written in 1961 by a then little-known barrister who was also editor of a Conservative publication, *Crossbow*, put forward a number of ideas which were later to characterize the philosophy of Thatcherism. Geoffrey Howe, who became Chancellor of the Exchequer and Foreign Secretary under Margaret Thatcher, argued in 1961 that Conservatism should naturally strive for a reduction in the role of the state in society, which necessitated a reduction in public expenditure and public services. Outrage at poverty in a civilized society should not lead Tories down the false road to income redistribution. A non-progressive tax policy should lie at the heart of Conservative economic management. Replacing the concept of universality of social entitlements with a systematically selective policy of welfare benefits should target public protection and public services towards those who needed them and avoid supplying those who were able to help themselves. For example, family allowances were a flat-rate statutory right which was too small to help the needy and superfluous income to those who were sufficiently prosperous to not require it yet were given it anyway. Howe suggested that a tax credit or negative tax system would serve as an effective modern method of means-testing, in order to send money where it was needed most and avoid spending it unnecessarily. Howe also proposed cutting pensions to the actuarial amount subscribed, and he suggested a voucher system for health and education so that individuals could choose services; a competitive principle would be introduced into their supply. He argued for the abolition of free school milk – an idea which Thatcher notoriously instituted as Education Minister under the administration of Edward Heath in 1974, saving a small amount of public money but creating widespread public hostility against her. Howe wanted to replace council-house building with rent and rate subsidies and to allow people who opted for private health insurance to opt out of paying towards the National Health Service. In the 1961 pamphlet, Geoffrey Howe articulated the future ideology of the British Tory Party, which would clearly delineate the blue water between themselves, social democracy and socialism. In 1961, however, very few ears were listening, either within or outside the British Tory Party ranks (Timmins, 1995).

The vigorously individualist rhetoric of the 1980s New Right assault on 'New Jerusalem' ignored the changing structural determinants of poverty and disadvantage (Glennerster, 1995). In practice, however, governments, regardless of their rhetoric, could not. In Britain the gap between rhetoric and practical policy-making remained considerable. After their election to power in 1979 the Conservative Party did not place welfare policy at the centre of their agenda until their third term of office, after the 1988 general election. Before that they altered welfare policy at the margins, squeezed and pinched social expenditure, but did not attempt to translate much of their bold rhetoric into reality. Instead they concentrated on controlling the money supply, cutting direct taxation, fighting the unions and privatizing the public sector. Some of the earliest Conservative reforms in social policy attempted to cut costs. Earnings-related unemployment and sickness benefit and pensions were abolished in 1979. Geoffrey Howe re-established social security on Beveridge's flat-rate basis. The value of pensions was to be subsequently linked to prices instead of earnings. Council-house building was more or less stopped during this period and replaced by a system of rent subsidies and rate rebates to individuals and families. While budget cuts in education removed local authorities' obligations to provide free school meals, milk and transport for school children, new money had to be found to fund an 'assisted places scheme' which would pay the fees of selected pupils to attend independent schools. It was intended to find some of the money by making the largest cut in spending on higher education since the war. In 1981, universities had their budgets cut by 8.5 per cent which, over three years, amounted to a 13 per cent reduction. Ten thousand academic and non-academic jobs were eliminated, largely through early retirements and voluntary redundancies, but student numbers continued to rise (Timmins, 1995; Glennerster, 1995).

Reductions in higher education funding created a politically treacherous minefield which faced the Tories because the middle-class investment in the welfare state required a subtle approach to social policy. Although middle

England, which now incorporated a wide range of affluent manual as well as white-collar workers and professionals, was no longer prepared to pay for 'the care of strangers', they nevertheless showed little taste for losing the universal services from which they benefited. Good-quality free school and university education for their children was one public provision which they were not prepared to see undermined. State pensions turned out to be another benefit which they were not prepared to give up. But perhaps the most popular of all the universal services which, as Le Grand pointed out, the middle classes enjoyed more than any other, was the National Health Service, which marshalled their greatest loyalty (Le Grand, 1982). The Chancellor in Margaret Thatcher's second administration, Nigel Lawson, stated in his memoirs that the NHS 'is the closest thing the English have to a religion, with those who practise in it regarding themselves as a priesthood. This made it quite extraordinarily difficult to reform' (Timmins, 1995: 453). While Margaret Thatcher believed that the NHS should exist to serve the 'great accidents and terrible diseases' and to serve the poor, she thought that those who could afford to pay for health care should be made to do so. Nevertheless, the British love affair with what the Americans liked to call 'socialized medicine' led her in 1982 to commit her government publicly to making sure that the NHS was safe in their hands. This was a wise action, because in 1980 a report on health standards commissioned by the previous Labour government was published, which put the question of 'inequality' back on to the public agenda. The Black Report demonstrated substantial differentials in health, morbidity and mortality rates between classes 1–3 and 4–5. Inequalities in health reflected an incipient divided nation in standards of living. Despite government attempts to stifle the report, it was widely publicized and became highly influential, not only in Britain but internationally. It remained an uncomfortable reminder of the importance of ideas, which belonged to a previous era, that health was largely determined by socio-economic conditions (Timmins, 1995; Glennerster, 1995).

Some initial moves were made in Britain in the 1980s to try and support the growth of private medicine. While private health insurance grew along with private hospitals, private medicine could only compete with the NHS at the margins. As private health insurance grew, so too did beliefs that the Tories intended to destroy the NHS. By 1987 the Institute of Economic Affairs set up a unit to explore ways of completely privatizing the NHS. However, even when Thatcher decided to begin implementing radical public welfare policies in housing and education after her election to a third term of government in 1988, she still remained cautious with regard to the health service. In effect, under the administration of both Norman Fowler and Kenneth Clarke as Ministers of Health, investment in the National Health Service increased, together with the proportion of GNP spent on health care overall. The NHS was to be the centre of some major political and organizational battles, but despite Tory desires to move from a tax-funded to either an insurance-funded system or market-provided health care by the time they left office, the publicly owned and funded statutory health service in Britain remained intact (Timmins, 1995; Glennerster, 1995).

An initial report on changing the financial basis of the NHS commissioned by the first Tory Secretary of State for Health and Social Security under Thatcher, Patrick Jenkin, illustrated the financial dilemma. Even if you moved health to private finance for the middle classes, a large tax-funded service would have to remain to cover the poor, the chronically sick and children. The middle classes would still be paying for this service through taxation and yet would have no access to it. In addition, they would be paying for private health insurance. It was the second Health and Social Security Secretary, Norman Fowler, who recognized that it was political suicide to consider changing the funding basis of the service at that time. Without dismissing the idea of privatization altogether, Fowler conveniently shelved the issue. However, in September 1981 an economic review completed by a Cabinet Office think-tank, the Central Policy Review Staff, put forward a plan for massive cuts in public spending to accommodate projected growth of 1 per cent. These proposals included privatizing health care. A rebellion of remaining 'wet' – centre-right – Cabinet ministers removed the proposals from the government agenda and leaked them to the press. This caused Fowler to declare again publicly that the NHS would continue to be funded on the basis of taxation (Timmins, 1995; Glennerster, 1995; Klein, 1989).

When Nigel Lawson became Chancellor in the re-elected government in 1983, he instituted a £500 million cut to the budgets of the biggest-spending ministries. Most of this was found by cutting and altering the basis of various social security benefits. The government superannuation pensions scheme, SERPS, was also abolished, but in the long run that cost a large amount in repayments. In 1983, the Tory pledge to honour Labour's NHS spending plans from 1979 ended, and health now faced a new financial squeeze which health authorities tried to gain through efficiency drives. This resulted in closed beds and wards in hospitals. The adverse publicity stimulated the central administration to try and evaluate costs and institute some form of accounting for performance. Annual reviews of performance against budgets for each region were instituted, which led to district reviews and the introduction of performance indicators. Health authorities were encouraged to put ancillary services up for tender and contract them out to the cheapest provider (Klein, 1989).

These measures led to major manpower reductions. The cuts caused bitter controversy, but as yet left the managerial hierarchy and the medical staff largely unaffected. Despite the cuts, however, overall spending on the health service was not reducing but actually rising. The government nevertheless faced major difficulties in assessing performance and accounting for costs as a result of the massively complex administrative structure of the NHS, which had no clear line of managerial command or responsibility. The managing director of the Sainsbury's supermarket chain, Roy Griffiths, was requested to investigate the management structure of the NHS in 1983. His report announced that 'if Florence Nightingale were alive and carrying her lamp through the corridors of the NHS today she would almost certainly be searching for the people in charge'. Griffiths proposed a new managerial structure to replace the existing administrative maze, which would involve doctors in running budgets, cost improvement programmes being established, the effectiveness of treatments being evaluated in both clinical and cost terms, and budget targets being set at every level. He also proposed that a new central management body be set up to overlook the entire structure. A new line-management system was subsequently introduced, which provided the central government with a lever to control the system. Medical staff resisted the change, in which they were replaced by managers as the organizers of the health service. Suspicion between the medical profession and the government grew until the doctors identified themselves as the front-line campaigners defending the NHS. The scepticism between the government and other professions grew at an equal rate. Hostility towards the government increased among dons, teachers, scientists and even lawyers. However, Kenneth Clarke, an ex-lawyer who was now Minister for Health under Fowler, treated professional organizations straightforwardly as trade unions. When he won a major battle with the BMA over the introduction of a limited list of drugs available on prescription, doctors no less than the defeated miners lost a level of power in their industry which they were never quite to regain (Klein, 1989). The BMA continued to fight a propaganda war against the government, claiming that a two-tier service was the logical conclusion of the direction in public policy. Nevertheless, no further major new initiatives were taken regarding health policy until after the Tories' election to a third term of government in 1988.

By 1987 the financial squeeze on the British health service had grown into a looming crisis. Each year, when their money ran out, health authorities started to close hospital beds from about January and put off paying their suppliers until the beginning of the next financial year in April. After five years, however, their budget deficits were extensive, amounting collectively to about £400 million, which made the NHS technically bankrupt. With an election year, the crisis in the NHS was played down and almost ignored by Thatcher's new Secretary of State for Health and Social Security, John Moore. His inactivity and acquiescence to Lawson's further spending restrictions in the 1987 round led to the need to withdraw free dental and eye check-ups completely, and to allow hospitals to make profits on patients. This caused a public furore but did little to stem the flow of financial debt. By the end of 1988, 4,000 beds had been closed. When David Barber, a baby with a hole in his heart, failed to receive an operation in time to save his life – surgery had been cancelled five times due to lack of supply of intensive-care nurses in hospitals in Birmingham – the NHS crisis became the most volatile and pressing political issue faced by the new government. The Royal Colleges of Physicians and Surgeons demanded the government act to save the service and find alternative funding. Tony Newton, Minister for Health under Moore, announced an extra £101 million to alleviate the fiscal disaster, but most of it went on repairing hospital roofs damaged during a hurricane in October 1987. After a policy review, headed by Thatcher herself, which drifted, decisive action was taken by the newly created Secretary of State for Health, Kenneth Clarke, in 1988. Clarke proposed creating an internal market within the NHS which separated purchasers from providers (Timmins, 1995; Strong and Robinson, 1990).

The idea of the internal market was originated by an American health management specialist from Stanford University who had once worked for the Johnson administration, Professor Alain Enthoven. He had been invited by the Nuffield Hospital Trust in 1984 to make a 'sympathetic' investigation into the NHS. After his investigation was completed, Enthoven advocated introducing an 'internal market' to create competition within the state system which would undermine the monopoly of power operated by its suppliers but would still retain its state-funded basis. Health authorities would be freed to purchase and sell services among themselves and the private sector. They would purchase services for their resident populations from the hospital offering the best deal in terms of cost, quality and convenience, whether it was within or outside their district. The dollars, in theory at least, would follow the patient (Timmins, 1995; Strong and Robinson, 1990).

In the final version worked out by Clarke and his colleagues, not only would local health authorities become purchasers but general practitioners would be offered the opportunity to become fundholders, choosing to buy services for their patients from any set of services which they thought the most effective and cost-efficient. GP practices which did not choose to become independent fundholders would have their patients' services purchased for them by the local health authority. Hospitals were offered the opportunity of becoming self-governing independent trusts, which would have to manage their own budgets and supply their services at a competitive price to purchasers. In the 1989 White Paper, *Working for Patients*, the internal market was announced as allowing money to follow the patient. The BMA claimed the reforms laid the groundwork for dismantling the service, but Clarke insisted that the NHS would remain a service available to all, free of charge and funded by taxation but reorganized internally on competitive lines. In the end the co-operation of the medical profession with the new scheme was extensive, with 57 hospitals opting to become Trusts in December 1990 and 306 GP practices choosing to become fundholders by 1991. These numbers subsequently grew extensively. The reforms also brought substantial new funding which, after a further boost in 1991, allowed it to rise by 6.6 per cent. The 'purchaser/provider split' model was reproduced in the field of community care, with local authorities being given the power to put out services for tender. In addition, they were charged with the responsibility of planning future provision. The greatest shortfall in this field, however, continued to be the failure to provide sufficient community services to cater for patients released from long-stay institutions which were closed down (Timmins, 1995).

Paradoxically, the Thatcher administration made a public service which she would have liked to abolish into an ever more attractive bargain to the middle classes. A state-funded free service remained in place, but with the monopoly of power which had accrued to its suppliers broken by competition. The purchaser/provider split and the social market economy became a new model for welfare provision, which was adopted beyond the NHS and beyond Britain itself. By the 1990s, however, renewed enthusiasm existed within the British Tory government, elected for a fourth term, for bringing social policy further into line with the critical rhetoric on reform. Under John Major, who succeeded Margaret Thatcher as prime minister in 1990 and won the general election in 1992, the Secretary of State for Social Security Peter Lilley announced that major structural reform was needed to prevent social security spending from exceeding economic growth. Michael Portillo, a new Treasury minister, announced in 1992 the government's intention to shift the boundaries between public and private spending, with plans allowing people to opt out of compulsory unemployment and health insurance and abolishing child benefit, mortgage interest relief and maternity allowances. New ideas were floated to require people to take out a mortgage to insure themselves against unemployment. Michael Howard, the Home Secretary, and John Redwood, the Secretary of State for Wales, attacked single mothers as a major cost on public spending and as a threat to traditional family structures and social stability. The Chancellor of the Exchequer, Norman Lamont, did not overtly support the new proposals but did nothing to dismiss them. After he fell from office as the result of Britain's expulsion from the Exchange Rate Mechanism in 1993, he was replaced by Kenneth Clarke, who announced, largely to his right-wing colleagues, that he was not in the business of dismantling the welfare state (Timmins, 1995; Glennerster, 1995).

Portillo nevertheless continued to warn under-forties that they should make their own private provision for pensions, and Lilley projected that the welfare society of the future would be based around provision made by individuals, families and companies rather than the state. The rhetoric was translated into major cuts to unemployment and sickness benefits in 1994 which aimed to save £2.5 billion over three years. These were the first cuts to contributory benefits that the Conservatives had introduced in seventeen years of government. Pension age for women was equalized to 65, which saved a further £3.5 billion a year. Within an annual social security budget of £260 billion, these sums were extremely small. These measures continued to prove that the massive edifice of the welfare state could not be dismantled but only eroded incrementally, even by those who had the greatest will in the world to do so. In the meantime, economic uncertainty began to affect a new proportion of the electorate. Unemployment had fallen substantially by the end of the 1980s, but began to soar again as persistent recession followed a boom–bust economic cycle at the end of Margaret Thatcher's period of office (Timmins, 1995; Glennerster, 1995).

However, unemployment now struck not manual workers in heavy industries but white-collar workers in service industries and professions. In 1992 John Kenneth Galbraith published an analysis of the *Culture of Contentment* which created a secure uncaring affluent majority in advanced industrial societies. In Britain, by 1995 the contented society was turning into an insecure majority who were anxious about their employment futures, homes and possessions. By the time of the election in 1997, the sacrilegious phrase of 'full employment' re-entered the political rhetoric of the centre-right of the Conservative Party and the new vision of social democracy offered by New Labour. Chancellor Clarke initiated 'workstart' as a method for trying to get the long-term and young unemployed back to work. Once New Labour won electoral victory in 1997, 'welfare-to-work' became one of the first policies to be implemented, funded by a 'windfall tax' on excessive profits accumulated by privatized national industries. By the late 1990s in Britain, the right-wing onslaught on the welfare state found itself limited to incremental change. The centre-right and social democratic consensus, by contrast, began implementing practical policies to try and change social behaviour and attack the 'culture of dependency' by turning entitlements into rights, earned on condition of responsible behaviour (Timmins, 1995; Glennerster, 1995).

The language of conditional citizenship, economic monetarism and new forms of welfare rationalization have all been employed to try and square the circle of social policy and public expenditure in Europe and beyond, but strategies for resolving the 'crisis' in welfare have varied in different national contexts (George and Taylor-Gooby (eds), 1996). In Germany, the Social Democratic (SPD) government responded to global inflationary conditions in the late 1970s by allowing the Bundesbank to dictate monetary policy to control inflation. This meant accepting increased unemployment and restrictions on social spending. The administrations of both Chancellors Schmidt and Kohl reduced company taxation and reduced state contributions to social insurance, which affected a wide range of benefits. Uprating of pensions was delayed and means testing was introduced for various family benefits. Health insurance and unemployment benefits were cut, along with public education, housing and social assistance. Throughout the 1980s the industrial sector of the German economy remained strong through manpower cuts and renewed export orientation, but the strength of the industrial economy marginalized workers in other sectors, such as service provision. Germany also underdeveloped the post-industrial base of its economy. Despite cuts to the social state there was no desire, as in Thatcher's England and Reagan's United States, 'to roll back the state'. The central state aimed instead to direct intervention more effectively. This meant that Kohl's administration made no attempt to denationalize the social state and transfer social security to a private insurance basis. Private insurance remained deeply unpopular with the German electorate (Lawson, 1996).

Demographic and social changes in Germany further contributed to redirecting policy in the 1990s. Apart from the common demographic transition to a longer-living but increasingly chronically sick population, higher immigration – from political asylum-seekers rather than industrial migration – became a new factor to be taken into account by the German social security system. The immigrant population who could claim social entitlements lacked the same civil rights as German citizens, and lacked political power without the right to vote. As a result, they developed into a structural underclass. Of far greater significance than even these changes, however, the unification of Germany following the collapse of Communism in 1989 changed the parameters of economic and social policy. In order to re-create the collapsed East German economy, social insurance contributions were raised by 3 per cent to transfer funds to support labour market programmes and pensions. This was followed by the creation of a 'solidarity contribution' which was effectively a new tax on Western middle-class Germans to pay for Eastern economic regeneration. In 1994 an extensive package of severe social benefits cuts affecting many of the services provided by the *Länder* and local authorities was introduced, along with cuts in education, children's allowances and West German labour programmes. These affected the poorest and weakest sections of the population, such as asylum-seekers, but aimed to achieve a DM100 billion saving (Lawson, 1996).

Despite these measures, social spending constituted 34 per cent of GDP in what would have been the old Federal Republic and 70 per cent of the GDP of Eastern Germany. The share funded by employers fell from 33 per cent to 30 per cent by the mid-1990s, along with the contributions made by the *Länder* and local taxation. Employees, however, increased the proportion of their contribution to the social state from 20 per cent in the 1970s to 30 per cent in the 1990s. Despite its costs, public protection for German workers and their dependants continued to be funded through compulsory state insurance. Significant changes were instituted, however, into means-tested assistance provided by local authorities. The massive increase in their responsibilities which occurred as unemployment rose and the effects of unification were felt placed a huge strain on the economic resources of the regional and local authorities. While the shame of receiving public assistance prevented large proportions of those in need from claiming it, neither the *Länder*, the local authorities nor the voluntary agencies could cope with the rise in numbers: 4.6 million members of the population were receiving benefits by the early 1990s. As a result an increasingly divided society emerged in Germany, between the affluent secure employed and those outside secure employment who were increasingly pauperized. Immigrant populations especially became increasingly ghettoized while incomes among the affluent consistently rose (Lawson, 1996).

After returning to power with a reduced majority in 1994, the Kohl CDU/CSU coalition sought to maintain public protection funded through insurance, but tried to reform the guiding principles of social policy through *Umbau*, or restructuring the social state. The Kohl government explored the possibility of making interventions into long-term unemployment by encouraging 'self-responsibility' through new workfare programmes, family policies and preventive health programmes. Kohl also committed himself to reducing the level of bureaucracy and the 'tyranny of experts' in social administration. However, among his further right-wing opponents, the Free Democratic Party advocated a much more radical programme, such as reducing social security benefits to a minimum supplemented by private insurance. Such initiatives were taken up by a liberal and right-wing alliance with the intention of beginning *Abbau*, or dismantling the social state. The employers' association, the BDA, called for a major reduction in state pensions and sickness benefits with a significant increase in patient charges for medical services. At the other end of the political spectrum, new alliances between the left and representatives of the Church considered reviving some of the socially effective features of the old

GDR system, such as benefits for women, the elimination of status distinctions among the workforce and polyclinics in health care. New coalitions between the left reasserted the need for redistributive economic policies and full-employment programmes. The left and the Church have more recently demanded a restructuring of social security based upon citizenship rather than employment. This has presented the Social Democratic Party (SDP) with a major dilemma, since it has traditionally staunchly defended the insurance system. Despite these divisions, the social state has remained substantially intact in unified Germany even though further cuts and enhanced workfare are likely in the future. The dangers of regional economic divisions and the growth of a disenfranchised underclass, however, pose a threat to the capacity of the social state to provide a basic level of public protection and social stability (Lawson, 1996).

The election of left-wing governments in France in the early 1980s, dedicated to redistributing wealth, meant that social spending continued to increase throughout the decade despite the attempts of the centre-right government to curb spending after 1986. Throughout the 1980s France's level of spending on social security remained the second highest in Europe, after Luxembourg, amounting to a quarter of GDP. The system continued to be funded by employer and employee contributions, with only a small contribution from the state. The proportion of employer contributions remained among the highest, after Italy, in Europe and acted as a damper on wages. The high level of spending was in part a response to demographic changes creating greater demand, but also the result of the use of welfare policy designed to redistribute wealth. In the early 1980s the left-wing government raised the minimum wage by 55 per cent and the minimum income for the elderly by 65 per cent. Family allowances, unemployment benefit and housing benefits were also increased. By 1982 new measures were introduced to curb spending, beginning with reductions to unemployment benefit. Contributions were raised and ceilings on employer contributions for health insurance were abolished. Income taxes were raised and then reduced in the mid-1980s and a general tax levy of 1.05 per cent, *contribution sociale généralisée*, was reintroduced in 1990 largely to fund new family allowance payments. At one time biased towards those with large families, the reformed family allowance system increased benefits for the second child and raised levels awarded to single parents. Family allowances were paid from five months before birth and for three months afterwards. They continued on a means-tested basis up to the child's third birthday (Hantrais, 1996).

In 1982 attempts were made to contain health costs by freezing doctors' fee levels and pharmaceutical prices along with sickness benefit. Charges for hospital beds were introduced in 1983 and the following year public hospitals were required to conform to strict new budgets. A restricted list of medicines was established and reimbursements to patients were reduced. In 1985 an attempt to restructure the management of the health system was successfully resisted by the medical profession, who forced the government to abandon their plans. Further economy measures were introduced in 1988, and by the end of the decade spending on health appeared to have been curbed even though deficits were still high. The result of these changes, however, was to begin to create a two-tier system of health. Access to comprehensive care became available only to those who had voluntary or private health insurance, while only a minimum service remained to serve the poorest sectors of the community.

When a right-wing government was elected in France in 1993, it tried to introduce reforms to the private school system and to introduce a workfare programme for the young unemployed. These measures provoked social disorder which echoed the unrest of 1968. The French population demonstrated emphatically that they were wedded to their system of social security but were unwilling to accept tax increases except for funding family policy. The dilemma for French policy-makers in the 1990s, therefore, was how to afford to maintain levels of welfare for a population whose demographic trends were steadily increasing demand. By the year 2000 France is likely to have 20.5 per cent of its population over 60 years of age. Until now France has been shielded somewhat from the common demographic shift to an ageing population by the effects of two world wars on its population levels and pronatalist policies pursued earlier in the century. Furthermore, a social security system based upon employment insurance has placed a pressure upon wages which could compromise the international competitive capacity of French industry. The insurance principle, together with increased private funding of social security, has begun to create a three-tier system of public protection in France in which the securely, high-waged employed are covered by employment insurance supplemented by additional private or voluntary schemes; the insecurely lower-paid employed have no additional schemes to top up benefits; and the long-term unemployed or never-employed are pauperized by dependency on a means-tested public assistance minimum. Left-wing policies improved working conditions and extended part-time working, but raised unemployment. The post-1993 right-wing government's attempt to reduce the working week and increase flexible work-time had similar effects. Governments of all political persuasions have tried to introduce job-creating schemes and workfare, but none have been able to make anything more than marginal incremental changes to the welfare system as a whole. As in Germany and Britain, internal ideological agendas appeared less able to determine policy than international economic forces.

For some time Sweden seemed to be the exception to this rule. As mentioned earlier, Sweden apparently escaped the effects of global trends in economic competition and inflation throughout the 1980s (Fry, 1979). By 1989, however, there were already signs that the devaluation of the kröner in 1982 had simply delayed a financial crisis which was about to explode. After the deregulation of financial markets in the mid-1980s Sweden experienced the pattern of credit boom followed by recession which was common among all European states in the late 1980s. By 1989 Sweden's overheated economy had an inflation rate above 10 per cent and unemployment below 2 per cent. The Social Democratic government began to institute social spending curbs by cutting benefits, but these failed to bring the economy back under control. In 1991 their public support had dwindled to 28 per cent and the country elected a minority right-wing coalition government. The national debt stood by this time at 80 per cent of GDP, and the budget deficit at 14 per cent of GDP. A negative growth rate for three years between 1988 and 1991, plus unemployment levels which began to reach comparable levels with other European states of 15–20 per cent, exacerbated the situation. Economic analysts identified the large edifice of Sweden's generous welfare system and the high levels of public expenditure – especially the high level of earnings-related benefits – as the cause of the crisis. The growth of public expenditure had been aggravated by increased demand from demographic changes, changes in family patterns and rising unemployment. Those living on state benefits rose from 2.7 million in 1972 to 4.7 million in 1992 out of a population of 8.7 million. Left-wing analysts pointed to other factors which had contributed to the crisis, such as imprudent foreign investment by Swedish enterprises in the early 1980s and massive credit losses incurred by the banks who had required the state to bail them out. Deregulation also made the currency more vulnerable to speculation. Nevertheless, even those on the left agreed that unemployment had been kept at a detrimentally low level and benefits had risen too high (Gould, 1993; Gould, 1996; Stephens, 1996).

In 1992 the new government introduced a package of public expenditure cost-cutting measures, in which sickness benefit received the biggest reduction from 90 per cent of income to 65 per cent for the second and third days of sickness to 80 per cent for the rest of one year and 70 per cent thereafter. Employers were given the responsibility of administering sick pay for the first fourteen days and also of investigating the claimant's need for rehabilitation in order to return to work after eight weeks. The possibility of employers, unions or voluntary societies taking over the complete administration of sickness benefit was also explored. The health services themselves cost 10 per cent of GDP by 1990 and employed 10 per cent of the workforce. Although it had a high international reputation, the system was re-evaluated in the wake of the financial crisis. Overmanned – especially with doctors – because it was overly hospital-based, the system was perceived to require substantial reform. The Bourgeois government, inspired by Enthoven's theories, introduced an internal market based upon a pricing mechanism, similar to that introduced by the British government in the late 1980s. Further rationalization and cost-cutting resulted in hospital closures, redundancies and substantial increases in charges for visits to the doctor, prescriptions and hospital stays. As a result there has been a growth in private health insurance comparable to that of France and Germany. Levels of visits to the doctor and referrals to specialists have significantly reduced. Finally, the Bourgeois government began to explore ways to return family practice to the private sector (Gould, 1993; Gould, 1996; Stephens, 1996).

By 1994, however, the Bourgeois government appeared to have gone as far as the Swedish electorate would allow them in dismantling state-funded health care, or indeed the welfare state as a whole. The preference for state-funded over private health care remained high, with a poll indicating that enthusiasm for market-based medicine had reduced from 48 per cent of the population in 1991 to only 22 per cent in 1994. The Social Democratic Party was returned to power in 1994, but with an entirely new agenda for reduced public spending and low inflation as their primary goal. They coupled these policies with a reduction in tax advantages for the highest paid. Also, some of the policies of the Bourgeois government were reversed, including the encouragement given to the growth of private medicine. Nevertheless, the Social Democratic government continued to pursue policies of severe cuts to the public benefits system. In 1994 Sweden joined the European Union and the impact of the single market and currency exchange controls upon its economy and public-sector spending is yet to be clearly seen (Gould, 1996; Stephens, 1996).

The idea of using 'managed competition', which was taken up to different extents in Britain and Sweden, was also highly influential in American proposals for health reform in the 1990s. The absence of health insurance from the social security legislation of 1935 meant that from the 1940s employers in the United States increasingly offered health insurance to their employees. However, whereas this initially meant providing quite cheap coverage for young healthy workers, by the 1960s these workers were older, sicker and more costly. In 1965, business spending on health benefits climbed from 2.2 per cent to 8.3 per cent of salaries and from 8.4 per cent to 56.4 per cent of pre-tax corporate profits. As health costs began to impede American competitiveness internationally, especially within the context of the world inflationary markets of the 1980s, employers began to adopt various strategies to try and reduce health costs. Some shifted costs towards older employees and retirees, others dropped coverage of dependants or imposed 'managed care' through institutions like health maintenance organizations (HMOs) upon their workforce. Some employers stopped hiring employees with known histories of expensive medical conditions, and others stopped hiring full-time employees altogether and hired work out on contract to smaller firms who employed only part-time employees, with no coverage (Skocpol, 1996).

These changes occurred concurrently with increased competitiveness within the insurance industry itself. Small insurance companies began 'cherry picking', offering cheap premiums to young healthy employees. Bigger companies began offering differential rates to different age groups of employees and occupational groups, and increasing their exclusion clauses for those with various types of medical and lifestyle histories. By the 1980s, fewer Americans were insured at an ever increasing cost. The numbers of uninsured grew to dramatic proportions. Furthermore, as white-collar unemployment grew with recession at the end of the decade, a much broader band of Americans experienced 'episodes' of being without health insurance. During the period of 'Reaganomics', middle-class anxieties over job and health security were ignored while the administration concentrated on foreign policy. During the Bush administration, however, rising public concerns over health insurance put the issue on the political agenda. In 1992, 38 million Americans had no health insurance. Of all Americans under 65 years of age, 17.4 per cent had no health insurance. In 1991 a youthful politically impregnable Republican Senator in Pennsylvania, John Heinz, was killed in a helicopter crash. In the 'by-election' that followed, his seat was won by a 60-

year-old Democrat from the Kennedy era, Harris Wofford, who had made health insurance the centrepiece of his campaign, asking, 'If criminals have the right to a lawyer, why don't the sick have the right to a doctor?' (Skocpol, 1996).

Following Wofford's election success in 1992, health reform bills proliferated in the Senate and in the House of Representatives. Organizations beyond Capitol Hill also put forward plans for reform. Even the American Medical Association, as we have seen the most fierce opponent of federal intervention into health care, put forward plans for new regulations to try and reduce costs and increase coverage. By 1992, three basic plans were being offered by a variety of promoters: market-oriented reforms aiming at incremental modifications of private health insurance markets; single payer tax-financed plans to cover all citizens; and universal health coverage called 'play or pay'. The Bush administration attempted to develop a market-orientated health reform proposal. This involved promoting but not guaranteeing insurance coverage through new regulations of the insurance market and tax relief. Limits would be placed on price variations offered between insurance companies, and the law would require companies to take all applicant groups and eliminate exclusion of customers who suffered from pre-existing medical conditions. A tax voucher system would help low-income earners to purchase health insurance and thereby try to extend coverage. Bush's 1992 plan intended to set up purchasing pools for small businesses and to introduce new regulations on insurance company practices and malpractice awards in order to reduce costs. Bush also wanted to encourage 'managed-care' forms of health service delivery, such as HMOs, in order to further competitive market efforts to hold down costs. Bush remained vague about how he intended to finance the reforms, which would have cost about $35 billion a year, but hinted that the money would be found from reducing the Medicare and Medicaid programmes. Bush's plan was dismissed by Democrats because the financing was vague, it did not guarantee universal coverage and did not tackle the question of reducing insurance and medical costs (Skocpol, 1996; Wiscman, 1993).

At the same time, various progressive Democrats were promoting their own health reform proposals based upon the Canadian model that became known as the 'single payer' scheme. Single payer offered universal coverage financed by payroll or general taxes, but medical services would continue to be provided by a variety of doctors, hospitals and clinics, most of which would be privately run. This system would essentially provide state-regulated compulsory insurance funded through payroll deductions and taxation, but would allow the market to continue to control the supply of services and patients to choose services independently. This scheme was powerfully supported by a number of policy analysts, such as Theodore Marmor and Rashi Fein. Single payer was also supported by some grassroots organizations, such as Citizen Action and Consumers' Union, and by a small maverick group of doctors called Physicians for a National Health Program. The single payer scheme would have been able to pay for universal coverage by saving on the cost of administration. The bulk of insurance companies' profits are spent not on medical care but on administration and advertising. In the 1980s, the Canadians had combined public financing with global budget limits and negotiated payments with physicians and hospitals for services. This system had massively reduced the costs of care. Many of those proposing single payer schemes in the United States suggested that they should be organized through state rather than federal administration to reduce the level of bureaucracy. The threat to powerful interests in the health care market, such as private health insurance companies and organized medicine, made the single payer model fraught with political insecurity. Also, the upheaval for white-collar employees switching from employer-based premiums to payroll deductions or new taxes brought the political viability of the scheme seriously into doubt, especially given the trouble that President Bush was experiencing from his broken 'read my lips' promises on taxation (Skocpol, 1996).

The system that became the most popular in 1992 with politicians, policy advisors and pundits was the 'play or pay' model. This managed to gather a consensus from both policy-makers and vested 'stakeholder' groups in the medical market as a 'middle of the road' reform. Play or pay would involve the federal government in requiring all employers either to play in the employer health system by offering health insurance for all employees, or else to pay a quit-tax to help subsidize expanded governmental coverage for the uninsured. An expanded public programme would replace cover for all non-elderly Americans who were either not employed or not insured by their employers. This system tried to universalize coverage while still preserving the principle of mixed public and private insurance. Progressive Democrats criticized the model for not including mechanisms to control costs directly and suggested that employers might dump previously insured workers into an inferior public-financed programme. Conservative Republicans, on the other hand, accused the play or pay scheme of being simply a stepping-stone to instituting the single payer model. The play or pay model, however, gathered a momentum of support throughout 1992 and received such prestigious backing from various quarters that it became accepted as the starting point for legislative reform.

When Bill Clinton entered the presidential race he decided to make health reform a prominent feature of his campaign. He opted for a health reform plan which mixed the play or pay model with federal regulation of costs. When Bush subsequently started identifying play or pay as 'socialized medicine' Clinton decided to explore new avenues of policy development. Clinton chose to take up a new policy initiative being explored by the Democratic Insurance Commissioner for California, John Garamendi. Garamendi worked with Theodore Zelman, who headed a California Commission on insurance coverage, and Paul Starr, a professor of sociology from Princeton who had written extensively on the history of health care provision in the United States. Garamendi, Zelman and Starr developed a policy which mixed some of the features of the market-orientated features with the concept of universal coverage in a system of inclusive managed competition. This plan was based on Enthoven's ideas, which had already been applied in Britain and Sweden. Enthoven proposed that universal health coverage could be achieved by making it mandatory for all employers to make payroll contributions for their workers, to pay for health insurance premiums. After that, managed competition would create a market which would minimize health costs. He suggested that tax relief for employers' contributions to health insurance should be capped at the lowest price level available in the region. Any employer who provided insurance above this level would pay the difference in after-tax dollars. As a result, employers would have to seek the most economically efficient care, such as that offered by HMOs, which would keep costs down (Skocpol, 1996).

Enthoven's theories of welfare provision based upon a social market were incorporated into but modified by the Garamendi–Zelman–Starr proposals. The GZS plan would achieve managed competition through regional health alliances. All employers, unless they were very large companies, would be required to join an alliance which would have to approve all health insurance purchases. Insurers would have to compete for approval by an alliance on the basis of offering the most comprehensive cover for the lowest premium. Low-cost efficiency in service delivery would be promoted by encouraging the development of HMOs or integrated networks of physicians and hospitals. Government subsidies would provide coverage for the unemployed and assist small businesses. Prices would be publicly regulated through budget caps.

By the time that Clinton was elected to office in November 1992 this basic plan was already in place. Public and political enthusiasm for health reform was at a peak. All that was required was that the details of legislation should be worked out through a process which would maximize the participation of all interest groups and parties. In order to do this, the Clinton administration set up a task force in September 1993 headed by First Lady Hillary Clinton and Clinton's closest advisor, Ira Magaziner. After one year, however, the momentum for reform had been lost and the task force failed to get even a highly modified bill passed through Congress. Media commentators suggested that the personalities and political attitudes of the task force planners were responsible for health reform failure. Some pundits disregarded the swell of public enthusiasm for reform and suggested that it was foolhardy to even attempt to institute inclusive health insurance in the first place. The reasons for the failure of the reforms, however, were much more broadly structural. Health reform had been moved down the scale of political priorities by events which dominated the first period of the Clinton presidency. Foreign policy, including the long negotiations around the North American Free Trade Agreement, dominated the President's agenda in late 1993. Beyond this, fragmentation among the 'parliamentary' Democratic Party failed to build a middle-class coalition to support the planned reforms. In part this resulted from changes to the pluralistic structure of American politics. At one time, large bloc-groups dominated the interests represented by the two political parties, such as trade union and employer organizations. Since the Second World War, however, America had witnessed the growth of non-partisan advocacy groups, such as the environmental lobby, which were sometimes organized around one issue, such as the protection of abortion rights. This created a type of 'hyper-pluralism' within the American political process which made it harder to mobilize bloc support behind a major federal reform, especially one that would affect one-seventh of the total economy. While attempts were made to mobilize support through the advocacy system it did not manage to overcome political fragmentation within the Congressional Democratic Party itself, divided among progressives, moderates and conservatives. Democratic support of their own reform, therefore, remained politically vulnerable to organized and co-ordinated opposition.

Co-ordinated opposition gathered force between 1993 and 1994. First, the Health Insurance Association of America (HIAA) began a television campaign of 'Harry-and-Louise' advertisements which showed an average middle-class couple bothered and bewildered by uncertainties about choice of physician, changes to their payroll taxes and the cost of complex new bureaucracies created by the reforms. The advertisements suggested that the average American was going to pay more for less choice and quality of health care. The HIAA subsequently founded a grassroots activist group, the Coalition for Health Insurance Choices, that attempted to enlist the support of local business leaders to oppose reform. This grassroots activism mirrored the successful campaign executed by the AMA in 1948–1950 when it used posters in doctors' surgeries to oppose the Truman reforms. Nevertheless, stakeholder opposition lacked unity. Different interest groups focused upon individual aspects of the Clinton plan which affected them particularly. The extreme right wing of the Republican Party, however, managed to turn fragmented stakeholder opposition to various parts of the plan into an ideological crusade against health reform as a whole (Skocpol, 1996).

The right wing of the Congressional Republican Party, led by Newt Gingrich and Dick Armey, moved on from accusing the Clinton plan of being an extravagant bureaucratic nightmare to arguing that there was no health care crisis in the United States at all. The right wing of the Republican Party decided to use their attack on the Clinton health plan as a model for their election crusade in 1994. In November 1993, the Project for the Republican Future was launched to create a framework for a new Republicanism. New Republicanism not only opposed the idea of big-government policies but challenged the very premises on which they were based. The Project for the Republican Future was chaired by William Kristol, who had been Vice President Dan Quayle's chief aide. He was a Harvard Ph.D. and the son of the conservative intellectuals Irving Kristol and Gertrude Himelfarb. Kristol memorialized 'Republican Leaders', telling them that the Clinton health plan not only undermined the breadth and quality of the current health care system in the United States but also represented a serious threat to the Republican Party. If health care reform was successful, it would legitimize middle-class dependence upon government for security and regulation. It would reinstate the Democrats as the 'generous protectors of middle-class interests'. Kristol pointed out that the Clinton plan had become vulnerable as the result of the failure to capitalize on the initial wave of support for reform, and that the time was ripe for an aggressive and uncompromising campaign of opposition. Kristol argued that initial piecemeal Republican opposition should be replaced by all-out war against health reform as part of a new Republican strategy which intended to replace the welfare state with free-market initiatives.

All-out opposition to the Clinton reform was rapidly taken up by a network of anti-government conservative think-tanks and Republican organizations. Kristol's arguments became popularized in the right-wing publication the *Policy Review* in an article entitled 'Clinton's Frankenstein', which characterized the plan as undiscriminating, massively bureaucratic, expensive, coercive and based upon rationing. Clinton's Frankenstein was taken up by the national press and the *Reader's Digest* as Republican opposition stepped up into a national campaign. Right-wing radio talk programmes, such as the Rush Limbaugh show, represented Clinton's plan as a take-over of the American health care system by welfare state liberals, and began to demonize Hillary Clinton as the evil queen of socialized medicine. New Republicanism took its all-out war against health reform to grassroot advocacy organizations such as the right-wing Christian Coalition. New Republicans also targeted their campaign at moderates who were prepared to compromise within the Republican Party and among the representatives of employers and the insurance industry, and within the AMA. When the AMA joined with the AFL-CIO and the American Association of Retired Persons to launch their own publicity campaign in support of universal health coverage, they became the subject of a bitter attack from Newt Gingrich. He accused the leadership of the AMA of being out of touch with its own rank-and-file membership. The Republican Party used local branches of the National Federation of Business Interests to try and influence individual groups of physicians at a local level to oppose the reform. In the face of such a powerfully concerted campaign for all-out opposition, moderate Republicans and moderately Republican organizations such as the Chamber of Commerce and the AMA, which were prepared to make compromises with the plan, retreated. The retreat of moderates prepared to compromise and the failure of the Democrats to mobilize an effective pro-reform campaign in the face of such powerfully organized all-out opposition began to undermine public confidence in the Clinton plan by the spring of 1994. By then, opinion polls showed that the majority of Americans wanted to put off legislation and allow the debate to continue. When a modified bill was presented to Congress in the summer of 1994, the reform had already been defeated and it failed to pass into law. The Clinton reform was defeated by a combination of factors. First, changing an existing massively complex health care delivery system was riddled with uncertainty, which was reflected in the failure to mobilize a coherently united campaign to support reform. Second, public sensitivity to the uncertainties plus the electorate's fears of increased taxation were exacerbated by a co-ordinated political campaign of aggressive all-out opposition (Skocpol, 1996).

The new Republican strategy appeared to be working according to plan when the defeat of health care reform was followed by overwhelming success for the Republicans in the 1994 Congressional elections. The return of Clinton to the White House in 1996, however, demonstrated the volatility of American politics in the late 1990s. By the time that Clinton was re-elected, the tide of both public opinion and practical Congressional politics turned decisively against the aggressive message of new Republicanism and returned to a more traditional middle ground. While health reform was not reinstated on to the federal legislative agenda, various aspects of the Clinton proposals were put into place at state and local levels. Managed competition and managed care, with a growth in HMOs, was taken up incrementally in different regions from 1994.

HEALTH AND WELFARE STATES IN TRANSITION

The transition to a post-industrial society has raised the prospect of something which intellectuals since the 1970s have been calling 'the end of ideology' and the development of global economic and political convergence. In the early 1970s, Daniel Bell posited that the 'convergence' of capitalism and Communism would result in a universalization of values, ending the twentieth-century ideological war between liberalism and Marxism (Bell, 1974; Bell, 1974a). Recently historians such as Eric Hobsbawm have echoed Bell's arguments, suggesting at least that there have been no winners of the ideological wars which have taken place in the twentieth century (Hobsbawm, 1991). Capitalism requires collectivist social policies to sustain it. The ideals of the 'October Revolution' were endlessly eroded in the old Communist systems which have now been overtaken by a desperate race to embrace free-market economic reform and political democracy (Klein, 1993; Esping-Anderson, 1997). Some historical commentators such as Francis Fukuyama have interpreted these events as bringing about the end of historical transformation itself and establishing a permanent and universal perpetuation of the liberal economic system and liberal democratic state (Fukuyama, 1992).

Some commentators have recast this thesis as the end of 'meta' or 'grand' narratives in a post-modern world (Mishra, 1993). Post-modernist intellectual discourses claim that the structural basis of 'modern' industrial society is rapidly disappearing. For example, the collapse of Communism and the failure of capitalism to survive without social and economic planning has proved the historicist assumptions of socialism and the evolutionary assumptions of economic liberalism to be dead ducks. The survival of the welfare state, more or less intact with only incremental changes at the margins, could be offered as evidence that a convergence of politics has been responsible for these developments. The recent downsizing of welfare strategies across nation-states could suggest that, as a result, social policy in the post-modern world is globally converging, driven by its own internal imperatives regardless of ideological conflicts (Mishra, 1993).

However, the concept of global convergence in welfare policy is contradicted by contemporary empirical reality no less than the individual historical development of welfare states has undermined Marshall's original citizenship as a teleological accumulative process (Esping-Anderson, 1997). The patterns of social citizenship development in mature industrial democracies are not reproduced in later industrializing societies. Later industrial economies have followed divided paths to social security, creating a variety of welfare models. Yet there are opportunities for powerful forces to effect convergence in economic and social policy, as can be seen from the influence of international agencies in the reconstruction of the economic systems of states in the former Eastern bloc after the collapse of Communism (Esping-Anderson, 1997).

In Latin America two models of welfare states are emerging, offering a range of neo-liberal and social democratic options for social policy. During the 1980s international financial conditions encouraged the dominance of a neo-liberal financial hegemony among some Latin American governments, such as Chile and, to a lesser extent, Argentina, which led them to pursue market-determined individualistic and inegalitarian models of social policy. However, as the social costs of inequality upon social cohesion began to take effect, other Latin American governments, such as Brazil and Costa Rica, have taken up social democratic market-correcting social policy programmes (Huber, 1997).

By the 1970s Chile had a fragmented system of social security which offered comprehensive coverage to 60–70 per cent of its population. A chaotic administrative system of 350 withholding funds and 150 different programmes meant that its costs were high. It was also inegalitarian, providing pensions which were eight times higher for military personnel and five times higher for bank employees than for blue-collar workers. While the Allende government planned to introduce a comprehensive welfare state, it was only able to extend coverage to the self-employed and improve access to benefits. Pinochet's regime achieved reform through ruthless repression of political dissent, eliminating the most glaring privileges enjoyed by some sectors but exempting the military and the police from reforms. Uniform benefits were introduced for the unemployed, along with uniform minimum pensions, family allowances and uniform entitlement to health care.

The economic crisis experienced by Latin America as a whole changed the direction of social policies not only in Chile but throughout the continent. From before the Second World War, Latin American economies had relied upon import substitution industrialization (ISI) for growth, which increased urbanization, creating a large group of workers in tertiary and service occupations. The international financial crisis of the mid-1970s, plus an exhaustion of the ISI model of growth, precipitated chronic balance of payment deficits in a number of Latin American economies, to the extent that they were unable to serve their debt burdens. Solutions to the dramatic prospect of bankruptcy for a number of states were sought in a complete reorientation of economic policy and political structures. Under the new dominating influence of the economic neo-liberalism of the International Monetary Fund, most states abandoned the ISI model and attempted to generate new export-led industrial economies with massively downsized states. ISI had been administered by large state apparatuses which, in the opinion of the IMF, were grossly bloated and inefficient, even corrupt. Shrinking states and liberalizing economies by deregulating trade through lowering tariffs and eliminating import controls, removing controls on foreign exchange, relaxing restrictions on financial institutions and foreign investment, and eliminating price controls and subsidies together with the privatization of state enterprises allowed the IMF to ensure that the market was able to dictate reorientation from ISI to export-led growth. In social policy severe austerity measures were introduced. In many Latin American countries these reforms necessitated large redundancies in employment in both the public and private sector, dramatic cutbacks in social expenditure and the elimination of price subsidies even for basic foods, transportation and utilities. Massive rises in unemployment and astronomical price rises, sometimes overnight, together with vast reductions in social expenditures, led to great increases in poverty and economic stagnation for a period in all the core Latin American states. As economic reorientation began to take effect, however, and activity recovered, different Latin American states began to redefine the structure of their systems of social protection. The existing systems of social security in most Latin American states were poorly equipped to deal with the consequences of the economic crises of the 1980s (Huber, 1997).

Even before the interventions of the IMF, the Pinochet government had been instituting a radical neo-liberal programme of economic reform in Chile. These economic reforms were part of an overall political strategy to repress all pre-existing political institutions and to destroy the social basis of the left. The regime sought to create a depoliticized atomized society where there would be no basis for collective action and a dramatically reduced role for the state. Deindustrialization followed these policies, but a consumption boom was stimulated by relaxation on foreign borrowing and import controls. In 1983 boom turned to bust with the Chilean government taking up a standard IMF package (Foxley, 1986).

As an emergency measure, the government took over banks and their debts to prevent them from bankruptcy, but reprivatized them as soon as the crisis began to subside. Reliance on the market had always characterized the Pinochet regime's social policy, so that even before the crisis expenditure on housing, social security and health had dramatically declined. In the wake of the economic crisis the Pinochet regime instituted an emergency employment programme with subsidies to employers for hiring new workers, together with a large expansion in public assistance which provided health and nutritional subsidies for the very poor, especially for mothers and infants. Means-tested free school lunches were established, along with pre-school day centres for poor children with health and nutritional problems. As a result the new levels of poverty created in the crisis were not reflected in higher infant mortality rates, but the effectiveness of these programmes was due largely to the structure of coverage achieved by the public health service established under the old pre-Pinochet system (Huber, 1997).

Comprehensive reform of the pension system was delayed by conflict between corporatist-orientated and neo-liberal technocrats, but policy was finally dictated by the latter when a new system of compulsory private insurance was instituted for wage and salary earners in 1980. Under the new system every employed individual and self-employed individual had to pay into an account administered by a non-profit private pension fund (AFP) and the eventual value of the pension would be determined by the individual's contributions, together with the level of performance of the private investment. The value of pensions under the new scheme depends, therefore, on the overall performance of the Chilean economy. Neither the state nor employers contribute to the scheme (Huber, 1997).

Privatization also took place in health care, along with reorganization of the public system. Membership of a private pension scheme makes an individual eligible to join a private health plan, although premiums are too high even for most middle-income groups. By 1990, 16 per cent of the population were affiliated with ISAPRES (private health plans) yet the ISAPRES spend four times the amount on health care as the public system and still make substantial profits. Most middle- and lower-income groups remained with the public system, which also served the destitute. Investment and salaries in the public medicine system had greatly reduced since the 1980s and thus a two-tier system of health services has emerged.

Payroll social security contributions were eliminated under the Pinochet government and not reintroduced by the democratic governments. Chile's economic integration into the world market has been achieved by a new export-led economy but at the price of higher levels of poverty and reduced levels of social security (Vergara, 1994). The weakening of the power of organized labour led to increased informal employment with low wages, employment insecurity and no social insurance for unemployment or disability. This has created a highly flexible labour market, based on subcontracted short-term, often part-time, employment but with high levels of overall employment. The weakness of the labour movement has also meant that the democratic governments have had no power to force a change in social policy. The Aylwin democratic government increased taxation to provide a legal minimum wage and to enable it to continue to provide a safety net of social security for the very poorest, but has not put a system of social insurance on the political agenda (Huber, 1997; Diamond and Valdés-Prieto, 1994).

Aspects of the neo-liberal market-determined model of social policy constructed in Chile have been adopted, in part, in other Latin American states recovering from the economic crises of the 1980s, such as Argentina. Costa Rica and Brazil, however, responded differently to economic reorientation (Smith *et al.* (eds), 1994). The political agenda of Brazil's President Vargas before the Second World War included a corporatist programme of state-promoted organized labour and control. Social security was established for all sectors of the urban working class as part of this programme. Social security units administered by the state to various occupational categories also offered health care and housing loans. The institutes, which were vehicles for political patronage, were never unified into one system even when partial democracy was restored after the war. Organized labour was significantly weakened when a military regime assumed power in 1964, however, and its representation in the administration of social insurance was abolished when six major social security institutes were merged into one. Military and civil servants kept their own privileged funds. While the regime aimed to undermine the power of the urban labour force, it attempted to institute an inclusionary corporatist project in relation to rural workers, establishing a system for them of flat-rate benefits of half of the highest national minimum salary and free access to health care. Cash and health benefits were administered by officially recognized rural syndicates of workers and employers, and the scheme was funded by payroll taxes on urban employers and a tax on the value of agricultural products. By the late 1970s, 70–80 per cent of the urban workforce and in theory the entire rural workforce were covered by Brazil's system of social security, but payments to rural workers were minimal and inadequate (Malloy, 1979).

Brazil's political history resisted the neo-liberal impulse of the 1980s and both military and later democratic governments adopted a much greater statist approach to social security. However, when a new democratic republic was created in 1985, although the statist impulse remained strong, the traditional role of patronage in Brazilian politics inhibited redistributive policies. When the Brazilian government had been forced to take new austerity measures in exchange for the assistance of the IMF in 1982, the country experienced deep recession until growth began to recover in 1984–1985. This was followed by massive inflation which the Sarney democratic government attempted to control with a prices and wages freeze. This policy remained in force for too long and the budget deficit remained out of control, along with inflation, which returned in 1987. When President Collor was elected in 1990, his government began a neo-liberal offensive to try and bring inflation and the budget deficit under control, introducing rapid liberalization and privatization along with conventional austerity measures. His impeachment in 1992 halted his programme, however, and inflation and the budget deficit have yet to be conquered (Huber, 1997).

When the Sarney government gave the administration of the social security system to progressive technocrats among the political opposition (PMDB), major universalizing reforms were introduced. Contributions made by the lowest income groups were reduced in order to encourage more of the marginal population without coverage into the system. Funding for these reduced contributions and increased benefits to the poorest sections were found by reducing privileges such as time-for-service and special pensions enjoyed by the highest paid. Controls on charges for private health care by providers were introduced, and attempts were made to rebalance the public system towards preventive rather than therapeutic medicine. These reforms were opposed by influential high-paid occupational groups and the Finance Ministry. Some privileges were reintroduced, and indirect sales taxes were imposed in order to finance increased spending on social security. In 1987 free health care was provided to all sectors of the population, but the differential availability of services and facilities, particularly in the poorest areas, limited the universalizing effect of these measures. In the same year, health reformers launched a campaign to create a unified and decentralized health system which would transfer resources and responsibilities to the local state level, aimed at bringing about a better co-ordination of health and social security for the poorest sections of the community. However, decentralization resulted largely in state governments reducing their overall health expenditures while increasing medical salaries in order to compete with the private sector for personnel. Decentralization failed to prevent private medicine driving up the costs of public health care (Luiz and Araújo, 1997). Although health care became a right of democratic citizenship in Brazil, its actual universalization was limited since access to health care was severely lacking among the poorest sections of the community. In the area of social security also, non-payment of contributions still left many low-income groups without coverage for unemployment and disability and without a pension. Further reforms remained hampered by the perpetuation of political patronage which resulted in over-staffed agencies filled with government supporters. The newly elected president, Fernando Henrique Cardoso, has attempted to address these institutional defects by strengthening Congressional party coalitions. The direction of policy remains aimed at universalization of social protection with new strategies aimed at combating poverty and hunger and providing a basic income to 7 million poor families who remain without any existing means of support (Huber, 1997).

Diversity within Latin American welfare systems reflects the divergent political and cultural histories of its nation-states. Diversity in East Asia equally reflects the history of individual states, yet long-shared cultural traditions such as Confucianism differentiate East Asian welfare overall from Western traditions. Reliance on mutual aid within the extended family is a Confucian ideal which has determined much of the history of welfare provision in states such as Japan, Taiwan and Korea. The process of economic 'modernization' in East Asia since the Second World War involved the adoption of Western patterns of industrial development and financial organization. Although in Japan the new constitution imposed by the American occupational government after the war introduced a system of welfare ostensibly based upon Western ideology, the reaffirmation of Confucian ideals in relation to welfare provision in all three countries has been a feature of the resistance to the Westernization of values and beliefs (Jones, 1993).

The rapid expansion of East Asian economies such as Japan, Taiwan and Korea since the Second World War was achieved by a largely youthful population imbued with Confucian beliefs in the importance of self-reliance, individual success and hard work for the benefit of the community. The rate of expansion, together with age of the population, meant that social welfare and protection were largely secured through full and increasingly affluent employment. Mainly low levels of unionization meant that organized labour was absent as a political force pressing for welfare reform.

In the 1960s Japan began to expand its social protection programmes through the introduction of welfare for the mentally disabled, national health insurance and a national pension scheme, public assistance for the aged and maternal and child welfare. A campaign to improve the 'quality of life' in the 1970s saw further expansion of these programmes and increasing public concern over issues like pollution and traffic accidents. Feminist groups also began to emerge in the 1960s who highlighted the issue of discrimination by both employers and the state. The move towards welfare expansion was halted in 1974, however, following the oil crisis. Between 1975 and 1985 unemployment expanded three-fold, resulting in an increase in expenditure which provoked a backlash in the 1980s. A new political rhetoric in the 1980s concerned with the 'reconsideration of welfare' stressed the cost of social welfare to the competitiveness of the economy. A political consensus between the Ministry of Health and Welfare and the Finance Ministry agreed that social expenditure had to be curtailed. In 1981 fiscal reforms reduced the levels of state social expenditure, shifting the burden of welfare costs back to the individual by placing surcharges on health care for the elderly, reducing the level of coverage of health insurance, increasing the age of eligibility for pensions from 60 to 70 for men and 55 to 60 for women, and imposing a 3 per cent indirect sales tax. In the 1990s, however, the prospect of increasingly ageing populations has raised the question of social welfare to a higher political priority. Japan anticipates that the number of retired people will more than double in the next two decades, with 25 per cent of its population being over 65 by 2020. The number of people over 80 is expected to be three times the contemporary level. Although savings levels in Japan, Taiwan and Korea are very high, such a major demographic transition poses serious questions for future social expenditure. Recently the Japanese government has attempted to address some of these questions by reasserting the value of volunteer activity as a return to traditional, i.e. Confucian, methods of welfare provision. The government encouraged the development of 'residential participation organizations' such as quasi state-funded voluntary mutual-aid service banks run by the government and local communities to help increase both individual and local community participation in welfare organization and provision (Goodman and Peng, 1997).

Some American analysts have proposed that two different welfare systems have emerged within industrial societies, the America-Pacific and the European. However, the 1980 welfare reforms in Japan reflected anxieties about the dangers of too much Westernization and were an attempt to avoid the economic difficulties experienced by Western economies as the result of the high costs of their welfare states. Japanese scholars became concerned with redefining Japan's identity and role among the world's industrial economies. Rather than a neo-liberal assault, the Japanese welfare reforms of the 1980s were an extension of traditional values concerning welfare as mutual aid and filial responsibility, which meant that statutory social assistance always remained highly stigmatized. Although the individual welfare histories of Taiwan and Korea have different components, to an extent they share some of the same underlying cultural determinants. The percentage of GDP spent on social expenditure in all three countries is significantly less than their European counterparts. Even where universal rights have been established, for example in health care in Japan and Korea, this is funded through public agencies which collect insurance premiums with a limited government subsidy. The state's role is therefore one of a regulator rather than a provider (Goodman and Peng, 1997; Jones, 1993).

Amid the story of international diversity in welfare policy, a force promoting economic and welfare convergence in the last quarter of the twentieth century has been the IMF. The IMF has been able to translate neo-liberal economic philosophy, largely derived from political thought in the United States, into the conditions and terms of financial aid to failing economies. Nowhere is its influence currently being felt more powerfully than in the states of Central and Eastern Europe following the collapse of Communism. Here the transition to democratic economic liberal societies has produced a crisis in social protection, but current trends indicate that an international neo-liberal language of welfare already influencing transformations in the United States and Western Europe is being translated into solutions to the social policy crisis experienced in many post-Communist European societies, by the conditions and terms offered by the IMF in exchange for economic aid. Yet the future direction of social policy amid what collectively constitutes a vast region is still unresolved (Standing, 1997).

While the analytical value of considering Central and Eastern Europe collectively is minimal, it can provide some insights into some of the major issues faced by societies experiencing major transformation following the collapse of Communism. Under Communism, social protection was largely ensured through policies of full secure low-income employment supported by services administered through state enterprises, such as health services, with low levels of income transfers in the form of unemployment or disability benefits or pensions. While pensions were provided for men after the age of 60 and for women after the age of 55, they were set at such a low percentage of the average income, which was close to the level of the minimum income, that most pensioners continued to work to subsidize them even if they were also in receipt of disability benefit. Unemployment benefit was rarely taken up, not only because unemployment was considered to be parasitical but also because there was guaranteed opportunity for work, often in vast state-owned enterprises employing many thousands of workers. The level of funding of enterprises was often linked to the numbers employed and therefore most enterprises frequently maintained a number of job vacancies to attract more workers. In the former Soviet Union there were many 'company towns' in which two such enterprises making a wide range of goods would employ the entire population. This system provided economic security but at the expense of an inflexible labour market, encouraged by the requirement of residence permits for workers, which was necessary for a dynamic economy. A further feature of the system was that complete integration did not prevent stratification within the labour force. Stratification often followed gender lines and was in terms of disability. Standards of living were maintained with low wages with little variation (except among the most privileged elite such as party bureaucrats), through substantial food and other price subsidies together with state housing provision (B. Deacon, 1993; Standing, 1997).

The growing inefficiency of this system, which eventually led to its collapse, left minimal systems of social security in place to cope with the massive rises in poverty and deprivation which followed. As the countries of the former Eastern bloc were plunged into a global economy in which, after 1989, they could not compete, the three pillars on which the previous system was based were eradicated – guaranteed employment, social protection via price subsidies, and enterprise-based social benefits in the form of goods and services. The reform of the Eastern and Central European economies was subsequently dictated largely by international agencies, and so too were labour market reform and social policy. In order to cap inflation, which rose out of control with the removal of price subsidies, tax-based incomes policies imposed punitive taxes upon employers offering average wage increases above a designated level. This created a new class of working poor, whose wages could barely provide subsistence as prices soared, with the result that the level of the minimum wage dramatically dropped. This directly affected social transfer payments since the minimum wage was often used as the floor against which benefits and pensions were set (Standing, 1997).

The safety net of public protection became increasingly eroded as markets restructured, mass poverty expanded and dramatic levels of inequality deepened through unemployment and the devaluation of real wages, pensions and benefits between 1990 and 1992. This was encouraged by policies designed to reduce the costs of social protection through greater reliance on employment-related market-determined social insurance and targeted means-tested social assistance. As in Western Europe, unemployment benefit in the former Communist bloc countries was perceived as a 'passive' social policy which might encourage idleness. In its place, the IMF have proposed a workfare 'active' social policy which offers training and work opportunities to the unemployed instead of benefits. Like industrial societies everywhere, countries in the former Eastern bloc face the prospect of pensions for ever ageing populations, and reforms here have been following Chilean lines with the creation of a new compulsory private contribution scheme coupled with residual entitlements for those covered only by the old scheme. Attempts are being made in some states, such as the Czech Republic, Slovakia and Hungary, to transfer the previous state-funded system to one based on private health insurance. Where the state-funded system has been left intact, the shock therapies of the new budgeting programmes have had a devastating effect on the reduction of services and the run-down of numbers of medical personnel employed, whose salaries have fallen rapidly in relation to those in the newly emergent private sector of medicine. The tightening of wages of public-sector salaries in health and education has caused an internal brain drain of doctors and teachers leaving their professions to earn more as company executives. The long-term consequences of such developments are yet to be realized (Standing, 1997).

Some states who started from a stronger economic position, such as the Czech Republic and rich enclaves like Slovakia, have made the transition to liberalized economies with far less difficulty than others. But the impact of economic transformation upon others, such as the old nuclear military states of the Ukraine, Belarus and the Russian Federation, is alarming. The average life expectancy of men in the Russian Federation dropped by seven years from 65 to 58 between 1989 and 1995. In Hungary, Poland and other republics, it has also fallen by between five and two years. The average age of life for women has anomalously dropped only slightly, which poses intriguing questions to be researched. Means-tested social assistance targeted at the very poorest appears to be seriously inadequate to serve as a minimal safety net when up to 50 per cent of those eligible fail to apply out of the wish to avoid the degradation of stigma. One Russian cabinet minister was quoted in 1993 as suggesting that instead of widespread public revolt over such massive deprivation people 'are just going into their homes and dying' (Standing, 1997: 250). The social anarchy emerging from such rapid transformations with such severe effects has created economic opportunities for exploiters who have become figures of hate, such as the shadowy characters of the new 'Mafia' of old state functionaries who have become commercial barons, traders making monopoly profits, successful partici-pants in the ever expanding informal economy and organized criminals. Under the current influence of the neo-liberal philosophies of the international agen-cies directing change, however, there seems little opportunity for individual states to choose alternative social democratic routes to the resolution of their social protection crises (Standing, 1997).

While powerful forces effecting a degree of globalization of economic and social reform can be observed in areas such as the states of the former Eastern bloc, ideological battles over health and social policy, both within and between nation states, illustrate the persistence of diversity. Furthermore, assumptions about a postmodern global convergence of social policy ignore the extent to which welfare states are consistently in transition. Changing policy directions and priorities led President Clinton to announce in 1997 that 'welfare as we know it' will be completely transformed by the early years of the twenty-first century. While policy-makers in the European Union are tentatively resurrecting employment as an economic priority over monetary control, they are also care-fully considering innovative models of welfare privatization in industrializing economies such as Chile for future inspiration. The growth of state intervention into health care provision in the twentieth century did not eliminate the role of market mechanisms and voluntary agencies. A variety of mixed economies of health provision persists, contextualized by national cultures and political organi-zations. Within this context of such historical flux and uncertainty, a postmodernist international globalization of health care is yet to be realized.

Part 4

Preparing for the twenty-first century

In the twentieth century collective action in relation to the health of populations has not been confined either to the prevention or management of disease. In Chapter 13 we probe the way in which fitness has been positively promoted in the twentieth century and examine how it has influenced new standards for the health of populations in the twenty-first century. Since before the Second World War, older ideas about the cultivation of individual health have been reinvigorated in new ideologies which have reinvented the individual body as a map of social and economic relations. The social construction of the fit body through state action, voluntaristic and entrepreneurial enterprise is explored here in order to question what postmodern societies require of individuals to allow them to claim legitimately to be fit to live in the twenty-first century. Finally, the Epilogue links some of the themes explored throughout the book to the latest developments in forging new perspectives on the health of populations.

13 Being fit to live in the twenty-first century: healthy bodies and somatic maps

Sanitary reform provided industrial societies with clean water, effective sewage and refuse removal. Premature mortality from 'filth' diseases subsequently declined. Rising standards of living combined with improved hygienic environments reduced the threat of lethal infections. In England, when continuing high levels of chronic ill health were discovered among the population following the 1904 Report on Physical Deterioration, the focus of British public health policy began to change towards personal health services. Similar developments happened elsewhere as an epidemiological transition took place in industrial societies from acute infectious diseases to chronic illnesses. Furthermore, new intellectual influences such as bacteriology, social biology and 'imperial competition' encouraged the development of preventive medicine 'from the social standpoint', in Newsholme's phrase. As we have seen in Chapter 10, on the one hand this led to a new concern with human reproduction and health care provision for mothers and infants and to hygiene and health education for children. On the other hand, in Chapters 11 and 12 we saw how the changing demographic structures of advanced industrial societies bound the health of populations to the costs of medical provision.

In this chapter we discuss yet further consequences of a type of preventive medicine from the social standpoint that, paradoxically, aimed to reduce chronic disease through the individualization of health care responsibility. This chapter examines how the influence of social science helped to develop a new managerial ethos in preventive medicine that focused on individual lifestyles as the source of social health. This approach starkly contrasted the political solutions of nineteenth-century state medicine or sanitary reform to population health improvement. The chapter also explores how these developments were paralleled by a new commercialization of individual health.

From the early twentieth century, health care became increasingly integrated into the collective provision of social welfare. As industrial societies in the twentieth century experienced epidemiological transition, so the function of public health administration became redefined by the conceptualization of health as social relations. One consequence of the socio-medical model of prevention was the identification of healthy living as a central goal. Was this new gospel of individual health responsibility as successful at achieving its goals as the

nineteenth-century sanitary revolution? Where it had been pursued most vigorously, the sanitary revolution succeeded in reducing premature mortality from
infectious diseases by the end of the nineteenth century. Did the management of
population health through the individualization of health responsibility achieve
as much in the twentieth? Did these new approaches to community health
through increased individual responsibility succeed in producing 'fitter' populations? This chapter examines the impact of these developments upon the
construction of a new somatic map in the twentieth century.

State and public health authorities did not have a monopoly in producing
strategies for creating healthy populations in the most affluent societies in history.
Ideals of health stimulated utopian philosophies and were also exploited by
commercial interests. A mass health culture turned selling health, fitness and
physical beauty into big business, and in the process medicine, social science and
commercial culture succeeded in fetishizing health and commodifying sexuality
in the construction of a reified healthy body. As a result, somatic obsession
allowed bodies to function as tools of social, economic and political differentiation wherein elite bodies became a social source of power.

CHRONIC INFECTION

One of the most powerfully symbolic representations of the epidemiological
transition at the turn of the twentieth century was the predominance of tuberculosis. Tuberculosis had been gradually retreating in both Europe and North
America from the early nineteenth century (Smith, 1988; Bryder, 1988). As
infant mortality from gut infections, smallpox and the other pandemics of the
nineteenth century declined, the persistent prevalence of tuberculosis among the
adult populations in industrial societies became more distinctively visible (Dubos,
1987; Rosenkrantz (ed.), 1994). Tuberculosis became a central issue of the population health in the first half of the twentieth century, stimulating new
approaches to its prevention and reduction.

At the end of the First World War, tuberculosis accounted for about a sixth of
all deaths in France and up to a quarter of mortality in some large urban
centres. The Rockefeller Foundation targeted it in a public health campaign in
1917. The campaign used a dispensary system for tracing cases, assisting
patients' families, providing disinfection and disseminating public education
about reducing the risk of spreading the disease. Sanatoria were also employed
to isolate patients and attempt to assist them to recover. Each *département* was
required by law to establish a tuberculosis dispensary from 1916, but the state
provided no additional funding for them and did not make TB a notifiable
disease. As a result, by the end of 1917 there were still only twenty-three tuberculosis dispensaries (Barnes, 1995; Ramsey, 1994).

Together with the American Red Cross, the Rockefeller workers established
model programmes in areas with high rates of tuberculosis infection. The
Foundation's campaign relied heavily upon public health nurses and encouraged

the creation of schools for training them. The Rockefeller mission assisted the state in building sanatoria in each *département*. In 1923 the Rockefeller mission handed control of the programme to the French National Committee for Defence against Tuberculosis. By this time the great majority of *départements* had permanent anti-TB programmes. The medical staff working in the dispensaries and sanatoria were salaried employees, and professionalization of nursing was encouraged by increased opportunities for specialist training and state certification (Barnes, 1995; Ramsey, 1994).

The tuberculosis dispensary and sanatorium system in France had been modelled on the methods which originated in Germany. The first sanatorium had been set up in the nineteenth century at Nordach in the Black Forest. Like Nordach, the subsequent sanatoria created in Germany and Switzerland were superior rest and recovery homes for the bourgeois sufferer. They were luxurious hotels in exquisite locations that offered rarefied air and social atmosphere, along with a variety of therapeutics (Bryder, 1988). Fictionalized in the famous novel by Thomas Mann, the elite continental sanatoria were magic mountain retreats in which to suffer and think, regardless of whether you recovered or not. In *The Magic Mountain*, Mann utilized the romantic representation of tuberculosis as an occupational hazard of artistic sensitive bourgeois creativity which had mythologized the disease from the early nineteenth century (Sontag, 1979). The romantic mythologization of the disease, however, bore little resemblance to the experience of even middle- and upper-class sufferers and was utterly contradicted by the reality faced by working-class patients.

Below Mann's fictional Magic Mountain, state-funded sanatoria throughout Europe provided anything but a holiday for their inmates. Most of these institutions did not even provide their patients with comfort and warmth as part of a vigorous therapeutic regime which believed that either enforced rest plus fresh air or graduated labour plus fresh air would cure the disease. As in France and Germany, sanatoria treatment in Britain was funded by the state. The 1911 National Insurance Act made provision for sanatorium benefit to be paid to all those hospitalized. Hospitalization was compulsory for anyone chosen by their GP local health officer who was in receipt of either Poor Law relief or state sickness benefit (Bryder, 1988; Smith, 1988).

In the late nineteenth century, medical officers of health had demanded that local authorities be compelled to provide isolation hospitals for highly infectious tuberculosis sufferers in the late stage of the disease (Watkins, 1984). The sanatoria in Britain, however, were established not primarily as isolation hospitals but as therapeutic environments that would offer treatment to cure patients in the early stages of the disease. Despite the identification of the bacteriological origin of the disease by Robert Koch in 1884, early twentieth-century clinical treatments were imbued with a folklorish belief in the value of fresh clean air because of the traditional association of TB with habitation of dark damp squalid domestic environments and industrial polluted towns. Enforced bedrest best accompanied fresh air for those in whom the disease was substantially developed. This meant lying on verandas in the sunshine or the snow, summer and winter, regardless of the temperature. Some of the British state sanatoria were built without windows or heating in order that the patients might constantly benefit from the value of exposure to the elements. In some cases this meant patients' beds had to have snow removed from them by the nursing staff (Bryder, 1988; Smith, 1988).

Another therapeutic regime favoured by the clinical staff of the British state sanatoria was graduated labour for those in the earlier stages of the disease. Clinicians in charge of sanatoria, such as Marc Patterson at Frimley, were concerned that working-class patients should not develop habitual idleness and become ill-equipped to return to an active labouring existence when they left the sanatorium. In addition, a new theory of auto-inoculation advocated active work for stimulating the body's immunity system and allowing the patient's physiology to cure itself. The graduated labour schemes introduced into British sanatoria amounted to a pick-axe cure for consumptives. Patients were required to grad-uate from gardening to mixing concrete, laying roads and building swimming pools. Dietary regimes assumed that if the patient could manage to increase in weight then this would also bring about a cure, so patients were fed foods with a high starch content (Bryder, 1988; Smith, 1988).

Cure rates did not match expectations despite the fact that patients were sent back to their communities before they became terminal. The level of mortality among sanatoria patients within five years of leaving the institution was about 85 per cent. Their lack of immediate success forced the sanatoria hospitals and specialist medical staff to explore new avenues for treatment. Modern surgery appeared to offer hope in the form of an operation which would collapse a diseased lung and provide it with complete rest. Pneumothorax was popularized throughout the sanatorium movement. Despite its dangers and painful conse-quences patients eagerly opted for the surgery, either in the hope of a cure or in the belief that this at least was the most scientific approach to the disease (Bryder, 1988; Smith, 1988).

Sanatoria housed a tiny percentage of the tuberculosis population in Britain and elsewhere. There is no evidence that they contributed to the decline of the disease before the introduction of the vaccine, the BCG, developed in France by 1921 (Barnes, 1995; Ramsey, 1994). TB was more or less eliminated after the antibiotic cure, streptomycin, became available in 1946. In recent times, rising levels of poverty have seen the return of TB. Some populations, such as AIDS sufferers, have become specially vulnerable to TB infection. The most worrying development is the appearance of new antibiotic-resistant strains.

Much historical debate has tried to identify the cause of TB's retreat. Improved standards of living and nutrition status clearly played a major role. Other factors were important in the British context. Working-class sufferers in the latter stages of the disease were often too weak to continue working and thereby fell into destitution. Their isolation in the workhouse removed them from their family and immediate community, giving them less opportunity to infect others. Isolation of poor patients increasingly reduced the risk of infection to the community as a whole over time (Smith, 1988).

The sanatoria service in Britain provided an economic and administrative model on which a state-funded health service could be based (Bryder, 1988). In France also it stimulated new debates about the provision of health care through state insurance. Tuberculosis provision brought hospital administration into the arena of public authority. Public health regulation of hospital administration subsequently increased in the inter-war years in Britain, France and Germany. In France and Britain public health shifted away from the orientation of public hygiene and embraced a medical model.

PHYSICIANS TO THE COMMUNITY

A medical model of public health service also developed in the United States at the turn of the twentieth century. In Chapter 9 we saw how US public health originated as a philanthropic cause until bacteriology stimulated the creation of a new scientific model of preventive medicine. The New Public Health made prevention a biomedical discipline (Fee, 1987). The medical model of prevention was institutionalized in practice by the commissioned corps of officers of the US Public Health Service. The first law establishing any kind of collective provision of health care in the United States was an Act for the Relief of Sick and Disabled Seamen, passed in 1798 (Williams, 1951). Hospital provision for sailors evolved into a large commissioned corps of medical officers in the Marine Hospital Service headed by a Supervising Surgeon-General. The hospital service had fallen into decay by the 1870s, until Surgeon-General John Woodworth instituted radical improvements and turned the dissipated hospital fund into a systematic and regulated hospital service. An enthusiastic supporter of the fledgling public health reform movement and the American Public Health Association, Woodworth campaigned for federal regulation of quarantine. After Woodworth's death in 1879 the succeeding Surgeon-General, John B. Hamilton, planned to turn the marine hospital system into a public health service with wide-ranging activities. By virtue of political manoeuvres made by various succeeding Surgeons-General, this goal was achieved when the MHS was transformed into the US Public Health Service in 1902. The creation of this service defeated the chance to create a federal public health system with national policies and directives (Williams, 1951; Mullan, 1989).

The work of sanitary reform was largely accomplished through local initiative and organization but the Surgeon-General was given the power to demand annual meetings of all states' public health authorities and to ensure the universalization of standards. The US Public Health corps of medical officers were not part of the engineering revolution of states' public health reform. Their role was that of a physician to the community using biomedical theory to inform the management of disease among the population collectively. This was exemplified by their role as the medical managers of immigration restriction. One officer, Dr Samuel Grubb, identified the role of the public health officer as that of a detective, comparable to a federal agent, seeking out the criminal activity of infectious diseases (Mullan, 1989). The US Public Health Service fulfilled this role in screening immigrants both for physical diseases and for mental disorder and retardation (Williams, 1951).

By the early twentieth century the service had generated a number of different divisions dealing, in addition to immigration control, with rural health and epidemic disease prevention. John B. Hamilton had established a hygiene laboratory in one room on Statten Island in 1887; this was moved to be near the new headquarters of the service in Washington D.C. in 1891 by Surgeon-General Walter Wyman. The hygiene laboratory became the National Institutes of Health, which is now probably the world's largest funded and most prestigious biomedical laboratory organization together with its sister institution, the Centre for Disease Control in Atlanta (Mullan, 1989).

The aim of the first Surgeon-General, John Maynard Woodworth, in adopting the military structure was to prevent appointments becoming sinecures and spoils, and to establish instead an organization of professionals. Despite this ethic of separating professionalism from politics, the history of the service has been inherently political. Surgeons-General have been keen political operators. Surgeon-General Wyman effectively prevented the Progressive movement's attempt to establish a federal national health department when he secured the 1912 legislation establishing the service as the only federal health agency. President Taft's appointment as Surgeon-General, Rupert Blue, acquired his political skills when dealing with California's 1906 plague epidemic which followed the earthquake (Mullan, 1989).

Plague had first broken out in San Francisco in 1900 when Joseph Kinyoun was seconded from his directorship of the Hygiene Laboratory to manage the epidemic. A battle subsequently ensued between the public health and local government authorities in San Francisco, along with civil unrest among the Chinese community. Volatile public hostilities took place between Kinyoun and California governor Henry T. Cage, who publicly denied the existence of the epidemic. Battles were fought over the institution of quarantine and sanitary improvement in Chinatown which were only resolved when an independent commission ruled that plague was present. The state authorities subsequently agreed to institute public health measures on condition that Kinyoun left California. The controversial history of plague control in San Francisco left Blue a political minefield to negotiate but, in contrast to Kinyoun, he did so with public acclaim and managed to eradicate the epidemic from the city. In 1916 Blue was the only Surgeon-General to also become president of the American Medical Association. He used his position to support the Progressives' policy proposals for the introduction of national health insurance. Subsequent Surgeons-General have equally reflected the political spirit of their era, such as Blue's successor, President Wilson's choice of Hugh S. Cumming. A conservative with aristocratic bearing, Cumming in contrast to Blue, represented a philosophy of strategic complacency. He allowed the state authorities to dominate prevention and resisted any attempt to expand any interventionist role for the service into the provision of social welfare services. Under Cumming's tenure the USPHS became heavily involved in the expansion of epidemiological and biostatistical investigations which steered the service away from the ideological conflicts surrounding health care provision. Cummings hoped to repeat Blue's achievement of becoming the president of the AMA, and his conservative politics always represented the interests of organized medicine, which led him, for example, to oppose the Sheppard–Towner Act in 1921. Cumming did not succeed in his aim to become AMA president, but he did manage to avoid the elimination of the USPHS by politicians who wanted public health to be expanded either at the local state level or through the creation of a federal health department. The only social medical involvement of the service during this period was confined to the management of rehabilitation centres for drug addicts, clinics for venereal disease sufferers and the Veterans' Bureaux of psychiatric hospitals (Mullan, 1989).

The USPHS was given a new role in welfare provision under the 1935 Social Security Act. Although Roosevelt resisted including health insurance in his New Deal programme, the Social Security Act re-established grants in aid to states for maternal and child welfare services. The USPHS used these funds to establish local health departments. When Cumming finished his term in 1936, Roosevelt replaced him with the pioneer of venereal disease control, Thomas Parran, as Surgeon-General. Parran pursued a much more interventionist role for the USPHS and under his direction the programme for establishing local health departments was vigorously supported. Parran also worked with the Farm Security Administration to help organize medical co-operatives to provide care for poor rural farming families. The USPHS helped to draft the ill-fated National Health Plan produced by the Interdepartmental Committee for Health and Welfare. Parran pledged the allegiance of the USPHS to the idea of health insurance but was the last Surgeon-General to involve the service so directly in the politics of national health care provision (Mullan, 1989; Brandt, 1987).

Changes in the political colour of White House administrations were matched by choice of Surgeon-General appointments. Thomas Parran was replaced by Leonard Scheele in 1947, who had a dramatically different political orientation from his predecessor. He absented the USPHS from the political debates surrounding the attempt of the Truman administration to institute a national health programme through the Murray–Wagner–Dingell Bill in 1948. Scheele did not assist the government's defence against the AMA's campaign against 'state medicine', and when asked by Oscar Ewing from the Federal Security Agency to appear in a TV debate to argue the case for the bill he refused, suggesting that it would compromise his status as a professional officer of the corps. Scheele concentrated instead on expanding the NIH's programme of medical research and facilitated its amalgamation with the National Heart Institute and National Institute of Dental Health, making it the plural National Institutes of Health. He secured $40 million to build a research hospital on campus, added a further four research institutes to its organization and secured a growth of its research budget from $37 million to $100 million within the first seven years of his administration (Mullan, 1989).

Despite the conservative politics of the USPHS leadership in the 1950s, the service acquired a further social medical role in the administration of health services for the Native American population. Health care for the Amerindian population had been poorly provided for by the Bureaux of Indian Affairs since 1849. By the Second World War, army recruitment among the Indian population revealed epidemic tuberculosis up to levels, for example, of 10 per cent among Alaska Natives. The National Tuberculosis Association, together with the AMA, the American Public Health Association and the Association of State and Territorial Health Officials, began a campaign in 1949 to have responsibility for Indian health care transferred to the USPHS. The transfer of authority from the BIA eventually took place in 1955 with new funding and the reorganization of services under the direction of the USPHS.

In the reorganization of health services for the poor and the elderly under Lyndon Johnson's programme for the Great Society, the USPHS was largely by-passed, along with the local health departments which were overtaken by grants in aid offered by the Office of Economic Opportunity to fund new neighbour-hood health centres. The USPHS found itself increasingly marginalized from the debates surrounding the Medicare and Medicaid programmes, and when they became law in 1965 responsibility for them was placed within the Department of Health, Education and Welfare. The USPHS nevertheless managed to survive subsequent federal governments of various political persuasions despite overt efforts by the Nixon administration to abolish it. The service now functions as an emergency service which can be called upon by local authorities when faced by health crises, and as a sort of National Health Service for the Native American population. Perhaps its most influential role emanates from the Centre for Disease Control based at Atlanta. The corps of commissioned officers are now a tiny minority within a huge number of 'civilian' personnel who work as scientific researchers, public health nurses and administrators. The USPHS's political influence was given a new lease of life when the AIDS epidemic began to threaten to become the major epidemic disease of the late twentieth century. In the early 1980s Surgeon-General C. Everett Koop forced a reluctant President Ronald Reagan to publicly acknowledge the disease and provide funds for education to prevent it, for diagnostic and treatment services for its victims and for research into the possibility of creating a vaccine (Mullan, 1989).

Although marginalized within the politics of medical service provision, the US Public Health Service never fulfilled an alternative role of a sanitary organization providing environmental health regulation. Throughout the twentieth century it was a corps of medical officers providing medical management, either in moments of health crisis or as a social service to the poorest and underprivileged American populations who could not participate in the medical free market economy. In addition, and as a separate wing of its organization, the USPHS oversaw the development of biomedical research. As a result of the medicalization of public health, it was relegated to the periphery of the politics of health care in the post-war era in the US.

In Britain the public health system had always been run by doctors who had perceived it as 'state medicine' and 'preventive medicine' from the middle of the nineteenth century. Chadwick's sanitary 'idea' was not instituted by engineers, as he had envisaged. The health of populations, while informed by broader philosophies of philanthropic and political social reform, had nevertheless been a medical speciality in Britain throughout the nineteenth century. When the first specialist training in public health work was introduced in Britain, it was a post-graduate diploma for which only fully qualified doctors were eligible to study (Porter, 1991).

From the time that medical officers of health were made compulsory appointments to every sanitary district in Britain in 1872, rivalry and overlapping functions were feared by local general practitioners. Overlapping increased as medical officers of health began to use public health laboratory diagnostic testing for infectious diseases such as diphtheria. The notification of infectious diseases also added a statutory administrative burden to a general practitioner's responsibilities for which he was not recompensed, and hostility and non-co-operation could sometimes result within a local health district. As the new sociological environmentalism underlying public health practice identified more and more groups at risk and targeted them for state-funded services, so the territory of the general practitioner was increasingly threatened. The institution of state-funded ante- and post-natal services, the public registration of midwives, health visitors for mothers and infants, baby clinics, health inspection and clinic provision for schoolchildren and state hospitals for tuberculosis patients all encroached further into the clinical field. As state-funded health care provision expanded before the Second World War in Britain, so the administrative power of the public health officer was enhanced. The 1929 Local Government Act officially abolished the nineteenth-century Poor Law and replaced it with a new system of means-tested welfare provision called National Assistance. The old workhouse infirmaries now became local authority hospitals for those in receipt of assistance, and these were placed under the control of the local medical officer of health. The use of local health authority hospitals expanded in the inter-war period with the stigma of pauperism somewhat removed from them, and they provided increasingly efficient therapeutics. The popularity of local authority hospitals, as we saw in the last chapter, seriously compromised the viability of the voluntary hospital sector to the point where many institutions were on the verge of bankruptcy by the Second World War (Lewis, 1986).

By the time that the National Health Service was being planned in Britain, deep professional divisions existed between clinical and preventive medicine. Clinicians loathed the expansion of authority of medical officers of health. MOHs themselves were absorbed in an unwieldy managerial quagmire of an excessively complex and uncoordinated system of services. Rationalization was needed, but public health as an academic discipline and professional speciality did not address this question directly. Public health failed to redefine its function as a specialized practice of disease prevention and management in a world in epidemiological transition. On the one hand lifted up by new powers of political and administrative control in health care, and on the other bogged down in the management of an inefficient system of services, public health professionals lost the opportunity to develop their specialism intellectually in order to meet the challenges presented to them by the epidemic rise of chronic disease (Lewis, 1986; Webster, 1988).

After the establishment of the NHS the managerial role of public health officers increased. In the post-war years, local health officers found themselves trying to co-ordinate an ever widening range of community services from environmental regulation to social work administration. By the end of the 1960s a new concept was emerging of public health as community service planning. The expansion of this role ultimately led to the replacement of public health officers with practitioners of a new discipline called 'community medicine' (Jefferys, 1986).

Implementing community health planning involved major conflicts with different factions of health providers, especially at times when the elite branch of the clinical profession felt their autonomy compromised. Community medicine as a discipline increasingly experienced difficulties in defining its constituency and faced mounting problems of implementation in practice (Warren, 1997). At a critical juncture in the history of community medicine in Britain, a new lethal pandemic emerged in the Western world, which raised the question of reviving the comprehensive statutory functions of nineteenth-century public health authorities for modern British society. In other societies the advent of AIDS has raised similar questions.

These questions have arisen because, prior to the advent of AIDS, public hygiene since the Second World War concentrated on reinstating the individual's responsibility for their own health and the health of others. One central focus of preventive medicine in the post-war period became the mass communication of personal health care advice for the individual to take responsibility not only for limiting their vulnerability to chronic disease, such as coronary failure or lung cancer, but also to preserve their youth and raise their level of athletic fitness. Equally the individual has been urged to become aware of the responsibilities each has for the health of the other, for example through publicity about passive smoking. The new era of missionary health evangelism, especially successful in the United States, owes more, however, to long traditions of personal health cultures and the methods of clinical prevention than to state medicine.

In both Britain and the United States the organization of public health became increasingly confused with the management and delivery of public medical services. Public health as a conceptual system lost the opportunity to redefine its preventive function in a world of epidemiological, technological, economic and political transition. Such a conceptual revolution regarding the prevention and social management of health behaviour and disease was being formed elsewhere, within clinical medicine itself, and led to new intellectual and educational experiments.

SOCIAL MEDICINE AND THE NEW SOCIETY

By the middle of the twentieth century, dramatic reductions in infectious diseases and the creation of health care provision together with a general rise in affluence created new patterns of disease distribution and life expectancy in Western societies. The demographic pyramid changed shape. Both the birth and mortality rates declined. Fewer and fewer productive members of the population began supporting more and more elderly and chronically sick people. A longer life did not necessarily mean a sweeter one. Old age did not come alone, it brought with it arthritis, cancer, senility, poverty, loneliness. Even being affluent did not make you immune to the new epidemics of chronic disorders. Life in the fast lane produced neuroses, stomach ulcers and coronary heart disease (Kiple (ed.), 1993).

The epidemiological and demographic transitions of the twentieth century presented medicine with new challenges. The laboratory had revealed the causes of infectious disease, which had assisted their prevention. By the 1940s it had also produced the means, antibiotics, by which to cure them once contracted. Experimental science had also escalated the technological development of clinical medicine in the twentieth century. It had not, however, done anything to assist the understanding, prevention or cure of chronic disease. By the 1930s some clinicians began to think that medicine must reorientate itself to cope with the challenge of chronic sickness. The doctor must take on a new role, develop a new perspective, be trained in a different way, practise a new sort of medicine which would synthesize both prevention and cure.

The social hygiene movements of the early twentieth century had begun to create a new pathway for medicine, as Arthur Newsholme had put it, 'from the social standpoint'. But in the inter-war years experiments in social medicine in the Soviet Union illustrated much greater potential for amalgamating the social and medical sciences. The social hygiene movement in the post-revolutionary Soviet state moved beyond the bounds of social hygiene in its neighbouring European states (Solomon and Hutchinson (eds), 1990). While openly acknowledging its debt to the development of social medicine and social hygiene in Germany, Soviet social hygiene prioritized the sociological context of health and illness over and above its biological determinants. The sociologicalization of health and disease in Soviet social hygiene was linked to its political status. After the Revolution, physicians and public health experts were integrated into the new regime as part of what Lenin described as a feature of the state's need for 'bourgeois specialists' to help construct the future society. Social organization, therefore, was the goal for all applied expertise in the service of the state and thus it became the primary methodological and intellectual focus of study. Identifying the relationship between health, illness, medicine and society, and constructing medicine as a social science, was a political goal (Solomon, 1994).

A sociological approach to the analysis of disease and the practice of preventive and therapeutic medicine was incorporated into the reform of medical education after the Revolution. Social hygiene became a major feature of the state's medical curriculum. The state had been responsible for medical training and had controlled qualification under the Tsarist regime, and continued to do so after 1917. The first departments of social hygiene were subsequently established in the three Moscow faculties in 1922, and within five years fifteen further departments had been established in medical schools throughout the Russian republic. A research institute for social hygiene was opened in Moscow in 1923 (Solomon, 1994).

Both bourgeois and Bolshevik physicians had ideological motivations which drew them into the sociological understanding of disease. For the Marxists, ill health and disease were expressions of socio-economic inequality. For the bourgeois physicians or *Pirogovtsy*, understanding the social roots of disease was a legacy of the *zemstvo* system of health centres set up under the Tsars in the mid-nineteenth century. Both groups believed that the improvement of material conditions would result in lower disease and death rates. Soviet social hygiene strove to achieve its own distinctive methodology and establish an independent standing as a scientific discipline. Practitioners and teachers of social hygiene claimed that the scientific and distinctive status of their discipline was based upon an innovative amalgamation of medicine with the social sciences. Despite the fact that academic sociology was abolished in Soviet universities from the early 1920s, the discipline of social hygiene relied heavily upon the methods and approaches of the early work of the Chicago School of Sociology. By 1926–1927, the research agenda of the Soviet hygiene field included studies on nutrition, birth, death, migration, leisure, education, housing and sexology. In addition to the gathering of social statistics on these topics, social hygiene investigators employed anthropometry, demography, structured questionnaires and social surveys. Soviet social hygiene was an overtly prescriptive as well as a descriptive science. Its goal was to identify the cause of inequality of health and recommend the route to correcting it. Its explicit identity as an academic discipline was, in the words of the Commissar of Public Health, N.A. Semashko, as 'the hygiene of the underprivileged'. Nevertheless, social hygiene researchers did not confine themselves to a class analysis of health alone, but examined other socio-historical variables, such as the effects of urbanization, occupational patterns, culture, sub-culture and the family. The new discipline linked the medical school with the aims of the Bolshevik Revolution and provided medicine with legitimacy in the new order. It aimed to create a new breed of social physicians within the Soviet system whose priority was preventive rather than therapeutic medicine. The programme of social hygiene became threatened by the budgetary problems which accompanied rapid industrialization at the end of the 1920s. It was an experiment in the politicization of medicine which did not survive intact into the 1930s (Solomon, 1994). Nevertheless, it was a model which was matched by attempts to develop a new academic discipline of social medicine in both Europe and the United States.

The relationship between sociology and medicine in the twentieth century has led to intellectual alliances and conflicts, institutional and educational experiments, the founding and disappearance of new academic disciplines and the creation of new journals, for example the journal *Medicine and Social Science*. Beyond the Soviet republic, various attempts to institutionalize social medicine took place in Europe. In France the social hygiene movement became absorbed into the development of social services on the one hand and expanded in the field of family and preventive medicine on the other. Various clinics and health centres were set up by a number of municipalities. Within the university faculties, some academics explored the possible methods and central principles of social medicine. Pierre Delore at Lyons attempted to link the rise of social medicine to the neo-Hippocratic movement which gained popularity throughout Europe during the 1920s and 1930s. This was concerned to reassert the principles of the clinical *art* of medicine in the face of the increasing technologicalization of practice resulting from the influence of the experimental sciences. In this context Etienne Burnet gave a lecture series on 'Experimental Medicine and Social Medicine' at the Collège de France in 1935. Numerous courses were developed in French medical faculties on social hygiene and social medicine, and Jacques Parisot, at Nancy, became professor of hygiene and social medicine in 1920. He also created the Parisot Institute, which established connections between departmental and municipal health authorities and agencies and university teaching and research departments. Parisot also edited a journal, *Revue d'hygiène et de médecine sociales*. The long association in France between legal medicine and public health was extended into the field of social medicine by J. Leclercq, who taught forensic medicine at Lille. After taking up his chair in 1925, he amalgamated his teaching of forensic, industrial and social medicine and founded the *Institut de médecine légale et de médecine sociale* in 1934. Between 1934 and 1938, Leclerq edited the *Archives de l'Institut de Médecine légale et de Médecine sociale de Lille*. No department of social medicine was created in France before the Second World War, but numerous volumes on the subject were produced by academics who attempted to integrate it into their teaching within institutes of hygiene and medical schools (Sand, 1952).

A chair in social medicine was established in Belgium with the assistance of funding from the Rockefeller Foundation. René Sand took up the post at Brussels University in 1945. Sand had been developing the concept of a new academic discipline of prevention from the 1930s, trying to integrate the principles of social medicine into an analysis of what he called 'the human economy'. He wrote a number of treatises on the history of social medicine in which he defined the modern discipline as 'medical sociology' (Sand, 1952).

Before Sand had taken up his post, however, there had been earlier experiments in the institutional integration of the medical and social sciences in the United States and in Britain. At Yale University in 1931, the Institute of Human Relations was created under the direction of James Angell, Milton Winternitz and Robert Hutchins. It aimed to facilitate interdisciplinary research into the crucial social and economic problems of the times. It was to be the vehicle through which Yale could become a new type of university which would interact with the world outside its walls, address social issues and play a part in helping to resolve them. Turning medicine into a social science was part of this programme (Viseltear, 1997).

Winternitz, the dean of Yale's medical school, believed that specialization had divided up the 'organism' of medicine and the patient had become distributed into parts. Medicine had lost sight of the fact that individuals were both biological and sociological beings, who lived in society where they worked, married, had children, were happy and unhappy and encountered disease. The new programme of medical education in the Institute would combine sociological, psychological and clinical training to produce 'social physicians'. They would practise a new type of medicine which Winternitz called 'clinical sociology'.

Despite enthusiasm, idealism and $7 million of funding from the Russell Sage Foundation, the Institute ultimately foundered. Senior faculty stuck to individual research and conflict replaced co-operation. The doubts aired by Abraham Flexner at the outset of the venture proved to be ungraciously far-sighted. Winternitz's idealism for instituting preventive humanistic medicine at Yale failed to attract the interests of the students, who were more dazzled by developments in neurophysiology, pharmacology, endocrinology and surgical and medical interventions. Winternitz 'retired' his directorship of the Institute and the medical school in 1935 and the interdisciplinary programme for medical education retired with him, until it was revived in more recent times under the curriculum reforms proposed in the 1980s (Viseltear, 1997).

No comparable developments in medical education took place in Britain during the 1920s and 1930s. The British Medical Association had created a section for 'medical sociology' at its annual conference in 1913. However, no serious recommendations to change the medical curriculum occurred until 1939, when Sir Arthur McNaulty, the second Chief Medical Officer to the Ministry of Health, proposed that a new chair of social medicine should be established at his old university of Oxford. In 1942 a Committee of the Royal College of Physicians concluded that social medicine should be integrated into all future plans for revision of the medical curriculum. Sir E. Farquahar Buzzard, the regius professor of medicine at Oxford and chairman of the medical advisory committee to the Nuffield Provincial Hospitals Trust, together with the Trust's chairman, the banker Sir William Goodenough, and the third Chief Medical Officer of the Ministry of Health, Sir William Jameson, were critically influential, not only in establishing the new Institute at Oxford, but also in making social medicine a central issue in proposals for the general reform of medical education during and after the war (Oswald, 1991; Oswald, 1997).

Buzzard believed that doctors needed to develop a much greater orientation to preventive medicine and the preservation of health. He thought that new teaching programmes in social medicine for pre-clinical students would help to reconstruct the general practitioner as a health provider rather than a therapeutic technician. Through his influence upon Lord Nuffield as his personal physician and upon the Trust as chairman, in 1942 Buzzard successfully negotiated an endowment to establish the new Institute of Social Medicine. John Ryle, also a member of the medical advisory committee to the Nuffield Provincial Hospitals Trust, was invited to take its first chair (Oswald, 1991; Oswald, 1997).

The Institute was founded as both a research and a teaching institution. It provided courses in social medicine for medical students and lectures which were open to all graduate students and to medical social workers and health visitors. By 1946 Ryle suggested that social medicine was reforming the pre-clinical curriculum by 'placing a stronger emphasis on principles and paying close attention to social factors in aetiology'. The Institute's courses stressed the value of statistical methods and what Ryle termed 'social diagnosis and the importance of social case-taking in follow-up inquiries of hospitalized sickness' (Porter, 1992; Porter, 1993; Porter, 1996).

From the outset Ryle established major research projects. He had three senior members of staff and a number of junior faculty. A wide range of research projects were pursued at the Institute: a child health survey; a radiographic survey of child development; numerous statistical analyses, such as the correlation between skin cancer or TB with occupational and other social factors, and the analysis of the correlation between stillbirth rate and nutritional factors; a large survey of peptic ulcer among the employees of Morris Motors; an investigation of fluorine hazards to humans and animals; a survey of uncertified illness among local factory women; and the Institute co-operated with the MRC research on goitre and iodine prophylaxis. Ryle added more staff every year and continually hosted numerous visiting scholars from abroad (Porter, 1992; Porter, 1993).

As in the Soviet Union, social medicine in Britain was affiliated to a set of political objectives. For Ryle, the role of the physician in society and the role of science in creating a new social order were holistically bound together. In this context the marriage of the social and medical sciences was part of a broader aim of creating a medicine of society for society. Social medicine exemplified the politics of the radical scientific and medical intelligentsia of the late 1930s and 1940s. Emerging from the politics of science and ethics, the mission of social medicine was to facilitate progressive human social and biological evolution. As an expression of scientific humanism, social medicine aimed to fulfil the ethical dictates of the modern evolutionary synthesis and be part of the rising tide of corporate welfarism. John Ryle believed that this could be achieved by changing clinical medicine into a new discipline of holistic socio-biology of health and disease. Such a task demanded a marriage between medicine and the social sciences, but one which was devoted to a holistic rather than a mechanistic or positivist epistemology. Before Ryle died, however, positivism in the form of highly quantitative research into population health had already begun to dominate the new discipline (Porter, 1996).

The British Journal of Social Medicine was founded and edited by the professor of social medicine at Edinburgh, Francis Crew, and the biologist Lancelot Hogben in 1947, and was dedicated to analysing the 'numerical, structural and functional changes of human populations in their biological and medical aspects'. The editors suggested that the methods of social medicine 'must necessarily be statistical, involving the use of numerical data obtained either from official sources or from special field investigations, and interpreted in the light of established findings of the laboratory and of the clinic'. Furthermore, the new journal was emphatic about separating pure research from politics: 'This Journal is not meant to provide a platform for those who wish to present their views concerning the place of social medicine in the organizational set-up of medicine as a whole' (Porter, 1997).

The need to separate the research-based academic discipline from the practical concerns of service provision left social medicine in a weak position when the reorganization of the National Health Service was being planned in the late 1960s. By that stage a new term, 'community medicine', was becoming increasingly popular. It described an intellectual union between academic social medicine and practical service provision. In 1969 the Royal Institute of Public Health and Hygiene renamed its journal *Community Health* in order to address the question: 'What is public health and hygiene in the 1970s?' By 1970 a government Green Paper which explored the future reorganization of the National Health Service began using the term 'community physician' to replace the medical officer of health (Porter, 1997).

As in other national contexts, the institutional career of social medicine as an academic discipline in Britain following the Second World War was mixed at best. But medicine from the social standpoint had various legacies for the development of health care in the late twentieth century. Certainly the 'religion of rationalism' envisaged by Ryle was expressed in numerous health ideologies, some of which were translated into new moral imperatives regarding personal health and fitness.

HEALTH AND THE INDIVIDUAL: MEDICINE, SOCIAL SCIENCE AND COMMERCIAL CULTURE

State-funded strategies to improve the health of populations in advanced industrial societies since the Second World War increasingly individualized health protection. Market mechanisms reinforced this trend. Individualizing health protection, however, has encouraged the growth of self-preoccupation and even obsession with personal well-being. This has led some public commentators to characterize the late twentieth century as an epoch which has produced the 'I' or 'Me' generation, introspective, selfish and lacking communal consciousness.

From the time that the physician and iconoclast Bernard de Mandeville satirized the rise of hypochondriacal society in 1711 to the time that Jane Austen illustrated it in *Sanditon* in 1817, the eighteenth century invented a culture of sensibility which required you to be sick to get ahead. At the century's end the Bristol doctor who invented a pneumatic institute, Thomas Beddoes, despised the way in which life in the fast lane in the *fin de siècle* involved flaunting an array of fashionable diseases of civilization. Two hundred years later, at the end of the twentieth century, fashionable society became obsessed not with disease but with health. In the 1990s diseased bodies belong to the socially dysfunctional and economically inadequate. The beautiful people at the cosmopolitan heart of the affluent society strive to have low heartbeat rates and toned muscles, abstain from degenerate poisons like tobacco and fill their bodies with 'health foods' organically grown, humanely killed and naturally processed without chemical additives. The macrobiotic muscle-bound revolution took off among the healthy wealthy chattering classes. From the mid-1980s, bran sales went up, cigarettes were sold cheaply to the Third World, business in the gymnasium started to boom and anyone who wanted to be a citizen preparing for the twenty-first century began jogging in Central Park (Porter, 1998).

Health-obsessed society did not happen overnight, however. Health has become a priority of the cosmopolitan citizen of the affluent society over a period of time. Making health a priority of an affluent lifestyle was a central goal of 'medicine from the social standpoint' as part of a take-over of 'the corporate management of communal life'. Social medicine aimed to achieve this goal by educating patients and people about how to maximize their health status in order to reduce the chances of contracting disease. But beyond the world of professional medicine, the task of creating a mass health culture was taken up by private enterprise. John Harvey Kellogg viewed his breakfast cereals not just as a tasty option but as part of a mission to bring sufficient roughage to the diet of the American nation. Industrial capitalism had replaced idealized healthy agri-cultural labourers and huntin' and fishin' landowners with the sickly urban proletariat, sedentary office workers and neurotically stressed executive-entrepreneurs (Boyle, 1993). It was time to make up for it. You didn't have to go on being a seven-stone shivering weakling getting sand kicked in your face – commercial help was at hand. Charles Atlas and his contemporary Bernarr Macfadden had muscle-building programmes and exercise philosophies to turn you into the superman who was really living inside you. From these early begin-nings, healthy living, eating and exercise became a vast industry servicing Western society with a new moral code – be well or go to the wall at your own hand. There's no excuse. Strive or take a dive in your social mobility. Shape up or ship out of the affluent society.

There has been a downside. Gain often does require pain. Business executives gave themselves heart attacks on the squash courts and women began dying from silicone leaking from their breast implants. Because health carries its own imper-ative for beauty, it is always represented in a certain form – a bodily shape, size, proportion and, sinisterly, skin tone. The competition to be healthy in the twen-tieth century has been historically bound to the competition to be beautiful. The twentieth-century idealized beautiful healthy body can trace its heritage back to eugenically inspired inter-war utopian movements promoting nude sun-bathing, social hygiene and the production of a blond-haired blue-eyed race. Ironically, however, the contradictions of late twentieth-century health-obsessed culture are reflected in the representation of bodily distortion. Muscle-bound man does not look like a Vesalius drawing but is an 'Incredible Hulk' of testosterone-treated flesh. Equally paradoxical, elite health culture embraces the self-defeating consumption both of health foods to prevent physiological degeneration and of designer narcotics – either on prescription or from the illegal market – to relieve the stress of modern life. How did procuring health and beauty become such a dangerous pursuit?

PROCURING COMMUNITY HEALTH THROUGH INDIVIDUAL HEALTHY LIFESTYLES

Let's begin with new health strategies employed by the state. At the beginning of the century, state concerns with health in industrialized societies were driven by the goals of building economic strength and military might. These goals stimulated a new interrogation of the effects of social conditions and social behaviour upon physical deterioration, resulting in a range of social policies to provide personal health services for the most vulnerable in order to alleviate the effects of structural deprivation. But a number of these goals proved to be chimerical as demographic and epidemiological transitions produced ever longer-living chronically sick populations with ever declining fertility. From the mid-century, states in post-industrial societies began to employ new strategies to address the ever rising costs of providing health care, produced by demographic change. Propaganda campaigning now aimed to influence social behaviour and to educate citizens into adopting healthy lifestyles. The alliance between medicine, social science and public policy in trying to modify social behaviour altered the social contract of health between the modern state and its citizens. The emphasis between the obligations of the state and the obligations of the individual in democratic societies changed throughout the course of the twentieth century as post-industrial affluent societies modified their aims. The promotion of the healthy body became a rearguard action to reduce the exponentially increasing costs of redeeming chronically broken bodies in an ever ageing demographic structure.

Making health a priority of a modern lifestyle extended the concept of health as a right of citizenship which was created by the French and American Revolutionaries in the eighteenth century. As we saw in Chapter 3, Thomas Jefferson announced that despotism produced diseased populations and democracy would generate health among its free citizens. In 1791 the Constituent Assembly of the French Revolution declared health, along with work, as one of the rights of man. However, if health citizenship was a right, it was also an obligation. As Ludmilla Jordanova has pointed out, the *idéologue* Constantine Volney reminded the citizen of the new republic that his body was an economic unit belonging to the community, and that he had a social-political duty to lead a healthful temperate existence in order to ensure his value for the commonwealth (Jordanova, 1982). Democratic states in the late twentieth century reasserted this feature of the social contract of health by making it an individual responsibility. Using public information to persuade individuals to take up prescribed 'healthy' lifestyles employed a vast array of expertise to prevent chronic disease in a variety of fields, including the prevention of cardio-vascular disease, digestive disorders and above all the prevention of lung cancer and related diseases from smoking.

The practice of smoking tobacco has always had an ambiguous moral status from the time that it was first introduced to European society in the sixteenth century. Initially a botanical curiosity and a general herbal remedy, by the seventeenth century tobacco had become a substantial commercial trade and smoking a new social practice. The successful colonization and cultivation of tobacco crops by English settlers in the Chesapeake colonies and by the Spanish and Dutch elsewhere in the Americas supported the economic growth of tobacco production (Goodman, 1993; Goodman, 1998). From its earliest importation into Europe, tobacco had its enemies and supporters. James I attacked tobacco in his tract *Counterblaste*. Early modern paintings sometimes pictured tobacco as a symbol of moral degeneration (Harley, 1998). By the nineteenth century anti-smoking had become another prohibitionist cause which linked immorality and ill health (Hilton and Nightingale, 1998; see also Berridge, 1979; Harrison, 1995). Throughout these periods tobacco was equally associated with manly sociability and camaraderie (Cockerell, 1998).

The first scientific argument correlating cigarette consumption with rising levels of lung cancer was forwarded by Richard Doll and Austin Bradford Hill in their now famous study of lung cancer in twenty London hospitals, 'Smoking and Carcinoma of the Lung', published in the *BMJ* in 1950. Later they confirmed their original tentative conclusions with an analysis of the causes of death of doctors between 1951 and 1956 in relation to non-smoking, present smoking and ex-smoking groups at that date (Doll and Hill, 1950; Doll and Hill, 1956). In 1947 Bradford Hill had been commissioned by Britain's Medical Research Council to investigate the cause of increased mortality from lung cancer. At that time there was a general assumption that atmospheric pollution might be responsible, because of the urban–rural gradient in mortality and an inverse correlation with the recorded hours of sunshine in large towns. The study was set up within the current enthusiasm for the new paradigm of social medicine. Bradford Hill and Doll met while Hill was working for an MRC committee, chaired by John Ryle, which was supervising the MRC's study of peptic ulcer. Some argued against the environmental pollution explanation since the Clean Air Act had reduced pollution levels. Increased tobacco consumption was suggested by some as an alternative (Doll, 1998).

Although smoking was considered a habit rather than a dependency in the strict psychological definition of addiction, it was represented as an individual responsibility (Berridge, 1998). The anti-smoking campaign in Britain and the United States which followed the Doll and Hill results exemplified the new message of the clinical model of social medicine that the key to the social management of chronic illnesses – such as lung cancer – was individual prevention, raising health consciousness and promoting self-health care. The model of prevention through education of the individual gathered momentum following in the wake of the anti-smoking campaign. Subsequent post-war campaigns offered lifestyle methods for preventing heart disease, various forms of cancer, liver disease, digestive disorders, venereal disease and obesity. Both self-screening and public health technical and laboratory screening have been promoted for breast and cervical cancer.

This model of prevention was grounded in a new legitimate authority acquired by epidemiology in the post-war period. The analysis of the relationship between smoking and lung cancer gave epidemiology a new credence within the biomedical model of chronic disease. It became a critical heuristic device and legitimated a new approach to prevention which highlighted the role of individual behaviour and lifestyle in sharp contrast to the preventive model promoted by nineteenth-century epidemiology, which focused on social structural methods of preventing epidemics. The latter approach, however, was revived when in 1981 T. Hirayama published the results of a study which demonstrated that non-smoking wives of heavy smokers had a higher risk of contracting lung cancer than the wives of non-smokers (Brandt, 1998). The campaign to prevent 'passive smoking' in Britain and above all in the United States of America subsequently took on the increasingly draconian authoritarian character of a nineteenth-century campaign to prevent infectious disease. Civil liberties were increasingly eroded in the attempt to reduce the effects of passive smoking among the community. Like all such public health campaigns, the collective benefit of state action penalizes and stigmatizes a specific social group who are represented as social pariahs and failures and moral inferiors, reprobates and inadequates.

The first government to ban tobacco-smoking publicly was Prussia in the early nineteenth century, when it became an offence to smoke in the street. Prussian street smokers would have their tobacco seized from them by the Prussian police. One act of protest at the time of the revolution itself was to blow smoke in a policeman's face. Following the revolution the smoking ban was lifted. Before the Second World War, the Third Reich instituted an anti-smoking campaign on the grounds that it was not only unhealthy but un-German and countered the National Socialist athletic ideal of the healthy body (Smith and Edgar, 1996). In the post-war period anti-smoking has been less forcefully promoted in continental Europe than in the Anglo-Saxon context.

The prevention of substance abuse in Britain and the United States has been represented as a 'war' against degenerate behaviour. However, the success of the Anglo-American state in its ongoing 'battles' is mixed. Smoking has been reduced in both national contexts but alcohol consumption remains high. Even the consumption of narcotics appears to be growing, despite the heavy international legal sanctions against their production, sale, distribution and consumption. The state has employed punitive actions to prevent smoking, such as banning cigarette advertising from television, placing compulsory health warnings on cigarette packets and extracting high levels of indirect taxation on the sale of tobacco. But there has been no legal prohibition of tobacco consumption. In Britain and America the state has not yet risked completely opposing market demand. The last time the state took on consumers – by instituting alcohol prohibition in the United States – it was defeated. Thus expert administrators seek to reduce the costs of tobacco-related diseases upon the community, but the state does not risk challenging the right to consume cigarettes. It is interesting to note that the force of consumer demand, even in the case of narcotics, may possibly reverse existing state policy in the future. Leading advocates for the legalization of narcotics in the United States are represented in both the Republican and the Democratic Parties. The individualistic emphasis of the new social contract of health between the modern state and its citizens allows the right to consume to remain a priority. The obligation to remain healthy continues to be a subordinate value to the right of every citizen in a free market democracy to be a consumer. The lack of legal prohibition upon the sale of tobacco serves the state's claim that ill health is an individual liberty. Ill health is an individual responsibility which the state interferes with less and less in order to reduce the costs of state intervention. As a result, those who choose ill health face the consequences with less and less state assistance. Private health insurance for cigarette smokers has high premiums, but is increasingly necessary because smokers find it harder and harder to be treated by state-provided services. The first heavy smokers who were refused treatment in the British National Health Service made headline news; now such practices are becoming standard.

The mixed messages involved in the prevention of substance abuse, including tobacco consumption, have been fully represented in the campaigns against a new lethal infectious virus appearing in the early 1980s (Berridge, 1998), Human Immune-Deficiency Virus, which leads to a fatal syndrome commonly referred to as AIDS. The emergence of a new killer infection in the early 1980s reawakened all the public health concerns associated with an earlier era. AIDS was initially compared to dramatic historical invasions of the past such as plague and cholera (Gilman, 1995). The initial impact of AIDS upon both popular, political and expert perceptions raised familiar issues regarding the right of the state to police and regulate the spread of infection through surveillance, notification, screening and quarantine (Porter and Porter, 1989). Those who favoured authoritarian intervention in numerous national contexts called for the institution of compulsory testing, identity cards for people who were HIV-positive and their isolation. Most of these goals were not taken up by national policy-makers, but the question of identity cards came closest to realization in local contexts such as California and Bavaria. The epidemiological association of the disease initially with male homosexuals stimulated some to demand the recriminalization of homosexuality. Even though this was not achieved anywhere, homophobic discrimination was more readily expressed in various political measures during the 1980s, such as the British government's outlawing of educational material for schoolchildren which acknowledged the equal social status of the gay community.

As in the smoking campaign, epidemiology played a significant role in determining public policy (Berridge, 1996). Initial predictions of an epidemic spreading throughout the modern promiscuous heterosexual community stimulated the creation of education campaigns to promote prevention by encouraging the use of prophylactics, using a mixture of fear and sympathy. Many of the early campaigns were not specifically targeted at groups at greater or lesser risk. Awareness within the gay male community facilitated the control of the spread of the virus. The epidemiological course of the epidemic changed direction and the nature of the disease became reconceptualized as more experience was gained of it. By the late 1980s its transmission through needle-sharing among impoverished intravenous drug users meant that the disease became increasingly a disease spread by poverty and social despair rather than unprotected sexual intercourse (Gilman, 1995). Also, the length of time between contracting the HIV virus, the onset of the AIDS syndrome and the death of the sufferer lengthened as more effective therapeutic treatment was developed to slow the physiological progress of the disease in the individual. By the 1990s AIDS began to be perceived as a chronic disease among minority high-risk groups rather than an epidemic infection (Fee and Fox (ed.), 1992). Activist groups representing the interests of victims campaigned for the allocation of resources for prevention and management of the disease, but the initial high level of funding provided for the search for a vaccine and cure declined as the mass epidemic did not emerge in the dramatic way that had been originally expected.

AIDS victims have suffered legal and social discrimination in the popular mind and by official agencies. Even taking an HIV test can result in the subsequent failure to obtain personal insurance. The public knowledge of its contraction can mean that the individual sufferer fails to continue to gain employment or shelter. Its association with sexual activity has re-created the representations of degeneracy which were made of syphilitics and other venereal disease victims since the fifteenth century (Gilman, 1988). The implication of bodily and spiritual corruption has persisted as a powerful contemporary trope. Its association with the consumption of illegal substances has equally resulted in the characterization of disease victims as self-destructive degenerates. Even victims who were characterized as 'innocent', such as children and haemophiliacs who contracted the disease through heredity or blood transfusions, experienced as much hostile discrimination as popular sympathy (Gilman, 1995). Some observers, such as the political campaigner for gay rights and author Simon Whatney, argued that AIDS promoted a cultural eroticization of the diseased body (Whatney, 1987). Others have suggested that media health campaigns in a variety of national contexts which represented homosexuality as a legitimate sexual preference assisted in emancipating the social status of this group which has been relentlessly historically discriminated against (Gilman, 1995).

Medicine from the social standpoint ironically promoted a new model of prevention which emphasized the responsibility of the individual for their own health behaviour. It has been a model which utilized medical and social scientific analysis of health and illness to maximize health chances by encouraging individuals to change their lifestyles. The social contract of health promoted by medicine from the social standpoint has been illustrated in post-war public health campaigns from anti-smoking to AIDS prevention. The practice of medicine as a social science has mirrored the role that social science has played in providing the conceptual basis for new methods of social and individual managerialism in post-war society generally. The state and its public health agencies have not, however, had a monopoly on the promotion of health through lifestyle management. Health promotion through lifestyle education has also been successfully commercialized.

PHYSICAL CULTURE AND RACIAL SUPREMACY

The state was not the only force promoting responsible health citizenship in the twentieth century. A variety of utopian philosophies advocated their own ideals of health and alternative lifestyles. Furthermore, the commercial potential of the commodification of the healthy body was taken up by enterprising entrepreneurs in Europe and the United States. New intellectual and commercial discourses surrounding health adopted their own moral tones imbued with cultural anxieties about imperial strength and weakness which were linked to beliefs about the biological determinants of social progress and regression. The moral value of biological progress was vividly expressed in both utopian and commercial promotion of physical culture.

Victorian educational movements had attempted to establish muscular Christianity through the institution of games and athletics in British and American public schools. Regulated games were co-opted into creation of strong character within Thomas Arnold's educational system at Rugby School in the early nineteenth century. Subsequently Victorian teachers, curates and social reformers looked to organized games and sports such as football, cricket and fencing as a means of indoctrinating English upper-class schoolboys into a culture of muscular Christianity wherein godliness was equated with manliness. Victorian reformers such as Charles Kingsley and Cardinal Newman believed that on the playing fields of Eton, Westminster, Harrow, Charterhouse and the like, the English upper class would be socialized into an authoritarian disciplined social order which would prepare them for their role as rulers of an imperial nation. The value of sports for teaching discipline and building virtuous character was also taken up as an educational cause suitable for the lower orders, and thus physical education featured prominently in the Education Act of 1870, which instituted universal compulsory education in Britain (Haley, 1978).

In America the value of physical education was advocated by various social reformers. Heavily influenced by the British example, organized sports were instituted in private schools in the United States from the 1860s. But American physical culture in the United States was also influenced by continental European gymnastics. At the end of the eighteenth century a revival of the Greek system of athletics was instituted in Saxony by two rival physical philosophers, Gutsmuths and Jahn. Gutsmuths published a handbook of gymnastic movements in 1793 but Jahn developed a more muscularly demanding system which he called *Turnen*. Turnen became a popular system of exercise within German culture throughout the nineteenth century and promoted a German romantic philosophy of health, vigour and patriotic ethnic identity. The Gutsmuths system, however, was taken up in Scandinavia and developed by a Swedish virtuoso, Peter Henrik Ling. Ling had cured his own paralysed arm by taking up fencing, and then became preoccupied with the therapeutic and hygienic value of exercise. A child of the Enlightenment and a firm believer in the mechanical philosophy of knowledge, he attempted to apply the laws of motion to the human body to analyse the effects of movement upon the physiology of the internal organs.

> Every organ and texture can, accordingly, be placed directly or indirectly under a regulated and defined influence of mechanical stimulus devised in the most varied forms of motion either communicated [passive movements] consisting of pressure, friction, 'kneeding', vibration, percussion, ligatures etc. or voluntary [active movements] consisting of flexion, extension, torsion, rotation etc.
>
> (Georgii, 1854: 9)

Ling's system of gymnastic movements attempted to invoke physiological harmony through the creation of a motor music of the body by inventing 'a language of *nudges* to remind the brain, liver, spleen and all the organs of their neglected duties'. The Jahn system of Turnen was also concerned with movement and harmony but emphasized a more athletic system requiring and building strength. While the Ling system used movements designed to provide, for example, enhanced military dexterity for fencing or bayonet fighting, or to achieve poetic physiological harmony, the Turnen system used the parallel bars to build strength and agility in the upper body. Both of these systems remained powerfully influential in physical education reform campaigns and physical culture movements in both Britain and the United States throughout the nineteenth and into the twentieth century (McIntosh, 1981; Smith, 1974; Green, 1986).

Before the Civil War, Ling's system of gymnastics had been taken up in the United States and was popularized as a method of indoor training, 'callisthenics', especially appropriate for women, by campaigners for female health and educational reform such as Catherine Beecher. Turnen was exported to the United States along with the expansion of German immigration after the Civil War. Both Swedish and German gymnastics were promoted in the United States by reformers such as the American of Welsh descent, Dio Lewis, who set up a Normal Institute for Physical Education at Boston in 1861. Lewis's school was the first establishment to provide training for teachers in physical education, who became in ever greater demand as physical education became incorporated into both school and higher education in the United States from the 1880s (Green, 1986).

From the 1880s physical education was increasingly professionalized in the

United States. For example, separate gymnasiums and departments of physical education were introduced into women's colleges run by specially trained and licensed teachers. In Britain, the Ling system was introduced into schools after the 1907 Education Act, replacing military drill in the exercise yard. From 1895 the American Physical Education Association provided a professional organization for educationalists and had its own journal, the *American Physical Education Review*. In Britain a similar body, the British College of Physical Education, was founded in 1891, and the Gymnastic Teachers' Institute and National Society of Physical Education were created in 1897. These organizations provided examination and qualification for teachers and eventually amalgamated to form the British Association for Physical Training in 1916 (Park, 1992).

In the late nineteenth and early twentieth century, exercise regimes like callisthenics were taken up by health reformers who incorporated them into holistic utopian philosophies of health and social progress. New exercise movements such as eurhythmics were linked to dietary and sexual reform, dress reform, nude sunbathing, mountain climbing, hiking and sea bathing in a variety of utopian philosophies of physical culture and alternative lifestyles. Many of the new health philosophies were associated with alternative healing movements such as hydropathy and homeopathy and became inspired by eugenics. By the inter-war years a variety of physical culture movements in continental Europe and in the United States were linked via eugenics to ideals of racial improvement expressed within nationalistic contexts (Whorton, 1982). In inter-war Germany, National Socialism stressed the importance of personal health improvement to the collective well-being of the *volk*. As mentioned above, the Nazis powerfully disapproved of practices which threatened to poison the Tutonic germ plasm, like alcoholism and tobacco-smoking. Germany led the field in the development of new gymnastic techniques. The Nazis incorporated health utopianism within an expansive ecological philosophy which supported conservationism and the peasant movement on the one hand, led by Richard Walter Darre, and promoted alternative healing on the other. Darre linked 'blood and soil' into a *volkish* ecological philosophy and used it to promote the political interests of peasant farmers within the Nazi administration. The Nazis supported the introduction of alternative healing theories into medical education and made it compulsory for students to study medical history, including the study of the alchemical theories of Paracelsus (Proctor, 1988).

In the United States health was linked to the politics of conservation during the Progressive era. President Teddy Roosevelt popularized his 'strenuous life' philosophy for invigorating the nation. Roosevelt was a president who became a folk hero of the sporting life and who promoted the idea that a somatic map of national progress was to be found in the vigour of the new American male. The Olympian examples of American muscle and brawn began to redefine the image of the well-developed male body. The American sportsmen who triumphed in the first Olympiads at the turn of the century were athletes of bulk, and contrasted sharply with the sinewy athletic sportsmen of the playing field in the early Victorian era. The image of the svelte Greek athlete which had characterized the somatic ideal from antiquity, through the Renaissance and up to the early nineteenth century was challenged by this late nineteenth-century representation of muscular mass and power (Green, 1986).

Entrepreneurs absorbed racial and nationalistic ideologies into their various sales pitches for the healthy body. One of the many spectacular attractions at the World Trade Fair in 1893 was Eugene Sandow's displays of physical strength. By this date Sandow had become an international showman through his world tours of demonstrations of extraordinary physical feats. Sandow represented the new distinctive American Herculean body which demonstrated its physical superiority the following year at the first modern Olympiad, staged in Athens. By the time of the second Olympic Games, held at St Louis in 1904, the identification of American physical with economic and industrial strength had been reinforced from the very top of the political structure. A second-generation immigrant from the mid-West, Sandow built a career as a strong man in the tradition of the funfair freak, but through the commercial aptitude of Florenz Ziegfeld for creating visual spectacle Sandow became an extravagantly successful business between 1890 and 1897 (Chapman, 1994).

Sandow moved to England in 1897 after an exhausting world tour, broken in health, but after a short period of recuperation began to commercialize his system of physical training through the establishment of an Institute of Physical Culture at 32a St James' Street in London in 1897. He founded *Sandow's Magazine* in 1899 and published numerous volumes which he considered to be textbooks for a new lifestyle. In large tomes such as *Strength and How to Obtain it*, published in 1899, and *Life is Movement*, published in 1919, Sandow attempted to represent himself primarily as an educator and saviour-by-example of the deteriorating stock of the industrial nations. He advocated the elimination of disease through muscle-building. Sandow had hoped to play a direct political role in the development of physical education in schools in England, lobbying George Newman at the Education Department and giving evidence to the Interdepartmental Committee on Physical Deterioration. He wanted the 1907 Education Act to advocate his system of physical training for schools. By that stage, the Ling method of gymnastic training had powerful promoters in Britain among female teachers in women's physical training colleges and high schools and among army drill sergeants who had been sent to study the value of the Swedish system for military training. Despite his disappointment, Sandow continued to proselytize the importance of muscular development for the prevention of disease and physical deterioration. As he explained in *Life is Movement*, muscles could make a disease-proof body through the invigoration of what he called the 'Alpha of life', the living cell.

> Through the cell ... we can reach, cultivate, train, develop and reconstruct every part and organ of the human body and every cell of the body is dependent on, kept alive and maintained in health and power by the movement of the voluntary muscles.... *To keep all these cells in perfectly balanced strength*

*is the true secret of health, vitality and resistant power to disease....*This I contend we can only do by the balanced physical movement of the voluntary muscles.

(Sandow, 1922: 151)

Civilization had created an artificial sedentary human existence which was responsible for the creation of disease. The only way to redeem human health was by counteracting this process with vigorous exercise which would build muscular strength.

Sandow was not alone in his advocacy of muscle-building for the prevention of disease and the acquisition of perfect health. An even more adept entrepreneur emerged from the United States in the self-styled professor of 'kinesitherapy', Bernarr Macfadden. Macfadden, the son of an alcoholic father and tubercular mother in the mid-West, became one of the most notorious entrepreneurial crusaders for fitness, clean living and sexual efficiency of the early twentieth century. According to his chosen biographers, his attendance at the Chicago World Fair in 1893 had convinced him of his mission to develop and spread the gospel of physical culture. He emulated the muscle-building programme of Sandow but commercialized his own system with extravagant financial success. A brilliant self-publicist, he advertised his philosophical brand of physical culture through his own magazine, *Physical Culture*, which he founded in 1899, having taken over an existing publication which had had various titles since the 1830s, including the *Water-Cure Journal* between 1845 and 1861. He began his own 'healthatoriums', founded the first physical culture competitions in the late 1890s and published many volumes on physical training, eating for fitness and above all how to achieve sexual efficiency. In this Macfadden allied himself with the Progressivist philosophy of health, fitness and the war against prudery as the basis for building a revitalized society. Abolishing the wall of silence about sexuality and encouraging sexually fulfilling marriage – which would produce healthy offspring – was the lynch-pin of Macfadden's physical culture philosophy. Building physical strength and beauty was the route to achieving what he referred to as the 'well-sexed' woman and man who would, through their uninhibited and loving union in marriage, produce the children on which the nation could build its future. Macfadden was a eugenic advocate of national racism, supported immigration restriction and promoted pseudoanthropological assertions of Nordic superiority. He eventually became one of Mussolini's biggest fans (Whorton, 1982).

But his radical, almost reckless, pursuit of his own branch of physical culture reform broke with and offended convention. His proposed reforms for feminine physique and sexuality eventually caused the offices of his New York publishing company to be raided by Anthony Comstock and the Society for the Suppression of Vice in 1905 (Todd, 1987). Comstock confiscated posters which advertised the 'Mammoth Physical Culture Exhibition', to be held at Madison Square Gardens that year, which depicted the winners of physique competitions dressed in union-suits and leopardskin loincloths. Later publications on health, beauty and sexual advice for women which displayed images of bare breasts were also prosecuted for obscenity. The mixture of exercise and dietary peda-gogy and visual erotica, however, made Macfadden a fortune. The distribution of *Physical Culture* escalated to over 100,000 within its first year of publication. He combined this with the invention of gadgets and gimmicks for physical training, dieting and weight-gain to achieve a highly profitable commercial enterprise. In the process Macfadden did contribute to revolutionizing the social profile of the female form from the fainting, corseted, distortedly wasp-wasted Victorian beauty to the robust, fully-figured, fit physical culture girl of the twentieth century. The robust Rubenesque was physically enhanced, however, in order to fulfil her primary – and supremely significant – social biological role of healthy motherhood. Virulently against allopathic medicine, Macfadden provided an encyclopaedia of self-help health advice for achieving virile manhood and supreme motherhood upon which a nation could build its future, even if he did break the obscenity laws to do so (Macfadden, 1900; Macfadden, 1902).

Before the Second World War the promotion of muscular strength, physical fitness, dietary and sexual reform remained linked in utopian and entrepreneurial physical culture philosophies. Various physical culture reformers all embraced this agenda while emphasizing their own particular programmes, such as John Harvey Kellogg and Mary Wood-Allen's concern with fibre consumption, Horace Fletcher's obsession with mastication, and advocates of 'Muscular Vegetarianism' (Whorton, 1982). The commercial exploitation of erotica was legitimated within the language of progressive sexual reform, and health dictatorship was justified as an educative necessity for the prevention of disease, race survival and nation-building. National and personal health were bound within physical culture patriotism in the years before the Second World War. In Britain and America it was the man in the street's duty to make sure that the Anglo-Saxon, English-speaking nations did not become or remain seven-stone weaklings getting sand kicked in their faces. The self-styled 'Founder of the Fastest Health, Strength and Physique Building System', Charles Atlas, goaded his potential clientele into taking up his 'dynamic tension' system of muscle-building by shaming them for being only 'half-alive', flat-chested and enfeebled, unable to deliver a 'knockout defence' when insulted. The rhetoric of his adver-tisement campaigns echoed the concerns of the physical culture movement with race suicide and fears of imperial decline. Physical culture movements in Britain and the United States had, however, strong competitors for becoming Charles Atlas's 'lion in the jungle' who made 'every other animal sit up and take notice as soon as he lets out a roar' (Atlas, 1930: 3). Physical culture movements in conti-nental Europe equally appealed to the identity between the vigorously healthy body of the individual and the vigorous strength of the nation. The most emphatic expression of the equation between bodily and national-racial strength was voiced in pre-war Germany. In this respect the healthy body became reified into a metonymical trope for the international culture of racial and national competition before the Second World War.

THE FETISHISM OF COMMODITIES AND THE
REIFICATION OF THE FIT BODY

Physical culture expanded slowly after the Second World War up to the late 1970s and then made an exponential leap. As organized sports and competitive games became an ever greater mass spectator form of leisure activity, so the culture of getting fit took off in the 1980s. Sports-clothes manufacturers expanded their markets to provide casual attire which provided both comfort and an athletic fashion. The fashionability of track suits and running shoes reached murderous proportions in the 1990s, with American teenagers killing each other to steal a pair of Nike pumps to own for themselves. Fashionable athleticism gave new life to fitness culture expressed in new leisure activities such as jogging and gymnasium training. This renewed popular interest in the body-building cults of the pre-war era and set up new images of the ideal bodily shape and appearance.

The representation of racial supremacy through muscular strength and physical fitness declined in post-war cults of the healthy body, but the links between fitness-building and lifestyle reform persisted. Like Sandow, the entrepreneurial giant who created bodybuilding as a professional sport in the post-war period, Jo Weider promoted his system of muscle-building as a mission to create a new lifestyle. The Weider international commercial empire now dominates the market in bodybuilding, gym clubs, sports-wear and equipment, food supplements and vitamin products, and produces its own library of magazines and training manuals. The empire also controls the international professional competitions which include the 'Mr Olympia', 'Ms Olympia' and the new 'Ms Fitness' titles. When describing his magazine, *Muscle and Fitness*, Weider suggested that: 'I think of *Muscle and Fitness* as more than a magazine. I think of it as a textbook – a textbook about the Weider Bodybuilding Lifestyle' (Weider, 1988: 7).

Parts of this mission reverberated some of the themes of an earlier era such as Macfadden's insistence that building muscular strength was the cure for impotence (Macfadden, 1900). Macfadden, Kellogg and Atlas had all suggested that what the world needed then was 'virile men', 'Real Men' and 'he-men', and that their own particular brand of fitness fetishism would achieve it (Macfadden, 1900; Kellogg, 1894; Atlas, 1930). In the 1980s Armand Tanny – a one time Mr USA – writing in Weider's magazine, was concerned to counteract the effects of modern lifestyles, including the gender revolution, on male potency.

> Men are particularly apprehensive when it comes to sex….Inhibited sexual desire may result from marital problems, a deteriorating relationship, depression, stress, major life changes and the sexual revolution… [because]… new female freedom in the sexual revolution has created pressures that have caused some males to retreat from sex.
>
> (Tanny, 1988: 81)

Tanny, like his predecessor Macfadden, brought a reassuring message to his reader that the situation could be rectified through bodybuilding – especially with your partner. But unlike Macfadden or Sandow, who were restricted to vague references about the effects of movement on cellular metabolism, Tanny was able to incorporate bits of the modern science of endocrinology into his discussion.

> Bodybuilding, like many forms of vigorous exercise, is an aphrodisiac. Certainly the lean shapely muscular look of the bodybuilder's body is a psychological turn-on. But there is more to it than that. At the physiological level, scientists have found that vigorous exercise stimulates the production of the hormone responsible for the sex drive in both men and women, testosterone....When you are bodybuilding at an optimum level of exertion, you are likely to have the most testosterone at your disposal for both exercise and sex.
>
> (Tanny, 1988: 81)

Tanny, like every other modern competitive bodybuilder, should know, because endocrinology has become central to the construction of the muscularly extraordinary. Since Soviet weight-lifters, such as Vasily Stepanov, began using anabolic steroids to build strength in the early 1950s, testosterone has become a crucial weapon in the cold war of hard flesh.

The physiological consequences of taking human growth hormones are not yet fully known. Apart from distorting normal muscle proportions, the side effects have included a variety of pathological conditions from acne to liver damage. The aim of the contemporary bodybuilding cult, however, is not to produce the perfectly healthy human form or even a human form at all. The current criteria for achieving the most highly prized bodybuilding title, Mr Olympia, is body bulk which is also 'cut'. The title-holder in 1997, Dorian Yates, is the perfect example of the contemporary bodybuilding ideal, weighing in at over 250lb with a body-fat ratio of 2 per cent. A qualified doctor, Yates presumably has worked out how to keep the human body functioning on such an abnormally imbalanced proportion of lean to fat tissue. Arnold Schwarzenegger, the Hollywood film-star who won the Mr Olympia title several times in the 1980s, would not even come close to achieving it now. The goals of bodybuilding have changed since Schwarzenegger's day, taking on a new postmodernist 'post-human' tonality. As one of the currently most popular bodybuilding magazines, *Ironman*, illustrates, the desired goal of the contemporary competitive body-builder is to look 'alien' – or, in the lingo of the locker-room, to look 'freaky'. As T.C. Louoma, writing in the first edition of the British publication of *Ironman* in 1992, highlights, the competition between bodybuilders is to look 'out of this world'. Louoma tells us that

> On a recent episode of *Star Trek: the Next Generation* Warf the Klingon had to have back surgery. When the cameras zoomed in on his weird, reptilian-looking back, however, I was disappointed. Oh, Warf's back had its share of

bumps, lumps and bony protuberances, all right, but it looked a lot less alien than, say, Lee Haney's or Vince Taylor's back....Of all the hypetrophied bodyparts on a bodybuilder's physique, it is, perhaps, the back that looks the freakiest, the most alien.... It's tough to acquire that freaky look from the rear because this bodypart is just plain hard to work.

(Louoma, 1992: 33)

It is perhaps ironic that the contemporary bodybuilding cult, which can trace its heritage back to the role of the 'freak' strong-man in the nineteenth-century funfair, chooses to revive this particular Victorian value. The success of *Ironman* depends, as its British editor and publisher Dave McInerney points out, upon its ability to deliver the freakiest show in town. McInerney recalls the moment when he decided to take on the British publication of *Ironman*, which had been published in the United States since 1936.

The day after the British Grand Prix, John Balik [one of *Ironman*'s photographers] took a train from Nottingham to Birmingham to meet up with me, prior to his departure back to L.A. Sitting alongside John on the train were a group of bodybuilders, all with their noses stuck in one bodybuilding magazine. That magazine was *Ironman*. When John asked them what they liked about the mag, they echoed the opinions that both John and myself had about the attraction of the magazine. They loved the large, often freaky images and the hardcore training articles. They had only one complaint; namely that they had difficulty obtaining it at news stands in the U.K. John informed them, to their delight, that soon all that would be changing; and how right he was!

(McInerney, 1992: 5)

The alien look of professional bodybuilders cannot be achieved without the illegal use of growth hormones. The use of male sex hormones in building bodies that look like tower blocks expresses the contradictions of contemporary somatic obsession in bodily distortion. This contradiction results from the way in which the fetishization of health has become a commodification of the erotic body in late twentieth-century culture. Medicine, the state, voluntary action and commercial enterprise have constructed a collective physical culture of the healthy body in the twentieth century. The relationship between health and human reproduction has been a persistent and central theme of the social construction of the healthy body, expressed most vividly in a discourse of soft pornographic erotica. Prior to the Second World War, the physical-culture movement recruited erotica into the race for national-racial supremacy. In the post-war period the erotization of health has become an objective in its own right. One of the central goals of the healthy body was, from the beginning of the twentieth century, to become sexually attractive and supremely reproductively efficient. In the late twentieth century, the sexually desirable body *defines* elite health status.

The bodybuilding cult generated an offspring in the 1980s which secured a massively successful market. 'Fitness training' is a muscle-toning and aerobic exercise system which is not just the preoccupation of the alienated who want to look like aliens. Its goal is the construction of a designer body whose defining characteristic is sexual desirability. The world of fitness training has its own commercialized regimen and dietetics, literature and specialized knowledge for sale to all who wish to turn their dreams of looking like a 'Hollywood Babe' or 'Himbo' into a reality. Magazines such as *Fit Body* advertise a commercially driven culture which is bringing the fashionable elite into the expensive health club dressed in their designer kits in order to acquire a designer-desirable body. The designer-desirable body is not constructed through anabolic steroids and does not aim to build bulk. By contrast, its goal is the reduction of fat and the construction of 'shape', and the way to achieve it is through work – working out in the gym, in the aerobics class, the swimming-pool club, the squash court, etc. The designer body aims for toned muscles which have a clear definition. The desirable body of the late twentieth century is a designer commodity, which can be purchased by those with sufficient resources by employing a personal nutritionist, a personal trainer, an aromatherapeutic masseur and the best plastic surgeon in town. It is also a moral achievement, because you have to purchase it with your own labour. You have to work and work out to achieve the sensual ideal.

The defining characteristic of the designer body is sexual attractiveness. This is the official criterion on which the recently established 'Ms Fitness' competitions are judged (*Fit Body*, 1995: Supplement). And while its social construction is commercially driven, the designer body obeys all the laws of health which are promoted by medical and state health education. Acquiring the designer body requires low-fat organically purified dietary regimes, strictly controlled vigorous exercise plans, extremely temperate designer-drug abuse – of alcohol, cocaine, dope, etc. – safe tanning and safe sex. The designer body is disease-free and socially emancipating. 'Feminist' articles on fitness tell their readers that the first step for women wishing to take control over their female destiny begins with learning to become physically powerful and stretching their physical endurance. The fetishization of health has become inherently bound to the reification of sexuality in the designer body commodity, which is desirable but not desiring. It is an ultimately narcissistic expression.

But the designer body also bears the social and economic relations of power. Elite social status in late twentieth-century society requires your body, your economic activity, your lifestyle to be sexually attractive. Merchant banking has been one of the world's most boring occupations for centuries, but its elite economic power is now reaffirmed in the capacity it gives to its practitioners for purchasing sexy tropes such as Porsches, apartments in Chelsea or Manhattan, Chanel suits, and membership of the most expensive health club closest to the financial trading centre. The last is essential, because among other things crucial business deals are frequently negotiated on the squash court or in the bar afterwards. However, while your lifestyle and body have to be sexy in order to qualify for cosmopolitan elite social and economic status, your sex-life may be a complete contradiction of appearances. And therein lies the reification of sexuality from sexual activity, its fetishization in a commodity – the designer body.

The designer form of the healthy body is a social map of economic power in late twentieth-century society. Competitive bodybuilding is pursued by a range of social and economic groups, including a high proportion of working-class men and women. The gay community is also strongly represented within the bodybuilding world. But distorted structures of the bodybuilt body represent the contradictions of a sub-culture of somatic obsession. By contrast, the designer-toned body idealized by the leisure, fitness and entertainment industry is one of the new qualifications for membership to the cosmopolitan social and economic elite, and you have to at least strive to achieve it even to apply.

Furthermore, it serves as a moral instruction to the powerless masses and economically disadvantaged. Its message is that achieving health, beauty and desirability is your own responsibility and your social duty, because the economic elite and their political servants insist that society – especially them – can or will no longer pay to provide health for all. With ever longer-living unproductive proportions of the population growing as standards of living rise, the modern state, as we saw in Chapter 12, is redrawing the boundaries of its obligations to provide health as a right of citizenship, especially to the most economically vulnerable. 'Be well or go to the wall' is relentlessly communicated through the political scaling-down of public health care and service provision. It is a message which is reinforced by the moral disgust which is bestowed upon the diseased, broken, abused, self-indulged or neglected body. A recent survey quoted in the *Independent* showed that 90 per cent of a sample of women selected in the United States count a previous rape conviction in a prospective partner as being less unattractive than obesity. It is unnecessary to reiterate the renowned discrimination experienced by disease victims such as cancer and AIDS patients.

The commercialization of health makes striving for health and perfect bodily desirability a moral qualification for elite citizenship in the affluent society of the twenty-first century. The commodified healthy body is a somatic trope of economic and political power in post-industrial society. It is a classic representation of what Karl Marx identified as the personal and social alienation induced by the fetishism of commodities in a capitalist economic order (Marx, 1977–1984).

Epilogue

In ancient societies collective action regarding the health of populations was reserved for promoting the comfort of elites. Despite the expansion of public actions in many societies to try and preserve the health of both rich and poor, inequalities in health belligerently persist both within and between industrial and non-industrial societies in the late twentieth century. Historical continuities, however, cannot mask the forces of social transformation which are constantly at work. The question of population health has been both the subject of and the stimulus to change, and continues to be a major social question to be addressed by national and international governments.

In the early chapters, we have seen how the question of population health moved from a narrow concern with patrician comfort to political actions to control epidemic disease among the masses. While the rationale for epidemic disease control was preventing social disorder it also stimulated new social concerns about the health and welfare of the poor. From early modern times, disease prevention became increasingly bound to broader issues of social welfare, especially as concerns with health, rather than disease prevention, began to dominate discourses from the nineteenth century. Ironically, as the spectre of epidemic infectious diseases gradually reduced in the twentieth century, new attention was paid to the role that individual behaviour played in the achievement of population health. In recent times individual lifestyles became a primary concern overshadowing debates about the structural causes of health inequalities. Since the 1980s, as public health practice increasingly focused on the responsibilities of individuals, so the contract of health between governments and their citizens in advanced industrial societies began to change. Shifts in the modern – or postmodern – social contract of health have been contextualized within a re-evaluation of the role of social welfare in industrial and industrializing societies.

Nowhere has the redrawing of welfare boundaries been more dramatic than in the United States, which has pioneered the replacement of welfare with workfare. Equally radical restructuring has taken place in health care delivery through market-driven reforms. The failure of the Clinton health reform programme meant that the issues which stimulated its development remained yet to be addressed. American health care costs continued to threaten to rise to 18 per cent of GDP by the turn of the century. Approximately 15 per cent of the population remained without health insurance. The insecurities of the middle classes over the continuation of their health coverage were not dispersed. In an attempt to curb costs, employers continued to modify or eliminate the options that they offered their employees on health care coverage. Middle-class employees continued to face the risk that their existing coverage would diminish and that if they changed jobs their health coverage would be severely compromised. Furthermore, the private insurance sector became increasingly risk-selective and more adept at avoiding payment (Barer *et al.*, 1995).

In the wake of failed national reform, market-driven transformations increased the development of managed care in order to contain costs and improve access to care (Brook, 1997). Since 1995, state governments have become increasingly responsible for regulating the new system and initiating reform. Managed care is a system of prepayment for comprehensive health care coverage, provided by companies which control costs by curbing use. Managed care uses primary-care physicians as gatekeepers, who limit patient access to specialists and operate financial incentives to limit treatment. Managed care is provided through health management organizations and insurance health plans which physicians or groups of physicians and hospitals contract into, either receiving capitation fees or sharing financial risks with the managed care organization (Miller, 1997; Woods, 1997). Many states have also replaced their fee-for-service system of applying Medicaid with managed care programmes for a variety of eligible groups, especially those receiving Aid for Dependent Children/Temporary Assistance for Need Families (Epstein, 1997).

Managed care has improved access to care for those who remained previously un- or under-insured, increased the use of primary and preventive care, raised efforts to measure the quality of care and reduced the incentives to over-treat which were exacerbated by fee-for-service methods. It has, however, been widely criticized, especially by the American medical profession, for reducing the quality of care and interfering in the doctor–patient relationship. As a result, state policy-makers have been forced to introduce a wide range of regulatory legislation to ensure 'patient protection'. These Acts have become identified as 'patient bill of rights' Acts by some and as 'anti-managed care Acts' by others. Initial piecemeal legislation was replaced by more comprehensive regulation, called for by consumer groups, physicians and other health care professionals. Many state policies enacted between 1995 and 1996 introduced laws which expanded the level of information which health plans must provide to enrollees, and placed new requirements upon plans to provide proper grievance and appeal procedures. Some state legislation charted entirely new territory in order to respond to the new medical market-place. Some states passed laws providing patients with direct access to specialists, prohibiting gag clauses and granting physicians the right to plan information about their practices. A variety of states enacted legislation to control financial incentives for reducing care by prohibiting plans which: reward physicians for providing less than medically necessary and appropriate care; induce physicians to limit medically necessary services; limit services, reduce length of stay or the use of alternative treatment settings. Length of hospital stay became a nationally controversial issue because managed care reduced the length of stay after childbirth from 3.9 days to 2.1 days, and others refused in-patient care to post-mastectomy patients (Miller, 1997).

In the view of some members of the medical profession, while not eliminating all methods for limiting care much of the state-enacted legislation has eliminated the worst abuses, especially with regard to their most treasured area of autonomy, the doctor–patient relationship. In this respect physicians were particularly concerned to be free to offer on a private basis treatment not covered by insurance plan. This required laws which banned the gagging rules employed by numerous plans. Anti-gag laws banned the rules operated by some plans which prevented physicians from discussing treatment options not offered by the plan or from revealing the plan's limitations to his patients (Miller, 1997).

State-managed care regulation also stimulated federal legislation. Congress passed a law in July 1996 creating a statutory length of maternity stay of 48 hours. The Health Care Financing Administration adopted new regulations in December 1996 limiting the gagging rules which could be operated by plans (Woods, 1997). Future federal legislation will address improved access to emergency treatment and allow greater freedom for consumers with regard to grievance procedures (Miller, 1997).

States have registered the advantages gained for their Medicaid patients who have been enrolled in managed care. TennCare and MinnesotaCare have claimed much greater coverage for their previously uninsured or under-insured populations which is already being reflected in improved perinatal and child health among the poorest of their populations, who were disadvantaged under the fee-for-service system (Wayne *et al.*, 1998; Call *et al.*, 1997). Medicaid managed care has also required state regulation, however, to prevent the development of HMOs or plans providing inferior care for Medicaid patients only.

The American Association of Health Plans attempts to institute self-regulation within the managed care industry and address the concerns and controversies surrounding it (Woods, 1997). While some members of the American medical profession see many new opportunities opening up in what they believe is the 'industrialization of health care' (Kleinke, 1997), others despair of the domination of a profit-driven health care delivery system (Ad Hoc Committee to Defend Health Care, 1997). In 1997 in the *Journal of the American Medical Association*, a group of over 2,000 'physicians and nurses from across the spectrum of our profession' from Massachusetts warned that 'shadows darken our calling and threaten to transform healing from a covenant into a business contract' (Ad Hoc Committee to Defend Health Care, 1997: 1733). They claim that market medicine treats patients as profit centres and industrial commodities, reducing the time spent with each as pressure increases to improve 'throughput'. Market medicine encourages physicians to shun the sickest and most unprofitable, and threatens to fire health carers who suggest alternative treatments. As non-profit hospitals, visiting-nursing agencies and hospices created by state or voluntary funding are taken over by Wall Street companies, vital community services have been diminished. Non-profit health care providers forced to compete in the new market have to either change policy or face bankruptcy. The Massachusetts physicians claim that the ranks of the uninsured continue to grow while safety-net hospitals and clinics shrink and public health programmes are eroded. Even the insured find it difficult to gain access to emergency treatment or treatment for expensive illnesses. The headlong rush towards profit-driven care needs to be contained by a new public dialogue on health care, in which the Massachusetts practitioners want the voices of professionals and patients to be heard as much as those of the powerful financial health care organizations (Ad Hoc Committee to Defend Health Care, 1997).

Managed competition in health care has received criticism beyond the United States where it has been applied to the problem of containing costs. Some critics have identified inevitable 'traps' which managed care has fallen into wherever it has been applied, for example in Russia and Chile (Curtis *et al.*, 1997; Vergara, 1997). Some policy analysts have claimed that the application of an internal market of managed competition into previously state-planned health systems produced 'traps' which can be observed both in Britain and in the US. These traps include wide geographical variations in levels of provision; significant numbers not covered by the new insurance system, leaving them without access; reduced access for those unable to afford prescribed medicines; limited patient choice as the result of the formation of local oligarchies; vast reduction in the promotion of preventive medicine; and difficulties in regulating managed markets which are driven by profit incentives rather than standards of care (Curtis *et al.*, 1997). As discussed in Chapter 12, in Chile resources once used to run state clinics have been transferred to profit-making medical enterprises, Institutions of Provisional Health (ISAPRES), which resemble HMOs in the United States. However, by the late 1990s ISAPRES provide coverage for only 12 per cent of the population. They exclude the elderly, the chronically infirm and individuals with large families, who must rely upon vastly reduced levels of care in a massively underfunded public sector (Vergara, 1997).

Market-driven resolutions to contain the costs of health care highlight the problems faced by the attempt to redraw the social contract of health within the neo-liberal model of welfare. Social democratic welfare states equally face the question of reconfiguring the social contract of health, which involves balancing cost containment against reducing health inequalities.

The most recent developments in British policy-making highlight some dimensions of the new social contract of health being established within a social democratic rhetoric. Despite the claims by some commentators that a new consensus of 'Blairjorism' has developed in Britain – a convergence between the ideologies of Tony Blair, leader of the New Labour Party since 1994, and John Major, the last Conservative prime minister – since their election to government in 1996 New Labour have been attempting to impose their own rhetoric on redefining the welfare state. For example, in their Green Paper, *Our Healthier Nation* (Dobson and Jowell, 1998), the New Labour government offers the British public a 'new contract for health' which involves a partnership between the individual and society. The New Labour government has chosen to readdress questions raised by Sir Douglas Black, which were ignored and buried by the Tory government when he presented them in his report on health inequalities in 1980 (Black, 1981). The current Minister of Health, Frank Dobson, and the newly created Minister of Public Health, Tessa Jowell, acknowledge that good health is an individual and social need which is unevenly distributed among Britain's population. The government White Paper, *The New NHS. Modern. Dependable* (Department of Health, 1997), outlined New Labour's proposals for creating an integrated health service to provide for the needs of the sick. *Our Healthier Nation* sets out government proposals to prevent illness and reduce health inequalities.

The New Labour health ministers acknowledge that in tackling the root causes of avoidable illness, 'in recent times the emphasis has been on trying to get people to live healthy lives' (Dobson and Jowell, 1998: 2). The New Labour government wants to try a new approach with 'far more attention and Government action concentrated on the things which damage people's health which are beyond the control of the individual' (Dobson and Jowell, 1988: 2). In particular, *Our Healthier Nation* reasserts the importance of structural inequalities, arguing that poor people die sooner because their health is compromised by low incomes, unemployment, poor housing and social exclusion. Population health is compromised in areas with poor social facilities and where people are intimidated by high levels of crime and disorder. The poor and industrial workers are also often exposed to greater risks from environmental pollution and occupational hazards. New Labour's 'New Contract for Health' aims to 'improve the health of the population as a whole by increasing the length of people's lives and the number of years people spend free from illness' and 'to improve the health of the worst off in society and to narrow the health gap' (Dobson and Jowell, 1998). The new health contract intends that government and 'national players', local authorities, organizations and communities and individuals all play a part in trying to achieve these goals. *Our Healthier Nation* offers a vision of a government attempting to implement an integrated strategy for tackling inequality, ill health and disease which involves government action in everything from improved education and health care services to better public transport and stricter regulations to reduce environmental and industrial pollution.

In their plans for both public health and health care service reform, New Labour avoid appeals to the competitive spirit and to self-help, and use a language which emphasizes the need for co-operation and partnership and offers a holistic vision. In *The New NHS. Modern. Dependable*, the co-operative health contract is reinforced with plans to replace the internal market within the NHS with an integrated system of health planning between regional, local and primary care organizations. Old Labour's vision of creating an egalitarian society through central state planning to redistribute wealth has been replaced by New Labour's rhetoric of devolved power-sharing, partnerships and democratic participation. But while reopening the question of the structural causes to health inequalities, the New Labour Party continue to maintain New Right emphases on the social responsibilities and obligations of individuals and local communities in the 'new health contract'. The extent to which rhetorics designed for government consultation exercises are translated into policies which are implemented remains subject to restraints which New Labour refuse to attack no less than the New Right, namely the unwillingness of voters to pay higher taxes. The language of the 'new contract for health' may have changed. Whether New Labour actualizes changes in health policy which substantively contrast with those enacted by Britain's neo-liberal Tories remains to be seen.

The intentions behind New Labour's 'new contract for health' have been cautiously welcomed by medical, public health and social policy professionals, but they continue to reserve judgement until the new policies are put into practice (McKee and Sheldon, 1998; Horton, 1998; Jacobson and Yen, 1998; Shapiro *et al.*, 1998). The public health lobby appear to particularly welcome the possibility of finding a new role in the reduction of health inequalities, encouraged by the creation of a new Minister for Public Health (Horton, 1998). From the time of the Acheson Report in 1988, morale within the British public health profession has diminished as public health medicine became stranded between an underfunded system for the controlling of communicable diseases and an ill-defined role in the promotion of health and healthy living (Kisely and Jones, 1997). Gaps and uncertainties remain in New Labour's proposals but the opportunity to participate in the consultation process has been welcomed (Horton, 1998).

Cautious enthusiasm is mixed with a significant amount of scepticism with regard to the 'new contract for health' being constructed in Britain. Similar debates surrounding health care and public health reform continue throughout the Western and Eastern European communities. Here, as within industrialized and industrializing societies throughout the world, the pressures of demographic transformations and epidemiological transitions force policy-makers, professionals and the public to participate in the debate surrounding the health of populations. The outcome of those debates in the twenty-first century will depend, as it has always done, on national histories and cultures, international developments and political will.

Bibliography

INTRODUCTION

Adorno, Theodor and Horkheimer, Max (1972) *Dialectic of Enlightenment* translated by John Cumming (London, Allen Lane; first edition 1947).

Appleby, Joyce, Hunt, Lynn and Jacob, Margaret (1994) *Telling the Truth About History* (London, Norton).

Appleby, Joyce, Covington, Elizabeth, Hoyt, David, Latham, Michael and Sneider, Allison (eds) (1996) *Knowledge and Postmodernism in Historical Perspective* (London, Routledge).

Armstrong, David (1983)*The Political Anatomy of the Body* (Cambridge, Cambridge University Press).

Barker, T. and Drake, M. (eds) (1982) *Population and Society in Britain 1850–1980* (London, Batsford Academic and Educational).

Bell, Daniel (1974) *The End of Ideology* (London, Heinemann Educational Books).

Bernstein, Richard J. (1983) *Beyond Objectivism and Relativism: Science, Hermeneutics, and Praxis* (Oxford, Basil Blackwell).

Berridge, Virginia (1996) *AIDS in the UK: The Making of a Policy, 1981–1994* (Oxford, Oxford University Press).

Berridge, Virginia and Strong, P. (eds) (1993) *AIDS and Contemporary History* (Cambridge, Cambridge University Press).

Bourke, Joanna (1996) *Dismembering the Male: Men's Bodies, Britain and the Great War* (London, Reaktion).

Briggs, Asa (1961) 'Cholera and Society in the Nineteenth Century', *Past and Present* 19: 76–96.

Burns, Timothy (ed.) (1994) *After History?: Francis Fukuyama and His Critics* (London, Rowman and Littlefield).

Carmichael, Ann G. (1983) 'Infection, Hidden Hunger and History', *Journal of Interdisciplinary History* 14: 249–264.

Cippola, C.M. (1979) *Faith, Reason and the Plague. A Tuscan Story of the Seventeenth Century* (Brighton, Harvester).

Clark, George L., Forbes, D. and Francis, R. (eds) *Multiculturalism, Difference and Postmodernism* (Melbourne, Longman Cheshire).

Coleman, William (1982) *Death is a Social Disease* (Madison, Wisc., University of Wisconsin Press).

——(1987) *Yellow Fever in the North. The Methods of Early Epidemiology* (Madison, Wisc., University of Wisconsin Press).

Crosby, Alfred W. (1986) *Ecological Imperialism. The Biological Expansion of Europe. 900–1900* (London, Cambridge University Press).

Eagleton, Terry (1996) *The Illusions of Postmodernism* (Oxford, Blackwell Publishers).

Elias, Norbert (1994) *The Civilizing Process* (Oxford, Basil Blackwell; first edition 1939).

Evans, Peter B., Rueschemeyer, Dietrich and Skocpol, Theda (eds) *Bringing the State Back In* (Cambridge, Cambridge University Press).

Evans, R.J. (1987) *Death In Hamburg. Society and Politics in the Cholera Years 1830–1910* (Oxford, Clarendon Press).

Fee, E. and Fox, D. (1989) *AIDS: The Burdens of History* (Berkeley, Ca., University of California Press).

——(1992) *AIDS: The Making of a Chronic Disease* (Berkeley, University of California Press).

Finer, S. (1952) *The Life and Times of Edwin Chadwick* (London, Methuen).

Foucault, Michel (1970) *The Order of Things. An Archeology of the Human Sciences* (London, Tavistock).

Fraser Brockington, Colin (1956) *A Short History of Public Health* (London, Churchill).

Frazer, William (1950) *History of English Public Health 1834–1939* (London, Ballière, Tindall and Cox).

Fukuyama, Francis (1992) *The End of History and the Last Man* (London, Hamish Hamilton).

Gilman, Sander (1988) *Disease and Representation. Images of Illness from Madness to AIDS* (Ithaca, Cornell University Press).

——(1989) *Sexuality: An Illustrated History* (New York, Wiley).

——(1995) *Health and Illness. Images of Difference* (London, Reaktion).

Hobsbawm, Eric (1991) *The Age of Extremes. The Short Twentieth Century 1914–1991* (London, Michael Joseph).

Kiple, Kenneth F. (ed.) (1993) *The Cambridge World History of Human Disease* (Cambridge, Cambridge University Press).

Lambert, R. (1963) *John Simon and British Sanitary Administration* (London, Macgibbon and Key).

Landers, John (1987) 'Mortality and Metropolis: The Case of London 1625–1825', *Population Studies* 41: 59–76.

Lewis, R.A. (1952) *Edwin Chadwick and the Public Health Movement* (London, Longmans and Green).

McKeown, T. (1976a) *The Role of Medicine – Dream, Mirage or Nemesis* (London, Nuffield Provincial Trust).

——(1976b) *The Modern Rise of Population* (London, Edward Arnold).

——(1983) 'Food, Infection and Population', *Journal of Interdisciplinary History* 14: 227–247.

McNeill, W. (1976) *Plagues and Peoples* (New York, Doubleday).

Mannheim, Karl (1991) *Ideology and Utopia: An Introduction to the Sociology of Knowledge* translated by Louis Wirth and Edward Shils with preface by Louis Wirth (London, Routledge; first edition 1936).

Mennell, Stephen (1989) *Norbert Elias and the Human Self-Image* (Oxford, Basil Blackwell).

Morris, R.J. (1976) *Cholera 1832. The Social Response to an Epidemic* (London, Croom Helm).

Newman, Sir George (1932) *The Rise of Preventive Medicine* (London, Oxford University Press).

Newsholme, Sir Arthur (1927) *The Evolution of Preventive Medicine* (London, Baillière, Tindall and Cox).

Oddy, D.J. (1983) 'The Health of the People', *Journal of Interdisciplinary History* 14: 121–139.

Outram, Dorrinda (1989) *The Body and the French Revolution: Sex, Class and Political Culture* (New Haven, Yale University Press).

Pelling, M. (1978) *Cholera Fever and English Medicine 1825–1865* (Oxford, Oxford University Press).

Porter, Dorothy (ed.) (1994) *The History of Health and the Modern State* (Amsterdam and Atlanta, Rodopi).

Porter, Dorothy and Porter, Roy (1989) *Patient's Progress. The Dialectics of Doctoring in 18th Century England* (Cambridge, Polity Press).

Porter, Roy and Porter, Dorothy (1988) *In Sickness and In Health: the British Experience 1650–1850* (London, Fourth Estate Books).

Riley, James C. (1989) *Sickness, Recovery and Death: A History and Forecast of Ill Health* (London: Macmillan).

Rosen, George (1958) *The History of Public Health* (New York, MD Publications).

Rosenberg, C. (1962) *The Cholera Years 1832, 1849 and 1866* (Chicago, University of Chicago Press).

——(1992) 'What is an Epidemic? AIDS in Historical Perspective' in Charles Rosenberg (ed.) *Explaining Epidemics and Other Studies in the History of Medicine* (Cambridge, Cambridge University Press).

Sand, René (1952) *The Advance to Social Medicine* (London, Staples Press).

Showalter, Elaine (1986) *The Female Malady: Women, Madness, and English Culture, 1830–1980* (New York: Pantheon Press).

Slack, P. (1985) *The Impact of Plague in Tudor and Stuart England* (London, Routledge and Kegan Paul).

Szreter, Simon (1988) 'The Importance of Social Intervention in Britain's Mortality Decline c1850–1914: A Reinterpretation of the Role of Public Health', *Social History of Medicine* 1: 1–37.

——(1996) *Fertility, Class and Gender in Britain 1860–1940* (Cambridge, Cambridge University Press).

Topolski, Jerry (ed.) (1994) *Historiography Between Modernism and Postmodernism: Contributions to the Methodology of Historical Research* (Amsterdam, Rodopi).

Turner, Bryan S. (1984) *The Body and Society. Explorations in Social Theory* (Oxford, Basil Blackwell).

——(1992) *Regulating Bodies. Essays in Medical Sociology* (London, Routledge).

Weber, Max (1979) *Economy and Society. An Outline of Interpretative Sociology* translated by Ephraim Fischoff (Berkeley, University of California Press).

Weindling, Paul (1989) *Health, Race and German Politics Between National Unification and Nazism 1870–1945* (Cambridge, Cambridge University Press).

Woods, R. (1987) 'Approaches to the Fertility Transition in Victorian England', *Population Studies* 41: 283–311.

Woods, R., Waterson, P.A. and Woodward, J.H. (1988) 'The Causes of Rapid Infant Mortality', *Population Studies* 42: 343–366.

Wrigley, E.A. and Schofield, R.S. (1981) *The Population History of England 1541–1871* (London, Edward Arnold).

1 HEALTH AND MORALITY IN THE ANCIENT WORLD

Allen, N. (1990) 'Hospice to Hospital in the Near East', *Bulletin of the History of Medicine* 64: 446–462.

Amundsen, D.W. (1977) 'Images of the Physician in Classical Times', *Journal of Popular Culture* 11: 643–655.

——(1982) 'Medicine and Faith in Early Christianity', *Bulletin of the History of Medicine* 56: 326–350.

Amundsen, D.W. and Ferngren, G.B. (1986) 'The Early Christian Tradition' in R.L. Numbers and D.W. Amundsen (eds) *Caring and Curing, Health and Medicine in the Western Medical Tradition* (New York, Macmillan) 40–64.

Bray, Francesca (1988) 'Chinese Medicine' in W.F. Bynum and Roy Porter (eds) *Companion Encyclopedia of the History of Medicine*, 2 vols (London, Routledge) 728–754.

Brown, Peter (1978) *The Making of Late Antiquity* (Cambridge, Mass., Harvard University Press).

——(1988) *The Body and Society* (New York, Knopf, 1988).

——(1992) *Power and Persuasion in Late Antiquity. Towards a Christian Empire* (Madison, Wisc., University of Wisconsin Press).

Bruun, Chister (1991) *The Water Supply of Ancient Rome. A Study of Roman Imperial Administration* (Helsinki, Societas Scientiarium Fennica).

Bylebyl, J. (1971) 'Galen on the Non-natural Causes of the Variation in the Pulse', *Bulletin of the History of Medicine* 45: 482–485.

Cockburn, Aiden (1977) 'Where Did Our Infectious Diseases Come From? The Evolution of Infectious Diseases', *CIBA Foundation Symposium* 49: 103–112.

Cohen, Mark Nathan (1989) *Health and the Rise of Civilization* (Newhaven, Yale University Press

Cohn-Haft, Louis (1956) *The Public Physicians of Ancient Greece* (Northampton, Ma., Smith College).

Conrad, Lawrence (1992) *Epidemic Disease in Formal and Popular Thought in Early Islamic Society* (Berlin, Walter de Gruyer).

Davies, R.W. (1989) *Service in the Roman Army* edited by David Breeze and Valerie A. Maxfield (Edinburgh, Edinburgh University Press).

Douglas, Mary (1974) *Purity and Danger: an Analysis of Concepts of Pollution and Taboo* (London, Routledge and Kegan Paul).

Edelstein, L. (1967a) *Ancient Medicine* (Baltimore, Johns Hopkins University Press).

——(1967b) 'The Hippocratic Physician' in O. Temkin and C.L. Temkin (eds) *Ancient Medicine* (Baltimore, Johns Hopkins University Press) 87–110.

——(1967c) 'Empiricism and Skepticism in the Teaching of the Greek Empiricist School' in O. Temkin and C.L. Temkin (eds) *Ancient Medicine* (Baltimore, Johns Hopkins University Press) 195–203.

Edelstein, L. and Edelstein, E.J. (eds) (1943) *Asclepius*, 2 vols (Baltimore, Johns Hopkins University Press).

Epler, Dean C. (1988) 'The Concept of Disease in an Ancient Chinese Medical Text, the *Discourse on Cold-Damage Disorders (Shang-han Lun)*', *Journal of the History of Medicine and Allied Sciences* 43: 8–35.

Estes, John Worth (1989) 'Egyptian Healers' in John Worth Estes (ed.) *Medical Skills of Ancient Egypt* (Canton, MA, Science History Publications) 13–26.

Ferngren, G.B. (1992) 'Early Christianity and Healing', *Bulletin of the History of Medicine* 66: 1–15.

Garrison, Fielding H. (1929) *An Introduction to the History of Medicine* (Philadelphia, W.B. Saunders; fourth edition).

Glacken, J. (1967) *Traces on the Rodian Shore: Nature and Culture in Western Thought from Ancient Times to the End of the Eighteenth Century* (Berkeley, University of California Press).

Greer, R. (1974) 'Hospitality in the First Five Centuries of the Church', *Medieval Studies* 10: 29–48.

Grmeck, M.D. (1989) *Diseases of the Ancient Greek World* (Baltimore, Johns Hopkins University Press).

Horden, P. (1985) 'The Byzantine Welfare State: Image and Reality', *Society of the Social History of Medicine Bulletin* 37: 7–10.

——(1992) 'Disease, Dragons and Saints: the Management of Epidemics in the Dark Ages' in Terence Ranger and Paul Slack (eds) *Epidemics and Ideas. Essays on the Historical Perception of Pestilence* (Cambridge, Cambridge University Press) 45–76.

Jackson, R. (1988) *Doctors and Diseases in the Roman Empire* (London, British Museum).

Jarcho, Saul (1970) 'Galen's Six Non-Naturals: a Bibliographic Note and Translation', *Bulletin of the History of Medicine* 44: 372–377.

Jones, Colin (1993) 'Charity Before 1850' in W.F. Bynum and Roy Porter (eds) *Companion Encyclopedia of the History of Medicine*, 2 vols (London, Routledge, 1993) 1469–1479.

Jones, W.H.S. (1957) 'Ancient Roman Folk Medicine', *Journal of the History of Medicine and Allied Sciences* 12: 459–472.

Kiple, Kenneth (1993a) 'Preface' in Kenneth Kiple (ed.) *The Cambridge World History of Human Disease*, 5 vols (Cambridge, Cambridge University Press) 1–7.

——(1993b) 'The Ecology of Disease' in W.F. Bynum and Roy Porter (eds) *Companion Encyclopedia of the History of Medicine*, 2 vols (London, Routledge) 357–411.

Kroll, J. and Bachrach, B. (1986) 'Sin and the Etiology of Disease in Pre-Crusade Europe', *Journal of the History of Medicine and Allied Sciences* 41: 395–414.

Lloyd, G.E.R. (1979) *Magic, Reason and Experience* (Cambridge, Cambridge University Press).

——(ed.) (1983) *Hippocratic Writings* translated by J. Chadwick and W.N. Mann (Harmondsworth, Penguin Classics).

——(1987) *The Revolutions of Wisdom* (Berkeley, University of California Press).

Longrigg, J.N. (1980) 'The Great Plague of Athens', *History of Science* 18: 209–225.

——(1992) 'Epidemic, Ideas and Classical Athenian Society' in Terence Ranger and Paul Slack (eds) *Epidemics and Ideas. Essays on the Historical Perception of Pestilence* (Cambridge, Cambridge University Press) 21–44.

——(1993) *Greek Rational Medicine* (London, Routledge).

McKeown, Thomas (1988) *The Origin of Human Disease* (Oxford, Basil Blackwell).

MacKinney, L.C. (1937) *Early Medieval Medicine* (Baltimore, Johns Hopkins University Press).

McNeill, William (1976) *Plagues and Peoples* (New York, Anchor Press, Doubleday).

Miller, Geneve (1962) ' "Airs, Waters and Places" in History', *Journal of the History of Medicine and Allied Sciences* 17: 129–140.

Miller, T.S. (1985) *The Birth of the Hospital in the Byzantine Empire* (Baltimore, Johns Hopkins University Press).

Numbers, R.L. and Amundsen, D.W. (eds) *Caring and Curing, Health and Medicine in the Western Medical Tradition* (New York, Macmillan).

Nutton, Vivien (1981a) *Galen, Problems and Prospects* (London, The Wellcome Institute).

——(1981b) 'Continuity or Rediscovery? The City Physician in Classical Antiquity and Medieval Italy' in A. W. Russell (ed.) *The Town and State Physician in Europe* (Wolfenbüttel, Herzong August Bibliothek) 11–25.

——(1983) 'The Seeds of Disease: An Explanation of Contagion and Infection from the Greeks to the Renaissance', *Medical History* 27: 1–34.

——(1985) 'Murders and Miracles: Lay Attitudes Towards Medicine in Classical Antiquity' in Roy Porter (ed.) *Patients and Practitioners* (Cambridge, Cambridge University Press) 23–53.

——(1988) *From Democedes to Harvey* (London, Routledge).

Park, K. (1992) 'Medicine and Society in Medieval Europe, 500–1500' in A. Wear (ed.) *Medicine in Society* (Cambridge, Cambridge University Press) 59–90.

Parker, R. (1983) *Miasma* (Oxford, Oxford University Press).

Parkin, T.G. (1992) *Demography and Roman Society* (Baltimore, Johns Hopkins University Press).

Pelling, Margaret (1993) 'Contagion, Germ Theory/Specificity' in W.F. Bynum and Roy Porter (eds) *Companion Encyclopedia of the History of Medicine*, 2 vols (London, Routledge) 309–334.

Philips, J.H. (1980) 'The Emergence of the Greek Medical Profession in the Roman Republic', *Transactions of the College of Physicians of Philadelphia* 2: 267–275.

Preuss, J. (1978) *Biblical and Talmudic Medicine* (New York, Sanhedrin Press).

Rather, L. (1968) 'The "Six Things Non-Natural": a Note on the Origins and Fate of a Doctrine and a Phrase', *Clio Medica* 3: 337–347.

Risse, Guenter (1986) 'Imhotep and Medicine: a Re-evaluation', *Western Journal of Medicine* 144: 622–624.

Ritter, E.K. (1965) 'Medical Expert (asipu) and Physician (asu). Notes on Two Complementary Professions in Babylonian Medicine', *Assyriological Studies* 16: 299–321.

Robinson, Olivier F. (1992) *Ancient Rome City Planning and Administration* (London, Routledge).

Rosen, George (1958) *The History of Public Health* (New York, MD Publications).

Sallares, R. (1991) *The Ecology of the Ancient Greek World* (London, Duckworth).

Sheils, W.J. (ed.) (1982) *The Church and Healing* (Oxford, Basil Blackwell).

Smith, W.D. (1979) *The Hippocratic Tradition* (Ithaca, Cornell University Press).

Staden, Heinrich von (ed. and trans.) (1989) *Herophilus: The Art of Medicine in Early Alexandria* (Cambridge, Cambridge University Press).

Temkin, O. (1977) *The Double Face of Janus* (Baltimore, Johns Hopkins University Press).

Temkin, O. and Temkin, C.L. (eds) (1967) *Ancient Medicine* (Baltimore, Johns Hopkins University Press).

Unschuld, Paul U. (1985) *Medicine in China: A History of Ideas* (Berkeley, University of California Press).

Wear, Andrew (1993) 'The History of Personal Hygiene' in W.F. Bynum and Roy Porter (eds) *Companion Encyclopedia of the History of Medicine*, 2 vols (London, Routledge) 1283–1308.

Weymouth, A. (1938) *Through the Leper Squint: A Study of Leprosy from Pre-Christian Times to the Present Day* (London, Selwyn and Blount).

Whitney, Jerome (1996) *Healing and Resonance in Ancient Egypt* (London, Open Door).

Zysk, K.G. (1985) *Religious Healing in the Veda* (Philadelphia, PA., American Philosophical Society).

——(1991) *Asceticism and Healing in Ancient India: Medicine in the Buddhist Monastery* (New York, Oxford University Press).

2 PESTILENCE AND PUBLIC ORDER IN MEDIEVAL EUROPE

Alexander, J.T. (1980) *Bubonic Plague in Early Modern Russia* (Baltimore, Johns Hopkins University Press).

Allbutt, Clifford T. (1905) *The Relations of Medicine and Surgery to the End of the Sixteenth Century*, (London, Macmillan).

Amundsen, Darrel W. (1979) 'Medicine and Surgery as Art or Craft: The Role of Schematic Literature in the Separation of Medicine and Surgery in the Middle Ages', *Transactions and Studies of the College of Physicians of Philadelphia* (series 5) 1 (1): 43–57.

Appleby, A.P. (1980) 'The Disappearance of Plague: A Continuing Puzzle', *Economic History Review* 33: 161–173.

Arano, Louisa Cogliati (1976) *The Medieval Health Handbook. Tacuinum Sanitatis* (New York, George Braziller).

Arno, Karlen (1995) *Plague's Progress. A Social History of Man and Disease* (London, Gollancz).

Arrizabalaga, Jon (1993) 'Syphilis' in Kenneth F. Kiple (ed.) *The Cambridge World History of Human Disease* (Cambridge University Press)1025–1033.

Bar-Sela, Ariel, Hoff, Hebbel E. and Faris, Elias (1964) 'Moses Maimonides' Two Treatises on Regimen and Health', *Transactions of the American Philosophical Society* (NS) 54: part 4.

Bloch, Marc (1973) *The Royal Touch. Sacred Monarchy and Scrofula in England and France* translated by J.E. Anderson (London, Routledge and Kegan Paul).

Bridbury, A.R. (1973) 'The Black Death', *Economic History Review* 26: 557–592.

Britnell, R.H. (1986) *The Commercialization of English Society 1000–1500* (Cambridge, Cambridge University Press).

Brody, Saul Nathaniel (1974) *The Disease of the Soul: Leprosy in Medieval Literature* (Ithaca, NY, Cornell University Press).

Brucker, Gene (1977) *The Civic World of Renaissance Florence* (Princeton, Princeton University Press).

Bullough, V. (1966) *The Development of Medicine as a Profession: The Contribution of the Medieval University to Modern Medicine* (Basel/New York, Karger).

Cambell, Bruce M.S. (ed.) (1991) *Before the Black Death. Studies in the 'Crisis' for the Early Fourteenth Century* (Manchester, Manchester University Press).

Cameron, Gruner O. (1930) *A Treatise on the Cannon of Avicenna, Incorporating a Translation of the First Book* (London, Luzac).

Camporasi, P. (1988) *The Incorruptible Flesh: Bodily Mutation and Mortification in Religion and Folklore* (Cambridge, Cambridge University Press).

Carmichael, A.G. (1986) *Plague and the Poor in Renaissance Florence* (Cambridge, Cambridge University Press).

——(1993a) 'Bubonic Plague' in Kenneth F. Kiple (ed.) *The Cambridge World History of Human Disease* (Cambridge University Press) 628–631.

——(1993b) 'Leprosy' in K. Kiple (ed.) *The Cambridge World History of Human Disease* (Cambridge, Cambridge University Press) 834–840.

Cipolla, C.M. (1973) *Cristofano and the Plague: A Study of Public Health in the Age of Galileo* (Berkeley, University of California Press).

——(1976) *Public Health and the Medical Profession in the Renaissance* (Cambridge, Cambridge University Press).

——(1979) *Faith, Reason and the Plague. A Tuscan Story of the Seventeenth Century* (Brighton, Harvester).

——(1981) *Fighting the Plague in Seventeenth-century Italy* (Madison, University of Wisconsin Press).

Coban, Alan Balfour (1975) *The Medieval Universities: Their Development and Organization* (London, Methuen).

Cohn, Samuel Kline (1980) *The Labouring Classes in Renaissance Florence* (London, Academic Press).

Conrad, L. (1992) *Epidemic Disease in Formal and Popular Thought in Early Islamic Society* (Berlin, Walter de Gruyter).

——(1995) 'The Arab-Islamic Medical Tradition' in L. Conrad, Michael Neve, Vivian Nutton, R.M. Porter and Andrew Wear (eds) *The Western Medical Tradition 800 BC–1800* (Cambridge, Cambridge University Press) 89–138.

Crosby, Alfred (1972) *The Columbian Exchange: Biological and Cultural Consequences of 1492* (Westport, CT, Greenwood Press).

Defoe, Daniel (1990) *A Journal of the Plague Year*, edited by Louis Landa with a new introduction by David Roberts (Oxford, Oxford University Press; first edition 1722).

Dols, Michael W. (1977) *The Black Death in the Middle East* (Princeton, Princeton University Press).

Flinn, Michael (1981) *The European Demographic System 1500–1800* (Brighton, Harvester).

Garcia-Ballester, Luis, French, Roger, Arrizabalaga, Jon and Cunningham, Andrew (eds) (1994) *Practical Medicine from Salernao to the Black Death* (Cambridge, Cambridge University Press).

Garrison, F.H. (1929) *An Introduction to the History of Medicine* (Philadelphia, W.B. Saunders; fourth edition).

Gilman, Sander (1988) *Disease and Representation: Images of Illness from Madness to AIDS*, (Ithaca, Cornell University Press).

——(1989) *Sexuality: An Illustrated History* (New York, Wiley).

Gottfried, Robert S. (1983) *The Black Death. Natural and Human Disaster in Medieval Europe* (London, Hale).

Grmeck, M.D. (1989) *Diseases of the Ancient Greek World* (Baltimore, Johns Hopkins University Press).

Haller, John (1993) 'Ergotism' in Kenneth F. Kiple (ed.) *The Cambridge World History of Human Disease* (Cambridge University Press) 718–719.

Hannaway, Caroline (1993) 'Environment and Miasmata' in W.F. Bynum and Roy Porter (eds) *Companion Encyclopedia of the History of Medicine*, 2 vols (London, Routledge) 292–308.

Hatcher, J. (1994) 'England in the Aftermath of the Black Death', *Past and Present* 144: 3–35.

Henderson, John (1988) 'Epidemics in Renaissance Florence: Medical Theory and Government Response' in N. Bulst and R. Delort (eds) *Maladies et société (XIIe–XVIIe siècles)* (Paris, Editions du Centre national de la recherche) 165–186.

——(1989) 'The Hospitals of Late-medieval and Renaissance Florence' in Lindsay Granshaw and Roy Porter (eds) *The Hospital in History* (London, Routledge).

Horden, P. (1988) 'A Discipline of Relevance: The Historiography of the Later Medieval Hospital', *Social History of Medicine* 1: 259–274.

Howard-Jones, N. (1977) 'Fracastoro and Henle: A Reappraisal of Their Contribution to the Concept of Communicable Diseases', *Medical History* 21: 61–68.

Kristeller, P.O. (1945) 'The School of Salerno: Its Development and its Contribution to the History of Learning', *Bulletin of the History of Medicine* 17: 143–159.

Kunke, La Verne (1993) 'Disease Ecologies of the Middle East and North Africa' in Kenneth F. Kiple (ed.) *The Cambridge World History of Human Disease* (Cambridge, Cambridge University Press) 453–462.

Lopez-Pinero, Maria (1981) 'The Medical Profession in Sixteenth-Century Spain' in Andrew Russell (ed.) *The Town and State Physician in Europe from the Middle Ages to the Enlightenment* (Wolfenbuttel, Herzog August Bibliothek) 85–98.

Martines, Lauro (1983) *Power and Imagination. City-states in Renaissance Italy* (Harmondsworth, Penguin; first edition Allen Lane, 1979).

Miller, T.S. (1978) 'The Knights of Saint John and the Hospitals of the Latin West', *Speculum* 53: 709–733.

Nicholas, David (1997a) *The Growth of the Medieval City from Late Antiquity to the Early Fourteenth Century* (London, Longman).

——(1997b) *The Later Medieval City, 1300–1500* (London, Longman).

Nutton, V. (1990) 'The Reception of Fracastoro's Theory of Contagion. The Seed that Fell Among Thorns', *Osiris* 6: 196–234.

O'Neill, Ynez Violé (1993) 'Diseases of the Middle Ages' in Kenneth F. Kiple (ed.) *The Cambridge World History of Human Disease* (Cambridge, Cambridge University Press) 270–279.

Ormrod, Mark and Lindley, Phillip (eds) (1996) *The Black Death In England* (Stamford, Watkins).

Ottosson, P.G. (1984) *Scholastic Medicine and Philosophy* (Naples, Bibliopolis).

Palmer, R. (1978) *The Control of Plague in Venice and Northern Italy, 1348–1600* (Ph.D. thesis, University of Kent).

——(1981) 'Physicians and the State in Post-medieval Italy' in Andrew Russell (ed.) *The Town and State Physician in Europe from the Middle Ages to the Enlightenment* (Wolfenbuttel, Herzog August Bibliothek) 47–61.

——(1982) 'The Church, Leprosy and Plague in Medieval and Early Modern Europe' in W. J. Shiels (ed.) *The Church and Healing: Papers Read at the Twentieth Summer Meeting and the Twenty-first Winter Meeting of the Ecclesiastical History Society* (Oxford, Oxford University Press) 79–101.

——(1991) 'Health, Hygiene and Longevity in Medieval and Renaissance Europe' in Yosio Kawakita, Shizu Sakai and Yasuo Ostura (eds) *Proceedings of the 12th International*

Symposium on the Comparative History of Medicine – East and West (Tokyo, Ishiyaku, EuroAmerica).

Park, Catherine (1985) *Doctors and Medicine in Early Renaissance Florence* (Princeton, Princeton University Press).

——(1993) 'The Black Death' in Kenneth F. Kiple (ed.) *The Cambridge World History of Human Disease* (Cambridge: Cambridge University Press) 612–615.

Pelling, M. (1993) 'Contagion, Germ Theory/Specificity' in W.F. Bynum and Roy Porter (eds) *Companion Encyclopedia of the History of Medicine*, 2 vols (London, Routledge) 309–334.

Platt, C. (1986) *King Death, The Black Death and its Aftermath in Late-Medieval England* (London, UCL Press).

Pullan, Brian (1971) *Rich and Poor in Renaissance Venice. The Social Institutions of a Catholic State to 1620* (Oxford, Blackwell).

——(1988) 'Support and Redeem: Charity and Poor Relief in Italian Cities from the Fourteenth to the Seventeenth Century', *Continuity and Change* 3: 177–208.

——(1992) 'Plague and Perceptions of the Poor in Early Modern Italy' in Terence Ranger and Paul Slack (eds) *Epidemics and Ideas. Essays on the Historical Perception of Pestilence* (Cambridge, Cambridge University Press) 101–125.

Quetel, Claude (1990) *History of Syphilis* (Cambridge, Polity Press).

Rawcliffe, Carol (1984) 'The Hospitals of Later Medieval London', *Medical History* 28: 1–21.

Razell, Peter (1994) *Essays in English Population History* (London, Caliban Books).

Richards, P. (1977) *The Medieval Leper and His Northern Heirs* (Cambridge, Cambridge University Press).

Rigby, S.H. (1995) *English Society in the Later Middle Ages. Class, Status and Gender* (London, Macmillan).

Rosen, George (1958) *A History of Public Health* (New York, MD Publications).

Rosenthal, Franz (1990) *Science and Medicine in Islam* (Aldershot, Variorum).

Rotberg, R.J. and Rabb, T.K.(eds) (1985) *Hunger and History. The Impact of Changing Food Production and Consumption Patterns on Society* (Cambridge, Cambridge University Press).

Scarborough, J. (ed.) (1983) *Symposium on Byzantine Medicine* (Washington D.C., Dumbarton Oaks Library).

Siraisi, N.G. (1987) *Avicena in Renaissance Italy. The Canon and Medical Teaching in Italian Universities after 1500* (Princeton, Princeton University Press).

——(1990) *Medieval and Early Renaissance Medicine: An Introduction to Knowledge and Practice* (Chicago, University of Chicago Press).

Slack, P. (1981) 'The Disappearance of Plague: An Alternative View', *Econonomic History Review* 34: 469–476.

——(1985) *The Impact of Plague in Tudor and Stuart England* (London, Routledge and Kegan Paul).

Smith, R.M. (ed.) (1984) *Land, Kinship and Life-Cycle* (Cambridge, Cambridge University Press).

Twigg, Graham (1984) *The Black Death. A Biological Reappraisal* (London, Batsford Academic and Educational).

Vigarello, George (1988) *Concepts of Cleanliness. Changing Attitudes in France since the Middle Ages* (Cambridge, Cambridge University Press).

Walter, John and Schofield, Roger (eds) (1989) *Famine, Disease and the Social Order in Early Modern Society* (Cambridge, Cambridge University Press).

Wear, Andrew (1995) 'Medicine in Early Modern Europe, 1500–1700' in L. Conrad, Michael Neve, Vivian Nutton, Roy Porter and Andrew Wear (eds) *The Western Medical Tradition 800 BC–1800* (Cambridge, Cambridge University Press) 215–361.

Webster, C. (ed.) (1979) *Health, Medicine and Mortality in the Sixteenth Century* (Cambridge, Cambridge University Press).

Ziegler, P. (1997) *The Black Death* (London, The Folio Society; first edition Collins, 1969).

3 ENLIGHTENMENT DISCOURSE AND HEALTH

Arrizabalaga, Jon (1993) 'Syphilis' in Kenneth F. Kiple (ed.) *The Cambridge World History of Human Disease* (Cambridge, Cambridge University Press) 1025–1033.

Ashburn, P.M. (1947) *The Ranks of Death: A Medical History of the Conquest of America* (New York, Coward-McCann).

Bahmueller, C.F. (1981) *The National Charity Company. Jeremy Bentham's Silent Revolution* (Berkeley, University of California Press).

Baker, Keith Michael (1982) *Condorcet. From Natural Philosophy to Social Mathematics* (Chicago, University of Chicago Press).

Beier, Lucinda McCray (1987) *Sufferers and Healers. The Experience of Illness in Seventeenth Century England* (London, Routledge).

Bonnar, James (1966) *Malthus and His Work* (reprinted facsimile, London, Frank Cass; first edition 1885).

Borsay, P. (1989) *The English Urban Renaissance: Culture and Society in the Provincial Town 1660–1770* (Oxford, Oxford University Press).

Brooke, J.H. (1991) *Science and Religion. Some Historical Perspectives* (Cambridge, Cambridge University Press).

Brucker, Gene (1977) *The Civic World of Renaissance Florence* (Princeton, Princeton University Press).

Buikstra, Jane E. (1993) 'Diseases of the Pre-Columbian Americas' in K. F. Kiple (ed.) *The Cambridge World History of Human Disease* (Cambridge, Cambridge University Press) 305–317.

Carmichael, Anne G. (1993a) 'Diseases of the Middle Ages' in Kenneth F. Kiple (ed.) *The Cambridge World History of Human Disease* (Cambridge, Cambridge University Press) 270–279.

——(1993b) 'Sweating Sickness' in Kenneth F. Kiple (ed.) *The Cambridge World History of Human Disease* (Cambridge, Cambridge University Press) 1023–1025.

Carr, Craig L. (ed.) (1994) *The Political Writings of Samuel Pufendorf* translated by Michael J. Seidler (Oxford, Oxford University Press).

Carrigan, J.A. (1988) 'Yellow fever: scourge of the South' in T. L. Savitt and J. H. Young (eds) *Disease and Distinctiveness in the American South* (Knoxville, University of Tennessee Press) 55–78.

Clarke, G. (ed.) (1987) *John Bellers. His Life, Times and Writings* (London, Routledge and Kegan Paul).

Clarkson, L. (1975) *Death, Disease and Famine in Pre-Industrial England* (Dublin, Gill and Macmillan).

Corfield, P.J. (1982) *The Impact of English Towns 1700–1800* (Oxford, Oxford University Press).

Crosby, Alfred W. (1972) *The Colombian Exchange: Biological and Cultural Consequences of 1492* (Westport, Conn., Greenwood).

——(1986) *Ecological Imperialism. The Biological Expansion of Europe. 900–1900* (London, Cambridge University Press).

Daston, Lorraine J. (1988) *Classical Probability in the Enlightenment* (Princeton, Princeton University Press).

Delacy, Margaret (1986) *Prison Reform in Lancashire, 1700–1850: A Study in County Administration* (Stanford, Stanford University Press).

Dewhurst, Kenneth (1966) *Dr Sydenham 1624–1689* (Berkeley, Ca., University of California Press).

Dickson, P.G.M. (1987) *Finance and Government Under Maria Theresa*, 2 vols (Oxford, Oxford University Press).

Dinwiddy, J.R. (1989) *Bentham* (Oxford, Oxford University Press).

Duffy, John (1990) *The Sanitarians. A History of American Public Health* (Chicago, University of Illinois Press).

Einstein, Alan O. (1991) *The Greatest Happiness Principle: An Examination of Utilitarianism* (New York, Garland).

Evans, R.J.W. (1979) *The Making of the Habsburg Monarchy, 1550–1700* (Oxford, Oxford University Press,)

Eyler, John (1979) *Victorian Social Medicine. The Ideas and Methods of William Farr* (Baltimore, Johns Hopkins University Press.

Finer, S. (1952) *The Life and Times of Edwin Chadwick* (London, Methuen).

Flew, Anthony (1986) *David Hume. Philosopher of Moral Science* (Oxford, Basil Blackwell).

Flinn, Michael (1981) *The European Demographic System 1500–1800* (Brighton, Harvester).

Foucault, Michel (1977) *Discipline and Punish: The Birth of the Prison* (London, Tavistock).

——(1990) *The History of Sexuality. Volume 1: An Introduction* (London, Vintage Books; first English translation 1978).

Fox, Christopher, Porter, Roy and Wokler, Alan (eds) (1995) *Inventing Human Science. Eighteenth Century Domains* (Berkeley, University of California Press).

Frängsmyr, Tore, Heilbron, J.L. and Rider, Robin (eds) (1990) *The Quantifying Spirit in the Eighteenth Century* (Berkeley, California University Press).

Gawthrop, Richard L. (1993) *Pietism and the Making of Eighteenth-Century Prussia* (Cambridge, Cambridge University Press).

Gay, Peter (1967–9) *The Enlightenment: An Interpretation*, 2 vols (New York, Knopf).

Gigerenzer, Gerd, Swijtink, Zeno, Porter, Theodore, Daston, Lorraine, Beatty, John and Krüger, Lorenz (eds) (1989) *The Empire of Chance. How Probability Changed Science and Everyday Life* (Cambridge, Cambridge University Press).

Greenwood, Major (1948) *Medical Statistics from Graunt to Farr* (Cambridge, Cambridge University Press).

Hacking, Ian (1990) *The Taming of Chance* (Cambridge, Cambridge University Press).

Halévy, Elie (1972) *The Growth of Philosophical Radicalism* translated by Mary Morris (London Faber 1972; first edition 1934, first English translation 1952).

Hannaway, Caroline (1972) 'The *Société royale de médecine* and epidemics in the Ancien Regime', *Bulletin of the History of Medicine* 46: 257–273.

Harrington, G.J. (1965) 'Epidemic Typhus and History', *Marquette Medical Review* 31: 147–190.

Hilton, Boyd (1988) *The Age of Atonement. The Influence of Evangelicalism on Social and Economic Thought, 1785–1865* (Oxford, Oxford University Press).

Himelfarb, G. (1984) *The Idea of Poverty. England in the Early Industrial Age* (New York, Knopf).

Hopkins, Donald R. (1983) *Princes and Peasants: Smallpox in History* (Chicago, University of Chicago Press).

James, Patricia (1979) *Population Malthus. His Life and Times* (London, Routledge and Kegan Paul).

Johannisson, Karin (1988) 'Why Cure the Sick? Population Policy and Health Programs Within Eighteenth-Century Swedish Mercantilism' in Anders Brändström and Lars-Göran Tedebrand (eds) *Society, Health and Population during the Demographic Transition* (Stockholm, Almqvist and Wiksell).

——(1994) 'The People's Health: Public Health Policies in Sweden' in Dorothy Porter (ed.) *The History of Public Health and the Modern State* (Amsterdam and Atlanta, Rodopi) 165–182.

Jordanova, L.J. (1981) 'Policing Public Health in France 1780–1815' in T. Ogawa (ed.) *Public Health* (Tokyo, Tanaguchi Foundation) 12–32.

——(1982) 'Guarding the Body Politic: Volney's Catechism of 1793' in Francis Barker *et. al.* (eds) *1789: Reading Writing Revolution. Proceedings of the Essex Conference on the Sociology of Literature, July 1981* (Colchester, University of Essex) 12–21.

Kiple, Kenneth F. (ed.) (1993a) *The Cambridge World History of Human Disease* (Cambridge, Cambridge University Press).

——(1993b) 'The Ecology of Disease' in *Companion Encyclopedia of the History of Medicine*, 2 vols (London, Routledge) 357–411.

Lesky, Erna (1976) Introduction to *A System of Complete Medical Police. Selections from Johann Peter Franck* translated by E. Vilim (Baltimore, Johns Hopkins University Press).

Leslie, Margaret (1972) 'Mysticism Misunderstood: David Hartley and the Idea of Progress', *Journal of the History of Ideas* 33: 625–632.

Letwin, Shirley (1993) *The Pursuit of Certainty. David Hume, Jeremy Bentham, John Stewart Mill, Beatrice Webb* (Aldershot, Gregg Revivals).

Lindemann, Mary (1990) *Patriots and Paupers: Hamburg 1712–1830* (New York, Oxford University Press).

——(1996) *Health and Healing in Eighteenth Century Germany* (Baltimore, Johns Hopkins University Press).

Livingston, Donald and Martin, Marie (eds) (1991) *Hume as Philosopher of Society, Politics and History* (Rochester NY, University of Rochester Press).

McNeill, William (1976) *Plagues and Peoples* (New York, Doubleday).

Manuel, Frank (ed.) (1965) *The Enlightenment* (Englewood Cliffs NJ, Prentice Hall).

Melton, Edgar (1995) 'The Prussian Junkers' in H.M. Scott, *The European Nobilities in the Seventeenth and Eighteenth Century*, 2 vols (London, Longman) 1: 71–109.

Miller, G. (1981) 'Putting Lady Mary in Her Place: A Discussion of Historical Causation', *Bulletin of the History of Medicine* 55: 2–16.

Munch, Ragnhild (1995) *Gesundheitswesen im 18. und 19. Jahrhundert das Berliner Beispiel* (Berlin, Akademie Verlag).

Oestreich, Gerhard (1982) *Neostoicism and the Early Modern State* (Cambridge, Cambridge University Press).

Ogberg, Barbara Bowen (1976) 'David Hartley and the Association of Ideas', *Journal of the History of Ideas* 37: 441–454.

Porter, Dorothy (1994) 'Introduction' in D. Porter (ed.) *The History of Health and the Modern State* (Amsterdam, Rodopi) 1–44.

Porter, Roy and Porter, Dorothy (1988) *In Sickness and in Health. The British Experience 1650–1850* (London, Fourth Estate).

——(1989) *Patient's Progress. Doctors and Doctoring in Eighteenth Century England* (Cambridge, Polity Press).

Porter, Roy (1991) 'Cleaning up the Great Wen: Public Health in Eighteenth Century London' in W.F. Bynum and Roy Porter (eds) *Living and Dying in London: Medical History Supplement No. 11* (London, Wellcome Institute) 61–75.

Porter, Theodore (1986) *The Rise of Statistical Thinking, 1820–1900* (Princeton, Princeton University Press).

Quennell, Peter (1988) *The Pursuit of Happiness* (London, Constable).

Quetel, Claude (1990) *History of Syphilis* translated by Judith Bradock and Brian Pike (London, Polity Press).

Raeff, M. (1983) *The Well-Ordered Police State* (New Haven, Yale University Press, 1983).

Ramsey, Matthew (1988) *Professional and Popular Medicine in France, 1770–1830. The Social World of Medical Practice* (Cambridge, Cambridge University Press).

——(1994) 'Public Health in France' in Dorothy Porter (ed.) *The History of Public Health and the Modern State* (Amsterdam and Atlanta, Rodopi) 45–118.

Razell, Peter (1977) *The Conquest of Smallpox: The Impact of Inoculation on Smallpox Mortality in Eighteenth Century England* (Firle, Sussex, Caliban Books).

Riley, James C. (1987) *The Eighteenth Century Campaign to Avoid Disease* (Basingstoke: Macmillan).

——(1989) *Sickness, Recovery and Death: A History and Forecast of Ill Health* (London: Macmillan).

Riley, Patrick (ed.) (1981) *The Political Writings of Leibniz* translated and edited by Patrick Riley (Cambridge, Cambridge University Press; first edition 1972).

Rosen, George (1952) 'Political Order and Human Health in Jeffersonian Thought', *Bulletin of the History of Medicine* 26: 32–44.

——(1974) *From Medical Police to Social Medicine. Essays on the History of Health Care* (New York, Science History Publications).

Russell, A. (ed.) (1981) *The Town and State Physician in Europe from the Middle Ages to the Enlightenment: Europe* (Wolfenbüttel, Herzong August Bibliothek).

Scarre, G. (1995) *Utilitarianism* (London, Routledge).

Scott, William Robert (1900) *Francis Hutchison. His Life, Teaching and Position in the History of Philosophy* (Cambridge, Cambridge University Press).

Semple, Janet (1993) 'Bentham's Utilitarianism and the Provision of Medical Care' in Dorothy Porter and Roy Porter (eds) *Doctors, Politics and Society: Historical Essays* (Amsterdam and Atlanta, Rodopi) 30–46.

Smith, C.U.M. (1987) 'David Hartley's Newtonian Neuropsychology', *Journal of the History of the Behavioural Sciences* 23: 123–136.

Smith, G. (1985) 'Prescribing the Rules of Health: Self-Help and Advice in Late Eighteenth Century England' in Roy Porter (ed.) *Patients and Practitioners: Lay Perceptions of Medicine in Pre-Industrial Society* (Cambridge and New York, Cambridge University Press) 249–282.

Soloway, Richard Allen (1982) *Birth Control and the Population Question in England, 1877–1930* (Chapel Hill, University of North Carolina Press).

Stannard, David (1993) 'Disease, Human Migration and History' in Kenneth F. Kiple (ed.) *The Cambridge World History of Human Disease* (Cambridge, Cambridge University Press) 35–42.

Taylor, William Leslie (1965) *Francis Hutchison and David Hume as Predecessors of Adam Smith* (Durham NC, Duke University Press).

Tomaselli, S. (1989) 'Moral Philosophy and Population Questions in Eighteenth-Century Europe' in Michael S. Teitelbaum and Jay M. Winter (eds) *Population and Resources in Western Intellectual Traditions* (Cambridge, Cambridge University Press) 7–29.

Vigarello, George (1988) *Concepts of Cleanliness. Changing Attitudes in France Since the Middle Ages* (Cambridge, Cambridge University Press).

Vyverberg, Henry (1989) *Human Nature, Cultural Diversity and the French Enlightenment* (Oxford, Oxford University Press).

Wear, Andrew (1987) 'Interfaces: Perceptions of Health and Illness in Early Modern England' in R. Porter and A. Wear (eds) *Problems and Methods in the History of Medicine* (London, Routledge) 230–255.

——(1993) 'The History of Personal Hygiene' in W.F. Bynum and Roy Porter (eds) *Companion Encyclopedia of the History of Medicine* (London, Routledge) 1283–1308.

Weiner, Dora (1970) 'Le droit de l'homme à la santé: une belle idée devant l'Assemblée constituante: 1790–1791', *Clio Medica* 5: 208–223.

——(1974) 'Public Health Under Napoleon: the Conseil de salubrité de Paris, 1802–1815', *Clio Medica* 9: 271–284.

——(1993) *The Citizen-Patient in Revolutionary and Imperial Paris* (Baltimore, Johns Hopkins University Press).

Weitzman, A.J. (1975) 'Eighteenth Century London: Urban Paradise or Fallen City?', *Journal of the History of Ideas* 36: 469–480.

Whaley, Joachim (1981) 'The Protestant Enlightenment in Germany' in Roy Porter and Mikulas Teich (eds) *The Enlightenment in National Context* (Cambridge, Cambridge University Press) 106–117.

Whelan, Frederick G. (1991) 'Population and Ideology in the Enlightenment', *History of Political Thought* 7: 35–72.

White, Brenda (1983) 'Medical Police: Politics and Police, the Fate of John Roberton', *Medical History* 27: 407–472.

Winch, Donald (1987) *Malthus* (Oxford, Oxford University Press).

Woods, R. and Woodward, J. (eds) (1989) *Urban Disease and Mortality in 19th Century England* (London, Batsford Academic).

Wrigley, E.A. (1989) 'The Limits to Growth: Malthus and the Classical Economists' in Michael S. Teitelbaum and Jay M. Winter (eds) *Population and Resources in Western Intellectual Traditions* (Cambridge, Cambridge University Press) 30–48.

Wylie, John A.H. and Collier, Leslie H. (1981) 'The English Sweating Sickness (*sudor anglicus*). A Reappraisal', *Journal of the History of Medicine and Allied Sciences* 36: 425–445.

Zinsser, Hans (1942) *Rats, Lice and History* (London, Routledge; first edition 1935).

4 SOCIAL SCIENCE AND THE QUANTITATIVE ANALYSIS OF HEALTH

Abrams, Philip (1968) *The Origins of British Sociology: 1834–1914* (Chicago, Chicago University Press).

Ackerknecht, Erwin (1948) 'Hygiene in France, 1815–1848', *Bulletin of the History of Medicine* 22: 117–155.

——(1952) 'Villermé and Quetelet', *Bulletin of the History of Medicine* 26: 317–329.

Baker, K.M. (1982) *Condorcet From Natural Philosophy to Social Mathematics* (Chicago, University of Chicago Press).

Blaug, Mark (ed.) (1991a) *Henry Thornton (1770–1815) Jeremy Bentham (1748–1832) James Lauderdale (1759–1839) Simonde de Sismondi (1773–1842). Pioneers in Economics 15* (Aldershot, Edward Elgar).

——(ed.) (1991b) *Jean-Baptiste Say (1776–1832). Pioneers in Economics 15* (Aldershot, Edward Elgar).

Boardman, Philip (1978) *The Worlds of Patrick Geddes, Biologist, Town Planner, Re-educator, Peace-warrior* (London, Routledge and Kegan Paul).

Canguilhem, George (1989) *The Normal and the Pathological* (reprinted, New York, Zone Books; first edition 1943, revised 1966).

Chinn, Carl (1995) *Poverty Amidst Prosperity. The Urban Poor in England, 1834–1914* (Manchester, Manchester University Press).

Coleman, William (1982) *Death is a Social Disease* (Madison, University of Wisconsin Press).

Cowherd, Raymond G. (1977) *Political Economists and the English Poor Laws: A Historical Study of the Influence of Classical Economics on the Formation of Social Welfare Policy* (Athens, Ohio, Ohio University Press).

Cullen, M.J. (1975) *The Statistical Movement in Early Victorian Britain. The Foundation of Empirical Social Research* (New York, Barnes and Noble, Hassocks, Harvester).

Daston, Lorraine J. (1981) 'Mathematics and the Moral Sciences: the Rise and Fall of the Probability of Judgments, 1785–1840' in H.N. Jahnke and M.Otte (eds) *Epistemological and Social Problems of the Sciences in the Early Nineteenth Century* (Dordrecht, Reidel).

——(1988) *Classical Probability in the Enlightenment* (Princeton, Princeton University Press).

Disraeli, Benjamin (1983) *Sybil, or, The Two Nations*, introduction by Patrick Cormack (London, Folio Society; first edition 1845).

Easson, Betty R. and McIntyre, J.E. (1978) *Early Victorian Society. The Two Nations* (Glasgow, Blackie).

Engels, Friedrich (1985) *The Origin of the Family, Private Property and the State* (Harmondsworth, Penguin).

Eyler, John (1979) *Victorian Social Medicine. The Ideas and Methods of William Farr* (Baltimore, Johns Hopkins University Press).

Foucault, Michel (1970) *The Order of Things. An Archeology of the Human Sciences* (London, Tavistock).

——(1972) *The Archeology of Knowledge* translated by A. M. Sheridan Smith (London, Tavistock).

Gallagher, Catherine (1987) 'The Body Versus the Social Body in the Works of Thomas Malthus and Henry Mayhew' in Catherine Gallagher and Thomas Laqueur (eds) *The Making of the Modern Body. Sexuality and Society in the Nineteenth Century* (Berkeley, University of California Press) 83–106.

Giddens, Anthony (1990) *Durkheim* (London, Fontana).

Gigerenzer, Gerd, Swijtink, Zeno, Porter, Theodore, Daston, Lorraine, Beatty, John and Krüger, Lorenz (eds) (1989) *The Empire of Chance* (Cambridge, Cambridge University Press).

Goldman, Lawrence (1986) 'The Social Science Association, 1857–1886: A Context for Mid-Victorian Liberalism', *The English Historical Review* CI: 95–134.

——(1987) 'A Peculiarity of the English? The Social Science Association and the Absence of Sociology in Nineteenth Century Britain', *Past and Present* 114: 133–171.

Gordon, Scott (1991) *The History and Philosophy of Social Science* (London, Routledge).

Grey-Turner, E. and Sutherland, F.M. (1981) *History of the British Medical Association, vol. I, 1832–1931, vol. II, 1932–1981* (London, British Medical Association).

Hacking, Ian (1990) *The Taming of Chance* (Cambridge, Cambridge University Press).

Hardy, Anne (1993) 'Lyon Playfair and the Idea of Progress: Science and Medicine in Victorian Parliamentary Politics' in Dorothy Porter and Roy Porter (eds) *Doctors, Politics and Society: Historical Essays* (Amsterdam and Atlanta, Rodopi) 81–106.

Harrison, John F.C. (1979) *Early Victorian Britain, 1832–51* (London, Fontana).

Hawthorn, Geoffrey (1976) *Enlightenment and Despair. A History of Sociology* (Cambridge, Cambridge University Press).

Houwart, Eddy (1993/4) 'Medical Statistics and Sanitary Provisions: A New World of Social Relations and Threats to Health', *Tractrix. Yearbook for the History of Science, Medicine, Technology and Mathematics* 5: 1–33.

Hughes, H. Stuart (1979) *Consciousness and Society. The Reorientation of European Social Thought 1890–1930* (Brighton, Sussex, Harvester).

Ionescu, Ghita (ed.) (1976) *Saint-Simon, Claude-Henri de Rouvroy. The Political Thought of Saint-Simon* (Oxford, Oxford University Press).

Kunitz, Stephen (1993) 'Diseases and European Mortality Decline, 1700–1900' in Kenneth Kiple (ed.) *The Cambridge World History of Human Diseases* (Cambridge, Cambridge University Press) 287–293.

Lester, David (ed.) (1994) *Emile Durkheim: Le Suicide One Hundred Years Later* (Philadelphia, Charles Press).

Lukes, Steven (1973) *Emile Durkheim. His Life and Work: A Historical and Critical Study* (Harmondsworth, Penguin).

Macleod, Roy (1968) 'The Anatomy of State Medicine: Concept and Application' in F.N.L. Poynter (ed.) *Medicine and Science in the 1860s* (London, Wellcome Institute) 199–227.

Macleod, Roy and Collins, P. (eds) (1981) *The Parliament of Science. The British Association for the Advancement of Science, 1821–1981* (Northwood, Northwood Science Reviews).

Manuel, Frank (1956) *The New World of Henri Saint-Simon* (Cambridge, Mass., Harvard University Press).

Matthews, J. Rosner (1995) *Quantification and the Quest for Medical Certainty* (Princeton, NJ, Princeton University Press).

Metz, Karl H. (1984) 'Social Thought and Social Statistics in the Early Nineteenth century. The Case of Sanitary Statistics in England', *International Review of History*, 29: 254–273.

Mill, J.S. (1961) *Auguste Comte and Positivism* (reprinted, Ann Arbor; Michigan; first edition 1865).

Morrell, J. and Thackray, A. (1981) *Gentlemen of Science. Early Years of the British Association for the Advancement of Science* (Oxford, Oxford University Press).

Newsholme, Arthur (1923) *The Elements of Vital Statistics* (London, Allen and Unwin; first edition 1892).

Peel, J.D.Y. (ed.) (1972) *Herbert Spencer On Social Evolution. Selected Writings* (Chicago, The University of Chicago Press).

Pelling, Margaret (1978) *Cholera Fever and English Medicine 1825–1865* (Oxford, Oxford University Press).

Pickering, Mary (1993) *Auguste Comte: An Intellectual Biography* (Cambridge, Cambridge University Press).

Porter, Dorothy (1993) 'Public Health' in W. F. Bynum and Roy Porter (eds) *The Routledge Encyclopaedia of the History of Medicine* (London, Routledge) 1231–1261.

——(1997) 'Introduction' in Dorothy Porter (ed.) *Social Medicine and Medical Sociology in the Twentieth Century* (Amsterdam and Atlanta, Rodopi) 1–33.

Porter, Theodore (1986) *Rise of Statistical Thinking 1820–1900* (Princeton, Princeton University Press).

——(1990) 'Natural Science and Social Theory' in R.C. Olby, G.N. Cantor, J.R.R. Christie and M.J.S. Hodge (eds) *Companion to the History of Modern Science* (London, Routledge) 1024–1044.

Roberts, David (1979) *Paternalism in Early Victorian England* (New Brunswick, NJ, Rutgers University Press).

Shepherd, David E. (1995) *John Snow. Anaesthetist to a Queen and Epidemiologist to a Nation. A Biography* (Cornwall, PE, Canada, York Point Publishing).

Shryock, Richard H. (1979) *The Development of Modern Medicine. An Interpretation of the Social and Scientific Factors Involved* (Madison, Wisc., University of Wisconsin Press).

Spencer, Herbert (1969) *The Principles of Sociology* edited by Stanislav Andreski (abridged edition) (London, Macmillan; first edition 1876).

——(1996) *The Study of Sociology* with a new introduction by Michael Taylor (London, Routledge/Thoemmes; second edition 1873).

Stanlis, Peter J. (1991) *Edmund Burke: The Enlightenment and Revolution* (New Brunswick, Transaction Publishers).

Thompson, Kenneth (ed.) (1976) *Auguste Comte: The Foundation of Sociology* (London, Nelson).

——(1990) *Emile Durkheim* (London, Routledge).

Turner, J.H. (1995) *Herbert Spencer. A Renewed Appreciation* (London, Sage Publications).

Watkins, Dorothy (1984) *The English Revolution in Social Medicine 1889–1911* (University of London, Ph.D. thesis).

Young, G. M. (1977) *Portrait of an Age: Victorian England* (London, Oxford University Press. Annotated edition by George Kitson Clark with biographical memoir by Sir George Clark).

Zeitlin, Irving M. (1968) *Ideology and the Development of Sociological Theory* (Englewood, NJ, Prentice-Hall).

5 EPIDEMICS AND SOCIAL DISLOCATION IN THE NINETEENTH CENTURY

Ackerknecht, Erwin H. (1948) 'Anti-Contagionism Between the Wars', *Bulletin of the History of Medicine* 22: 562–593.

——(1953) *Rudolf Virchow, Doctor, Statesman, Anthropologist* (Madison, Wisconsin, Wisconsin University Press).

Baldry, Peter (1976) *The Battle Against Bacteria. A Fresh Look* (Cambridge, Cambridge University Press).

Blake, John B. (1968) 'Yellow Fever in Eighteenth-Century America', *Bulletin of the History of America* 44: 673–686.

Bourdelais, Patrice and Raulot, Jean-Yves (1987) *Une peur bleue: Histoire du choléra en France, 1832–1854* (Paris, Payot).

Brock, Thomas D. (1988) *Robert Koch: A Life in Medicine and Bacteriology* (Madison, Wisc., Science Technical Publishers).

Chevalier, Louis (1958) *Le Choléra: La Première épidemie du XIX siècle* (La Roche-sur-Yon, La Roche-sur-Yon)

Coleman, William (1982) *Death is a Social Disease* (Madison, University of Wisconsin Press).

——(1987) *Yellow Fever in the North. The Methods of Early Epidemiology* (Madison, University of Wisconsin Press).

Connolly, S.J. (1983) 'The Blessed Turf: Cholera and Popular Panic in Ireland, June 1832', *Irish History Studies* 23: 214–232.

Cooter, Roger (1982) 'Anticontagionism and History's Medical Record' in P. Wright and A. Treacher (eds) *The Problem of Medical Knowledge* (Edinburgh, Edinburgh University Press) 87–108.

Corbin, Alain (1986) *The Foul and the Fragrant: Odor and the French Social Imagination* (Cambridge, Mass., Harvard University Press).

Crosby, Alfred W. (1986) *Ecological Imperialism. The Biological Expansion of Europe. 900–1900* (London, Cambridge University Press).

Delacy, Margaret (1986) *Prison Reform in Lancashire, 1700–1850: A Study in County Administration* (Stanford, Stanford University Press).

Delaporte, François (1986) *Disease and Civilization* (Cambridge, Mass., MIT Press).

Duffy, John (1966) *The Sword of Pestilence. The New Orleans Yellow Fever Epidemic of 1853* (Baton Rouge, Louisiana State University Press).

——(1968) *A History of Public Health in New York City 1625–1866* (New York, Russell Sage Foundation).

——(1990) *The Sanitarians. A History of American Public Health* (Chicago, University of Illinois Press).

Durey, Michael (1979) *The Return of the Plague. British Society and the Cholera 1831–2* (London, Gill and Macmillan).

Evans, Richard J. (1987) *Death In Hamburg. Society and Politics in the Cholera Years 1830–1910* (Oxford, Clarendon Press).

——(1988) 'Epidemics and Revolutions: Cholera in Nineteenth Century Europe', *Past and Present* 120: 123–146.

Eyler, John (1979) *Victorian Social Medicine. The Ideas and Methods of William Farr* (Baltimore, Johns Hopkins University Press).

Farley, John (1977) *The Spontaneous Generation Controversy from Descartes to Oparin* (Baltimore, Johns Hopkins University Press).

Foster, G.M. (1981) 'Typhus Disaster in the Wake of War: The American-Polish Relief Expedition, 1919–1920', *Bulletin of the History of Medicine* 55: 221–232.

Foster, W.D. (1970) *A History of Medical Bacteriology and Immunology* (London, Heinemann).

Geison, Gerald L. (1995) *The Private Science of Louis Pasteur* (Princeton, Princeton University Press).

Geiston, A.L. and Jones, T.C. (1977) 'Typhus Fever: Report of an Epidemic in New York City in 1847', *Journal of Infectious Diseases* 136: 813–821.

Hamlin, Christopher (1990) *A Science of Impurity. Water Analysis in Nineteenth Century Britain* (Bristol, Adam Hilger).

——(1992) 'Predisposing Causes and Public Health in Early Nineteenth Century Medical Thought', *Social History of Medicine* 5: 43–70.

Hannaway, Caroline (1993) 'Environment and Miasmata' in W.F. Bynum and Roy Porter (eds) *Companion Encyclopedia of the History of Medicine*, 2 vols (London, Routledge) 292–308.

Harden, Victoria A. (1993a) 'Rickettsial Diseases' in Kenneth F. Kiple (ed.) *The Cambridge World History of Human Disease* (Cambridge, Cambridge University Press) 981–982.

——(1993b) 'Typhus, Epidemic' in Kenneth F. Kiple (ed.) *The Cambridge World History of Human Disease* (Cambridge, Cambridge University Press) 1080–1084.

Hardy, Anne (1984) 'Water and the Search for Public Health in London in the Eighteenth and Nineteenth Centuries', *Medical History* 28: 250–282.

——(1988) 'Urban Famine or Urban Crisis? Typhus in the Victorian City', *Medical History* 32: 401–425.

——(1993) *The Epidemic Streets. Infectious Disease and the Rise of Preventive Medicine 1856–1900* (Oxford, Clarendon Press).

Harrington, G.J. (1965) 'Epidemic Typhus and History', *Marquette Medical Review* 31: 147–190.

Himelfarb, Gertrude (1984) *The Idea of Poverty. England in the Early Industrial Age* (New York, Knopf).

Howard-Jones, Norman (1972) 'Cholera Therapy in the Nineteenth Century', *Journal of the History of Medicine and Allied Sciences* 27: 373–395.

Hudson, Robert P. (1983) *Disease and Its Control, The Shaping of Modern Thought* (Westport, Conn., Greenwood).

——(1993) 'Concepts of Disease in the West' in Kenneth F. Kiple (ed.) *The Cambridge World History of Human Disease* (Cambridge, Cambridge University Press) 45–52.

Kiple, Kenneth, F. (ed.) (1993) *The Cambridge World History of Human Disease* (Cambridge, Cambridge University Press).

Kunitz, Stephen J. (1983) 'Speculations on the European Mortality Decline', *Economic History Review*, 2nd series, 36: 349–364.

——(1984) 'Mortality Change in America, 1620–1920', *Human Biology* 56: 559–582.

Landers, John and Reynolds, Vernon (eds) (1990) *Fertility and Resources* (Cambridge, Cambridge University Press).

Latour, Bruno (1986) *Microbes: The Pasteurization of France* translated by Alan Sheridan and John Law (Cambridge, Mass., Harvard University Press).

Logan, J.S. (1989) 'Trench fever in Belfast, and the nature of the "relapsing fevers" in the United Kingdom in the 19th century', *Ulster Medical Journal* 58: 83–88.

Longmate, Norman, (1966) *King Cholera: The Biography of a Disease* (London, Hamish Hamilton).

Luckin, Bill (1971) 'The Final Catastrophe – Cholera in London, 1866', *Medical History* 21: 32–42.

——(1984) 'Evaluating The Sanitary Revolution: Typhus and Typhoid in London' in R. Woods and J. Woodward (eds) *Urban Disease and Mortality in 19th Century England* (London, Batsford Academic) 111–116.

——(1986) *Pollution and Control: A Social History of the Thames in the Nineteenth Century* (Bristol, Adam Hilger).

McGrew, Roderik E. (1965) *Russia and the Cholera, 1823–1832* (Madison, Wisc., Wisconsin University Press).

McKeown, Thomas (1976) *The Modern Rise of Population* (London, Edward Arnold).

McNeill, William (1976) *Plagues and Peoples* (New York, Doubleday).

Morris, R.J. (1976) *Cholera 1832 The Social Response to an Epidemic* (London, Croom Helm).

Pelling, Margaret (1978) *Cholera Fever and English Medicine 1825–1865* (Oxford, Oxford University Press).

——(1993) 'Contagion, Germ Theory/Specificity' in W.F. Bynum and Roy Porter (eds) *Companion Encyclopedia of the History of Medicine*, 2 vols (London, Routledge) 309–334.

Porter, Dorothy (1985) 'Theories of Disease in the Work of Edmund Parkes', *Bulletin of the Society for the Social History of Medicine* 37: 40–42.

——(1991) 'Stratification and its Discontents: Professionalization and the English Public Health Service, 1848–1914' in E. Fee and Roy Acheson (eds) *Health that Mocks the Doctors' Rules. A History of Education in Public Health* (Oxford, Oxford University Press) 83–113.

Ranger, Terrance and Slack, Paul (eds) (1992) *Epidemics and Ideas. Essays in the Historical Perceptions of Pestilence* (Cambridge, Cambridge University Press).

Razell, P.E. (1974) 'An Interpretation of the Modern Rise of Population: A Critique', *Population Studies* 28: 5–17.

Reid, Robert (1974) *Microbes and Men* (London, BBC Publications).

Richardson, Ruth (1988) *Death, Dissection and the Destitute* (Harmondsworth, Penguin).

Risse, G. (1979) 'Epidemics and Medicine: The Influence of Disease Upon Medical Thought and Practice', *Bulletin of the History of Medicine* 54: 505–519.

——(1985) 'Typhus Fever in Eighteenth Century Hospitals: New Approaches to Medical Treatment', *Bulletin of the History of Medicine* 59: 176–195.

Rosenberg, Charles (1962) *The Cholera Years 1832, 1849 and 1866* (Chicago, University of Chicago Press).

——(1989) 'Disease in History. Frames and Framers', *Milbank Quarterly* 67: 1–15.

——(1992) *Explaining Epidemics and Other Studies in the History of Medicine* (Cambridge, Cambridge University Press).

Shryock, Richard H. (1972) 'Germ Theories in Medicine Prior to 1870: Further Comments on Continuity in Science', *Clio Medica* 7: 81–109.

Slack, Paul (1985) *The Impact of Plague in Tudor and Stuart England* (London, Routledge and Kegan Paul).

——(1992) 'Introduction' in Paul Slack (ed.) *Epidemics and Ideas. Essays on the Historical Perception of Pestilence* (Cambridge, Cambridge University Press) 1–20.

Smith, D.C. (1980) 'Gerhard's Distinction Between Typhoid and Typhus and its Reception in America, 1833–1860', *Bulletin of the History of Medicine* 54: 368–375.

Snowden, Frank M. (1995) *Naples in the Time of Cholera, 1884–1911* (Cambridge, Cambridge University Press).

Spink, Wesley, M. (1978) *Infectious Diseases. Prevention and Treatment in the Nineteenth and Twentieth Centuries* (Minneapolis, University of Minnesota Press).

Szreter, Simon (1988) 'The Importance of Social Intervention in Britain's Mortality Decline c.1850–1914: a Re-interpretation of the Role of Public Health', *Social History of Medicine* 1: 1–37.

Tauber, Alfred and Chernyak, Leon (1991) *Metchnikoff and the Origins of Immunology* (New York, Oxford University Press).

Vernon, K. (1990) 'Pus, Sewage, Beer and Milk: Microbiology in Britain, 1870–1940', *History of Science* 28: 289–325.

Watkins, Dorothy (1985) 'Explanations of Disease and the Technology of Hygiene in Parke's *Manual*, 1864–1873', *Bulletin of the Society for the Social History of Medicine* 37: 40–42.

Webster, Charles (1985) 'Two Hundredth Anniversary of the 1784 Report on Fever at Radcliffe Mill', *Society for the Social History of Medicine Bulletin* 7: 36–65.

Winter, Jay M. (1982) 'The Decline of Mortality in Britain 1870–1950' in T. Barker and M. Drake (eds) *Population and Society in Britain 1850–1980* (London, Batsford Academic and Educational) 100–120.

Wohl, Anthony (1983) *Endangered Lives. Public Health in Victorian Britain* (London, Dent).
Woods, R. and Woodward, J. (eds) (1984) *Urban Disease and Mortality in Nineteenth Century England* (New York, St Martin's Press).
Woodward, T.E. (1973) 'A Historical Account of the Rickettsia Disease', *Journal of Infectious Diseases* 127: 583–594.
Wrigley, E.A. and Schofield, R.S. (1981) *The Population History of England 1541–1871* (London: Edward Arnold).
Zinsser, Hans (1935) *Rats, Lice, and History* (Boston, for Atlantic Monthly Press by Little, Brown).

6 PUBLIC HEALTH AND THE MODERN STATE: FRANCE, SWEDEN AND GERMANY

Ackerknecht, Erwin H. (1953) *Rudolf Virchow: Doctor, Statesman and Anthropologist* (Madison, Wisc., University of Wisconsin Press).
——(1967) *Medicine at the Paris Hospital, 1794–1848* (Baltimore, Johns Hopkins University Press).
Ackerman, E.B. (1990) *Health Care in the Parisian Countryside 1800–1914* (New Brunswick, Transaction Publishers).
Beyer, Alfred (1956) *Max von Pettenkofer* (Berlin, Berlag Volk und Gesundheit).
Boyd, Byron A. (1991) *Rudolf Virchow: The Scientist as Citizen* (New York, Garland).
Brandstrom, Anders and Tedebrand, Lars-Goran (eds) (1988) *Society, Health and Population During the Demographic Transition* (Stockholm, Almqvist and Wiksell International).
Coleman, William (1982) *Death is a Social Disease* (Madison, University of Wisconsin Press).
——(1987) *Yellow Fever in the North. The Methods of Early Epidemiology* (Madison, University of Wisconsin Press).
Elwitt, Sanford (1986) *The Third Republic Defended: Bourgeois Reform in France 1880–1914* (Baton Rouge, Louisiana State University Press).
Evans, R.J. (1987) *Death In Hamburg. Society and Politics in the Cholera Years 1830–1910* (Oxford, Clarendon Press).
Faure, Olivier (1989) 'Les Politiques sociales de la santé au XIXe siècle', *Cahiers de la recherche en travail social* 16: 29–38.
Goubert, Jean-Pierre (1989) *The Conquest of Water: The Advent of Health in the Industrial Age* translated by Andrew Wilson (Princeton, NJ, Princeton University Press).
Hannaway, Caroline (1981) 'From Private Hygiene to Public Health: A Transformation in Western Medicine in the Eighteenth and Nineteenth Centuries' in T. Ogawa (ed.) *Public Health* (Tokyo, Tanaguchi Foundation) 108–127.
Heidenheimer, Arnold J. and Elvander, Nils (eds) (1980) *The Shaping of the Swedish Health System* (London, Croom Helm).
Heuerkamp, C. (1985) 'The History of Smallpox Vaccination in Germany: A First Step in the Medicalization of the General Public', *Journal of Contemporary History* 20: 617–635.
Hildreth, Martha Lee (1987) *Doctors, Bureaucrats and Public Health in France* (New York, Garland).
Johannisson, Karin (1994) 'The People's Health: Public Health Policies in Sweden' in Dorothy Porter (ed.) *The History of Public Health and the Modern State* (Amsterdam and Atlanta, Rodopi) 165–182.
La Berge, Anne (1984) 'The Early Nineteenth-Century French Public Health Movement: The Disciplinary Development and Institutionalization of *hygiène publique*', *Bulletin for the History of Medicine* 58: 363–379.

——(1988) 'Edwin Chadwick and the French Connection', *Bulletin of the History of Medicine* 62: 23–41.
——(1992) *Mission and Method: The Early Nineteenth-Century French Public Health Movement* (Cambridge, Cambridge University Press).
La Berge, Anne and Feingold, Mordechai (eds) (1994) *French Medical Culture in the Nineteenth Century* (Amsterdam and Atlanta, Rodopi).
Latour, Bruno (1986) *Microbes: The Pasteurization of France* translated by Alan Sheridan and John Law (Cambridge, Mass., Harvard University Press).
Mitchell, Alan (1991) 'The Function and Malfunction of Mutual Aid Societies in Nineteenth Century France' in Jonathan Barry and Colin Jones (eds) *Medicine and Charity Before the Welfare State* (London, Routledge) 149–171.
Ramsey, Matthew (1994) 'Public Health in France' in Dorothy Porter (ed.) *The History of Public Health and the Modern State* (Amsterdam and Atlanta, Rodopi) 45–118.
Sand, René (1952) *The Advance to Social Medicine* (London, Staples Press).
Steudler, François (1986) 'The State and Health in France', *Social Science and Medicine* 22: 211–221.
Virchow, Rudolf (1986) *Public Health Reports* edited by L. J. Rather, 2 vols (Maryland, Science History Publications) vol. I, 307–319.
Weindling, Paul (1984) 'Was Social Medicine Revolutionary? Virchow on Famine and Typhus in 1848', *Bulletin of the Society for the Social History of Medicine* 34: 13–18.
——(1994) 'Public Health in Germany' in Dorothy Porter (ed.) *The History of Public Health and the Modern State* (Amsterdam and Atlanta, Rodopi) 119–131.
Wilson, Dorothy (1979) *The Welfare State in Sweden. A Study in Comparative Social Administration* (London, Heinemann).

7 PUBLIC HEALTH AND CENTRALIZATION: THE VICTORIAN BRITISH STATE

Barrington, Ruth (1987) *Health, Medicine and Politics in Ireland 1900–1970* (Dublin, Institute of Public Administration).
Barry, Jonathan and Jones, Colin (eds) (1991) *Medicine and Charity Before the Welfare State* (London, Routledge).
Brundage, Anthony (1988) *England's 'Prussian Minister': Edwin Chadwick and the Politics of Government Growth, 1832–1854* (University Park, Pa., Penn State University Press).
Clark, G. Kitson (1959) 'Statesmen in Disguise: Reflections on the History of the Neutrality of the Civil Service', *Historical Journal* 2: 19–39.
Crowther, M.A. (1981) *The Workhouse System 1834–1929* (London, Batsford Academic and Educational Press).
——(1984) 'Paupers or Patients? Obstacles to Professionalization in the Poor Law Medical Service Before 1914', *Journal of the History of Medicine* 39: 33–54.
Edsall, N.C. (1971) *The Anti-Poor Law Movement, 1834–1844* (Manchester, Manchester University Press).
Evans, Eric J. (ed.) (1978) *Social Policy 1830–1914: Individualism, Collectivism and the Origins of the Welfare State* (London, Routledge and Kegan Paul).
Eyler, John M. (1992) 'The Sick Poor and the State: Arthur Newsholme on Poverty, Disease and Responsibility' in Charles Rosenberg and Janet Golden (eds) *Framing Disease* (New Brunswick, Rutgers University Press) 275–297.
Finer, S. (1952) *The Life and Times of Edwin Chadwick* (London, Methuen).
——(1972) 'The Transmission of Benthamite Ideas 1820–50' in Gillian Sutherland (ed.) *Studies in the Growth of Nineteenth-Century Government* (London, Routledge and Kegan Paul) 11–32.

Flinn, Michael (1965) 'Introduction' in Edwin Chadwick, *Report on the Sanitary Condition of the Labouring Classes of Great Britain, 1842* edited by M. Flinn (reprinted, Edinburgh, Edinburgh University Press).

Fraser, D. (1973) *The Evolution of the British Welfare State. A History of Social Policy Since the Industrial Revolution* (London, Macmillan).

Fraser Brockington, Colin (1956) *A Short History of Public Health* (London, Churchill).

Frazer, William (1947) *Duncan of Liverpool. Being an Account of the Work of Dr W. H. Duncan Medical Officer of Health of Liverpool 1847–63* (London, Hamish Hamilton Medical Books).

——(1950) *History of English Public Health 1834–1939* (London, Ballière, Tindall and Cox).

Hamlin, Christopher (1990) *A Science of Impurity. Water Analysis in Nineteenth-Century Britain* (Bristol, Adam Hilger).

——(1997) *Public Health and Social Justice in the Age of Chadwick* (Cambridge, Cambridge University Press).

Hardy, Anne (1984) 'Water and the Search for Public Health in London in the Eighteenth and Nineteenth Centuries', *Medical History* 28: 250–282.

——(1993) *The Epidemic Streets. Infectious Disease and the Rise of Preventive Medicine 1856–1900* (Oxford, Clarendon Press).

Himelfarb, Gertrude (1984) *The Idea of Poverty. England in the Early Industrial Age* (New York, Knopf).

Hobsbawm, Eric J. (1962) *The Age of Revolution 1749–1848* (New York, Mentor Books).

Hodgkinson, Ruth (1967) *The Origins of the National Health Service. The Medical Services of the New Poor Law, 1836–1871* (London, Wellcome Institute).

Hollis, P. (ed.) (1973) *Class and Conflict in Nineteenth-Century England* (London, Routledge and Kegan Paul).

James, Patricia (1979) *Population Malthus. His Life and Times* (London, Routledge and Kegan Paul).

Jones, Gareth Stedman (1983) *Languages of Class: Studies in English Working-Class History 1832–1982* (Cambridge, Cambridge University Press).

Lambert, Royston (1963) *John Simon and British Sanitary Administration* (London, Macgibbon and Key).

Lewis, R.A. (1952) *Edwin Chadwick and the Public Health Movement* (London, Longmans and Green).

Lubenow, William C. (1971) *The Politics of Government Growth: Early Victorian Attitude Toward State Intervention 1833–1848* (Newton Abbot, David and Charles).

Luckin, Bill (1984) 'Evaluating the Sanitary Revolution: Typhus and Typhoid in London' in R. Woods and J. Woodward (eds), *Urban Disease and Mortality in 19th Century England* (London, Batsford Academic) 111–116.

——(1986) *Pollution and Control: A Social History of the Thames in the Nineteenth Century* (Bristol, Adam Hilger).

MacDonagh, Oliver (1958) 'The Nineteenth-Century Revolution in Government: A Reappraisal', *Historical Journal* 1: 52–67.

McKeown, Thomas (1976a) *The Modern Rise of Population* (London, Edward Arnold).

——(1976b) *The Role of Medicine – Dream, Mirage or Nemesis* (London, Nuffield Provincial Trust).

Macleod, Roy (1967) 'The Frustration of State Medicine 1880–1907', *Medical History* 11: 15–40.

——(1968) 'The Anatomy of State Medicine: Concept and Application' in F.N.L. Poynter, *Medicine and Science in the 1860s* (London, Wellcome Institute) 199–227.

Morris, R.J. (1976) *Cholera 1832. The Social Response to an Epidemic* (London, Croom Helm).

Pelling, Margaret (1978) *Cholera Fever and English Medicine 1825–1865* (Oxford, Oxford University Press).

Pickstone, John (1985) *Medicine and Industrial Society. A History of Hospital Development in Manchester and its Region* (Manchester, Manchester University Press).

Porter, Dorothy (ed.) (1990a) 'The Ghost of Edwin Chadwick', *British Medical Journal* 301 (4 August): 252.

——(1990b) 'How Soon is Now? Public Health and the *BMJ*', *British Medical Journal* 301: 738–740.

——(1994) 'Introduction' in D. Porter (ed.) *The History of Public Health and the Modern State* (Amsterdam and Atlanta, Rodopi) 1–45.

——(1997) 'Public Health and Centralisation: The Victorian State' in Walter Holland, Roger Detels and George Knox (eds) *Third Oxford Text Book of Public Health*, 2 vols (Oxford, Oxford University Press) vol. 1, 19–34.

Porter, D. and Porter, R. (1988) 'The Politics of Prevention: Anti-Vaccinationism and Public Health in Nineteenth-Century England', *Medical History* 32: 231–252.

Roberts, David (1969) 'Jeremy Bentham and the Victorian Administrative State', *Victorian Studies* 2: 193–210.

——(1979) *Paternalism in Early Victorian England* (New Brunswick, NJ, Rutgers University Press).

Rose, Michael (1991) *The Relief of Poverty* (London, Macmillan).

Rosenberg, Charles (1962) *The Cholera Years 1832, 1849 and 1866* (Chicago, University of Chicago Press).

Shryock, R.H. (1979) *The Development of Modern Medicine. An Interpretation of the Social and Scientific Factors Involved* (Madison, University of Wisconsin Press).

Smith, F.B. (1979) *The People's Health 1830–1910* (London, Croom Helm).

Szreter, Simon (1988) 'The Importance of Social Intervention in Britain's Mortality Decline c.1850–1914: a Re-Interpretation of the Role of Public Health', *Social History of Medicine* 1: 1–37.

Thompson, Edward (1970) *The Making of the English Working Class* (Harmondsworth, Penguin).

Watkins, D.E. (1984) *The English Revolution in Social Medicine, 1989–1911* (Ph.D. thesis, University of London).

Webb, R.K. (1993) 'Thomas Southwood Smith. The Intellectual Sources for Public Services', in Dorothy Porter and Roy Porter (eds) *Doctors and Politics* (Amsterdam, Rodopi).

Webster, Charles (1988) *Problems of Health Care, The National Health Service Before 1957* (London, H.M.S.O.).

Williams, K. (1981) *From Pauperism to Poverty* (London, Routledge and Kegan Paul).

Wohl, A.S. (1975) *The Eternal Slum. Housing and Social Policy in Victorian London* (London, Edward Arnold).

——(1984) *Endangered Lives. Public Health Reform in Victorian Britain* (London, Methuen).

Woods, R. and Woodward, J. (eds) (1984) *Urban Disease and Mortality in 19th Century England* (London, Batsford Academic).

8 THE ENFORCEMENT OF HEALTH AND RESISTANCE

Baxby, Derek (1981) *Jenner's Smallpox Vaccine: The Riddle of Vaccinia Virus and Its Origin* (London, Heinemann Educational).

Beardsley, E.H. (1976) 'Allied Against Sin: American and British Responses to Venereal Disease in World War I', *Medical History* 20: 189–202.

Brand, Jeanne (1965) *Doctors and the State. The British Medical Profession and Government Action in Public Health, 1870–1912* (Baltimore, Johns Hopkins University Press).

Brandt, Allan (1987) *No Magic Bullet. A Social History of Venereal Disease in the United States since 1880* (New York, Oxford University Press).

——(1992) 'Sexually Transmitted Diseases', in W. F. Bynum and R. Porter (eds) *Encyclopaedia of the History of Medicine* (London, Routledge) 562–584.

Cooter, Roger (ed.) (1988) *Studies in the History of Alternative Medicine* (London, Macmillan).

Eyler, John (1997) *Sir Arthur Newsholme and State Medicine 1885–1935* (Cambridge, Cambridge University Press).

Fraser, S.M. (1980) 'Leicester and Smallpox: The Leicester Method', *Medical History* 24: 315–332.

Hardy, Anne (1983) 'Smallpox in London. Factors in the Decline of the Disease in the Nineteenth Century', *Medical History* 27: 111–138.

Henderson, Donald (1976) 'The Eradication of Smallpox', *Scientific American* 235: 25–33.

Hopkins, Donald R. (1983) *Princes and Peasants: Smallpox in History* (Chicago, University of Chicago Press).

Kaufman, Martin (1967) 'The American Anti-Vaccinationists and their Arguments', *Bulletin of the History of Medicine* 41: 463–483.

Lambert, Royston (1963) *John Simon and British Sanitary Administration* (London, Macgibbon and Key).

Leavitt, J.W. (1976) 'Politics and Public Health: Smallpox in Milwaukee, 1894–1895', *Bulletin of the History of Medicine* 50: 553–568.

Luckin, Bill (1977) 'The Decline of Smallpox and the Demographic Revolution of the Nineteenth Century', *Social History* 6: 793–797.

Mchugh, Paul (1982) *Prostitution and Victorian Social Reform* (London, Croom Helm).

Mercer, A.J. (1985) 'Smallpox and Epidemiological-Demographic Change in Europe: The Role of Vaccination', *Population Studies* 39: 287–307.

Mill, John Stuart (1986) *On Liberty* (Harmondsworth, Penguin Classics; first edition 1859).

Mooney, Graham (1997) ' "A Tissue of the Most Flagrant Anomalies", Smallpox Vaccination and the Centralization of Sanitary Administration in Nineteenth-Century London', *Medical History* 41: 261–290.

Mort, Frank (1987) *Dangerous Sexualities: Medico-Moral Politics in England Since 1830* (London, Routledge and Kegan Paul).

Porter, Dorothy (1985) 'Theories of Disease in the Work of Edmund Parkes', *Bulletin of the Society for the Social History of Medicine* 37: 40–42.

——(1991a) 'Stratification and its Discontents: Professionalisation and Conflict in the British Public Health Service', in Elizabeth Fee and Roy Acheson (eds) *The History of Education in Public Health. Health that Mocks the Doctors' Rules* (Oxford, Oxford Medical Publications) 83–113.

——(1991b) ' "Enemies of the Race": Biologism, Environmentalism and the Public Health in Edwardian England', *Victorian Studies* 34 (2): 159–178.

Porter, D. and Fee, E. (1992) 'Public Health, Preventive Medicine and Professionalisation in England and America, 1848–1914' in A. Wear (ed.) *The History of Medicine in Society* (Cambridge, Cambridge University Press) 249–275.

Porter, D. and Porter, R. (1988) 'The Politics of Prevention: Anti-Vaccinationism and Public Health in Nineteenth-Century England', *Medical History* 32: 231–252.

——(1989) 'The Enforcement of Health' in E. Fee and D. Fox (eds) *AIDS: The Burdens of History* (Berkeley, Ca., University of California Press) 97–121.

Razell, Peter (1980) *Edward Jenner's Cowpox Vaccine: The History of a Medical Myth* (Firle, Sussex).

Smith, F.B. (1990) 'The Contagious Diseases Acts Reconsidered', *Social History of Medicine* 3: 197–217.

Walkowitz, J. (1980) *Prostitution and Victorian Society: Women, Class and the State* (Cambridge, Cambridge University Press).

Watkins, Dorothy E. (1984) *The English Revolution in Social Medicine, 1989–1911* (Ph.D. thesis, University of London).

9 LOCALIZATION AND HEALTH SALVATION IN THE UNITED STATES

Anderson, Letty (1984) 'Hard Choices: Supplying Water to New England', *Journal of Interdisciplinary History* 15: 211–234.

Brandt, Allan (1987) *No Magic Bullet. A Social History of Venereal Disease in the United States since 1880* (New York, Oxford University Press).

Brewer, Paul W. (1975) 'Voluntarism on Trial: St. Louis Response to the Cholera Epidemic of 1849', *Bulletin of the History of Medicine* 49: 102–122.

Brieger, Gert H. (1966) 'Sanitary Reform in New York City: Stephen Smith and the Passage of the Metropolitan Health Bill', *Bulletin of the History of Medicine* 40: 407–429.

Brogan, Hugh (1985) *Longman History of the United States of America* (London, Longman).

Brown, E. Richard (1979) *Rockefeller Medicine Men. Medicine and Capitalism in America* (Berkeley, University of California Press).

Cassedy, James (1962) *Charles V. Chapin and the Public Health Movement* (Cambridge, Mass., Harvard University Press).

——(1984) *American Medicine and Statistical Thinking, 1800–1860* (Cambridge, Mass., Harvard University Press).

Chapman, Carlton B. (1994) *Order Out of Chaos. John Shaw Billings and America's Coming of Age* (Boston, Boston Medical Library).

Colburn, David R. and Pozzetta, George E. (eds) (1983) *Reform and Reformers in the Progressive Era* (Westport, Conn., Greenwood).

Davis, Allen F. (1984) *Spearheads for Reform. The Social Settlements and the Progressive Movement, 1890–1914* (New Brunswick, NJ, Rutgers University Press).

Delaporte, François (1991) *The History of Yellow Fever. An Essay on the Birth of Tropical Medicine* (Cambridge, Mass., MIT Press).

Duffy, John (1966) *The Sword of Pestilence. The New Orleans Yellow Fever Epidemic of 1853* (Baton Rouge, Louisiana State University Press).

——(1968–1974) *A History of Public Health in New York City 1625–1866*, 2 vols (New York, Russell Sage Foundation).

——(1990) *The Sanitarians. A History of American Public Health* (Urbana and Chicago, University of Illinois Press).

Ellis, John (1970) 'Businessmen and Public Health in the Urban South During the Nineteenth Century: New Orleans, Memphis and Atlanta', *Bulletin of the History of Medicine* 44: 197–212; 346–371.

Ettling, John (1981) *The Germ of Laziness: Rockefeller Philanthropy and Public Health in the New South* (Cambridge, Mass., Harvard University Press).

Fee, Elizabeth (1987) *Disease and Discovery. A History of the Johns Hopkins School of Hygiene and Public Health, 1916–1939* (Baltimore, Johns Hopkins University Press).

Galishoff, Stuart (1988) *Newark, The Nation's Unhealthiest City 1832–1895* (New Brunswick, Rutgers University Press).

Harrell, L.D.S (1966) 'Preventive Medicine in the Mississippi Territory, 1799–1802', *Bulletin of the History of Medicine* 40: 365–375.

Leavitt, Judith W. (1982) *The Healthiest City. Milwaukee and the Politics of Health Reform* (Princeton, NJ, Princeton University Press).

Marcus, Alan (1979) 'Disease Prevention in America: From a Local to a National Outlook, 1880–1910', *Bulletin of the History of Medicine* 53: 184–203.

Melosi, Martin V. (ed.) (1980) *Pollution and Reform in American Cities, 1870–1930* (Austin, University of Texas Press).

Mullan, Fitshugh (1989) *Plagues and Politics. The Story of the United States Public Health Service* (New York, Basic Books).

Porter, Dorothy and Fee, Elizabeth (1992) 'Public Health, Preventive Medicine and Professionalization in England and America, 1848–1914' in A. Wear (ed.) *The History of Medicine in Society* (Cambridge, Cambridge University Press) 249–275.

Rimini, Robert V. (1976) *The Revolutionary Age of Andrew Jackson* (New York, Harper and Row).

——(1984) *Andrew Jackson and the Course of American Democracy, 1835–1845* (New York, Harper and Row).

Roe, Daphene (1973) *A Plague of Corn. The Social History of Pellagra* (Ithaca, Cornell University Press).

Rosen, George (1988) 'Urbanization, Occupation and Disease in the United States, 1870–1920. The Case of New York City', *Journal of the History of Medicine and Allied Sciences* 43: 391–425.

Rosenberg, Charles (1962) *The Cholera Years 1832, 1849 and 1866* (Chicago, University of Chicago Press).

Rosenberg, Charles and Smith-Rosenberg, Carol (1968) 'Pietism and the Origins of the American Public Health Movement', *Journal of the History of Medicine and Allied Sciences* 23: 6–34.

Rosenkrantz, B.G. (1972) *Public Health and the State. Changing Views in Massachusetts, 1842–1936* (Cambridge, Mass., Harvard University Press).

——(1974) 'Cart Before Horse: Theory, Practice and Professional Image in American Public Health', *Journal of the History of Medicine and Allied Sciences* 29: 55–73.

——(1985) 'The Search for Professional Order in Nineteenth Century American Medicine' in J. Leavitt and R. Numbers (eds) *Sickness and Health in America. Readings in the History of Medicine and Public Health* (Madison, University of Wisconsin Press) 219–232.

Savitt, Todd and Young, James Havery (eds) (1988) *Disease and Distinctiveness in the American South* (Knoxville, University of Tennessee Press).

Thomas, H. (1968) 'Yellowjack, The Yellow Fever Epidemic of 1878 in Memphis, Tennessee', *Bulletin of the History of Medicine* 42: 241–263.

Thompson, J.A. (1979) *Progressivism* (Durham, Elvet Riverside, University of Durham, British Association for American Studies).

Waring, Joseph Ioor (1966) 'Asiatic Cholera in South Carolina', *Bulletin of the History of Medicine* 40: 459–475.

Warner, Margaret (1985) 'Hunting the Yellow Fever Germ: The Principle and Practice of Etiological Proof in Late Nineteenth-Century America', *Bulletin of the History of Medicine* 59: 361–382.

Wasserman, Manfred (1975) 'The Quest for a National Health Department in the Progressive Era', *Bulletin of the History of Medicine* 49: 353–380.

Watson, Richard L. (1982) *The Development of National Power in the United States 1900–1919* (Washington, D.C., University Press of America).

10 THE QUALITY OF POPULATION AND FAMILY WELFARE: HUMAN REPRODUCTION, EUGENICS AND SOCIAL POLICY

Allan, Garland E. (1991) 'Old Wine in New Bottles: From Eugenics to Population Control in the Work of Raymond Pearl' in Keith R. Benson, Jane Maienschein and Ronald

Rainger (eds) *The Expansion of American Biology* (New Brunswick, Rutgers University Press) 195–230.

Andreski, Stanislav (ed.) (1971) *Herbert Spencer: Structure, Function and Evolution* (London, Michael Joseph).

Armstrong, David (1983) *The Political Anatomy of the Body* (Cambridge, Cambridge University Press).

Bannister, Robert (1979) *Social Darwinism: Science and Myth in British-American Social Thought* (Philadelphia, Temple University Press).

Bock, Gisela (1991) 'Antinatalism, Maternity and Paternity in National Socialist Racism' in Gisela Bock and Pat Thane, *Maternity and Gender Policy. Women and the Rise of the European Welfare States 1880s–1950s* (London, Routledge) 233–255.

——(1997) 'Sterilization and "Medical" Massacres in National Socialist Germany' in Manfred Berg and Geoffrey Cocks (eds) *Medicine and Modernity. Public Health and Medical Care in Nineteenth and Twentieth-Century Germany* (Cambridge, Cambridge University Press)149–172.

Bowler, Peter (1989) *Evolution. The History of an Idea* (Berkeley, University of California Press; revised edition, first edition 1983).

Bryder, Linda (1994) 'A New World? Two Hundred Years of Public Health in Australia and New Zealand' in D. Porter (ed.) *The History of Public Health and the Modern State* (Amsterdam and Atlanta, Rodopi) 313–334.

Buttafuoco, Annarita (1991) 'Motherhood as a Political Strategy: The Role of the Italian Women's Movement in the Creation of the *Cassa Nazionale di Maternià*' in Gisela Bock and Pat Thane, *Maternity and Gender Policy. Women and the Rise of the European Welfare States 1880s–1950s* (London, Routledge) 178–195.

Cassel, Jay (1994) 'Public Health in Canada' in D. Porter (ed.) *The History of Public Health and the Modern State* (Amsterdam and Atlanta, Rodopi) 276–312.

Chamberlin, J. Edward and Gilman, Sander (eds) (1985) *Degeneration. The Dark Side of Progress* (New York, Guildford, Columbia University Press).

Cohen, M. and Hanagan, M. (1991) 'The Politics of Gender and the Making of the Welfare State: A Comparative Perspective', *Journal of Social History* 24: 469–484.

Davies, Celia (1988) 'The Health Visitor as Mother's Friend', *Social History of Medicine* 1: 39–60.

Davin, Anna (1978) 'Imperialism and the Cult of Motherhood', *History Workshop Journal* 5: 9–66.

Digby, Anne (1996) 'Poverty, Health and the Politics of Gender in Britain, 1870–1948' in Anne Digby and John Stewart (eds) *Gender, Health and Welfare* (London, Routledge) 67–90.

Dwork, Deborah (1987) *War is Good for Babies and Other Young Children. A History of the Infant and Child Welfare Movement in England 1898–1918* (London, Tavistock).

Evans, Richard J. (1997) 'In Search of German Social Darwinism. The History and Historiography of a Concept' in Manfred Berg and Geoffrey Cocks (eds) *Medicine and Modernity. Public Health and Medical Care in Nineteenth and Twentieth-Century Germany* (Cambridge, Cambridge University Press) 55–79.

Eyler, John (1997) *Sir Arthur Newsholme and State Medicine, 1885–1935* (Cambridge, Cambridge University Press).

Farrell, Lyndsey A. (1985) *The Origins and Growth of the English Eugenics Movement, 1865–1925* (New York, Garland Publishing).

Forrest, D.W. (1974) *Francis Galton. The Life and Work of a Victorian Genius* (London, Paul Elek).

Freeden, Michael (1979) 'Eugenics and Progressive Thought: a Study in Ideological Affinity', *The Historical Journal* 22 (3): 645–671.

Geison, Gerald (1969) 'Darwin and Heredity: The Evolution of His Hypothesis of Pangenesis', *Journal of the History of Medicine and Allied Sciences* 24: 251–263.

Glass, D.V. (1936) *The Struggle for Population* (Oxford, Clarendon Press).

Haller, Mark (1984) *Eugenics: Hereditarian Attitudes in American Thought* (New Brunswick, NJ, Rutgers University Press).

Hirst, J.D. (1981) ' "A Failure Without Parallel": The School Medical Service and the London County Council 1907–12', *Medical History* 25: 281–300.

Hoggart, Lesley (1996) 'The Campaign for Birth Control in Britain in the 1920s' in Anne Digby and John Stewart (eds) *Gender, Health and Welfare* (London, Routledge) 141–166.

Hollis, Patricia (1987) *Ladies Elect. Women in Local Government, 1865–1914* (Oxford, Clarendon Press).

Johannisson, Karin (1994) 'The People's Health: Public Health Policies in Sweden' in Dorothy Porter (ed.) *The History of Public Health and the Modern State* (Amsterdam and Atlanta, Rodopi) 165–182.

Jones, Greta (1980) *Social Darwinism and English Thought: The Interaction between Biological and Social Theory* (Brighton, Harvester Press).

——(1986) *Social Hygiene in Britain* (London, Croom Helm).

Jones, Helen (1994) *Health and Society in Twentieth-Century Britain* (London, Longman).

Kelly, Hugh (1996) *The Gothic Body. Sexuality, Materialism and Degeneration at the Fin de Siècle* (Cambridge, Cambridge University Press).

Kevles, Daniel (1968) 'Testing the Army's Intelligence: Psychologists and the Military in World War I', *Journal of American History* 55: 565–581.

——(1985) *In the Name of Eugenics. Genetics and the Uses of Human Heredity* (New York: Knopf).

Koven, Seth and Michel, Sonya (eds) (1983) *Mothers of a New World: Maternalist Politics and the Origins of Welfare States* (London, Routledge).

——(1990) 'Womanly Duties: Maternalist Politics and the Origins of Welfare States in France, Germany, Great Britain and the United States', *American Historical Review* XCV: 1095–1108.

Ladd-Taylor, M. (1994) *Mother-Work. Women, Children, Welfare and the State, 1890–1930* (Urbana and Chicago, University of Illinois Press).

Leavitt, Judith W. (1986) *Brought to Bed: Childbearing in America 1750–1950* (Oxford, Oxford University Press).

Lewis, Jane (1980) *The Politics of Motherhood. Child and Maternal Welfare in England 1900–1939* (London, Croom Helm).

——(1983) *Women's Welfare, Women's Rights* (London, Croom Helm).

——(1991) *Women and Social Action in Victorian and Edwardian England* (Brighton, Wheatsheaf).

——(1994) 'Gender, the Family and Women's Agency in the Building of "Welfare States": The British Case', *Social History* 19: 37–55.

——(1996a) 'The Boundaries Between Voluntary and Statutory Social Service in the Nineteenth and Early Twentieth Centuries', *Historical Journal* 39: 155–177.

——(1996b) 'Gender and Welfare in the Late Nineteenth and Early Twentieth Centuries' in Anne Digby and John Stewart (eds) *Gender, Health and Welfare* (London, Routledge) 208–228.

Loudon, I.S.L. (1992) *Death in Childbirth: An International Study of Maternal Care and Maternal Mortality 1800–1950* (London, Oxford University Press).

Ludmerer, Kenneth (1972) 'Genetics, Eugenics and the Immigration Restriction Act of 1924', *Bulletin of the History of Medicine* 46: 59–81.

MacKenzie, Donald (1981) *Statistics in Britain, 1865–1930* (Edinburgh: Edinburgh University Press).

Macnicol, John (1980) *The English Movement for Family Allowances* (London, Heinemann).

——(1989) 'Eugenics and Campaign for Voluntary Sterilization in Britain Between the Wars', *Social History of Medicine* 2: 147–170.

Marks, Lara (1996) *Metropolitan Maternity. Maternal and Infant Welfare Services in Early Twentieth-Century London* (Amsterdam and Atlanta, Rodopi).

Mazumdar, Pauline (1992) *Eugenics, Genetics and Human Failings* (London, Routledge).

Nordau, Max Simon (1993) *Degeneration*, reprinted with a new introduction by George L. Mosse (Lincoln, University of Nebraska Press, translated into English from the second edition in 1895).

Offen, Karen (1991) 'Body Politics: Women, Work and the Politics of Motherhood in France, 1920–1950' in Gisela Bock and Pat Thane, *Maternity and Gender Policy. Women and the Rise of the European Welfare States 1880s–1950s* (London, Routledge) 138–159.

Ohlander, Ann-Sofie (1991) 'The Invisible Child? The Struggle for a Social Democratic Family Policy in Sweden, 1900–1960s' in Gisela Bock and Pat Thane, *Maternity and Gender Policy. Women and the Rise of the European Welfare States 1880s–1950s* (London, Routledge) 60–71.

Paul, Diane (1984) 'Eugenics and the Left', *Journal of the History of Ideas* 45: 567–590.

Pederson, Susan (1993) *Family Dependence and the Origins of the Welfare State. Britain and France 1914–1945* (Cambridge, Cambridge University Press).

Peel, J.D.Y. (ed.) (1972) *Herbert Spencer on Social Evolution. Selected Writings* (Chicago, University of Chicago Press).

Pick, Daniel (1989) *Faces of Degeneration. A European Disorder, c.1848–1918* (Cambridge, Cambridge University Press).

Pickens, Donald, K. (1968) *Eugenics and the Progressives* (Nashville, Vanderbilt University Press).

Porter, Dorothy (1991a) ' "Enemies of the Race": Biologism, Environmentalism and the Public Health in Edwardian England', *Victorian Studies* 34 (2): 159–178.

——(1991b) 'Stratification and its Discontents: Professionalisation and Conflict in the British Public Health Service' in Elizabeth Fee and Roy Acheson (eds) *The History of Education in Public Health. Health that Mocks the Doctors' Rules* (Oxford, Oxford Medical Publications) 83–113.

——(forthcoming) *Medicine and Social Science in Britain in the Twentieth Century*.

Proctor, Robert N. (1988) *Racial Hygiene. Medicine Under the Nazis* (Cambridge, Mass., Harvard University Press).

Ramsey, Matthew (1994) 'Public Health in France' in Dorothy Porter (ed.) *The History of Public Health and the Modern State* (Amsterdam and Atlanta, Rodopi) 45–118.

Saraceno, Chiara (1991) 'Redefining Maternity and Paternity: Gender, Pronatalism and Social Policies in Fascist Italy' in Gisela Bock and Pat Thane, *Maternity and Gender Policy. Women and the Rise of the European Welfare States 1880s–1950s* (London, Routledge) 196–212.

Searle, Geoffrey R. (1971) *The Quest for National Efficiency. A Study in British Politics and Political Thought, 1899–1914* (Berkeley, University of California Press).

——(1976) *Eugenics and Politics in Britain 1900–1914* (Leyden, Noordhoff).

Skocpol, Theda (1992) *Protecting Soldiers and Mothers. The Political Origins of Social Policy in the United States* (Cambridge, Mass., Harvard University Press).

Smith, F.B. (1979) *The People's Health 1830–1910* (London, Croom Helm).

Soloway, Richard Allen (1982) *Birth Control and the Population Question in England, 1877–1930* (Chapel Hill, University of North Carolina Press).

——(1990) *Demography and Degeneration* (Chapel Hill, University of North Carolina Press).

Stewart, John (1996) ' "The Children's Party, Therefore the Women's Party." The Labour Party and Child Welfare in Inter-War Britain' in Anne Digby and John Stewart (eds) *Gender, Health and Welfare* (London , Routledge) 167–188.

Szreter, Simon (1996) *Fertility, Class and Gender in Britain 1860–1940* (Cambridge, Cambridge University Press).

Thane, Pat (1991) 'Visions of Gender in the Making of the British Welfare State: The Case of Women in the British Labour Party and Social Policy, 1906–1945' in Gisela

Bock and Pat Thane (eds) *Maternity and Gender Policy. Women and the Rise of the European Welfare States 1880s–1950s* (London, Routledge) 93–118.

Watkins, Dorothy E. (1984) *The English Revolution in Social Medicine* (Ph.D. thesis, University of London).

Weindling, Paul (1989) *Health, Race and German Politics Between National Unification and Nazism 1870–1945* (Cambridge, Cambridge University Press).

——(1990) 'Eugenics and the Welfare State During the Weimar Republic' in W.R. Lee and Eve Rosenhaft (eds) *The State and Social Change in Germany, 1880–1980* (Munich, Berg) 131–160.

11 HEALTH AND THE RISE OF THE CLASSIC WELFARE STATE

Altenstetter, Christa (1982) *The Implementation of National Health Insurance Seen from the Perspective of General Sickness Funds (AOKs) in the Federal Republic of Germany, 1955–1975* (Berlin, Wissenschaftszentrum).

Anderson, Odin W. (1975) *Blue Cross Since 1929. Accountability and the Public Trust* (Cambridge, Mass., Ballinger).

——(1985) *Health Services in the United States. A Growth Enterprise Since 1875* (Ann Arbor, Michigan, Health Administration Press).

Ashford, Douglas (1986) *The Emergence of Welfare States* (Oxford, Basil Blackwell).

Burrow, James G. (1977) *Organized Medicine in the Progressive Era: The Move Toward Monopoly* (Baltimore, Johns Hopkins University Press).

Cadenhead, Ivie E. (1974) *Theodore Roosevelt. The Paradox of Progressivism* (Woodbury, NY, Barron's Educational).

Cavallo, Sandra (1991) 'The Motivations of Benefactors: An Overview of Approaches to the Study of Charity' in Jonathan Barry and Colin Jones (eds) *Medicine, Charity and the Welfare State* (London, Routledge) 46–62.

Clarke, John, Cochrane, Allan and Smart, Carol (1992) *Ideologies of Welfare: From Dreams to Disillusion* (London, Routledge).

Clarke, Peter (1990) *The Keynesian Revolution in the Making 1924–1936* (Oxford, Clarendon Press).

Crowther, M.A. (1988) *British Social Policy 1914–1945* (London, Macmillan).

Culpitt, Ian (1992) *Welfare and Citizenship. Beyond the Crisis of the Welfare State?* (London, Sage).

Daunton, Martin (1996) 'Payment and Participation: Welfare and State Formation in Britain 1900–1951', *Past and Present* 150: 169–216.

Deakin, Nicholas (1994) *The Politics of Welfare. Continuities and Change* (London, Harvester/Wheatsheaf).

Digby, Anne (1996) 'Medicine and the English State, 1901–1948' in S.J.D. Green and R. C. Whiting, *The Boundaries of the State in Modern Britain* (Cambridge, Cambridge University Press) 213–231.

Ekirch, Arthur A. (1974) *Progressivism in America. A Study of the Era from Theodore Roosevelt to Woodrow Wilson* (New York, New Viewpoints).

Esping-Anderson, Gosta (1990) *The Three Worlds of Welfare Capitalism* (Cambridge, Polity Press).

——(1997) 'After the Golden Age? Welfare State Dilemmas in a Global Economy' in Gosta Esping-Anderson (ed.) *Welfare States in Transition. National Adaptations in Global Economies* (London, Sage) 1–31.

Evans, Peter, Rueschemeyer, Dietrich and Skocpol, Theda (eds) (1985) *Bringing the State Back In* (Cambridge, Cambridge University Press).

Finlayson, Geoffrey (1994) *Citizen, State, and Social Welfare in Britain 1830–1990* (Oxford, Clarendon Press).

Fox, Daniel (1986) *Health Policies, Health Politics, The British and American Experiences* (Princeton, NJ, Princeton University Press).

——(1993) *Power and Illness. The Failure and Future of American Health Policy* (Berkeley and Los Angeles, University of California Press).

Fraser, Derek (1973) *The Evolution of the British Welfare State. A History of Social Policy Since the Industrial Revolution* (London, Macmillan).

Gilbert, Bentley (1966)*The Evolution of National Insurance in Great Britain. The Origins of the Welfare State* (London, Michael Joseph).

Greenleaf, W.H. (1983) *The British Political Tradition: Volume 1. The Rise of Collectivism* (London, Methuen).

Grey, Michael R. (1989) 'Poverty, Politics and Health: The Farm Security Administration Medical Care Program, 1935–1945', *Journal of the History of Medicine and Allied Sciences* 44: 320–350.

Harris, Jose (1992) 'Political Thought and the Welfare State 1870–1940: An Intellectual Framework for British Social Policy', *Past and Present* 135: 116–141.

——(1994) *Private Lives, Public Spirit: Britain 1870–1914* (Oxford, Oxford University Press).

——(1996) 'Political Thought and the State' in S.J.D. Green and R.C. Whiting (eds) *The Boundaries of the State in Modern Britain* (Cambridge, Cambridge University Press) 15–29.

Harvey, Elizabeth (1993) *Youth and the Welfare State in the Weimar Republic* (Oxford, Clarenden Press, 1993).

Heidenheimer, Arnold J. and Elvander, Nils (eds) (1980)*The Shaping of the Swedish Health System* (London, Croom Helm).

Hennock, E.P. (1987) *British Social Reform and German Precedents. The Case of Social Insurance 1880–1914* (Oxford, Clarendon Press).

Hirshfield, D. (1970) *The Lost Reform: The Campaign for Compulsory Health Insurance in the United States from 1932 to 1943* (Cambridge, Mass., Harvard University Press).

Hollingsworth, J. Rogers, Hage, Gerald and Hanneman, Robert A. (1990) *State Intervention in Medical Care. Consequences for Britain, France, Sweden and the United States, 1890–1970* (Ithaca, Cornell University Press).

Honigsbaum, Frank (1989) *Health, Happiness and Security. The Creation of the National Health Service* (London, Routledge).

——(1993) 'Christopher Addison: a Realist in Pursuit of Dreams' in Dorothy Porter and Roy Porter (ed.) *Doctors, Politics and Society: Historical Essays* (Amsterdam and Atlanta, Rodopi) 229–246.

Jacobs, Lawrence R. (1993) *The Health of Nations. Public Opinion and the Making of American and British Health Policy* (Ithaca, Cornell University Press).

Labisch, Alfons (1997) 'From Traditional Individualism to Collective Professionalism: State, Patient, Compulsory Health Insurance, and the Patient Doctor Question in Germany, 1883–1931' in Manfred Berg and Geoffrey Cocks (eds) *Medicine and Modernity. Public Health and Medical Care in Nineteenth and Twentieth-Century Germany* (Cambridge, Cambridge University Press) 35–54.

Law, Sylvia (1976) *Blue Cross. What Went Wrong?* (New Haven, Conn., Yale University Press).

Lawson, Roger (1996) 'Germany: Maintaining the Middle Way' in Vic George and Peter Taylor-Gooby (eds) *European Welfare Policy. Squaring the Welfare Circle* (London, Macmillan Press) 31–50.

Milles, Dietrich (1990) 'Industrial Hygiene: A State Obligation? Industrial Pathology as a Problem in German Social Policy' in W. R. Lee and Eve Rosenhaft (eds) *The State and Social Change in Germany, 1880–1980* (Munich, Berg) 161–199.

Mitchell, Alan (1991a) *The Divided Path: The German Influence on Social Policy Reform in France After 1870* (Chapel Hill, The University of North Carolina Press).

——(1991b) 'The Function and Malfunction of Mutual Aid Societies in Nineteenth Century France' in Jonathan Barry and Colin Jones (eds), *Medicine and Charity Before the Welfare State* (London, Routledge) 149–171.

Mommsen, W.J. and Mock, Wolfgang (eds) (1981) *The Emergence of the Welfare State in Britain and Germany 1850–1950* (London, Croom Helm).

Numbers, Ronald (1978) *Almost Persuaded: American Physicians and Compulsory Health Insurance* (Baltimore, Johns Hopkins University Press).

Pickstone, John V. (1985) *Medicine and Industrial Society. A History of Hospital Development in Manchester and Its Regions, 1752–1946* (Manchester, Manchester University Press).

Poen, M. (1979) *Harry S. Truman Versus the Medical Lobby. The Genesis of Medicare* (Columbia, University of Missouri Press).

Ramsey, Matthew (1994) 'Public Health in France' in D. Porter (ed.) *The History of Public Health and the Modern State* (Amsterdam and Atlanta, Rodopi) 45–118.

Rosen, George (1983) *The Structure of American Medical Practice 1875–1941* (Philadelphia, University of Pennsylvania Press).

Rowbotham, Sheila (1994) 'Interpretations of Welfare and Approaches to the State, 1870–1920' in Ann Oakley and A. Susan Williams (eds), *The Politics of the Welfare State* (London, UCL Press) 18–36.

Skocpol, Theda (1985) 'Bringing the State Back In: Strategies of Analysis in Current Research' in Peter B. Evans, Dietrich Rueschemeyer and Theda Skocpol (eds) *Bringing the State Back In* (Cambridge, Cambridge University Press) 3–43.

Starr, Paul (1982) *The Social Transformation of American Medicine* (New York, Basic Books).

Thane, Pat (1985) *The Foundations of the Welfare State* (London, Longmans).

Thompson, J.A. (1979) *Progressivism* (Durham, Elvet Riverside, University of Durham, British Association for American Studies).

Vogel, Ursula and Moran, Michael (1991) 'Introduction' in Ursula Vogel and Michael Moran (eds) *The Frontiers of Citizenship* (London, Macmillan).

Webster, Charles (ed.) (1985) 'Health, Welfare and Unemployment During the Depression', *Past and Present* 109: 104–130.

——(1988) *Problems of Health Care, The National Health Service Before 1957* (London, H.M.S.O.).

——(1991) *Aneurin Bevan on the National Health Service* (Oxford, The Wellcome Unit for the History of Medicine).

Weindling, Paul (ed.) (1985) *The Social History of Occupational Health* (London, Croom Helm).

——(1990) 'Eugenics and the Welfare State During the Weimar Republic' in W. R. Lee and Eve Rosenhaft (eds) *The State and Social Change in Germany, 1880–1980* (Munich, Berg) 131–160.

——(1991) 'The Modernization of Charity in Nineteenth-Century France and Germany' in Jonathan Barry and Colin Jones (eds) *Medicine and Charity Before the Welfare State* (London, Routledge) 190–206.

——(1994) 'Public Health in Germany' in Dorothy Porter (ed.) *The History of Public Health and the Modern State* (Amsterdam and Atlanta, Rodopi) 119–131.

Weir, Margaret, Orloff, Shola Ann and Skocpol, Theda (eds) (1988) *The Politics of Social Policy in the United States* (Princeton, NJ, Princeton University Press).

Weiss, John (1983) 'Origins of the French Welfare State: Poor Relief in the Third Republic 1871–1914', *French Historical Studies* 13: 47–78.

Wilson, Dorothy (1979) *The Welfare State in Sweden. A Study in Comparative Social Administration* (London, Heinemann).

12 CONDITIONAL CITIZENSHIP: THE NEW POLITICAL ECONOMY OF HEALTH

Allardt, Erik (1986) 'The Civic Conception of the Welfare State in Scandinavia' in Richard Rose and Rei Shiratori (eds) *The Welfare State East and West* (New York, Oxford, Oxford University Press).

Apple, N. (1980) 'The Rise and Fall of Full Employment Capitalism', *Studies in Political Economy. A Socialist Review* 4: 5–39.

Barbalet, J.M. (1988) *Citizenship* (Milton Keynes, Open University Press).

Barnett, Correlli (1986) *The Audit of War: The Illusion and Reality of Britain as a Great Nation* (London, Macmillan).

Bell, Daniel (1974a) *The Coming of Post-Industrial Society. A Venture in Social Forecasting* (London, Heinemann Educational Books).

——(1974b) *The End of Ideology* (London, Heinemann Educational Books).

Butler, A. (1993) 'The End of the Post-War Consensus', *Political Quarterly* 64: 435–446.

Castles, Francis G. (1978) *The Social Democratic Image of Society: A Study of the Achievements and Origins of Scandinavian Social Democracy in Comparative Perspective* (London, Routledge and Kegan Paul).

Castles, Francis G. and Mitchell, D. (1991) *Three Worlds of Welfare Capitalism or Four?* (Canberra, Australian National University Press).

Clarke, John, Cochrane, Allan and Smart, Carol (1992) *Ideologies of Welfare: From Dreams to Disillusion* (London, Routledge).

Culpitt, Ian (1992) *Welfare and Citizenship, Beyond the Crisis of the Welfare State?* (London, Sage).

Cutler, Tony, Williams, Karel and Williams, John (1986) *Keynes, Beveridge and Beyond* (London, Routledge and Kegan Paul).

Deacon, Alan (1992) 'Whose Obligations? Work and Welfare in the 1990s', *Benefits* 5: 14–17.

——(1996) 'The Dilemmas of Welfare: Titmuss, Murray and Mead' in S.J.D. Green and R.C. Whiting (eds) *The Boundaries of the State in Modern Britain* (Cambridge, Cambridge University Press) 191–213.

Deacon, Bob (1993) 'Developments in East European Social Policy' in Catherine Jones (ed.) *New Perspectives on the Welfare State in Europe* (London, Routledge) 177–197.

Deakin, Nicholas (1994) *The Politics of Welfare: Continuities and Change* (London, Harvester).

Dean, Hartley and Taylor-Gooby, Peter (1992) *The Dependency Culture* (London, Harvester Wheatsheaf).

Diamond, Peter and Valdés-Prieto, Salvador (1994) 'Social Security Reforms' in B.P. Bosworth, Rudiger Dornbusch and Raul Labán (eds) *The Chilean Economy: Policy Lessons and Challenges* (Washington, DC, Brookings Institution) 257–320.

Digby, Anne (1989) *British Welfare Policy. Workhouse to Workfare* (London, Faber).

Esping-Anderson, Gosta (1990) *The Three Worlds of Welfare Capitalism* (Cambridge, Polity Press).

——(1997) 'After the Golden Age? Welfare State Dilemmas in a Global Economy' in Gosta Esping-Anderson (ed.) *Welfare States in Transition. National Adaptations in Global Economies* (London, Sage, 1997) 1–31.

Fee, Elizabeth and Fox, D.M. (eds) (1988) *AIDS: The Burdens of History* (Berkeley, University of California Press).

——(1992) *AIDS. The Making of a Chronic Disease* (Berkeley, University of California Press).

Flora, Peter (1986) (ed.) *Growth to Limits: the Western European Welfare State Since World War II* (Berlin, de Gruyter).

Fox, Daniel, M. (1986) *Health Policies, Health Politics, The British and American Experiences* (Princeton, NJ, Princeton University Press).

——(1993) *Power and Illness. The Failure and Future of American Health Policy* (Berkeley and Los Angeles, University of California Press).

Foxley, Alejandro (1986) 'The Neoconservative Economic Experiment in Chile' in J. Samuel Valenzuela and Arturo Valenzuela (eds) *Military Rule in Chile* (Baltimore, Johns Hopkins University Press).

Friedman, Kathi F. (1981) *Legitimation of Social Rights and the Western Welfare State: A Weberian Perspective* (Chapel Hill, University of North Carolina Press).

Friedman, M. and Friedman, R. (1980) *Free to Choose* (Harmondsworth, Penguin).

Friedman, R., Gilbert, Neil and Sherer, Moshe (eds) (1987) *Modern Welfare States* (London, Harvester-Wheatsheaf).

Fry, John (ed.) (1979) *Limits of the Welfare State: Critical Views on Post-War Sweden* (Farnborough, Hants., Saxon House).

Fukuyama, Francis (1992) *The End of History and the Last Man* (London, Hamish Hamilton).

George, Vic and Miller, Stewart (1994) '2000 and Beyond: A Residual or Citizens' Welfare State?' in Vic George and Stewart Miller (eds) *Social Policy Towards 2000. Squaring the Welfare Circle* (London, Routledge) 215–225.

George, Vic and Taylor-Gooby, Peter (eds) (1996) *European Welfare Policy. Squaring the Welfare Circle* (London, Macmillan Press).

Giddens, Anthony (1982) 'Class Division, Class Conflict and Citizenship Rights' in Anthony Giddens, *Profiles and Critiques and Social Theory* (London, Macmillan).

Gilbert, Neil (1983) *Capitalism and the Welfare State: Dilemmas of Social Benevolence* (New Haven, Conn., Yale University Press).

Ginsburg, Norman (1979) *Class, Capital and Social Policy* (London, Macmillan).

Girod, Roger, Laubier, Patrick de and Gladstone, Alan (eds) (1985) *Social Policy in Western Europe and the USA 1950–80* (Basingstoke, Macmillan in association with Institute for Labour Studies).

Glennerster, Howard (1995) *British Social Policy Since 1945* (Oxford, Blackwell).

Glennerster, Howard and Matsaganis, M. (1992) *The English and Swedish Health Care Reforms* (London, London School of Economics).

Goffman, Erving (1968) *Stigma. Notes on the Management of Spoiled Identity* (Harmondsworth, Penguin; first published 1963).

Goodman, Roger and Peng, Ito (1997) 'The East Asian Welfare States: Peripatetic Learning, Adaptive Change and Nation-Building' in Gosta Esping-Anderson (ed.) *Welfare States in Transition. National Adaptations in Global Economies* (London, Sage) 192–224.

Gough, Ian (1979) *The Political Economy of the Welfare State* (London, Macmillan).

Gould, Arthur (1993) 'The End of the Middle Way? The Swedish Welfare State in Crisis' in Catherine Jones (ed.) *New Perspectives on the Welfare State in Europe* (London, Routledge) 157–176.

——(1996) 'Sweden: The Last Bastion of Social Democracy' in Vic George and Peter Taylor-Gooby (eds) *European Welfare Policy. Squaring the Welfare Circle* (London, Macmillan Press) 72–94.

Graubard, Stephen R. (ed.) (1986) *Norden: The Passion for Equality* (Oslo, Norwegian University Press).

Green, David G. (1993) *Reinventing Civil Society: The Rediscovery of Welfare Without Politics* (London, Institute of Economic Affairs).

Gutman, Amy (ed.) (1988) *Democracy and the Welfare State* (Princeton, NJ, Princeton University Press).

Habermas, Jurgen (1989) *The New Conservatism. Cultural Criticism and the Historical Debate* edited and translated by S. W. Nicholson (Cambridge, Polity Press).

Hall, Peter (1986) *Governing the Economy: The Politics of State Intervention in Britain and France* (Oxford, Oxford University Press).

——(1989) *The Political Power of Economic Ideas. Keynesianism Across Nations* (Princeton, NJ, Princeton University Press).

Hantrais, Linda (1996) 'France: Squaring the Welfare Triangle' in Vic George and Peter Taylor-Gooby (eds) *European Welfare Policy. Squaring the Welfare Circle* (London, Macmillan) 51–71.

Harrington, Michael (1987) 'Mitterrand's Term: A Balance Sheet. Where the French Socialists Succeeded and Failed', *Dissent* 34: 82–92.

Harris, Jose (1992) 'Political Thought and the Welfare State 1870–1940: An Intellectual Framework for British Social Policy', *Past and Present* 135: 116–141.

——(1996) 'Political Thought and the State' in S.J.D. Green and R.C. Whiting (eds) *The Boundaries of the State in Modern Britain* (Cambridge, Cambridge University Press) 15–29.

Heater, D. (1990) *Citizenship* (Harlow, Longman).

Heclo, H. and Madsden, H. (1987) *Policy and Politics in Sweden* (Philadelphia, Temple University Press).

Heidenheimer, Arnold J. and Elvander, Nils (eds) (1980) *The Shaping of the Swedish Health System* (London, Croom Helm).

Hennessy, Peter (1992) *Never Again: Britain 1954–51* (London, Cape).

Hobsbawm, Eric (1991) *The Age of Extremes. The Short Twentieth Century 1914–1991* (London, Michael Joseph).

Huber, Evelyne (1997) 'Options for Social Policy in Latin America: Neo-liberal versus Social Democratic Models' in Gosta Esping-Anderson (ed.) *Welfare States in Transition. National Adaptations in Global Economies* (London, Sage, 1997) 141–191.

Ignatieff, Michael (1984) *The Needs of Strangers* (London, Chatto and Windus).

Jacobs, Lawrence R. (1993) *The Health of Nations. Public Opinion and the Making of American and British Health Policy* (Ithaca, Cornell University Press).

Jones, Catherine (1993) 'The Pacific Challenge. Confucian Welfare States' in Catherine Jones (ed.) *New Perspectives on the Welfare State in Europe* (London, Routledge) 198–217.

Kavanagh, D. and Seldon, A. (1989) *Consensus Politics from Attlee to Thatcher* (Oxford, Blackwell).

Klein, Rudolf (1989) *The Politics of the National Health Service* (London, Longmans; second edition).

——(1993) 'O'Goffe's Tale, Or What We Can Learn from the Success of the Capitalist Welfare States' in Catherine Jones (ed.) *New Perspectives on the Welfare State in Europe* (London, Routledge) 1–17.

Lawson, Roger (1996) 'Germany: Maintaining the Middle Way' in Vic George and Peter Taylor-Gooby (eds) *European Welfare Policy. Squaring the Welfare Circle* (London, Macmillan Press) 31–50.

Le Grand, Julian (1982) *The Strategy of Equality: Redistribution and the Social Services* (London, Allen and Unwin).

Leibfried, Stephan (1993) 'Towards a European Welfare State?' in Catherine Jones (ed.) *New Perspectives on the Welfare State in Europe* (London, Routledge) 157–176.

Lewin, Leif (1988) *Ideology and Strategy: A Century of Swedish Politics* (Cambridge, Cambridge University Press).

Lister, Ruth (1997) *Citizenship. Feminist Perspectives* (London, Macmillan).

Lowe, Rodney (1990) 'The Second World War, Consensus, and the Foundation of the Welfare State', *Twentieth Century British History* 1: 152–182.

——(1993) *The Welfare State in Britain Since 1945* (London, Macmillan).

——(1994) 'Lessons from the Past: The Rise and Fall of the Classic Welfare State in Britain, 1945–76' in Ann Oakley and A. Susan Williams (eds.) *The Politics of the Welfare State* (London, UCL Press) 37–53.

Luiz, José and Araújo, A.C. (1997) 'Attempts to Decentralise in Recent Brazilian Health Policy: Issues and Problems, 1988–1994', *International Journal of Health Services* 27: 109–124.

Malloy, James (1979) *The Politics of Social Security in Brazil* (Pittsburgh, Pittsburgh University Press).

Marcuse, Herbert (1972) *One Dimensional Man* (London, Abacus).

Marshall, T.H. (1950) *Citizenship and Class and Other Essays* (Cambridge, Cambridge University Press).

Mead, Lawrence (1986) *Beyond Entitlement. The Social Obligations of Citizenship* (New York, Free Press).

Mishra, Ramesh (1984) *The Welfare State in Crisis* (Brighton, Wheatsheaf Books).

——(1990) *The Welfare State in Capitalist Society* (London, Harvester-Wheatsheaf).

——(1993) 'Social Policy in a Post-Modern World' in Catherine Jones (ed.) *New Perspectives on the Welfare State in Europe* (London, Routledge) 18–42.

Murray, Charles (1984) *Losing Ground. American Social Policy, 1950–1980* (New York, Basic Books).

Offe, Claus (1984) *The Contradictions of the Welfare State* (London, Hutchinson).

Olson, S.E. (1990) *Social Policy and Welfare State in Sweden* (Lund, Arkiv).

Parker, Julia (1975) *Social Policy and Citizenship* (London, Macmillan).

Plant, Raymond, Lesser, Harry and Taylor-Gooby, Peter (1980) (eds) *Political Philosophy and Social Welfare: Essays on the Normative Basis of Welfare Provision* (London, Routledge and Kegan Paul).

Ringen, Stein (1987) *The Possibility of Politics: A Study in the Political Economy of the Welfare State* (Oxford, Clarendon).

Seldon, A. (1994) 'Consensus: A Debate Too Long?', *Parliamentary Affairs* 47: 501–515.

Skocpol, Theda (1996) *Boomerang, Clinton's Health Security Effort and the Turn Against Government in U.S. Politics* (New York, Norton).

Smith, William C., Acuría, Carlos H. and Gamarra, Eduardo A. (eds) (1994) *Democracy, Markets and Structural Reform in Latin America: Argentina, Bolivia, Brazil, Chile and Mexico* (New Brunswick, NJ, Transaction Books).

Standing, Guy (1997) 'Social Protection in Central and Eastern Europe: A Tale of Slipping Anchors and Torn Safety Nets' in Gosta Esping-Anderson (ed.) *Welfare States in Transition. National Adaptations in Global Economies* (London, Sage) 192–224.

Starr, Paul (1982) *The Social Transformation of American Medicine* (New York, Basic Books).

Stephens, John (1996) 'The Scandinavian Welfare States: Achievements, Crisis and Prospects' in Gosta Esping-Anderson (ed.) *Welfare States in Transition. National Adaptations in Global Economies* (London, Sage) 32–65.

Strong, Philip and Robinson, Jane (1990) *The NHS Under New Management* (Milton Keynes, Open University Press).

Swaan, Abram de (1988) *In Care of the State: Health Care, Education and Welfare in Europe and the USA in the Modern Era* (Cambridge, Polity).

Timmins, Nicolas (1995) *The Five Giants. A Biography of the Welfare State* (London, Harper-Collins).

Titmuss, R. M. (1968) *Commitment to Welfare* (London, George Allen and Unwin).

Turner, Bryan (1986) *Citizenship and Capitalism: The Debate over Reformism* (London, Allen and Unwin).

——(1993) 'Contemporary Problems in the Theory of Citizenship' in Bryan Turner (ed.) *Citizenship and Social Theory* (London, Sage) 1–18.

Vergara, Pilar (1994) 'Market Economy, Social Welfare and Democratic Consolidation in Chile' in William C. Smith, Carlos H. Acuría and Eduardo A. Gamarra (eds) *Democracy, Markets and Structural Reform in Latin America: Argentina, Bolivia, Brazil, Chile and Mexico* (New Brunswick, NJ, Transaction Books) 237–262.

Webster, Charles (1988) *The Health Services Before the War. Volume I: Problems of Health Care, The National Health Service Before 1957* (London, H.M.S.O.).

——(ed.) (1991) *Aneurin Bevan on the National Health Service* (Oxford, The Wellcome Unit for the History of Medicine).

——(1994) 'Conservatives and Consensus: the Politics of the National Health Service, 1951–64' in Ann Oakley and A. Susan Williams (eds) *The Politics of Welfare* (London, UCL Press) 54–73.

——(1996) *The Health Services Since the War. Volume II: Government and Health Care, The National Health Service 1958–1979* (London, H.M.S.O.).

Wilensky, Harold L. (1976) *The New Corporatism, Centralization and the Welfare State* (London, Sage Publications).

Wilson, Dorothy (1979) *The Welfare State in Sweden. A Study in Comparative Social Administration* (London, Heinemann).

Wiseman, M. (1993) 'Welfare Reform in the States. The Bush Legacy', *Focus* 15, 1: 18.

13 BEING FIT TO LIVE IN THE TWENTY-FIRST CENTURY: HEALTHY BODIES AND SOMATIC MAPS

Armstrong, David (1983) *The Political Anatomy of the Body* (Cambridge, Cambridge University Press).

Atlas, Charles (1930) *Charles Atlas, Founder of the Fastest Health, Strength and Physique Building System* (London, Charles Atlas Ltd).

Barnes, David S. (1995) *The Making of a Social Disease: Tuberculosis in Nineteenth-Century France* (Berkeley, University of California Press).

Beecher, Catherine (1856) *Physiology and Callisthenics for Schools and Families* (New York, Harper and Broths).

Berridge, Virginia (1979) 'Morality and Medical Science; Concepts of Narcotic Addiction in Britain', *Annals of Science* 36: 67–85.

——(1996) *Aids in the UK. The Making of a Policy, 1981–1994* (Oxford, Oxford University Press).

——(1998, forthcoming) 'Science and Policy: the Case of Post War British Smoking Policy' in Stephen Lock and E. M. Tansey (eds) *Ashes to Ashes* (Amsterdam and Atlanta, Rodopi).

Berryman, Jack W. and Park, Roberta J. (eds) (1992) *Sport and Exercise Science. Essays in the History of Sports Medicine* (Urbana and Chicago: University of Illinois Press).

Boyle, T. Coraghessan (1993) *The Road to Wellville* (Harmondsworth, Penguin).

Brandt, Alan (1987) *No Magic Bullet. A Social History of Venereal Disease in the United States since 1880* (New York, Oxford University Press).

——(1998 forthcoming) 'Blow Some My Way; Passive Smoking, Risk, and American Culture' in Stephen Lock and E. M. Tansey (eds) *Ashes to Ashes* (Amsterdam and Atlanta, Rodopi).

Bryder, Linda (1988) *Below the Magic Mountain* (Oxford, Oxford University Press).

Burnham, John (1985) 'American Medicine's Golden Age: What Happened to It' in J. Leavitt and R. Numbers (eds) *Sickness and Health in America. Readings in the History of Medicine and Public Health* (Madison, University of Wisconsin Press) 248–258.

Chapman, David L. (1994) *Sandow the Magnificent* (Urbana and Chicago: University of Illinois Press).

Cockerell, Hugh (1998, forthcoming) 'Tobacco and Victorian Literature' in Stephen Lock and E. M. Tansey (eds) *Ashes to Ashes* (Amsterdam and Atlanta, Rodopi).

Department of Health and Social Security (1976) *Prevention and Health: Everybody's Business* (London: H.M.S.O.).

Doll, Richard and Hill, Austin Bradford (1950) 'Smoking and Carcinoma of the Lung', *British Medical Journal* ii: 739–748.

——(1956) 'Lung Cancer and Other Causes of Death in Relation to Smoking', *British Medical Journal* ii: 1071–81.

——(1998, forthcoming) 'The First Reports on Smoking and Lung Cancer' in Stephen Lock and E. M. Tansey (eds) *Ashes to Ashes* (Amsterdam and Atlanta, Rodopi).

Doyal, Leslie (1981) *The Political Economy of Health* (Boston, South End Press).

Dubos, René (1987) *The White Plague. Tuberculosis, Man and Society* (New Brunswick, NJ, Rutgers University Press).

Fee, Elizabeth (1987) *Disease and Discovery. A History of the Johns Hopkins School of Hygiene and Public Health, 1916–1939* (Baltimore, Johns Hopkins University Press).

Fee, E. and Fox, D. (eds) (1992) *AIDS: The Making of a Chronic Disease* (Berkeley and Los Angeles, University of California Press).

Fit Body (1995) 'The 1995 Tropicana Ms. Fitness British Championships', [16-page supplement] August/September.

Georgii, Augustus (1854) *A Biographical Sketch of the Swedish Poet and Gymnasiarch Peter Henry Ling* (London, Ballière).

Gilman, Sander (1988) *Disease and Representation. Images of Illness from Madness to AIDS* (Ithaca, Cornell University Press).

——(1995) *Health and Illness. Images of Difference* (London, Reaktion Books).

Goodman, J. (1993) *Tobacco in History. The Cultures of Dependence* (London, Routledge).

——(1998, forthcoming) 'Webs of Drug Dependence: Towards a Political History of Tobacco' in Stephen Lock and E. M. Tansey (eds) *Ashes to Ashes* (Amsterdam and Atlanta, Rodopi).

Green, Harvey (1986) *Fit for America. Health, Fitness, Sport and American Society* (Baltimore, Johns Hopkins University Press).

Haley, Bruce (1978) *The Healthy Body in Victorian Culture* (Cambridge, Mass., Harvard University Press).

Harley, David (1998, forthcoming) 'The Moral Symbolism of Tobacco in Dutch Genre Painting' in Stephen Lock and E. M. Tansey (eds) *Ashes to Ashes* (Amsterdam and Atlanta, Rodopi).

Harrison, Brian (1995) *Drink and the Victorians: The Temperance Question in England, 1815–1872* (Keele University Press Reprint).

Hilton, Matthew and Nightingale, Simon (1998, forthcoming) ' "A Microbe of the Devil's Own Make": Religion and Science in the British Anti-Tobacco Movement, 1853–1908' in Stephen Lock and E. M. Tansey (eds) *Ashes to Ashes* (Amsterdam and Atlanta, Rodopi).

Jefferys, Margot (1986) 'The Transition from Public Health to Community Medicine: The Evolution and Execution of a Policy', *Society for the Social History of Medicine Bulletin* 39: 47–63.

Jordanova, L.J. (1982) 'Guarding the Body Politic: Volney's Catechism of 1793' in Francis Barker *et al.* (eds) *1789: Reading Writing Revolution. Proceedings of the Essex Conference on the Sociology of Literature, July 1981* (Colchester, University of Essex) 12–21.

Kellogg, J.H. (1894) *Man The Masterpiece or, Plain Truths Plainly Told, Boyhood, Youth, and Manhood* (London, International Tract Society).

Kiple, Kenneth (ed.) (1993) *The Cambridge World History of Human Disease* (Cambridge, Cambridge University Press).

Lewis, Jane (1986) *What Price Community Medicine. The Philosophy, Practice and Politics of Public Health Since 1919* (Brighton, Sussex, Harvester).

Lock, Stephen and E. M. Tansey (eds) (1998, forthcoming) *Ashes to Ashes. A Wellcome Symposium on the History of Tobacco-Smoking* (Amsterdam and Atlanta, Rodopi).

Luoumo, T.C. (1992) 'Alien Back Attack', *Ironman. For Ultimate Fitness*, November: 32–39.

MacFadden, Bernarr (1900) *The Virile Powers of Superb Manhood. How Developed, How Lost, How Regained* (New York, The Physical Culture Publishing Company).

——(1902) (editor and proprietor) *Physical Development. Special Edition for England* 3, 1.

McInerney, Dave (1992) 'Editorial', *Ironman. For Ultimate Fitness* November: 5.

McIntosh, Peter C. (1981) *Physical Education in England Since 1800* (London, Bell).

McIntosh, Peter C. *et al.* (eds) (1981) *Landmarks in the History of Physical Education* (London, Routledge and Kegan Paul).

Mangan, J.A. (1981) *Athleticism in the Victorian and Edwardian Public School. The Emergence and Consolidation of an Educational Ideology* (Cambridge: Cambridge University Press).

Marx, Karl (1977–1984) *Capital* translated from the Third German Edition by Samuel Moore and Edward Aveling and edited by Friedrich Engels (London, Lawrence and Wishart, 1956–1959; 1977–1984 Printings).

Means, Richard K. (1962) *A History of Health Education in the United States* (London, Henry Kimpton).

Mullan, F. (1989) *Plagues and Politics. The Story of the United States Public Health Service* (New York, Basic Books).

Oswald, Nigel (1991) 'A Social Health Service Without Doctors', *Social History of Medicine* 4: 295–315.

——(1997) 'Training Doctors for the National Health Service. Social Medicine, Medical Education and the GMC, 1936–1948' in Dorothy Porter (ed.) *Social Medicine and Medical Sociology in the Twentieth Century* (Amsterdam and Atlanta, Rodopi) 59–80.

Park, Roberta (1992) 'Athletes and their Training, 1800–1914' in Jack W. Berryman and Roberta J. Park (eds) *Sports and Exercise Science. Essays in the History of Sports Medicine* (Urbana and Chicago, University of Illinois Press) 64–84.

Petersen, Alan and Bunton, Robin (eds) (1997) *Foucault, Health and Medicine* (London, Routledge).

Porter, Dorothy (1991) 'Stratification and its Discontents: Professionalization and Conflict in the British Public Health Service' in Elizabeth Fee and Roy Acheson (eds) *The History of Education in Public Health. Health that Mocks the Doctors' Rules* (Oxford, Oxford Medical Publications) 83–113.

——(1992) 'Changing Disciplines: John Ryle and the Making of Social Medicine in Twentieth Century Britain', *History of Science* 30: 119–147.

——(1993) 'John Ryle: Doctor of Revolution?' in Dorothy Porter and Roy Porter (eds) *Doctors, Politics and Society: Historical Essays* (Amsterdam, Rodopi) 229–247.

——(1996) 'Social Medicine and the New Society: Medicine and Scientific Humanism in Mid-Twentieth Century Britain', *Journal of Historical Sociology* 9: 168–187.

——(1997) 'The Decline of Social Medicine in Britain in the 1960s' in Dorothy Porter (ed.) *Social Medicine and Medical Sociology in the Twentieth Century* (Amsterdam and Atlanta, Rodopi) 97–119.

——(1998, forthcoming) 'The Healthy Body in the Twentieth Century' in Roger Cooter and John Pickstone (eds) *Twentieth Century Medicine* (London, Harwood Academic Publications).

Porter, D. and Porter, R. (1989) 'The Enforcement of Health: The English Debate' in E. Fee and D. Fox (eds) *AIDS: The Burdens of History* (Berkeley and Los Angeles, University of California Press) 97–121.

Proctor, Robert N. (1988) *Racial Hygiene: Medicine under the Nazis* (Cambridge, Cambridge University Press).

Ramsey, Matthew (1994) 'Public Health in France' in Dorothy Porter (ed.) *The History of Public Health and the Modern State* (Amsterdam and Atlanta, Rodopi) 45–118.

Rosenkrantz, Barbara Gutmann (ed.) (1994) *From Consumption to Tuberculosis: A Documentary History* (New York, Garland).

Rothman, Sheila M. (1994) *Living in the Shadow of Death: Tuberculosis and the Social Experience of Illness in American History* (New York, Basic Books).

Ryle, John A. (1994) *Changing Disciplines* (New Brunswick, Transaction Publishers; first edition 1948).

Sand, René (1952) *The Advance to Social Medicine* (London, Staples Press).

Sandow, Eugene (1922) *Life is Movement. The Physical Reconstruction and Regeneration of the People. (A Diseaseless World)* (London, The Family Encyclopaedia of Health, 1922, 1st edn 1919).

Smith, David W. (1974) *Stretching Their Bodies. The History of Physical Education* (London and Vancouver, Newton Abbot).

Smith, F.B. (1988) *The Retreat of T. B. 1850–1950* (London, Croom Helm).

Smith, George, Davy and M. Egger (1996) 'Smoking and Health Promotion in Nazi Germany', *Journal of Epidemiology and Community Medicine* 50: 109–110.

Solomon, Susan Gross (1990) 'Social Hygiene in Soviet Medical Education 1922–30', *Journal for the History of Medicine and Allied Sciences* 4: 607–643.

——(1994) 'The Expert and the State in Russian Public Health: Continuities and Changes Across the Revolutionary Divide' in Dorothy Porter (ed.) *The History of Public Health and the Modern State* (Amsterdam and Atlanta, Rodopi) 183–224.

Solomon, Susan Gross and Hutchinson, John F. (eds) (1990) *Health and Society in Revolutionary Russia* (Bloomington, Indiana University Press).

Sontag, Susan (1979) *Illness as a Metaphor* (London, Allen Lane).

Starr, Paul (1982) *The Social Transformation of American Medicine* (New York, Basic Books).

Tanny, Armand (1988) 'Sex and Fitness. How Bodybuilding Cures Impotence', *Muscle and Fitness* July.

Todd, Jan (1987) 'Bernarr Macfadden: Reformer of the Feminine Form', *Journal of Sport History* 14: 61–75.

Turner, Bryan S. (1984) *The Body and Society. Explorations in Social Theory* (Oxford, Basil Blackwell).

——(1987) *Medical Power and Social Knowledge* (London, Sage).

——(1992) *Regulating Bodies. Essays in Medical Sociology* (London, Routledge).

Viseltear, Arthur J. (1997) 'Milton C. Winternitz and the Yale Institute for Human Relations: A Brief Chapter in the History of Social Medicine' in Dorothy Porter (ed.) *Social Medicine and Medical Sociology in the Twentieth Century* (Amsterdam and Atlanta, Rodopi; first published *Yale Journal of Biology and Medicine* 57 (1984): 869–889) 32–58.

Walvin, James (1978) *Leisure and Society, 1830–1950* (London, Longman).

Warren, Michael (1997) *The Genesis of the Faculty of Community Medicine, Now the Faculty of Public Health Medicine* (Kent, Centre for Health Service Studies, University of Kent).

Watkins, Dorothy E. (1984) *The English Revolution in Social Medicine* (Ph.D. thesis, University of London).

Watney, Simon (1987) *Policing Desire: Pornography, AIDS and the Media* (London, Methuen).

Webster, Charles (1988) *The Health Services Before the War. Volume I: Problems of Health Care, The National Health Service Before 1957* (London, H.M.S.O.).

Weider, Jo (1988) 'Editorial', *Muscle and Fitness* July: 7.

Whorton, James C. (1982) *Crusaders for Fitness. The History of American Health Reformers* (Princeton, Princeton University Press).

Williams, Ralph C. (1951) *The United States Public Health Service, 1798–1950* (Washington, Commissioned Officers Association of the United States Public Health Service).

EPILOGUE

Ad Hoc Committee to Defend Health Care (1997) 'For Our Patients, Not for Profits. A Call to Action', *Journal of the American Medical Association* 278: 1733–1738.

Barer, Morris L., Marmor, Theodore R. and Morrison, Ellen M. (1995) 'Health Care Reform in the United States: On the Road to Nowhere (Again)?', *Social Science and Medicine*, 41: 453–460.

Black, Sir Douglas (1981) *Inequalities in Health* (Birmingham, University of Birmingham).

Brook, Robert H. (1997) 'Managed Care is Not the Problem, Quality Is', *Journal of the American Medical Association* 278: 1612–1614.

Call, Kathleen Thiede, Lurie, Nicole, Jonk, Yvonne, Feldman, Roger and Finch, Michael D. (1997) 'Who is Still Uninsured in Minnesota? Lessons from State Reform Efforts', *Journal of the American Medical Association* 278: 1191–1195.

Curtis, Sarah, Petukhova, Natasha, Sezonova, Galina and Netsenko, Nadia (1997) 'Caught in the "Traps of Managed Competition"? Examples of Russian Health Care Reforms from St. Petersburg and the Leningrad Region', *International Journal of Health Services* 27: 661–686.

Department of Health (1997) *The New NHS. Modern. Dependable* (London, H.M.S.O., Cmd. 3807).

Dobson, Frank and Jowell, Tessa (1998) *Our Healthier Nation. A Contract for Health* (London, H.M.S.O., Cmd. 3852).

Epstein, Arnold (1997) 'Medicaid Managed Care and High Quality. Can We Have Both?' *Journal of the American Medical Association* 278: 1617–1625.

Horton, Richard (1998) 'Our Healthier Nation, Possibly', *The Lancet* 351: 463.

Jacobson, Bobbie and Yen, Laurann (1998) 'Health Action Zones Offer the Possibility of Radical Ideas which Need Rigorous Evaluation', *British Medical Journal* 316: 164.

Kisely, S. and Jones, J. (1997) 'Acheson Revisited: Public Health Medicine Ten Years After the Acheson Report', *Public Health* 111: 361–364.

Kleinke, J.O. (1997) 'The Industrialization of Health Care', *Journal of the American Medical Association* 278: 1456–1457.

McKee, Martin and Sheldon, Trevor (1998) 'Measuring Performance in the NHS. Good That It's Moved Beyond Money and Activity but Many Problems Remain', *British Medical Journal* 316: 322.

Miller, Tracy E. (1997) 'Managed Care Regulation. In the Laboratory of the States', *Journal of the American Medical Association* 278: 1102–1109.

Shapiro, Jonathan, Black, Nick, Wyatt, Jeremy and Griffiths, Sian (1998) 'The New NHS: Commentaries on the White Paper. Encouraging Responsibility: Different Paths to Accountability', *British Medical Journal* 316: 296–304.

Vergara, P. (1997) 'In Pursuit of "Growth with Equity": The Limits of Chile's Free-Market Social Reforms', *International Journal of Health Services* 27: 207–215.

Wayne, Ray A., Gigante, Joseph, Mitchel, Edward F., Jr, and Hickson, Gerald B. (1998) 'Perinatal Outcomes Following Implementation of TennCare', *Journal of the American Medical Association* 279: 314–316.

Woods, David (1997) 'Meet Ms Managed Care', *British Medical Journal* 315: 628.

Index

$\mathcal{E}$thics

FOR THE
INFORMATION
AGE FIFTH EDITION